A Sample of Commentary About John Taylor Gatto's Teaching Ca[reer] by
Students, Parents, Administrators and Colleagues:

"John Gatto has rendered a record of ability, energy, dedication, and selflessness"... "A most outstanding classroom teacher"... "Many students have remarked he is the best teacher they ever had"... "Intellectual curiosity unmatched"... "John did an exemplary job"... "A flair for teaching"... "A teacher with rare gifts"... "The excitement John generated was infectious"... "His keen intelligence, his encyclopedic range of knowledge, his verve and enthusiasm make him, to say the least, an unusual individual"... "Your class was a major highlight"... "A pleasure working with you"... "You make good things happen"... "Your work was inspired"... "Thank you for the innumerable contributions you have made to our school community"..."Outstanding"... "Students are constantly challenged intellectually"... "You provide your students with one of the greatest gifts that anyone can give another—confidence and a sense of power"... "Your actions constantly demonstrate your commitment"... "Working with you is both exciting and revitalizing"... "An outstanding professional and scholar"... "Your exceptional achievement brings honor not only to yourself but to the entire District. We are fortunate indeed to have you"..."You are certainly an outstanding winner"... "I am sure there are not many with your recognizably outstanding gifts"... "Creative, imaginative, and outstanding"... "A tribute to your leadership"... "The entire school is indebted to you"... "Inspiring our children to such heights of creativity"... "Your masterful direction, your inspiration"... "Because of Mr. Gatto's enthusiasm and voluntary contributions of time and expertise, the original concept was developed"... "As usual in your classes the lesson was an exercise in thought"... "You are truly an outstanding teacher, equipped with a mind of rare vision and originality, aided and abetted by great enthusiasm"... "Your teaching style is superb"... "The experiment you conducted with your English classes was certainly a grand success"... "Your presentation was delightful, highly informative, and most entertaining"... "An exhilarating experience, not only for the students but also for your colleagues"... "The real reward for your efforts is not this meager letter but rather the abundant tribute of the several hundred students you taught and inspired"... "The lesson exhibited the tremendous respect you have for the intelligence and ability of these 8th graders"... "John Gatto's instructor rating was the highest in the Department of Education at Queens and, in fact, the highest on the Queens College campus. Although John Gatto's students consistently rated his teaching as more valuable than the courses he taught, they gave the courses he taught the highest rating in the department as well"... "To a wonderful teacher"... "The course was great"... "To my cherished friend and counselor"... "I can say with some authority that John was the finest teacher this student ever had. Thanks, John"... "You treated me like my father"... "You're great and we all love you"... "You are my favorite human being"... "Thank you for being a good friend as well as a teacher"... "You've really opened my eyes and made me see things in new ways"... "Personally Mr. Gatto and my father are the only successful educators I have come across in my 9 years of lousy education"... "Bronx Science drains your brain of ideas and tries to fill it with routines. I wish I hadn't come here. This school is terrible—even the Honors English. Why don't you start a school? I'd love to go to it and be thinking in school rather than whatever it is I do here"... "I learned more about life and education in one year I had with Gatto than in all my previous years in school"... "John Gatto taught both of my children. We realized something was different. Mr. Gatto pulled out all the stops. My daughter said, 'Mr. Gatto is the best teacher I ever had from 1st through 12th grade. He made me question what I was learning.'" "I am very grateful he was their teacher"... "A great person, far superior to other teachers I've had"... "He enhances everyone's self-worth"... "John Gatto is beyond description, fascinating"... "Packed with a quality of innovation"... "The most striking appeal"... "Emanates warmth"... "A true asset"

FROM
AMONG

MY

SCRAP-

BOOK

PICTURES,

SOME

OF THE MANY

OF
MY
LIFE.

HEROES
AND
HEROINES

VALE
ATQUE
VALE

SOME ADVANCE COMMENTS ABOUT

The Underground History of American Education

I count John Gatto among my heroes.
>—Robert Bly
>(letter to *The Journal of Family Life*)

Your ideas are splendid. I just hope someone is listening.
>—Christopher Lasch
>*Revolt of the Elites; True and Only Heaven*
>(letter to author)

Gatto is the most interesting writer on education today.
>—PreserveNet Home Page

This book is brilliant. When I finished it I felt like I'd just gone fifteen rounds with the champ. This book is unlike any other, for my money the best approach to an understanding of the mythology of public education in America around.
>—Chris Mercogliano
>Director, The Albany Free School

Gatto's voice is strong and unique, a Socrates of the educational world. Don't deny yourself the blood-curdling pleasure of reading this perverse history of American education as a design for a real life. I loved this book!
>—Thomas Moore
>*Care of the Soul; Soul Mates*

I've loved John Gatto's work ever since I first encountered his astounding essays in *The Sun*. This analysis of schooling is presented with daring, panache, and a humorous passion that leaps off the page. I give this book a standing ovation! Bravo!
>—Christiane Northrup, M.D.
>*Women's Bodies, Women's Wisdom*

The emotional effect of *Underground History* cannot be overstated. It reminds me of the reporter watching the Hindenburg burst into flames who cried, "Oh, the *humanity*!" Gatto is crying here, "Oh, the *Children*!" This is the most important education book of my lifetime.
>—Michael Farris
>President, Home School Legal
>Defense Association

These pages burn with insight and controversy. You cannot read this book without changing the way you look at schools.
>—Pat Farenga, President
>*John Holt Associates*

Anyone interested in the fate of our schools should make this book a priority. Gatto's insistence on calling a spade a spade in recognizing the bases on which modern schooling has been built leaves no doubt that our well-being requires us to leave behind the concept of institutional education as a social good.

—Dan Greenberg
Co-founder, *The Sudbury Valley School*

Gatto tells us straight up what's wrong with school in his powerful trademark blend of passion and hard thinking. Grounded in a careful study of history, crafted out of the context of his own brilliant 30-year teaching career, this book will validate your own shadowy intuition about schooling.

—Grace Llewelyn
The Teenage Liberation Handbook

John Taylor Gatto is the most famous schoolteacher in the United States for good reasons!

—*The Independence Institute*

He paints a scathing picture of caring people's best intentions undermined....examines the psychology, economics, sociology, anthropology, and politics of modern institutionalized forced schooling, concluding it cannot be reformed because it is doing exactly what it is designed to do. Don't miss this inspiring rebel educator.

—*The Open Center*
New York City

The Underground History of American Education is the *Blair Witch Project* of educational critiques. I predict it will prove to be an indigestible lump in the throat of the school establishment. A triumph!

—Roland Legiardi-Laura
Director, *The Nuyorican Poet's Café*
Founder, *The Fifth Night Film Project*

How does he probe so deeply the complex issues surrounding our schools when so many experts can hardly penetrate the surface at all? Here a master lecturer works his magic to cast the issues surrounding our schools in a new light. An examination of the assumptions behind compulsory schooling is the goal of this book. Haunting. A minor classic.

—Eric Schultes
The Whitehead Institute, M.I.T.

I can honestly say there are few things I've read recently, or probably ever, that provoked me to exclaim "This is so RIGHT!" with such alarming regularity.

—Chersteen Anderson
Director, *Sisters Under the Skin*

Thought-provoking, entertaining, and intelligent. Based on years of reading education books I was expecting a drowsy read of little or no content. Was I surprised! Wonderful.

—Judith Current
Teacher, Colorado

Gatto does my heart good. I know parents who were so heavily influenced by his words they pulled their kids out of public school. He is inspirational.

—Libby Bartley
Mother, South Carolina

In my opinion this is one of the most important books on education ever written. Gatto takes us on a journey, tracing the development of his own thinking about government schooling. Here is the whole story, the hidden agendas, the true believers, the dumbing down. If you care at all about children, you'll be livid as you read.

—Cathy Duffy
THE LINK

The most powerful, important, moving, and in many places, beautiful manuscript I have ever read. It is a book I know will change the people who read it.

—John Strohmeier
Publisher, Berkeley Hills Books
Author, *Divine Harmony: The Life and Teachings
of Pythagoras*

This book is the *Silent Spring* of American education.

—Diane Flynn Keith
Publisher, "Homefires"

A breathtaking work of scholarship and encyclopedic scope...history accompanied by an incisive and illuminating narrative. Gatto delivers for our consideration an astonishing cast of cranks while revealing the nest of special interests which profit from schools just as they are. This marvelous book should be required reading for anyone interested in the frightening truth about the enterprise we call "education."

—Adam Robinson, co-founder, *The Princeton Review*
Author, *What Smart Students Know*

John Taylor Gatto's voice is a singular antidote to stale convention.

—David Guterson
Author, *Snow Falling on Cedars*

A brilliant educational renegade.

—Borders Bowie

The most innovative teacher in Manhattan's best and worst schools...unique...one of this country's underground heroes.

—Educational Reform Group, Inc.
Sheffield, Massachusetts

Mr. Gatto is an adventure not to be missed.

—L.I.G.H.T. Long Island Education Conference

John Taylor Gatto

THE UNDERGROUND HISTORY OF AMERICAN EDUCATION

A Schoolteacher's Intimate Investigation Into

The Problem Of Modern Schooling

THE OXFORD VILLAGE PRESS • NEW YORK

Portions of various chapters have appeared in *The Wall Street Journal, UTNE Reader, The Sun, The Whole Earth Review, YES!* A Journal of Sustainable Futures, *Sköle, The Journal of Family Life, Homefires, The Link, The Independent Family, San Francisco Chronicle, Miami Herald, Pittsburgh Post-Gazette,* and elsewhere. Certain parts of the text have been previewed on Pacifica, National Public Radio, and in public addresses given before a wide variety of audiences in the continental United States, Hawaii, Alaska, and overseas.

Published by The Oxford Village Press, 725 McDonough Road, Oxford, New York 13830 in cooperation with The Odysseus Group, a tax-exempt, non-profit organization dedicated to enhancing the debate about the education of the young. The Odysseus Group is recognized by the IRS and can accept contributions, which are tax-deductible. It is located at 295 East 8th Street, New York, New York 10009.

THE UNDERGROUND HISTORY OF AMERICAN EDUCATION

To order personal copies from the publisher, please add $4.00 shipping to the price of the first copy and $1.00 for each additional copy. Send check or money order to: The Oxford Village Press, P.O. Box 562, Oxford, New York 13830. New York State residents should add appropriate tax. Wholesale orders: **SAN:** 247-7696.

First paperback edition prior to publication, June 30, 2000. This edition has been prepared for distribution to press, reviewers, wholesale book buyers, and for sale at Mr. Gatto's lectures. The market first edition will be issued on January 31, 2001.

Publisher's Cataloging-in-Publication Data

Gatto, John Taylor.
   The underground history of American education:
a schoolteacher's intimate investigation into the
problem of modern schooling / John Taylor Gatto.
   — 1st ed.
      p. cm.
      Includes bibliographical references and index.
      LCCN : 00-130611
      ISBN : 0-945-70005-9 (hbk.)
      ISBN : 0-945-70004-0 (pbk.)

      1. Education—United States—History.
   2. Education—Evaluation. 3. Education—Philosophy.
   4. Education—Experimental methods—History.
   5. Education and state—United States. 6. Education
   —Aims and objectives—History.   I. Title.

LA205.G38 2000   370.973
                    QBI00-296

Manufactured in the United States of America

Typing by: Sylvia McNitt and Julie Bennack
Interior by: Janet MacAdam
Jacket by: Maria Whitworth
Proofreading by: Eleanor Nauen, Cathy Duffy, Sherry Rothman, and Tom McPherren
Index by: Rick Hurd

DISCLAIMER
This book is not intended to be legal advice, readers assume full responsibility for any specific application of the contents to their particular concerns. Critical references to people or organizations are the private judgement of the author, entered in the spirit of a search for truth, not as insults. Keep in mind the possibility of error and reflect independently in every instance.

The Oxford Village Press

The Odysseus Group, Inc.

For my wife, Janet MacAdam, an extraordinary woman,

daughter of Thomas James MacAdam,

a seafaring man of Ayr, and

Doris Cuthbertson Brown,

one of eight adventurous sisters from Glasgow.

With love and gratitude from the green river Monongahela

to blue Oyster Bay, until death do us part.

Three Outlooks

On

The Human Condition,

Each Of Which

Demands

A Different Kind

Of Schooling

To

Achieve

I

The Behaviorist

Individuals will be more and more deeply embedded in complex hierarchical structures. Their interaction will be mediated by the interaction of the many socio-cultural unities which they and their primary groups jointly form. The more you organize, the more you regiment. To create the fully organized human society is to create the fully regimented human cog.

> — B.F. Skinner, as his position is characterized
> by scientific humanist Erwin Laszlo in
> *The Systems View of the World.*

II

The Scientific Humanist

We have enormous control capabilities. As we manipulate the organs and cells of our body through medicines and surgery, so we can manipulate the many strands of social and ecological relations around us. We know fairly clearly what constitutes organic health for our biological system; now we must likewise learn the norms of our manifold ecologic, economic, political and cultural systems. The supreme challenge of our age is to specify, and learn to respect, *the objective norms of existence* within the complex and delicately balanced hierarchic order.

> — Erwin Laszlo, *The Systems View of the World*

III

The Human Being

Only here in America were the common folk of the Old World given a chance to show what they could do on their own, without a master to push and order them about. History contrived an earth-shaking joke when it lifted by the nape of the neck lowly peasants, shopkeepers, laborers, paupers, jailbirds, and drunks from the midst of Europe, dumped them on a vast virgin continent and said: Go to it, it is yours!

> — Eric Hoffer, *The Ordeal of Change* (Hoffer
> was a migrant farm worker for ten years,
> then became a San Francisco longshoreman)

Contents

The shocking possibility that dumb people don't exist in sufficient numbers
to warrant the millions of careers devoted to tending them will seem incredible
to you. Yet that is my central proposition: the mass dumbness which justifies
official schooling first had to be dreamed of; it isn't real.

Bianca, You Animal, Shut Up! • I Quit, I Think • The New Individualism •
School As Religion • He Was Square Inside And Brown • The New
Dumbness • Putting Pedagogy To The Question • Author's Note •

PART ONE
Of Schooling, Education, And Myself

Our official assumptions about the nature of modern childhood are dead wrong,
as history amply demonstrates. Children allowed to take responsibility and given
a serious part in the larger world are always superior to those merely permitted to
play and be passive. At the age of 12, Admiral Farragut got his first command.
I was in fifth grade when I learned of this. Had Farragut gone to my school he
would have been in seventh.

A Nation From The Bottom Up • You Had To Do It Yourself • No Limit To Pain
For Those Who Allow It • The Art Of Driving • Two Approaches To Discipline •
The Schools Of Hellas • The Fresco At Herculaneum • The Seven Liberal Arts •
The Platonic Ideal • Oriental Pedagogy • Counter-Attack On Democracy • How
Hindu Schooling Came To America (I) • How Hindu Schooling Came To America (II) •
How Hindu Schooling Came To America (III) • Braddock's Defeat • Ben Franklin •
George Washington • Montaigne's Curriculum •

Chapter Two
An Angry Look At Modern Schooling

The secret of American schooling is that it doesn't teach the way children learn and it isn't supposed to. It took seven years of reading and reflection to finally figure out that mass schooling of the young by force was a creation of the four great coal powers of the nineteenth century. On April 11, 1933, Max Mason, president of the Rockefeller Foundation, announced to insiders that a comprehensive national program was underway to allow, in Mason's words, "the control of human behavior."

A Change In The Governing Mind • Extending Childhood • The Geneticist's Manifesto • Participatory Democracy Put To The Sword • Bad Character As A Management Tool • An Enclosure Movement For Children • The Dangan • Occasional Letter Number One • Change Agents Infiltrate • Bionomics • Waking Up Angry •

Chapter Three
Eyeless In Gaza

Something strange has been going on in government schools, especially where the matter of reading is concerned. Abundant data exists to show that by 1840 the incidence of complex literacy in the United States was between 93 and 100 percent wherever such a thing mattered. Yet compulsory schooling existed nowhere. Between the two world wars, schoolmen seem to have been assigned the task of terminating our universal reading proficiency.

The School Edition • Intellectual Espionage • Looking Behind Appearances • The Sudbury Valley School • Bootie Zimmer • False Premises • A System Of State Propaganda • The Ideology Of The Text • The National Adult Literacy Survey • Name Sounds, Not Things • The Meatgrinder Classroom • The Ignorant Schoolmaster • Frank Had A Dog; His Name Was Spot • The Pedagogy Of Literacy • Dick And Jane •

Chapter Four
I Quit, I Think

I lived through the great transformation which turned schools from often useful places into laboratories of state experimentation with the lives of children, a form of pornography masquerading as pedagogical science. Yet all theories of child-rearing talk in averages, and the evidence of your own eyes and ears tells you that average men and women don't really exist—except as a statistical conceit.

Wadleigh, The Death School • Dr. Caleb Gattegno, Expert • Intimidation • Hector Of The Feeble-Mind • Hector Isn't The Problem • One Lawyer Equals 3000 Reams Of Paper • The Great Transformation • Education As A Helix Sport • I'm Outta Here! •

PART TWO
The Foundation Of Schooling

Chapter Five
True Believers And The Unspeakable Chautauqua   93

From start to finish, school as we know it is a tale of true believers and how they took the children to a land faraway. All of us have a tiny element of true believer in our makeups. You have only to reflect on some of your own wild inner urges and the lunatic gleam that comes into your own eyes on those occasions to begin to understand what might happen if those impulses were made a permanent condition.

Munsterberg And His Disciples • The Prototype Is A Schoolteacher • Teachers College Maintains The Planet • A Lofty, Somewhat Inhuman Vision • Rain Forest Algebra • Godless, But Not Irreligious • An Insider's Insider • Compulsion Schooling • De-Moralizing School Procedure • William Torrey Harris • Cardinal Principles • The Unspeakable Chautauqua •

Chapter Six
The Lure Of Utopia   115

Presumably humane utopian interventions like compulsion schooling aren't always the blessing they appear to be. For instance, Sir Humphrey Davy's safety lamp saved thousands of coalminers from gruesome death, but it wasted many more lives than it rescued. That lamp alone allowed the coal industry to grow rapidly, exposing miners to mortal danger for which there is no protection. What Davy did for coal producers, forced schooling has done for the corporate economy.

So Fervently Do We Believe • The Necessity Of Detachment • Enlarging The Nervous System • Producing Artificial Wants • The *Parens Patriae* Powers • The Plan Advances • Children's Court • Mr.Young's Head Was Pounded To Jelly • William Rainey Harper • Death Is Executed • The Three Most Popular Books • No Place To Hide • The Irony Of The Safety Lamp •

Chapter Seven
The Prussian Connection   131

In 1935, at the University of Chicago's experimental school where John Dewey had once held sway, Howard C. Hill, head of the social science department, published an inspirational textbook called *The Life and Work of the Citizen*. The title page clearly shows four cartoon hands symbolizing law, order, science, and the trades interlocked to form a perfect swastika. By1935, Prussian pattern and Prussian goals had embedded themselves so deeply into the vitals of institutional schooling that hardly a soul noticed the traditional purposes of the enterprise were being abandoned.

The Land Of Frankenstein • The Long Reach Of The Teutonic Knights • The Prussian Reform Movement • Travelers' Reports • Finding Work For Intellectuals • The Technology Of Subjection •

A dramatic shift to mass production and mass schooling occurred in the same heady rush. Mass production could not be rationalized unless the population accepted massification. In a democratic republic, school was the only reliable long-range instrument available to accomplish this. Older American forms of schooling would not have been equal to the responsibility which coal, steam, steel, and machinery laid upon the national leadership. Coal demanded the schools we have and so we got them—as an ultimate act of rationality.

Coal At The Bottom Of Things • The Demon Of Overproduction • The Quest For Arcadia • Managerial Utopia • The Positive Method • Plato's Guardians • Far-Sighted Businessmen • Coal Gives The Coup De Grâce • The Spectre Of Uncontrolled Breeding • Global Associations Of Technique • Labor Becomes Expendable • Burying Children Alive • The End Of Competition • America Is Massified • German Mind Science •

"In the past," Frederick Taylor wrote, "Man has been first. In the future, System must be first." The thought processes of the standardized worker had to be standardized, too, in order to render him a dependable consumer. Scientific management spread rapidly from the factory into the schools to seek this goal.

Frederick W. Taylor • The Adoption Of Business Organization By Schools • The Ford System And The Kronstadt Commune • The National Press Attack On Academic Schooling • The Fabian Spirit • The Open Conspiracy • An Everlasting Faith • Regulating Lives Like Machinery • The Gary Plan • The Jewish Student Riots • The Rockefeller Report • Obstacles On The Road To Centralization •

PART THREE
A Personal Interlude

The great destructive myth of the twentieth century was the aggressive contention that a child could not grow up correctly in the unique circumstances of his own family. Forced schooling was the principal agency broadcasting this attitude.

The Character Of A Village • Singing And Fishing Were Free • The Greatest Fun Was Watching People Work • Sitting In The Dark • I Hung Around A Lot In Monongahela • Shooting Birds • On Punishment • Separations • Principles • Walking Around Monongahela • The College Of Zimmer And Hegel •

PART FOUR
Metamorphosis

Chapter Eleven
The Crunch

The experience of global war gave official school reform a grand taste for what was possible. Government intervention was proclaimed the antidote for all dissent. In every nook and cranny of American life new social organizations flourished, all feeding on intervention into personal sovereignty and family life. A new republic was here at last just as Herbert Croly announced, and government school was its church.

The Struggle For Homogeneity • Eugenics Arrives • Mr. Hitler Reads Mr. Ford • Racial Suicide • The Passing Of The Great Race • The Poison Of Democracy • The American Protective League • Guaranteed Customers • Industrial Efficiency • High-Pressure Salesmanship • A New Collectivism •

Chapter Twelve
Daughters Of The Barons of Runnemede

The new-compulsion school institution was assigned the task of fixing the social order into place, albeit with the cautions of Pareto and Mosca kept in mind. Society was to reflect the needs of modern corporate organization and the requirements of rational evolution. The best breeding stock had to be protected and displayed. The supreme challenge was to specify who was who in the new hierarchical order.

The Scientifically Humane Future • Exclusive Heredity • Divinely Appointed Intelligence • The Paxton Boys • Soldiers For Their Class • Organizing Caste • Your Family Tree • The Fatal Sound Shift • Our Manifest Destiny • The Lost Tribes • Unpopular Government • Kinship Is Mythical • The Machine Gun Builds Hotchkiss • Fountains Of Business Wealth • The General Education Board And Friends •

Chapter Thirteen
The Empty Child

The basic hypothesis of utopia-building is that structure of personhood can be broken and reformed again and again. The notion of empty children was the most important concept which inspired the social architects and engineers to believe that schools could indeed be remade into socialization laboratories.

Miss Skinner Commits Self-Slaughter • Behaviorists • Plasticity • Elasticity • Emptiness: The Master Theory • A Metaphysical Commitment • The Limits Of Behavioral Theory • Reality Engages The Banana • Programming The Empty Child • Dr. Watson Presumes • Cleaning The Canvas • Therapy As Curriculum • The New Thought Tide • To Abolish Thinking • Wundt! • Napoleon Of Mind Science • What Is Sanity? • Bending The Student To Reality • Paying Children To Learn •

God was pitched out of forced schooling on his ear after WWII. This wasn't because
of any constitutional proscription—there was none that anyone had been able to find
in over a century and a half—but because the political state and corporate economy
considered the Western spiritual tradition too dangerous a competitor. And it is.

The Problem Of God • Spirits Are Dangerous • Foundations Of The Western
Outlook • Codes Of Meaning • The Scientific Curriculum • *Everson v. Board
of Education* (1947) • Judaism • The Dalai Lama And The Genius Of The West •
Religion And Rationality • The Illusion Of Punishment •

None of the familiar school sequences is defensible according to the rules of
evidence, all are arbitrary; most grounded in superstition or aesthetic prejudice
of one sort or another. Pestalozzi's basic "Simple to Complex" formulation, for
instance, is a prescription for disaster in the classroom.

An Arena Of Dishonesty • The Game Is Crooked • Psychopathic Programming •
What Really Goes On • Pathology As A Natural Byproduct • A Critical Appraisal •
Vox Populi • The Systems Idea In Action •

PART FIVE
The Problem Of Modern Schooling

Spare yourself the anxiety of thinking of this school thing as a conspiracy, even
though the project is indeed riddled with petty conspirators. It was and is a fully
rational transaction in which all of us play a part. We trade the liberty of our kids
and our free will for a secure social order and a very prosperous economy. It's a
bargain in which most of us agree to become as children ourselves, under the same
tutelage which holds the young, in exchange for food, entertainment, and safety.
The difficulty is that the contract fixes the goal of human life so low that students
go mad trying to escape it.

Two Social Revolutions Become One • The Fear Of Common Intelligence •
The Cult Of Forced Schooling • Disinherited Men And Women • Serving
The Imperial Virus • Quill-Driving *Babus* • The Release From Tutelage •

At the heart of the durability of mass schooling is a brilliantly designed power fragmentation system which distributes decision-making so widely among so many warring interests that large-scale change is impossible without a guidebook. Few insiders understand how to steer this ship and the few who do may have lost the will to control it.

The only conceivable way to break out of this trap is to repudiate any further centralization of schooling in the form of national goals, national tests, national teaching licenses, school-to-work plans, and the rest of the utopian package which accompanies these. Schooling must be desystematized, the system must be put to death. Adam Smith has correctly instructed us for more than two centuries now that the wealth of nations is the product of freedom, not of tutelage. The connection between the corporate economy, national politics, and schooling is a disease of collectivism which must be broken if children are to become sovereign, creative adults, capable of lifting a free society to unimaginable heights. The rational management model has damaged the roots of a free society and the free market it claims to defend.

What has happened in our schools was foreseen long ago by Jefferson. We have been recolonized silently in a second American Revolution. Time to take our script from this country's revolutionary start, time to renew traditional hostility toward hierarchy and tutelage. We became a unique nation from the bottom up, that is the only way to rebuild a worthy concept of education.

Prologue

Bianca, You Animal, Shut Up!

Our problem in understanding forced schooling stems from an inconvenient fact: that what wrong it does from a human perspective is right from a systems perspective. You can see this in the case of six-year-old Bianca, who came to my attention because an assistant principal screamed at her in front of an assembly, "BIANCA, YOU ANIMAL, SHUT UP!" Like the wail of a banshee, this sang the school doom of Bianca. Even though her body continued to shuffle around, the voodoo had poisoned her.

Do I make too much of this simple act of putting a little girl in her place? It must happen thousands of times everyday in schools all over. I've seen it many times; if I were painfully honest I'd admit to *doing* it many times. Schools are *supposed* to teach kids their place. That's why we have graded classes. In any case it wasn't your own little Janey or mine.

Most of us tacitly accept the pragmatic terms of public school which allow every kind of psychic violence to be inflicted on Bianca in order to fulfill the prime directive of the system: putting children in their place. It's called "social efficiency." But I get this precognition, this flash-forward to a moment far in the future when your little girl, having left her comfortable home, wakes up to a world where Bianca is her enraged meter maid, or the passport clerk Jane counts on for her emergency ticket out of the country, or the strange lady who lives next door.

I picture this animal Bianca grown large and mean, the same Bianca who didn't go to school for a month after her little friends took to whispering, "Bianca is an animal. Bianca is an animal," while Bianca, only seconds earlier a human being like themselves, sat choking back tears, struggling her way through a reading selection by guessing what the words meant.

In my dream I see this fiend manufactured by schooling regarding Janey as a vehicle for vengeance. In a transport of passion she:

1) Gives Jane's car a ticket before the meter runs out.
2) Throws away Jane's passport application after Jane leaves the office.

3) Plays heavy metal music through the thin partition which separates Bianca's apartment from Jane's while Jane pounds frantically on the wall for relief.
4) All the above.

You aren't compelled to loan your car to anyone who wants it, but you are compelled to surrender your school-age child to strangers who process children for a livelihood, even though one in every nine schoolchildren is terrified of physical harm happening to them in school, terrified with good cause; about 33 are murdered there every year.[1] Your great-great-grandmother didn't have to surrender her children. What happened?

If I demanded you give up your television to an anonymous, itinerant repairman who needed work you'd think I was crazy; if I came with a policeman who forced you to pay that repairman even after he broke your set—you would be outraged. Why are you so docile when you give up your child to a government agent called a schoolteacher?

I want to open up concealed aspects of modern schooling such as the deterioration it forces in the morality of parenting. You have no say at all in choosing your teachers. You know nothing about their backgrounds or families. And the state knows little more than you do. This is as radical a piece of social engineering as the human imagination can conceive. What does it mean?

One thing you do know is how unlikely it will be for any teacher to understand the personality of your particular child or anything significant about your family, culture, religion, plans, hopes, dreams. In the confusion of school affairs even teachers so disposed don't have opportunity to know those things. How did this happen?

Before you hire a company to build a home you would, I expect, insist on detailed plans showing what the finished structure was going to look like. Building a child's mind and character is what public schools do, their justification for prematurely breaking family and neighborhood learning. Where is documentary evidence to prove this assumption that trained and certified professionals do it better than people who know and love them can? There isn't any.

The cost in New York State for building a well-schooled child in the year 2000 is $200,000 per body when lost interest is calculated. That capital sum invested in the child's name over the past twelve years would have delivered a million dollars to each kid as a nest egg to compensate for having no school. The original $200,000 is more than the average home in New York costs. You wouldn't build a home without some idea what it would look like when finished, but you are compelled to let a corps of perfect strangers tinker with your child's mind and personality without the foggiest idea what they want to do with it.

Law courts and legislatures have totally absolved school people from liability. You can sue a doctor for malpractice, not a schoolteacher. Every homebuilder is accountable to customers years after the home is built; not schoolteachers, though. You can't sue a priest, minister, or rabbi either; that should be a clue.

If you can't be guaranteed even minimal results by these institutions, not even physical safety; if you can't be guaranteed *anything* except that you'll be arrested if you fail to surrender your kid, just what does the *public* in public schools mean?

---

[1] From 1992 through 1999, 262 children were murdered in school.

What exactly is public about public schools? That's a question to take seriously. If schools were public as libraries, parks, and swimming pools are public, as highways and sidewalks are public, then the public would be satisfied with them most of the time. Instead, a situation of constant dissatisfaction has spanned many decades. Only in Orwell's "Newspeak" as perfected by legendary spin doctors of the twentieth century such as Ed Bernays or Ivy Lee, or by great advertising combines, is there anything public about public schools. That's been the case for about 40 years.

I Quit, I Think

In the first year of the last decade of the twentieth century during my thirtieth year as a school teacher in Community School District 3, Manhattan, after teaching in all five secondary schools in the district, crossing swords with one professional administration after another as they strove to rid themselves of me, after having my license suspended twice for insubordination and terminated covertly once while I was on medical leave of absence, after the City University of New York borrowed me for a five-year stint as a lecturer in the Education Department (and the faculty rating handbook published by the Student Council gave me the highest ratings in the department my last three years), after planning and bringing about the most successful permanent school fund-raiser in New York City history, after placing a single eighth grade class into 30,000 hours of volunteer community service, after organizing and financing a student-run food cooperative, after securing over a thousand apprenticeships, directing the collection of tens of thousands of books for the construction of private student libraries, after producing four talking job dictionaries for the blind, writing two original student musicals, and launching an armada of other initiatives to reintegrate students within a larger human reality, I quit.

I was New York State Teacher of the Year when it happened. An accumulation of disgust and frustration which grew too heavy to be borne finally did me in. To test my resolve I sent a short essay to *The Wall Street Journal* titled, "I Quit, I Think." In it I explained my reasons for deciding to wrap it up even though I had no savings and not the slightest idea what else I might do in my mid-fifties to pay the rent. In its entirety it read like this:

Government schooling is the most radical adventure in history. It kills the family by monopolizing the best times of childhood and by teaching disrespect for home and parents. The whole blueprint of school procedure is Egyptian, not Greek or Roman. It grows from the theological idea that human value is a scarce thing, represented symbolically by the narrow peak of a pyramid.

That idea passed into American history through the Puritans. It found its "scientific" presentation in the bell curve, along which talent supposedly apportions itself by some Iron Law of Biology. It's a religious notion, School is its church. I offer rituals to keep heresy at bay. I provide documentation to justify the heavenly pyramid.

Socrates foresaw if teaching became a formal profession, something like this would happen. Professional interest is served by making what is easy to do seem hard; by subordinating the laity to the priesthood. School is too vital a jobs-project, contract giver and protector of the social order to allow itself to be "re-formed." It has political allies to guard its marches, that's why reforms come and go without changing much. Even reformers can't imagine school much different.

David learns to read at age four; Rachel, at age nine: In normal development, when both are 13, you can't tell which one learned first—the five-year spread means nothing at all. But in school I label Rachel "learning disabled" and slow David down a bit, too. For a paycheck, I adjust David to depend on me to tell him when to go and stop. He won't outgrow that dependency. I identify Rachel as discount merchandise, "special education" fodder. She'll be locked in her place forever.

In 30 years of teaching kids rich and poor I almost never met a learning disabled child; hardly ever met a gifted and talented one either. Like all school categories, these are sacred myths, created by human imagination. They derive from questionable values we never examine because they preserve the temple of schooling.

That's the secret behind short-answer tests, bells, uniform time blocks, age grading, standardization, and all the rest of the school religion punishing our nation. There isn't a right way to become educated; there are as many ways as fingerprints. We don't need state-certified teachers to make education happen—that probably guarantees it won't.

How much more evidence is necessary? Good schools don't need more money or a longer year; they need real free-market choices, variety that speaks to every need and runs risks. We don't need a national curriculum or national testing either. Both initiatives arise from ignorance of how people learn or deliberate indifference to it. I can't teach this way any longer. If you hear of a job where I don't have to hurt kids to make a living, let me know. Come fall I'll be looking for work.

The New Individualism

The little essay went off in March and I forgot it. Somewhere along the way I must have gotten a note saying it would be published at the editor's discretion, but if so, it was quickly forgotten in the press of turbulent feelings that accompanied my own internal struggle. Finally, on July 5, 1991, I swallowed hard and quit. Twenty days later the *Journal* published the piece. A week later I was studying invitations to speak at NASA Space Center, the Western White House, the Nashville Center for the Arts, Columbia Graduate Business School, the Colorado Librarian's Convention, Apple Computer, and the financial control board of United Technologies Corporation. Eight years later, still enveloped in the orbit of compulsion schooling, I had spoken 700 times in 50 states and seven foreign countries. I had no agent and never advertised, but a lot of people made an effort to find me just the same.

My hunch is it wasn't so much what I was saying that kept the lecture round unfolding, but that a teacher was speaking out at all and the curious fact that I represented nobody except myself.

In the great school debate, this is unheard of. Every single voice allowed regular access to the national podium is the mouthpiece of some association, corporation, university, agency, or institutionalized cause. The poles of debate blocked out by these ritualized, figurehead voices are extremely narrow. Each has a stake in continuing forced schooling much as it is.

As I traveled, I discovered a universal hunger, often unvoiced, to be free of managed debate. A desire to be given untainted information. Nobody seemed to have any maps where this thing had come from or why it acted as it did, but the ability to smell a rat was alive and well all over America.

Exactly what John Dewey heralded at the onset of the twentieth century has indeed happened, our once highly individualized nation has evolved into a centrally managed village, an agora made up of huge special interests which regard individual voices as irrelevant. The masquerade is managed by having collective agencies speak through particular human beings. Dewey said this would mark a great advance in human affairs, but the net effect is to reduce men and women to the status of functions in whatever sub-system they are placed. Public opinion is turned on and off in laboratory fashion. All this in the name of social efficiency, one of the two main goals of forced schooling.

Dewey called this transformation "the new individualism." When I stepped into the job of schoolteacher in 1961, the new individualism was sitting in the driver's seat all over urban America, a far cry from my own school days on the Monongahela when the Lone Ranger and not Sesame Street was our nation's teacher, and school things weren't nearly so oppressive. But gradually they became something else in that euphoria after WWII when easy money, easy travel, and easy laughs provided by the new non-stop theater, television, masked a deliberate conversion of formal education into an instrument of the leviathan state. Who made that happen and why is part of the story I have to tell.

School As Religion

Nothing about school is what it seems, not even boredom. To show you what I mean is the burden of this long essay. My book represents a try at arranging my own thoughts in order to figure out what 50 years of classroom confinement (as student and teacher) add up to for me. You'll encounter a great deal of speculative history here. This is a personal investigation of why school is a dangerous place. It's not so much that anyone there sets out to hurt children; more that all of us associated with the institution are stuck like flies in the same great web your kids are. We buzz frantically to cover our own panic but have little power to help smaller flies.

Looking backward on a 30-year teaching career full of rewards and prizes, somehow I can't completely believe that I spent my time on earth institutionalized; I can't believe that centralized schooling is allowed to exist at all as a gigantic indoctrination and sorting machine, robbing people of their children. Did it really happen? Was this my life? God help me.

School is a religion. Without understanding the holy mission aspect you're certain to misperceive what takes place as a result of human stupidity or venality or even class warfare. All are present in the equation, it's just that none of these matter very much—even without them school would move in the same direction. Dewey's *Pedagogic Creed* statement of 1897 gives you a clue to the zeitgeist:

Every teacher should realize he is a social servant set apart for the maintenance
of the proper social order and the securing of the right social growth. In this way
the teacher is always the prophet of the true God and the usherer in of the true
kingdom of heaven.

What is "proper" social order? What does "right" social growth look like? If you don't know you're
like me, not like John Dewey who did, or John D. Rockefeller, his patron, who did, too.

Somehow out of the industrial confusion which followed the Civil War, powerful men and
dreamers became certain what kind of social order America needed. This realization didn't arise as
a product of public debate as it should have in a democracy, but as a distillation of private
discussion. Their ideas contradicted the original American charter but that didn't disturb them. They
had a stupendous goal in mind—the rationalization of everything. The end of unpredictable history
and its transformation into something orderly.

From mid-century onwards certain utopian schemes to retard maturity in the interests of a
greater good were put into play, following roughly the blueprint Rousseau laid down in the book
Emile. At least rhetorically. The first goal, to be reached in stages, was an orderly, scientifically
managed society, one in which the best people would make the decisions, unhampered by democratic
tradition. After that, human breeding, the evolutionary destiny of the species, would be in reach.
Universal institutionalized formal forced schooling was the prescription, extending the dependency
of the young well into what had traditionally been early adult life. Individuals would be prevented
from taking up important work until a relatively advanced age. Maturity was to be inhibited.

During the post-Civil War period, childhood was extended about four years. Later, a special
label was created to describe very old children. It was called *adolescence*, a phenomenon hitherto
unknown to the human race. The infantilization of young people didn't stop at the beginning of the
twentieth century; child labor laws were extended to cover more and more kinds of work, the age
of school leaving set higher and higher. The greatest victory for this utopian project was making
school the only avenue to certain occupations. The intention was ultimately to draw all work into the
school net. By the 1950s it wasn't unusual to find graduate students well into their 30s, running
errands, waiting to start their lives.

He Was Square Inside And Brown

Barbara Whiteside showed me a poem written by a high school senior in Alton, Illinois, two
weeks before he committed suicide:

> He drew... the things inside that needed saying.
> Beautiful pictures he kept under his pillow.
> When he started school he brought them...
> To have along like a friend.
>
> It was funny about school, he sat at a square brown desk
> Like all the other square brown desks... and his room

Was a square brown room like all the other rooms, tight
And close and stiff.
He hated to hold the pencil and chalk, his arms stiff
His feet flat on the floor, stiff, the teacher watching
And watching. She told him to wear a tie like
All the other boys, he said he didn't like them.
She said it didn't matter what he liked. After that the class drew.
He drew all yellow. It was the way he felt about
Morning. The Teacher came and smiled, "What's this?
Why don't you draw something like Ken's drawing?"
After that his mother bought him a tie, and he always
Drew airplanes and rocketships like everyone else.
He was square inside and brown and his hands were stiff.
The things inside that needed saying didn't need it
Anymore, they had stopped pushing... crushed, stiff
Like everything else.

After I spoke in Nashville, a mother named Debbie pressed a handwritten note on me which I read on the airplane to Binghamton, N.Y.:

We started to see Brandon flounder in the first grade, hives, depression, he died every night after he asked his father, "Is tomorrow school, too?" In second grade the physical stress became apparent. The teacher pronounced his problem Attention Deficit Syndrome. My happy, bouncy child was now looked at as a medical problem, by us as well as the school.

A doctor, a psychiatrist, and a school authority all determined he did have this affliction. Medication was stressed along with behavior modification. If it was suspected that Brandon had not been medicated he was sent home. My square peg needed a bit of whittling to fit their round hole, it seemed.

I cried as I watched my parenting choices stripped away. My ignorance of options allowed Brandon to be medicated through second grade. The tears and hives continued another full year until I couldn't stand it. I began to homeschool Brandon. It was his salvation. No more pills, tears, or hives. He is thriving. He never cries now and does his work eagerly.

The New Dumbness

Ordinary people send their children to school to get smart, but what modern schooling teaches is dumbness. It's a religious idea gone out of control. You don't have to accept that, though, to realize this kind of economy is put in danger by too many smart people who understand too much.

I won't ask you to take that on faith. Be patient. I'll let a famous American publisher explain to you the secret of our global financial success in just a little while. Be patient.

Old-fashioned dumbness used to be simple ignorance, now it is transformed from ignorance; into permanent mathematical categories of relative stupidity like "gifted and talented," "mainstream," "special ed." Categories in which learning is rationed for the good of a system of order. Dumb people are no longer merely ignorant. Now they are indoctrinated, their minds conditioned with substantial doses of commercially prepared disinformation dispensed for tranquilizing purposes.

Jacques Ellul, whose essay *Propaganda* is a reflection on the phenomenon, warned us that prosperous children are more susceptible than others to the effects of schooling because they are promised more lifelong comfort and security for yielding wholly:

> Critical judgment disappears altogether, for in no way can there ever be
> *collective* critical judgment....The individual can no longer judge for himself
> because he inescapably relates his thoughts to the entire complex of values
> and prejudices established by propaganda. With regard to political situations,
> he is given ready-made value judgments invested with the power of the truth
> by...the word of experts.

The new dumbness is particularly deadly to middle and upper-middle class kids already made shallow by multiple pressures to conform imposed by the outside world on their usually lightly rooted parents. When they come of age, they are certain they must know something because their degrees and licenses say they do. They remain so convinced until an unexpectedly brutal divorce, a corporate downsizing in mid-life, or panic attacks of meaninglessness manage to upset the precarious balance of their incomplete humanity, their stillborn adult lives. Alan Bullock, the English historian, said Evil was a state of incompetence. If true, our school adventure has filled the twentieth century with evil.

Ellul puts it this way:

> The individual has no chance to exercise his judgement either on principal
> questions or on their implication; this leads to the atrophy of a faculty not
> comfortably exercised under [the best of] conditions....Once personal judgment
> and critical faculties have disappeared or have atrophied, they will not simply
> reappear when propaganda is suppressed...years of intellectual and spiritual
> education would be needed to restore such faculties. The propagandee, if
> deprived of one propaganda, will immediately adopt another, this will spare him
> the agony of finding himself *vis a vis* some event without a ready-made opinion.

Once the best children are broken to such a system they disintegrate morally, becoming dependent on group approval. A National Merit Scholar in my own family once wrote that her dream was to be "a small part in a great machine." It broke my heart. What kids dumbed down by schooling can't do is to think for themselves or ever be at rest very long without feeling crazy; stupefied boys and girls reveal dependence in many ways easily exploitable by their knowledgeable elders.

According to all official analysis, dumbness isn't *taught* (as I claim), but is *innate* in a great percentage of what has come to be called "the workforce." *Workforce* itself is a term that should tell you much about the mind that governs modern society. According to official reports, only a small fraction of the population is capable of what you and I call mental life: creative thought, analytical thought, judgmental thought, a trio occupying the three highest positions on Bloom's *Taxonomy of Educational Objectives*. Just how small a fraction would shock you. According to experts, the bulk of the mob is hopelessly dumb, even dangerously so. Perhaps you're a willing accomplice to this social coup which revived the English class system. Certainly you are if your own child has been rewarded with a "gifted and talented" label by your local school. This is what Dewey means by "proper" social order.

If you believe nothing can be done for the dumb except kindness, because it's biology (the bell-curve model); if you believe capitalist oppressors have ruined the dumb because they are bad people (the neo-Marxist model), if you believe dumbness reflects depraved moral fiber (the Calvinist model), or that it's nature's way of disqualifying boobies from the reproduction sweepstakes (the Darwinian model), or nature's way of providing someone to clean your toilet (the pragmatic elitist model), or that it's evidence of bad karma (the Buddhist model), if you believe any of the various explanations given for the position of the dumb in the social order we have, then you will be forced to concur *that a vast bureaucracy is indeed necessary to address the dumb*. Otherwise they would murder us in our beds.

The shocking possibility that dumb people don't exist in sufficient numbers to warrant the careers devoted to tending to them will seem incredible to you. Yet that is my proposition: Mass dumbness first had to be imagined, it isn't real.

Once the dumb are wished into existence, they serve valuable functions: as a danger to themselves and others they have to be watched, classified, disciplined, trained, medicated, sterilized, ghettoized, cajoled, coerced, jailed. To idealists they represent a challenge, reprobates to be made socially useful. Either way you want it, hundreds of millions of perpetual children require paid attention from millions of adult custodians. An ignorant horde to be schooled one way or another.

Putting Pedagogy To The Question

More than anything else, this book is a work of intuition. The official story of why we school doesn't add up today any more than it did yesterday. A few years before I quit, I began to try to piece together where this school project came from, why it took the shape it took, and why every attempt to change it has ended in abysmal failure.

By now I've invested the better part of a decade looking for answers. If you want a conventional history of schooling, or education as it is carelessly called, you better stop reading now. Although years of research in the most arcane sources are reflected here, throughout it's mainly intuition that drives my synthesis.

This is in part a private narrative, the map of a schoolteacher's mind as it tracked strands in the web in which it had been wrapped; in part a public narrative, an account of the latest chapter in an ancient war: the conflict between systems which offer physical safety and certainty at the cost of suppressing free will, and those which offer liberty at the price of constant risk. If you keep both plots in mind, no matter how far afield my book seems to range, you won't wonder what a chapter on coal or one on private hereditary societies has to do with schoolchildren.

What I'm most determined to do is start a conversation among those who've been silent up until now, and that includes schoolteachers. We need to put sterile discussions of grading and testing, discipline, curriculum, multiculturalism and tracking aside as distractions, as mere symptoms of something larger, darker, and more intransigent than any problem a problem-solver could tackle next week. Talking endlessly about such things encourages the bureaucratic tactic of talking around the vital, messy stuff. In partial compensation for your effort, I promise you'll discover what's in the mind of a man who spent his life in a room with children.

Give an ear then to what follows. We shall cross-examine history together. We shall put pedagogy to the question. And if the judgment following this *auto da fe* is that only pain can make this monster relax its grip, let us pray together for the courage to inflict it.

Reading my essay will help you sort things out. It will give you a different topological map upon which to fix your own position. No doubt I've made some factual mistakes, but essays since Montaigne have been about locating truth, not about assembling facts. Truth and fact aren't the same thing. My essay is meant to mark out crudely some ground for a scholarship of schooling, my intention is that you not continue to regard the official project of education through an older, traditional perspective, but to see it as a frightening chapter in the administrative organization of knowledge—a text we must vigorously repudiate as our ancestors once did. We live together, you and I, in a dark time when all official history is propaganda. If you want truth, you have to struggle for it. This is my struggle. Let me bear witness to what I have seen.

Author's Note

With conspiracy so close to the surface of the American imagination and American reality, I can only approach with trepidation the task of discouraging you in advance from thinking my book the chronicle of some vast diabolical conspiracy to seize all our children for the personal ends of a small, elite minority.

Don't get me wrong, American schooling has been replete with chicanery from its very beginnings[2], indeed it isn't difficult to find various conspirators *boasting* in public about what they pulled off. But if you take that tack you'll miss the real horror of what I'm trying to describe, that what has happened to our schools was inherent in the original design for a planned economy and a planned society laid down so proudly at the end of the nineteenth century. I think what happened

---

[2] For instance, school superintendents *as a class* are virtually the stupidest people to pass through a graduate college program, ranking 51 points below the elementary school teachers they normally "supervise," (on the Graduate Record Examination), and about 80 points below secondary-school teachers; while teachers themselves as an aggregate finish seventeenth of twenty occupational groups surveyed. The reader is of course at liberty to believe this happened accidentally, or that the moon is composed of blue, not green, cheese as is popularly believed.

would have happened anyway—without the legions of venal, half-mad men and women who schemed so hard to make it as it is. If I'm correct, we're in a much worse position than we would be if we were merely victims of an evil genius or two.

If you obsess about conspiracy, what you'll fail to see is that we are held fast by a form of highly abstract thinking fully concretized in human institutions which has grown beyond the power of the managers of these institutions to control. If there is a way out of the trap we're in, it won't be by removing some bad guys and replacing them with good guys.

Who are the villains, really, but ourselves? People can change, but systems cannot without losing their structural integrity. Even Henry Ford, a Jew-baiter of such colossal proportions he was lionized by Adolf Hitler in *Mein Kampf*, made a public apology and denied to his death bed he had ever intended to hurt Jews—a too strict interpretation of Darwin made him do it! The great industrialists who gave us modern compulsion schooling inevitably found their own principles subordinated to systems-purposes, just as happened to the rest of us.

Take Andrew Carnegie, the bobbin boy, who would certainly have been as appalled as the rest of us at the order to fire on strikers at his Homestead plant. But the system he helped to create was committed to pushing men until they reacted violently or dropped dead. It was called "the Iron Law of wages." Once his colleagues were interested in the principles of the Iron Law, they could only see the courage and defiance of the Homestead strikers as an opportunity to provoke a crisis which would allow the steel union to be broken with state militia and public funds. Crushing opposition is the obligatory scene in the industrial drama, whatever it takes, and no matter how much individual industrial leaders like Carnegie might be reluctant to do so.

My worry was about finding a prominent ally to help me present this idea that inhuman anthropology is what we confront in our institutional schools, not conspiracy. The hunt paid off with the discovery of an analysis of the Ludlow Massacre by Walter Lippmann in the *New Republic* of January 30, 1915. Following the Rockefeller slaughter of up to 47, mostly women and children in the tent camp of striking miners at Ludlow, Colorado, a Congressional investigation was held which put John D. Rockefeller Jr. on the defensive. Rockefeller agents had employed armored cars, machine guns, and fire bombs in his name. As Lippmann tells it, Rockefeller was charged with having the only authority to authorize such a massacre, but also with too much indifference to what his underlings were up to. "Clearly," said the industrial magnate, "both cannot be true."

As Lippmann recognized, this paradox is the worm at the core of all colossal power. *Both indeed could be true.* For ten years Rockefeller hadn't even seen this property; what he knew of it came in reports from his managers he scarcely could have read along with mountains of similar reports coming to his desk each day. He was compelled to rely on the word of others. Drawing an analogy between Rockefeller and the czar of Russia, Lippmann wrote that nobody believed the czar himself performed the many despotic acts he was accused of; everyone knew a bureaucracy did so in his name. But most failed to push that knowledge to its inevitable conclusion: If the czar tried to change what was customary he would be undermined by his subordinates. He had no defense against this happening because it was in the best interests of all the divisions of the bureaucracy, including the army, that it—not the czar—continue to be in charge of things. The czar was a prisoner of his own subjects. In Lippmann's words:

> This seemed to be the predicament of Mr. Rockefeller. I should not believe he
> personally hired thugs or wanted them hired. It seems far more true to say that

his impersonal and half-understood power has delegated itself into unsocial forms, that it has assumed a life of its own which he is almost powerless to control....His intellectual helplessness was the amazing part of his testimony. Here was a man who represented wealth probably without parallel in history, the successor to a father who has, with justice, been called the high priest of capitalism....Yet he talked about himself on the commonplace moral assumptions of a small businessman.

The Rockefeller Foundation has been instrumental through the century just passed (along with a few others) in giving us the schools we have. It imported the German research model into college life, elevated service to business and government as the goal of higher education, not teaching. And Rockefeller-financed University of Chicago and Columbia Teachers College have been among the most energetic actors in the lower school tragedy. There is more, too, but none of it means the Rockefeller family "master-minded" the school institution, or even that his foundation or his colleges did. All became in time submerged in the system they did so much to create, almost helpless to slow its momentum even had they so desired.

Despite its title, *Underground History* isn't a history proper, but a collection of materials toward a history, embedded in a personal essay analyzing why mass compulsion schooling is unreformable. The history I have unearthed is important to our understanding; it's a good start, I believe, but much remains undone. The burden of an essay is to reveal its author so candidly and thoroughly that the reader comes fully awake. You are about to spend 25-30 hours with the mind of a schoolteacher, but the relationship we should have isn't one of teacher to pupil but rather that of two people in conversation. I'll offer ideas and a theory to explain things and you bring your own experience to bear on the matters, supplementing and arguing where necessary. Read with this goal before you and I promise your money's worth. It isn't important whether we agree on every detail.

A brief word on sources. I've identified all quotations and paraphrases and given the origin of many (not all) individual facts, but for fear the forest be lost in contemplation of too many trees, I've avoided extensive footnoting. So much here is my personal take on things that it seemed dishonest to grab you by the lapels that way: of minor value to those who already resonate on the wavelength of the book, useless, even maddening, to those who do not.

This is a workshop of solutions as well as an attempt to frame the problem clearly, but be warned: they are perversely sprinkled around like raisins in a pudding, nowhere grouped neatly as if to help you study for a test—except for a short list at the very end. The advice there is practical, but strictly limited to the world of compulsion schooling as it currently exists, not to the greater goal of understanding how education occurs or is prevented. The best advice in this book is scattered throughout and indirect, you'll have to work to extract it. It begins with the very first sentence of the book where I remind you that what is right for systems is often wrong for human beings. Translated into a recommendation, that means that to avoid the revenge of Bianca, we must be prepared to insult systems for the convenience of humanity, not the other way around.

PART ONE

Of Schooling,
Education,
And Myself

Public education as it was in the late nineteenth century and is now has not grown from known seventeenth century seeds; it was a new and unexpected genus whose ultimate character could not have been predicted, and whose emergence troubled well-disposed, high-minded people.

— Bernard Bailyn

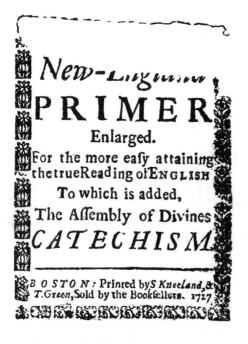

CHAPTER ONE

The Way

It Used To Be

Whoever controls the image and information of the past determines what and how future generations will think; whoever controls the information and images of the present determines how those same people will view the past.[1]

— George Orwell, *1984* (1949)

Take at hazard one hundred children of several educated generations and one hundred uneducated children of the people and compare them in anything you please; in strength, in agility, in mind, in the ability to acquire knowledge, even in morality—and in all respects you are startled by the vast superiority on the side of the children of the uneducated.

— Count Leo Tolstoy, "Education and Children" (1862)

A Nation From The Bottom Up

***ESTABLISHING SHOT*:**

Fifty children of different ages are teaching each other while the schoolmaster hears lessons at his desk from older students. An air of quiet activity fills the room. A wood stove crackles in the corner. What drove the nineteenth century school world celebrated in Edward Eggleston's classic, *The Hoosier Schoolmaster*, was a society rich with concepts like duty, hard work, responsibility, and self-reliance; a society overwhelmingly local in orientation although never so provincial it couldn't be fascinated by the foreign and exotic. But when tent Chautauqua with its fanfare about modern marvels left town, conversation readily returned to the text of local society.

---

[1] This is Toynbee's paraphrase of Orwell's "Who controls the past controls the future; who controls the present controls the past."

Eggleston's America was a special place in modern history, one where the society was more central than the national political state. Words can't adequately convey the stupendous radicalism hidden in our quiet villages, a belief that ordinary people have a right to govern themselves. A confidence that they can.

Most revolutionary of all was the conviction that personal rights can only be honored when the political state is kept weak. In the classical dichotomy between liberty and subordination written into our imagination by Locke and Hobbes in the seventeenth century, America struggled down the libertarian road of Locke for awhile while her three godfather nations, England, Germany, and France, followed Hobbes and established leviathan states through the eighteenth and nineteenth centuries. Toward the end, America began to follow the Old World's lead.

For Hobbes, social order depended upon state control of the inner life, a degree of mental colonization unknown to the tyrants of history whose principal concern had been controlling the *bodies* of their subjects. But the sheer size of an America without national roads or electronic networks ensured that liberty would be nurtured outside the ring of government surveillance. Then, too, many Americans came out of the dissenting religious sects of England, independent congregations which rejected church/state partnerships. The bulk of our population was socially suspect anyway, even our gentry was second and third string by English standards, gentlemen without inheritances, the rest a raggle-taggle band of wastrels, criminals, shanghaied boys, poor yeomanry, displaced peasants.

Benet, the poet, describes our founding stock:

> The disavouched, hard-bitten pack
> Shipped overseas to steal a continent
> with neither shirts nor honor to their back.

George Bernanos in *Last Essays* observes that America, unlike other nations, was built from the bottom up. Francis Parkman made the same observation a century earlier. What America violently rejected in its early republic was the Anglican "Homily On Obedience" set down by English established-church doctrine in the Tudor state of 1562, a doctrine likening order in Heaven with the English social order on Earth—fixed and immutable:

> The sun, moon, stars, rainbows, thunder, lightning, clouds, and all the birds
> of the air do keep their order. The earth, trees, seeds, plants, herbs, corn,
> grass, and all manner of beasts keep themselves in order.... Every degree of
> people in their vocations, callings and office has appointed to them their duty
> and order.

The theological utopia such a principle moves toward was well established in the Britain of the German Georges by 1776 as well as in the three North German states of Prussia, Saxony, and Hanover, all to play an important role along with England in twentieth century American forced schooling. The same divine clock, superficially secularized, was marking time in the interlude of Enlightenment France, the pre-revolutionary utopia which potently affected American school thought also. Hobbes and his doctrine of mental colonization eclipsed Locke everywhere else, but not in America.

You Had To Do It Yourself

CUT TO:

Abe Lincoln, by the fireplace in a log house. "An American," Francis Grund remarked in 1837, "is almost from his cradle brought up to reflect on his condition and from the time he is able to act, employed with the means of improving it."

Lincoln, hardly a slouch as writer, speaker, or thinker, packed 50 weeks of formal schooling into his entire life over the twelve-year period 1814 to 1826. Even that little seemed a waste to his relatives. Unless you want to argue that those few weeks made a decisive difference to Abe, we need to look elsewhere for his education. Clifton Johnson thinks it happened this way:

> He acquired much of his early education at home. In the evening he would pile sticks of dry wood into the brick fireplace. These would blaze up brightly and shed a strong light over the room, and the boy would lie down flat on the floor before the hearth with his book in front of him. He used to write his arithmetic sums on a large wooden shovel with a piece of charcoal. After covering it all over with examples, he would take his jack-knife and whittle and scrape the surface clean, ready for more ciphering. Paper was expensive and he could not afford a slate. Sometimes when the shovel was not at hand he did his figuring on the logs of the house walls and on the doorposts, and other woodwork that afforded a surface he could mark on with his charcoal.

In Lincoln's Illinois and Kentucky, only reading, writing, and ciphering "to the Rule of Three" were required of teachers, but in New England the business often attracted ambitious young men like Noah Webster, confident and energetic, merely pausing on their way to greater things. Adam Gurowski, mid-nineteenth century traveler in our land, took special notice of the superiority of American teachers. Their European brethren were, he said, "withered drifters" or "narrowed martinets."

Young people in America were expected to make something of themselves, not to prepare themselves to fit into a pre-established hierarchy. Every foreign commentator notes the early training in independence, the remarkable precocity of American young, their assumption of adult responsibility. Tom Nichols, a New Hampshire schoolboy in the 1820s, recalls in his memoir how electrifying the air of expectation was in early American schools:

> Our teachers constantly stimulated us by the glittering prizes of wealth, honors, offices, and distinctions, which were certainly within our reach—there were a hundred avenues to wealth and fame opening fair before us if we only chose to learn our lessons.

Overproduction, overcapacity, would have been an alien concept to that America, something redolent of British mercantilism. Our virgin soil and forests undermined the stern doctrine of Calvinism by paying dividends to anyone willing to work. As Calvinism waned, contrarian attitudes emerged which represented a new American religion. First, the conviction that opportunity was available to all; second, that failure was the result of defective character, not predetermination or bad placement on a biological bell curve.

Character flaws could be remedied, *but only from inside*. You had to do it yourself by courage, determination, honesty, and hard work. Don't discount this as hot air; it marks a critical difference between Americans and everyone else. Teachers had a place in this process of self-creation, but it was an ambiguous one: anyone could teach, it was thought, just as anyone could self-teach. Secular schools, always a peripheral institution, were viewed with ambivalence, although teachers were granted some value—if only gratitude for giving mother a break. In the southern and middle colonies, teachers were often convicts serving out their sentences, their place in the social order caught in this advertisement of Washington's day:

> RAN AWAY. A servant man who followed the occupation of Schoolmaster.
> Much given to drinking and gambling.

Washington's own schoolmaster, "Hobby," was just such a bondsman. Tradition has it he laid the foundation for national greatness by whipping the devil out of Washington.

Whipping and humiliation seem to have always been an eternal staple of schooling. Evidence survives from ancient Rome, Montaigne's France, Washington's Virginia—or my own high school in western Pennsylvania in the 1950s, where the teacher's personalized paddle hung prominently at the entrance to many a classroom, not for decoration but for use. The football coach, and, if I recall correctly, the algebra teacher, had paddles electrified by addition of a dry cell battery with which to prod the recalcitrant.

Something in the structure of schooling calls forth violence. While latter-day schools don't allow energetic physical discipline, certainly they are state-of-the-art laboratories in humiliation, as your own experience should remind you. In my first years of teaching I was told over and over that humiliation was my best friend, more effective than whipping. I witnessed this theory in practice through my time as a teacher. If you were to ask me now whether physical or psychological violence does more damage I would reply that slurs, aspersion, formal ranking, insult, and inference are far and away the more deadly. Nor does law protect the tongue-lashed.

Early schools in America were quick with cuff or cane, but local standards demanded fairness. Despotic teachers were often quarry themselves, as Washington Irving's "Legend of Sleepy Hollow" warns us. Listen to the fate of schoolmaster Thomas Beveridge at the hands of the upperclass Latin School in Philadelphia eleven years before the Revolution:

> He arrives, enters the school, and is permitted to proceed until he is supposed
> to have nearly reached his chair at the upper end of the room, when instantly
> the door, and every window shutter is closed. Now shrouded in utter darkness
> the most hideous yells that can be conceived are sent forth from three score of
> throats; and Ovids and Virgils and Horaces, together with the more heavy metal
> of dictionaries, are hurled without remorse at the astonished preceptor, who,
> groping and crawling under cover of the forms, makes the best of his way to the
> door. When attained, a light is restored and a death-like silence ensues.

Every boy is at his lesson: No one has had a hand or a voice in the recent atrocity.[2]

In the humbler setting of rural Indiana recreated by Eggleston for *Hoosier Schoolmaster* (1871), we can easily see that passage of more than a century (and the replacement of rich kids by farmer's sons and daughters) hasn't altered classroom dynamics:

> When Ralph looked round on the faces of the scholars—the little faces full of mischief and curiosity, the big faces full of an expression which was not further removed than second-cousin from contempt—when young Hartsook looked into these faces, his heart palpitated with stage fright. There is no audience so hard to face as one of schoolchildren, as many a man has found to his cost.

While Ralph was applying to a trustee of the school committee for this job, a large ugly bulldog sniffed at his heels, causing a young girl to "nearly giggle her head off at the delightful prospect of seeing a new schoolteacher eaten up by the ferocious brute." Weary, discouraged, "shivering with fear," he is lectured:

> You see, we a'n't none of your soft sort in these diggin's. It takes a man to boss this deestrick...if you git licked, don't come to us. Flat Crick don't pay no 'nsurance, you bet! ...it takes grit to apply for this school. The last master had a black eye for a month.

No Limit To Pain For Those Who Allow It

One of the most telling accounts of schooling ever penned comes directly from the lips of a legendary power broker, Colonel Edward Mandel House, one of these grand shadowy figures in American history. House had a great deal to do with America's entry into WWI as a deliberate project to seize German markets in chemicals, armor plate and shipping, an aspect of our bellicosity rarely mentioned in scholastic histories. When peace came, House's behind-the-scenes maneuvering in the League of Nations debacle contributed to its repudiation. His management of President Wilson led to persistent stories that Wilson was little more than a puppet of the Colonel.

In his memoirs, *The Intimate Papers of Colonel House*, we get a glimpse of elite American schooling in the 1870s. House's early years were school-free. He was brought up after the Civil War around Houston, Texas:

> My brother James, six years older than I, was the leader....We all had guns and pistols... there were no childish games excepting those connected with war. [House was nine at the time.] In the evening around the fireside there were told tales of daring deeds that we strove to emulate.... I cannot

---

[2] This incident was memorialized by Beveridge's pupil, Alexander Graydon.

remember the time when I began to ride and to shoot.... I had many narrow
escapes. Twice I came near killing one of my playmates in the reckless use
of firearms. They were our toys and death our playmate.

At the age of fourteen House was sent to school in Virginia. The cruelty of the other boys
made an immense impression on his character, as you can sift from this account:

I made up my mind at the second attempt to haze me that I would not permit it.
I not only had a pistol but a large knife, and with these I held the larger, rougher
boys at bay. There was no limit to the lengths they would go in hazing those
who would allow it. One form I recall was that of going through the pretense of
hanging. They would tie a boy's hands behind him and string him up by the neck
over a limb *until he grew purple in the face*. None of it, however, fell to me. What
was done to those who permitted it is almost beyond belief.

At the Hopkins Grammar School in New Haven at the age of seventeen, during the Hayes-Tilden
campaign of 1876, House began to "hang around" political offices instead of "attending to studies."
He came to be recognized and was given small privileges. When the election had to be ultimately
settled by an Electoral Commission he was allowed to "slip in and out of hearings at will." House
again:

All this was educational in its way, though not the education I was placed in Hopkins
Grammar School to get, and it is no wonder that I lagged at the end of my class. I
had no interest in desk tasks, but I read much and was learning in a larger and more
interesting school.

House's story was written over and over in the short, glorious history of American education
before schooling took over. Young Americans were allowed close to the mechanism of things. This
rough and tumble practice kept social class elastic and American achievement in every practical field
superb.

The Art Of Driving

Now come back to the present while I demonstrate that the identical trust placed in ordinary
people 200 years ago still survives where it suits managers of our economy to allow it. Consider the
art of driving, which I learned at eleven. Without everybody behind the wheel, our sort of economy
would be impossible, so everybody *is* there, IQ notwithstanding. With less than 30 hours of
combined training and experience, a hundred million people are allowed access to vehicular weapons
more lethal than pistols or rifles. Turned loose without a teacher, so to speak. Why are those
shocking acts of trust committed by our government (in comparison to the tight grip imposed on state
near-monopoly schooling)?

An analogy will illustrate just how radical this trust really is. What if I proposed that we hand
three sticks of dynamite and a detonator to anyone who asked for them. All an applicant would need
is money to pay for the explosives. You'd have to be an idiot to agree with my plan—at least based
on the assumptions you picked up in school about human nature and human competence.

And yet gasoline, a spectacularly mischievous explosive, dangerously unstable and with the intriguing characteristic as an assault weapon that it can flow under locked doors and saturate bulletproof clothing, is available to anyone with a container. Five gallons of gasoline has the destructive power of a stick of dynamite.[3] The average tank holds fifteen gallons, yet no background check is necessary for dispenser or dispensee. As long as gasoline is freely available, gun control is beside the point.

Push on. Why do we allow access to a portable substance capable of incinerating houses, torching crowded theaters, or even turning skyscrapers into infernos? We haven't even considered the battering ram aspect of cars—why are novice operators allowed to command a ton of metal capable of hurtling through school crossings at up to two miles a minute? Why do we give the power of life and death this way to everyone?

It should strike you at once that our unstated official assumptions about human nature are dead wrong. Average people *are* competent and responsible; universal motoring proves that. The efficiency of motor vehicles as terrorist instruments would have written a tragic record long ago if people were inclined to terrorism. But almost all auto mishaps are accidents.

I know it's difficult to accept this because the spectre of global terrorism is a favorite cover story of governments, but the truth is substantially different from the tale the public is sold. According to the U.S. State Department, 1995 was a near-record year for terrorist murders; it saw 300 worldwide (200 at the hand of the Tamil Tigers in Sri Lanka) compared to 400,000 cigarette deaths in the U.S. alone. When we consider our assumptions about human nature that keep children in a condition of confinement and limited options, we need to reflect on driving and things like almost non-existent global terrorism.

Notice how quickly people learn to drive well. Early failure is efficiently corrected, usually self-corrected, because the terrific motivation of staying alive and in one piece steers driving improvement. If the grand theories of Comenius and Herbart about learning by incremental revelation, or those lifelong nanny rules of Owens, Maclure, Pestalozzi, and Beatrice Webb, or those calls for precision in human ranking of Thorndike and Hall, or those nuanced interventions of Yale and Columbia Teachers College were actually as essential as their proponents claimed, this libertarian miracle of motoring would be unfathomable.

Now consider the intellectual component of driving. It isn't all just hand-eye-foot coordination. First-time drivers make dozens, no, hundreds, of continuous hypotheses, plans, computations, and fine-tuned judgments every day they drive. They do this skillfully without being graded because if they don't, organic provision exists in the motoring universe to punish them. There isn't any court of appeal from your own stupidity on the road.

I could go on: think of licensing, maintenance, storage, adapting machine and driver to seasons and daily conditions. Carefully analyzed, driving is as impressive a miracle as walking, talking, or reading, but this only shows the inherent weakness of analysis since we know almost everyone learns to drive well in a few hours. The way we used to be as Americans, learning everything, breaking down social class barriers, is the way we might be again without forced schooling. Driving proves that to me.

---

[3] Actually more than that if carefully mixed with air in proper proportions and suitably contained.

Two Approaches To Discipline

Rules of the Stokes County School November 10, 1848
Wm. A. Chaffin, Master

	OFFENSE	*LASHES*
1.	Boys & Girls Playing Together	4
2.	Quarreling	4
3.	Fighting	5
4.	Fighting at School	5
5.	Quarreling at School	3
6.	Gambling or Betting at School	4
7.	Playing at Cards at School	10
8.	Climbing for every foot over three feet up a tree	1
9.	Telling Lies	7
10.	Telling Tales Out of School	8
11.	Nick Naming Each Other	4
12.	Giving Each Other ILL Names	3
13.	Fighting Each Other in Time of Books	2
14.	Swearing at School	8
15.	Blackguarding Each Other	6
16.	For Misbehaving to Girls	10
17.	For Leaving School Without Leave of the Teacher	4
18.	Going Home With Each Other without Leave of Teacher	4
19.	For Drinking Spiritous Liquors at School	8
20.	Making Swings & Swinging on Them	7
21.	For Misbehaving when a Stranger is in the House	6
22.	For Wearing Long Finger Nails	2
23.	For not Making a Bow when a Stranger Comes in	3
24.	Misbehaving to Persons on the Road	4
25.	For not Making a Bow when you Meet a Person	4
26.	For Going to Girl's Play Places	3
27.	For Going to Boy's Play Places	4
28.	Coming to School with Dirty Face and Hands	2
29.	For Calling Each Other Liars	4
30.	For Playing Bandy	10
31.	For Bloting Your Copy Book	2
32.	For Not Making a bow when you go home	4
33.	For Not Making a bow when you come away	4
34.	Wrestling at School	4
35.	Scuffling at School	4
36.	For Weting each Other Washing at Play Time	2
37.	For Hollowing and Hooping Going Home	3

Whatever you might think of this in light of Dr. Spock and Piaget or the Yale Child Study folks, it must be apparent civility was honored and we can be sure nobody ever played Bandy a second time! I've yet to meet a parent in public school who ever stopped to calculate the large, sometimes lifelong price their children pay for the privilege of being rude and ill-mannered at school. I haven't met a public school parent yet who was properly suspicious of the state's endless forgiveness for bad behavior for which the future will be merciless.

At about the same time Master Chaffin was beating the same kind of sense into young tarheels that convict Hobby had beaten into little Washington, Robert Owens, a Scottish industrialist usually given credit for launching utopian socialism, was constructing his two-volume *Life*. This autobiography contains "Ten Rules of Schooling," the first two of which show a liberalization occurring in nineteenth century educational thought:

1st Rule—No scolding or punishment of the Children.

2nd Rule—Unceasing kindness in tone, look, word, and action, to all children without
            exception, by every teacher employed so as to create a real affection and
            full confidence between the teachers and the taught.

The Owenite colony had what we now call a theory of *holistic* schooling as its foundation, Owens was a genuine messiah figure and his colony operated in a part of Indiana which was removed from prying eyes. New Harmony, as it was called, was the center of the transatlantic upperclass world's fascinated attention in its short existence. Yet it fell apart in three years, slightly less time than it took for John Dewey's own Lab School to be wrecked by Owenite principles unmistakably enough to suggest to Dewey it would be the better if he got out of Chicago. And so he did, transferring to Teachers College in Manhattan, where in time, his Lincoln School carried on the psychological traditions of New Harmony before it, too, ultimately failed.

The Schools Of Hellas

Wherever it occurred, schooling through the eighteenth and nineteenth centuries (up until the last third of the nineteenth) heavily invested its hours with language, philosophy, art, and the life of the classical civilizations of Greece and Rome. In the grammar schools of the day, little pure grammar as we understand it existed; they were places of classical learning. Early America rested easily on a foundation of classical understanding, one subversive to the normal standards of English class society. The lessons of antiquity were so vital to the construction of every American institution it's hardly possible to grasp how deep the gulf between then and now is without knowing a little about those lessons. Prepare yourself for a surprise.

For a long time, for instance, classical Athens distributed its most responsible public positions by *lottery*: army generalships, water supply, everything. The implications are awesome— trust in everyone's competence was assumed; it was their version of universal driving. Professionals existed but did not make key decisions; they were only technicians, never well regarded because prevailing opinion held that technicians had enslaved their own minds. Anyone worthy of citizenship was expected to be able to think clearly and to welcome great responsibility. As you reflect on this, remember our own unvoiced assumption that anyone can guide a ton of metal traveling at high speed with three sticks of dynamite sloshing around in its tanks.

When we ask what kind of schooling was behind this brilliant society which has enchanted the centuries ever since, any honest reply can be carried in one word: None. After writing a book searching for the hidden genius of Greece in its schools, Kenneth Freeman concluded his unique study *The Schools of Hellas* in 1907 with this summary, "There were no schools in Hellas." No place boys and girls spent their youth attending continuous instruction under command of strangers. Indeed, nobody did homework in the modern sense; none could be located on standardized tests. The tests that mattered came in living, striving to meet ideals that local tradition imposed. The word *sköle* itself means leisure, leisure in a formal garden to think and reflect. Plato in *The Laws* is the first to refer to school as learned discussion.

The most famous school in Athens was Plato's Academy, but in its physical manifestation it had no classes or bells, it was a well-mannered hangout for thinkers and seekers, a generator of good conversation and good friendship, things Plato thought lay at the core of education. Today we might call such a phenomenon a *salon*. Aristotle's Lyceum was pretty much the same, although Aristotle delivered two lectures a day—a tough one in the morning for intense thinkers, a kinder, gentler version of the same in the afternoon for less ambitious minds. Attendance was optional. And the famous Gymnasium so memorable as a forge for German leadership later on was in reality only an open training ground where men 16 to 50 were free to participate in high-quality, state- subsidized instruction in boxing, wrestling, and javelin.

The idea of schooling free men in anything would have revolted Athenians. Forced training was for slaves. Among free men, learning was self-discipline, not the gift of experts. From such notions Americans derived their own academies, the French their *lycees*, and the Germans their *gymnasium*. Think of it: In Athens, instruction was unorganized even though the city-state was surrounded by enemies and its own society engaged in the difficult social experiment of sustaining a participatory democracy, extending privileges without precedent to citizens, and maintaining literary, artistic, and legislative standards which remain to this day benchmarks of human genius. For its 500-year history from Homer to Aristotle, Athenian civilization was a miracle in a rude world; teachers flourished there but none were grounded in fixed buildings with regular curricula under the thumb of an intricately layered bureaucracy.

There were no schools in Hellas. For the Greeks, study was its own reward. Beyond that few cared to go.

The Fresco At Herculaneum

Athens' neighbor, Sparta, was a horse of a different color. Society in Sparta was organized around the concept of cradle-to-grave formal training. The whole state was a universal schoolhouse, official prescriptions for the population filled every waking minute and the family was employed as a convenience for the state. Sparta's public political arrangements were an elaborate sham, organized nominally around an executive branch with two legislative bodies, but ultimate decision-making was in the hands of *ephors*, a small elite who conducted state policy among themselves. The practical aspect of imitation democracy figures strongly in the thought of later social thinkers such as Machiavelli (1532) and Hobbes (1651), as well as in minds nearer our own time who had influence on the shape of American forced schooling.

Spartan ideas of management entered American consciousness through classical studies in early schooling, through churches, and also through interest in the German military state of Prussia, which consciously modeled itself after Sparta. As the nineteenth century entered its final decades American university training came to follow the Prussian/Spartan model. Service to business and the political state became the most important reason for college and university existence after 1910. No longer was it primarily about developing the mind and character of the young but instead about molding those things as instruments for use by others.

Here is an important clue to the philosophical split which formed the foundation of modern schooling and to an important extent still does. The small farmers, crafts folk, trades people, little town and city professionals, little industrialists, and older manorial interests took a part of their dream of America from democratic Athens or from republican Rome (not the Rome of the emperors). This comprised a significant proportion of ordinary America. But the new urban managerial elites pointed to a future based on Spartan outlook. When the instructional system of Athens transferred to Imperial Rome, a few schools we would recognize began to appear. The familiar punishment practices of colonial America can be found anticipated vividly in the famous fresco at Herculaneum, showing a Roman schoolboy being held by two of his classmates while the master advances carrying a long whip.

Roman schools must have started discipline early in the morning for we find the poet Martial cursing a school for waking him up at cock's crow with shouts and beatings; Horace immortalizes pedagogue Orbilius for whipping a love of old poets into him. But we shouldn't be misled by these school references; what few schools there were in Rome were for boys of prosperous classes, and even most of these relied upon tutors, tradition, and emulation, not school.

The word *pedagogues* is Latin for a specialized class of slave assigned to walk a student to the schoolmaster; over time the slave was given additional duties, his role was enlarged to that of drill master, a procedure memorialized in Varro's *instituit pedagogus, docet magister*, which I translate in rusty altar-boy Latin as, "The master creates instruction, the slave pounds it in." A key to modern schooling is this: free men were never pedagogues. And yet we often refer to the science of modern schooling as *pedagogy*. The unenlightened parent who innocently brings matters of concern to the pedagogue, whether that poor soul is called schoolteacher, principal, or superintendent, is usually beginning a game of frustration which will end in no fundamental change. A case of barking up the wrong tree in a dark wood where the right tree is far away and obscure.

Pedagogy is social technology for winning attention and cooperation (or obedience) while strings are attached to the mind and placed in the hands of an unseen master. This may be done holistically, with smiles, music, and light-duty simulations of intellection, or it can be done harshly with rigorous drills and competitive tests. The quality of self-doubt aimed for in either case is similar.

Pedagogy is a useful concept to help us unthread some of the mysteries of modern schooling. That it is increasingly vital to the social order is testified to by the quiet teacher-pay revolution that has occurred since the 1960s. As with police work (to which pedagogy bears important similarities), school pay has become relatively good, its hours of labor short, its job security first rate. Contrast this with the golden years of one-room schooling where pay was subsistence only and teachers were compelled to board around to keep body and soul together. Yet there was no shortage then of applicants and many sons of prominent Americans began their adult lives as schoolteachers.

With the relative opulence of today, it would be simple to fill teaching slots with accomplished men and woman if that were a goal. A little adjustment in what are rationally indefensible licensing requirements would make talented people, many performance-tested adults in their 50s and 60s, available to teach. That there is not such fluid access is a good sign the purpose of schooling is more than it appears. The year in, year out *consistency* of mediocre teacher candidates demonstrates clearly that the school institution actively seeks, nurtures, hires, and promotes the caliber of personnel it needs.

The Seven Liberal Arts

When Rome dissolved in the sixth century, Roman genius emerged as the Universal Christian Church, an inspired religious sect grown spontaneously into a religious vehicle which invested ultimate responsibility for personal salvation in the sovereign individual. The Roman church hit upon schooling as a useful adjunct, and so what few schools could be found after the fall of Rome were in ecclesiastical hands, remaining there for the next eleven or twelve centuries. Promotion inside the Church began to depend on having first received training of the Hellenic type. Thus a brotherhood of thoughtful men was created from the demise of the Empire and from the necessity of intellectually defining the new mission.

As the church experimented with schooling, students met originally at the teacher's house, but gradually some church space was dedicated for the purpose. Thanks to competition among church officials, each Bishop strove to offer a school and these, in time to be called Cathedral schools, attracted attention and some important sponsorship, each being a showcase of the Bishop's own educational taste.

When the Germanic tribes evacuated northern Europe, overrunning the south, cathedral schools and monastic schools trained the invading leadership—a precedent of disregarding local interests which has continued ever after. Cathedral schools were the important educational institutions of the Middle Ages; from them derived all the schools of western Europe, at least in principle.

In practice, however, few forms of later schooling would be the intense intellectual centers these were. The Seven Liberal Arts made up the main curriculum: lower studies were composed of grammar, rhetoric, and dialectic. Grammar was an introduction to literature, rhetoric an introduction to law and history, dialectic the path to philosophical and metaphysical disputation. Higher studies included arithmetic, geometry, music, and astronomy. Arithmetic was well beyond simple calculation, entering into descriptive and analytical capacities of numbers and their prophetic use (which became modern statistics); geometry embraced geography and surveying; music covered a broad course in theory; astronomy prepared entry into physics and advanced mathematics.

Between the eleventh and the fourteenth centuries, an attempt to reduce the influence of emotionality in religion took command of church policy. Presenting the teachings of the church in scientific form became the main ecclesiastical purpose of school, a tendency called *scholasticism*, which produced as its products great skill in analysis, in comparison and contrasts, in classifications and abstraction, as well as famous verbal hairsplitting—like how many angels could dance on the head of a pin. Scholasticism became the basis for future upperclass schooling.

The Platonic Idea

The official use of common schooling was invented by Plato; after him the idea languished, its single torchbearer the Church. Educational offerings from the church were intended for, though not completely limited to, those young whose parentage qualified them as a potential Guardian class. You would hardly know this from reading any standard histories of Western schooling intended for the clientele of teacher colleges.

Intense development of the Platonic ideal of comprehensive social control through schooling suddenly reappeared 2000 years later in eighteenth century France at the hands of a philosophical *cultus* known to history as *philosophes*, enthusiastic promoters of the bizarre idea of mass forced schooling. Most prominent among them, a self-willed man named Jean Jacques Rousseau. To add piquancy to Rousseau's thought, you need be aware he chose to give his own five offspring away to strangers at birth. If any man captures the essence of enlightenment transformation, it is Rousseau.

The Enlightenment "project" was conceived as a series of stages, each further leveling mankind, collectivizing ordinary humanity into a colonial organism like a volvox. The penetration of this idea, at least on the periphery of our own Founders' consciousness, is captured in the powerful mystery image of the pyramid on the obverse of our Great Seal.[4] This was only one of many colors present at America's beginning, of course, and not the most important, a fact we can infer because the pyramid was kept out of public notice until 1935. Then suddenly it appeared on the back of our one dollar bill, and a profound change in political management was thus signaled.

Oriental Pedagogy

The ideal of a leveling Oriental pedagogy expressed through government schooling was promoted by Jacobin orators of the French National Convention in the early 1790s, the commencement years of our own republic. The notion of forced schooling was irresistible to French

---

[4] The eye-topped pyramid. This notion is taken specifically from religious and philosophical prescriptions of Hinduism, Buddhism, and Confucianism which occupied a prominent position in English thought during the last half of the eighteenth century, perhaps because major fortunes were coming from contact with the East. The mentality of Oriental rulers fascinated the thrones of Europe. For instance, a Chinese court minister had propounded a strategy known as "The Policy of Keeping People Dumb." Such thinking inspired similar notions in the West.

radicals, an enthusiasm whose foundation had been laid in preceding centuries by utopian writers like Harrington (*Oceania*), More (*Utopia*), Bacon (*New Atlantis*), Campanella (*City of the Sun*), and in other speculative fantasy embracing the fate of children. Cultivating a collective social organism was considered the ingredient missing from feudal society, an ingredient which would allow the West the harmony and stability of the East.

Utopian schooling isn't ever about learning in the traditional sense; it's about the transformation of human nature. The core of the difference between Occident and Orient lies in the power relationship between privileged and ordinary, and in respective outlooks on human nature. In the West, a metaphorical table is spread by society; the student decides how much to eat; in the East, the teacher makes that decision. The Chinese character for school shows a passive child with hands pouring knowledge into his empty head.

To mandate outcomes centrally would be a major step in the destruction of Western identity. Management by objectives, whatever those objectives might be, is a technique of corporate subordination, not of education. Charlemagne, whose awareness of Asia was sharpened in mortal combat was, along with Alfred, the first secular potentate in the West to beat the drum for universal schooling. It was easy to ignore Plato's gloomy forecast that however attractive utopia appears in imagination, human nature will not live easily with the degree of synthetic constraint it requires.

Counter-Attack On Democracy

By standards of the time, America was utopia already. No grinding poverty, no dangerous national enemies, no indigenous tradition beyond a general spirit of exuberant optimism, a belief the land had been touched by destiny, a conviction Americans could accomplish anything. Jay wrote to Jefferson in 1787, "The enterprise of our country is inconceivable," inconceivable, that is, to those accustomed to keeping the common population on a leash—namely English, Germans, and French. Our colonial government was the creation of the Crown, of course, but soon a fantastic idea began to circulate, a belief that people might create or destroy governments at their will.

The empty slate of the new republic made it vulnerable to advanced utopian thinking. While in England and Germany, temptation was great to develop and use Oriental social machinery to bend mass population into an instrument of elite will, in America there was no hereditary order or traditional direction, we were a nation awash in literate, self-reliant men and women, the vast majority with an independent livelihood or ambitions toward getting one. Americans were inventors and technicians without precedent, entrepreneurs unlocked from traditional controls, dreamers, confidence men, flim-flam artists. There never was a social stew quite like it.

The practical difficulties these circumstances posed to utopian governing would have been insuperable except for one seemingly strange source of enthusiasm for such an endeavor in the business community. That puzzle can be solved by considering how the promise of democracy was a frightening *terra incognita* to men of substance. To look to men like Sam Adams or Tom Paine as directors of the future was like looking down the barrel of a loaded gun, at least to people of means, so the men who had begun the Revolution were eased out by the men who ended it.

As early as 1784, a concerted effort was made by the Boston business community to overthrow town meetings, replacing them with a professionally managed corporation. Joseph Barrell, a wealthy merchant, claimed citizen safety could be enhanced this way,—and besides, "a great number of very respectable gentlemen" wished it. Timothy Dwight, longtime president of Yale after 1795, and a pioneer in modern education (advocating science as the center of curriculum), fought a mighty battle against advancing democracy. Democracy was hardly the sort of experiment men of affairs would willingly submit their lives and fortunes to for very long.

This tension explains much how our romance with forced schooling came about; it was a way to stop democracy aborning as Germany had done. Much ingenuity was expended on this problem in the early republic, particularly by so-called liberal Christian sects like Unitarians and Universalists. If you read relics of these debates preserved from select lyceums, private meetings at which minutes were kept, journals, recollections of drawing room conversations and club discussions, you see that what was shaping up was an attempt to square the circle, to give the appearance that the new society was true to its founding promise, while at the same time a sound basis could be established for the meritorious to run things. Once again, the spirit of Sparta was alive with its ephors and its reliance on forced instruction. In discussions, speeches, sermons, editorials, experimental legislation, letters, diaries, and elsewhere, the ancient idea of mass forced schooling was called forth and mused upon.

How Hindu Schooling Came To America (I)

By the end of the first quarter of the nineteenth century, a form of school technology was up and running in America's larger cities, one in which children of lower-class customers were psychologically conditioned to obedience under pretext that they were learning reading and counting (which may also have happened). These were the Lancaster schools, sponsored by Governor DeWitt Clinton of New York and prominent Quakers like Thomas Eddy, builder of the Erie Canal. They soon spread to every corner of the nation where the problem of an incipient proletariat existed. Lancaster schools are cousins of today's school factories. What few knew then or realize now is that they were also a Hindu invention, designed with the express purpose of retarding mental development.

How Hindu schooling came to America, England, Germany, and France at just about the same time is a story which has never been told. A full treatment is beyond the scope of this book, but I'll tell you enough to set you wondering how an Asiatic device specifically intended to preserve a caste system came to reproduce itself in the early republic, protected by influentials of the magnitude of Clinton and Eddy. Even a brief dusting off of schooling's Hindu provenance should warn you that what you know about American schooling isn't much. First, a quick gloss on the historical position of India at the time of the American Revolution—for Lancaster schools were in New York two decades after its end.

India fell victim to Western dominance through nautical technology in the following fashion: When medieval Europe broke up after its long struggle to reconcile emergent science with religion, five great ocean powers appeared to compete for the wealth of the planet: Portugal, Spain, France, the Netherlands, and England. Portugal was the first to sail for wealth, enriching itself and leaving colonies in India, China, and South America, but its day in the sun was short. Spain emerged as the next global superpower, but after 1600, her character decayed rapidly from effects of the wealth of the Americas and Spain went into a long decline. Holland's turn followed. That Spain nation had the advantage of great coherence: a strong commercial class in control of its politics before that happened anywhere else. It monopolized the carrying trade of Europe with globe-trotting merchant ships and courageous military seamanship, yet as with Portugal before it, the Dutch population was too small, its internal resources too anemic for its dominance to extend very long.

Beginning in the seventeenth century, England and France gradually built business in the East, both balked for a time by the Dutch who controlled the spice trade of the Indies. Three naval wars with the Dutch made the Royal Navy master of the seas, in the process developing tactics of sea warfare that made it dominant for the next two centuries. By 1700, only France and England remained as global sea powers with impressive fighting capability, and during the last half of that century these giants slugged it out directly in Canada, India, and in the territory which is today the U.S., with the result that France went permanently into eclipse.

In India, the two contended through their commercial pseudopodia, the British and French East India Companies: each maintained a private army to war on the other for tea, indigo, turmeric, ginger, quinine, oilseeds, silk, and that product which most captivated British merchants with its portability and breakaway profit potential—opium. At Plassey, Chandernagor, Madras, and Wandiwash, this long corporate rivalry ended. The French abandoned India to the British. The drug monopoly was finally England's.

Out of this experience and the observations of a wealthy young Anglican chaplain in India, the formula for modern schooling was discovered. Perhaps it was no more than coincidence this fellow held his first gainful employment as a schoolteacher in the United States; on the other hand, perhaps his experience in a nation which successfully threw off British shackles sensitized him to the danger an educated population poses to plutocracies.

How Hindu Schooling Came To America (II)

Andrew Bell, the gentlemen in question, used to be described in old editions of the *Britannica* as "cold, shrewd, self-seeking." He might not have been the most pious cleric. Perhaps like his contemporary, Parson Malthus, he didn't really believe in God at all, but as a young man following the flag he had an eye out for the main chance. Bell found his opportunity when he studied the structure Hindus arranged for training the lower castes, about 95 percent of the Indian population. It might well serve a Britain which had driven its peasantry into ruin in order to create an industrial proletariat for coal-driven industry.

Bell was fascinated by the *purposeful* nature of Hindu schooling. It seemed eminently compatible with the goals of the English state church. So as many another ambitious young man has done throughout history when he stumbles upon a little-known novelty, he swiped it. Before we turn to details of the Hindu method, and how Bell himself was upstaged by an ambitious young Quaker who beat him into the school market with a working version of Bell's idea, you should understand a little about Hindu religion.

After the British military conquest of India (in reality a merchant conquest) nothing excited the popular mind and the well-bred mind alike more than Hindu religion with its weird (to Western eyes) idols and rituals. Close analysis of Sanskrit literature seemed to prove that some kind of biological and social link had existed between the all-conquering Aryans from whom the Hindus had descended and Anglo-Saxons, which might explain theological similarities between Hinduism and Anglicanism. The possibilities suggested by this connection eventually provided a powerful psychic stimulus for creation of class-based schooling in the United States. Of course such a development then lay far in the future.

The caste system of Hinduism or Brahminism is the Anglican class system pushed to its imaginative limits. A five-category ranking (each category further subdivided) apportions people into a system similar to that found in modern schools. Prestige and authority is reserved for the three highest castes although they only comprise five percent of the total; inescapable servility is assigned the lowest caste, a pariah group outside serious consideration. In the Hindu system one may *fall* into a lower caste, *but one cannot rise.*

When the British began to administer India, Hindus represented 70 percent of a population well over a hundred million. Contrast this with an America of perhaps three million. In the northern region, British hero Robert Clive was president of Bengal where people were conspicuously lighter-skinned than the other major Indian group, having features not unlike those of the British.

Hindu castes looked like this:

The upper five percent was divided into three "twice-born" groups.

1. Brahmins—Priests and those trained for law, medicine, teaching, and other professional occupations.

2. The warrior and administrative caste.

3. The industrial caste, which would include cultivators and mercantile groups.

The lower 95 percent was divided into:

1. The menial caste.

2. Pariahs, called "untouchables."

The entire purpose of Hindu schooling was to preserve the caste system. Only the lucky five percent received an education which gave perspective on the whole, a key to understanding. In actual practice, warriors, administrators, and most of the other leaders were given much diluted insight into the driving engines of the culture, so that policy could be kept in the hands of Brahmins. But what of the others, the "masses" as Western socialist tradition would come to call them in an echoing tribute to the Hindu class idea? The answer to that vital question launched factory schooling in the West.

Which brings us back to Andrew Bell. Bell noticed that in some places Hinduism had created a mass schooling institution for children of the ordinary, one inculcating a curriculum of self-abnegation and willing servility. In these places hundreds of children were gathered in a single gigantic room, divided into phalanxes of ten under the direction of student leaders with the whole ensemble directed by a Brahmin. In the Roman manner, paid pedagogues drilled underlings in the memorization and imitation of desired attitudes and these underlings drilled the rest. Here was a social technology made in heaven for the factories and mines of Britain, still uncomfortably saturated in older yeoman legends of liberty and dignity, one not yet possessing the perfect proletarian attitudes mass production must have for maximum efficiency. Nobody in the early years of British rule had made a connection between this Hindu practice and the pressing requirements of an industrial future. Nobody that is until a 34-year-old Scotsman arrived in India as military chaplain.

How Hindu Schooling Came To America (III)

Young Bell was a go-getter. Two years after he got to India he was superintendent of the male orphan asylum of Madras. In order to save money Bell decided to try the Hindu system he had seen and found it led students quickly to docile cooperation, like parts of a machine. Furthermore, they seemed relieved not to have to think, grateful to have their time reduced to rituals and routines as Frederick Taylor was to reform the American workplace a hundred years later.

In 1797, Bell, now 42, published an account of what he had seen and done. Pulling no punches, he praised Hindu drill as an effective *impediment* to learning writing and ciphering, an efficient *control* on reading development. A twenty-year-old Quaker, Joseph Lancaster, read Bell's pamphlet, thought deeply on the method, and concluded, ironically, it would be a cheap way to *awaken* intellect in the lower classes, ignoring the Anglican's observation (and Hindu experience) that it did just the opposite.

Lancaster began to gather poor children under his father's roof in Borough Road, London, to give them rudimentary instruction without a fee. Word spread and children emerged from every alley, dive, and garret, craving to learn. Soon a thousand children were gathering in the street. The Duke of Bedford heard about Lancaster and provided him with a single enormous schoolroom and a few materials. The monitorial system, as it was called, promised to promote a mental counterpart to the productivity of factories.

Transforming dirty ghetto children into an orderly army attracted many observers. The fact that Lancaster's school ran at tiny cost with only one employee raised interest, too. Invitations arrived to lecture in surrounding towns, where the Quaker expounded on what had now become *his* system. Lancaster schools multiplied under the direction of young men he personally trained. So talked about did the phenomenon become, it eventually attracted the attention of King George III himself, who commanded an interview with Joseph. Royal patronage followed on the stipulation that every poor child be taught to read the Bible.

But with fame and public responsibility, another side of Lancaster showed itself—he became vain, reckless, improvident. Interested noblemen bailed him out after he fell deeply in debt, and helped him found the British and Foreign School Society, but Lancaster hated being watched over and soon proved impossible to control. He left the organization his patrons erected, starting a private school which went bankrupt. By 1818 the Anglican Church, warming to Bell's insight that schooled ignorance was more useful than unschooled stupidity, set up a rival chain of factory schools that proved to be handwriting on the wall for Lancaster. In the face of this competition he fled to America where his fame and his method had already preceded him.

Meanwhile, in England, the whole body of dissenting sects gave Lancaster vociferous public support, thoroughly alarming the state church hierarchy. Prominent church laymen and clergy were not unaware that Lancaster's schools weren't playing by Hindu rules—the prospect of a literate underclass with unseemly ambitions was a window on a future impossible to tolerate. Bell had been recalled from his rectory in Dorset in 1807 to contest Lancaster's use of Hindu schooling. In 1811, he was named superintendent of an organization to oppose Lancaster's British and Foreign School

Society, "The National Society for Promoting the Education of the Poor in the Principles of the Established Church." Since those principles held that the poor were poor because the Lord wanted it that way, the content of the society's schooling leaves little about which we need to speculate. Bell was sent to plant his system in Presbyterian Scotland while the patronage advantage of Bell-system schools contained and diminished the reach of Lancaster. For his services to the state, Bell was eventually buried in Westminister Abbey.

At first, Lancaster was welcomed warmly in the U.S., but his affection for children and his ability to awaken pride and ambition in his charges made him ultimately unacceptable to important patrons who were much more interested in spreading Bell's dumbed-down method, without its Church of England baggage attached. Fortunately for their schemes, Lancaster grew even more shiftless, unmethodical, and incapable of sustained effort (or principled action). In the twenty years he had yet to live, Lancaster ranged from Montreal to Caracas, disowned by Quakers for reasons I've been unable to uncover. He once declared it would be possible to teach illiterates to read fluently in 20 to 90 days, which is certainly true. At the age of 60 he was run over by a carriage in New York and died in a few hours.

But while he died outcast, his system outlived him, or at least a system bearing his name did, albeit more Bell's than Lancaster's. It accustomed an influential public to expect streets to be clear of the offspring of the poor and to expenditures of tax money to accomplish this end. The first Lancaster school was opened in New York City in 1806; by 1829 the idea had spread to the Mexican state of Texas with stops as far west as Cincinnati, Louisville, and Detroit. The governors of New York and Pennsylvania recommended general adoption to their legislatures.

What exactly was a "Lancaster" school? Its essential features involved one large room stuffed with from 300 to 1000 children under the direction of a single teacher. The children were seated in rows. The teacher was not there to teach but to be "a bystander and inspector;" students, ranked in a paramilitary hierarchy, did the actual teaching:

> What the master says should be done. When the pupils as well as the schoolmaster, understand how to act and learn on this system, the system, not the master's *vague discretionary, uncertain judgment*, will be in practice. In common school the authority of the master is personal, and the rod is his scepter. His absence is an immediate signal for confusion, but in a school conducted on my plan when the master leaves the school, the business will *go on as well in his absence as in his presence....*

Here, without forcing the matter, is our modern *pedagogus technologicus*, harbinger of future computerized instruction. In such a system, teachers and administrators are forbidden to depart from instructions elsewhere written. But while dumbing children down was the whole of the government school education in England, it was only part of the story in America, and a minor one until the twentieth century.

Braddock's Defeat

Unless you're a professional sports addict and know that Joe Montana, greatest quarterback of the modern era, went to Waverly school in Monongahela, or that Ron Neccai, only man in modern baseball history to strike out every batter on the opposing team for a whole game did, too, or that Ken Griffey, Jr. went to its high school as well, you can be forgiven if you never heard of Monongahela. But once upon a time at the beginning of our national history, Monongahela marked the forward edge of a new nation, a wilder West than ever the more familiar West became. Teachers on a frontier cannot be bystanders.

Custer's Last Stand in Montana had no military significance. Braddock's Last Stand near Monongahela, on the other hand, changed American history forever because it proved that the invincible British could be taken. And 21 years later we did take them, an accomplishment the French and Spanish, their principal rivals, had been unable to do. Why that happened, what inspiration allowed crude colonials to succeed where powerful and polished nations could not, is so tied up with Monongahela I want to bring the moment back for you. It will make a useful reference point, you'll see, as we consider the problem of modern schooling. Without Braddock's defeat we would never have had a successful American revolution, without getting rid of the British, the competence of ordinary people to educate themselves would never have had a fair test.

In July of 1755, at the age of 23, possessing no university degrees, the alumnus of no military academy, with only two years of formal schooling under his belt, half-orphan George Washington was detailed an officer in the Virginia militia to accompany an English military expedition moving to take the French fort at the forks of the Monongahela and Allegheny, the point that became Pittsburgh. His general, Edward Braddock, was an aristocrat commanding a well-equipped and disciplined force considerably superior to any possible resistance. Braddock felt so confident of success, he dismissed the advice of Washington to put aside traditional ways of European combat in the New World.

On July 9, 1755, two decades and one year before our Revolution commenced under the direction of the same Washington, Braddock executed a brilliant textbook crossing of the Monongahela near the present Homestead High Bridge by Kennywood amusement park. With fife and drum firing the martial spirit, he led the largest force in British colonial America, all in red coats and polished metal across the green river into the trees on the farther bank. Engineers went ahead to cut a road for men and cannon.

Suddenly the advance guard was enveloped in smoke. It fell back in panic. The main body moved up to relieve, but the groups meeting, going in opposite directions, caused pandemonium. On both sides of the milling redcoats, woods crackled with hostile gunfire. No enemy could be seen, but soldiers were caught between waves of bullets fanning both flanks. Men dropped in bunches. Bleeding bodies formed hills of screaming flesh, accelerating the panic.

Enter George, the Washington almost unknown to American schoolchildren. Making his way to Braddock, he asked permission to engage the enemy wilderness fashion; permission denied. Military theory held that allowing commands to emanate from inferiors was a precedent more dangerous than bullets. The British were too well trained to fight out of formation, too superbly schooled to adapt to the changing demands of the new situation. When my grandfather took me to the scene of that battle years after on the way to Kennywood, he muttered without explanation, "Goddam bums couldn't think for themselves." Now I understand what he meant.

The greatest military defeat the British ever suffered in North America before Saratoga was underway. Washington's horse was shot from under him, his coat ripped by bullets. Leaping onto a second horse, his hat was lifted from his head by gunfire and the second horse went down. A legend was in the making on the Monongahela that day, passed to Britain, France, and the colonies by survivors of the battle. Mortally wounded, Braddock released his command. Washington led the retreat on his hands and knees, crawling through the twilight dragging the dying Braddock, symbolic of the imminent death of British rule in America.

Monongahela began as a town fourteen years later, crossing point for a river ferry connecting to the National Road (now Route 40) which began, appropriately enough, in the town of Washington, Pennsylvania. In 1791, leaders of the curious "Whiskey Rebellion" met in Monongahela about a block from the place I was born; Scotch-Irish farmers sick of the oppression of federal rule in the new republic spoke of forging a Trans-Allegheny nation of free men. Monongahela might have been its capital had they succeeded. We know these men were taken seriously back East because Washington, who as general never raised an army larger than 7,000 to fight the British, as president assembled 13,000 in 1794 to march into Western Pennsylvania to subdue the Whiskey rebels. Having fought *with* them as comrades, he knew the danger posed by these wild men of the farther forests was no pipedream. They were the descendants of the original pioneers who had broken into the virgin forest, a virulent strain of populism running through their character.

Monongahela appears in history as a place where people expected to make their own luck, a place where rich and poor talked face to face, not through representatives. In the 1830s it became a way station on the escape route from Horace Mann-style Whiggery, the notion that men should be bound minutely by rules and layered officialdom. Whiggery was a neo-Anglican governing idea grown strong in reaction to Andrew Jackson's dangerous democratic revolution. *Whigs* brought us forced schooling before they mutated into both Democrats and Republicans; history seemed to tell them that with School in hand their mission was accomplished. Thousands of Americans, sensibly fearing the worst, poured West to get clear of this new British consciousness coming back to life in the East, as if the spirit of General Braddock had survived after all. Many of the new pilgrims passed through Mon City on the road to a place that might allow them to continue seeing things their own way.

Each group passing through on its western migration left a testament to its own particular yearnings—there are no less than 23 separate religious denominations in Monongahela although less than 5,000 souls live in the town. Most surprising of all, you can find there world headquarters of an autonomous Mormon sect, one that didn't go to Nauvoo with the rest of Smith's band but decamped here in a grimier utopia. Monongahela Mormons never accepted polygamy. They read the Book of Morman a different way. From 1755 until the Civil War, the libertarianism of places like Monongahela set the tone for the most brilliant experiment in self-governance the modern world has ever seen. Not since the end of the Pippin Kings in France had liberty been so abundantly available for such a long time. A revolution in education was at hand as knowledge of the benefits of learning to the vigor of the spirit spread far and wide across America. The role of formal schooling in this transformation had some significance but it was far from decisive. Schooled or not, the United States was the best-educated nation in human history—because it had liberty.

When I was a schoolboy at the Waverly School in Monongahela, Peg Hill told us that David Farragut, the U.S. Navy's very first admiral, had been commissioned midshipman at the ripe old age of ten for service on the warship *Essex*. Had Farragut been a schoolboy like me he would have been in fifth grade when he sailed for the Argentine, rounding the Horn into action against British warships operating along the Pacific coast of South America.

Farragut left a description of what he encountered in his first sea fight:

> I shall never forget the horrid impression made upon me at the sight of the first man I had ever seen killed. It staggered me at first, but they soon began to fall so fast that it appeared like a dream and produced no effect on my nerves.

The poise a young boy is capable of was tested when a gun captain on the port side ordered him to the wardroom for primers. As he started down the ladder, a gun captain on the starboard side opposite the ladder was "struck full in the face by an 18-pound shot," his headless corpse falling on Farragut:

> We tumbled down the hatch together. I lay for some moments stunned by the blow, but soon recovered consciousness enough to rush up on deck. The captain, seeing me covered with blood, asked if I were wounded; to which I replied, "I believe not, sir." "Then," said he, "where are the primers?" This brought me to my senses and I ran below again and brought up the primers.

The *Essex* had success; it took prizes. Officers were dispatched with skeleton crews to sail them back to the U.S., and at the age of twelve, Farragut got his first command when he was picked to head a prize crew. I was in sixth grade when I read about that. Had Farragut gone to my school he would have been in seventh. You might remember that as a rough index how far our maturity had been retarded even 50 years ago. Once at sea, the deposed British captain rebelled at being ordered about by a boy and announced he was going below for his pistols (which as a token of respect he had been allowed to keep). Farragut sent word down with a steward that if the captain appeared on deck armed he would be summarily shot and dumped overboard. He stayed below.

So ended David Farragut's first great test of sound judgment. At fifteen, this unschooled young man went hunting pirates in the Mediterranean. Anchored off Naples, he witnessed an eruption of Vesuvius and studied the mechanics of volcanic action. On a long layover in Tunis, the American consul, troubled by Farragut's ignorance, tutored him in French, Italian, mathematics, and literature. Consider our admiral in embryo. I'd be surprised if you thought his education was deficient in anything a man needs to be reckoned with.

When I was a schoolboy in Monongahela, I learned how Thomas Edison left school early because the school thought him feeble-minded. He spent his early years peddling newspapers. Just before the age of twelve he talked his mother into letting him work on trains as a train-boy, a permission she gave which would put her in jail right now. A train-boy was apprentice of all work. Shortly afterwards a printer gave Edison some old type he was about to discard and the boy, successfully begging a corner for himself in the baggage car to set type, began printing a four-page newspaper the size of a handkerchief about the lives of the passengers on the train and the things that could be seen from its window.

Several months later, twelve-year-old Edison had 500 subscribers, earning a net profit monthly about 25 percent more than an average schoolteacher of the day made. When the Civil War broke out, the newspaper became a goldmine. Railroads had telegraph facilities so war news was available to Edison as quickly as to professional journalists, but he could move it into print sooner than they could. He sold the war to crowds at the various stops. "The Grand Trunk Herald" sold as many as 1,000 extra copies after a battle at prices per issue from a dime to a quarter, amassing for Edison a handsome stake. Unfortunately, at the same time he had been experimenting with phosphorus in the baggage car. One thing led to another and Edison set the train on fire; otherwise there might never have been a light bulb.

When I was a schoolboy in Monongahela, I learned with a shock that the men who won our Revolution were barely out of high school by the standards of my time: Hamilton was 20 in the retreat from New York; Burr, 21; Light Horse Harry Lee, 21; Lafayette, 19. What amounted to a college class rose up and struck down the British empire, afterwards helping to write the most sophisticated governing documents in modern history.

When I was a schoolboy in Monongahela, I learned the famous Samuel Pepys, whose *Diary* is a classic, wasn't just an old gossip but President of the Royal Society, the most prominent association of scientists in existence in the seventeenth century. He was also Secretary of the Admiralty. Why that's important to our investigation of modern schooling is this: *Pepys could only add and subtract right up to the time of his appointment to the Admiralty*, but then quickly learned to multiply and divide to spare himself embarrassment. I took a different lesson from that class than the teacher intended, I think.

At the age of five, when I entered the first grade, I could add, subtract, and multiply because dad used to play numbers games with my sister and me in the car. He taught me the mastery of those skills within a matter of a few hours, not years and years as it took in school. We did all calculations in our heads with such gusto I seldom use a pencil today even for much more intricate computation. Pepys verified my fathers's unstated premise: You can learn what you need, even the technical stuff, at the moment you need it or shortly before. Sam Pepys wasn't put in charge of Britain's sea defense because he knew how to multiply or divide but because he had good judgment, or at least it was thought so.

Ben Franklin

Ben Franklin was born in Milk Street, Boston, on January 17, 1706. His father had seventeen children (four died at birth) by two wives. Ben was the youngest. Josiah, the father, was a candlemaker, not part of the gentry. His tombstone tells us he was "without an estate or any gainful employment" which apparently means his trade didn't allow wealth to be amassed. But, as the talkative tombstone continues, "By constant labor and industry with God's blessing they maintained a large family comfortably, and brought up thirteen children and seven grandchildren reputably."

Writing to his own son at the age of 65, Franklin referred to his circumstances as "poverty and obscurity" from which he rose to a state of affluence, and to some degree, reputation. The means he used "so well succeeded" he thought posterity might like to know what they were. Some, he believed, "would find his example suitable to their own situations, and therefore, fit to be imitated."

At twelve he was bound apprentice to brother James, a printer. After a few years of that, and disliking his brother's authority, he ran away first to New York and soon after to Philadelphia where he arrived broke at the age of seventeen. Finding work as a printer proved easy, and through his sociable nature and ready curiosity he made acquaintance with men of means. One of these induced Franklin to go to London where he found work as a compositor and once again brought himself to the attention of men of substance. A merchant brought him back to Philadelphia in his early twenties as what might today be called an administrative assistant or personal secretary. From this association, Franklin assembled means to set up his own printing house which published a newspaper, *The Pennsylvania Gazette*, to which he constantly contributed essays.

At 26, he began to issue "Poor Richard's Almanac," and for the next quarter century the Almanac spread his fame through the colonies and in Europe. All this time he involved himself deeper and deeper in public affairs. He designed an Academy which was developed later into the University of Pennsylvania; he founded the American Philosophical Society as a crossroads of the sciences; he made serious researches into the nature of electricity and other scientific inquiries, carried on a large number of moneymaking activities; and involved himself heavily in politics. At the age of 42 he was wealthy. The year was 1748.

In1748, he sold his business in order to devote himself to study, and in a few years, scientific discoveries gave him a reputation with the learned of Europe. In politics, he reformed the postal system and began to represent the colonies in dealings with England, and later France. In 1757, he was sent to England to protest against the influence of the Penns in the government of Pennsylvania, and remained there five years, returning two years later to petition the King to take the government away from the Penns. He lobbied to repeal the Stamp Act. From 1767 to 1775, he spent much time traveling through France, speaking, writing, and making contacts which resulted in a reputation so vast it brought loans and military assistance to the American rebels and finally crucial French intervention at Yorktown, which broke the back of the British.

As a writer, politician, scientist, and businessman, Franklin had few equals among the educated of his day—though he left school at ten. He spent nine years as American Commissioner to France. In terms only of his ease with the French language, of which he had little until he was in his sixties, this unschooled man's accomplishments are unfathomable by modern pedagogical theory. In many of his social encounters with French nobility, this candlemaker's son held the fate of the new nation in his hands, because he (and Jefferson) were being weighed as emblems of America's ability to overthrow England.

Franklin's *Autobiography* is a trove of clues from which we can piece together the actual curriculum which produced an old man capable of birthing a nation:

> My elder brothers were all put apprentice to different trades. I was put to
> the grammar school at eight years of age, my father intending to devote
> me, as the tithe of his sons, to the services of the (Anglican) church. My
> early readiness in learning to read (which must have been very early, as I
> do not remember when I could not read) and the opinion of all his friends,
> that I should be a good scholar, encouraged him in this purpose...I continued,
> however, at grammar school not quite one year....

Young Ben was yanked from grammar school and sent to another type less ritzy and more nuts and bolts in colonial times: the "writing and arithmetic"school. There under the tutelage of Mr. Brownell, an advocate of "mild, encouraging methods," Franklin failed in arithmetic:

> At ten years old I was taken home to assist my father in his business....
> Accordingly I was employed in cutting wick for candles, filling the
> dipping mold and the molds for cast candles. Attending the shop, going
> on errands, etc. I disliked the trade, and had a strong inclination for the
> sea, but my father declared against it.

There are other less flattering accounts why Franklin left both these schools and struck out on his own at the age of ten—elsewhere he admits to being a leader of mischief, some of it mildly criminal, and to being "corrected" by his father—but causation is not our concern, only bare facts. Benjamin Franklin commenced school at third grade age and exited when he would have been in the fifth to become a tallow chandler's apprentice.

A major part of Franklin's early education consisted of studying father Josiah, who turns out, himself, to be a pretty fair example of education without schooling:

> He had an excellent constitution...very strong...ingenious...could draw
> prettily... skilled in music...a clear pleasing voice...played psalm tunes on
> his violin...a mechanical genius...sound understanding...solid judgment in
> prudential matters, both private and public affairs. In the latter, indeed, he
> was never employed, the numerous family he had to educate and the straitness
> of his circumstances keeping him close to his grade; but I remember well his
> being frequently visited by leading people, who consulted him for his opinion
> in affairs of the town or of the church...and showed a great deal of respect for
> his judgment and advice...frequently chosen an arbitrator between contending
> parties.

We don't need to push too hard to see a variety of informal training laboratories incidentally offered in this father/son relationship which had sufficient time to prove valuable in Franklin's own development, opportunities that would have been hard to find in any school.

Josiah drew, he sang, he played violin—this was a tallow chandler with sensitivity to those areas in which human beings are most human; he had an inventive nature ("ingenious") which must have provided a constant example to Franklin that a solution can be crafted *ad hoc* to a problem if a man kept his nerve and had proper self-respect. His good sense, recognized by neighbors who sought his judgment, was always within earshot of Ben. In this way the boy came to see the discovery process, various systems of judgment, the role of an active citizen who may become minister without portfolio simply by accepting responsibility for others and discharging that responsibility faithfully:

> At his table he liked to have as often as he could some sensible friend or
> neighbor to converse with, and always took care to start some ingenious
> or useful topic for discourse, which might tend to improve the minds of
> his children. By this means he turned our attention to what was good,
> just, and prudent in the conduct of life; and little or no notice was ever
> taken of what related to the victuals on the table...I was brought up in

such perfect inattention to those matters as to be quite indifferent what
kind of food was set before me.

No course of instruction or quantity of homework could deliver Franklin's facility with
language, only something like Josiah's incidental drills at the dinner table. We can see sharply
through Franklin's memoir that a tallow chandler can indeed teach himself to speak to kings.

And there were other themes in the family Franklin's educational armory besides arts, home
demonstrations, regular responsibility, being held to account, being allowed to overhear adults
solving public and private problems, and constant infusions of good conversation:

> He...sometimes took me to walk with him, and see joiners, bricklayers,
> turners, braziers, etc., at their work, that he might observe my inclination,
> and endeavor to fix it on some trade or other.... It has ever since been a
> pleasure to me to see good workmen handle their tools; and it has been
> useful to me, having learnt so much by it as to be able to do little jobs myself.

The largest single aspect of Franklin's educational foundation was (as it is for most of a
literate society) reading:

> From a child I was fond of reading, and all the little money that came into
> my hands was ever laid out in books. Pleased with *Pilgrim's Progress* my
> first collection was of John Bunyan's works in separate little volumes. I
> afterwards sold them to enable me to buy R. Burton's *Historical Collections*;
> they were small chapman's books, and cheap, 40 to 50 in all. My father's
> little library consisted chiefly of books in polemic divinity, most of which I
> read....*Plutarch's Lives* there was in which I read abundantly, and I still think
> that time spent to great advantage. There was also a book of Defoe's, called
> an *Essay on Projects*, and another of Dr. Mather's, called *Essays to Do Good*,
> which perhaps gave me a turn of thinking that had an influence on some of the
> principal future events in my life.

You might well ask how young Franklin was reading Bunyan, Burton, Mather, Defoe,
Plutarch, and works of "polemic divinity" before he would have been in junior high school. If you
were schooled in the brain development lore of academic pedagogy it might seem quite a *tour de
force*.

How do you suppose this son of a workingman with thirteen kids became such an effective
public speaker that for more than half a century his voice was heard nationally and internationally
on the great questions? He employed a method absolutely free, he argued with his friend Collins:

> Very fond we were of argument, and very desirous of confuting one another,
> which disputatious turn is based upon contradiction. [Here Franklin warns
> against using dialectics on friendships or at social gatherings] I had caught
> it [the dialectical habit] by reading my father's books of dispute about

religion.... A question was started between Collins and me, of the propriety of educating the female sex in learning, and their abilities to study. He was of the opinion that it was improper.... I took the contrary side.

Shortly after he began arguing, he also began reading the most elegant periodical of the day, Addison and Steele's *Spectator*:

> I thought the writing excellent and wished, if possible, to imitate it. With that in view I took some of the papers, and making short hints of the sentiment in each sentence, laid them by a few days, and then, without looking at the book, try'd to complete the papers again, by expressing each hinted sentiment at length, and as fully as it had been expressed before, in any suitable words that should come to hand. Then I compared my *Spectator* with the original, discovered some of my faults, and corrected them.

This method was hammered out while working a 60-hour week. In learning eloquence there's only Ben, his determination, and the *Spectator*, no teacher. For instance, while executing rewrites Franklin, came to realize his vocabulary was too barren:

> I found I wanted a stock of words...which I thought I should have acquired before that time if I had gone on making verses; since the continual occasion for words of the same import, but of different length, to suit the measure, or of different sound for the rhyme, would have laid me under a constant necessity of searching for variety, and also have tended to fix that variety in my mind and make me master of it.

As a good empiricist he tried a home cure for this deficiency:

> I took some tales and turned them into verse; and after a time when I had pretty well forgotten the prose, turned them back again. I also sometimes jumbled my collection of hints [his outline] into confusions and after some weeks endeavored to reduce them into the best order, before I began to form the full sentences and complete the paper. This was to teach me method in the arrangement of thoughts. By comparing my work afterwards with the original I discovered many faults and amended them; but I sometimes thought... I had been lucky enough to improve the method or the language....

By the time he was sixteen Franklin was ready to take up his deficiencies in earnest with full confidence he could by his own efforts overcome them. Here's how he handled that problem with arithmetic:

> Being on some occasion made asham'd of my ignorance in figures, which I had twice failed in learning when at school, I took Crocker's book of

Arithmetick, and went through the whole by myself with great ease. I also read Seller's and Shermy's book of Navigation and became acquainted with the geometry they contain....

This school dropout tells us he was also reading John Locke's *Essay Concerning Human Understanding*, as well as studying the arts of rhetoric and logic, particularly the Socratic method of disputation which so charmed and intrigued him that he abruptly dropped his former argumentative style, putting on the mask of "the humble inquirer and doubter:"

I found this method safest for myself and very embarrassing to those against whom I used it; therefore I took a delight in it, practis'd it continually, and grew very artful and expert in drawing people, even of superior knowledge, into concessions, the consequences of which they did not foresee, entangling them in difficulties out of which they could not extricate themselves, and so obtaining victories that neither myself nor my cause always deserved.

Might there be an instructive parallel between teaching a kid to drive as my uncle taught me to do at age eleven, and the incredible opportunities working class kids like Franklin were given to develop as quickly and as far as their hearts and minds allowed? We drive, regardless of our intelligence or characters, because the economy demands it; in colonial America through the early republic, a pressing need existed to get the most from everybody. Because of that need, unusual men and unusual women appeared in great numbers to briefly give the lie to traditional social order. In that historical instant, thousands of years of orthodox suppositions were shattered. In the words of Eric Hoffer, "Only here in America were common folk given a chance to show what they could do on their own without a master to push and order them about." Franklin and Edison, multiplied many times, were the result.

George Washington

A good yardstick to measure how far modern schooling has migrated from the education of the past is George Washington's upbringing in the middle eighteenth century. Although Washington descended from important families, his situation wasn't quite the easeful life that suggests. The death of his father left him, at eleven, without Ben Franklin's best rudder, and the practice of primogeniture, which vested virtually the entire inheritance in the first son (in order to stabilize social class) compelled Washington to either face the future as a ward of his brother, an unthinkable alternative for George, or take destiny into his own hands as a boy. You probably already know how that story turned out, but since the course he pursued was nearly schoolless, its curriculum is worth a closer look. For the next few minutes imagine yourself at "school" with Washington.

George Washington was no genius; we know that from too many of his contemporaries to quibble. John Adams called him "too illiterate, too unlearned, too unread for his station and reputation." Jefferson, his fellow Virginian, declared he liked to spend time "chiefly in action, reading little." It was an age when everyone in Boston, even shoeblacks, knew how to read and count; it was a time when a working class boy in a family of thirteen like Franklin couldn't remember when he didn't know how to read.

As a teenager, Washington loved two things, dancing and horseback riding. He studied both hard with no prompting, supplying his own motivation. Both studies paid off tremendously for the future president because the overpowering *grace* they communicated to his actions, a grace which counterpointed his large size, allowed him to physically command any gathering. Thanks to his twin obsessions he bore his responsibilities with the aspect of a champion athlete, and that saved his life during the Revolution when a British sharpshooter drew a bead but found himself unable to pull the trigger because his target bore itself so magnificently! George Mercer, a friend, described Washington as a young man in the following way:

> He is straight as an Indian, measuring six feet, two inches in his stockings
> and weighing 175 pounds.... His frame is padded with well developed muscles,
> indicating great strength.

British military superiority, including the best available war-making technology, would have made hash of a brainless commander in spite of his admirable carriage, so we need to analyze the curriculum which produced "America's Fabius"[5] as he was called.

Washington had no schooling until he was eleven, no classroom confinement, no blackboards. He arrived at school already knowing how to read, write, and calculate about as well as the average college student today. If that sounds outlandish, turn back to Franklin's curriculum and compare it with the intellectual diet of a modern gifted and talented class. Full literacy wasn't unusual in the colonies or early republic; many schools wouldn't *admit* students who didn't know reading and counting because few schoolmasters were willing to waste time teaching what was so easy to learn. It was deemed a mark of depraved character if literacy hadn't been attained by the matriculating student. Even the many charity schools operated by churches, towns, and philanthropic associations for the poor would have been flabbergasted at the great hue and cry raised today about difficulties teaching literacy. American experience proved the contrary.

In New England and the middle colonies where literacy was especially valued, it was universal, less in the South where it was not. But even there it was common. The unbelievable explosion of colleges in nineteenth century America was made possible because general literacy among all classes created conditions where advanced forms of learning appeared attractive even to ordinary people.

Following George to school at eleven to see what the schoolmaster had in store would reveal a skimpy menu of studies, yet one with a curious gravity: geometry, trigonometry, and surveying. You might regard that as impossible or consider it was only a dumbed-down version of those things, some kid's game akin to the many simulations one finds today in schools for prosperous children—simulated city-building, simulated court trials, simulated businesses—virtual realities to bridge the gap between adult society and the immaturity of the young. But if George didn't get the

---

[5] Washington's *critics* dubbed him "Fabius" after the Roman general who dogged Hannibal's march but avoided battle with the Carthaginian. Washington wore down British resolve by eroding the general belief in their invincibility, something he had learned on the Monongahela when Braddock's force was routed. Eventually the French became convinced Washington was on the winning side, and with their support America became a nation. But it was the strategy of Washington that made a French/American alliance possible at all.

real thing, how do you account for his first job as official surveyor for Culpepper County, Virginia, only 2,000 days after he first hefted a surveyor's transit in school?

For the next three years, Washington earned in modern purchasing power about $100,000 a year. It's probable his social connections helped this fatherless boy get the position, but in frontier society anyone would be crazy to give a boy serious work unless he actually could do it. Almost at once he began speculating in land; he didn't need a futurist to tell him which way the historical wind was blowing. By 21, he had leveraged his knowledge and income into 2,500 acres of prime land in Frederick County, Virginia.

Washington had no father as a teenager, and we know he was no genius, yet he learned geometry, trigonometry, and surveying when he would have been a fifth or sixth grader in our era. Ten years later he had prospered directly by his knowledge. His entire life was a work of art in the sense it was an artifice under his control. He even eventually freed his slaves without being coerced to do so. Washington could easily have been the first king in America but he discouraged any thinking on that score, and despite many critics, he was so universally admired the seat of government was named after him while he was still alive.

Washington attended school for exactly two years. Besides the subjects mentioned, at twelve and thirteen (and later) he studied frequently-used legal forms like bills of exchange, tobacco receipts, leases, and patents. From these forms, he was asked to deduce the theory, philosophy, and custom which produced them. By all accounts, this steeping in grown-up reality didn't bore him at all. I had the same experience with Harlem kids 250 years later, following a similar procedure in teaching them how to struggle with complex income tax forms. Young people yearn for this kind of guided introduction to serious things, I think. When that yearning is denied, schooling destroys their belief that justice governs human affairs.

By his own choice, Washington put time into learning deportment, how to be regarded a gentleman by other gentlemen; he copied a book of rules which had been used at Jesuit schools for over a century and with that, his observations, and what advice he could secure, gathered his own character. Here's rule 56 to let you see the flavor of the thing: "Associate yourself with men of good Quality if you Esteem your own reputation." Sharp kid. No wonder he became president.

Washington also studied geography and astronomy on his own, gaining a knowledge of regions, continents, oceans, and heavens. In light of the casual judgment of his contemporaries that his intellect was of normal proportions, you might be surprised to hear that by eighteen he had devoured all the writings of Henry Fielding, Tobias Smollett, and Daniel Defoe and read regularly the famous and elegant *Spectator*. He also read Seneca's *Morals*, Julius Caesar's *Commentaries*, and the major writing of other Roman generals like the historian Tacitus.

At sixteen the future president began writing memos to himself about clothing design, not content to allow something so important to be left in the hands of tradesmen. Years later he became his own architect for the magnificent estate of Mt. Vernon. While still in his twenties, he began to experiment with domestic industry where he might avoid the vagaries of international finance in things like cotton or tobacco. First he tried to grow hemp "for medicinal purposes," which didn't work out; next he tried flax—that didn't work either. At the age of 31, he hit on wheat. In seven years he had a little wheat business with his own flour mills and hired agents to market his own brand of flour; a little later he built fishing boats: four years before the Declaration was written he was pulling in 9,000,000 herring a year.

No public school in the United States is set up to allow a George Washington to happen. Washingtons in the bud stage are screened, browbeaten, or bribed to conform to a narrow outlook on social truth. Boys like Andrew Carnegie who begged his mother not to send him to school and was well on his way to immortality and fortune at the age of thirteen would be referred today for psychological counseling; Thomas Edison would find himself in Special Ed until his peculiar genius had been sufficiently tamed.

Anyone who reads can compare what the American present does in isolating children from their natural sources of education, modeling them on a niggardly last, to what the American past proved about human capabilities. The magnitude of the forced schooling institution's strange accomplishment has been monumental. No wonder history has been outlawed.

Montaigne's Curriculum

Between the fall of Rome in the late fifth century and the decline of monarchy in the eighteenth, secular schooling in any form was hardly a ripple on the societies of Europe. There was talk of it at certain times and places, but it was courtly talk, never very serious. What simple schooling we find was modestly undertaken by religious orders which usually had no greater ambition than providing a stream of assistants to the ecclesiastical bureaucracy, and perhaps molding the values of whatever future leaders proved susceptible; the few exceptions shouldn't be looked upon as the spark for our own schools. School was only a tiny blip on the radar until the last half of the eighteenth century.

If you and I are to have a productive partnership in this book you need to clear your mind of false history, the type that clogs the typical school chronicle written for teacher training institutes where each fact may be verifiable but the conclusions drawn from them are not. Turn to typical school history and you will learn about the alleged anticipation of our own schools by Comenius, of the reformed Latin Grammar School founded by Dean Colet at St. Paul's in London in 1510, of the "solitaries of Port Royal," whoever those lonely men may have been; each instance is real, the direction they lead in is false. What formal school experimentation the West provided touched only a tiny fraction of the population, and rarely those who became social leaders, let alone pioneers of the future.

You can disinter proclamations about schooling from Alfred's kingdom or Charlemagne's, but you can't find a scrap of hard evidence that the thing was ever seriously essayed. What talk of schooling occurs is the exclusive property of philosophers, secret societies, and a host of cranks, quacks, and schemers. What you never find anywhere is any popular clamor for a place to dump children called School. Yet while schooling is conspicuous by its absence, there's no shortage of intelligent commentary about *education*—a commodity not to be conflated with the lesser term until late in history.

Aeneas Sylvius Piccolomini, Pope Pius II, in his tract on *The Education of Children* (1451), prescribes the reading and study of classical authors, geometry and arithmetic "for training the mind and assuring rapidity of conceptions" and history and geography, adding "there is nothing in the world more beautiful than enlightened intelligence." The sixteenth century is filled with theories of education from men like Erasmus, Rabelais, and Montaigne; French schoolman Gabriel Compayre, in his *History of Pedagogy* (1885), holds all three in the highest regard:

> Erasmus, Rabelais, and Montaigne...before pretending to surpass them,
> even at this day, we should rather attempt to overtake them, and to equal
> them in their pedagogical precepts.

Like most educated men and women, Erasmus was his own teacher. He assigned politeness an important place in education:

> The tender mind of the child should...love and learn the liberal arts...be
> taught tact in the conduct of the social life...from the earliest be accustomed
> to good behavior based on moral principles.

Montaigne, who actually attended school at Guienne from the age of six until he was thirteen, bequeathed an image of late sixteenth century schooling amazingly modern in its particulars:

> Tis the true house of correction of imprisoned youth...do but come when
> they are about their lesson and you shall hear nothing but the outcries of
> boys under execution, with the thundering noise of their *Pedagogues*,
> drunk with fury, to make up the consort. A pretty way this to tempt these
> tender and timorous souls to love their book, with a furious countenance
> and a rod in hand.

What Montaigne requires of a student seeking education is the development of sound judgment, "if the judgment be not better settled, I would rather have him spend his time at tennis."

Montaigne was preoccupied with the training of judgement; he would have history learned so that facts have contexts and historical judgment a bearing on contemporary affairs; he was intrigued by the possibilities of *emulation* as were all the classical masters[6], and so informs us. He said we need to see the difference between teaching, "where Marcellus died," which is unimportant and teaching "why it was unworthy of his duty that he died there," which has great significance. For Montaigne, learning to judge well and speak well is where education resides:

> Whatever presents itself to our eyes serves as a sufficient book. The
> knavery of a page, the blunder of a servant, a table witticism...conversation
> with men is wonderfully helpful, so is a visit to foreign lands...to whet and
> sharpen our wits by rubbing them upon those of others.

And in *Gargantua* the physician Rabelais set out a pedagogy quite in harmony with the experience-based curriculum of John Locke.

When I started teaching, I was able to transfer principles of Montaigne to my classroom without any difficulty. They proved as useful to me in 1962 as they must have been to Montaigne

---

[6] Horace Mann and the entire inner coterie of mid-nineteenth to early-twentieth century schoolmen derided emulation or the imitation of notable models as an effective spring of learning; thus was the most ancient and effective motivation to learn—to become like someone admirable—put to death deliberately by institutional pedagogy.

in 1562, wisdom eternally sane, always cost-free. In contrast, the bloated lists of "aims," "motivations," and "methods" the New York City Board of Education supplied me with were worse than useless; many were dead wrong.

One important bit of evidence that the informal attitude toward schooling was beginning to break up in seventeenth century New England is found in the Massachusetts School Law of 1647, legislation attempting to establish a system of schools by government order and providing means to enforce that order. Talk like this had been around for centuries, but this was a significant enactment, coming from a theocratic utopia on the frontier of the known universe.

Yet for all the effort of New England Puritan leadership to make its citizenry uniform through schooling and pulpit, one of history's grand ironies is that orderly Anglican Virginia and post-Puritan Massachusetts were the prime makers of a revolution which successfully overthrew the regulated uniformity of Britain. And in neither the startling Declaration of Independence which set out the motives for this revolution nor in the even more startling Bill of Rights in which ordinary people claimed their reward for courageous service, is either the word *School* or the word *Education* even mentioned. At the nation's founding, nobody thought School a cause worth going to war for, nobody thought it a right worth claiming.

Four Architects of Modern Forced Schooling

Andrew Carnegie. An enthusiastic Darwinist and early proponent of planned economy and society, reunion with Great Britain. Beatrice Webb, the Fabian, called him "a slimy little reptile." Carnegie Endowments.

J. P Morgan. The foremost Anglican layman in the world Worked resolutely for the restoration of a class system in America, and Anglo-American sovereignty worldwide.

J. D. Rockefeller Sr. "Survival of the fittest is nature's way of producing beauty," said Rockefeller. As a principal stockholder in U.S. Steel, he approved of school experiments in Gary, Indiana, to dumb down curriculum, seek more effective means give of mind control. Rockefeller Foundation.

Henry Ford. "I regard Henry Ford as my inspiration," Hitler told a Detroit newspaper in 1931. In July, 1938, automaker Ford received the Grand Cross of the Golden Eagle, highest award the German government could a foreigner. Lenin acknowledged his debt to Ford's genius. Ford Foundation.

CHAPTER TWO

An Angry Look

At Modern Schooling

*Today's corporate sponsors want to see their money used in ways to
line up with business objectives.... This is a young generation of corporate
sponsors and they have discovered the advantages of building long-term
relationships with educational institutions.*
> — Suzanne Cornforth of Paschall & Associates,
> Public relations consultants. As quoted in
> *The New York Times*, July 15, 1998

A Change In The Governing Mind

Sometimes the best hiding place is right in the open. It took seven years of reading and reflection for me to finally figure out that mass schooling of the young by force was a creation of the four great coal powers of the nineteenth century. It was under my nose, of course, but for years I avoided seeing what was there because no one else seemed to notice. Forced schooling arose from the logic that fossil fuel in conjunction with high-speed machinery imposes on flesh and blood.

This simple reality is hidden from view by early philosophical and theological anticipations of mass schooling in various writings about social order and human nature. But you shouldn't be fooled any more than Charles Francis Adams was fooled when he observed in 1880 that what was being cooked up for kids unlucky enough to be snared by the newly proposed institutional school net combined characteristics of the cotton mill and the railroad with those of a state prison.

After the Civil War, utopian speculative analysis regarding isolation of children in custodial compounds where they could be subjected to deliberate molding routines began to be discussed seriously by the Northeastern policy elites of business, government, and university life. These discussions were inspired by a growing realization that the productive potential of machinery driven by coal was limitless. Railroad development made possible by coal, startling new inventions like the telegraph, seemed suddenly to make village life and local dreams irrelevant. A new governing mind was emerging in harmony with the new reality.

The principal motivation for this revolution in family and community life seems on the surface to be greed, but appearance concealed philosophical visions approaching religious exaltation in intensity—that effective early indoctrination of all children would lead to an orderly scientific society, one controlled by the best people, now freed from the obsolete strait-jacket of democratic traditions and historic American libertarian attitudes.

Forced schooling was the medicine to bring the whole continental population into conformity with these plans so it might be regarded as a "human resource." Managed as a "workforce." No more Ben Franklins or Tom Edisons could be allowed; they set a bad example. One way to manage this transformation was to see to it that individuals were prevented from taking up their working lives until an advanced age when the ardor of youth and its insufferable self-confidence had cooled.

Extending Childhood

From the beginning, there was purpose behind forced schooling, purpose which had nothing to do with what parents, kids, or communities wanted; but instead was forged out of what a highly centralized corporate economy and system of finance bent on internationalizing itself was thought to need; that, and what a strong, centralized political state needed, too. School was looked upon from the first decade of the twentieth century as a branch of industry and a tool of governance. For a considerable time, probably provoked by a climate of official anger and contempt directed against immigrants in the greatest displacement of people known to history, social managers of schooling were remarkably candid about what they were doing. This candor can be heard clearly in a speech Woodrow Wilson made to businessmen before the First World War:

> We want one class to have a liberal education. We want another class, a very
> much larger class of necessity, to forgo the privilege of a liberal education and
> fit themselves to perform specific difficult manual tasks.

By1917, the major administrative jobs in American schooling were under control of a group referred to in the press of that day as "the Education Trust." The first meeting of this trust included representatives of Rockefeller, Carnegie, Harvard, Stanford, the University of Chicago, and the National Education Association. The chief end, wrote Benjamin Kidd, the British evolutionist, in 1918, was to "impose on the young the ideal of subordination."

At first, the primary target was the tradition of independent livelihoods in America. Unless Yankee entrepreneurialism could be put to death, at least among the common population, the immense capital investments that mass production industry required for equipment weren't conceivably justifiable. Students were to learn to think of themselves as *employees* competing for the favor of management. Not as Franklin or Edison had once regarded themselves, as self-determined, free agents.

Only by a massive psychological campaign could the menace of *overproduction* in America be contained. That's what important men and academics called it. The ability of Americans to think as independent producers had to be curtailed. The writings of Alexander Inglis give an excellent *precis* of this successful project to curb the tendency of little people to compete with big companies. Overproduction became a controlling metaphor among the managerial classes from 1880 to 1930 and this affected the development of mass schooling profoundly.

I know how difficult it is for most of us who mow our lawns and walk our dogs to comprehend that long-range social engineering even exists, let alone that it began to dominate compulsion schooling nearly a century ago. Yet the 1934 edition of Ellwood P. Cubberley's *Public Education in the United States* is explicit about what happened and why. As Cubberley puts it:

> It has come to be desirable that children should not engage in productive labor. On the contrary, all recent thinking...[is] opposed to their doing so. Both the interests of organized labor and the interests of the nation have set against child labor....[1]

The statement occurs in a section of *Public Education* called "A New Lengthening of the Period of Dependence," in which Cubberley explains that "the coming of the factory system" has made extended childhood necessary by depriving children of the training and education that farm and village life once gave. With the breakdown of home and village industries, the passing of chores, and the extinction of the apprenticeship system by large-scale production with its extreme division of labor (and the "all conquering march of machinery"), an army of workers has arisen, said Cubberley, who know nothing.

Furthermore, modern industry needs such workers. Sentimentality could not be allowed to stand in the way of progress. According to Cubberley, with "much ridicule from the public press" the old book-subject curriculum was set aside, replaced by a change in purpose and "a new psychology of instruction which came to us from abroad." That last mysterious reference to a new psychology is to practices of dumbed-down schooling common to England, Germany, and France, the three major world coal-powers (other than the U.S.), each of which had already converted its common population into an industrial proletariat long before.

Arthur Calhoun's 1919 *Social History of the Family* notified the nation's academics what was happening. Calhoun declared that the fondest wish of utopian writers was coming true, the child was passing from its family "into the custody of community experts." He offered a significant forecast, that in time we could expect to see public education "designed to check the mating of the unfit." Three years later, Mayor John F. Hylan of New York said in a public speech that the schools had been seized as an octopus would seize prey, by "an invisible government." He was referring specifically to certain actions of the Rockefeller Foundation and other corporate interests in New York City which preceded the school riots of 1917.

The 1920s were a boom period for forced schooling as well as for the stock market. In 1928, a well-regarded volume called *A Sociological Philosophy of Education* claimed, "It is the business of teachers to run not merely schools but the world." A year later, the famous creator of educational psychology, Edward Thorndike of Columbia Teachers College, announced, "Academic subjects are of little value." His colleague at Teachers College, William Kirkpatrick, boasted in *Education and the Social Crisis* that the whole tradition of rearing the young was being made over by experts.

The Geneticist's Manifesto

Meanwhile, at the project offices of an important employer of experts, the Rockefeller Foundation, friends were hearing from president Max Mason that a comprehensive national program

---

[1] This is the same Ellwood P. Cubberley who wrote in his Columbia Teachers College Dissertation of 1905 that schools were to be factories "in which raw products, children, are to be shaped and formed into finished products...manufactured like nails, and the specifications for manufacturing will come from government and industry."

was underway to allow, in Mason's words, "the control of human behavior." This dazzling ambition was announced on April 11, 1933. Schooling figured prominently in the design.

Rockefeller had been inspired by the work of Eastern European scientist Hermann Müller to invest heavily in genetics. Müller had used x-rays to override genetic law, inducing mutations in fruit flies. This seemed to open the door to the scientific control of life itself. Müller preached that planned breeding would bring mankind to paradise faster than God. His proposal received enthusiastic endorsement from the greatest scientists of the day as well as from powerful economic interests.

Müller would win the Nobel Prize, reduce his proposal to a 1,500-word *Geneticists' Manifesto*, and watch with satisfaction as 22 distinguished American and British biologists of the day signed it. The state must prepare to consciously guide human sexual selection, said Müller. School would have to separate worthwhile breeders from those slated for termination.

Just a few months before this report, an executive director of the National Education Association announced that his organization expected "to accomplish by education what dictators in Europe are seeking to do by compulsion and force." You can't get much clearer than that.

WWII drove the project underground, but hardly retarded its momentum. Following cessation of global hostilities, school became a major domestic battleground for the scientific rationalization of social affairs through compulsory indoctrination. Great private corporate foundations led the way.

Participatory Democracy Put To The Sword

Thirty-odd years later, between 1967 and 1974, teacher training in the U.S. was covertly revamped through coordinated efforts of a small number of private foundations, select universities, global corporations, think tanks, and government agencies, all coordinated through the U.S. Office of Education and through key state education departments like those in California, Texas, Michigan, Pennsylvania, and New York.

Important milestones of the transformation were: 1) an extensive government exercise in futurology called *Designing Education for the Future*, 2) the *Behavioral Science Teacher Education Project*, and 3) Benjamin Bloom's multi-volume *Taxonomy of Educational Objectives*, an enormous manual of over 1,000 pages, which in time, impacted on every school in America. While other documents exist, these three are appropriate touchstones of the whole, serving to make clear the nature of the project underway.

Take them one by one and savor each: *Designing Education*, produced by the Education Department, redefined the term "education" after the Prussian fashion as "a means to achieve important economic and social goals of a national character." State education agencies would henceforth act as on-site federal enforcers, ensuring the compliance of local schools with central directives. Each state education department was assigned the task of becoming "an agent of change" and advised to "lose its independent identity as well as its authority," in order to "form a partnership with the federal government."

The second document, the gigantic *Behavioral Science Teacher Education Project*, outlined teaching reforms to be forced on the country after 1967. If you ever want to hunt this thing down, it bears the U.S. Office of Education Contract Number OEC-0-9-320424-4042 (B10). The document sets out clearly the intentions of its creators—nothing less than "impersonal manipulation" through schooling of a future America in which "few will be able to maintain control over their opinions," an America in which "each individual receives at birth a multi-purpose identification number" which enables employers and other controllers to keep track of underlings and to expose them to direct or subliminal influence when necessary. Readers learned that "chemical experimentation" on minors would be normal procedure in this post-1967 world, a pointed foreshadowing of the massive Ritalin interventions which accompany the practice of forced schooling at present.

The *Behavioral Science Teacher Education Project* identified the future as one "in which a small elite" will control all important matters, one where participatory democracy will largely disappear. Children are made to see, through school experiences, that their classmates are so cruel and irresponsible, so inadequate to the task of self-discipline, and so ignorant they need to be controlled and regulated for society's good. Under such a logical regime, school terror can only be regarded as good advertising. It is sobering to think of mass schooling as a vast demonstration project of human inadequacy, but that is at least one of its functions.

Post-modern schooling, we are told, is to focus on "pleasure cultivation" and on "other attitudes and skills compatible with a non-work world." Thus the socialization classroom of the century's beginning—itself a radical departure from schooling for mental and character development—can be seen to have evolved by 1967 into a full-scale laboratory for psychological experimentation.

School conversion was assisted powerfully by a curious phenomenon of the middle to late 1960s, a tremendous rise in school violence and general school chaos which followed a policy declaration (which seems to have occurred nationwide) that the disciplining of children must henceforth mimic the "due process" practice of the court system. Teachers and administrators were suddenly stripped of any effective ability to keep order in schools since the due process apparatus, of necessity a slow, deliberate matter, is completely inadequate to the continual outbreaks of childish mischief all schools experience.

Now, without the time-honored *ad hoc* armory of disciplinary tactics to fall back on, disorder spiraled out of control, passing from the realm of annoyance into more dangerous terrain entirely as word surged through student bodies that teacher hands were tied. And each outrageous event that reached the attention of the local press served as an advertisement for expert prescriptions. Who had ever seen kids behave this way? Time to surrender community involvement to the management of experts; time also for emergency measures like special education and Ritalin. During this entire period, lasting five to seven years, outside agencies like the Ford Foundation exercised the right to supervise whether "children's rights" were being given due attention, fanning the flames hotter even long after trouble had become virtually unmanageable.

The *Behavioral Science Teacher Education Project*, occurring at the peak of this violence, informed teacher-training colleges that under such circumstances, teachers had to be trained as therapists; they must translate prescriptions of social psychology into "practical action" in the classroom. As curriculum had been redefined, so teaching followed suit.

Third of the new gospel texts was Bloom's *Taxonomy,*[2] in his own words, "a tool to classify

---

[2] A fuller discussion of Bloom and the other documents mentioned here, plus many more, is available in the writings of Beverly Eakman, a former Department of Education employee, particularly her book, *The Cloning of the American Mind* (1998).

the ways individuals are to act, think, or feel as the result of some unit of instruction." Using methods of behavioral psychology, children would learn proper thoughts, feelings, and actions, and have their improper attitudes brought from home "remediated."

In all stages of the school experiment, testing was essential to localize the child's mental state on an official rating scale. Bloom's epic spawned important descendent forms: Mastery Learning, Outcomes-Based Education, and School to Work government-business collaborations. Each classified individuals for the convenience of social managers and businesses, each offered data useful in controlling the mind and movements of the young, mapping the next adult generation. But for what purpose? Why was this being done?

Bad Character As A Management Tool

A large piece of the answer can be found by reading between the lines of an article appearing in the June 1998 issue of *Foreign Affairs*. Written by Mortimer Zuckerman, owner of *U.S. News and World Report* (and other major publications), the essay praises the American economy, characterizing its lead over Europe and Asia as so structurally grounded no nation can possibly catch up for100 years. American workers and the American managerial system are unique.

You are intrigued, I hope. So was I. Unless you believe in master race biology, our advantage can only have come from training of the American young, in-school and out, training which produces attitudes and behavior useful to management. What might these crucial determinants of business success be?

First, says Zuckerman, the American worker is a pushover. That's my translation, not his, but I think it's a fair take on what he means when he says the American is indifferent to everything but a paycheck. He doesn't try to tell the boss his job. By contrast, Europe suffers from a strong "steam age" craft tradition where workers demand a large voice in decision-making. Asia is even worse off because, although the worker is silenced there, tradition and government interfere with what business can do.

Next, says Zuckerman, workers in America live in constant panic; they know companies here owe them nothing as fellow human beings. Fear is our secret supercharger, it gives management flexibility no other country has. In 1996, after five years of record profitability, almost half all Americans in big business feared being laid off. This fear keeps a brake on wages.

Next, in the U.S., human beings don't make decisions, abstract formulae do; management by mathematical rules makes the company manager-proof as well as worker-proof.

Finally, our endless consumption completes the charmed circle, consumption driven by non-stop addiction to novelty, a habit which provides American business with the only reliable domestic market in the world. Elsewhere, in hard times business dries up, but not here; here we shop till we drop, mortgaging the future in bad times as well as good.

Can't you feel in your bones Zuckerman is right? I have little doubt the fantastic wealth of American big business is psychologically and procedurally grounded in our form of schooling. The training field for these grotesque human qualities is the classroom. Schools train individuals to respond as a mass. Boys and girls are drilled in being bored, frightened, envious, emotionally needy, generally incomplete. A successful mass production economy requires such a clientele. A small business, small farm economy like that of the Amish requires individual competence, thoughtfulness, compassion, and universal participation; our own requires a managed mass of leveled, spiritless, anxious, familyless, friendless, godless, and obedient people who believe the difference between "Cheers" and "Seinfeld" is a subject worth arguing about.

The extreme wealth of American big business is the direct result of school training us in certain attitudes like a craving for novelty. That's what the bells are for. They don't ring so much as to say, "Now for something different."

An Enclosure Movement For Children

The secret of American schooling is that it doesn't teach the way children learn, and it isn't supposed to. School was engineered to serve a concealed command economy and an increasingly layered social order; it wasn't made for the benefit of kids and families as those people would define their own needs. That's what massive corporate subsidies which make a mockery of the free market tell you. School is the first impression children get of organized society. Like most first impressions it is the lasting one: Life is *dull* and *stupid*, only Coke provides relief. And other products, too, of course.

The decisive dynamics which make forced schooling poisonous to healthy human development aren't hard to spot. Work in classrooms isn't significant work; it fails to satisfy real needs pressing on the individual; it doesn't answer real questions experience raises in the young mind; it doesn't contribute to solving any problem encountered in actual life. The net effect of making all schoolwork external to individual longings, experiences, questions, and problems is to render the victim listless. This phenomenon has been well-understood at least since the time of the British enclosure movement which forced small farmers off their land into factory work. Growth and mastery come only to those who vigorously self-direct. Initiating, creating, doing, reflecting, freely associating, enjoying privacy—these are precisely what the structures of schooling are set up to prevent, on one pretext or another.

As I watched it happen, it took about three years to break most kids, three years confined to environments of emotional neediness with nothing real to do. In such environments, songs, smiles, bright colors, cooperative games, and other tension-breakers do the work better than angry words and punishments could. Years ago it struck me as more than a little odd that the Prussian government was the patron of Heinrich Pestalozzi, inventor of multicultural fun-and-games psychological elementary schooling and of Friedrich Froebel, inventor of kindergarten. It struck me as odd that J.P. Morgan's partner was instrumental in bringing Prussian schooling to the prostrate South after the Civil War. But after a while I began to see that behind the philanthropy lurked a rational economic purpose.

The strongest meshes of the school net are invisible. Constant bidding for a stranger's attention creates a chemistry producing the common characteristics of modern schoolchildren: whining, dishonesty, malice, treachery, cruelty. Unceasing competition for official favor in the dramatic fish bowl of a classroom delivers cowardly children, little people sunk in chronic boredom, little people with no apparent purpose for being alive. The full significance of the classroom as a dramatic environment, as *primarily* a dramatic environment, has never been properly acknowledged or examined.

The most destructive dynamic is identical to that which causes caged rats to develop eccentric or even violent mannerisms when they press a bar for sustenance on an aperiodic reinforcement schedule (one where food is delivered at random, but the rat doesn't suspect). Much of the weird behavior school kids display is a function of the aperiodic reinforcement schedule. And the endless confinement and inactivity slowly drives children out of their minds. Trapped children, like trapped rats, need close management. Any rat psychologist will tell you that.

The Dangan

In the first decades of the twentieth century, a small group of soon-to-be-famous academics, symbolically led by John Dewey and Edward Thorndike of Columbia Teachers College, Ellwood P. Cubberley of Stanford, G. Stanley Hall, and an ambitious handful of others, energized and financed by major corporate and financial allies like Morgan, Astor, Whitney, Carnegie, and Rockefeller, decided to bend government schooling to the service of business and the political state—as it had been done a century before in Prussia.

Cubberley delicately voiced what was happening this way: "The nature of the national need must determine the character of the education provided." National need, of course, depends upon point of view. The NEA in 1930 sharpened our understanding by specifying in a resolution of its Department of Superintendence that what school served was an "effective use of capital" through which our "unprecedented wealth-producing power has been gained." Pronouncements like this mark the degree to which the organs of schooling had been transplanted into the corporate body of the new economy when you look beyond the rhetoric of Left and Right.

It's important to keep in mind that no harm was meant by any designers or managers of this great project. It was only the law of nature as they perceived it, working progressively as capitalism itself did for the ultimate good of all. The real force behind school effort came from true believers of many persuasions, linked together mainly by their belief that family and church were retrograde institutions standing in the way of progress. Far beyond the myriad practical details and economic considerations there existed a kind of grail-quest, an idea capable of catching the imagination of dreamers and firing the blood of zealots.

The entire academic community here and abroad had been Darwinized and Galtonized by this time and to this contingent school seemed an instrument for managing evolutionary destiny. In Thorndike's memorable words, conditions for controlled selective breeding had to be set up before the new American industrial proletariat "took things into their own hands."

America was a frustrating petri dish in which to cultivate a managerial revolution, however, because of its historic freedom traditions. But thanks to the patronage of important men and institutions, a group of academics were enabled to visit mainland China to launch a modernization project known as the "New Thought Tide." Dewey himself lived in China for two years where pedagogical theories were inculcated in the Young Turk elements, then tested on a bewildered population which had recently been stripped of its ancient form of governance. A similar process was embedded in the new Russian state during the 1920s.

While American public opinion was unaware of this undertaking, some big-city school superintendents were wise to the fact that they were part of a global experiment. Listen to H.B. Wilson, superintendent of the Topeka schools:

The introduction of the American school into the Orient has broken up 40 centuries of conservatism. It has given us a new China, a new Japan, and is working marked progress in Turkey and the Philippines. The schools...are in a position to determine the lines of progress.

— *Motivation of School Work* (1916)

Thoughts like this don't spring full-blown from the heads of men like Dr. Wilson of Topeka. They have to be planted there.

The Western-inspired and Western-financed Chinese revolution, following hard on the heels of the last desperate attempt by China to prevent the British government market in narcotic drugs there, placed that ancient province in a favorable state of anarchy for laboratory tests of mind-alteration technology. Out of this period rose a Chinese universal tracking procedure called "The Dangan," a continuous lifelong personnel file exposing every student's intimate life history from birth through school and onwards. The Dangan constituted the ultimate overthrow of privacy. Today, nobody works in China without a Dangan.

By the mid-1960s preliminary work on an American Dangan was underway as information reservoirs attached to the school institution began to store personal information. A new class of expert like Ralph Tyler of the Carnegie endowments quietly began to urge collection of personal data from students and its unification in computer code to enhance cross-referencing. Surreptitious data gathering was justified by Tyler as "the moral right of institutions."

Occasional Letter Number One

Between 1896 and 1920, a small group of industrialists and financiers together with their private charitable foundations, subsidized university chairs, university researchers, and school administrators, and spent more money on forced schooling than the government itself did. Carnegie and Rockefeller, as late as 1915, were spending more themselves. In this laissez-faire fashion a system of modern schooling was constructed without public participation. The motives for this are undoubtedly mixed, but it will be useful for you to hear a few excerpts from the first mission statement of Rockefeller's General Education Board as they occur in a document called *Occasional Letter Number One* (1906):

> In our dreams...people yield themselves with perfect docility to our molding hands.
> The present educational conventions [intellectual and character education] fade
> from our minds, and unhampered by tradition we work our own good will upon a
> grateful and responsive folk. We shall not try to make these people or any of their
> children into philosophers or men of learning or men of science. We have not to
> raise up from among them authors, educators, poets or men of letters. We shall not
> search for embryo great artists, painters, musicians, nor lawyers, doctors, preachers,
> politicians, statesmen, of whom we have ample supply. The task we set before
> ourselves is very simple...we will organize children...and teach them to do in a perfect
> way the things their fathers and mothers are doing in an imperfect way....

This mission statement will reward multiple rereadings.

Change Agents Infiltrate

By 1971, the U.S. Office of Education was deeply committed to accessing private lives and thoughts of children. In that year it granted contracts for seven volumes of "change-agent" studies to the RAND Corporation. Change-agent training was launched with federal funding under the Education Professions Development Act. In time the fascinating volume *Change Agents Guide to Innovation in Education* appeared, following which grants were awarded to teacher training programs for the development of change agents. Six more RAND manuals were subsequently distributed enlarging the scope of change agentry.

In 1973, Catherine Barrett, president of the National Education Association said, "Dramatic changes in the way we raise our children are indicated, particularly in terms of schooling...we will be agents of change." By 1989, a senior director of the Mid-Continent Regional Educational Laboratory told the 50 governors of American states assembled to discuss government schooling that year, "What we're into is total restructuring of society." It doesn't get much plainer than that. There is no record of a single governor objecting.

Several years later Gerald Bracey, a leading government school advocate, claimed in an instructive essay that, realistically, we must continue to produce an uneducated social class. Overproduction was the bogey of industrialists in 1900; a century later underproduction made possible by dumbed-down schooling had still to keep that disease in check.

Bionomics

The crude power and resources to make twentieth century forced schooling happen as it did came from corporations, powerful families, university people derived from sons of the declining Protestant ministry, and the federal government. All this is easy enough to trace once you know it's there. But the soul of the thing was far more complex, an amalgam of ancient religious doctrine, utopian philosophy, and European/Asiatic strong-state politics mixed together and distilled. The great facade behind which this was happening was a new enlightenment: scientific scholarship in league with German research values brought to America in the last half of the nineteenth century. Modern German tradition always assigned universities the primary task of directly serving industry and the political state, but that was a radical contradiction of American tradition to serve the individual and the family.

Indiana University provides a sharp insight into the kind of science-fictional consciousness developing outside the mostly irrelevant debate conducted in the press about schooling, a debate proceeding on early nineteenth century lines. By 1900, a special discipline existed at Indiana for elite students, Bionomics. Invitees were hand-picked by college president David Starr Jordan, who created and taught the course. It dealt with the why and how of producing a new evolutionary ruling class, although that characterization, suggesting as it does kings, dukes, and princes, is somewhat misleading. In the new scientific era dawning the ruling class were those managers trained in the goals and procedures of new systems. Jordan did so well at Bionomics he was soon invited into the major leagues of university existence, (an invitation extended personally by rail tycoon Leland Stanford) to become first president of Stanford University, a school inspired by Andrew Carnegie's famous "Gospel of Wealth" essay. Jordan remained president of Stanford for 30 years.

Bionomics acquired its direct link with forced schooling in a fortuitous fashion. When he left Indiana, Jordan eventually reached back to get his star Bionomics protégé, Ellwood P. Cubberley, to become Dean of Teacher Education at Stanford. In this heady position, young Cubberley made himself a reigning aristocrat of the new institution. He wrote a history of American schooling which became the standard of the school business for the next 50 years; he assembled a national syndicate which controlled administrative posts from coast to coast. Cubberley was the man to see, the kingmaker in American school life until its pattern set in stone.

Did the abstract and rather arcane discipline of Bionomics have any effect on real life? Well, consider this: the first formal legislation making forced sterilization a legal act on planet Earth was passed, not in Germany or Japan, but in the American state of Indiana, a law which became official in the famous 1927 Supreme Court test case *Buck vs. Bell.* Justice Oliver Wendell Holmes wrote the majority opinion allowing 17-year-old Carrie Buck to be sterilized against her will to prevent her "degenerate offspring," in Holmes' words, from being born. Twenty years after the momentous decision, in the trial of German doctors at Nuremberg, Nazi physicians testified their precedents were American—aimed at combating racial degeneracy. The German name for forced sterilization was "the Indiana Procedure."

To say this bionomical spirit infected public schooling is only to say birds fly.[3] Once you know it's there, the principle jumps out at you from behind every school bush. It suffused public discourse in many areas where it had claimed superior insight. Walter Lippmann, in 1922, demanded "severe restrictions on public debate," in light of the allegedly enormous number of feeble-minded Americans. The old ideal of participatory democracy was insane, according to Lippmann.

The theme of scientifically controlled breeding interacted in a complex way with the old Prussian ideal of a logical society run by experts loyal to the state. It also echoed the idea of British state religion and political society that God Himself had appointed the social classes. What gradually began to emerge from this was a Darwinian caste-based American version of institutional schooling remote-controlled at long distance, administered through a growing army of hired hands, layered into intricate pedagogical hierarchies on the old Roman principle of divide and conquer. Meanwhile in the larger world, assisted mightily by intense concentration of ownership in the new electronic media, developments moved swiftly also.

In 1928, Edward Bernays, godfather of the new craft of spin control we call "public relations," told the readers of his book *Crystallizing Public Opinion* that "invisible power" was now in control of every aspect of American life. Democracy, said Bernays, was only a front for skillful wire-pulling. The necessary know-how to pull these crucial wires was available for sale to businessmen and policy people. Public imagination was controlled by shaping the minds of schoolchildren.

By 1944, a repudiation of Jefferson's idea that mankind had natural rights was resonating in every corner of academic life. Any professor who expected free money from foundations, corporations, or government agencies had to play the scientific management string on his lute. In

---

[3] The following questions were put to schoolchildren in the South Dearborn School District in Aurora, Indiana, in 1994 with which they were asked to: Strongly Agree/Agree/Disagree/Strongly Disagree: "I approve the practice of sterilizing the feeble-minded living in state institutions," and "I think it is unacceptable to society to use medical procedures to keep genetically defective humans alive so they can marry and reproduce."

1961, the concept of the political state as the sovereign principle surfaced dramatically in John F. Kennedy's famous Inaugural address in which his national audience was lectured, "Ask not what your country can do for you, but what you can do for your country."

Thirty-five years later Kennedy's lofty Romanized rhetoric and metaphor was replaced by the tough-talking wise guy idiom of *Time*, now instructing its readers in a 1996 cover story that "Democracy is in the worst interest of national goals." As *Time* reporters put it, "The modern world is too complex to allow the man or woman in the street to interfere in its management." Democracy was deemed a system for losers.

To a public desensitized to its rights and possibilities, frozen out of the national debate, to a public whose fate was in the hands of experts, the secret was in the open for those who could read entrails: the original American ideals had been repudiated by their guardians. School was best seen from this new perspective as the critical terminal on a production line to create a utopia resembling EPCOT Center, but with one important bionomical limitation: it wasn't intended for everyone, at least not for very long, this utopia.

Out of Johns Hopkins in 1996 came this chilling news:

> The American economy has grown massively since the mid 1960s, but
> workers' real spendable wages are no higher than they were 30 years ago.

That from a book called *Fat and Mean*, about the significance of corporate downsizing. During the boom economy of the 1980s and 1990s, purchasing power rose for 20 percent of the population and actually declined 13 percent for the other four-fifths. Indeed, after inflation was factored in, purchasing power of a working couple in 1995 was only eight percent greater than for a single working man in 1905; this steep decline in common prosperity over 90 years forced both parents from home and deposited kids in the management systems of daycare, extended schooling, and commercial entertainment. Despite the century-long harangue that schooling was the cure for unevenly spread wealth, exactly the reverse occurred—wealth was 250 percent more concentrated at century's end than at its beginning.

I don't mean to be inflammatory, but it's as if government schooling made people dumber, not brighter; made families weaker, not stronger; ruined formal religion with its hard-sell exclusion of God, set the class structure in stone by dividing children into classes and setting them against one another, and has been midwife to an alarming concentration of wealth and power in the hands of a fraction of the national community.

Waking Up Angry

Throughout most of my long school career I woke up angry in the morning, went through the school day angry, went to sleep angry at night. Anger was the fuel that drove me to spend 30 years trying to master this destructive institution.

CHAPTER THREE

Eyeless In Gaza

The deeds were monstrous, but the doer [Adolf Eichmann]....was quite ordinary, commonplace, and neither demonic nor monstrous. There was no sign in him of firm ideological convictions or of specific evil motives, and the only notable characteristic one could detect in his past behavior as well as in his behavior during the trial...was something entirely negative; it was not stupidity but thoughtlessness.... Might not the problem of good and evil, our faculty for telling right from wrong, be connected with our faculty for thought?
— Hannah Arendt, *The Life of the Mind*

The School Edition

I always knew schoolbooks and real books were different, most kids do, but I remained vague on any particular grounds for my prejudice until one day, tired of the simple-minded junior high school English curriculum, I decided to teach *Moby Dick* to eighth grade classes. A friendly assistant principal smuggled a school edition into the book purchases and we were able to weigh anchor the next fall.

What a book! Ishmael, the young seaman who relates Melville's novel, is a half-orphan by decree of Fate, sentenced never to know a natural home again. But Ahab is no accidental victim; he has consciously willed his own exile from a young wife and child, from the fruits of his wealth, and from Earth itself in order to pursue his vocation of getting even. Revenge on the natural order is what drives him.

War against God and family. To me it defines the essence of Americanness. It's no accident that America's three classic novels, *Moby Dick*, *The Scarlet Letter*, and *Huckleberry Finn*, each deal with ambiguous families, or that each is close in time to the creation of the others. America has been an inferno for families; Melville, Hawthorne, and Twain all knew this. By the mid-point of our first century as a nation, the near-universal American experience of homelessness found its voice. Ishmael is a half-orphan, Ahab an absentee father and husband, the harpooners expatriate men of color; Pearl a bastard, Hester an adulteress, the Reverend Dimmesdale a sexual predator and runaway father; Huck Finn, *de facto*, an adoptee, Jim a twice-uprooted African slave. When we think what our schools became we need to recall what a great pile of us are homeless. We itch for homes we can never have as long as we have institutions like school, television, corporation, and government *in loco parentis*.

Patricia Lines of the Department of Education, in trying honorably to discuss what the rank and file of homeschoolers actually *do*, finally declared it seems to be wrapped up closely with a feeling of "intense interest in the life of the community." Above anything else, she found *loyalty* to the warp and woof of family:

> Homeschoolers are tremendously *loyal* as family members, they are
> suspicious of television and other less intimate influences. They eat
> as a family, they socialize as a family, they attend church as a family,
> they become members of an extended...homeschooling community.

American great fiction is about individuals broken from family. The closest they come to satisfying the universal yearning is a struggle for surrogates—like the strange connection between Pearl, Hester, and the dark forest. America's most fascinating storytellers focus on the hollowness of American public life. We have no place to go when work is done. Our inner life long extinguished, our public work in remaking the world can never be done because personal *homework* isn't available to us. There's no institutional solace for this malady. In outrage at our lonely fate, we lay siege to the family sanctuary wherever it survives, as Ahab lay siege to the seas for his accursed Whale.

For this and other reasons long lost, I decided to teach *Moby Dick* to my eighth grade classes. Including the dumb ones. I discovered right away the white whale was just too big for 45-minute bell breaks; I couldn't divide it comfortably to fit the schedule. Melville's book is too vast to say just what the right way to teach it really is, it speaks to every reader privately. To grapple with it demanded elastic time, not the fixed bell breaks of junior high; indeed it offered so many choices of purpose—some aesthetic, some historical, some social, some philosophical, some theological, some dramatic, some economic—that compelling the attention of a room full of young people to any one aspect seemed willful and arbitrary.

Soon after I began teaching *Moby Dick* I realized the school edition wasn't a real book but a kind of disguised indoctrination providing all the questions, a scientific addition to the original text designed to make the book teacher-proof and student-proof. If you even *read* those questions (let alone answered them) there would be no chance ever again for a private exchange between you and Melville; the invisible editor would have preempted it.

The editors of the school edition provided a package of prefabricated questions and more than 100 chapter-by-chapter abstracts and interpretations of their own. Many teachers consider this a gift—it does the thinking for them. If I didn't assign these questions kids wanted to know why. Their parents wanted to know why. Unless everyone duly parroted the party line set down by the book editor, children used to getting high marks became scared and angry.

The school text of *Moby Dick* had been subtly denatured; it was worse than useless, it was dangerous. So I pitched it out and bought a set of undoctored books with my own money. The school edition of *Moby Dick* asked all the right questions so I had to throw it away. Real books don't do that. Real books demand people actively participate asking their own questions. Books that show you the best questions to ask aren't just stupid, they hurt the mind under the guise of helping it—exactly the way standardized tests do. Real books, unlike schoolbooks, can't be standardized. They are eccentric; no book fits everyone.

If you think about it, schooled people, like schoolbooks, are much alike. Some folks find that desirable for economic reasons. The discipline organizing our economy and our politics derives from mathematical and interpretive exercises, the accuracy of which depends upon customers being much alike and very predictable. People who read too many books get quirky. We can't have too much eccentricity or it would bankrupt us. Market research depends on people behaving *as if* they were alike. It doesn't really matter whether they *are* or not.

One way to see the difference between schoolbooks and real books like *Moby Dick* is to examine different procedures which separate librarians, the custodians of real books, from schoolteachers, the custodians of schoolbooks. To begin with, libraries are usually comfortable, clean and quiet. They are orderly places where you can actually read instead of just pretending to read.

For some reason libraries are never age-segregated, nor do they presume to segregate readers by questionable tests of ability any more than farms or forests or oceans do. The librarian doesn't tell me what to read, doesn't tell me what sequence of reading I have to follow, doesn't grade my reading. The librarian trusts me to have a worthwhile purpose of my own. I appreciate that and trust the library in return.

Some other significant differences between libraries and schools: the librarian lets me ask my own questions and helps me when I want help, not when she decides I need it. If I feel like reading all day long, that's okay with the librarian, who doesn't compel me to stop at intervals by ringing a bell in my ear. The library keeps its nose out of my home, it doesn't send letters to my family, it doesn't issue orders how I should use my reading time at home.

The library doesn't play favorites; it's a democratic place as seems proper in a democracy. If the books I want are available I get them even if that decision deprives someone more gifted and talented than I am. The library never humiliates me by posting ranked lists of good readers, it presumes good reading is its own reward and doesn't need to be held up as an object lesson to bad readers. One of the strangest differences between a library and a school is that you almost never see a kid behaving badly in a library.

The library never makes predictions about my future based on my past reading habits. It tolerates eccentric reading because it realizes free men and women are often very eccentric. Finally, the library has real books, not schoolbooks. I know the *Moby Dick* I find in the library won't have questions at the end of the chapter or be scientifically bowlderized. Library books are not written by collective pens. At least not yet.

Real books conform to the private curriculum of each author, not to the invisible curriculum of a corporate bureaucracy. Real books transport us to an inner realm of solitude and unmonitored mental reflection in a way schoolbooks and computer programs can't because that would jeopardize school routines devised to control behavior.

Intellectual Espionage

At the start of WWII millions of men showed up at registration offices to take low-level academic tests before being inducted.[1] The years of maximum mobilization were 1942 to1944; the fighting force had been mostly schooled in the 1930s, both those inducted and those turned away. Eighteen million men were tested; seventeen million, two-hundred-and-eighty-thousand of them were judged to have the minimum competence in reading required to be a soldier, a 96 percent literacy rate. Although this was a 2 percent fall-off from the 98 percent rate among *voluntary* military applicants ten years before, the dip was so small it didn't worry anybody.

WWII was over in 1945. Six years later another war began in Korea. Several million men were tested for military service but this time 600,000 were rejected. Literacy in the draft pool had dropped to 81 percent even though all that was needed to classify a soldier as literate was fourth grade reading proficiency. In the few short years from the beginning of WWII to Korea a terrifying problem of adult illiteracy had appeared. The Korean War group received most of *its* schooling in the 1940s, it had more years in school with more professionally trained personnel and more scientifically selected textbooks than the WWII men, yet it could not read, write, count, speak or think as well as the earlier, less-schooled contingent.

A third American war began in the mid-1960s. By its end in 1973 the number of men found non-inductible by reason of inability to read safety instructions, interpret road signs, decipher orders, and so on—the number found illiterate in other words—had reached 27 percent of the total pool. Vietnam-era young men had been schooled in the 1950s and the 1960s—much better schooled than either of the two earlier groups—but the 4 percent illiteracy of 1941 which had transmuted into the 19 percent illiteracy of 1952 had now had grown into the 27 percent illiteracy of 1970. Not only had the fraction of competent readers dropped to 73 percent but a substantial chunk of even those were only *barely* adequate; they could not keep abreast of developments by reading a newspaper, they could not read for pleasure, they could not sustain a thought or an argument, they could not write well enough to manage their own affairs without assistance.

Consider how much more compelling this steady progression of intellectual blindness is when we track it through Army admissions tests rather than college admissions scores and standardized reading tests which inflate apparent proficiency by frequently changing the way the tests are scored.

Looking back, abundant data exists from states like Connecticut and Massachusetts to show that by 1840 the incidence of complex literacy in the United States was between 93 and 100 percent wherever such a thing mattered. Everyone was literate, rich and poor alike. In Connecticut only one citizen out of every 579 was illiterate[2] and you probably don't want to know, not really, what people in those days considered literate; it's too embarrassing. Popular novels of the period give a clue: *Last of the Mohicans,* published in 1818, sold so well a contemporary equivalent would have to

---

[1] The discussion here is based on Regna Lee Wood's work printed in the U.S. Citizens' Alliance Educational Foundation newsletter, also in Chester Finn and Diane Ravitch's *Network News and Views,* and other places.

[2] Census of 1840.

move 10 million copies to match it. If you pick up an uncut version you find yourself in a dense thicket of philosophy, history, culture, manners, politics, geography, astute analysis of human motives and actions, all conveyed in data-rich periodic sentences so formidable only a determined and well-educated reader can handle it nowadays. Yet in 1818 we were a small-farm nation without colleges or universities to speak of. Could those simple folk have had more complex minds than our own?

By 1940, the literacy figure for all states stood at 96 percent for whites, 80 percent for blacks. Notice for all the disadvantages blacks labored under, four of five were still literate. Six decades later, at the end of the twentieth century, the National Adult Literacy Survey and the National Assessment of Educational Progress say 40 percent of blacks and 17 percent of whites can't read at all. Put another way, black illiteracy doubled, white illiteracy quadrupled. Before you think of anything else in regard to these numbers, think of this: we spend three to four times as much real money on schooling as we did 60 years ago, but 60 years ago virtually everyone, black or white, could read.

In their famous bestseller, *The Bell Curve*, prominent social analysts Charles Murray and Richard Herrnstein say that what we're seeing are the results of breeding in a high-tech society. Smart people naturally get together with smart people, dumb people with dumb people. As they have children generation after generation, the differences between the groups gets larger and larger. That sounds plausible and the authors produce impressive mathematics to prove their case, but their documentation shows they are entirely ignorant of the military data available to challenge their contention. The terrifying drop in literacy between World War II and Korea happened in a decade, and even the brashest survival-of-the-fittest theorist wouldn't argue evolution unfolds that way. *The Bell Curve* writers say black illiteracy (and violence) is genetically programmed, but like many academics they ignore contradictory evidence.

For example, on the matter of violence inscribed in black genes, the inconvenient parallel is to South Africa where 31 million blacks live, the same as the number who live in the United States. Compare numbers of blacks who died by violence in South Africa in civil war conditions during 1989, 1990, and 1991 with our own peacetime mortality statistics and you find that far from exceeding the violent death toll in the U.S. or even matching it, South Africa had proportionately less than one-quarter the violent death rate of American blacks. If more contemporary comparisons are sought, we need only compare the current black literacy rate in the U.S. (56 percent) with the rate in Jamaica (98.5 percent)—a figure considerably higher than the American white literacy rate (83 percent).

If not heredity, what then? Well, one change is indisputable, well-documented and easy to track. During WWII, American public schools massively converted to non-phonetic ways of teaching reading. On the matter of violence alone this would seem to have impact: according to the Justice Department, 80 percent of the incarcerated *violent* criminal population is illiterate or nearly so (and 67 percent of all criminals locked up). There seems to be a direct connection between the humiliation poor readers experience and the life of angry criminals.[3] As reading ability plummeted

---

[3] A particularly clear example of the dynamics hypothesized to cause the correlation can be found in Michael S. Brunner's monograph, "Reduced Recidivism and Increased Employment Opportunity Through Researched-Based Reading Instruction," United States Department of Justice (June, 1992). Brunner's recent book *Retarding*

in America after WWII, crime soared, so did out-of-wedlock births, which doubled in the 1950s and doubled again in the 60s when bizarre violence for the first time became commonplace in daily life.

When literacy was first abandoned as a primary goal by schools, white people were in a better position than black people because they inherited a 300-year-old American tradition of learning to read at home by matching spoken sound with letters, thus home assistance was able to correct the deficiencies of dumbed-down schools for whites. But black people had been forbidden to learn to read during slavery, and as late as 1930 only averaged three to four years of schooling so they were helpless when teachers suddenly stopped teaching children to read, they had no fall-back position. Not helpless because of genetic inferiority but because they had to trust school authorities to a much greater extent than white people.

Back in 1952 the Army quietly began hiring hundreds of psychologists to find out how 600,000 high school graduates had successfully faked illiteracy. Regna Wood sums up the episode this way:

> After the psychologists told the officers that the graduates weren't faking, Defense Department administrators knew that something terrible had happened in grade school reading instruction. And they knew it had started in the thirties. Why they remained silent, no one knows. The switch back to reading instruction that worked for everyone should have been made then. But it wasn't.

In 1882, fifth graders read these authors in their *Appleton School Reader*: William Shakespeare, Henry Thoreau, George Washington, Sir Walter Scott, Mark Twain, Benjamin Franklin, Oliver Wendell Holmes, John Bunyan, Daniel Webster, Samuel Johnson, Lewis Carroll, Thomas Jefferson, Ralph Waldo Emerson, and others like them. In 1995, a student teacher of fifth graders in Minneapolis wrote to the local newspaper, "I was told children are not to be expected to spell the following words correctly: back, big, call, came, can, day, did, dog, down, get, good, if, in, is, it, have, he, home, like, little, man, morning, mother, my, night, off, out, over, people, play, ran, said, saw, she, some, soon, their, them, there, time, two, too, up, us, very, water, we, went, where, when, will, would, etc. Is this nuts?"

America, written as a Visiting Fellow for the U.S. Department of Justice, is recommended. A growing body of documentation ties illiteracy causally to violent crime. A study by Dennis Hogenson "Reading Failure and Juvenile Delinquency" (Reading Reform Foundation) attempted to correlate teenage aggression with age, family size, numbers of parents present in home, rural versus urban environment, socio-economic status, minority group membership, and religious preference. None of these factors produced a significant correlation. But one did. As the author reports, "Only reading failure was found to correlate with aggression in both populations of delinquent boys." An organization of ex-prisoners testified before the Sub-Committee on Education of the U.S. Congress that in its opinion illiteracy was an important causative factor in crime "for the illiterate have very few honest ways to make a living." In 1994 the U.S. Department of Education acknowledged that two-thirds of all incarcerated criminals have poor literacy.

Looking Behind Appearances

Do you think class size, teacher compensation, and school revenue have much to do with education quality? If so, the conclusion is inescapable that we are living in a golden age. From 1955 to 1991 the U.S. pupil/teacher ratio dropped 40 percent, the average salary of teachers rose 50 percent (in real terms) and the annual expense per pupil, inflation adjusted, soared 350 percent. What other hypothesis then might fit this strange data I'm about to present?

Forget the 10 percent drop in SAT and Achievement Test scores the press beats to death with regularity; how do you explain the 37 percent decline since 1972 in students who score above 600 on the SAT? *This is an absolute decline not a relative one.* It is not affected by an increase in unsuitable minds taking the test or by an increase in the numbers. The absolute body count of smart students is down drastically with a test not more difficult than yesterday's but considerably less so.

What should be made of a 50 percent decline among the most rarefied group of test-takers, those who score above 750? Two-thousand, eight-hundred-and-seventeen American students reached this pinnacle in 1972; 1,438 did in 1994—*when kids took a much easier test.* Can a 50 percent decline occur in 22 years without signaling that some massive leveling in the public school mind is underway?[4] Between 1960 and 1998 the non-teaching bureaucracy of public schools grew 500 percent, but oversight was concentrated into fewer and fewer hands. The 40,520 school districts with elected boards this nation had in 1960 shriveled to 15,000 by 1998.

On the college rung of the school ladder something queer was occurring, too. Between 1960 and 1984 the quality of undergraduate education at America's 50 best-known colleges and universities altered substantially. According to a 1996 report by the National Association of Scholars, these schools stopped providing "broad and rigorous exposure to major areas of knowledge" for the average student, even at decidedly un-average universities like Yale and Stanford.

---

[4] The critics of schooling who concentrate on fluctuations in standardized test scores to ground their case against the institution are committing a gross strategic mistake for several reasons, the most obvious of which is that in doing so they must first implicitly acknowledge the accuracy of such instruments in ranking every member of the youth population against every other member, hence the justice of using such measures to allocate privileges and rewards. An even larger folly occurs because the implicit validation of these tests by the attention of school critics cedes the entire terrain of scientific pedagogy, armoring it against strong counter-measures by recruiting the opposition, in effect, to support teaching to the test. The final folly lies in the ease with which these measures can be rigged to produce whatever public effects are wanted.

In a real sense where your own child is concerned you might best forget scores on these tests entirely as a reliable measure of what they purport to assess. I wouldn't deny that *mass* movements in these scores in one direction or another indicate *something* is going on, and since the correlation between success *in schooling* and success on these tests is close, then significant score shifts are certainly measuring changes in understanding. This is a difficult matter for anyone to sort out since many desirable occupational categories (and desirable university seats even before that) are reserved for those who score well. The resultant linkage of adult income with test scores then creates the illusion these tests are separating cream from milk, but the results are rigged in advance by foreclosing opportunity to those screened out by the test! In a humble illustration, if you only let students with high scores on the language component of the SATs cut hair, eventually it would appear that verbal facility and grooming of tresses had some vital link with each other.

In 1964, more than half these institutions required a thesis or comprehensive for the bachelor's degree, by 1993 twelve percent did; over the same period, the average number of classroom days fell 16 percent, and requirements in math, natural science, philosophy, literature, composition, and history almost vanished. Rhetoric, most potent of the active literacies, *completely* vanished, and foreign language, once required at 96 percent of the great colleges, fell to 64 percent.

According to *The Journal of the American Medical Association*, (December 1995), 33 percent of all patients cannot read and understand instructions on how often to take medication, notices about doctor's appointments, consent forms, labels on prescription bottles, insurance forms, and other simple parts of self-care. They are rendered helpless by inability to read. Behind prison walls (where the nation's jailed population has tripled since 1980) the National Center for Education Statistics said in a 1996 report that 80 percent of all prisoners could not interpret a bus schedule, could not understand a news article or warranty instructions, read maps, schedules or payroll forms, or balance a checkbook. Forty percent could not calculate the cost of a purchase.

Once upon a time we were a new nation that allowed ordinary citizens to learn how to read well and encouraged them to read anything they thought would be useful. Close reading of tough-minded writing is still the best, cheapest, and quickest method known for learning to think for yourself. This invitation to commoners extended by America was the most revolutionary pedagogy of all.

Reading, and rigorous discussion of that reading in a way that obliges you to formulate a position and support it against objections, is an operational definition of education in its most fundamental civilized sense. No one can do this very well without learning ways of paying attention: from a knowledge of diction and syntax, figures of speech, etymology, and so on, to a sharp ability to separate the primary from the subordinate, understand allusion, master a range of modes of presentation, test truth, and penetrate beyond the obvious to the profound messages of text. Reading, analysis and discussion is the way we develop reliable judgment, the principal way we come to penetrate covert movements behind the facade of public appearances. Without the ability to read and argue we're just geese to be plucked.

Just as experience is necessary to understand abstraction, so the reverse is true. Experience can only be mastered by extracting general principles out of the mass of details. In the absence of a perfect universal mentor, books and other texts are the best and cheapest stand-ins, always available to those who know where to look. Watching details of an assembly line or a local election unfold isn't very educational unless you have been led in careful ways to analyze the experience. Reading is the skeleton key for all who lack a personal tutor of quality.[5]

Reading teaches nothing more important than the state of mind in which you find yourself *absolutely alone* with the thoughts of another mind, a matchless form of intimate rapport only

---

[5] In a fascinating current illustration of the power of books, black female tennis star Venus Williams' father acknowledged in a press interview for the Toronto *Globe* that he had, indeed, set out to create a tennis millionaire from his infant daughter even before her birth. Mr. Williams, who had no knowledge whatsoever of the game of tennis, and who was reared in a poor home in the South by his single mother, had his ambition piqued by witnessing a young woman on television receiving a $48,000 check for playing tennis successfully. At that moment he proposed to his wife that they set out to make their unborn children tennis millionaires. How did he learn the game? By reading books, he says, and renting videos. That, and common sense discipline, was all that Venus and sister Serena needed to become millionaire teenagers.

available to those with the ability to block out distraction and concentrate. Hence the urgency of reading *well* if you read for power.

Once you trust yourself to go mind-to-mind with great intellects, artists, scientists, warriors and philosophers you are finally free. In America, before we had forced schooling, an astonishing range of unlikely people knew reading was like the tresses of Samson, something to make them formidable, something that taught them rights and how to defend those rights, that helped them be self-determining and not intimidated by experts, that gave them insight into the ways of the human heart so they could not be cheated or fooled so easily, and that provided an inexhaustible store of useful knowledge, advice on how to do just about anything.

By 1812, Pierre DuPont was claiming barely four in a thousand Americans couldn't read well and that the young had disciplined skill in argumentation thanks to daily debates at the common breakfast table. If more evidence was needed, it could be found in the sale of five million copies of James Fenimore Cooper's complex and allusive novels by 1820 and an equal sale of Noah Webster's didactic *Speller*—both to a population of dirt farmers under 20 million in size.

In 1835, Richard Cobden announced there was six times as much newspaper reading in the United States as in England, and the census figures of 1840 gave fairly exact evidence that a sensational reading revolution had taken place without any exhortation on the part of public moralists and social workers but because common people had the initiative and freedom to learn. In North Carolina, the worst situation of any state surveyed, eight out of nine could still read and write.

In 1853, Per Siljestromm, a Swedish visitor, wrote, "In no country in the world is the taste for reading so diffuse as among the common people in America." The *American Almanac* observed grandly, "Periodical publications, especially newspapers, disseminate knowledge throughout all classes of society and exert an amazing influence in forming and giving effect to public opinion." It noted the existence of over 1,000 newspapers. In this nation of common readers, the spiritual longings of ordinary people shaped the public discourse. Ordinary people who could read, though not privileged by wealth, power, or position, could see through the fraud of social class or the even grander fraud of official expertise. That was the trouble.

Sam Blumenfeld, whose book *The New Illiterates* is the best introduction to what went wrong with reading in the U.S., once got a letter from a reader bursting with honest pride at the success she had imparting the alphabet code to her four children, ranging in age up to five. The author's method was the classic time-tested one of practice with letter sounds. She confided her three-year-old was working his way through a lesson alone:

> One day I found my three-year-old at the kitchen table reading S-am,
> Sam; m-an, man, and so on, completing Lesson 2 all by himself. I had
> not taught him. I had just taught him his letter sounds. He picked it up
> and did it himself. That's how simple it is.

The Sudbury Valley School

I know a school for kids age 3 to 18 that doesn't teach anybody to read, yet everyone who goes there learns to do it, most very well. It's the beautiful Sudbury Valley School, 20 miles west of Boston in the old Nathaniel Bowditch "cottage" (which looks suspiciously like a mansion), a place ringed by handsome outbuildings, a private lake, woods, and acres of magnificent grounds. Sudbury is a private school but with a tuition under $4,000 a year it's considerably cheaper than a seat in a New York City public school. At Sudbury kids teach themselves to read; they learn at many different ages, even into the teen years (though that's rare). When each kid is ready he or she self-instructs, if such a formal label isn't inappropriate for such a natural undertaking. During this time they are free to request as much adult assistance as needed. That usually isn't much.

In 30 years of operation, Sudbury has never had a single kid who didn't learn to read. All this is aided by a magnificent school library on open shelves where books are borrowed and returned on the honor system. About 65 percent of Sudbury kids go on to good colleges. The place has never seen a case of dyslexia. (That's not to say some kids don't reverse letters and such from time to time but such conditions are temporary and self-correcting unless institutionalized into a disease.) So Sudbury doesn't even teach reading yet all its kids learn to read and even like reading. What could be going on there that we don't understand?

Bootie Zimmer

The miracle woman who taught me to read was my mother, Bootie. Bootie never got a college degree but nobody despaired about that because daily life went right along then without too many college graduates. Here was Bootie's scientific method: she would hold me in her lap and read to me while she ran her finger under the words. That was it, except to read always with a lively expression in her voice and eyes, to answer my questions, and from time to time to give me some practice with different letter sounds. One thing more is important. For a long time we would *sing*, "A, B, C, D, E, F, G,.......H, I, J, K, LMNOP..." and so on, every single day. We learned to love each letter. She would read tough stories as well as easy ones; truth is I don't think she could readily tell the difference anymore than I could. The books had some pictures but only a few; words made up the center of attention. Pictures have nothing at all to do with learning to love reading except too many of them will pretty much guarantee that it never happens.

Over 50 years ago my mother Bootie Zimmer chose to teach me to read well. She had no degrees, no government salary, no outside encouragement, yet her private choice to make me a reader was my passport to a good and adventurous life. Bootie, the daughter of a Bavarian printer, said "Nuts!" to the Prussian system. She voted for her own right to decide, and for that I will always be in her debt. She gave me a love of language and it didn't cost much. Anybody could have the same, if schooling hadn't abandoned its duty so flagrantly.

False Premises

The religious purpose of modern schooling was announced clearly by the legendary University of Wisconsin sociologist Edward A. Ross in 1906 in his famous book, *Social Control*. Your librarian should be able to locate a copy for you without much trouble. In it Ed Ross wrote these words for his prominent following:

> Plans are underway to replace community, family, and church with
> propaganda, education, and mass media....the State shakes loose from

Church, reaches out to School.... People are only little plastic lumps of
human dough.

There you have it in a nutshell. The whole problem with modern schooling. It rests on a nest
of false premises. People are *not* little plastic lumps of dough. They are not blank tablets as John
Locke said they were, they are not machines as La Mettrie hoped, not vegetables as Friedrich
Froebel, inventor of kindergartens, hypothesized, not organic mechanisms as Wilhelm Wundt taught
every psychology department in America at the turn of the century, nor are they repertoires of
behaviors as Watson and Skinner wanted. They are not, as the new crop of systems thinkers would
have it, mystically harmonious microsystems interlocking with grand macrosystems in a dance of
atomic forces. I don't want to be crazy about this; locked in a lecture hall or a bull session there's
probably no more harm in these theories than reading too many Italian sonnets all at one sitting, but
each of these suppositions sprung free as a foundation for school experiments leads to frightfully
oppressive practices.

One of the ideas that empty child thinking led directly to was the notion that human breeding
could be enhanced or retarded as plant and animal breeding was—by scientific gardeners and
husbandmen. Naturally the time scale over which this was plotted to happen was quite long.
Nobody expected it to be like breeding fruit flies, but it was a major academic, governmental, and
even military item generously funded until Hitler's proactive program (following America's lead)
grew so embarrassing by 1939 that our own projects and plans became more circumspect.

Back at the beginning of the twentieth century, the monstrously influential Edward Thorndike
of Columbia Teachers College said that school would establish conditions for "selective breeding
before the masses take things into their own hands." The religious purpose of modern schooling was
embarrassingly evident back when Ross and Thorndike were on center stage, but they were
surrounded by many like-minded friends. Another major architect of standardized testing, H.H.
Goddard, said in his book *Human Efficiency* (1920) that government schooling was about "the
perfect organization of the hive." He said standardized testing was a way to make lower classes
recognize their own inferiority. Like wearing a dunce cap, it would discourage them from breeding
and having ambition. Goddard was head of the Psychology Department at Princeton, so imagine the
effect he had on the minds of the doctoral candidates he coached, and there were hundreds. We
didn't leave the religious purpose of modern schooling back in the early years of the century. In
April of 1996, Al Shanker of the AFT said in his regular *New York Times* split page advertisement
that every teacher was really a priest.

A System Of State Propaganda

Something strange is going on in schools and has been going on for quite some time.
Whatever it is does not arise from the main American traditions. As closely as I can track the thing
through the attitudes, practices, and stated goals of the shadowy crew who make a good living
skulking around educational "laboratories," think tanks, and foundations, we are experiencing an
attempt, successful so far, to reimpose the strong-state, strong social class attitudes of England and
Germany on the United States—the very attitudes we threw off in the American Revolution. And
in this counter-revolution the state churches of England and Germany have been replaced by the
secular church of forced government schooling.

Advertising, public relations, and stronger forms of quasi-religious propaganda are so pervasive in our schools, even in "alternative" schools, that independent judgment is suffocated in mass-produced secondary experiences and market-tested initiatives. One of the many new corporations formed to dig gold from our conditions of schooling, Lifetime Learning Systems, announced to its corporate clients, "School is the ideal time to influence attitudes, build long-term loyalties, introduce new products, test-market, promote sampling and trial usage—and above all—to generate immediate sales."

Arnold Toynbee, the establishment's favorite historian in mid-twentieth century America, said in his monumental *Study of History* that the original promise of universal education had been destroyed *as soon as the school laws were passed*, a destruction caused by "the possibility of turning education to account as a means of amusement for the masses" and a means of "profit for the enterprising persons by whom the amusement is purveyed." This opportunistic conversion quickly followed mass schooling's introduction when fantastic profit potential set powerful forces in motion:

> The bread of universal education is no sooner cast upon the water than
> a shoal of sharks arises from the depths and devours the children's bread
> under the educator's very eyes.

In Toynbee's analysis "the dates speak for themselves":

> The edifice of universal education was, roughly speaking, completed...
> in 1870; and the Yellow Press was invented twenty years later—as soon,
> that is, as the first generation of children from the national schools had
> acquired sufficient purchasing power—by a stroke of irresponsible genius
> which had divined that the educational labour of love could be made to
> yield a royal profit....

But vultures attending the inception of forced compulsion schooling attracted more ferocious predators:

> [The commercial institutions that set about at once to prey on forced mass
> schooling] attracted the attention of the rulers of modern...national states.
> If press lords could make millions by providing idle amusement for the
> half-educated, serious statesman could draw, not money perhaps, but power
> from the same source. The modern dictators have deposed the press lords
> and substituted for crude and debased private entertainment an equally crude
> and debased system of state propaganda.

The Ideology Of The Text

Looking back on the original period of school formation in her study of American history textbooks, *America Revised*, Frances Fitzgerald remarked on the profound changes that emerged following suggestions issued by sociologists and social thinkers in the later nineteenth and early twentieth centuries. The original history of our institutions and the documents which protect our unique liberties gradually began to be effaced. Fitzgerald raises the puzzle of textbook alteration:

> The ideology that lies behind these texts is rather difficult to define....
> it does not fit usual political patterns....the texts never indicate any line
> of action....authors avoid what they choose to and some of them avoid
> main issues....they fail to develop any original ideas....they confuse social
> sciences with science....clouds of jargon....leave out ideas....historical
> names are given no character, they are cipher people....*there are no
> conflicts, only "problems"*....

Indeed, the texts are nearly unreadable and that may be their purpose.

The National Adult Literacy Survey

In 1982, Anthony Oettinger, a member of the private discussion group called the Council on Foreign Relations, asked an audience of communications executives this question: "Do we really have to have everybody literate—writing and reading in the traditional sense—when we have means through our technology to achieve a new flowering of oral communication?" Oettinger suggested "our idea of literacy" is "obsolete." Eighty-three years earlier John Dewey had written in "The Primary Education Fetish" that "the plea for the predominance of learning to read in early school life because of the great importance attaching to literature seems to be a perversion."

For the balance of this discussion I'm going to step into deeper water, first reviewing what reading in a Western alphabet really means and what makes it a reasonably easy skill to transmit or to self-learn, and then trying to tackle what happened to deprive the ordinary person of the ability to manage it very well. I want to first show you *how*, then answer the more speculative question *why*.

The National Adult Literacy Survey represents 190 million U.S. adults over age sixteen with an average school attendance of 12.4 years. The survey is conducted by the Educational Testing Service of Princeton, New Jersey. It ranks adult Americans into five levels. Here is its 1993 analysis:

1) Forty-two million Americans over the age of sixteen can't read. Some of this group can write their names on Social Security cards and fill in height, weight, and birth spaces on application forms.

2) Fifty million can recognize printed words on a fourth and fifth grade level. They cannot write simple messages or letters.

3) Fifty-five to sixty million are limited to sixth, seventh, and eighth grade reading. A majority of this group could not figure out the price per ounce of peanut butter in a 20-ounce jar costing $1.99 when told they could round the answer off to a whole number.

4)   Thirty million have ninth and tenth grade reading proficiency. This group (and all preceding) cannot understand a simplified written explanation of the procedures used by attorneys and judges in selecting juries.

5)   About 3.5 percent of the 26,000-member sample demonstrated literacy skills adequate to do traditional college study, a level 30 percent of all U.S. high school students reached in 1940, and which 30 percent of secondary students in other developed countries can reach today. This last fact alone should warn you how misleading comparisons drawn from international student competitions really are, since the samples each country sends are small elite ones, unrepresentative of the entire student population. But behind the bogus superiority a real one is concealed.

6)   Ninety-six and a half percent of the American population is mediocre to illiterate where deciphering print is concerned. This is no commentary on their intelligence, but without ability to take in primary information from print and to interpret it they are at the mercy of commentators who tell them what things mean. A working definition of immaturity might include those who excessively require others to tell them what things mean.

Certainly it's possible to argue that bad readers aren't victims at all but perpetrators, cursed by inferior biology to have only shadows of intellect. That's what bell curve theory, evolutionary theory, aristocratic social theory, eugenics theory, strong-state political theory, and some kinds of theology are about. All agree most of us are inferior, if not downright dangerous. The integrity of such theoretical outlooks— at least where reading was concerned—took a stiff shot on the chin from America. Here democratic practice allowed a revolutionary generation to learn how to read. Those granted the opportunity took advantage of it brilliantly.

Name Sounds, Not Things

So how was the murder of American reading ability pulled off? I'll tell you in a second, but come back first to classical Greece where the stupendous invention of the alphabet by Phoenicians was initially understood. The Phoenicians had an alphabetic language used to keep accounts, but the Greeks were the first to guess correctly that revolutionary power could be unleashed by transcending mere lists, using written language for the permanent storage of analysis, exhortation, visions, and other things. After a period of experiment the Greeks came up with a series of letters to represent sounds of their language. Like the Phoenicians, they recognized the value of naming each letter in a way distinct from its sound value—as every human being has a name distinct from his or her personality, as numbers have names for reference.

Naming sounds *rather than things* was the breakthrough! While the number of things to be pictured is impossibly large, the number of sounds is strictly limited. In English, for example, most people recognize forty-four.[6] Also, communicating abstractions in picture language is a subtlety

---

[6] The "problem" with English phonics has been wildly exaggerated, sometimes by sincere people but most often by those who make a living as guides through the supposed perils of learning to read. These latter constitute a

requiring more time and training to master than is available for most of us. Greeks now could organize ambitious concepts abstractly in written language, communicating accurately with each other over space and time much more readily than their competitors.

According to Mitford Mathews:[7]

> The secret of their phenomenal advance was in their conception of the nature of a word. They reasoned that words were sounds or combinations of ascertainable sounds, and they held inexorably to the basic proposition that writing, properly executed, was a guide to sound.

Learning sound-sight correspondences comes first in an alphabetic language. Competence with the entire package of sounds corresponding to alphabet symbols comes quickly. After that anything can be read and its meaning inquired after. The substantial speaking vocabulary kids bring to school (6,000-10,000 words) can now be read at once, and understood.

When the Romans got the alphabet through the Etruscans they lost the old letter *names* so they invented new ones making them closer to the letter sounds. That was a significant mistake which causes confusion in novice readers even today. Through conquest the Latin alphabet spread to the languages of Europe; Rome's later mutation into the Universal Christian Church caused Latin, the language of church liturgy, to flow into every nook and cranny of the former empire.

The Latin alphabet was applied to the English language by Christian missionaries in the seventh century. While it fused with spoken English this was far from a perfect fit. There were no single letters to stand for certain sounds. Scribes had to scramble to combine letters to approximate sounds that had no companion letter. This matching process was complicated over centuries by repeated borrowings from other languages and by certain massive sound shifts which still occupy scholars in trying to explain.

Before the spread of printing in the sixteenth century, not being able to read wasn't much of a big deal. There wasn't much to read. The principal volume available was the Bible, from which

---

vast commercial empire with linkages among state education departments, foundations, publishers, authors of school readers, press, magazines, education journals, university departments of education, professional organizations, teachers, reading specialists, local administrators, local school boards, various politicians who facilitate the process and the U.S. offices of education, defense and labor.

The problem, which American families once largely solved for themselves, is this: in English, a Latin alphabet has been imposed on a Germanic language with multiple non-Germanic borrowings, and it doesn't quite fit. Our 44 sounds are spelled 400+ different ways. That sounds horrible, but in reality in the hands of even a mediocre teacher, its only annoying; in the hands of a good one, a thrilling challenge. Actually 85 percent of the vast word stock of English can be read with knowledge of only 70 of the phonograms. A large number of the remaining irregularities seldom occur and can be remastered on an as-needed basis. Meanwhile a whole armory of mnemonic tricks like "If a 'c' I chance to spy, place the 'e' before the "i" exist to get new readers over the common humps. Inexpensive dictionaries, spell-check typewriters, computers, and other technology are readily available these days to silently coach the fearful, but in my experience, that "fear" is neither warranted nor natural. Instead it is engendered. Call it good business practice.

[7] Mitford Mathews, *Teaching to Read Historically Considered (1966)*. A brief, intelligent history of reading. A number of other good treatments are available for the newcomer.

appropriate bits were read aloud by religious authorities during worship and on ceremonial occasions. Available texts were in Latin or Greek, but persistent attempts to provide translations was a practice thought to contain much potential for schism. An official English Bible, the Authorized King James Version, appeared in 1611, preempting all competitors in a bold stroke which changed popular destiny.

Instantly, the Bible became a universal textbook, offering insights both delicate and powerful, a vibrant cast of characters, brilliant verbal pyrotechnics and more to the humblest rascal who could read. Talk about a revolutionary awakening for ordinary people! The Bible was it, thanks to the dazzling range of models it provided in the areas of exegesis, drama, politics, psychology, characterization, plus the formidable reading skills it took to grapple with the Bible. A little more than three decades after this translation, the English king was deposed and beheaded. The connection was direct. Nothing would ever be the same again because too many good readers had acquired the proclivity of thinking for themselves.

The magnificent enlargement of imagination and voice that the Bible's exceptional catalogue of language and ideas made available awakened in ordinary people a powerful desire *to read* in order to read the Holy Book without a priest's mediation. Strenuous efforts were made to discourage this, but the Puritan Revolution and Cromwell's interregnum sent literacy surging. Nowhere was it so accelerated as in the British colonies in North America, a place already far removed from the royal voice.

Printing technology emerged. Like the computer in our own day, it was quickly incorporated into every corner of daily life. But there were still frequent jailings, whippings, and confiscations for seditious reading as people of substance came to realize how dangerous literacy could be.

Reading offered many delights. Cravings to satisfy curiosity about this Shakespeare fellow or to dabble in the musing of Lord Bacon or John Locke were now not difficult to satisfy. Spelling and layout were made consistent. Before long, prices of books dropped. All this activity multiplied pressure on illiterate individuals to become literate. The net result of printing (and Protestantism, which urged communicants to go directly to the Word, eliminating the priestly middleman), stimulated the spread of roving teachers and small proprietary and church schools. A profession arose to satisfy demand for a popular way to understand what uses to make of books, and from this a demand to understand many things.

The Meatgrinder Classroom

The first schoolman to seriously challenge what is known today as phonics was Friedrich Gedike, a disciple of Rousseau, director of a well-known gymnasium in Prussia. In 1791 he published the world's first look/say primer, *A Children's Reader Without the ABC's and Spelling*. The idea was to eliminate drill. Kids would learn through pictures following suggestions the legendary mystic and scholar Comenius set down in his famous *Orbis Pictus* of 1657.

After a brief splash and three editions, the fashion vanished for an excellent reason: As good as it sounds in theory, it doesn't work well at all in practice (although here and there exceptions are encountered and infuriatingly enough it can *seem* to work in the early years of first and second grade). Soon after that the rapidly developing reading power in phonetically trained children makes them capable of recognizing in print their entire speaking and listening vocabulary, while look/say trained readers can only read without error words they have memorized as whole shapes, a relative handful.

This is devilishly complex terrain. Gedike's theory held that when enough words are ingested and recognized, the student *can figure out for himself* the 70 key phonograms of the English language. Indeed this is the only credible explanation which *could* account for the well-known phenomenon of children who teach themselves to read handily without the use of any system at all. I have no doubt children occasionally learn to read this way. Yet if true, how do we account for the grotesque record of whole word instruction for over a century and a half in every conceivable school setting?

Money, time, attention, and caring adults in profusion, all have been available to make this alternative method work to teach reading proficiency, yet its record in competition with the old-fashioned alphabet system is horrifying. What might account for this?

I have a hunch based on a decade of ruminating. Since no one has yet bothered to assemble a large group of self-taught good readers and asked them how it happened, let my hunch serve as a working hypothesis for you to chew upon at your leisure. Consider first the matter of *time*. The average five-year-old can master all of the 70 phonograms in six weeks. At that point he can *read* fluently just about anything. Can he *understand* everything? No, of course not. But also no synthetic barrier to understanding is being interposed by weird-looking words to be memorized whole, either. Paulo Freire taught ignorant *campesinos* with no tradition of literacy at all to read in 30 hours. They were adults, with different motivations than children, but when he showed them a sentence and they realized it said, "The land belongs to the tiller," they were hooked. That's Jesuit savvy for you.

Back to this matter of *time*. By the end of the fourth grade, phonics-trained students are at ease with an estimated 24,000 words. Whole-word trained students have memorized about 1,600 words and can successfully guess at some thousands more, but also *unsuccessfully* guess at thousands, too. One reigning whole-word expert has called reading, "a psycho-linguistic guessing game" in which the reader is not extracting the writer's meaning but constructing a meaning of his own.

Now while there is an attractive side to this that is ignored by critics of whole language (and I number myself among these), the value doesn't begin to atone for the theft of priceless reading time and guided practice. As long as whole-language kids are retained in a hothouse environment, shielded from linguistic competition, things seem idyllic, but once mixed together with phonetically trained kids of similar age and asked to avail themselves of the intellectual treasure locked up in words, the result is not so pretty. Either the deficient kid must retreat from the field with a whopping sense of inferiority, or worse, he must advance aggressively into the fray claiming books are overrated, that thinking and judgment are merely matters of opinion. The awful truth is that circumstances hardly give us the luxury of testing Gedike's hypothesis about kids being able to deduce the rules of language from a handful of words. Humiliation makes mincemeat of most of them long before the trial is fairly joined.

So, the second hunch I have is that where whole word might work when it works at all is in a comfortable, protected environment without people around to laugh meanly at the many wretched mistakes you must make on the way to becoming a Columbus of language. But in case you hadn't noticed, schools *aren't* safe places for the young to guess at the meanings of things. Only an imbecile would pretend that school isn't a pressure-cooker of psycho-drama. Wherever children are gathered into groups by compulsion, a pecking order soon emerges in which malice, mockery, intimidation of the weak, envy, and a whole range of other nasty characteristics hold sway, like that famous millpond of Huxley's, whose quiet surface mirroring fall foliage conceals a murderous subterranean world whose law is eat or be eaten.

That's melodramatic, I suppose, yet 30 classroom years and a decade more as a visitor in hundreds of other schools have shown me what a dramatic meatgrinder the peaceful classroom really is. Bill is wondering whether he will be beaten again on the way to the lunchroom; Molly is paralyzed with fear that the popular Jean will make loud fun of her prominent teeth; Ronald is digging the point of a sharpened pencil into the neck of Herbert who sits in front of him, all the while whispering he will get Herb good if he gets Ron in trouble with the teacher; Alan is snapping a rubber band at Flo; Ralph is about to call Leonard "trailer park trash" for the three-hundredth time that day, not completely clear he knows what it means, yet enjoying the anguish it brings to Leonard's face; Greta, the most beautiful girl in the room, is practicing ogling shyer boys, then cutting them dead when she evokes any hopeful smiles in response; Willie is slowly shaken down for a dollar by Phil, and Mary's single mom at home has just received an eviction notice.

Welcome to another day in an orderly, scientific classroom. Teacher may have a permanent simper pasted on her face but it's deadly serious, the world she presides over, a bad place to play psycho-linguistic guessing games which involve sticking one's neck out in front of classmates as the rules of language are empirically derived. A method that finds mistakes to be "charming stabs in the right direction" may be onto something person-to-person or in the environment of a loving home but it's dynamically unsuited to the forge of forced schooling.

The Ignorant Schoolmaster

After Gedike, the next innovator to hit on a reading scheme was Jean Joseph Jacotot, a grand genius, much misunderstood. A professor of literature at nineteen, Jacotot discovered a method of teaching non-speakers of French the French language beginning not with primers but with Fenelon's *Telemachus*. Jacotot read aloud slowly while students followed his reading in a dual translation—to their own familiar language and to Fenelon's spoken French. Then the process was repeated. After the group reading, each student individually dismantled the entire book into parts, into smaller parts, into paragraphs, into sentences, into words, and finally into letters and sounds. This followed the "natural" pattern of scientists it was thought, beginning with wholes, and reducing them to smaller and smaller elements.

Jacotot has a reputation as a whole-word guru but any resemblance to contemporary whole-word reading in Jacotot is illusion. His method shifts the burden for analysis largely from the shoulders of the teacher to the student. The trappings of holistic non-competitiveness are noticeably absent. Penalty for failure in his class was denial of advancement. Everyone succeeded in Jacotot's system, but then, his students were highly motivated, self-selected volunteers, all of college age.

From Jacotot we got the idea anybody can teach anything. His was the concept of the ignorant schoolmaster. It should surprise no one that the ideas of Jacotot interested Prussians who brought his system back to Germany and modified it for younger children. For them, however, a *book* seemed too impractical a starting point, perhaps a *sentence* would be better or a *single* word. Eventually it was the latter settled upon. Was this the genesis of whole-word teaching which eventually dealt American reading ability a body blow?

The answer is a qualified *No*. In the German "normal word" method the whole word was not something to be memorized but a specimen of language to be analyzed into syllables. The single word was made a self-conscious vehicle for learning letters. Once letter sounds were known, reading instruction proceeded traditionally. To a great extent, this is the method my German mother used with my sister and myself to teach us to read fluently before we ever saw first grade.

Frank Had A Dog; His Name Was Spot

Two flies now enter the reading ointment in the persons of Horace Mann and his second wife, Mary Peabody. There is raw material here for a great intrigue novel: in the early 1830s, a minister at Hartford, Thomas Gallaudet, invented a sight-reading, look-say method to use with the deaf. Like Jacotot, Gallaudet was a man of unusual personal force and originality. He served as director at the asylum for the education of the deaf and dumb in Hartford. Deaf mutes couldn't learn a sound-symbol system, it was thought, so Gallaudet devised a sight-reading vocabulary of 50 whole words which he taught through pictures. Then his deaf students learned a manual alphabet which permitted them to indicate letters with their fingers and communicate with others.

Even in light of the harm he inadvertently caused, it's hard not to be impressed by Gallaudet. In Gallaudet's system, writing transmuted from a symbolic record of *sounds* to a symbolic record of *pictures*. Gallaudet had reinvented English as ancient Babylonian! One of Gallaudet's former teachers, William Woodbridge, now editor of the *American Annals of Education*, received a long, detailed letter in which Gallaudet described his flash-card method and demanded that education be regarded as a science like chemistry: "Mind, like matter, can be made subject to experiment." Fifty words could be learned by memory *before* introducing the alphabet. By removing the "dull and tedious" normal method, great interest "has [been] excited in the mind of the little learner."

Historically, three important threads run together here: 1) that learning should be scientific, and learning places a laboratory; 2) that words be learned ideographically; 3) that relieving boredom and tedium should be an important goal of pedagogy. Each premise was soon pushed to extremes. These themes institutionalized would ultimately require a vast bureaucracy to enforce. But all this lay in the future.

Gallaudet had adopted the point of view of a deaf-mute who had to make his way without assistance from sound to spoken language. Samuel Blumenfeld's analysis of what was wrong in this is instructive:

> It led to serious confusions in Gallaudet's thinking concerning two very
> different processes; that of learning to speak one's native language and
> that of learning to read it. In teaching the deaf to read by sight he was also
> teaching them language by sight for the first time. They underwent two
> learning processes, not one. But a normal child came to school already
> with the knowledge of several thousand words in his speaking vocabulary,
> with a much greater intellectual development which the sense of sound
> afforded him. In learning to read it was not necessary to teach him what he

already knew, to repeat the process of learning to speak. The normal child
did not learn his language by learning to read. He learned to read in order
to help him expand his *use* of the language....

In 1830, Gallaudet published *The Child's Picture Defining and Reading Book,* a book for
non-deaf children, seeking to generalize his method to all. In its preface, the book sets down for the
first time basic whole-word protocols. Words will be taught as representing objects and ideas, not
as sounds represented by letters.

He who controls language controls the public mind, a concept well understood by Plato.
Indeed, the manipulation of language was at the center of curriculum at the Collegia of Rome, in the
Jesuit academies, and the private schools maintained for children of the influential classes; it made
up an important part of the text of Machiavelli; it gave rise to the modern arts and sciences of
advertising and public relations. The whole-word method, honorably derived and employed by men
like Gallaudet, was at the same time a tool to be used by any regime or interest with a stake in
limiting the growth of intellect.

Gallaudet's primer, lost to history, was published in 1836. One year later, the Boston School
Committee was inaugurated under the direction of Horace Mann. Although no copies of the primer
have survived, Blumenfeld tells us, "From another source we know that its first line was, *Frank had
a dog; his name was Spot.*" On August 2, 1836, Gallaudet's primer was adopted by the Boston
Primary School Committee on an experimental basis. A year later a report was issued pronouncing
the method a success on the basis of *speed in learning* when compared to the alphabet system, and
of bringing a "pleasant tone" to the classroom by removing "the old unintelligible, and irksome mode
of teaching certain arbitrary marks, or letters, by certain arbitrary sounds."

A sight vocabulary *is* faster to learn than letters and phonograms, but the gain is a Trojan
horse; only after several years have passed does the sight reader's difficulty learning words from
outside sources begin to become apparent. By that time conditions made pressing by the social
situation of the classroom and demands from the world at large combine to make it hard to retrace
the ground lost.

Mann endorsed Gallaudet's primer in his *Second Annual Report* (1838). His endorsement,
Gallaudet's general fame and public adulation, erroneous reports circulating at the time that mighty
Prussia was using a whole word system, and possibly the prospect of fame and a little profit, caused
Mann's own wife, Mary Tyler Peabody—whose family names were linked to a network of powerful
families up and down the Eastern seaboard—to write a whole-word primer. The Mann family was
only one of a host of influential voices being raised against the traditional reading instructions in the
most literate nation on Earth. In Woodbridge's *Annals of Education,* a steady tattoo was directed
against spelling and the alphabet method.

By the time of the Gallaudet affair, both Manns were under the spell of phrenology, a now
submerged school of psychology and the brainchild of a German physician. Francois Joseph Gall,
in working with the insane, had become convinced he had located the *physical site* of personality
traits like love, benevolence, acquisitiveness, and many more. He could provide a map of their
positions inside the skull! These faculties signaled their presence, said Gall, by making bumps on
the visible exterior of the cranium. The significance of this to the future of reading is that among
Gall's claims was: *too much reading causes insanity.* The Manns agreed.

One of Gall's converts was a Scottish lawyer named George Combe. On October 8, 1838, Mann wrote in his diary that he had met "the author of that extraordinary book, *The Constitution of Man*, the doctrines of which will work the same change in metaphysical science that Lord Bacon wrought in natural." The book was Combe's. Suddenly the Mann project to downgrade reading acquired a psychological leg to accompany the political, social, economic, and religious legs it already possessed. Unlike other arguments against enlightenment of ordinary people—all of which invoked one or another form of class interest—what psychological phrenology offered was a scientific argument based on the supposed best interests of the child. Thus a potent weapon fell into pedagogy's hands which would not be surrendered after phrenology was discredited. If one psychology could not convince, another might. The scientific case, by appearing to avoid any argument from special interest, took the matter of who should learn what out of the sphere of partisan politics into a loftier realm of altruism.

Meanwhile Combe helped Mann line up his great European tour of 1843, which was to result in the shattering *Seventh Report* to the Boston School Committee of 1844. (The *Sixth* had been a plea to phrenologize classrooms!) This new report said: "I am satisfied our greatest error in teaching children to read lies in beginning with the alphabet." Mann was attempting to commit Massachusetts children to the hieroglyphic system of Gallaudet. The result was an outcry from Boston's schoolmasters, a battle that went on in the public press for many months culminating (on the schoolmaster's side) in this familiar lament:

> Education is a great concern; it has often been tampered with by vain theorists;
> it has suffered from the stupid folly and the delusive wisdom of its treacherous
> friends; and we hardly know which have injured it most. Our conviction is, that
> it has much more to hope from the collected wisdom and common prudence of
> the community than from the suggestions of the individual. Locke injured it by
> his theories, and so did Rousseau, and so did Milton. All their plans were too
> splendid to be true. It is to be advanced by conceptions, neither soaring above
> the clouds, nor groveling on the earth—but by those plain, gradual, productive,
> common sense improvements, which use may encourage and experience suggest.
> We are in favor of advancement, provided it be towards usefulness....
>
> We love the secretary but we hate his theories. They stand in the way of substantial
> education. It is impossible for a sound mind not to hate them.

The Pedagogy Of Literacy

Between Mann's death and the great waves of Italian immigration after the 1870s, the country seemed content with McGuffey readers, Webster Spelling Books, *Pilgrim's Progress*, the Bible, and the familiar alphabet method for breaking the sound code. But beginning about the year 1880 with the publication of Francis W. Parker's *Supplementary Reading for Primary Schools* (and his *Talks on Pedagogics*, 1883), a new attack on reading was mounted.

Parker was a loud, affable, flamboyant teacher with little academic training himself, a man forced to resign as principal of a Chicago teachers college in 1899 for reasons not completely honorable. Shortly thereafter, at the age of 62, he was suddenly selected to head the School of Education at Rockefeller's new University of Chicago,[8] a university patterned after great German research establishments like Heidelberg, Berlin, and Leipzig.

As supervisor of schools in Boston in a former incarnation, Parker had asserted boldly that learning to read was learning a vocabulary which can be instantly recalled as ideas when certain symbolic signposts are encountered. Words are learned, he said, by repeated acts of association of the word with the idea it represents.

Parker originated the famous Quincy Movement, the most recognizable starting point for progressive schooling. Its reputation rested on four ideas: 1) *group activities* in which the individual is submerged for the good of the collective; 2) *emphasis on the miracles of science (as opposed to traditional classical studies* of history, philosophy, literature); 3) *informal instruction* in which teacher and student dress casually, call each other by first names, treat all priorities as very flexible, etc; 4) *the elimination of harsh discipline* as psychologically damaging to children. Reading was not stressed in Parker schools.

Parker's work and that of other activists antagonistic to reading received a giant forward push in 1885 from one of the growing core of America's new "psychologists" who had studied with Wilhelm Wundt at Leipzig. James McKeen Cattell boldly announced he had *proven*, using the tachistoscope, *that we read whole words and not letters*. Cattell's lusty ambition can be heard in his cry of triumph:

> These results are important enough to prove those to be wrong who hold with
> Kant that psychology can never become an exact science.

Until 1965 no one bothered to check Cattell's famous experiment with the tachistoscope. When they did it was found Cattell had been dead wrong. People read letters, not words.

It was out of the cauldron of Columbia Teacher's College that the most ferocious advocate of whole word therapy came: Edward Burke Huey was his name, his mentor, G. Stanley Hall. In 1908 they published an influential book, *The Psychology and Pedagogy of Reading*, which laid out the revolution ahead in a way that sent a message of bonanzas to come to the new educational book publishing industry. Publishing was a business just beginning to reap fantastic profits from contracts with the new factory schools. Centralized management was proving a pot of gold for lucky book contractors in big cities. The message was this: "Children should be taught to read English as if it were Chinese: ideographically."

Huey was even more explicit: he said *children learned to read too well and too early and that was bad for them*:

> He must not, by reading adult grammatical and logical forms, begin exercises
> in mental habits which will violate his childhood.

As Blumenfeld (to whom I owe much of the research cited here) explains, Huey concocted a novel

---

[8] Mrs. Anita McCormick Blaine, daughter of the inventor of the harvesting machine, became his patron, *purchasing* the College of Education for him with a contribution of one million dollars.

justification based on Darwinian evolution for jettisoning the alphabet system:

> The history of the language in which picture-writing was long the main means
> of written communication has here a wealth of suggestions for the framers
> of the new primary course. It is not from mere perversity that the boy chalks
> or carves his records on a book and desk.... There is here a correspondence
> with, if not a direct recapitulation of the life of the race; and we owe it to the
> child to encourage his living through the best there is in this pictography stage....

Dick And Jane

As many before him, Huey missed entirely the brilliant Greek insight that *reading* and *understanding* are two different things. Good reading is the fluent and effortless cracking of the symbol-sound code which puts understanding within easy reach. Understanding is the translation of that code into meaning.

It is for many people a natural and fairly harmless mistake. Since they read for meaning, the code-cracking step is forgotten. Forgotten, that is, by those who read well. For others, self-disgust and despair engendered by halting progress *in decoding sounds* sets into play a fatal chain of circumstances which endangers the relationship to print for a long time, sometimes wrecking it forever. If decoding is a painful effort, filled with frustrating errors, finally a point is reached when the reader says in effect, *to the devil with it.*

Another piece of dangerous philosophy is concealed inside whole word practice—the notion that a piece of writing is only an orange one squeezes in order to extract something called meaning, some bit of data. The sheer luxury of putting your mind in contact with the greatest minds of history across time and space, *feeling* the rhythm of their thought, the sallies and retreats, the marshaling of evidence, the admixture of humor or beauty of observation and many more attributes of power and value language possesses, has something in common with being coached by Bill Walsh in football or Toscanini in orchestra conducting. *How* these men say what they say is as important as the translation of their words into yours. The music of language is what poetry and much rhetoric is about, the literal meaning often quite secondary. Powerful speech depends on this understanding.

By 1920, the sight-word method was being used in new wave progressive schools. In 1927, another professor at Columbia Teacher's College, Arthur Gates, laid the foundation for his own personal fortune by writing a book called *The Improvement of Reading*, which purported to muster 31 experimental studies proving that sight reading was superior to phonics. All these studies are either trivial or highly ambiguous at best and at times, in a practice widely encountered throughout higher education research in America, Gates simply draws the conclusions he want from facts which clearly lead elsewhere.

But his *piece de resistance* is a comparison of first grade deaf pupils tutored in the whole word method with Detroit first graders. The scores of the two groups are almost identical, causing Gates to declare this a most convincing demonstration. Yet it had been well known for almost a century that deaf children taught with a method created expressly for deaf children only gain a temporary advantage which disappears quickly. In spite of this cautionary detail Gates called this "conclusive proof" *that normal children taught this way would improve even faster*!

Shortly after the book's publication, Arthur Gates was given the task of authoring Macmillan's basal reader series, a pure leap into whole word method by the most prestigious education publisher of them all. Macmillan was a corporation with wide-reaching contacts able to enhance an author's career. In 1931, Gates contributed to the growth of a new reading industry by writing an article for *Parents* magazine, "New Ways of Teaching Reading." Parents were told to abandon any residual loyalty they might have to the barren, formal older method and to embrace the new as true believers. A later article by a Gates associate was expressly tailored for "those parents concerned because children do not know their letters." It explained, "the modern approach to reading," eliminated the boredom of code-cracking.

With its finger in the wind, the large educational publisher, Scott, Foresman, ordered a revision of its Elson Basic Readers drawn on the traditional method, a series which had sold 50 million copies to that date. To head up the mighty project, the publisher brought in William S. Gray, dean of the University of Chicago College of Education, to write its all new whole-word pre-primer and primer books marking the debut of two fictional young Americans who would change millions of minds into mush during their long tenure in school classrooms. Their names were Dick and Jane.

After Gates and Gray, most major publishers fell into line with other whole word series and in the words of Rudolf Flesch, "inherited the kingdom of American education," with its fat royalties. Blumenfeld does the student of American schooling a great service when he compares this original 1930 Dick and Jane with its 1951 successor:

"In 1930, the Dick and Jane *Pre-Primer* taught 68 sign words in 39 pages of story text, with an illustration per page, a total of 565 words—and a Teacher's Guidebook of 87 pages. In 1951, the same book was expanded to 172 pages with 184 illustrations, a total of 2,603 words—and a Guidebook of 182 pages to teach a sight vocabulary of only 58 words!" Without admitting any disorder, the publisher was protecting itself from this system, and the general public, without quite knowing why, was beginning to look at its schools with unease.

By 1951, entire public school systems were bailing out on phonics and jumping on the sight-reading bandwagon. Out of the growing number of reading derelicts poised to begin tearing the schools apart which tormented them, a giant remedial reading industry was spawned, a new industry completely in the hands of the very universities who had with one hand written the new basal readers, and with the other taught a generation of new teachers about the wonders of the whole word method.

Mute evidence Scott, Foresman wasn't just laughing all the way to the bank, but was actively trying to protect its nest egg in *Dick and Jane,* was its canny multiplication of words intended to be learned. In 1930, the word *look* was repeated eight times; in 1951, 110 times; in the earlier version *oh* repeats twelve times, in the later 138 times; in the first, *see* gets 27 repetitions, in the second, 176.[9]

---

[9] 1955 proved to be a year of great frustration to the reading combine because of the publication of Rudolf Flesch's hostile *Why Johnny Can't Read* which precisely analyzed the trouble and laid it at the doorstep of the reading establishment. The book was a hot seller for over a year, continuing to reverberate through the reading world for a long time thereafter. In 1956, 56,000 reading professionals formed a look/say defense league called the International Reading Association." It published three journals as bibles of enthusiasm; *The Reading Teacher, The Journal of*

The famous Dr. Seuss of *Cat in the Hat* fame, America's best-selling controlled scientific vocabulary, children's book author, put the mindlessness of all this before the public in an interview he gave in 1981:

> I did it for a textbook house and they sent me a word list. That was due to the Dewey revolt in the twenties, in which they threw out phonics reading and went to a word recognition as if you're reading a Chinese pictograph instead of blending sounds or different letters. I think killing phonics was one of the greatest causes of illiteracy in the country.
>
> Anyway they had it all worked out that a healthy child at the age of four can only learn so many words in a week. So there were two hundred and twenty-three words to use in this book. I read the list three times and I almost went out of my head. I said, " I'll read it once more and if I can find two words that rhyme, that'll be the title of my book." I found "cat" and "hat" and said, the title of my book will be *The Cat in the Hat*.

For the 41 months beginning in January of 1929 and concluding in June of 1932, there were 88 articles written in various pedagogical journals on the subject of reading difficulties and remedial teaching; in the 41 months beginning in July of 1935 and concluding in December of 1938, the number rose almost 200 percent to 239. The first effects of the total victory of whole word reading philosophy were being reflected in academic journals as the once mighty reading Samson of America was led eyeless to Gaza with the rest of the slaves.

Reading, The Reading Research Quarterly. Between 1961 and 1964, a new generation of academics shape-shifted look/say into psycholinguistics under the leadership of Frank Smith, an excellent writer when not riding his hobby horse, and Kenneth and Yetta Goodman, senior authors at Scott, Foresman who had been widely quoted as calling reading "a psycholinguistic guessing game." From 1911 to 1981, there were 124 legitimate studies attempting to prove Cattell and the other whole-word advocates right. Not a single one confirmed whole word reading as effective.

The Author in his last year of teaching. Staging a publicity event at Tri-Star Films
to illustrate the principle of *quid pro quo.*

CHAPTER FOUR

I Quit,

I Think

The master's face goes white, then red. His mouth tightens and opens
and spit flies everywhere....
What will I do, boys?
Flog the boy, sir.
Till?
Till the blood spurts, sir.

> — Frank McCourt. Writing of Ireland's
> schools as they were in the 1940s.

Wadleigh, The Death School

One day after spending nearly my entire life inside a school building as student and teacher, I quit. But not before I saw some things you ought to know. McCourt is right, spit flies everywhere in the classroom and school, children mock us because of it. The smell of saliva. I had forgotten until I returned as a teacher. Put the cosmic aspect aside and come back again into school with me. See it from the inside with grownup eyes.

On my first day back to school I was hired to substitute in a horrible place, Wadleigh Junior High School, nicknamed "the death school" by regulars at the West End Tavern near Columbia. Jean Stapleton (Archie Bunker's wife Edith) had gone there as a young girl; so had Anäis Nin, celebrated diarist and pornographer. Some palace revolution long before I got there had altered the nature of this school from an earnest, respectable Victorian lock-up to something indescribable. During my teaching debut at Wadleigh, I was attacked by a student determined to bash my brains out with a chair.

Wadleigh was located three blocks from that notorious 110th street corner in Harlem made famous by a bestseller of the day, *New York Confidential*, which called it "the most dangerous intersection in America." I mention danger as the backdrop of my teaching debut because two kinds of peril were in the air that season: one, phony as my teaching license, was the "Cuban Missile Crisis," the other, only too genuine, was a predicament without any possible solution, a deadly brew compounded from 1,200 black teenagers penned inside a gloomy brick pile six hours a day with a white guard staff misnamed "faculty" manning the light towers and machine-gun posts. This faculty was charged with dribbling out something called "curriculum" to inmates, a gruel so thin Wadleigh might rather have been a home for the feebleminded than a place of education.

My own motive in being there was a personal quest. I was playing hooky from my real job as a Madison Avenue ad writer flogging cigarettes and shaving cream, a fraternity boy's dream job. Not a single day without Beefeater Martinis, then the preferred adman's tipple, not a morning without headache, not a single professional achievement worth the bother. I was hardly a moralist in those days, but I wasn't a moron either. A future composed of writing 50 words or so a week, drunk everyday, hunting sensation every night, had begun to make me nervous. Sitting around the West End one weekend I decided to see what schoolteaching was like.

Harlem then was an ineffable place where the hip white in-crowd played in those last few moments before the fires and riots of the 1960s broke out. Black and white still pretended it was the same high-style Harlem of WWII years, but a new awareness was dawning among teenagers. Perhaps Mama had been sold a bill of goods about the brighter tomorrow progressive America was arranging for black folks, but the kids knew better.

"The natives are restless." That expression I heard a half-dozen times in the single day I spent at Wadleigh, the Death School. Candor was the style of the moment among white teachers (who comprised 100 percent of the faculty) and with administrators in particular. On some level, black kids had caught on to the fact that their school was a liar's world, a jobs project for seedy white folk. The only blacks visible outside Harlem and its outrigger ghettos were maids, laborers, and a token handful stuffed into make-work government occupations, in theater, the arts, or civil service.

The notable exception consisted of a small West Indian business and professional elite which behaved itself remarkably like upperclass whites, exhibiting a healthy dose of racial prejudice, itself built on skin color and gradations, lighter being better. British manners made a difference in Harlem just as they did elsewhere. The great ad campaigns of the day were overwhelmingly British. Men in black eye patches wearing Hathaway shirts whose grandfathers fought at Mafeking, "curiously delicious" Schweppes "Commander Whitehead" ads, ads for Rolls cars where the loudest noise you heard was the ticking of the electric clock. The British hand in American mid-twentieth-century life was noticeably heavy. Twelve hundred Wadleigh black kids had no trouble figuring out what recolonization by the English meant for *them*.

I had no clue of this, of course, the day I walked into a school building for the first time in nine years, a building so dark, sour, and shabby it was impossible to accept that anyone seriously thought kids were better held there than running the streets.

Consider the orders issued me under which I traveled to meet eighth graders on the second floor:

> Good morning, Mr. Gatto. You have typing. Here is your program.
> Remember, THEY MUST NOT TYPE! Under no circumstances are
> they allowed to type. I will come around unannounced to see that you
> comply. DO NOT BELIEVE ANYTHING THEY TELL YOU about
> an exception. THERE ARE NO EXCEPTIONS.

Picture the scene: an assistant principal, a man already a living legend throughout the school district, a man with a voice of command like Ozymandias, dispatching young Gatto (who only yesterday wrote the immortal line "Legs are in the limelight this year" for a hosiery ad) into the dark tunnels of the Death School with these words:

> Not a letter, not a numeral, not a punctuation mark from those keys
> or you will never be hired here again. Go now.

When I asked what I should do instead with the class of 75, he replied, "Fall back on your resources!"

Off I went up the dark stairs, down the dark corridor. Opening the door I discovered my dark class in place, an insane din coming from 75 old black Underwoods, Royals, Smith Coronas: CLACKA! CLACKA! CLACKA! CLICK! CLICK! CLACK! DING! SLAM! CLACK! Seven hundred and fifty black fingers dancing *around under the typewriter covers*. One-hundred and fifty hammering hands clacking louder by far than I could bellow: STOP....TYPING! NO *TYPING* ALLOWED! DON'T TYPE! STOP! STOP! STOP I SAY! PUT THOSE COVERS ON THE MACHINES!

The last words were intended for the most flagrant of the young stenographers who had abandoned any pretense of compliance. By unmasking their instruments they were declaring war. In self-defense, I escalated my shouting into threats and insults, the standard tactical remedy of teachers in the face of impending chaos, kicked a few chairs, banged an aluminum water pitcher out of shape, and was having some success curtailing rogue typers when an ominous chant of OOOOOHHHHHH! OOOOOOOOOOHHHHHH! warned me some other game was now afoot.

Sure enough, a skinny little fellow had arisen in the back of the room and was bearing down on me, chair held high over his head. He had heard enough of my deranged screed, just as Middlesex farmers had enough of British lip and raised *their* chairs at Concord and Lexington. I too raised a chair and was backing my smaller opponent down when all of a sudden I caught a vision of both of us as a movie camera might. It caused me to grin and when I did the whole class laughed and tensions subsided.

"Isn't this a typing period?" I said, "WHY DON'T YOU START TYPING?" Day One of my 30-year teaching career concluded quietly with a few more classes to which I said at once, "No goofing off! Let's TYPE!" And they did. All the machines survived unscathed.

I had never thought much about kids up to that moment, even fancied I didn't like them, but these bouts of substitute teaching raised the possibility I was reacting adversely not to youth but to invisible societal directives ordering young people to act childish whether they want to or not. Such behavior provides the best excuse for mature oversight. Was it possible I *did* like kids, just not the script written for them?

There were other mysteries. What kind of science justified such sharp distinctions among classes when even by the house logic of schooling it was obvious that large numbers of students were misplaced? Why didn't this bother teachers? Why the apparent indifference to important matters like these? And why was the mental ration doled out so sparingly? Whenever I stepped up my own pace and began cracking the mental whip all manner of kids responded better than when I followed the *prescribed* dopey curriculum. Yet if that were so, why this skimpy diet instead?

The biggest mystery lurked in the difference between the lusty good will of first, second, and to some extent third graders—even in Harlem—the bright, quick intelligence and good will always so abundant in those grades, and the wild change fourth grade brought in terms of sullenness, dishonesty, and downright mean spirit.

I knew *something* in the school experience was affecting these kids, but what? It had to be hidden in those first, second and third grade years which appear so idyllic even in Harlem. What surfaced by fourth grade was the effect of a lingering disease running rampant in the very utopian interlude when they were laughing, singing, playing, and running round in the earlier grades. And kids who had been to kindergarten seemed worse than the others.

But schoolwork came as a great relief to me in spite of everything after studying Marlboro cigarette campaigns and Colgate commercials. In those days I was chomping at the bit to have work that involved real responsibility; this imperative made me decide to throw ambition to the winds at least for the moment and teach. Plenty of time to get rich later on, I thought.

In New York City in the 1960s, becoming a teacher was easier than you could imagine or believe (it still is). It was a time of rich cash harvests for local colleges giving two-week teacher courses for provisional certification; nearly everyone passed and permanent license requirements could be met on the job. At the end of summer I had a license to go to school and get paid for it. Whether I could actually teach was never an issue with anyone. Kids assigned to me had no choice in the matter. That following autumn I found regular work at William J. O'Shea Junior High whose broken concrete playground sat in plain view of the world-famous Museum of Natural History, diagonally across Columbus Avenue to the northeast. It was a playground my kids and I were later to use to make the school rich by designing and arranging for a weekend flea market to be held there. But that came long afterwards.

Dr. Caleb Gattegno, Expert

I began to schoolteach as an engineer would, solving problems as they arose. Because of my upbringing and because of certain unresolved contradictions in my own character I had a great private need not just to have a *job* but to have *work* that would allow me to build the unbuilt parts of myself, to give me competence and let me feel my life was one being lived instead of it living me. I brought to those first years an intensity of watchfulness probably uncommon in those who grow up untroubled. My own deficiencies provided enough motivation to want to make something worthwhile happen.

Had I remained a problem-solver I would have drowned in life for sure, but a habit of mind that demands things in context sensitized me to the culture of schooling as a major element in my work and that wariness eventually allowed me to surmount it. The highest school priorities are administrative coherence, student predictability, and institutional stability; children doing well or poorly are incidental to the main administrative mission. Hence teachers are often regarded as instruments which respond best if handled like servants made to account for the silverware. In order to give these vertical relationships strength, the horizontal relationships among teachers—collegiality—must be kept weak.

This divide-and-conquer principle is true of any large system. The way it plays itself out in the culture of schooling is to bestow on some few individuals *favor*, on some few *grief*, and to approach the large middle with a carrot in one hand, a stick in the other with these dismal examples illuminating the discourse. In simple terms, some are bribed into loyalty, but seldom so securely they become complacent, others sent despairing but seldom without hope since a crumb might eventually fall their way. Those whose loyalties are purchased function as spies to report staff defiance or as cheerleaders for new initiatives.

I used to hear from granddad that a man's price for surrendering shows you the dirt floor of his soul. A short list of customary teacher payoffs includes: 1) assignment to a room on the shady side of the building; 2) or one away from playground noise; 3) a parking permit; 4) the gift of a closet as a private office; 5) the tacit understanding one can solicit administrative aid in disciplinary situations without being persecuted afterwards; 6) first choice of textbooks from the available supply in the book room; 7) access to the administrators' private photocopy machine; 8) a set of black shades for your windows so the room can be sufficiently darkened to watch movies comfortably; 9) privileged access to media equipment so *machines* could be counted on to take over the teaching a few days each week; 10) assignment of a student teacher as a private clerk; 11) the right to go home on Friday a period or two early in order to beat the weekend rush; 12) a program with first period (or first and second) free so the giftee can sleep late while a friend or friendly administrator clocks them in.

Many more "deals" than this are available, extra pay for certain cushy specialized jobs or paid after-school duty are major perks. Thus is the ancient game of divide and conquer played in school. How many times I remember hearing, "Wake up, Gatto. Why should I bother? This is all a big joke. Nobody cares. Keep the kids quiet, that's what a good teacher is. I have a life when I get home from this sewer." Deals have a lot to do with that attitude and the best deals of all go to those who establish themselves as experts. As did Dr. Caleb Gattegno.

A now long-forgotten Egyptian intellectual, Caleb Gattegno had a brief vogue in the 1960s as inventor of a reading system based on the use of nonverbal color cues to aid learning. He was brought to the middle school where I worked in 1969 to demonstrate how his new system solved seemingly intractable problems. This famous man's *demonstration* made such impact on me that 30 years later I could lead you blindfolded to the basement room on West 77th Street where 25 teachers and administrators crammed into the rear lane of a classroom in order to be touched by this magic. Keep in mind it was only the demonstration I recall, I can't remember the idea at all. It had something to do with color.

Even now I applaud Gattegno's courage if nothing else. A stranger facing a new class is odds-on to be eaten alive, the customary example of this situation is the hapless substitute. But in his favor another classroom advantage worked besides his magical color technology, the presence of a crowd of adults virtually guaranteed a peaceful hour. Children are familiar with adult-swarming through the twice-a-year-visitation days of parents. Everyone knows by some unvoiced universal etiquette to be on best behavior when a concentration of strange adults appears in the back of the room.

On the appointed day, at the appointed hour, we all assembled to watch the great man put children through their paces. An air of excitement filled the room. From the publicity buildup a permanent revolution in our knowledge of reading was soon to be put on display. Finally, with a full retinue of foundation officers and big bureaucrats, Dr. Caleb Gattegno entered the arena.

I can't precisely say *why* what happened next happened. The simple truth is I wasn't paying much attention. But suddenly a babble of shouting woke me. Looking up, I saw the visiting expert's face covered with blood! He was making a beeline through the mob for the door as if desperate to get there before he bled to death.

As I later pieced together from eyewitness accounts, Dr. Gattegno had selected a student to cooperate with his demonstration, a girl with a mind of her own. She didn't *want* to be the center of attention at that moment. When Gattegno persisted her patience came to an end. What I learned in a Harlem typing class years earlier, the famous Egyptian intellectual now learned in a school in the middle of some of the most expensive real estate on earth.

Almost immediately after she raked her long fingernails down his well-educated cheeks, the doctor was off to the races, exiting the room quickly, dashing up the staircase into Egyptian history. We were left milling about, unable to stifle cynical remarks. What I failed to hear was a single word of sympathy for his travail, then or later. Word of the incident traveled quickly through the three-story building, the event was postmortemed for days.

I should be ashamed to say it but I personally felt traces of amusement at his plight, at the money wasted, at the temporary chagrin of important people. Not a word was ever said about Gattegno again in my presence. I read a few pages of his slim volume and found them intelligent, but for some unaccountable reason I couldn't muster interest enough to read on. Probably because there isn't any trick teaching children to read by very old-fashioned methods. That makes it difficult to work up much enthusiasm for novelty. Truth to tell, the reading world doesn't *need* a better mousetrap. If you look up his work in the library, I'd appreciate it if you dropped me a postcard explaining what his colorful plan was all about.

Intimidation

New teachers and even beleaguered veterans are hardly in any position to stand back far enough to see clearly the bad effect the dramatic setting of the building—its rules, personalities, and hidden dynamics—has on their own outlook and on children's lives. About one kid in five in my experience is in acute torment from the intimidation of peers, maybe more are driven to despair by the indifference of official machinery. What the hounded souls can't possibly see is that from a system standpoint, they are the problem with their infernal whining, not their persecutors.

And for every one broken by intimidation, another breaks himself just to get through the days, months, and years ahead. This huge silent mass levels a moral accusation lowly teachers become conscious of only at their peril because there is neither law nor institutional custom to stop the transgressions. Young, idealistic teachers burn out in the first three years because they can't solve administrative and collegial indifference, often concluding mistakenly that consciously-willed policies of actual human beings—a principal here, a department head or union leader there—are causing the harm when indifference is a system imperative; it would collapse from its contradictions if too much sensitivity entered the operating formula.

I would have been odds-on to become one of these martyrs to inadequate understanding of the teaching situation but for a fortunate accident. By the late sixties I had exhausted my imagination inside the conventional classroom when all of a sudden a period of phenomenal turbulence descended upon urban schoolteaching everywhere. I'll tell you more about this in a while, but for the moment, suffice it to say that supervisory personnel were torn loose from their moorings, superintendents, principals and all the rest, flung to the wolves by those who actually direct American schooling. In this dark time, local management cowered. During one three-year stretch I can remember, we had four principals and three superintendents. The net effect of this ideological bombardment, which lasted about five years in its most visible manifestation, was to utterly destroy the utility of urban schools. From my own perspective all this was a godsend. Surveillance of teachers and administrative routines lost their bite as school administrators scurried like rats to escape the wrath of their unseen masters while I suddenly found myself in possession of a blank check to run my classes as I pleased as long as I could secure the support of key parents.

Hector Of The Feeble-Mind

See 13-year-old Hector Rodriguez[1] as I first saw him: slightly built, olive-skinned, short, with huge black eyes, his body twisting acrobatically trying to slip under the gated defenses of the skating rink on the northern end of Central Park one cold November day. Up to that time I had known Hector for several months but had never really *seen* him, nor would I have seen him then but for the startling puzzle he presented by gatecrashing with a fully-paid admission ticket in his pocket. Was he nuts?

This particular skating rink sits in a valley, requiring patrons to descend several flights of concrete steps to reach the ice. When I counted bodies at the foot of the stairs, Hector was missing. I went back up the stairs to find Hector wedged in the bars of the revolving security gate. "You little imbecile," I screamed. "Why are you sneaking in? You have a ticket!" No answer, but his expression told me his answer. It said, "Why shout? I know what I'm doing, I have principles to uphold." He actually looked offended at my lack of understanding.

Hector was solving a problem. Could the interlocking bars of the automatic turnstile be defeated? What safer way to probe than with a paid ticket in hand in case he got caught. Later as I searched school records for clues to understand this boy, I discovered in his short transit on Earth he had already left a long outlaw trail behind him. And yet, although none of his crimes would have earned more than a good spanking a hundred years earlier, now they helped support a social-service empire. By substituting an excessive response for an appropriate (minimal) reaction, behavior we sought to discourage has doubled and redoubled. It is implicit in the structure of institutional logic that this happens. What's bad for real people is the very guarantee of institutional amorality.

At the time of this incident, Hector attended one of the 55 lowest-rated public schools (academically) in New York State, part of a select group threatened with takeover by state custodians. Seven of the nine rapists of the Central Park jogger—a case that made national headlines some years back—were graduates of the school. Of the thirteen classes in Hector's grade, a full nine were of higher rank than the one he was in. Hector might be seen at twelve as an exhausted salmon swimming upstream in a raging current trying to sweep away his dignity. We had deliberately unleashed such a flood by assigning about 1,100 kids in all, to five *strictly* graduated categories:

First Class was called "Gifted and Talented Honors."
Second Class was called "Gifted and Talented."
Third Class was called "Special Progress."
Fourth Class was called "Mainstream."

---

[1] Not his real name.

Fifth Class was called "Special Ed." These last kids had a cash value to the school three times higher than the others, a genuine incentive to find fatal defects where none existed.

Hector was a specimen from the doomed category called Mainstream, itself further divided into alphabetized sub-categories—A, B, C, or D. Worst of the worst above Special Ed would be Mainstream D where he reported. Since Special Ed was a life sentence of ostracism and humiliation at the hands of the balance of the student body, we might even call Hector "lucky" to be Mainstream, though as Mainstream D, he was suspended in that thin layer of mercy just above the truly doomed. Hector's standardized test scores placed him about three years behind the middle of the rat-pack. This, and his status as an absolute cipher, (where school activities, sports, volunteer work, and good behavior were concerned) would have made it difficult enough for anyone prone to be his advocate, but in Hector's case, he wasn't just behind an eight-ball, he was six feet under one.

Shortly after I found him breaking and entering (the skating rink), Hector was arrested in a nearby elementary school with a gun. It was a fake gun but it looked pretty real to the school secretaries and principal. I found out about this at my school faculty Christmas party when the principal came bug-eyed over to the potato salad where I camped, crying, GATTO, WHAT HAVE YOU DONE TO ME?, his exact words. Hector had been dismissed for holiday only that morning; he then hightailed it immediately to his old elementary school, still in session, to turn the younger children loose, to free the pint-sized slaves like a modern Spartacus. Come forward now one year in time: Hector in high school, second report card. He failed every subject, and was absent enough to be cited for truancy. But you could have guessed that before I told you because you read the same sociology books I do.

Can you see the Hector trapped inside these implacable school records? Poor, small for his age, part of a minority, not accounted much by people who matter, dumb, in a super-dumb class, a bizarre gatecrasher, a gunslinger, a total failure in high school. Can you see Hector? Certainly you think you do. How could you not, the system makes it so easy to classify him and predict his future.

What is society to do with its Hectors? This is the boy, multiplied by millions, that school people have been agonizing about in every decade of the twentieth century. This is the boy who destroyed the academic mission of American public schooling, turning it into a warehouse operation, a clinic for behavioral training and attitude adjustment. Hector's principal said to the *Christian Science Monitor* when it made a documentary film about my class and Hector's, "Sure the system stinks, but John (Gatto) has nothing to replace it. And as bad as the system is, it's better than chaos." But is the only alternative to a stifling system really chaos?

Hector Isn't The Problem

The country has been sold a bill of goods that the problem of modern schooling is Hector. That's a demon we face, that misperception. Under its many faces and shape-shifting rhetoric, forced schooling itself was conceived as the front line in a war against chaos. Horace Mann wrote once to Reverend Samuel May, "Schools will be found to be the way God has chosen for the reformation of the world." School is the beginning of the process to keep Hector and his kind in protective custody. Important people believe with the fervor of religious energy that civilization can only survive if the irrational, unpredictable impulses of human nature are continually beaten back, confined until their demonic vitality is sapped.

Read Merle Curti's *Social Ideas of the Great Educators*, a classic which will never be allowed to go out of print as long as we have college courses as gatekeeper for teacher certification. Curti shows that every single one of the greats used this Impending Chaos argument in front of financial tycoons to marshal support for the enlargement of forced schooling.

I don't want to upset you, but I'm not sure. I have evidence Hector isn't what school and society make him out to be, data that will give a startlingly different picture. During the period when the skating incident and school stickup occurred, Senator Bob Kerrey of Nebraska was putting together an education plank in order to run for his party's presidential nomination. To that end, his office called me to inquire whether I could meet with the Senator to discuss an article I wrote which had been printed in the *Congressional Record*. It was agreed we would meet for breakfast at Manhattan's famous Algonquin Hotel, site of the famous literary Roundtable. Hector and his close friend Kareem would join us.

Our conference lasted three hours without any bell breaks. It was cordial but businesslike with the Senator asking hard questions and his assistant, a vivacious attractive woman, taking notes. Hector dominated the discussion. Concise, thoughtful, inventive, balanced in his analysis, graceful in his presentation with the full range of sallies, demurs, illustrations, head-cocking, and gestures—you might expect from a trained conversationalist. Where had he learned to handle himself that way? Why didn't he act this way in school?

As time passed, Hector gravitated bit by bit to the chair where the woman I thought to be Kerrey's assistant was sitting. Hector perched in a natural posture on its arm, still apparently intent on the verbal give and take, but I noticed he cast a smoldering glance directly down at the lady. By a lucky accident I got a snapshot of him doing it. It turned out she was the movie star Debra Winger! Hector was taking both Washington *and* Hollywood in stride while eating a trencherman's breakfast at a class hotel! He proved to be a valuable colleague in our discussion too, I think the Senator would agree.

In April of the following year, Hector borrowed $15.00 from me to buy pizza for a young woman attending Columbia University's School of International Affairs. As far as Hector was concerned, being a graduate student was only her cover—in his world of expertise as a knowledgeable student of the comic book industry (and a talented self-taught graphic artist), she was, in reality, a famous writer for Marvel Comics. The full details of their liaison are unknown to me but a brilliant piece of documentary film footage exists of this young woman giving a private seminar to Hector and Kareem under an old oak tree on the Columbia campus. What emerged from the meetings between writer and diminutive holdup man was a one-day-a-week private workshop at her studio just north of Wall Street.

In November of that same year, utterly unknown to his school (where he was considered a dangerous moron), all gleaming in white tie, tails and top hat, Hector acted as master of ceremonies for a program on school reform at Carnegie Hall complete with a classical pianist and a lineup of distinguished speakers, including the cantankerous genius Mary Leue, founder of the Albany Free School, and several of my former students.

The following spring, just after he produced his unblemished record of failure as a high school freshman, Hector came to me with a job application. An award-winning cable television show was packaging kids into four-person production teams to make segments for a television magazine format hour like *60 Minutes*. Hector wanted to work there.

I sprang the bad news to him right away: "Your goose is cooked, I said. You'll sit down in that interview and they'll ask you how you're doing in school. You'll say, Listen, I'm failing all my subjects and oh, another thing, the only experience I have with TV is watching it until my eyeballs bug out—unless you count the time they filmed me at the police station to scare me. Why would they want to scare me? I think it was because I held up an elementary school and they didn't want me to do it again."

"So you're dead the minute they run your interview on any conventional lines. But you might have a slim chance if you don't follow the form sheet. Don't do what other kids will. Don't send in an application form. Guidance counselors will pass these out by the thousands. Use a typed résumé and a cover letter the way a real person would. And don't sent it to some flunky, call up the station, find out who the producer of the show is, say in a letter that you're not the greatest *sit-down* student in the world because you have your own ideas, but that you've come to understand film through an intense study of comic art and how it produces its effects. All that's true, by the way. Mention casually you have a private apprenticeship with one of the big names in the comic business and that you've done consultation work for the famous Nuyorican Poet's Café...."

"I have?" asked Hector.

"Sure. Don't you remember all those times you sat around with Roland chewing the fat when he was trying to shoot his film last year? Roland's one of the founders of the Nuyorican. And toss in your MC-ship at Carnegie Hall, that ought to set you apart from the chumps. Now let's get on with that résumé and cover letter. As sure as I'm sitting here they'll, only get one cover letter and résumé. That should buy you an interview.

"The only way you can squeak through that interview though is to convince someone *by your behavior* you can do the job better than anyone else. They'll be staring the spots off your every move, your clothing, your gestures, trying to see into your soul. Your goose is cooked if you get caught in a grilling."

"You mean I'll shift around, Hector asked, and get an attitude in my voice, don't you?"

"Right, just before the shifty look comes into your eyes!" I said.

We both laughed.

"So, what do I do?" Hector asked.

"The only thing you *can* do is quietly take over the interview. By quietly, I mean in a way they won't understand what's happening. You and I will just sit here until we figure out every single question they might ask, and every single *need* they might have which they won't tell you about, and every single *fear* they have that some aspect of your nature will screw up *their* project. Remember they're not hiring a kid to be nice people, they're hiring a kid because that's the gimmick of their show. So what you must do is to show by your commanding presence, impeccable manners, vast range of contacts, and dazzling intelligence that their fears are groundless.

"You're going to show them you love work for its own sake, that you don't watch the time clock, that you *can* take orders when orders make sense, that you are a goldmine of ideas, that you're fun to be around. You'll have to master all this quickly because I have a hunch you'll be called in right after your letter arrives. Can you do it?"

Six weeks later Hector started his new job.

One Lawyer Equals 3000 Reams of Paper

Once, a long time ago, I spoke before the District 3 School Board in Manhattan to plead that it not retain a private lawyer when all the legal work a school district is legitimately entitled to is provided free by the city's corporation counsel. In spite of this, the district had allocated $10,000 to retain a Brooklyn law firm. This is standard technique with boards everywhere which seek legal advice to get rid of their "enemies." They either prefer to conceal this from the corporation counsel or fear such work might be rejected as illegitimate. One school board member had already consulted with these same attorneys on five separate occasions pursuing some private vendetta, then submitting bills for payment against the school funds of the district. Sometimes this is simply a way to toss a tip to friends.

My argument went as follows:

In order to emphasize the magnitude of the loss this waste of money would entail—emblematic of dozens of similar wastes every year—I want to suggest some alternate uses for this money which will become impossible once it's spent on a lawyer none of the kids need. It would buy:

Three thousand reams of paper, 1,500,000 sheets. In September six of the schools in District 3 opened a school year without any paper at all. Letters from the principals of these schools to the school board, of which my wife has photocopies, will attest to this. It would buy enough chemicals and lab specimens to run the entire science program at I.S 44 and Joan of Arc, nearly 2,000 copies of *The Complete Works of William Shakespeare* as discounted by Barnes and Noble in hardcover, enough sewing machines and fabrication supplies to offer six modern dressmaking classes. In light of the fact New York City's fashion industry is a major employer, it would seem a saner use of the funds. How many musical instruments, how much sports equipment, wood, ceramic materials, art supplies does $10,000 buy? The Urban League's "Children Teach Children" reading project could be put in the district, displacing armies of low-utility, $23-an-hour consultants. With $10,000 we could pay our own students $1-an-hour—receive better value—and see our money in the pockets of kids, not lawyers. Invested in stock or even 30-year treasury notes as a scholarship fund, this money would return in perpetuity enough interest yearly to pay a kid's way through City University. The money in question would buy 50,000 pens. Eight computer installations. Two hundred winter coats for kids who are cold.

I concluded with two suggestions, first: a referendum among parents to find out whether they would prefer one of the options above or a lawyer; second: to buy 10,000 lottery tickets so we all could have a thrill out of this potlatch instead of the solitary thrill a Brooklyn lawyer would have banking our check.

Four years later, I appeared before the same school board, with the following somewhat darker statement:

On September 3, 1986, my teaching license which I had held for 26 years, was terminated secretly while I was on medical leave of absence for degenerative arthritis. The arthritis was contracted by climbing 80 steps a day to the third floor for more than a year—at the express request of the co-directors—with a badly broken hip held together by three large screws.

Although papers for a medical leave of absence were signed and filed, these documents were destroyed at the district level, removed from central board medical offices. The current management apparently was instructed to deny papers had ever been filed, allowing the strange conclusion I had simply walked away from a quarter century of work and vanished.

The notice terminating my teaching license was sent to an address where I hadn't lived for twenty-two years. It was returned marked "not known at this address." This satisfied the board's contractual obligation to notify me of my imminent dismissal, however nominally.

When I returned to work from what I had no reason to assume wasn't an approved leave, I was informed by personnel that I no longer worked for District 3, and that I could not work anywhere because I no longer had a teaching license. This could only be reinstated if my building principal would testify he knew I had properly filed for leave. Since this would involve the individual in serious legal jeopardy, it isn't surprising my request for such a notice was ignored.

From September 1987 to April of 1988 my family was plunged into misery as I sought to clear my name. Although I had personal copies of my leave forms at the first hearing on this matter, my building principal and the district personnel officer both claimed their signatures on the photocopies were forgeries. My appeal was denied.

Just before the second hearing in March, a courageous payroll secretary swore before a public official that my leave extensions had always been on file at Lincoln, signed by school authorities. She testified that attempts had been made to have her surrender these copies, requests she refused. Production of her affidavit to this at my third hearing caused an eventual return of my license and all lost pay. At the moment of disclosure of that affidavit during a third grievance hearing, the female co-director shouted in an agitated voice, "The District doesn't want him back!"

I am asking for an investigation of this matter because my case is far from the only time this has happened in District 3. Indeed, all over New York this business is conducted so cynically that administrators violate basic canons of decency and actual law with impunity because they know the system will cover for them no matter how culpable their behavior.

No comment was ever forthcoming from that Board of Education. Two years after my restoration, I was named New York City Teacher of the Year. Two years after that, New York State Teacher of the Year. A year later, after addressing the Engineer's Colloquium at NASA Space Center, invitations poured in to speak from every state in the union and from all over the world. But the damage my family had sustained carried lasting effects.

Yet I proved something important, I think. On looking back at the whole sorry tapestry of the system as it revealed itself layer by layer in my agony, what was most impressive wasn't its horrifying power to treat myself and my family without conscience or compassion, but its incredible *weakness* in the face of opposition. Battling without allies for 30 years, far from home and family, without financial resources, with no place to look for help except my native wit, nor for courage except to principles learned as a boy in a working-class town on the Monongahela river, I was able to back the school creature into such a corner it was eventually driven to commit crimes to get free of me.

What that suggests is cause for great hope. A relative handful of people could change the course of schooling significantly by resisting the suffocating advance of centralization and standardization of children, by being imaginative and determined in their resistance, by exploiting manifold weaknesses in the institution's internal coherence: the disloyalty its own employees feel toward it. It took 150 years to build this apparatus; it won't quit breathing overnight. The formula is to take a deep breath, then select five smooth stones and let fly. The homeschoolers have already begun.

The Great Transformation

I lived through the great transformation which turned schools from often useful places (if never the essential ones school publicists claimed) into laboratories of state experimentation. When I began teaching in 1961, the social environment of Manhattan schools was a distant cousin of the western Pennsylvania schools I attended in the 1940s, as Darwin was a distant cousin of Malthus.

Discipline was the daily watchword on school corridors. A network of discipline referrals, graded into an elaborate catalogue of well-calibrated offenses, was etched into the classroom heart. At bottom, hard as it is to believe in today's school climate, there was a common dedication to the intellectual part of the enterprise. I remember screaming (pompously) at an administrator who marked on my plan book that he would like to see evidence I was teaching "the whole child" that I didn't teach *children* at all, I taught the discipline of the English language! Priggish as that sounds, it reflects an *attitude* not uncommon among teachers who grew up in the 1940s and before. Even with much slippage in practice, Monongahela and Manhattan had a family relationship. About schooling at least. Then suddenly in 1965 everything changed.

Whatever the event is that I'm actually referring to—and its full dimensions are still only partially clear to me—it was a nationwide phenomenon simultaneously arriving in all big cities coast to coast, penetrating the hinterlands afterwards. Whatever it was, it arrived all at once, the way we see national testing and other remote-control school matters like School-to-Work legislation appear in every state today at the same time. A plan was being orchestrated, whose nature it will be the burden of upcoming chapters to unmask.

Think of this thing for the moment as a course of discipline dictated by coaches outside the perimeter of the visible school world. It constituted psychological restructuring of the institution's mission, but traveled under the guise of a public emergency which (the public was told) dictated *increasing* the intellectual content of the business! Except for its nightmare aspect, it could have been a scene from farce, a swipe directly from Orwell's *1984* and its fictional telly announcements that the chocolate ration was being raised every time it was being lowered. This reorientation did not arise from any democratic debate, or from any public clamor for such a peculiar initiative; the public was not consulted or informed. Best of all, those engineering the makeover denied it was happening.

I watched fascinated, as over a period of 100 days, the entire edifice of public schooling was turned upside down. I know there was no advance warning to low-level administrators like principals, either, because I watched my first principal destroy himself trying to stem the tide. A mysterious new deal was the order of the day.

Suddenly children were to be granted "due process" before any sanction, however mild, could be invoked. A formal schedule of hearings, referees, advocates, and appeals was set up. What might on paper have seemed only a liberal extension of full humanity to children was actually the starting gun for a time of unbridled madness. To understand this better, reflect a minute on the full array of ad hoc responses to wildness, cruelty, or incipient chaos teachers usually employ to keep the collective classroom a civil place at all. In a building with 100 teachers, the instituting of an adversarial justice system meant that inside of several weeks the building was an insane asylum.

Oddly enough, this changeover made administrative duty easier and so was not entirely unwelcome to a cynical class of low-level managers. Where once supervisory intercession had constituted a regular and often-employed link in the ladder of referral (as it was called), in the new order, administrators were excused from minute-to-minute discipline and were granted power to assume that incidents were a teacher's fault, to be duly entered on the Cumulative Record File, the pedagogical equivalent of the Chinese Dangan.

There was a humorous aspect to what transpired over the next few years. I had no particular trouble keeping a lid on things, but for teachers who counted upon support from administrative staff it was a different story. Now, if they asked for a hand, often they were pressured to resign, or formally charged with bad classroom management, or worst of all, transferred to an even more hideous school in expectation they would eliminate themselves.

Most, under such tension, took the hint and quit. A few had to be pushed. I remember a magnificent math teacher, an older black woman with honors and accomplishments to her name, much beloved and respected by her classes, singled out for public persecution probably because she acted as an intractable moral force, a strong model teacher with strong principles. Daily investigative teams from the district office watched her classes, busily took notes in the back of her room, challenged her style of presentation openly while children listened. This went on for two weeks, then her students began to be called one by one to the school office and closely questioned about the woman's behavior. Some were coached to watch her during the lesson, coached to look for telltale signs she was a racist! Parents were called and offered an option of withdrawing their kids from her classes. Broken by the ordeal, one day she vanished.

When my wife was elected to the district school board, one of her first actions was to gain access to the superintendent's private files without his knowledge. Some of those records concerned details of official harassments. Dozens of employees had been similarly purged, and dozens more were "under investigation" in this gulag on West 95th Street. Contacting these people in private, it became clear they were far from the worst teachers around. Indeed some were the best. Their relative prowess had emboldened them to speak out on policy matters and so marked them for elimination.

One principal, whose school was the most successful reading environment in the district, received similar treatment, ultimately sentenced to an official Siberia in Harlem, given no duties at all for the two years more he lasted before quitting. His crime: allegedly striking a girl although there were no witnesses to this but the girl, a student who admitted breaking into the light-control panel room in the auditorium where the offense is supposed to have occurred. His real crime was his refusal to abandon phonetic reading methodology and replace it with a politically mandated whole-word substitute.

I escaped the worst effects of the bloodbath. Mostly I minded my business trying to ignore the daily carnage. In truth I had no affection for the old system being savaged, and chaos made it easier for me to try out things that worked. On balance, I probably did my best work during those turbulent years as a direct result of the curious smokescreen they provided.

But accounts are not so simple to balance overall. If I regarded run-of-the-mill school administrators as scared rabbits or system flunkies, the reformers I saw parading daily through the building corridors like storm troopers made my skin crawl.

On several occasions, energetic efforts were made by these people to recruit my assistance as an active ally. All such appeals I politely refused. True belief they had, but for all of it they seemed like savages to me, inordinately proud of their power to cause fear, as willing to trample on decencies as the people they were harassing. However, it seemed just possible something good might actually emerge from the shakeup underway. About that, I was dead wrong. As the project advanced, schools became noticeably worse. Bad to begin with, now they mutated into something horrible.

What shape began to emerge was a fascinating echo of the same bureaucratic cancer which dogged the steps of the French, Russian, and Chinese revolutions. Do-nothing administrators and non-teaching teachers multiplied like locusts. With them came an entirely new class of school-teacher, one aggressively ignorant, cynical and often tied to local political clubs. New categories of job description sprang up like weeds.

My own school fell victim to a politically correct black gym teacher imported from New England to be its principal. Two school-wide riots followed his installation, mass marches on city hall transpired in which local politicians instrumental in the man's selection used schoolchildren as unwitting cadres to lobby their favorite schemes in newsworthy, children's crusade fashion.

A small band of old-fashioned teachers fought rearguard actions against this, but time retired them one by one until, with only an occasional exception, the classrooms of Community School District 3, in one of the most prosperous neighborhoods on earth, became lawless compounds, job projects for the otherwise unemployable.

I need to wrap this up so we can get on with things. You have to miss the story of the Hell's Angel math teacher who parked his Harley Hog outside the door of his classroom, and when the principal objected, told him in front of startled witnesses, that if the man didn't shut his mouth, the number-crunching cyclist would come to his home that evening, pour gasoline under his front door, and set fire to his home. I'll have to skip the hair-raising stories of not one but three junior high teachers I knew quite well who married their students. Each, spotting a likely 13-year-old, wooed the respective girl in class and married her a few years later. They took the more honorable course, hardly the outcome of most teacher/student romances I was privy to. I have to skip the drug habits of staff in each of the buildings I worked in and other lurid stuff like that. In the midst of the unending dullness of institutional schooling, human nature cracks through the peeling paint as grass through cement. I have to skip all that. Suffice it to say, my life experience taught me school isn't a very wholesome environment in which to confine children.

Education As A Helix Sport

Here's a principle of real education to carry you through the moments of self-doubt. Education is a helix sport, a unique personal project like seatless unicycle riding over trackless wilderness, a sport that avoids rails, rules, and programmed confinement. The familiar versions of this are cross-country skiing, sailing, fox-hunting, gliding, skateboarding, surfing, solitary mountain climbing, thousand-mile walks, things like that. I think of education as one, too.

In a helix sport the players search for a new relationship with themselves. They endure pain and risk to achieve this goal. Helix sports are free of expert micro-management. Experts can't help you much in that moment of truth when a mistake might leave you dead. Helix sports are a revolt against predestination.

Bringing children up properly is a helix sport forcing you to realize no boy or girl on Earth is just like another. If you do understand this you also understand there can exist no reliable map to tell you all you need to do. Process kids like sardines and don't be surprised when they come out oily and dead. In the words of the Albany Free School, if you don't make it up as you go along, you aren't doing it right.

The managerial and social science people who built forced schooling had no scruples about making your kids fit into their scheme. It's frightening to the spirit to be treated this way. A young lady from Tucson wrote me, "Now that I'm nearly 25, I can hardly remember why I began to be afraid to go to school." I wrote back she was afraid because her instincts warned her the school business had no use for the personal growth she sought. All pedagogical theory is based on stage theories of human development. All stage theories of child rearing talk in averages. The evidence of your own eyes and ears must show you that average men and women don't really exist. Yet they remain the basis of social theory, although useless to tell you anything valuable about your own implacably non-abstract child.

I'm Outta Here!

One day, after thirty years of this, I took a deep breath and quit.

PART TWO

The Foundations
Of Schooling

[Administration] covers the surface of society with a network of small complicated rules, minute and uniform, through which the most original minds and the most energetic characters cannot penetrate, to rise above the crowd. The will of man is not shattered, but softened, bent, guided; men are seldom forced by it to act, but they are constantly restrained from acting; such a power does not destroy, but it prevents existence; it does not tyrannize, but it compresses, extinguishes, and stupefies a people, till each nation is reduced to be nothing better than a flock of timid and industrious animals, of which government is the shepherd.
— Alexis de Tocqueville, *Democracy in America*

Frederick Winslow Taylor
The High Priest of True Belief in Modern Times

Taylor, schooled in Germany as a boy, scion of a prosperous Philadelphia Quaker family turned Anglican, imported the systems of Prussia and Saxony into the American industrial/ commercial workplace where they swiftly spread into government schooling, mainline protestant churches, journalism, politics, and mass entertainment. He is shown to the left of Andrew Carnegie's daughter, the flower girl, (upper right) and (bottom) in physiognomic transition.

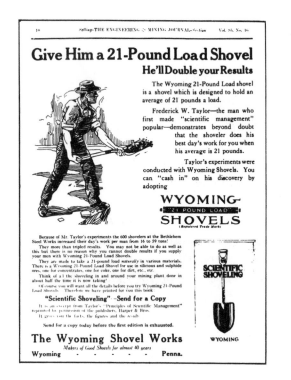

CHAPTER FIVE

True Believers And

The Unspeakable Chautauqua

A very small group of young psychologists around the turn of the century were able to create and market a system for measuring human talent that has permeated American institutions of learning and influenced such fundamental social concepts as democracy, sanity, justice, welfare, reproductive rights, and economic progress. In creating, owning, and advertising this social technology the testers created themselves as professionals.

> — Joanne Brown, *The Definition of a Profession*:
> *The Authority of Metaphor in the History of*
> *Intelligence Testing*

I have undertaken to get at the facts from the point of view of the business men—citizens of the community who, after all, pay the bills and, therefore, have a right to say what they shall have in their schools.

> — Charles H. Thurber, from an Address at the
> Annual Meeting of the National Education
> Association, July 9, 1897

Munsterberg And His Disciples

The self-interested have had a large hand conceiving and executing twentieth century schooling, yet once that's said, self-interest isn't enough to explain the *zeal* in confining other people's children in rooms, locked away from the world, the infernal *zeal* which keeps forcing its way to the surface in this business like a toadstool. Among millions of normal human beings professionally associated with the school adventure, a small band of true believers has been loose from the beginning, brothers and sisters whose eyes gleam in the dark, whose heartbeat quickens at the prospect of acting as "change agents" for a purpose larger than self-interest.

For true believers, children are test animals. The strongest belt in the engine of schooling is the strand of true belief. True believers can be located by their rhetoric; it reveals a scale of philosophical imagination which involves plans for you and me. All you need know about Mr. Laszlo, whose faith song is cited on page xiii of this book, is that the "we" he joins himself to, the "masters who manipulate," doesn't really include the rest of us, except as objects of the exercise. Here is a true believer in full gallop. School history is crammed with wild-eyed orators, lurking just behind the lit stage. Like Hugo Munsterberg.

One of those in on the birth of twentieth-century mass schooling was Hugo Munsterberg, recent émigré to America in 1892 from Wilhelm Wundt's laboratory of physiological psychology at Leipzig in Saxony and Harvard Professor of Psychology. Munsterberg taught his students to look at schools as social laboratories suitable for testing theory, not as aggregates of young people pursuing their own purposes. The St. Louis Exposition of 1904 showcased his ideas for academics all over the world, and the popular press made his notions familiar to upper middle classes horrified by the unfamiliar family ways of immigrants and eager to find ways to separate immigrant children from those alien practices of their parents.

Munsterberg's particular obsession lay in quantifying the mental and physical powers of the population for central government files, so policymakers could manage the nation's "human resources" efficiently. His students became leaders of the "standardization" crusade in America. Munsterberg was convinced racial differences could be reduced to numbers, equally convinced it was his sacred duty to the Aryan race to do so. Aryanism crackled like static electricity across the surface of American university life in those days, its implications part of every corporate board game and government bureau initiative.

One of Munsterberg's favorite disciples, Lillian Wald, became a powerful advocate of medical incursions into public schools. The famous progressive social reformer wrote in 1905: "It is difficult to place a limit upon the service which *medical inspection* should perform,"[1] continuing, "Is it not logical to conclude that physical development...should so far as possible *be demanded*?" One year later, immigrant public schools in Manhattan began performing tonsillectomies and adenoidectomies *in school* without notifying parents. *The New York Times* (June 29, 1906) reported that "Frantic Italians"—many armed with stiletto knives—"stormed" three schools, attacking teachers and dragging children from the clutches of the true believers into whose hands they had fallen. Think of the conscience which would ascribe to itself the right to operate on children at official discretion and you will know beyond a doubt what a true believer smells like.

Even a cursory study of the history of the school institution turns up true belief in rich abundance. In a famous book, *The Proper Study of Mankind* (1948), paid for by the Carnegie Corporation of New York and the Russell Sage Foundation, the favorite principle of true believers since Plato makes an appearance: "A society could be completely made over in something like 15 years, the time it takes to inculcate a new culture into a rising group of youngsters." Despite the spirit of profound violence hovering over such seemingly bloodless, abstract formulae, this is indeed the will-o'-the-wisp pursued throughout the twentieth century in forced schooling—not intellectual development, not character development, but the inculcation of a new synthetic culture in children, one designed to condition its subjects to a continual adjusting of their lives by unseen authorities.

---

[1] Forced medical inspection had been a prominent social theme in northern Germany since at least 1750.

It's true only a numerically small fraction of those who direct institutional schooling are actively aware of its ideological bent, but we need to see that without consistent generalship from that knowledgeable group in guiding things, the evolution of schooling would long ago have lost its coherence, degenerating into battles between swarms of economic and political interests fighting over the treasure-house hermetic pedagogy represents. One of the hardest things to understand is that true believers—dedicated ideologues—are useful to *all* interests in the school stew by providing a salutory continuity to the enterprise.

Because of the predictable greed embedded in human nature, some overarching "Guardian" vision, one indifferent to material gain, seems necessary to prevent marketplace chaos. True believers referee the school game, establishing its goals, rules, penalties; they negotiate and compromise with other stakeholders—and strangely enough, above all else, they can be trusted to continue being their predictable, dedicated, selfless selves. Pragmatic stakeholders need them to keep the game alive; true believers need pragmatists as cover. Consider this impossibly melodramatic if you must. I know myself that parts of my story sound like leaves torn from *Ragtime*. But from start to finish this is a tale of true believers and how by playing on their pipes they took all the children away.

The Prototype Is A Schoolteacher

One dependable signal of a true believer's presence is a strong passion for *everyone's* children. Find nonstop, abstract interest in the collective noun "children," the kind of love Pestalozzi or Froebel had, and you've flushed the priesthood from its lair. Eric Hoffer tells us the prototype true believer is a schoolteacher. Mao was a schoolteacher, so was Mussolini, so were many other prominent warlike leaders of our time, including Lyndon Johnson. In Hoffer's identification, the true believer is characterized by inner fire, "a burning conviction we have a holy duty to others." Lack of humor is one touchstone of true belief.

The expression "true believer" itself is from a fifth century book, *The City of God*, occurring in a passage where St. Augustine urges holy men and women to abandon fear and go at their sacred work fervently. True Believer is a psychological frame you'll find useful to explain individuals who relentlessly pursue a cause indifferent to personal discomfort, indifferent to the discomfort of others.[2] All of us show a tiny element of true belief in our makeup, usually just enough to recognize the lunatic gleam in the eye of some purer zealot when we meet face to face. But in a century which displaces us from hand-to-hand encounters with authority—removing us electronically, bureaucratically, and institutionally—the truly and dangerously mad have been given the luxury of full anonymity. We have to judge their presence by the fallout.

Horace Mann exemplifies the type. From start to finish he had a mission. He spoke passionately at all times. He wrote notes *to himself* about "breaking the bond of association among workingmen." To graduates of Antioch College he harangued, "Be ashamed to die until you have won some victory for humanity." A few cynical critics snipe at Mann for lying about his imaginary school tour of Prussia (which led to the adoption of Prussian schooling methodologies in America), but those cynics miss the point. For the great ones, the goal is everything; the end justifies *any*

---

[2] For instance, how else to get a handle on the Columbia Teachers College bureau head who delivered himself of this sentence in *Education Week*, March 18, 1998, in an essay called *Altering Destinies*: "Program officials consider no part of a student's life off limits."

means. Mann lived and died a social crusader. His second wife (the Peabody) paid him this tribute posthumously: "He was all afire with Purpose."

Al Shanker, longtime president of the American Federation of Teachers, said in one of his last Sunday advertisements in *The New York Times* before his death: "Public schools do not exist to please Johnny's parents. They do not even exist to ensure that Johnny will one day earn a good living at a job he likes." No other energy but true belief can explain what Shanker might have had in mind.

Teachers College Maintains The Planet

A beautiful example of true belief in action crossed my desk recently from the alumni magazine of my own alma mater, Columbia University. Written by the director of Columbia's Institute for Learning Technologies, a bureau at Teachers College, graduates were informed by this mailing that the education division now regarded itself as bound by "a contract with posterity." Something in the tone warned me against dismissing this as customary institutional gas. Seconds later I learned (with some shock) that Teachers College felt *obligated* to take a commanding role "maintaining the planet." The next extension of this strange idea was even more pointed. Teachers College now interpreted its mandate, I was told, as one compelling it "to distribute itself all over the world and to teach every day, 24 hours a day."

To gain perspective, try to imagine the University of Berlin undertaking to distribute itself among the 50 American states, to be present in this foreign land 24 hours a day, swimming in the minds of Mormon children in Utah and Baptist children in Georgia.   Any university intending to become global like some nanny creature spawned in Bacon's ghastly utopia, *New Atlantis*, is no longer simply in the business of education, at least not at staff level. Columbia Teachers College had become an aggressive evangelist by its own announcement, an institution of true belief selling a doctrine I can only guess at. I held its declaration in my hand for a while after I read it. Thinking.

Let me underline what you just heard. Picture some U.N. thought police dragging reluctant Serbs to a loudspeaker to listen to Teachers College rant. Most of us have no frame of reference in which to fit such a picture. Narcosis in the face of true belief is a principal reason the disease progressed so far through the medium of forced schooling without provoking much major opposition. Only after a million home schooling families and an equal number of religiously oriented private-school families emerged from their sleep to reclaim their children from the government in the 1970s and 1980s, in direct response to an epoch of flagrant social experimentation in government schools, did true belief find ruts in its road.

Columbia, where I took an undergraduate degree, is the last agency I would want maintaining *my* planet. For decades it was a major New York slumlord indifferent to maintaining its own neighborhood, a terrain much smaller than the globe. Columbia has been a legendary bad neighbor to the community for the 40 years I've lived near my alma mater. So much for its qualifications as Planetary Guardian. Its second boast is even more ominous, I mean that goal of intervening in mental life "all over the world," teaching "every day, 24 hours a day."

Teaching what? Shouldn't we ask? The trouble with recognizing true belief is that it wears a reasonable face in modern times.

A Lofty, Somewhat Inhuman Vision

Take a case reported by the Public Agenda Foundation which produced the first-ever survey of educational views held by teacher-college professors. To their surprise, the authors discovered that the majority of 900 randomly selected professors of education it interviewed did not regard a teacher's struggle to maintain an orderly classroom or to cope with disruptive students as major problems! The education faculty was generally unwilling to attend to these matters seriously in their work, believing that widespread alarm among parents stemming from worry that graduates can't spell, can't count accurately, can't sustain attention, can't write grammatically (or write at all), was only caused by views of life "outmoded and mistaken."

While 92 percent of the public thinks basic reading, writing, and math competency is "absolutely essential" (according to an earlier study by Public Agenda), education professors did not agree. In the matter of mental arithmetic, which a large majority of ordinary people, including some schoolteachers, consider very important, about 60 percent of education professors think cheap calculators make that goal obsolete.

The word "passion" appears more than once in the report from which this data is drawn, as in the following passage:

Education professors speak with passionate idealism about their own, sometimes lofty, vision of education and the mission of teacher education programs. The passion translates into ambitious and highly-evolved expectations for future teachers, expectations that often differ dramatically from those of parents and teachers now in the classroom. "The soul of a teacher is what should be passed on from teacher to teacher," a Boston professor said with some intensity. "You have to have that soul to be a good teacher."

It's not my intention at this moment to recruit you to one or another side of this debate, but only to hold you by the back of the neck as Uncle Bud once held mine and point out this vehicle has no brake pedal—ordinary parents and students have no way to escape the embrace of this passion. Twist and turn as they might, they will be subject to any erotic curiosity inspired love arouses. In the harem of true belief, there is scant refuge from the sultan's lusty gaze.

Rain Forest Algebra

In the summer of 1997, a Democratic senator stood on the floor of the Senate denouncing the spread of what he called "whacko algebra"; one widely distributed math text referred to in that speech did not ask a question requiring algebraic knowledge *until page 107*. What replaced the boredom of symbolic calculation were discussions of the role of zoos in community life, or excursions to visit the fascinating Dogon tribe of West Africa. Whatever your own personal attitude toward "rain forest algebra" as it was snidely labeled, you would be hard-pressed not to admit one thing: its problems are almost computation-free. Whether you find the mathematical side of social issues relevant or not isn't in question. Your attention should be fixed on the existence of minds, nominally in charge of number enlightenment for your children, which consider a private agenda more important than numbers.

One week last spring, the entire math homework in fifth grade at middle-class P.S. 87 on the upper west side of Manhattan consisted of two questions:[3]

1. Historians estimate that when Columbus landed on what is now the island of Hati (this is the spelling in the question) there were 250,000 people living there. In two years this number had dropped to 125,000. What fraction of the people who had been living in Hati when Columbus arrived remained? Why do you think the Arawaks died?

2. In 1515 there were only 50,000 Arawaks left alive. In 1550 there were 500. If the same number of people died each year, approximately how many people would have died each year? In 1550 what percentage of the original population was left alive? How do you feel about this?

Tom Loveless, professor at the Kennedy School of Government at Harvard, has no doubt that National Council of Teachers of Mathematics standards have deliberately de-emphasized math skills, and he knows precisely *how* it was done. But like other vigorous dissenters who have tried to arrest the elimination of critical intellect in children, he adduces no motive for the awesome project which has worked so well up to now. Loveless believes that the "real reform project has begun: writing standards that declare the mathematics children will learn." He may be right, but I am not so sanguine.

Elsewhere there are clues which should check premature optimism. In 1989, according to Loveless, a group of experts in the field of math education launched a campaign "to change the content and teaching of mathematics." This new math created state and district policies which "tend to present math reform as religion" and identify as sinful behaviors teacher-delivered instruction, individual student desk work, papers corrected for error. Teachers are ordered to keep "an elaborate diary on each child's 'mathematical disposition.'"

Specific skills de-emphasized are: learning to use fractions, decimals, percents, integers, addition, subtraction, multiplication, division—all have given way to working with manipulatives like beans and counting sticks (much as the Arawaks themselves would have done) and with calculators. Parents worry themselves sick when fifth graders can't multiply 7 times 5 without hunting for beans and sticks. Students who learn the facts of math deep down in the bone, says Loveless, "gain a sense of number unfathomable to those who don't know them."

The question critics should ask has nothing to do with computation or reading ability and everything to do with this: how does a fellow human being come to regard ordinary people's children as experimental animals? What impulse triggers the pornographic urge to deprive kids of volition, to fiddle with their lives? It is vital you consider this or you will certainly fall victim to impassioned appeals that you look at the worthiness of the *outcomes* sought and ignore the methods. This appeal

---

[3] A P. S. 87 parent, Sol Stern, brought this information to my attention, adding this assessment, "The idea that schools can starve children of factual knowledge and basic skills, yet somehow teach critical thinking, defies common sense." Mr. Stern in his capacity as education editor of New York's *City Journal* often writes eloquently of the metropolitan school scene.

to pragmatism urges a repudiation of principle, sometimes even on the grounds modern physics "proves" there is no objective reality.

Whether children are better off or not being spared the effort of thinking algebraically may well be a question worth debating, but if so, the burden of proof rests on the challenger. Short-circuiting the right to choice is a rapist's tactic or a seducer's. If, behind a masquerade of number study, some unseen engineer infiltrates the inner layers of a kid's consciousness—as is done in rainforest algebra, tampering with the way a child sees the larger world, then in a literal sense the purpose of the operation is to dehumanize the experimental subject by forcing him or her into a predetermined consensus.

Godless, But Not Irreligious

True believers are only one component of American schooling, as a fraction probably a small one, but they constitute a tail that wags the dog because they possess a blueprint and access to policy machinery, while most of the rest of us do not. The true believers we call great educators— Komensky, Mather, Pestalozzi, Froebel, Mann, Dewey, Sears, Cubberley, Thorndike, et.al.— were ideologues looking for a religion to replace one they never had or had lost faith in. They have been studied by some of the finest minds in the history of modern thought—Machiavelli, Tocqueville, Renan, William James to name a few—but the clearest profile of the type was set down by a onetime migrant farm worker who didn't learn to read until he was fifteen, Eric Hoffer. In *The True Believer*, a luminous modern classic, Hoffer tells us:

> Though ours is a godless age, it is the very opposite of irreligious. The true believer
> is everywhere on the march, shaping the world in his own image. Whether we line
> up with him or against him, it is well we should know all we can concerning his
> nature and potentialities.

It looks to me as if the energy to run this train was released in America from the stricken body of New England Calvinism when its theocracy collapsed from indifference, ambition, and the hostility of its own children. At the beginning of the nineteenth century, shortly after we became a nation, this energy gave rise to what Allan Bloom dubbed "the new American religion," eventually combining elements of old Calvinism with flavors of Anabaptism, Ranting, Leveling, Quakerism, rationalism, positivism, and the peculiar Unitarian spice: scientism.[4]

---

[4] This essay is packed with references to Unitarians, Quakers, Anglicans,and other sects because without understanding some of their natures, and ambitions, it is utterly impossible to comprehend where school came from and why it took the shape it did. Nevertheless it should be kept in mind that I am always referring to movements within these religions as they existed before the lifetime of any reader. Ideas set in motion long ago are still in motion because they took institutional form, but I have little knowledge of the modern versions of these sects, which for all I know are boiling a different kettle of fish.

Three groups descending from the seventeenth century Puritan Reformation in England have been principal influences on American schooling, providing shape, infrastructure, ligatures, and intentions, although only one is popularly regarded as Puritan—the New England Congregationalists. The Congregational mind *in situ*, first around the Massachusetts coast, then by stages in the astonishing Connecticut Valley displacement (when Yale became its critical resonator), has been exhaustively studied. But Quakers, representing the left wing of Puritan thought, and

Where the parent form of American Calvinism had preached the rigorous exclusion of all but a tiny handful deemed predestinated for salvation (the famous "Saints" or "justified sinners"), the descendent faith, beginning about the time of the Great Awakening of the 1740s, demanded universal *inclusion*, recruitment of *everyone* into a universal, unitarian salvation—whether they would be so recruited or not. It was a monumental shift which in time infiltrated every American institution. In its demand for eventual planetary unity the operating logic of this hybrid religion, although derived from a medley of Protestant sects and Judaism, was intensely *catholic* right down to its core.

After the Unitarian takeover of Harvard in 1805, orthodox Calvinism seemingly reached the end of its road, but so much explosive energy had been tightly bound into this intense form of sacred thought—an intensity which made every act, however small, brim with significance, every expression of personality proclaim an Election or Damnation—that in its structural collapse, a ferocious energy was released, a molten tornado which flashed across the Burned Over District of upstate New York, crossing the lakes to Michigan and other Germanized outposts of North America, and split there suddenly into two parts—one racing westward to California and the northwest territories, another turning southwest to the Mexican colony called Texas. Along the way, Calvin's by now much altered legacy deposited new religions like Mormonism and Seventh Day Adventism, raised colleges like the University of Michigan and Michigan State (which would later become fortresses of the new schooling religion) and left prisons, insane asylums, Indian reservations, and poorhouses in its wake as previews of the secularized global village it aimed to create.

School was to be the temple of a new, all-inclusive civil religion. Calvinism had stumbled, finally, from being too self-contained. This new American form, learning from Calvinism's failure, aspired to a multicultural super-system, world-girdling in the fullness of time. Calvinist origins armed school thinkers from the start with a utilitarian contempt for the notion of free will.

Brain-control experiments being explored in the psychophysical labs of Northern Germany in the last quarter of the nineteenth century attracted rich young men from thousands of prominent American families. Such mind science seemed to promise that tailor-made technologies could emerge to shape and control thought, technologies which had never existed before. Children, the new psychologies suggested, could be emptied, denatured, then reconstructed to more accommodating designs. H.G. Wells' *Island of Dr. Moreau* was an extrapolation-fable based on common university-inspired drawing room conversations of the day.

Unitarians—that curious mirror *obverse* of Calvinism—are much easier to understand when seen as children of Calvinist energy, too. These three together with the episcopacy in New York and Philadelphia, gathered in Columbia University and Penn, the Morgan Bank and elsewhere, have dominated the development of government schooling. Baptist Brown and Baptist Chicago are important to understand, too, and important bases of Dissenter variation like Presbyterian Princeton cannot be ignored, nor Baptist/Methodist centers at Dartmouth and Cornell, or centers of Freethought like Johns Hopkins in Baltimore and New York University in New York City—but someone in a hurry to understand where schooling came from and why it took the shape it did would not go far wrong by concentrating attention on the machinations of Boston, Philadelphia, Hartford, and New York City in school affairs from 1800 to 1850, or by simply examining the theologies of Congregationalism, Unitarianism, Hicksite and Gurneyite Quakerism, and ultimately the Anglican Communion, to discover how these, in complex interaction, have given us the forced schooling which so well suits their theologies.

David Hume's empirical philosophy, working together with John Locke's empiricism, had prepared the way for social thinkers to see children as blank slates—an opinion predominant among influentials long before the Civil War and implicit in Machiavelli, Bodin, and the Bacons. German psychophysics and physiological psychology seemed a wonderful manufactory of the tools a good political surgeon needed to remake the modern world. Methods for modifying society and all its inhabitants began to crystallize from the insights of the laboratory. A good living could be made by *saying* it was so, even if it weren't true. When we examine the new American teacher college movement at the turn of this century we discover a resurrection of the methodology of Prussian philosopher Herbart well under way. Although Herbart had been dead a long time by then, he had the right message for the new age: said Herbart, "Children should be cut to fit."

An Insider's Insider

A bountiful source of clues to what tensions were actually at work back then can be found in Ellwood P. Cubberley's celebratory history, *Public Education in the United States* (1919, revision 1934), the standard in-house reference for official school legends until revisionist writings appeared in the 1960s.

Cubberley was an insider's insider, in a unique position to know things neither public nor press could know. Although Cubberley always is circumspect and deliberately vague, he cannot resist showing more than he wants to; for example, the reluctance of the country to accept its new yoke of compulsion is caught briefly in this flat statement on page 564 of the 1934 revision:

> The history of compulsory-attendance legislation in the states has been much the same everywhere, and everywhere laws have been enacted only after overcoming strenuous opposition.

Reference here is to the period from 1852 to 1918 when the states, one by one, were caught in the compulsion net using the strategy of gradualism:

> *At first the laws were optional*...later the law was made state-wide but the compulsory period was short (ten to twelve weeks) and the age limits low, nine to twelve years. After this, struggle came to extend the time, often little by little...to extend the age limits downward to eight and seven and upwards to fourteen, fifteen or sixteen; to make the law apply to children attending private and parochial schools, and to *require* cooperation from such schools for the proper handling of cases; to institute *state* supervision of local enforcement; to connect school attendance enforcement with the child-labor legislation of the State through a system of working permits....[Emphasis added]

The extent to which proponents of centralized schooling were prepared to act covertly in defiance of majority will and in the face of extremely successful and inexpensive local school heritage is noteworthy. As late as 1901, after nearly a half-century of such legislation, first in

Massachusetts, then state by state in the majority of the remaining jurisdictions, Dr. Levi Seeley of Trenton Normal School could still thunder in his book, *Foundations of Education*, "while no law on the statute books of Prussia is more thoroughly carried out" (than compulsory attendance), and "in 1890, out of 5,300,000 Prussian children, only 645 slipped out of the truant officer's net," our own school attendance legislation is nothing more than "dead letter laws":

> We have been attempting compulsory education for a whole generation and cannot be said to have made much progress—Let us cease to require only 20 weeks of schooling, 12 of which shall be consecutive, thus plainly hinting that we are not serious in the matter....

Seeley's frustration clouded his judgment. Somebody was most certainly serious about mass confinement schooling to stay at it so relentlessly and expensively in the face of massive public repudiation of the scheme.

Compulsion Schooling

The center of the scheme was Massachusetts, the closest thing America had seen thus far to a theocracy. The chart below tellingly records the long gap between the Massachusetts' compulsion law of 1852 and those of the next set of accepting states; instructive also is the fellow-traveling of the District of Columbia, the seat of federal government.

Compulsory School Legislation

1852. Massachusetts	1875. Maine
1865. District of Columbia	New Jersey
1867. Vermont	1876. Wyoming Territory
1871. New Hampshire	1877. Ohio
Washington Territory	1879. Wisconsin
1872. Connecticut	1883. Rhode Island
New Mexico Territory	Illinois
1873. Nevada	Dakota Territory
1874. New York	Montana Territory
Kansas	
California	

Six other Western states and territories were added by 1890. Finally in 1918, 66 years after the Massachusetts force legislation, the forty-eighth state, Mississippi, enacted a compulsory school attendance law. Keep in mind Cubberley's words: everywhere there was "strenuous opposition."

De-Moralizing School Procedure

But a strange thing happened as more and more children were drawn into the net, a crisis of an unexpected sort. At first those primitive one-room and two-room compulsion schools—even the large new secondary schools like Philadelphia's Central High—poured out large numbers of trained, disciplined intellects. Government schoolteachers in those early days chose overwhelmingly to emulate standards of private academies, and to a remarkable degree they succeeded in unwittingly sabotaging the hierarchical plan being moved on line. Without a carefully trained administrative staff (and most American schools had *no* administrators) it proved impossible to regulate the dumbing-down process[5] promised by the German prototype. In addition, right through the 1920s, a skilled apprenticeship alternative was active in the U.S. representing a tradition still honored in our national success mythology.

Ironically then, the first crisis provoked by the new institution was a too-generous delivery of intellectually trained minds at exactly the moment when the national economy of independent livelihoods and democratic workplaces was beginning to vanish into centralized, professionally managed, accountant-driven, ladder-type corporations. The kind of graduate one- room schools featured represented a force antithetical to the logic of corporate life, a cohort trained to insist upon meritocracy.[6]

Immediate action was called for. Cubberley's celebratory history doesn't examine motives, but does uneasily record forceful steps taken just inside the new century to nip the career of intellectual schooling for the masses in the bud, replacing it with a different goal: the forging of "well-adjusted" citizens. I've added emphasis in the following so you can't miss what really happened:

> *Since 1900, and due more to the activity of persons concerned with social legislation and those interested in improving the moral welfare of children than to educators themselves*, there has been a general revision of the compulsory education laws of our States and the enactment of much new child-welfare...and anti-child-labor legislation....These laws have brought into the schools not only the truant and the incorrigible, who under former conditions either left early or were expelled, but also many children...who have no aptitude for book learning and many children of inferior mental qualities who do not profit by ordinary classroom procedures....Our schools

---

[5] It was not really until the period around 1914 that sufficient teacher training facilities, regulated texts, controlled certification, uniform testing, layered administrative cadres, and a sufficiently alienated public allowed the new age of schooling to tentatively begin.

[6] In conservative political theory dating back to Thucydides, meritocracy is seen as a box of trouble. It creates such a competitive flux no society can remain orderly and loyal to its governors because the governors can't guarantee preferment in licensing, appointments, grants, etc., in return. Meritocratic successes, having *earned* their place, are notoriously disrespectful. The most infamous meritocrat of history was Alcibiades, who ruined Athens, a cautionary name known to every elite college class, debating society, lyceum, or official pulpit in America.

have come to contain many children who...become a nuisance in the school
and *tend to demoralize school procedure.*

We're not going to get much closer to running face-to-face into the true believers and the self-interested parties which imposed forced schooling than in Cubberley's mysterious "persons concerned with social legislation." At about the time Cubberley refers to, Walter Jessup, president of the University of Iowa, was publicly complaining, "Now America demands we educate the whole.... It is a much more difficult problem to teach all children than to teach those who want to learn."

Common sense should tell you it isn't "difficult" to teach children who don't want to learn, it's impossible. Common sense should tell you "America" was demanding nothing of the sort. But somebody most certainly was insisting on universal indoctrination in class subordination. The forced attendance of children who want to be elsewhere, learning in a different way, meant the short happy career of academic public schooling was deliberately foreclosed, with "democracy" used as the excuse. The new *inclusive* pedagogy effectively doomed the bulk of American children.

What you should take away from this is the *deliberate* introduction of children who "demoralize school procedure," children who were accommodated prior to this legislation in a number of other productive (and not inferior) forms of training, just as Benjamin Franklin had been. Hofstadter and other social historians have mistakenly accepted at face value official claims that "democratic tradition"—the will of the people—imposed this anti-intellectual diet on the classroom. Democracy had nothing to do with it.

What we are up against is a strategic project supported by an uneasy coalition of elites, each with its own private goals in mind for the common institution. Among those goals was the urge to go to war against diversity, to impose orthodoxy on heterodox society. For an important clue how this was accomplished we return to Cubberley:

> The school reorganized its teaching along lines *dictated by the new psychology of instruction which had come to us from abroad....* Beginning about 1880 to 1885 our schools began to experience a new but steady change in purpose [though] it is only since about 1900 that any marked and rapid changes have set in.

The new psychology of instruction cited here is the new experimental psychology of Wilhelm Wundt at Leipzig which dismissed the very existence of mind as an *epiphenomenon.* Children were complex machines, capable of infinite "adjustments." Here was the beginning of that new and unexpected genus of schooling which Bailyn said "troubled well-disposed, high-minded people," and which elevated a new class of technocrat like Cubberley and Dewey to national prominence. The intention to sell schooling as a substitute for faith is caught clearly in Cubberley's observation: "However much we may have lost interest in the old problems of faith and religion, the American people has come to believe thoroughly in education." New subjects replaced "the old limited book subject curriculum, both elementary and secondary."

> This was done despite the objections of many teachers and citizens, and much ridicule from the public press. Many spoke sneeringly of the new subjects.

Cubberley provides an accurate account of the prospective new City on the Hill for which "public education" was to be a prelude, a City which rose hurriedly after the failed populist revolt of 1896 frightened industrial leaders: [Note: Emphases below added by author]

1) *The Spanish-American War of 1898 served to awaken us as a nation...It revealed to us something of the position we should be called on to occupy in world affairs....*

2) For the two decades following.... *the specialization of labor and the introduction of labor-saving machinery took place to an extent before unknown....* The national and state government were called upon to do many things for the benefit of the people never attempted before.

3) Since 1898, education has awakened a public interest before unknown.... Everywhere state educational commissions and city school surveys have evidenced a new critical attitude.... Much new educational legislation has been enacted; *permission has been changed to obligation*; minimum requirements have been laid down by the States in many new directions; and new subjects of instruction have been added by the law. Courses of study have been entirely made over and new types of textbooks have appeared..... A complete new system of industrial education, national in scope, has been developed.

4) New normal schools have been founded and higher requirements have been ordered for those desiring to teach. *College departments of education have increased from eleven in 1891 to something like five hundred today* [1919]. *Private gifts to colleges and universities have exceeded anything known before in any land.* School taxes have been increased, old school funds more carefully guarded, and new constitutional provisions as to education have been added.

5) *Compulsory education has begun to be a reality*, and child-labor laws to be enforced.

6) A new interest in child-welfare and child-hygiene has arisen, *evidencing a commendable desire to look after the bodies as well as the minds of children....*

Here in a brief progression is one window on the problem of modern schooling. It set out to build a new social order at the beginning of the twentieth century (and by 1970 had succeeded beyond all expectations) but in the process it crippled the democratic experiment of America, disenfranchising ordinary people, dividing families, creating wholesale dependencies, grotesquely extending childhoods. It emptied people of full humanity in order to convert them into human resources.

William Torrey Harris

If you have a hard time believing this revolution in the contract ordinary Americans had with their political state was intentionally provoked, it's time to meet William Torrey Harris, U.S.

Commissioner of Education from 1889 to 1906. Nobody, other than Cubberley, who rose out of the ranks of professional pedagogues ever had the influence Harris did. Harris standardized our schools and Germanized them. Listen as he speaks in 1906:

> Ninety-nine [students] out of a hundred are automata, careful to walk in prescribed paths, careful to follow the prescribed custom. This is not an accident but the result of substantial education, which, scientifically defined, is the subsumption of the individual.
> — *The Philosophy of Education* (1906)

Listen to Harris again, giant of American schooling, leading scholar of German philosophy in the Western hemisphere, editor/publisher of *The Journal of Speculative Philosophy* which trained a generation of American intellectuals in the ideas of the Prussian thinkers, Kant and Hegel, the man who gave America scientifically age-graded classrooms to replace successful mixed-age school practice:

> The great purpose of school can be realized better in dark, airless, ugly places.... It is to master the physical self, to transcend the beauty of nature. School should develop the power to withdraw from the external world.
> — *The Philosophy of Education* (1906)

Nearly a hundred years ago, this schoolman thought self-alienation was the secret to successful industrial society. Surely he was right. When you stand at a machine or sit at a computer you require an ability to withdraw from life, to alienate yourself without a supervisor. How else could that be tolerated unless prepared in advance by simulated Birkenhead drills? School, thought Harris, was sensible preparation for a life of alienation. Can you say he was wrong?

In exactly the years Cubberley of Stanford identified as the launching time for the school institution, Harris reigned supreme as the bull goose educator of America. His was the most influential voice teaching what school was to be in a modern, scientific state. School histories commonly treat Harris as an old-fashioned defender of high academic standards but this is grossly inadequate analysis; as a philosophical Hegelian Harris believed children were *property* and the state had a compelling interest in disposing of them as it pleased. Some would receive intellectual training, most not. Any distinction that can be made between Harris and later weak curriculum advocates (those interested in stupefaction for everybody) is far less important than substantial agreement in both camps that parents or local tradition could no longer determine the individual child's future.

Unlike any official schoolman until Conant, Harris had social access to important salons of power in the United States. Over his long career he furnished inspiration to the ongoing obsessions of Andrew Carnegie, the steel man who first nourished the conceit of yoking our entire economy to cradle-to-grave schooling. If you can find copies of *The Empire of Business* (1902) or *Triumphant Democracy* (1886) you will find remarkable congruence between the world Carnegie urged and the one our society has achieved.

Carnegie's "Gospel of Wealth" idea took his peers by storm at the very moment the great school transformation began—the idea that the wealthy owed society a duty to take over everything in the public interest was an uncanny echo of Carnegie's experience as a boy watching the elite establishment of Britain and the teachings of its state religion. It would require perverse blindness not to acknowledge a connection between the Carnegie blueprint, hammered into shape in the Greenwich Village salon of Mrs. Botta after the Civil War, and the explosive developments which restored the Anglican world view to our schools.

Of course, every upper class in history has specified what can be known. The defining characteristic of class control is that it establishes a grammar and vocabulary for ordinary people, and for subordinate elites, too. If the rest of us uncritically accept certain official concepts such as "globalization," then we have unwittingly committed ourselves to a whole intricate narrative of society's future, too, a narrative which inevitably drags an irresistible curriculum in its wake.

Since Aristotle, thinkers have understood that work is the vital theater of self-knowledge. Schooling in concert with a controlled workplace is the most effective way to foreclose the development of imagination ever devised. But where did these radical doctrines of true belief come from? Who spread them? We get at least part of the answer from the tantalizing clue Walt Whitman left when he said "only Hegel is fit for America." Hegel was the protean Prussian philosopher capable of shaping Karl Marx on one hand and J.P. Morgan on the other; the man who taught a generation of prominent Americans that history itself could be controlled by the deliberate provoking of crises. Hegel was sold to America in large measure by William Torrey Harris, who made Hegelianism his lifelong project and forced schooling its principal instrument in its role as a peerless *agent provocateor.*

Harris was inspired by the notion that correctly managed mass schooling would result in a population so dependent on leaders that schism and revolution would be things of the past. If a world state could be cobbled together by Hegelian tactical manipulation, and such a school plan imposed upon it, history itself would stop. No more wars, no civil disputes, just people waiting around pleasantly like the Eloi in Well's *The Time Machine*. Waiting for Teacher to tell them what to do. The psychological tool was alienation. The trick was to alienate children from themselves so they couldn't turn inside for strength, to alienate them from their families, religions, cultures, etc. so no countervailing force could intervene.

Carnegie used his own considerable influence to keep this expatriate New England Hegelian U.S. Commissioner of Education for 16 years, long enough to set the stage for an era of "scientific management" (or "Fordism" as the Soviets called it) in American schooling. Long enough to bring about the rise of the multi-layered school bureaucracy. But it would be a huge mistake to regard Harris and other true believers as merely tools of business interest; what they were about was the creation of a modern living faith to replace the Christian one which had died for them. It was their good fortune to live at precisely the moment when the dreamers of the empire of business (to use emperor Carnegie's label) for an Anglo-American world state were beginning to consider worldwide schooling as the most direct route to that destination.

Both movements, to centralize the economy and to centralize schooling, were aided immeasurably by the rapid disintegration of old-line Protestant churches and the rise from their pious ashes of the "Social Gospel" ideology, aggressively underwritten by important industrialists, who intertwined church-going tightly with standards of business, entertainment, and government. The experience of religion came to mean, in the words of Reverend Earl Hoon, "the best social programs money can buy." A clear statement of the belief that social justice and salvation were to be had through skillful consumption.

Shailer Mathews, dean of Chicago's School of Divinity, editor of *Biblical World*, president of the Federal Council of Churches, wrote his influential *Scientific Management in the Churches* (1912) to convince American Protestants they should sacrifice independence and autonomy and adopt the structure and strategy of corporations:

> If this seems to make the Church something of a business establishment, it is
> precisely what should be the case.

If Americans listened to the corporate message, Mathews told them they would feel anew the spell of Jesus.

In the decade before WWI, a consortium of private foundations drawing on industrial wealth began slowly working toward a long-range goal of lifelong schooling and a thoroughly rationalized global economy and society.

Cardinal Principles

Frances Fitzgerald, in her superb study of American textbooks, *America Revised*, notes that schoolbooks are superficial and mindless, that they deliberately leave out important ideas, that they refuse to deal with conflict—but then she admits to bewilderment. What could the plan be behind such texts? Is the composition of these books accidental or deliberate?

Sidestepping an answer to her own question, Fitzgerald traces the changeover to a pair of influential NEA reports published in 1911 and 1918 which reversed the scholarly determinations of the blue-ribbon "Committee of Ten" report of 1893. That Committee laid down a rigorous academic program for all schools and for all children, giving particular emphasis to history. It asserted, "*The purpose of all education is to train the mind.*" The NEA reports of 1911 and 1918 denote a conscious abandonment of this intellectual imperative and the substitution of some very different guiding principles. These statements savagely attack "the bookish curricula" which is "*responsible for leading tens of thousands of boys and girls away from pursuits for which they are adapted,*" toward pursuits for which they are not—like independent businesses, invention, white collar work, or the professions.

Books give children "*false ideals of culture.*" These reports urged the same kinds of drill which lay at the core of Prussian commoner schools. An interim report of 1917 also proposes that emphasis be shifted away from history to something safer called "social studies;" the thrust was away from any careful consideration of the past so that attention might be focused on the future. That 1918 NEA Report, "Cardinal Principles of Secondary Education," for all its maddening banality, was to prove over time one of the most influential education documents of the twentieth century. *It decreed that specified behaviors, health, and vocational training were the central goals of education, not mental development, not character, not godliness.*

Fitzgerald wrote she could not find a name for "the ideology that lies behind these texts." The way they handle history, for instance, is not history at all, "but a catechism... of American socialist realism." More than once she notes "actual *hostility* to the notion of intellectual training. Passion, in partnership with impatience for debate, is one good sign of the presence of true belief."

The most visible clue to the degree true belief was at work in mass schooling in the early decades of this century is the National Education Association's 1918 policy document. Written entirely in the strangely narcotic diction and syntax of official pedagogy which makes it almost impenetrable to outsiders, *Cardinal Principles* announced a new de-intellectualized curriculum to replace the famous recipe for high goals and standards laid out three decades before by the legendary Committee of Ten which declared the purpose of all education the training of the mind.

This new document contradicted its predecessor. It accused that older testament of "leading tens of thousands of boys and girls away from the pursuits for which they are adapted," giving them "false ideals of culture." The weight of such statements, full of dynamic assumptions and implications, cannot easily be felt through its abstract language, but if you recognize that its language conceals a mandate for the mass dumbing down of young Americans, then some understanding of the magnitude of the political coup which had occurred comes through the fog. The repudiation of the Committee of Ten was reinforced substantially by a companion report proposing that history, economics, and geography be dropped at once.

What *Cardinal Principles* gave proof of was that stage one of a silent revolution in American society was complete; children could now be taught anything, or even taught nothing in the part-time prisons of schooling, and there was little any individual could do about it. Bland generalities in the document actually served as potent talismans to justify the engineering of stupefaction. Local challenges could be turned back, local challengers demonized and marginalized, just by waving the national standards of *Cardinal Principles* as proof of one's legitimacy.

Venal motives as well as ideological ones were served by the comprehensive makeover of schooling, and palms incidentally greased in the transition soon found themselves defenders of it for their own material advantage. Schools quickly became the largest jobs project in the country, an enormous contractor for goods and services, one always willing to pay top dollar for bottom shelf merchandise in a dramatic reversal of economic theory. There are no necessary economies in large-scale purchasing;[7] school is proof of that.

Cardinal Principles assured mass production technocrats they would not have to deal with intolerable numbers of independent thinkers—thinkers stuffed with dangerous historical comparisons, who understood economics, who had insight into human nature through literary studies, who were made stoical or consensus-resistant by philosophy and religion, and given confidence and competence through liberal doses of duty, responsibility, and experience.

The appearance of *Cardinal Principles* signaled the triumph of forces which had been working since the 1890s to break the hold of complex reading, debate, and writing as the common heritage of children reared in America. Like the resourcefulness and habits of character toughness small farming conveyed, complex and active literacy produces a kind of character antagonistic to hierarchical, expert-driven, class-based society. As the nature of American society was moved deliberately in this direction, forges upon which a different kind of American had been hammered were eliminated. We see this process nearly complete in the presentation of *Cardinal Principles*.

We always knew the truth in America, that almost everyone can learn almost anything or be almost anything. But the problem with that insight is that it can't co-exist with any known form of modern social ordering. Each species of true belief expresses some social vision or another, some holy way to arrange relationships, time, values, etc., in order to drive toward a settlement of the great

---

[7] I remember the disbelief I felt the day I discovered that as a committee of one I could easily buy paper, milk, and any number of other school staples cheaper than my school district did.

question, "Why are we alive?" The trouble with a society which encourages argument, as America's did until the mid-twentieth century, is that there is no foreseeable end to the argument. No way to lock the door and announce that your own side has finally won. No certainty.

Our most famous true believers, the Puritans, thought they could build a City on the Hill and keep the riffraff out. When it became obvious *exclusion* wasn't going to work, their children and grandchildren did an about-face and began to move toward a totally *inclusive* society (though not a free one). It would be intricately layered into social classes like the old British system. This time God's will wouldn't be offered as reason for the way things were arranged by men, this time Science and Mathematics would justify things, and children would be taught to accept the inevitability of their assigned fates in the greatest laboratory of true belief ever devised: the Compulsion Schoolhouse.

The Unspeakable Chautauqua

One man left us a dynamic portrait of the great school project prematurely completed in miniature: William James, an insider's insider, foremost (and first) psychologist of America, brother of novelist Henry James. James' prestige as a most formidable Boston brahmin launched American psychology. Without him it's touch and go whether it would have happened at all. His *Varieties of Religious Experience* is unique in the American literary canon; no wonder John Dewey dropped Hegel and Herbart after a brief flirtation with the Germans and attached himself to James and his philosophy of pragmatism (which is the Old Norse religion brought up to date). But James was too deep a thinker to believe his own screed fully. In a little book called *Talks to Teachers,* which remains in print over a hundred years after it was written, James disclosed his ambivalence about the ultimate dream of schooling in America.

It was no Asiatic urge to enslave, no Midas fantasy of unlimited wealth, no conspiracy of class warfare but only the dream of a comfortable, amusing world for everyone, the closest thing to an Augustan pastoral you could imagine—the other side of British Imperial coin. England's William Morris and John Ruskin and perhaps Thomas Carlyle were the literary godfathers of this dream society to come, a society already realized in a few cloistered spots on earth, on certain great English estates and at the mother center of the Chautauqua movement in western New York.

In 1899, James spoke to an idealistic new brigade of teachers recruited by Harvard, men and women meant to inspirit the new institution then rising swiftly from the ashes of the older neighborhood schools, private schools, church schools, and home schools. He spoke to the teachers of the dream that the entire planet could be transformed into a vast Chautauqua. Before you hear what he had to say, you need to know a little about Chautauqua.

On August 10, 1878, John H. Vincent announced his plan for the formation of a study group to undertake a four-year program of guided reading for ordinary citizens. The Chautauqua Literary and Scientific Circle signed up 200 people its first hour, 8,400 by year's end. Ten years later, enrollment had grown to 100,000. At least that many more had completed four years or fallen out after trying. In an incredibly short period of time every community in the U.S. had somebody in it following the Chautauqua reading program. One of its teachers, Melvil Dewey, developed the Dewey Decimal System still in use in libraries.

The reading list was ambitious. It included Green's *Short History of the English People*, full of specific information about the original Anglo-Saxon tribes and their child-rearing customs—details which proved strikingly similar to the habits of upperclass Americans. Another Chautauqua text, Mahaffey's *Old Greek Life*, dealt with the utopia of Classical Greece. It showed how civilization could only rise on the backs of underclass drudges. Many motivations to "Go Chautauqua" existed: love of learning, the social urge to work together, the thrill of competition in the race for honorary seals and diplomas which testified to a course completed, the desire to keep up with neighbors.

The Chautauqua movement gave settlers of the Midwest and Far West a common Anglo-German intellectual heritage to link up with; this grassroots vehicle of popular education offered illustrations of principles to guide anyone through any difficulty. And in Chautauqua, New York itself, at the Mother Center, a perfect jewel of a rational utopia was taking shape, attended by the best and brightest minds in American society. You'll see it in operation just ahead with its soda pop fountains and model secondary schools.

The great driving force behind Chautauqua in its early years, as I've told you, was William Rainey Harper, a Yale graduate with a Ph.D. in philology, a man expert in ancient Hebrew, a prominent Freemason. Harper attracted a great deal of attention in his Chautauqua tenure. He would have been a prominent name on the national scene for that alone, even without his connection to the famous publishing family.

John Vincent, Chautauqua's founder, had been struck by the vision of a world-college described in Bacon's utopia, one crowded and bustling with international clientele and honored names as faculty. "Chautauqua will exalt the profession of teacher until the highest genius, the richest scholarship, and the broadest manhood and womanhood of the nation are *consecrated* to this service," Vincent once said:

> We expect the work of Chautauqua will be to arouse so much interest in the subject of general liberal education that by and by in all quarters young men and women will be seeking means to obtain such education in established resident institutions.... Our diploma, though radiant with thirty-one seals—shields, stars, octagons—would not stand for much at Heidelberg, Oxford, or Harvard...an American curiosity.... It would be respected not as conferring honor upon its holder, but as indicating a popular movement in favor of higher education.

Chautauqua's leaders felt their institution was a way station in America's progress to something higher.

By 1886 Chautauqua was well-known all over. The new University of Chicago, which Harper took over five years later, was patterned on the Chautauqua system, which in turn was superimposed over the logic of the German research university. Together with Columbia Teacher's College, Yale, Michigan, Wisconsin, Stanford, and a small handful more, Chicago would provide the most important *visible* leadership for American public school policy well into the twentieth century.

At the peak of its popularity, 8,000 American communities subscribed to Chautauqua's programmatic evangelism. The many tent-circuit Chautauquas simultaneously operating presented locals the latest ideas in social progress, concentrating on self-improvement and social betterment through active Reform with a capital "R." But in practice, entertainment often superseded educational values because the temptation to hype the box-office draw was insidious. Over time, Progress came to be illustrated *dramatically* for maximum emotional impact. Audience reactions were then studied centrally and adjustments made in upcoming shows using what had been learned. What began as education ended as show business. Its legacy is all over modern schooling in its spurious concept of *Motivation*.

Tent-Chautauqua did a great deal to homogenize the U.S. as a nation. It brought to the attention of America an impressive number of new ideas and concepts, always from a management perspective. What seemed even-handed was seldom that. The classic problem of journalism (like that of school teaching) is how to avoid influencing an audience to think a certain way by the use of psychological trickery. In this, Chautauqua failed, but even a partial list of developments credited to Chautauqua is impressive evidence of the influence of this early mass communication device, a harbinger of days ahead. For instance, we have Chautauqua to thank in some important part for the graduated income tax, for slum clearance as a business opportunity, juvenile courts, the school lunch program, free textbooks, a "balanced" diet, physical fitness, the Camp Fire Girls, the Boy Scout movement, pure food laws, and much, much more.

One of the most popular Chautauqua speeches was titled "Responsibilities of the American Citizen." The greatest responsibility was *to listen* to national leaders and get out of the way of progress. Ideas presented during Chautauqua Week were argued and discussed after the tents were gone. The most effective kind of indoctrination, according to letters which passed among Chautauqua's directors, is always "*self-inflicted.*" In the history of American orthodoxies, Chautauqua might seem a quaint sort of villain, but that's because technology soon offered a way through radio to "Chautauqua" on a grander scale, to Chautauqua *simultaneously* coast-to-coast. Radio inherited tent-Chautauqua, presenting us with model heroes and families to emulate, teaching us all to laugh and cry the same way. The great dream of utopians, that we all behave alike like bees in a hive or ants in a hill, was brought close by Chautauqua, closer by radio, even closer by television, and to the threshold of universal reality by the world-wide web.

The chapter in nineteenth century history, which made Chautauqua the harbinger of the new United States, is not well enough appreciated. Ideas like evolution, German military tactics, Froebel's kindergartens, Hegelian philosophy, cradle-to-grave schooling, and systems of complete medical policing were all grist for Chautauqua's mill—nothing was too esoteric to be popularized for a mass audience by the circuit of tent-Chautauqua. But above all, Chautauqua loved Science. Science was the commodity it retailed most energetically. A new religion for a new day.

The Chautauqua operation had been attractively planned and packaged by the former president of Masonic College (Georgia), William Rainey Harper. Dr. Harper left Chautauqua eventually to become Rockefeller's personal choice to head up a new German-style research university Rockefeller had brought into being in 1890 at the University of Chicago. He would eventually become an important early patron of John Dewey and other leading lights of pedagogy. But his first publicly acclaimed triumph was Chautauqua. Little is known of his work at Masonic College; apparently it was impressive enough to bring him to the attention of the most important Freemasons in America.

The real Chautauqua was not the peripatetic tent version but a beautiful Disney-like world: a village on a lake in upstate New York. William James went for a day to lecture at Chautauqua and "stayed for a week to marvel and learn,"—his exact words of self-introduction to those teachers he spoke to long ago at Harvard. What he saw at Chautauqua was the ultimate realization of all reasonable thought solidified into one perfect working community. Utopia for real. Here it is as James remembered it for students and teachers:

> A few summers ago I spent a happy week at the famous Assembly Grounds on the borders of Chautauqua Lake. The moment one treads that sacred enclosure, one feels one's self in an atmosphere of success. Sobriety and industry, intelligence and goodness, orderliness and reality, prosperity and cheerfulness pervade the air. It is a serious and studious picnic on a gigantic scale.

> Here you have a town of many thousands of inhabitants, beautifully laid out in the forest and drained, and equipped with means for satisfying all the necessary lower and most of the superfluous higher wants of man. You have a first class college in full blast. You have magnificent music—a chorus of 700 voices, with possibly the most perfect open-air auditorium in the world.

> You have every sort of athletic exercise from sailing, rowing, swimming, bicycling, to the ball field and the more artificial doings the gymnasium affords. You have kindergarten and model secondary schools. You have general religious services and special club-houses for the several sects. You have perpetually running soda-water fountains and daily popular lectures by distinguished men. You have the best of company and yet no effort.

> You have no diseases, no poverty, no drunkenness, no crime, no police. You have culture, you have kindness, you have equality, you have the best fruits of what mankind has fought and bled and striven for under the name of civilization for centuries. You have, in short, a foretaste of what human society might be were it all in the light with no suffering and dark corners.

Flickering around the edges of James' description is a dawning consciousness that something is amiss—like those suspicions of some innocent character on an old "Twilight Zone" show: it's so peaceful, so pretty and *clean...it....it looks* like Harmony, but I just have this terrible feeling that...*something is wrong...!*

When James left Chautauqua he realized he had seen spread before him the realization on a sample scale of all the ideals for which a scientific civilization strives: intelligence, humanity and order. Then why his violently hostile reaction? "What a relief" he said, "to be out of there." There was no sweat, he continued disdainfully, "in this unspeakable Chautauqua." "No sight of the everlasting battle of the powers of light with those of darkness." No heroism. No struggle. No strength. No "strenuousness."

James cried aloud for the sight of the human struggle, and in a fit of pessimism, he said to the schoolteachers:

> An irremediable flatness is coming over the world. Bourgeoisie and mediocrity, church sociables and teachers' conventions are taking the place of the old heights

and depths....The whole world, delightful and sinful as it may still appear for a moment to one just escaped from the Chautauquan enclosure, is nevertheless obeying more and more just those ideals sure to make of it in the end a mere Chautauqua Assembly on an enormous scale.

A mere Chautauqua assembly? Is that all this monument to intelligence and order adds up to? The full horror of this country's first theme park gave James an epiphany:

The scales seemed to fall from my eyes; and a wave of sympathy greater than anything I had ever before felt with the common life of common men began to fill my soul. It began to seem as if virtue with horny hands and dirty skin were the only virtue genuine and vital enough to take account of. Every other virtue poses; none is absolutely unconscious and simple, unexpectant of decoration or recognition like this. These are our soldiers, thought I, these our sustainers, these are the very parents of our lives.

Near the end of his life, James finally understood what the trap was, an overvaluation placed on order, rational intelligence, humanism, and material stuff of all sorts. The search for a material paradise is a flight away from humanity into the sterile non-life of mechanisms where everything *is* perfect until it becomes junk.

At the end of 1997, Chautauqua was back in the news. A young man living there had deliberately infected at least nine girls in the small town adjoining—and perhaps as many as 28—with AIDS. He picked out most of his victims from the local high school, looking for, as he put it, "young ladies...in a risk-taking mode." A monster like this AIDS predator could turn up anywhere, naturally, but I was struck by the irony that he had found the very protected lakeside hamlet with its quaint nineteenth century buildings and antique shops, this idyllic spot where so many of the true beliefs of rationality made their American debut, as the place to encounter women unprepared to know the ways of the human heart. "In a risk-taking mode" as he puts it in instructively sociological jargon.

Has over 100 years of the best rational thinking and innovation the Western world can muster made no other impact on the Chautauqua area than to set up its children to be preyed upon? A columnist for a New York paper, writing about the tragedy, argued that condom distribution might have helped, apparently unaware that the legitimization of birth control devices in the U.S. was just one of many achievements claimed by Chautauqua.

Other remarks the reporter made were more to the point of why we need to be skeptical whether *any* kind of schooling—and Chautauqua's was the best human ingenuity could offer—is sufficient to make good people or good places:

The area has the troubles and social problems of everywhere. Its kids are lonely in a crowd, misunderstood, beyond understanding and seeking love, as the song says, in all the wrong places.... Once, intact families, tightly knit neighborhoods and stay-at-home mothers enforced community norms. Now the world is the mall, mothers work, and community exists in daytime television and online chat rooms.

CHAPTER SIX

The Lure

Of Utopia

*Every morning when you picked up your newspaper you would read of
some new scheme for saving the world...soon all the zealots, all the
Come-Outers, all the transcendentalists of Boston gathered at the Chardon
Street Chapel and harangued each other for three mortal days. They talked
on nonresistance and the Sabbath reform, of the Church and the Ministry,
and they arrived at no conclusions. "It was the most singular collection of
strange specimens of humanity that was ever assembled," wrote Edmund
Quincy, and Emerson was even more specific: "Madmen, madwomen, men
with beards, Dunkers, Muggletonians, Come-Outers, Groaners, Agrarians,
Seventh-day Baptists, Quakers, Abolitionists, Calvinists, Unitarians, and
Philosophers, all came successively to the top and seized their moment, if not
their hour, wherein to chide, or pray, or preach or protest....There was something artificial about the Chardon Street debates, there was a hothouse
atmosphere in the chapel. There was too much suffering fools gladly, there
was too much talk, too much display of learning and of wit, and there was,
for all the talk of tolerance, an unchristian spirit.*
— Henry Steele Commager, *Theodore Parker*

So Fervently Do We Believe

The cries of true believers are all around the history of schooling, thick as gulls at a garbage
dump. As I wrote that, *USA Today* was telling the story of principal Debbie Reeves of the Barnwell
Elementary School in a wealthy Atlanta suburb, who delivered herself of this amazing statement for
publication: "I'm not sure you ever get to the point you have enough technology. We just believe
so fervently in it."

It's that panting excitement you want to keep an eye out for, that exaggeration of human
perfectibility that Tocqueville noticed in Americans 170 years ago. The same newspaper article

wanders through the San Juan Elementary School in the very heart of Silicon Valley. There, obsolete computers sit idle in neat rows at the back of a spacious media center where years ago a highly touted "open classroom" with a sunken common area drew similar enthusiasm. The school lacks resources for the frequent updates needed to boast state-of-the-art equipment. A district employee was quoted saying: "One dying technology on top of a former dying technology, sort of like layers of an archaeological dig."

America has always been a land congenial to utopian thought. The Mayflower Compact is a testimonial to this. Although its signers were trapped in history, they were ahistorical, too, capable of acts and conceptions beyond the imagination of their parents. The very thinness of constituted authority, the high percentage of males as colonists—homeless, orphaned, discarded, marginally unattached, uprooted males—encouraged dreams of a better time to come. Here was soil for a better world where kindly strangers take charge of children, loving and rearing them more skillfully than their ignorant parents had ever done.

Religion flourished in the same medium, too, particularly the Independent and Dissenting religious traditions of England. The extreme rationalism of the Socinian heresy and deism, twin roots of America's passionate romance with science and technology to come, flourished too. Most American sects were built on a Christian base, but the absence of effective state or church monopoly authority in early America allowed 250 years of exploration into a transcendental dimension no other Western nation ever experienced in modern history, leaving a wake of sects and private pilgrimages which made America the heir of ancient Israel—a place where everyone, even free thinkers, actively trusted in a god of some sort.

Without Pope or Patriarch, without an Archbishop of Canterbury, the episcopal principle behind state and corporate churches lacked teeth, allowing people here to find their own way in the region of soul and spirit. This turned out to be fortunate, a precondition for our laboratory policy of national utopianism which required that every sort of visionary be given scope to make his case. It was a matter of degree, of course. Most Americans, most of the time, were much like people back in England, Scotland, Scandinavia, Germany and Ireland from which domains they had originally derived. After all, the Revolution itself was prosecuted by less than a quarter of our population. But enough of the other sort existed as social yeast that nobody could long escape some plan, scheme, exhortation or tract designed to lead the faithful into one or another Promised Land. Old Testament principles reigned for the most part, not New, and the Prophets had a good part of the national ear.

From 1830 to 1900, over one thousand utopian colonies flourished around the country, colonies which mixed the races, like Fanny Wright's Neshoba in Tennessee, colonies built around intensive schooling like New Harmony in Indiana, colonies which encouraged free love and commonly shared sexual partners as did the Perfectionists at Oneida in upstate New York. In the wonderful tapestry of American utopian thought and practice, one unifying thread stands out clearly. Long before the notion of forced schooling became household reality, utopian architects universally recognized that schooling was the key to breaking with the past. The young had to be isolated, and drilled in the correct way of looking at things or all would fall apart when they grew up. Only the tiniest number of these intentional communities ever did solve that problem, and so almost all vanished after a brief moment. But the idea itself lingered on.

In this chapter I want to push a bit into the lure of utopia because this strain in human nature crisscrosses the growth curve of compulsion schooling at many junctures. Think of it as a search for the formula to change human nature in order to build paradise on Earth. Such an idea is in flagrant opposition to the dominant religion of the Western world, whose theology teaches that human nature is permanently flawed, that all human salvation must be *individually* undertaken.

Even if you aren't used to considering school this way, it isn't hard to see that a curriculum to reach the first end would have to be different from that necessary to reach the second, and the purpose of the educator is all important. It is simply impossible to evaluate what you see in a school without knowing its purpose, but if local administrators have no real idea why they do what they do—why they administer standardized tests for instance, then any statement of purpose made by the local school can only confuse the investigator. To pursue the elusive purpose or purposes of American schooling as they were conceived about a century ago requires that we wander afield from the classroom into some flower beds of utopian aspiration which reared their head in an earlier America.

The Necessity Of Detachment

In Hertzler's *History of Utopian Thought,* the influence of Francis Bacon's *New Atlantis* is traced, a book you need to know something about if you are ever to adequately understand the roots of modern schooling. Hertzler makes a good case from the testimony of its founders that the Royal Society itself[1] arose from the book's prophetic scheme of "Salomon's House," a world university assembling the best of universal mankind under its protection. One of its functions: to oversee management of everything.

New Atlantis had immense influence in England, Germany, Italy, and France. In France it was considered the principal inspiration of the *Encyclopedia* whose connection to the American Revolution is a close one. That story has been told too many times to bear repeating here. Suffice it to say that the very same triangle-encased eye that appears on the back of the American dollar appears as the center of Solomon's Temple in early eighteenth-century French artistic representations.

One consistent requirement of utopian procedure is *detachment* of its subjects from ordinary human affairs. Acting with detached intelligence is what utopians are all about, but a biological puzzle intrudes: detaching intelligence from emotional life isn't really possible. The feat has never been performed although imaginative writers are endlessly intrigued by the challenge it presents. Sherlock Holmes or Mr. Spock come to mind.

Utopian thinking is intolerant of variety or competition, so the tendency of modern utopians to enlarge their canvas to include the whole planet through multinational organizations becomes disturbing. Utopians regard national sovereignty as irrational and democracy as a disease unjustified by biological reality. We need one world they say, and that one world should (reasonably) be under direction of the best utopians. Democracy degrades the hierarchy necessary to operate rational polity. An aspect of nearly all utopias has been addiction to elaborate social machinery like schooling and to what we can call *marvelous machinery.* Excessive human affection between parents, children, husbands, wives, et. al., is suppressed to allow enthusiasm for machine magic to stand out in bold relief.

---

[1] It is useful to remember that Britain's Royal Society was founded not in the pursuit of pure knowledge and not by university dons but by practical businessmen and noblemen concerned with increased profits and lower wages.

Enlarging The Nervous System

There is a legend that in lost Atlantis once stood a great university in the form of an immense flat-topped pyramid from which star observations were made. In this university, most of the arts and sciences of the present world were contained. Putting aside that pleasant fancy which we can find clearly reflected on the obverse of our American Great Seal, almost any early utopia holds a profusion of inside information about things to come. In 1641 Bishop John Wilkins, a founder of the Royal Society, wrote his own utopia, *Mercury: or the Secret and Swift Messenger*. Every single invention Wilkins imagined has come about: "a flying chariot," "a trunk or hollow pipe that shall preserve the voice entirely," a code for communicating by means of noise-makers, etc. *Giphantia*, by de la Roche, unmistakably envisions the telephone, the radio, television, and dehydrated foods and drinks. Even the mechanisms suggested to make these things work are very like the actual ones eventually employed.

Marshall McLuhan once called on us to notice that all machines are merely *extensions* of the human nervous system, artifices which improve on natural apparatus, each a utopianization of some physical function. Once you understand the trick, utopian prophecy isn't so impressive. Equally important, says McLuhan, the use of machinery causes its natural flesh and blood counterpart to atrophy, hence the lifeless quality of the utopias. Machines dehumanize people wherever they are used and however sensible their use appears. In a correctly conceived demonology, the Devil would be perceived as a machine, I think. Yet the powerful, pervasive influence of utopian reform thinking on the design of modern states has brought utopian mechanization of all human functions into the councils of statecraft and into the curriculum of state schooling.

An important part of the virulent, sustained attack launched against family life in the United States, starting about 150 years ago, arose from the impulse to escape fleshly reality. Interestingly enough, the overwhelming number of prominent social reformers since Plato have been childless, usually childless men, in a dramatic illustration of escape-discipline employed in a living tableaux.

Producing Artificial Wants

Beginning about 1840, a group calling itself the Massachusetts School Committee held a series of secret discussions involving many segments of New England political and business leadership.[2] Stimulus for these discussions, often led by the politician Horace Mann, was the deterioration of family life the decline of agriculture was leaving in its wake.[3] A peculiar sort of

---

[2] Much light on these developments is shed by Michael Katz's *The Irony of Early School Reform* and by Joel Spring's historical writings. Both writers are recommended for a dense mine of information; both strike a good balance between the perspective supplied by their personal philosophies and reportage without allegiance to any particular dogma.

[3] The decline of American agriculture was part of a movement to replicate the centralized pattern found in Britain, which had deliberately destroyed its own small farm holdings by 1800. Agriculture had been conducted on a capitalist basis in Britain since the notorious enclosure movement prompted by the growing of farming. In its first stage, peasants were displaced to make room for large scale pasture farming. The second displacement transformed the small farmer into the "farm hand" or the factory worker.

dependency and weakness caused by mass urbanization was acknowledged by all with alarm. The once idyllic American family situation was giving way to widespread industrial serfdom. Novel forms of degradation and vice were appearing.

And yet a great opportunity was presented at the same time, too. Plato, Augustine, Erasmus, Luther, Calvin, Hobbes, Rousseau, and a host of other insightful thinkers, sometimes referred to at the Boston *Athenaeum* as "The Order of the Quest," all taught that without compulsory universal schooling the idiosyncratic family would never surrender its central hold on society allowing utopia to become reality. Family had to be discouraged from its function as a sentimental haven, pressed into the service of loftier ideals—those of the perfected State.

Mann saw that society's "guards and securities" had to increase because an unsuspected pathological phenomenon was following the introduction of mass production into life. It was producing "artificial wants." It was multiplying the temptation to accumulate *things*. But the barbarous life of the machine laborer made family ideals a hollow mockery. Morality could no longer be taught by such families. Crime and vice were certain to explode unless children could be pried away from their degraded custodians and civilized according to formulas laid down by the best minds.

Barnas Sears, Mann's Calvinist colleague, saw the rapid growth of commercial mass entertainment catering to dense urban settlements as "a current of sensuality sweeping everything before it." Former bucolics, who once looked to nature for entertainment, were now pawns in the hands of worldly wisemen vending commercial amusement. Urban confinement robbed men and women of their ability to find satisfaction outside the titillation of mechanical excitation. Whoever provided excitement became the master.

Mann's other colleague, George Boutwell, who would inherit the leadership of New England education from Sears, argued that a course must be selected from which there could be no turning back. Urbanization spelled the collapse of worker families; there was no remedy for it. Fathers were grossly diverted by non-agricultural labor from the custody and training of their children. Claims of a right to society and fashion led to neglect by mothers, too. "As in some languages there is no word which expresses the true idea of home," said Boutwell, "so in our manufacturing towns there are many persons who know nothing of its reality."

Mann proclaimed the State must assert itself as primary parent of children. If an infant's natural parents were removed—or if parental ability failed (as was increasingly certain)—it was the duty of government to step in and fill the parent's place. Mann noted Massachusetts had a long tradition of being "parental in government." His friend Sears described the State as "a nourishing

---

Capitalist farming was established in Britain side by side with a growing manufacturing industry which made it possible to rely on the import of foodstuffs from abroad. Freely imported food meant cheap food. Cheap food meant cheap labor. The development of factory farming in America (and Australia) provided an outlet for the investment of surplus capital at good rates of interest; hence the decline of small farming in America was hastened considerably by direct inducements from its former motherland. Although as late as 1934, 33 percent of American employment was still in agriculture (versus 7 percent in Great Britain), the curriculum of small farm, which encouraged resourcefulness, independence, and self-reliance, was fast giving way to the curriculum of government education which called for quite a different character.

mother, as wise as she is beneficent. Yet, should difficulties arise, the State might become stern—as befits a ruling *patriarch*."

The *Parens Patriae* Powers

The 1852 compulsory schooling legislation of Massachusetts represents a fundamental change in the jurisprudence of parental authority, as had the adoption act passed by the nearly identically constituted legislature just four years prior, the first formal adoption legislation anywhere on Earth since the days of the Roman Empire. Acts so radical could not have passed silently into practice unless fundamental changes in the status of husbands and wives, parents and children, had not already gravely damaged the prestige of the family unit.

These are clear signs as far back as 1796 that elements in the new American state intended to interpose themselves in corners of the family where no European state had ever gone before. In that year, the Connecticut Superior Court, representing the purest Puritan lineage of original New England, introduced "judicial discretion" into the common law of child custody and a new conception of youthful welfare hardly seen before outside the pages of philosophy books—the notion that each child had an *individual* destiny, a private "welfare" *independent of what happened to the rest of its family*.

A concept called "psychological parenthood" began to take shape, a radical notion without legal precedent which would be used down the road to support drastic forcible intervention into family life. It became one of the basic justifications offered during the period of mass immigration for a compulsion law intended to put children under the thrall of so-called scientific parenting in schools.

Judicial discretion in custody cases was the first salvo in a barrage of poorly understood court rulings in which American courts *made* law rather than interpret it. These rulings were formalized later by elected legislatures. Rubber-stamping the *fait accompli*, they marked a restructuring of the framework of the family ordered by a judicial body without any public debate or consent. No precedent for such aggressive court action existed in English law, only in the dreams and speculations of utopian writers and philosophers.

The 1840 case *Mercein v People* produced a stunning opinion by Justice Paige—a strain of radical strong-state faith straight out of Hegel:

> The moment a child is born it owes allegiance to the government of the country
> of its birth, and is entitled to the protection of the government.

As the opinion unrolled, Paige further explained "with the coming of civil society the father's sovereign power passed to the chief or government of the nation." A part of this power was then transferred back to both parents *for the convenience of the State*. But their guardianship was limited to the legal duty of maintenance and education, while absolute sovereignty remained with the State.

Not since John Cotton, teacher of the Boston church in the early Puritan period, had such a position been publicly asserted. Cotton, in renouncing Roger Williams, insisted on the absolute authority of magistrates in civil *and* religious affairs, the quintessential Anglican position. In later life he even came to uphold the power of judges over conscience and was willing to grant powers of life and death to authorities to bring about conformity. Thus did the Puritan rebellion rot from within.

A few years after the Paige ruling, American courts received a second radical authorization to intervene in family matters, "the best interest of the child" test. In 1847, Judge Oakley of New York City Superior Court staked a claim that such power "is not unregulated or arbitrary" but is "governed, as far as the case will admit, by fixed rules and principles." When such fixed rules and principles were not to be found, it caused no problem either, for it was only another matter subject to court discretion.

In the 54-year period separating Massachusetts' compulsion school law/adoption law and the founding of Children's Court at the beginning of the twentieth century in Chicago, the meaning of these decisions became increasingly clear. With opposition from the family-centered societies of tidewater and hill-country South diminished by civil war, the American state assumed the *parens patriae* powers of old-time absolute kings, the notion of the political state as the primary father. And there were signs it intended to use those powers to synthesize the type of scientific family it wanted, for the society it wanted. To usher in the future it wanted.

The Plan Advances

In the space of one lifetime, the United States was converted from a place where human variety had ample room to display itself into a laboratory of virtual orthodoxy—a process concealed by dogged survival of the mythology of independence. The cowboy and frontiersman continued as film icons until 1970, living ghosts of some collective national inspiration. But both died, in fact, shortly after Italian immigration began in earnest in the 1880s.

The crucial years for the hardening of our national arteries were those between 1845 and 1920, the immigration years. Something subtler than Anglo-Saxon revulsion against Celt, Latin, and Slav was at work in that period. A utopian ideal of society as an orderly social hive had been transmitting itself continuously through small elite bodies of men since the time of classical Egypt. New England had been the New World proving ground of this idea. Now New England was to take advantage of the chaotic period of heavy immigration and the opportunity of mass regimentation afforded by Civil War to establish this form of total State.

The plan advanced in barely perceptible stages, each new increment making it more difficult for individual families to follow an independent plan. Ultimately, in the second and third decades of the twentieth century—decades which gave us Adolf Hitler, Prohibition, mass IQ-testing of an entire student population, junior high schools, raccoon coats, Rudy Vallee, and worldwide depression, room to breathe in a personal, peculiar, idiosyncratic way just ran out. It was the end of Thomas Jefferson's dream, the final betrayal of democratic promise in the last new world on the planet.

When you consider how bizarre and implausible much of the conformist machinery put in place during this critical period really was—and especially how long and successfully all sorts of people resisted this kind of encroachment on fundamental liberty—it becomes clear that to understand things like universal medical policing, income tax, national banking systems, secret police, standing armies and navies which demand constant tribute, universal military training, standardized national examinations, the cult of intelligence tests, compulsory education, the organization of colleges around a scheme called "research" (which makes teaching an unpleasant inconvenience), the secularization of religion, the rise of specialist professional monopolies sanctioned by their state, and all the rest of the "progress" made in these 75 years, you have to find reasons to explain. Why then? Who made it happen? What was the point?

Children's Court

The very clear connection between all the zones of the emerging American hive-world are a sign of some organized intelligence at work, with some organized end in mind.[4] For those who can read the language of conventional symbolism, the philosophical way being followed represents the extraordinary vision of the learned company of deists who created the country coupled to the Puritan vision as it had been derived from Anglo-Normans—descendants of the Scandinavian/French conquerors of England—those families who became the principal settlers of New England. It is careless to say that bad luck, accident, or blind historical forces caused the trap to spring shut on us.

Of the various ways an ancient ideal of perfected society can be given life through institutions under control of the State, one is so startling and has been realized so closely it bears some scrutiny. As the hive-world was being hammered out in the U.S. after 1850, the notion of unique, irreplaceable natural families came increasingly to be seen as the major roadblock in the path of social progress toward the extraordinary vision of a machine-driven, utopian paradise. To realize such a theory in practice, families must be *on-trial* with each other constantly and with their neighbors, just as a politician is ever on trial. Families should be conditional entities, not categories absolute. This had been the operational standard of the Puritan settlement in America, though hardly of any other region (unless the Quaker/Pietist sections of the middle colonies who "shunned" outcasts, even if family). If, after testing, an original mother and father did not suit, then children should be removed and transferred to parent-surrogates. This is the basis of foster care and adoption.

By 1900, through the agency of the radical new Denver/Chicago "Children's Court," one important machine to perform this transfer function was in place. Children need not be wasted building blocks for the State's purpose just because their natural parents had been. The lesson the new machine-economy was teaching reinforced the spiritual vision of utopians: perfect interchangeability, perfect subordination. People could learn to emulate machines; by progressive approximations they might ultimately become as reliable as machinery. In a similar vein, husbands and wives were encouraged through easy divorce laws and easier and easier access to sexually explicit imagery to delay choosing marriage mates. With the mystery removed, the pressure to mate went with it, it was supposed. The new system encouraged "trials," trying on different people until a good fit was found.

---

[4] The paradox that a teenager in the year 2000 requires parental permission to be given Tylenol or have ears pierced but not, in some states, to have an abortion suggests the magnitude of the control imposed and at least a portion of its purpose.

Mr. Young's Head Was Pounded To Jelly

The most surprising thing about the start-up of mass public education in mid-nineteenth-century Massachusetts is how overwhelmingly parents of all classes soon complained about it. Reports of school committees around 1850 show the greatest single theme of discussion was conflict between the State and the general public on this matter. Resistance was led by the old yeoman class—those families accustomed to taking care of themselves and providing meaning for their own lives. The little town of Barnstable on Cape Cod is exemplary. Its school committee lamented, according to Katz's *Irony of Early School Reform*, that "the great defect of our day is the absence of governing or controlling power on the part of parents and the consequent insubordination of children. Our schools are rendered inefficient by the apathy of parents."

Years ago I was in possession of an old newspaper account which recounted the use of militia to march recalcitrant children to school there, but I've been unable to locate it again. Nevertheless, even a cursory look for evidence of state violence in bending public will to accept compulsion schooling will be rewarded: Bruce Curtis's book *Building the Education State 1836-1871* documents the intense aversion to schooling which occurred across North America, in Anglican Canada where leadership was uniform as well as in the U.S. where leadership was more divided. Many schools were burned to the ground and teachers run out of town by angry mobs. When students were kept after school, parents often broke into school to free them.

At Saltfleet Township in 1859 a teacher was locked in the school house by students who "threw mud and mire into his face and over his clothes," according to school records—while parents egged them on. At Brantford in 1863 the teacher William Young was assaulted to the point (according to his replacement) that "Mr. Young's head, face and body was, if I understand rightly, pounded literally to jelly." Curtis argues that parent resistance was motivated by a radical transformation in the intentions of schools—a change from teaching basic literacy to molding social identity.

The first effective American compulsory schooling in the modern era was a reform school movement which Know-Nothing legislatures of the 1850s put into the hopper along with their radical new adoption law. Objects of reformation were announced as follows: Respect for authority; Self-control; Self-discipline. The properly reformed boy "acquires a fixed character," one that can be planned for in advance by authority in keeping with the efficiency needs of business and industry.

Reform meant the total transformation of character, behavior modification, a complete makeover. By 1857, a few years after stranger-adoption was kicked off as a new policy of the State, Boutwell could consider foster parenting (the old designation for adoption) "one of the major strategies for the reform of youth."[5] The first step in the strategy of reform was for the State to become de facto parent of the child. That, according to another Massachusetts educator, Emory Washburn, "presents the State in her true relation of a parent seeking out her erring children."

---

[5] The reader will recall such a strategy was considered for Hester Prynne's child, Pearl, in Hawthorne's *Scarlet Letter*. That Hawthorne, writing at mid-century, chose this as a hinge for his characterization of the fallen woman Hester is surely no coincidence.

The 1850s in Massachusetts marked the beginning of a new epoch in schooling. Washburn triumphantly crowed that these years produced the first occasion in history "whereby a state in the character of a common parent has undertaken the high and sacred duty of rescuing and restoring her lost children...by the influence of the school." John Philbrick, Boston school superintendent, said of his growing empire in 1863, "Here is *real* home!" All schooling, including the reform variety, was to be in imitation of the best "family system of organization;" this squared with the prevalent belief that delinquency was not caused by external conditions—thus letting industrialists and slumlords off the hook—but by deficient homes.

Between 1840 and 1860, male schoolteachers were cleansed from the Massachusetts system and replaced by women. A variety of stratagems were used, including the novel one of paying *women* slightly *more* than men in order to bring shame into play in chasing men out of the business. Again the move was part of a well-conceived strategy: "Experience teaches that these boys, many of whom never had a mother's affection...need the softening and refining influence which woman alone can give, and we have, wherever practicable, substituted female officers and teachers for those of the other sex."

A state report noted the *frequency* with which parents coming to retrieve their own children from reform school were met by news their children had been given away to others, through the state's *parens patriae* power. "We have felt it to be our duty *generally* to decline giving them up to their parents and have placed as many of them as we could with farmers and mechanics," reads a portion of Public Document 20 for the state of Massachusetts, written in 1864. To recreate the feelings of parents on hearing this news is beyond my power.

William Rainey Harper

Three decades later at the University of Chicago, William Rainey Harper, former Chautauqua wizard, began a revolution that would change the face of American university education. Harper imported the university system of Germany into the U.S., lock, stock, and barrel. Undergraduate teaching was to be relegated to a form of Chautauqua show business, while research at the graduate level was where prestige academic careers would locate, just as Bacon's *New Atlantis* had predicted.

Harper, following the blueprint suggested by Andrew Carnegie in his powerful "Gospel of Wealth" essays, said the U.S. should work toward a unified scheme of education, organized vertically from kindergarten through university, horizontally through voluntary association of colleges, all supplemented by university extension courses available to everyone. Harper wrote in 1902:

> The field of education is at the present time in an extremely disorganized condition.
> But the forces are already in existence [to change that]. Order will be secured and
> a great new system established, which may be designated "The American System."
> The important steps to be taken in working out such a system are coordination,
> specialization and association.

Harper and his backers regarded education purely as a commodity. Thorstein Veblen describes Harper's revolution this way:

> The underlying business-like presumption accordingly appears to be that learning is a merchantable commodity, to be produced on a piece-rate plan, rated, bought and sold by standard units, measured, counted, and reduced to staple equivalence by impersonal, mechanical tests.

Harper believed modern business enterprise represented the highest and best type of human productive activity. He believed business had discovered two cosmic principles—techniques implicit in the larger concept of survival of the fittest: consolidation and specialization. Whatever will not consolidate and specialize must perish, he believed. The conversion of American universities into a system characterized by institutional giantism and specialization was not finished in Harper's lifetime, but went far enough that in the judgment of the *New York Sun*, "Hell is open and the lid is off!"

Harper's other main contribution to the corporatizing of U.S. scholarly life was just as profound. He destroyed the lonely vocation of great teacher by trivializing its importance. Research alone, objectively weighed and measured, subject to the surveillance of one's colleagues would, after Harper, be the *sine qua non* of university teaching:

> Promotion of younger men in the departments will depend more largely upon the results of their work as investigators than upon the efficiency of their teaching.... In other words, it is proposed to make the work of investigation primary, the work of giving instruction secondary.

Harper was the middleman who introduced the organization and ethics of business into the world of pedagogy. Harper-inspired university experience is now virtually the only ritual of passage into prosperous adulthood in the United States just as the Carnegie Foundation and Rockefeller's General Education Board willed it to be. Few young men or women are strong enough to survive this passage with their humanity wholly intact.

Death Is Executed

In 1932, John Dewey, now elevated to a position as America's most prominent educational voice, heralded the end of what he called "the old individualism." Time had come, he said, for *a new individualism* that recognized the radical transformation that had come in American society:

> Associations, tightly or loosely organized, more and more define opportunities, choices, and actions of individuals.

Death, a staple topic of children's books for hundreds of years because it poses a central puzzle for all children, nearly vanished as theme or event after 1916. Children were instructed indirectly there was no grief; indeed an examination of hundreds of those books from the transitional period between 1900 and 1916 reveals that Evil no longer had any reality either. There was no Evil, only bad attitudes, and those were correctable by training and adjustment therapies.

To see how goals of utopian procedure are realized, consider further the sudden change that fell upon the children's book industry between 1890 and 1920. Without explanations or warning, timeless subjects disappeared from the texts, replaced by what is best regarded as a political agenda. The suddenness of this change was signaled by many other indications of powerful social forces at work: the phenomenal overnight growth of "research" hospitals where professional *hospital-ity* replaced home-style sick care was one of these, the equally phenomenal sudden enforcement of compulsory schooling another.

Through children's books, older generations announce their values, declare their aspirations, and make bids to socialize the young. Any sudden change in the content of such books must necessarily reflect changes in *publisher* consciousness, not in the general class of book-buyer whose market preferences evolve slowly. What is prized as human achievement can usually be measured by examining children's texts; what is valued in human relationships, can be, too.

In the 30-year period from 1890 to 1920, the children's book industry became a *creator*, not a reflector, of values. In any freely competitive situation this could hardly have happened because the newly aggressive texts would have risked missing the market. The only way such a gamble could be safe was for total change to occur *simultaneously* among publishers. It was the insularity and collegiality of children's book publishing which allowed it this luxury.

One aspect of children's publishing that has remained consistent all the way back to 1721 is the zone where it is produced; today as nearly 300 years ago, the Northeast is where children's literature happens—inside the cities of Boston, New York, and Philadelphia. No industry shift has ever disturbed this cozy arrangement: over time, concentration became even more intense—Philadelphia was virtually eliminated in the early twentieth century leaving Boston and New York co-regents. In 1975 an unbelievable 87 percent of all titles available came from those two colonial cities while in 1876 it had been "only" 84 percent, a marvelous consistancy. For the past one hundred years these two cities have decided what American children will read.

Until 1875, about three quarters of all children's titles dealt with some aspect of the future—usually salvation. Over the next 40 years this idea vanished completely. As Comte and Saint-Simon had strongly advised, the child was to be relieved of concerning itself with the future. The future would be arranged *for* children and for householders by a new expert class, and the need to do God's will was now considered dangerous superstition by men in charge.

Another dramatic switch in children's books had to do with a character's dependence on *community* to solve problems and to give life meaning. Across the eighteenth and nineteenth century, strength, afforded by stable community life, was an important part of narrative action, but toward the end of the nineteenth century a totally new note of "self" was sounded. Now protagonists became more competent, more in control, their need for family and communal affirmation disappeared to be replaced by a new imperative—the quest for certification by *legitimate* authority. Needs now suddenly dominant among literary characters were so-called "expressive needs": exploring, playing, joy, loving, self-actualizing, *intriguing against one's own parents*. By the early twentieth century, a solid majority of all children's books focus on the individual child *free from the web of family and community*.

This model had been established by the Horatio Alger books in the second half of the nineteenth century; now with some savage modern flourishes (like encouraging *active* indifference to family) it came to totally dominate the children's book business. Children were invited to divide their interests from those of their families and to concentrate on private concerns. A few alarmed critical voices saw this as a strategy of "divide and conquer," a means to separate children from family so they could be more easily molded into new social designs. In the words of Mary Lystad, the biographer of children's literary history from whom I have drawn heavily in this analysis:

> As the twentieth century continued, book characters were provided more and
> more opportunities to pay attention to themselves. More and more characters
> were allowed to look inward to their own needs and desires.

This change of emphasis "was managed at the expense of others in the family group," she adds.

From 1796 to 1855, 18 percent of all children's books were constructed about the idea of conformity to some adult norm; but by 1896 emphasis on conformity had *tripled*. This took place in the 30 years following the Civil War. Did the elimination of the Southern pole of our national dialectic have anything to do with that? Yes, everything, I think. With tension between Northern and Southern ways of life and politics resolved permanently in favor of the North, the way was clear for triumphant American orthodoxy to seize the entire field. The huge increase in conformist themes increased even further as we entered the twentieth century and has remained at an elevated level through the decades since.

What is most deceptive in trying to fix this characteristic conformity is the introduction of an apparently libertarian note of free choice into the narrative equation. Modern characters are encouraged to self-start and to proceed on what appears to be an independent course. But upon closer inspection, that course is always toward a *centrally prescribed* social goal, never toward personal solutions to life's dilemmas. Freedom of choice in this formulation arises from the *feeling* that you have freedom, not from its actual possession. Thus social planners get the best of both worlds: a large measure of control without any kicking at the traces. In modern business circles, such a style of oversight is known as management by objectives.

Another aspect of this particular brand of regulation is that book characters are shown being *innovative*, but innovative only in the way they arrive at the same destination; their emotional needs for self-expression are met harmlessly in this way without any risk to social machinery. Much evidence of centralized tinkering within the factory of children's literature exists, pointing in the direction of what might be called Unit-Man—people as work units partially broken free of human *community* who can be moved about efficiently in various social experiments. Such an end University of Chicago president William Rainey Harper thought of as "laboratory research aimed at designing a rational utopia."

To mention just a few other radical changes in children's book content between 1890 and 1920: school credentials replace experience as the goal book characters work towards, and child labor becomes a label of condemnation in spite of its ancient function as the quickest, most reliable way to human independence—the way taken in fact by Carnegie, Rockefeller, and many others who were now apparently quite anxious to put a stop to it.

Children are encouraged *not to work at all* until the late teen years, sometimes not until their thirties. A case for the general superiority of youth working instead of idly sitting around in school confinement is often made prior to 1900, but never heard again in children's books after 1916. The universality of this silence is the notable thing, deafening in fact.

Protagonists' goals in the new literature, while apparently individualistic, are almost always found being pursued through social institutions—those ubiquitous "associations" of John Dewey— never through family efforts. Families are portrayed as good-natured dormitory arrangements or affectionate manager-employer relationships, but emotional commitment to family life is noticeably ignored. Significant family undertakings like starting a farm or teaching each other how to view life from a multi-age perspective are so rare the few exceptions stand out like monadnocks above a broad, flat plain.

The Three Most Popular Books

The three most influential books ever published in North America, setting aside the *Bible* and *The New England Primer*, were all published in the years of the utopian transformation of America which gave us government schooling: *Uncle Tom's Cabin, or Life Among the Lowly* (1852), a book which testifies to the ancient obsession of English-speaking elites with the salvation of the under classes. *Ben Hur* (1889), a book illustrating the Christian belief that Jews can eventually be made to see the light of reason and converted; and the last a pure utopia, *Looking Backwards* (1888), still in print more than 100 years later, translated into 30 languages.[6]

In 1944, three American intellectuals, Charles Beard, John Dewey, and Edward Weeks, interviewed separately, proclaimed Edward Bellamy's *Looking Backwards* second only to Marx's *Das Kapital* as the most influential book of modern times. Within three years of its publication, 165 "Bellamy Clubs" sprouted up. In the next 12 years, no less than 46 other utopian novels became best-sellers.

Was it Civil War, chaos, decades of mass immigration, or a frightening series of bloody national labor strikes shattering our class-free myths that made the public ready for stories of a better tomorrow? Whatever the cause or causes, the flowering of actual American utopianism took on real shape in the nineteenth century from famous ones like Owenite communities and Fourierian *phalansteres* or Perfectionist sexual stews like Oneida, right down to little-known oddities, like Mordecai Noah's *Ararat*, city of refuge for Jews. First they happened, then they were echoed in print, not the reverse. Nothing in the human social record matches the outburst of purely American longing for something better in community life, the account recorded in deeds *and* words in the first full century of our nationhood.

What Bellamy's book uncovered in middle-class/upper middle-class consciousness was revealing—the society Bellamy describes is a totally *organized* society, all means of production are in the hands of State parent-surrogates. The conditions of well-behaved, middle class childhood are

---

[6] Economist Donald Hodges' book, *America's New Economic Order*, traces the intellectual history of professionalism in management (John Kenneth Galbraith's corporate "Technostructure" in *The New Industrial State*) to *Looking Backwards* which described an emerging public economy similar to what actually happened. Hodges shows how various theorists of the utopian transition like John Dewey and Frederick Taylor shaped the regime of professional managers we live under.

recreated on a corporate scale in these early utopias. Society in Bellamy's ideal future has eliminated the reality of democracy, citizens are answerable to commands of industrial officers, little room remains for self-initiative. The State regulates all public activities, owns the means of production, individuals are transformed into a unit directed by bureaucrats.

Erich Fromm thought Bellamy had missed the strong similarities between corporate socialism and corporate capitalism—that both *converge* eventually in goals of industrialization, that both are societies run by a managerial class and professional politicians, both thoroughly materialistic in outlook; both organize human masses into a centralized system; into large, hierarchically arranged employment-pods, into mass political parties. In both, alienated corporate man—well-fed, well-clothed, well-entertained—is governed by bureaucrats. Governing has no goals beyond this. At the end of history men are not slaves, but robots. This is the vision of utopia seen complete.

No Place To Hide

How could the amazing lives of George Washington, Andrew Jackson, John D. Rockefeller, Margaret Fuller, Amy Lowell, my own immigrant McManuses, Gattos, Zimmers, Hoffmans, and Dagastinos, have added up to this lifeless utopia? Like a black hole it grew, although no human being flourishes under such a regime or rests easily inside the logic of hundreds of systems intermeshing into one master system, all demanding obedience from their human parts. This is a religious vision, Ezekial's wheels within wheels, a nightmare come to life.

In a *New York Times* description of the first "Edison Project" school in Sherman, Texas—a system of proprietary schools supplying a home computer for every child, e-mail, longer school days and years, and "the most high-tech school in America" (as Benno Schmidt, ex-Yale president put it)—the local superintendent gloated over what he must have regarded as the final solution to the student-control issue: " Can you imagine what this means if you're home sick? The teacher can just put stuff in the student's e-mail,....There's no place to hide anymore!"

The Irony Of The Safety Lamp

Have I made too much of this? What on earth is wrong with wanting to help people, even in institutionalizing the helping urge so it becomes more reliable? Just this: the helping equation is not as simple as utopians imagined. I remember the shock I felt on many occasions when my well-meant intercession into obvious problems a kid was having were met with some variation of the angry cry, "Leave me alone!" as if my assistance would actually make things worse. It was baffling how often that happened, and I was a well-liked teacher. Is it possible there are hills that nature or God demands we climb alone or become forever the less for having been carried over them?

The plans true believers lay down for our lives may be "better" than our own when tested against some official standard, but to deny anyone a personal struggle is to strip humanity from their lives; what are we left with after our struggles are taken away but some unspeakable Chautauqua, a liar's world driven by the dishonest promise that if only all rules are followed, a good life will ensue? Inconvenience, discomfort, hurt, defeat, and tragedy are inevitable accompaniments of our time on Earth; we learn to manage trouble by managing trouble, not by turning our burden over to another. Think of the mutilated spirit that victims of over-protective parents carry long after they are grown and gone from home. What should make you suspicious about School is its relentless *compulsion*. Why should this rich brawling, utterly successful nation ever have needed to resort to *compulsion* to order people into school classes—unless advocates of force-schooling were driven by peculiar philosophical beliefs not commonly shared?

Another thing should concern you, that the consequences of orthodox mass schooling have never been thought through. Consider Sir Humphrey Davy, who invented the coal mine safety lamp in 1813 after an 1812 explosion in the Felling mine, northern England, in which 92 boys and men were killed. Davy's assignment to sainthood comes from his announcement that the sole object of his enterprise was to "serve the cause of humanity"—a declaration given credibility by his refusal to patent the device.

No one denies that the safety lamp decreased the danger of explosion relative to older methods of illumination, but who can deny either that *many more miners have died as the indirect result of Davy's invention*? Davy's safety lamp was a great curse. It alone allowed the coal industry to grow rapidly, bringing vastly more men into the mines than before, opening deeper tunnels, exposing miners to mortal dangers, of which fire-damp is only one, dangers for which there is no protection. The chief effect of the safety lamp was to increase the wealth of coal mine owners. It wasted many more lives than it saved.

Serving the cause of humanity through schooling may also turn out to be a stranger matter than it appears, another Davy lamp in different costume.

CHAPTER SEVEN

The Prussian

Connection

Prussian Fire-Discipline

On approaching the, enemy the marching columns of Prussians wheeled in succession to the right or left, passed along the front of the enemy until the rear company had wheeled. Then the whole together wheeled into line facing the enemy. These movements brought the infantry into two long well-closed lines, parade-ground precision obtained thanks to remorseless drilling. With this movement was bound up a fire-discipline more extraordinary than any perfection of maneuver. "Pelotonfeuer" was opened at 200 paces from the enemy and continued up to 30 paces when the line fell on with the bayonet. The possibility of this combination of fire and movement was the work of Leopold, who by sheer drill made the soldier a machine capable of delivering (with flintlock muzzle-loading muskets) five volleys a minute. The special Prussian fire-discipline gave an advantage of five shots to two against all opponents. The bayonet attack, if the rolling volleys had done their work, was merely, "presenting the cheque for payment," as a German writer put it.

          — Encyclopedia Britannica, 11th edition, "Prussia"

The Land Of Frankenstein

The particular utopia American believers chose to bring to the schoolhouse was Prussian. The seed that became American schooling, twentieth century style, was planted in 1806 when Napoleon's amateur soldiers bested the professional soldiers of Prussia at the battle of Jena. When your business is renting soldiers and employing diplomatic extortion under threat of your soldiery, losing a battle like that is pretty serious. Something had to be done.

  The most important immediate reaction to Jena was an immortal speech, the "Address to the German Nation" by the philosopher Fichte—one of the influential documents of modern history leading directly to the first workable compulsion schools in the West. Other times, other lands talked about schooling, but all failed to deliver. Simple forced training for brief intervals and for narrow purposes was the best that had ever been managed. This time would be different.

In no uncertain terms Fichte told Prussia the party was over. Children would have to be disciplined through a new form of universal conditioning. They could no longer be trusted to their parents. Look what Napoleon had done by banishing sentiment in the interests of nationalism. Through forced schooling, everyone would learn that "work makes free," and working for the State, even laying down one's life to its commands, was the greatest *freedom* of all. Here in the genius of semantic redefinition[1] lay the power to cloud men's minds, a power later packaged and sold by public relations pioneers Edward Bernays and Ivy Lee in the seedtime of American forced schooling.

Prior to Fichte's challenge any number of compulsion-school proclamations had rolled off printing presses here and there, including Martin Luther's plan to tie church and state together this way and, of course, the "Old Deluder Satan" law of 1642 in Massachusetts and its 1645 extension. The problem was these earlier ventures were virtually unenforceable, roundly ignored by those who smelled mischief lurking behind fancy promises of free education. People who wanted their kids schooled had them schooled even then; people who didn't didn't. That was more or less true for most of us right into the twentieth century; only 32 percent of American kids went past elementary school as late as 1920. If that sounds impossible, consider the practice in Switzerland today where only 23 percent of the student population goes to high school though Switzerland has the world's highest per capita income in the world.

Prussia was prepared to use bayonets on its own people as readily as it wielded them against others, so it's not all that surprising the human race got its first effective secular compulsion schooling out of Prussia in 1819, the same year Mary Shelley's *Frankenstein*, set in the darkness of far off Germany, was published in England. *Schule* came after more than a decade of deliberations, commissions, testimony, and debate. For a brief, hopeful moment, Humboldt's brilliant arguments for a high-level no-holds-barred, free-swinging, universal, intellectual course of study for all, full of variety, free debate, rich experience, and personalized curricula almost won the day. What a different world we would have today if Humboldt had won the Prussian debate, but the forces backing Baron vom Stein won instead. And that has made all the difference.

The Prussian mind, which carried the day, had a clear idea what centralized schooling should deliver: 1) Obedient soldiers to the army;[2] 2) Obedient workers for mines, factories, and farms; 3)

---

[1] Machiavelli had clearly identified this as a necessary strategy of state in 1532, and even explored its choreography.

[2] For an ironic reflection on the success of Prussian educational ideals, take a look at Martin Van Creveld's *Fighting Power* (Greenwood Press, 1982). Creveld, the world's finest military historian, undertakes to explain why German armies in 1914-1918 and 1939-1945, although heavily outnumbered in the major battles of both wars, consistently inflicted 30 percent more casualties than they suffered, whether they were winning or losing, on defense or on offense, no matter who they fought. They were better led, we might suspect, but the actual training of those field commanders comes as a shock. While American officer selection was right out of Frederick Taylor, complete with psychological dossiers and standardized tests, German officer training emphasized individual apprenticeships, week-long field evaluations, extended discursive written evaluations by senior officers who personally knew the candidates.

Well-subordinated civil servants, trained in their function; 4) Well-subordinated clerks for industry; 5) Citizens who thought alike on mass issues; 6) National uniformity in thought, word, and deed.

The area of individual volition for commoners was severely foreclosed by Prussian psychological training procedures drawn from the experience of animal husbandry and equestrian training, and also taken from past military experience. Much later, in our own time, the techniques of these assorted crafts and sullen arts became "discoveries" in the pedagogical pseudoscience of psychological behaviorism.

Prussian schools delivered everything they promised. Every important matter could now be worked out in advance confidently by leading families and institutional heads because well-schooled masses would concur with a minimum of opposition. This tightly schooled consensus in Prussia eventually combined the kaleidoscopic German principalities into a united Germany, after a thousand years as a nation in fragments. What a surprise the world would soon get from this successful experiment in national centralization! Under Prussian state socialism private industry surged, vaulting resource-poor Prussia up among world leaders. Military success remained Prussia's touchstone, even before the school law went into full effect, the army corps under Blücher destroyed Napoleon at Waterloo, miraculously bounding back from serious defeat at his hands just days before.[3]

The immense prestige earned from this triumph reverberated through an America not so lucky in its own fortunes of war, a country humiliated by a shabby showing against the British in the war of 1812. Even 30 years after Waterloo, so highly was Prussia regarded in America and Britain, the English-speaking adversaries selected the Prussian king to arbitrate our northwest border with Canada. Hence the Pennsylvania town "King of Prussia." Thirty-three years after Prussia made state schooling work, we borrowed the structure, style, and intention of those Germans for our own first compulsion schools.

The surprise is, while German state management was rigid and regulated with its common citizens, it was liberal and adventuresome with its elites. After WWII, and particularly after Vietnam, American elite military practice began to follow this German model. Ironically enough, America's elite private boarding schools like Groton had followed the Prussian lead from their inception as well as the British models of Eton and Harrow.

German elite war doctrine cut straight to the heart of the difference between the truly educated and the merely schooled. For the German High Command war was seen as an art, a creative activity, grounded in science. War made the highest demands on an officer's entire personality and the role of the individual in Germany was decisive. American emphasis, on the other hand, was doctrinal, fixated on cookbook rules. The U.S. officer's manual said: "Doctrines of combat operation are neither numerous nor complex. Knowledge of these doctrines provides a firm basis for action in a particular situation." This reliance on automatic procedure rather than on creative individual decisions got a lot of Americans killed by the book. The irony, of course, was that American, British, and French *officers* got the same lockstep conditioning in dependence that German foot soldiers did. There are some obvious lessons here which can be applied directly to public schooling.

[3] Napoleon assumed the Prussians were retreating in the direction of the Rhine after a defeat, but in truth they were only executing a feint. The French were about to overrun Wellington when Blücher's "Death's Head Hussars," driven beyond human endurance by their officers, reached the battlefield at a decisive moment. Not pausing to rest, the Prussians immediately went into battle, taking the French in the rear and right wing. Napoleon toppled, and Prussian discipline became the focus of world attention.

Traditional American school purpose—piety, good manners, basic intellectual tools, self-reliance, etc.—was scrapped to make way for something different. Our historical destination of personal independence gave way slowly to Prussian-purpose schooling, not because the American way lost in any competition of ideas, but because for the new commercial and manufacturing hierarchs, such a course made better economic sense.

This private advance toward nationalized schooling in America was partially organized, although little has ever been written about it; Orestes Brownson's journal identifies a covert national apparatus (to which Brownson briefly belonged) already in place in the decade after the War of 1812, one whose stated purpose was to "Germanize" America beginning in those troubled neighborhoods where the urban poor huddled, and where disorganized new immigrants made easy targets, according to Brownson. Enmity on the part of old-stock middle class and working class populations toward newer immigrants gave these unfortunates no appeal against the school sentence to which Massachusetts assigned them. They were in for a complete makeover, like it or not.

Much of the story, as it was being written by 1844, lies just under the surface of Mann's florid prose in his *Seventh Annual Report* to the Boston School Committee. On a visit to Prussia the year before, he had been much impressed (so he said) with the ease by which Prussian calculations could determine precisely how many thinkers, problem-solvers, and working stiffs the State would require over the coming decade, then how it offered the precise categories of training required to develop the percentages of human resource needed. All this was much fairer to Mann than England's repulsive episcopal system—schooling based on social class; Prussia, he thought, was republican in the desirable, manly, Roman sense. Massachusetts must take the same direction.

The Long Reach Of The Teutonic Knights

William H. Welch, an ambitious young Bostonian, told his sister in 1876 before setting off from America to Germany for study: "If by absorbing German lore I can get a little start of a few thousand rivals and thereby reduce my competition to a few hundred more or less it is a good point to tally." Welch did go off to Germany for the coveted Ph.D., a degree which at the time had its actual existence in any practical sense only there, and in due course his ambition was satisfied. Welch became first dean of Johns Hopkins Medical School and, later, chief adviser to the Rockefeller foundation on medical projects. Welch was one of thousands who found the German Ph.D. a blessing without parallel in late-nineteenth-century America. German Ph.D.s ruled the academic scene by then.

Prussia itself was a curious place, not an ordinary country unless you consider a land which by 1776 required women to register each onset of their menses with police ordinary. North America had been interested in Prussian developments since long before the American Revolution, its social controls being a favorite subject of discussion among Ben Franklin's[4] exclusive private discussion

---

[4] Franklin's great-grandson, Alexander Dallas Bache, became the leading American proponent of Prussianism in 1839. After a European school inspection tour lasting several years, his *Report on Education in Europe*, promoted heavily by Quakers, devoted hundreds of pages to glowing description of Pestalozzian method and to the German *gymnasium*.

group, the *Junta*. When the phony Prussian baron, Von Steuben, directed bayonet drills for the colonial army, interest rose even higher. Prussia was a place to watch, an experimental state totally synthetic like our own, having been assembled out of lands conquered in the last crusade. For a full century Prussia acted as our mirror, showing elite America what we might become with discipline.

In 1839, twelve years before the first successful school compulsion law was passed in the United States, a perpetual critic of Boston Whig leadership (Mann's own party) charged that proposals to erect German-style teacher seminaries in this country were a thinly disguised attack on local and popular autonomy. The critic Brownson[5] allowed that state regulation of teaching licenses was a necessary preliminary only if school were intended to serve as a psychological control mechanism for the state and as a screen for a controlled economy. If that was the game truly afoot, said Brownson, it should be reckoned an act of treason.

"Where the whole tendency of education is to create obedience," Brownson said, "all teachers must be pliant tools of government. Such a system of education is not inconsistent with the theory of Prussian society but the thing is wholly inadmissible here." He further argued that "according to our theory the people are wiser than the government. Here the people do not look to the government for light, for instruction, but the government looks to the people. The people give law to the government." He concluded that "to entrust government with the power of determining education which our children shall receive is entrusting our servant with the power of the master. The fundamental difference between the United States and Prussia has been overlooked by the board of education and its supporters."[6]

This same notion of German influence on American institutions occurred recently to a historian from Georgetown, Dr. Carroll Quigley.[7] Quigley's analysis of elements in German character which were exported to us occurs in his book, *Tragedy and Hope: A History of the World in Our Time*. Quigley traced what he called "the German thirst for the coziness of a totalitarian way of life" to the breakup of German tribes in the great migrations 1,500 years ago. When pagan Germany finally transferred its loyalty to the even better totalitarian system of Diocletian in post-Constantine Rome, that system was soon shattered, too, a second tragic loss of security for the Germans. According to Quigley, they refused to accept this loss. For the next 1,000 years, Germans made every effort to reconstruct the universal system, from Charlemagne's Holy Roman Empire right up to the aftermath of Jena in 1806. During that thousand year interval, other nations of the West developed individual liberty as the ultimate center of society and its principal philosophical reality. But while Germany was dragged along in the same process, it was never convinced that individual sovereignty was the right way to organize society.

---

[5] Brownson is the main figure in Christopher Lasch's bravura study of Progressivism, *The True and Only Heaven*, being offered there as the best fruit of American democratic orchards, a man who, having seemingly tried every major scheme of meaning the new nation had to offer, settled on trusting ordinary people as the best course into the future.

[6] "In Opposition to Centralization" (1839).

[7] Quigley holds the distinction of being the only college professor ever to be publicly honored by a major party presidential candidate Bill Clinton in his formal acceptance speech for the presidential nomination.

Germans, said Quigley, wanted freedom from the need to make decisions, the negative freedom that comes from a universal totalitarian structure which gives security and meaning to life. The German is most at home in military, ecclesiastical, or educational organizations, ill at ease with equality, democracy, individualism or freedom. This was the spirit that gave the West forced schooling in the early nineteenth century, so spare a little patience while I tell you about Prussia and Prussianized Germany whose original mission was expressly religious but in time became something else.

During the thirteenth century, the Order of Teutonic Knights set about creating a new state of their own. After 50 turbulent years of combat, the Order successfully Christianized Prussia by the efficient method of exterminating the entire native population and replacing it with Germans. By 1281, the Order's hold on lands once owned by the heathen Slavs was secure. Then something of vital importance to the future occurred—the system of administration selected to be set up over these territories was not one patterned on the customary European model of dispersed authority, but instead was built on the logic of Saracen *centralized* administration, an Asiatic form first described by crusaders returned from the Holy Land. For an example of these modes of administration in conflict, we have Thucydides' account of the Persian attempt to force the pass at Thermopylae. Persia with its huge bureaucratically subordinated army arrayed against self-directed Leonidas and his 300 Spartans. This image of free will and personal determination in conflict with a highly trained and specialized military bureaucracy was passed down to 60 generations of citizens in Western lands as an inspiration and model. Now Prussia had established an Asiatic beachhead on the northern fringe of Europe, one guided by a different inspiration.

Between the thirteenth and nineteenth centuries, the Order of Teutonic Knights evolved by gradual stages into a highly efficient, secular civil service. In 1525, Albert of Brandenberg declared Prussia a secular kingdom. By the eighteenth century, under Frederick the Great, Prussia became a major European power in spite of its striking material disadvantages. From 1740 onwards, it had been feared throughout Europe for its large, well-equipped, and deadly standing army, comprising a formulaic one percent of the population. After centuries of debate, the one percent formula became the lot of the United States military, too, a gift of Prussian strategist von Clausewitz to America. By 1740, the mature Prussian state-structure was almost complete. During the reigns of Frederick I and his son Frederick II, Frederick the Great, the modern absolute state was fashioned there by means of immense sacrifices imposed on the citizenry to sustain permanent mobilization.

The historian Thomas Macauley wrote of Prussia during these years: "The King carried on warfare as no European power ever had, he governed his own kingdom as he would govern a besieged town, not caring to what extent private property was destroyed or civil life suspended. The coin was debased, civil functionaries unpaid, but as long as means for destroying life remained, Frederick was determined to fight to the last." Goethe said Frederick "saw Prussia as a concept, the root cause of a process of abstraction consisting of norms, attitudes and characteristics which acquired a life of their own. It was a unique process, supra-individual, an attitude depersonalized, motivated only by the individual's duty to the State." Today it's easy for us to recognize Frederick as a systems theorist of genius, one with a real country to practice upon.

Under Frederick William II, Frederick the Great's nephew and successor, from the end of the eighteenth century on into the nineteenth, Prussian citizens were deprived of all rights and privileges.

Every existence was comprehensively subordinated to the purposes of the State, and in exchange the State agreed to act as a good father, giving food, work, and wages suited to the people's capacity, welfare for the poor and elderly, and universal schooling for children. The early nineteenth century saw Prussian state socialism arrive full-blown as the most dynamic force in world affairs, *a powerful rival to industrial capitalism*, with antagonisms sensed but not yet clearly identified. It was the moment of schooling, never to surrender its grip on the throat of society once achieved.

The Prussian Reform Revolt

The devastating defeat by Napoleon at Jena triggered the so-called Prussian Reform Movement, a transformation which replaced cabinet rule (by appointees of the national leader) with rule by permanent civil servants and permanent government bureaus. Ask yourself which form of governance responds better to public opinion and you will realize what a radical chapter in European affairs was opened. The familiar three-tier system of education emerged in the Napoleonic era, one private tier, two government ones. At the top, one-half of one percent of the students attended *Akadamiensschulen*[8] where, as future policy makers, they learned to think strategically, contextually, in wholes; they learned complex processes, useful knowledge, studied history, wrote copiously, argued often, read deeply, and mastered tasks of command.

The next level, *Realsschulen*, was intended mostly as a manufactory for the professional proletariat of engineers, architects, doctors, lawyers, career civil servants, and such other assistants as policy thinkers at times would require. From five to seven-and-a-half percent of all students attended these "real schools," learning in a superficial fashion how to think in context, but mostly learning how to manage materials, men, and situations—to be problem solvers. This group would also staff the various policing functions of the state, bringing order to the domain. Finally, at the bottom of the pile, a group between 92 and 94 percent of the population attended "people's schools" where they learned obedience, cooperation and correct attitudes along with rudiments of literacy and official state myths of history.

This universal system of compulsion schooling was up and running by 1819, and soon became the eighth wonder of the world, promising for a brief time—in spite of its exclusionary layered structure—liberal education for all. But this early dream was soon abandoned, this particular utopia had a different target than human equality, it aimed instead for frictionless efficiency. From its inception *Volksschule*, the people's place, heavily discounted reading; reading produced dissatisfaction it was thought. The Bell-school remedy was called for: a standard of virtual illiteracy formally taught under state church auspices. Reading offered too many windows onto better lives, too much familiarity with better ways of thinking. It was a gift unwise to share with those permanently consigned to low station.

---

[8] I've exaggerated the *neatness* of this tripartite division in order to make clear its functional logic. The system as it actually grew in those days without an electronic technology of centralization was more whimsical than I've indicated, dependent partially on local tradition and resistance, partially on the ebb and flow of fortunes among different participants in the transformation. In some places, the "academy" portion didn't occur in a separate institution, but as a division inside the Realsschulen, something like today's "gifted and talented *honors*" programs as compared to the common garden variety "gifted and talented" pony shows.

Heinrich Pestalozzi, an odd[9] Swiss-German school reformer, was producing at this time a non-literary, experience-based pedagogy, strong in music and industrial arts, which was attracting much favorable attention in Prussia. Here seemed a way to keep the poor happy without arousing in them hopes of drastically changing the social order. Pestalozzi claimed ability to mold the poor "to accept all the efforts peculiar to their class." He offered them love in place of ambition. By employing psychological means in the training of the young, class warfare might be avoided.

A curiously prophetic note for the future development of scientific school teaching was that Pestalozzi himself could barely read. Not that he was a dummy; those talents simply weren't important in his work. He reckoned his own semi-literacy an advantage in dealing with children destined *not* to find employments requiring much verbal fluency. Seventeen agents of the Prussian government acted as Pestalozzi's assistants in Switzerland, bringing insights about the style of schooling they saw there home to northern Germany.

While Pestalozzi's raggedy schools lurched clumsily from year to year, a nobleman, von Fellenberg, refined and systematized the Swiss reformer's disorderly notes, hammering the funky ensemble into clarified plans for a worldwide system of industrial education for the masses. As early as 1808, this non-academic formulation was introduced into the United States under Joseph Neef, formerly a teacher at Pestalozzi's school. Neef, with important Quaker patronage, became the principal schoolmaster for Robert Owen's pioneering work-utopia at New Harmony, Indiana. Neef's efforts there provided high-powered conversational fodder to the fashionable Unitarian drawing rooms of Boston in the decades before compulsory legislation was passed. And when it did pass, all credit for the political victory belonged to those Unitarians.

Neef's influence resonated across the U.S. after the collapse of New Harmony, through lectures given by Robert Owen's son (later a congressman, then referee of J.P. Morgan's legal contretemps with the U.S. Army[10]), and through speeches and intrigues by that magnificent nineteenth century female dynamo, Scottish emigre Fanny Wright, who demanded the end of family life and its replacement by communitarian schooling. The tapestry of school origins is one of paths crossing and recrossing and more apparent coincidences than seems likely.

Together, Owens and Wright created the successful Workingman's Party of Philadelphia which seized political control of that city in 1829. The party incorporated strong compulsion schooling proposals as part of its political platform. Its idea to place working class children under the philosophical discipline of highly skilled craftsmen—men comparable socially to the yeomanry of pre-enclosure England—would have attracted favorable commentary in Philadelphia where banker Nicholas Biddle was locked in struggle for control of the nation's currency with working class hero

---

[9] Pestalozzi's strangeness comes through in almost all the standard biographical sketches of him despite universal efforts to emphasize his saintliness. Anthony Sutton in a recent study claims Pestalozzi was also director of a secret lodge of "illuminated" freemasonry—with the code name "Alfred." If true, the Swiss "educator" was even stranger than I sensed initially.

[10] Morgan sold back to the army its own defective rifles (which had been auctioned as scrap) at a 1,300 percent profit. After a number of soldiers were killed and maimed, young Morgan found himself temporarily in hot water. Thanks to Owens his penalty was the return of about *half* his profit!

Andrew Jackson. Biddle's defeat by Jackson quickly moved abstract discussions of a possible social technology to control working class children from the airy realms of social hypothesis to policy discussions about immediate reality. In that instant of maximum tension between an embryonic financial capitalism and a populist republic struggling to emerge, the Prussian system of pedagogy came to seem perfectly sensible to men of means and ambition.

Travelers' Reports

Information about Prussian schooling was brought to America by a series of travelers' reports published in the early nineteenth century. First was the report of John Griscom, whose book *A Year in Europe* (1819) highly praised the new Prussian schools. Griscom was read and admired by Thomas Jefferson and leading Americans whose intellectual patronage drew admirers into the net. Pestalozzi came into the center of focus at about the same time through the letters of William Woodbridge to *The American Journal of Education*, letters which examined this strange man and his "humane" methods through friendly eyes. Another important chapter in this school buildup came from Henry Dwight[11] whose *Travels in North Germany* (1825) praised the new quasi-religious teacher seminaries in Prussia where prospective teachers were screened for correct attitudes toward the State.

The most influential report, however, was French philosopher Victor Cousin's to the French government in 1831. This account by Cousin, France's Minister of Education, explained the administrative organization of Prussian education in depth, dwelling at length on the system of people's schools and its far-reaching implications for the economy and social order. Cousin's essay applauded Prussia for discovering ways to contain the danger of a frightening new social phenomenon, the industrial proletariat. So convincing was his presentation that inside of two years after its publication, French national schooling was drastically reorganized to meet Prussian *Volksschulen* standards. French children could be stupefied as easily as German ones.

Across the Atlantic, a similar revolution took place in the brand new state of Michigan. Mimicking Prussian organization, heavily Germanic Michigan established the very first State Superintendency of Education.[12] With a state minister and state control entering all aspects of schooling, the only missing ingredient was compulsion legislation.

---

[11] Of the legendary Dwight family which bankrolled Horace Mann's forced schooling operation. Dwight was a distant ancestor of Dwight D. Eisenhower.

[12] This happened under the direction of William Pierce, a man as strange in his own way as Pestalozzi. Pierce had been a Unitarian minister around Rochester, New York, until he was forced to flee across the Great Lakes to escape personal harm during the anti-Masonic furor just before the first Jackson election. Pierce was accused of concealing a lodge of Illuminati behind the facade of his church. When his critics arrived with the tar and feathers, the great educator-to-be had already flown the coop to Michigan, his tools of illumination safely in his kit and a sneer of superior virtue on his noble lip. Some say a local lady of easy virtue betrayed the vigilante party to Pierce in exchange for a few pieces of Socinian silver, but I cannot confirm this reliably. How he came to be welcomed so warmly in Michigan and honored with such a high position might be worth investigating.

On Cousin's heels came yet another influential report praising Prussian discipline and Prussian results, this time by the bearer of a prominent American name, the famous Calvin Stowe whose daughter Harriet Beecher Stowe, conscience of the abolition movement, was author of its sacred text, *Uncle Tom's Cabin*. Stowe's report to the Ohio legislature attesting to Prussian superiority was widely distributed across the country, the Ohio group mailing out 10,000 copies and the legislatures of Massachusetts, Michigan, Pennsylvania, North Carolina and Virginia each reprinting and distributing the document.

The third major testimonial to Prussian schooling came in the form of Horace Mann's *Seventh Report to the Boston School Committee* in 1843. Mann's *Sixth Report*, as noted earlier, had been a paean to phrenology, the science of reading head bumps, which Mann argued was the only proper basis for curriculum design. The *Seventh Report* ranked Prussia first of all nations in schooling, England last. Pestalozzi's psychologically grounded form of pedagogy was specifically singled out for praise in each of the three influential reports I've recited, as was the resolutely non-intellectual subject matter of Prussian *Volksschulen*. Also praised were mild Pestalozzian discipline, grouping by age, multiple layers of supervision, and selective training for teachers. Wrote Mann, "There are many things there which we should do well to imitate."[13]

Mann's *Report* strongly recommended radical changes in reading instruction from the traditional alphabet system which had made America literate to Prussia's hieroglyphic-style technique. In a surprising way, this brought Mann's *Report* to general public attention because a group of Boston schoolmasters attacked his conclusions about the efficacy of the new reading method and a lively newspaper debate followed. Throughout nineteenth century Prussia, its new form of education seemed to make that warlike nation prosper materially and militarily. While German science, philosophy, and military success seduced the whole world, thousands of prominent young Americans made the pilgrimage to Germany to study in its network of research universities, places where teaching and learning were always subordinate to investigations done on behalf of business and the state. Returning home with the coveted German Ph.D., those so degreed became university presidents and department heads, took over private industrial research bureaus, government offices, and the administrative professions. The men they subsequently hired for responsibility were those who found it morally agreeable to offer obeisance to the Prussian outlook, too; in this leveraged fashion the gradual takeover of American mental life managed itself.

For a century here, Germany seemed at the center of everything civilized; nothing was so esoteric or commonplace it couldn't benefit from the application of German scientific procedure. Hegel of Berlin University even proposed that history was really a scientific subject, displaying a progressive linear movement toward some mysterious end. Elsewhere, Herbart and Fechner were applying mathematical principles to learning, Müller and Helmholtz were grafting physiology to behavior in anticipation of the psychologized classroom, Fritsch and Hitzig applied electrical stimulation to the brain to determine the relationship of brain functions to behavior, and Germany itself was approaching its epiphany of unification under Bismarck.

---

[13] The fact is Mann arrived in Prussia *after the schools had closed for the summer*, so that he never actually saw one in operation. This did nothing to dampen his enthusiasm, nor did he find it necessary to enlighten his readers to this interesting fact. I'll mention this again up ahead.

When the spirit of Prussian *pelotonfeuer* crushed France in the lightning war of 1871, the world's attention focused intently on this hypnotic, utopian place. What could be seen to happen there was an impressive demonstration that endless production flowed from a Baconian liaison between government, the academic mind, and industry. Credit for Prussian success was widely attributed to its form of schooling. What lay far from casual view was the religious vision of a completely systematic universe which animated this Frankensteinian nation.

Finding Work For Intellectuals

The little North German state of Prussia had been described as "an army with a country," "a perpetual armed camp," "a gigantic penal institution." Even the built environment in Prussia was closely regimented: streets were made to run straight, town buildings and traffic were state-approved and regulated. Attempts were made to cleanse society of irregular elements like beggars, vagrants, and Gypsies, all this intended to turn Prussian society into "a huge human automaton" in the words of Hans Rosenberg. It was a state where scientific farming alternated with military drilling and with state-ordered meaningless tasks intended for no purpose but to subject the entire community to the experience of collective discipline—like fire drills in a modern junior high school or silent passing in the space between class periods. Prussia had become a comprehensive administrative utopia. It was Sparta reborn.

Administrative utopias spring out of the psychological emptiness which happens where firmly established communities are nonexistent and what social cohesion there is is weak and undependable. Utopia happens best where there is no other social and political life around which seems attractive or even safe. The dream of state power refashioning countryside and people is powerful, especially compelling in times of insecurity where local leadership is inadequate to create a satisfying social order, as must have seemed the case in the waning decades of the nineteenth century. In particular, the growing intellectual classes began to resent their bondage to wealthy patrons, their lack of any truly meaningful function, their seeming overeducation for what responsibilities were available, their feelings of superfluousness. The larger national production grew on wheels and belts of steam power. The more it produced unprecedented surpluses, the greater the number of intellectuals condemned to a parasitic role grew, and the more certain it became that some utopian experiment must come along to make work for these idle hands.

In such a climate it could not have seemed out of line to the new army of homeless men whose work was only endlessly thinking, to reorganize the entire world and to believe such a thing not impossible to attain. It was only a short step before associations of intellectuals began to consider it their *duty* to reorganize the world. It was then the clamor for universal forced schooling became strong. Such a need coincided with a corresponding need on the part of business to train the population as consumers rather than independent producers.

In the last third of the nineteenth century, a loud call for popular education arose from princes of industry, from comfortable clergy, professional humanists and academic scientists, those who saw schooling as an instrument to achieve state and corporate purposes. Prior to 1870, the only countries where everybody was literate were Prussia, its tiny adjacent neighbor states in Nordic Scandinavia, and the United States. Despite all projects of the Enlightenment, of Napoleon, of the parliaments of England and Belgium and of revolutionaries like Cavour, the vast majority of Europeans could neither read nor write. It was not, of course, because they were stupid but because circumstances of their lives and cultures made literacy a luxury, sometimes even impossible.

Steam and coal provided the necessary funds for establishing and maintaining great national systems of elementary schooling. Another influence was the *progressivism* of the liberal impulse, never more evident than in the presence of truly unprecedented abundance. Yes, it was true that to create that abundance it became necessary to uproot millions from their traditional habitats and habits, but one's conscience could be salved by saying that popular schooling would offer, *in time*, compensations for the proletariat. In any case, no one doubted Guizot's epigram: "The opening of every schoolhouse closes a jail."

For the enlightened classes, popular education after Prussia became a sacred cause, one meriting crusading zeal. In 1868, Hungary announced compulsion-schooling; in 1869, Austria; in 1872, the famous Prussian system was nationalized to all the Germanies; 1874, Switzerland; 1877, Italy; 1878, Holland; 1879, Belgium. Between 1878 and 1882, it became France's turn. School was made compulsory for British children in 1880. No serious voice questioned what was happening except Tolstoy's, and that Russian nobleman-novelist-mystic was easily ignored.

The school movement was strongest in Western and Northern Europe, the ancient lands of the Protestant Reformation, much weaker in Catholic Central and Southern Europe, virtually nonexistent at first in the Orthodox East. Enthusiasm for schooling is closely correlated with a nation's intensity in mechanical industry, and that closely correlated with its natural heritage of coal. One result passed over too quickly in historical accounts of school beginnings is the provision for a quasi-military noncommissioned officer corps of teachers, and a staff-grade corps of administrators to oversee the mobilized children. One consequence unexpected by middle classes (though perhaps not so unexpected to intellectual elites) was a striking increase in gullibility among well-schooled masses. Jacques Ellul is the most compelling analyst of this awful phenomenon, in his canonical essay, *Propaganda*. He fingers schooling as an unparalleled propaganda instrument; if a schoolbook prints it and a teacher affirms it, who is so bold as to demur?

The Technology Of Subjection

Administrative utopias are a peculiar kind of dreaming by those in power, driven by an urge to arrange the lives of others, organizing them for production, combat, or detention. The operating principles of administrative utopia are hierarchy, discipline, regimentation, strict order, rational planning, a geometrical environment, a production line, a cellblock, and a form of welfarism. Government schools and some private schools pass such parameters with flying colors. In one sense, administrative utopias are laboratories for exploring the technology of subjection and as such belong to a precise subdivision of pornographic art: total surveillance and total control of the helpless. The aim and mode of administrative utopia is to bestow order and assistance on an unwilling population: to provide its clothing and food. *To schedule it.* In a masterpiece of cosmic misjudgement, the phrenologist, George Combe, wrote Horace Mann on November 14, 1843:

The Prussian and Saxon governments by means of their schools and their just laws and rational public administration are doing a good deal to bring their people into a rational and moral condition. It is pretty obvious to thinking men that a few years more of this cultivation will lead to the development of free institutions in Germany.

Earlier that year, Mann had written to Combe (May 21, 1843): "I want to find out what are the results, as well as the workings of the famous Prussian system." Just three years earlier, with the election of Marcus Morton as governor of Massachusetts, a serious challenge had been presented to Mann and to his Board of Education and the air of Prussianism surrounding it and its manufacturer/politician friends. A House committee was directed to look into the new Board of Education and its plan to undertake a teachers college with $10,000 put up by industrialist Edmund Dwight. Four days after its assignment, the majority reported out a bill to kill the board! Discontinue the Normal School experiment, it said, and give Dwight his money back:

If then the Board has any actual power, it is a dangerous power, touching directly upon the rights and duties of the Legislature; if it has no power, why continue its existence at an annual expense to the commonwealth?

But the House committee did more; it warned explicitly that this board, dominated by a Unitarian majority of 7-5 (although Unitarians comprised less than 1 percent of the state), really wanted to install a Prussian system of education in Massachusetts, to put "a monopoly of power in a few hands, contrary in every respect to the true spirit of our democratical institutions." The vote of the House on this was the single greatest victory of Mann's political career, one for which he and his wealthy friends called in every favor they were owed. The result was 245 votes to continue, 182 votes to discontinue, and so the House voted to overturn the recommendations of its own committee. A 32-vote swing might have given us a much different twentieth century than the one we saw.

Although Mann's own letters and diaries are replete with attacks on orthodox religionists as enemies of government schooling, an examination of the positive vote reveals that from the outset the orthodox churches were among Mann's staunchest allies. Mann had general support from Congregational, Presbyterian, and Baptist clergymen. At this early stage they were completely unaware of the doom secular schooling would spell out for their denominations. They had been seduced into believing school was a necessary insurance policy to deal with incoming waves of Catholic immigration from Ireland and Germany, the cheap labor army which as early as 1830 had been talked about in business circles and eagerly anticipated as an answer to America's production problems.

The reason Germany, and not England, provided the original model for America's essay into compulsion schooling may be that Mann had a shocking experience in English class snobbery while in Britain, which left him reeling. Boston Common, he wrote, with its rows of mottled sycamore trees, gravel walks and frog ponds was downright *embarrassing* compared with any number of stately English private grounds furnished with stag and deer, fine arboretums of botanical specimens from far away lands, marble *floors* better than the *table tops* at home, portraits, tapestries, giant gold-frame mirrors. The ballroom in the Bullfinch house in Boston would be a butler's pantry in England, he wrote. When Mann visited Stafford House of the Duke of Cumberland, he went into culture shock:

> Convicts on treadmills provide the energy to pump water for fountains. I
> have seen equipages, palaces, and the regalia of royalty side by side with
> beggary, squalidness, and degradation in which the very features of humanity
> were almost lost in those of the brute.

For this great distinction between the layered orders of society, Mann held the Anglican church to blame. "Give me America with all its rawness and want. We have aristocracy enough at home and here I trace its foundations." Shocked from his English experience, Mann virtually willed that Prussian schools would provide him with answers, says his biographer Jonathan Messerli.

Mann arrived in Prussia when its schools were closed for vacation, he toured empty classrooms, spoke with authorities, interviewed vacationing schoolmasters, and read piles of dusty official reports. Yet from this nonexperience he claimed to come away with a strong sense of the professional competence of Prussian teachers! All "admirably qualified and full of animation!" His wife Mary, of the famous Peabodys, wrote home: "We have not seen a teacher *with a book in his hand* in all Prussia; no, not one!" This wasn't surprising, for they hardly saw teachers at all.

Equally impressive, he wrote, was the wonderful *obedience* of children; these German Kinder had "innate respect for superior years." The German teacher corps? "The finest collection of men I have ever seen—full of intelligence, dignity, benevolence, kindness and bearing.... "Never, says Mann, did he witness "an instance of harshness and severity. All is kind, encouraging, animating, sympathizing." On the basis of imagining this miraculous vision of exactly the Prussia he wanted to see, Mann made a special plea for changes in the teaching of reading. He criticized the standard American practice of beginning with the alphabet and moving to syllables, urging his readers to consider the superior merit of teaching entire words from the beginning. "I am satisfied," he said, "our greatest error in teaching lies in beginning with the alphabet."

The heart of Mann's most famous *Report to the Boston School Committee*, the legendary *Seventh*, rings a familiar theme in American affairs. It seems *even then we were falling behind!* This time behind the Prussians in education. In order to catch up, it was mandatory to create a professional corps of teachers, just as the Prussians had. And a systematic curriculum just as the Prussians had. Mann fervently implored the Board to accept his prescription...*while there was still time!*

That fall, the Association of Masters of the Boston Public Schools published their 150-page rebuttal of Mann's *Report*. They attacked the normal schools proposal as a vehicle for propaganda for Mann's "hot bed theories, in which the projectors have disregarded experience and observation." They belittled his advocacy of phrenology and charged Mann with attempting to excite the prejudices of the ignorant. Their second attack was against the teacher-centered non-book presentations of Prussian classrooms, insisting the psychological result of these was to break student potential "for forming the habit of independent and individual effort." The third attack was against the "word method" in teaching reading, and in defense of the traditional alphabet method. Lastly they attacked Mann's belief that interest was a better motivator to learning than discipline: "Duty should come first and pleasure should grow out of the discharge of it."

Sixty years later, amid a well-coordinated attempt on the part of industrialists and financiers to transfer power over money and interest rates from elected representatives of the American people to a "Federal Reserve" of centralized private banking interests, George Reynolds, president of the American Bankers Association, rose before an audience on September 13, 1909, to declare himself flatly in favor of a central bank modeled after the German Reichsbank. As he spoke, the schools of the United States were being forcibly rebuilt on Prussian lines.

On September 14, 1909, in Boston, the President of the United States, William Howard Taft, instructed the country that it should "take up seriously" the problem of establishing a centralized bank on the German model. As *The Wall Street Journal* put it, an important step in the education of Americans would soon be taken to translate the "realm of theory" into "practical politics," in pedagogy as well as finance.

Dramatic, symbolic evidence of what was working deep in the bowels of the school institution surfaced in 1935. At the University of Chicago's experimental high school, the head of the Social Science department, Howard C. Hill, published an inspirational textbook, *The Life and Work of the Citizen*. It is decorated throughout with the *fasces*, symbol of the fascist movement, an emblem binding government and corporation together as one entity. Mussolini had landed in America.

But it is the title page of this American textbook which grips the attention of the fascinated reader most. It shows four cartoon hands symbolizing Law, Order, Science, and the Trades interlocked to form a perfect swastika. The Prussian connection had entrenched itself deep into the vitals of American institutional schooling by then, too.

CHAPTER EIGHT

A Coal-Fired

Dream World

*Wanting coal we could not have smelted the iron needed to make
our engines, nor have worked our engines when we had got them.
But take away the engines and the great towns vanish like a dream.
Manufacturers give place to agriculture and pasture, and not ten
men can live where now ten thousand.*

— Thomas Huxley (1875)

*Coal introduced a new race of men who work with machinery instead
of their hands, who cluster together in cities instead of spreading over
the land, men who trade with those of other nations as readily as with
those of their own town...men whose market is no longer the city or
country but the world itself.*

— Henry DeBeers Gibbins (1903)

Coal At The Bottom Of Things

Where I grew up the hand of coal was everywhere. Great paddle-wheel boats pushed it up and down the river every day, driven by the heat of coal fire. Columns of barges—eight, ten, twelve to a boat—were as common a sight to me as police cars are to the modern Manhattan where I live a half-century later. Those barges glide majestically through my memory, piled high with coal gleaming in the sunshine, glistening in the rain, coal destined for steel mills, coke ovens, machine works, chemical plants, coal yards and coal chutes everywhere. Long before we saw the lead barges push the river aside, we saw plumes of smoke shoot above the willows on the riverbanks. As the big paddle-wheel went crashing by, orange clouds of sulfuric rip surged up in waves from the depths of the deep green river, an angry reminder this wasn't just water we were playing with.

On certain days the town sky darkened from coal smoke, the air so dark automobiles used headlights at midday. Some favorite games we played circled around coal: one called simply "walking the railroad ties" gave way naturally to its successor "walking the rails" as a fellow got better at the thing. But whether you hopped along the creosoted wood or teetered on the polished steel stretching in the mind to infinity, the object was to gather up black diamonds spilled from the coal cars.

At night we played ghostly games in and out of long rows of abandoned beehive coke ovens looking for all the world like Roman tombs. I can still hear the crunch of a battered shovel digging into the pyramid of coal in our basement and the creak of the cast iron gate on the furnace door opening to accept another load into the flames. Squinting through medieval view slits in the grate like an armored knight's helmet paid off with a shocking blast of superheated air. Nothing could be a more awe-inspiring introduction to power for a child.

Mother, puffing her Chesterfield, would often complain about dirty air as the cigarette smoldered, about the impossibility of keeping white clothes white for even a few hours, about her wish to live in the mountains where the air was clean. And Grandmother Mossie would say cryptically, her unfiltered Chesterfield cocked, "Smoke means work." Sometimes I heard men from the beer halls talking to Pappy (my granddad) about arcane matters which summoned up the same sacred utterance, "Smoke means work."

In science class at Ben Franklin Junior High, up in the clean mountains where Mother finally arrived, coal was waiting for me. I remember Mrs. Conn with sections of coal in which fantastic fossil shapes were embedded. In the same school, a music teacher, name now forgotten, taught us to sing the song he told us miners sang as they trudged to the pits each morning:

> (Sadly, Slowly)
> Zum, Gollie, Gollie, Gollie,
> ZUM Gaw-lee, Gaw-lee,
> Zum, Gollie, Gollie, Gollie,
> ZUM Gaw-lee, Gaw-lee.

Even as a boy I doubted that song was genuine because the miners I passed on the street were far from musical men, I loved the feeling of connection it awakened to a life far stranger than any fiction, a life going on deep inside the green hills around me while I sat at my desk in school.

Occasionally an abandoned mine, its hollow tunnels reaching out for miles like dark tentacles beneath the earth, would catch fire along an undug coal seam and burn for years, causing wisps of smoke to issue from unlikely rural settings, reminder of the fiendish world unseen below the vegetable landscape. Now and then a coal tunnel would collapse, entombing men alive down there—from which fate (all too easy to imagine for a boy with a penchant for crawling around in storm drains) the victims would sometimes be rescued on the front page of the *Sun-Telegraph*, and sometimes not. When a situation like that was pronounced hopeless and miners sat dying underground with no chance of rescue as sailors died in the hull of the *Arizona* at Pearl Harbor, I would stare at the black lumps I took for granted in a different light.

Another thing I clearly remember is that years after a mine was abandoned and the community far above had lost memory of its subterranean workings, occasionally an entire unsuspecting town would begin to slump into the pit. Frantic effort to shore up old tunnels would stretch out over months, even years, the progress of creeping disaster faithfully recorded in newspapers and street corner gossip as it marched house by house toward its inexorable conclusion.

Very interesting, I hear you mutter, what on earth does all this have to do with the problem of schooling? The answer is everything, but it will take some effort to see why, so deeply buried has been the connection between schooling in all its aspects and the nature of the nations's work.

The Demon Of Overproduction

Real school reforms have always failed, not because they represent bad ideas but because they stand for different interpretations of the purpose of life than the current management of society will allow. If too many people adopted such reforms a social and economic catastrophe would be provoked, one at least equal to that which followed the original imposition of centralized, collective life on men, women and children in what had been a fairly libertarian American society. Reverberations of this earlier change in schooling are still being heard. What else do you think the explosion of home schooling in recent years means?

The reason this cataclysm, out of which we got forced schooling, has been put to the question so very little by the groups it violently damaged is that the earlier storm had a confusing aspect to it. Those who suffered most didn't necessarily experience declining incomes. The cost of the metamorphosis was paid for in liberties: loss of freedom, loss of time, loss of significant human associations, including those with one's own children, loss of a spiritual dimension, perhaps. Losses difficult to pin down. Coal, and later oil, relentlessly forced a shift in crucial aspects of social life: our relations to nature, our relations to each other, our relations to ourselves. But nowhere was the impact greater than in the upbringing of children.

Colonial and Federal period economics in America emphasized those characteristics in children designed to lead to independent livelihoods—characteristics which have remained at the heart of the romantic image of our nation in the world's eyes and in our own. These characteristics, however, were recognized by thinkers associated with the emerging industrial/financial systems as danger signs of incipient *overproduction*. The very ingenuity and self-reliance that built a strong and unique America came to be seen as its enemy. Competition was recognized as a corrosive agent no mass production economy could long tolerate without bringing ruinous financial panics in its wake, engendering bankruptcy and deflation.

A preliminary explanation is in order. Prior to coal and the inventiveness coal inspired, no harm attended the very realistic American dream to have one's own business. A startling percentage of Americans did just that. Businesses were small and local, mostly subsistence operations like the myriad small farms and small services which kept home and hearth together across the land. Owning yourself was understood to be the best thing. The most radical aspect about this former economy was the way it turned ancient notions of social class privilege and ancient religious notions of exclusion on their ears.

Yet, well inside a single generation, godlike fossil fuel power suddenly became available. Now here was the rub, that power was available to industrialists but also at the same time to the most resourceful, tough-minded, independent, cantankerous, and indomitable group of ordinary citizens ever seen anywhere. A real danger existed that in the industrial economy being born, too many would recognize the new opportunity, thus creating far too much of everything for any market to absorb.

The result: prices would collapse, capital could not be protected. Using the positive method of analysis (of which more later), one could easily foresee that continuous generations of improved machinery (with never an end) might well be forthcoming once the commitment was made to let the coal genie completely out of the bottle. Yet in the face of a constant threat of overproduction, who would invest and reinvest and reinvest unless steps were taken to curtail promiscuous competition in the bud stage? The most efficient time to do that was *ab ovo*, damping down those qualities of mind and character which gave rise to the dangerous American craving for independence where it first began, in childhood.

The older economy scheduled for replacement had set up its own basic expectations for children. Even small farmers considered it important to toughen the mind by reading, writing, debate, and declamation, and to learn to manage numbers well enough so that later one might manage one's own accounts. In the older society, competition was the tough love road to fairness in distribution. Democracy, religion, and local community were the counterpoise to excesses of individualism. In such a universe, home education, self-teaching, and teacher-directed local schoolhouses served well.

In the waning days of this family-centered social order, an industrial replacement made necessary by coal lay waiting in the wings, but it was a perspective still unable to purge itself of excess competition, unable to sufficiently accept government as the partner it must have to suppress dangerous competition—from an all-too-democratic multitude.

Then a miracle happened or was arranged to happen. After decades of surreptitious Northern provocation, the South fired on Fort Sumter. Hegel himself could not have planned history better. America was soon to find itself shoehorned into a monoculture. The Civil War demonstrated to industrialists and financiers how a standardized population trained to follow orders could be made to function as a reliable money tree; even more, how the common population could be stripped of its power to cause political trouble. These war years awakened canny nostalgia for the British colonial past, and in doing so, the coal-driven society was welcomed for the social future it promised as well as for its riches.

The Quest For Arcadia

The great mistake is to dismiss too hastily the inducements industrial utopia offers. Defense of it on strictly humanistic grounds is usually discarded as hypocrisy, but after some reflection, I don't think it is. Remember that many philosophical and scientific minds were fellow travelers in the industrial procession. Like Adam Smith, they predicted that just beyond the grim factory smoke and the foul pits where men mined coal, a neo-Arcadian utopia beckoned—we have already witnessed its evanescent, premature embodiment in Chautauqua. This Arcadia would only be possible if men of great vision had the nerve and iron discipline to follow where rationality and science led. The crucial obstacle was this: an unknown number of generations would have to be sacrificed to industrial slavery before mankind could progress to its comfortable destiny. On the other side of that immoral divide, paradise might lie.

How to get there? Though Malthus and Darwin had shown the way to intellectually devalue human life and to do with protoplasm whatever needed to be done, the force of Western tradition, particularly Judeo-Christian tradition, was still too strong to brush aside. Into this paradox stepped Socialism. It was a happy coincidence that while one aspect of industrial imagination, the capitalist lobe, was doing the necessary dirty work of breaking the old order and reorganizing its parts, another, softer, aspect of the same industrial mind could sing the identical song in a different key to a different audience.

What socialists helped capitalism to teach was that the industrial promise was *true*, the road to riches could be followed through coal smoke to an eventual paradise on Earth. *Only the masters had to be changed.* In place of bosses would sit workers. Meanwhile, both sides agreed (Marx is particularly eloquent on this point) that many would have to suffer a great while until predictable advances in social re-ordering ultimately relieved their descendants.

Managerial Utopia

An angry letter to the *Atlantic Monthly* in its January 1998, issue by Walter Greene of Hatboro, Pennsylvania, protested the "myth of our failing schools," as he called it, on these grounds:

> We just happen to have the world's most productive work force, the largest
> economy, the highest material standard of living, more Nobel prizes than the
> rest of the world combined, the best system of higher education, the best
> high-tech medicine, and the strongest military. These things could not have
> been accomplished with second-rate systems of education.

On the contrary, the surprising truth is they could not have been accomplished *without* second-rate systems of education. But here it is, writ plain, the crux of an unbearable paradox posed by scientifically efficient schooling. It works. School, as we have it, does build national wealth, it does lead to endless scientific advances.

Where is Greene's misstep? It lies in the equation of material prosperity and power with *education* when our affluence is built on *schooling*. A century of relentless agit-prop has thrown us off the scent. The truth is that America's unprecedented global power and spectacular material wealth is a direct product of a third-rate educational system, upon whose *inefficiency* in developing intellect and character it depends. If we educated better we could not sustain the corporate utopia we have made. Schools build national wealth by tearing down personal sovereignty, morality, and family life. It's a trade-off.

This contradiction is not unknown at the top, but it is never spoken aloud as part of the national school debate. Unacknowledged, it has been able to make its way among us untroubled by protest. E.P. Thompson's classic, *The Making of the English Working Class,* is an eye-opening introduction to this bittersweet truth about "productive" work forces and national riches. When a Colorado coal miner testified before authorities in 1871 that eight hours underground was long enough for any man because "he has no time to improve his intellect if he works more," the coaldigger could hardly have realized his very deficiency was value added to the market equation.

What the nineteenth century in the coal-rich nations pointed toward was building infrastructure for managerial utopia, a kind of society in which unelected functional specialists make all decisions that matter. Formal periods of indoctrination and canonical books of instruction limit these specialists in their choices. The idea of managerial science is to embed managers so securely in abstract regulation and procedure that the fixed purpose of the endeavor becomes manager-proof.

Managerial utopias take tremendous effort to build. England's version of this political form was a millennium in the building. Such governance is costly to maintain *because it wastes huge amounts of human time* on a principle akin to the old warning that the Devil finds work for idle hands; it employs large numbers of incompetent and indifferent managers in positions of responsibility on the theory that *loyalty* is more important than ability to do the job. I watched this philosophy in action in public schools for 30 years.

Ordinary people have a nasty habit of consciously and unconsciously sabotaging managerial utopias, quietly trashing in whole or part, the wishes of managers. To thwart these tendencies, expensive vigilance is the watchword of large systems, and the security aspect of managerial utopia has to be paid for. Where did this money originally come from? The answer was from a surplus provided by coal, steam, steel, chemicals, and conquest. It was more than sufficient to pay for a mass school experiment. Society didn't slowly evolve to make way for coal-based economy. It was forcibly made over in double time like Prussians marching to battle Napoleon at Waterloo. An entirely successful way of life was forcibly ushered out.

Before anything could be *modern,* the damnable past had to be uprooted with its village culture, tight families, pious population, and independent livelihoods. Only a state religion had the power to do this—England and Germany were evidence of that—but America lacked one. A military establishment had power to do it, too. France, under the Directorate and Napoleon, was the most recent example of what physical force could accomplish in remaking the social order, but military power was still too dispersed and unreliable in America to employ it consistently against citizens.

As the established Protestant religion schismed and broke apart, however, America came into possession of something that would serve in its place—a kaleidoscope of utopian cults and a tradition of utopian exhortation, a full palette of roving experts and teachers, Sunday schools, lyceums, pulpits, and Chautauquas. It was a propitious time and place in which to aim for long-range management of public opinion through the utopian schooling vehicle Plato had described and that modern Prussia was actually using.

It takes no great insight or intelligence to see that the health of a centralized economy built around dense concentrations of economic power and a close business alliance with government can't tolerate any considerable degree of intellectual schooling. This is no vain hypothesis. The recent French Revolution was widely regarded as the work of a horde of underemployed intellectuals, the American uprising more of the same. As the nineteenth century wore on, the Hungarian and Italian revolutions were both financed and partially planned from the United States using cells of marginal intellectuals, third sons, and other malcontents as a volunteer fifth column in advance of the revolutionary moment back home. Ample precedent to fear the educated was there; it was recognized that historical precedent identified thoughtful schooling as a dangerous blessing.

The Positive Method

Most of the anti-intellectual shift in schooling the young was determined by attitudes and needs of prominent businessmen. The first exhibit for your perusal is the U.S. Bureau of Education's *Circular of Information* for April 1872, which centers around what it calls the "problem of educational schooling." With whose interests in mind, did the bureau view education as a problem?

The amazing answer is: from a big business perspective. By 1872, this still feeble arm of the federal government is seen filled with concern for large industrial employers at a time when those were still a modest fraction of the total economy.

According to this *Circular of Information*, "inculcating knowledge" teaches workers to be able to "perceive and calculate their grievances," thus making them "more redoubtable foes" in labor struggles. Indeed this was one important reason for Thomas Jefferson's own tentative support of a system of universal schooling, but something had been lost between Monticello and the Capitol. "Such an enabling is bound to retard the growth of industry," continues the *Circular*. There is nothing ambiguous about that statement at all, and the writer is correct, of course.

Sixteen years later (1888), we can trace the growth in this attitude from the much more candid language in the *Report of the Senate Committee on Education*. Its gigantic bulk might be summarized in this single sentence taken from page 1382:

> We believe that education is one of the principal causes of discontent of late
> years manifesting itself among the laboring classes....

Once we acknowledge that planned economies of nation or corporation are systems with their own operating integrity, quite sensibly antagonistic to the risks educated minds pose, much of formal schooling's role in the transformation that came is predictable. If education is indeed "one of the principal causes of discontent," it performs that subversive function innocently by developing intellect and character in such a way as to resist absorption into impersonal systems: *Here is the crux of the difference between education and schooling—the former turns on independence, knowledge, ability, comprehension, and integrity, the latter upon obedience.*

In *The Empire of Business* (1902), Andrew Carnegie, author of the Homestead siege which destroyed the steelworker's union, inveighs against "teachings which serve to imbue [children] with false ideas." From a transatlantic business perspective, education taught what was socially and economically useless, transmitting bad attitudes which turned students against the ripening scheme of centralized national management. Carnegie's new empire demanded that old-fashioned character be schooled out of children in a hurry. It would be a large mistake to assume this new empire of business Carnegie boasts of was only a new face on old style greed. While it did take away liberty and sovereignty, it put forth serious intellectual arguments for doing so. Ordinary people were promised what Walter Greene's outraged letter at the beginning of this chapter tells you they got: the best space program, the best high-tech medicine, the strongest military, the highest material standard of living. These things could not have been accomplished without a kind of forced schooling that terminated most independent livelihoods. That was the price paid for a gusher of easy prosperity.

To understand this paradox better requires some insight into what inspired such *certainty* among the architects of modern schooling that this disruption would work to produce material prosperity. Their faith that wealth would inevitably follow the social mechanization of the population is founded on a magnificent insight of Francis Bacon's, set down in startlingly clear prose back in the early seventeenth century. Thanks to the patronage of John Stuart Mill, the seeds Bacon planted grew into the cult of scientific Positivism by the mid-nineteenth century, a movement we associate today with the name of a Frenchman, Auguste Comte. It's hard to overestimate the influence Positivism had on the formation of mass schooling and on the shaping of an international corporate economy made possible by coal.

Positivism holds that if proper procedures are honored, then scientific marvels and inventions follow automatically. If you weigh and measure and count and categorize slowly and patiently, retaining the microscopic bits of data which can be confirmed, rejecting those that cannot, on and on and on and on, *then genius and talent are almost irrelevant*—improvements will present themselves regularly in an endless progression despite any fall-off in creative power. Advances in power and control are mainly a function of the amount of money spent, the quantity of manpower employed, and correct methodology.

Mankind can be freed from the tyranny of intelligence by faithful obedience to system! This is a shattering pronouncement, one made all the more difficult to resist because it seems to work. Even today, its full significance isn't widely understood nor is the implacable enmity it demands toward any spiritual view of humanity.

In the Positive method , the managerial classes of the late nineteenth century, including their Progressive progeny in the social management game, knew they had a mill to grind perpetual profits—financial, intellectual, and social. Since innovations in production and organization are a principal engine of social change, and since positive science has the power to produce such innovations without end, then even during the launch of our era of scientific management it had to be clear to its architects that nonstop social turbulence would be a daily companion of exercising this power. This is what the closet philosophy of Bionomics was there to explain. It preached that the evolutionarily advanced would alone be able to tolerate the psychic chaos—as for the rest, the fate of Cro-Magnon man and the Neanderthal were history's answer. And the circularity of this convenient proposition was lost on its authors.

Faced with the problem of dangerous educated adults, what could be more natural than a factory to produce safely stupefied children? You've already seen that the positive system has only limited regard for brainy people, so nothing is lost productively in dumbing down and leveling the mass population, even providing a dose of the same for "gifted and talented" children. And much can be gained in social efficiency. What motive could be more "humane" than the wish to defuse the social dynamite positive science was endlessly casting off as a byproduct of its success?

To understand all this you have to be willing to see there is no known way to stop the social mutilation positive science brings in its train. Society must forcibly be adapted to accept its own continuing disintegration as a natural and inevitable thing and taught to recognize its own resistance as a form of pathology to be expunged. Once an economic system becomes dependent on positive science, it can't allow any form of education to take root which might interrupt the constant accumulation of observations which produce the next scientific advance.

In simple terms, what ordinary people call religious truth, liberty, free will, family values, the idea that life is not centrally *about* consumption or good physical health or getting rich—all these have to be strangled in the cause of progress. What salves the positivistic soul to endure the agony it inflicts on others is its divine certainty that these bad times will pass. Evolution will breed out of existence unfortunates who can't tolerate this discipline.

This is the sacred narrative of modernity, its substitute for the message of the Nazarene. History will end in Chautauqua. School is a means to this end.

Plato's Guardians

Coal made common citizens dangerous for the first time. The Coal Age put inordinate physical power within the reach of common people. The power to destroy through coal-derived explosive products was an obvious dramatization of a cosmic leveling foreseen only by religious fanatics, but much more dangerous as power became the power coal unleashed to create and to produce—available to all.

The dangerous flip side of the power to produce isn't mere destruction, but over- production, a condition which could degrade or even ruin the basis for the new financial system. The superficial economic advantage that overproduction seems to confer—increasing sales by reducing the unit price of products through savings realized by positivistic gains in machinery, labor, and energy utilization—is more than offset by the squeezing of profits in industry, commerce, and finance. Capitalists would not/could not gamble on the huge and continuous investments which a positivistic science-based business system demands if profit could not be virtually guaranteed.

Now you can see the danger of competition. Competition pushed manufacturers to overproduction in self-defense. And for double jeopardy, the unique American entrepreneurial tradition *encouraged an overproduction of manufacturers*. This guaranteed periodic crises all along the line. Before the modern age could regard itself as mature, ways had to be found to control overproduction. In business, that was begun by the Morgan interests who developed a system of cooperative trusts among important business leaders. It was also furthered through the conversion of government from servant of the republic to servant of industry. To that end, the British government provided a clear model; Britain's military and foreign policy functioned as the right arm of her manufacturing interests.

But of what lasting value could controlling topical overproduction be—addressing it where and when it threatened to break out—when the ultimate source of overproduction in products and services *was the overproduction of minds* by American libertarian schooling and *the overproduction of characters* capable of the feat of production in the first place? As long as such a pump existed to spew limitless numbers of independent, self-reliant, resourceful, and ambitious minds onto the scene, who could predict what risk to capital might strike next? To minds capable of thinking cosmically like Carnegie's, Rockefellers's, Rothschild's, Morgan's, or Cecil Rhodes', real scientific control of overproduction must rest ultimately on the power to constrain the production of mentality. Here was a task worthy of immortals. Coal provided capital to finance it.

If the Coal Age promised anything thrilling to the kind of mind which thrives on managing the behavior of others, that promise would best be realized by placing control of everything important—food, clothing, shelter, recreation, the tools of war—in a relatively few hands, creating a new race of benevolent, godlike managers, not for their own good but the good of all. Plato had called such benevolent despots "guardians." Why these men would necessarily be benevolent nobody ever bothered to explain.

Abundant supplies of coal, and later oil, cried out for machinery which would tirelessly convert a stream of low value raw materials into a cornucopia of *things* which everyone would covet. Through the dependence of the all on the few, an instrument of management and of elite association would be created far beyond anything ever seen in the past. This powerful promise was, however, fragilely balanced atop the need to homogenize the population and all its descendent generations.[1] A mass production economy can neither be created nor sustained without a leveled population, one conditioned to mass habits, mass tastes, mass enthusiasms, predictable mass behaviors. The will of both maker and purchaser had to give way to the predestinated output of machinery with a one-track mind.

Nothing posed a more formidable obstacle than the American family. Traditionally a self-sufficient production unit for which the marketplace played only an incidental role, the American family manufactured its own food, cooked it and served it, made its own soap, its clothing, its transportation, its entertainment, health care, and old age assistance. It entered freely into cooperative associations with neighbors, not with corporations. For that way of life to continue as it has continued successfully for the modern Amish would have spelled curtains for corporate society.

Another factor which made ordinary citizens dangerous in a coal age was that coal gave rise to heavy industries whose importance for war-making made it imperative to have a workforce docile, dependable, and compliant. Too much was at stake to tolerate democracy. Coal-fired industry had such a complex organization it could be seriously disrupted by worker sabotage, and strikes could be fomented at any moment by a few dissident working men with some training in rhetoric and a little education. The heightened importance to high-speed industry of calculating mass labor as a predictable quality rendered nonconformity a serious matter.

The danger from ordinary people is greatly magnified by the positive philosophy which drives a mass production, corporate management epoch. While it was necessary to sensitize ordinary people to the primacy of scientific needs, and to do this partially by making the study of biology, chemistry, physics, and so forth formal school lessons, to go further and reveal the insights of Bacon and Comte about how easily and inevitably Nature surrenders her secrets to anybody in possession of a simple, almost moronic *method*, was to open Pandora's box. The revolutionary character of scientific discovery discussed earlier—that it requires neither genius nor expensive equipment and is within reach of anyone—had to be concealed.

It was through schooling that this revolutionary aspect of science (once known or at least suspected by tens of thousands of small, subsistence farming families and miscalled "Yankee ingenuity") was hidden right out in the open. Science teaching became from the start what it remains today: for the ordinary student a simplified history of scientific discovery, and for the better classes a simple instilling of knowledge and procedures. In this transmission of factual data and chronicles, the positive method remains unseen, unsuspected, and untaught.

Taught correctly, science would allow large numbers of young people to find and practice the most effective techniques of discovery. The real gift science confers is teaching how to reach potent conclusions by common powers of observation and reasoning. But if incidental overproduction was already a crisis item in the mind of the new social planners, you can imagine what hysteria any attempt to broadcast the secrets of discovery would have occasioned.

----

[1] Coal explains a part of the curious fact that modern Mexico is still not a mass society in spite of its authoritarian governing class and traditional ways, while the wealthy neighboring U.S. is. Mexico had no coal, and while it has recently acquired oil (and NAFTA linkage to the mass economy of North America) which will level its citizenry into a mass in time, centuries of individuation must first be overcome.

The General Education Board said it best when it said children had to be organized and taught in a way that would *not* make them "men of science."[2] To that end, science was presented in as authoritarian a form as Latin grammar, involving vast tracts of memorization. Children were taught that technical competence is bought and sold as a commodity; it does not presume to direct activities, or even to inquire into their purpose. When people are brought together to build a shopping mall, a dam, or an atomic bomb, nothing in the contract gives them latitude to question what they have been paid to do, or to stir up trouble with co-workers. Recruitment into the dangerous sciences was mostly limited to those whose family background made them safe. For the rest, science was taught in a fashion to make it harmless, ineffective, and even dull.

Now my job is to open a window for you into that age of economic transformation whose needs and opportunities gave us the schools we got and still have. Thorstein Veblen said back in 1904, just a year or two before the forced schooling project began to take itself seriously, that "any theoretical inquiry into cultural life as it is running into the future must take into account the central importance of the businessman and his work." Insofar as any theorist aims to explain aspects of modern life like schools, the line of approach has to be from the businessman's standpoint since it is from that perspective that the course of events is directed.

And while I urge the reader to remember that no notion of single causes can possibly account for schooling, yet the model of modern medicine—where the notion of single causes has been brilliantly productive—can teach us something. When medicine became "modern" at the end of the nineteenth century, it did so by embracing germ theory, a conception much less "factual" than it appears. The idea in germ theory is to trace specific pathologies to single instigators. Whatever its shortcomings, this narrowing of vision frequently revealed the direction in which successful treatment lay.

Just so, the important thing in viewing the development of the modern economy is not to find in it a conspiracy against children, but *to remain detached enough to ask ourselves how the development of forced schooling could have been any different than it was.* To understand the modern economy and modern schooling, we need to see how it grows organically from coal and oil.

Far-Sighted Businessmen

Coal has been used for thousands of years as domestic fuel, for most of that time only in the few spots where it cropped out on the surface or was washed ashore by the sea. Any kind of plant matter can become coal, but most of what we have is the gift of the earth as it existed 350 million years ago when rushes and ferns grew tall as trees. Decay, compression, heat, and a great deal of time makes the rock that burns. As it sits in your cellar it continues to putrefy, all coal gives off marsh gas or methane continuously. This is the reason coal mines blow up, a clue to even more explosive secrets locked inside its shiny blackness.

When infortuitously methane becomes mixed with five percent oxygen it creates a highly explosive mixture miners call "firedamp." Any bright eight-year-old could create this explosive with about five minutes training—one good reason why the mass development of intellect after the Coal Age became more problematic than it might appear on the surface. Though such a possibility was

---

[2] See head quote, Chapter Eleven, which states the vital proposition even more clearly.

never a central cause of the rush to school, it and other facts like it were details of consequence in the background of the tapestry.

Through the early years of the eighteenth century, enormous technical problems plagued the development of coal. Once quarrying gave way to underground mining and shafts went below the water table, seepage became a nightmare. And as underground workings extended further and further from the shaft, the problem of hauling coal from where it was mined back to the shaft, and from the shaft hoisted to the surface—distances between 500 and 1,000 feet in places—posed enormous technological challenges. As did the simple matter of illumination in the dark tunnels. Collections of marsh gas might be encountered at any turn, resulting in the sudden termination of miners and all their expensive equipment.

Solving these problems took two centuries, but that effort resulted in the invention of the steam engine and the railroad as direct solutions to the dilemmas of drainage and haulage under the earth. A simple pump, "the miner's friend" patented by Savery in 1699, became Newcomen's steam pump powered by water boiled over coal fires, driving a piston device which drained British coal mines for the next century. Priscilla Long says, "The up and down motion of this piston, transferred to the moving parts of machines and especially to the wheels of trains" changed global society. Newcomen's pump used so much coal it could only be used near coal mines, but James Watt's engine which came along at precisely the moment the Continental Congress was meeting in 1776, was superior in every way: efficient and capable of delivering a source of power *anywhere*.

Industries could now be located away from coal fields because the coal industry had invented the railroad—as a way to solve its other underground problem, moving the coal from the diggings to the surface. By the middle of the seventeenth century, the haulage problem had been partially solved by laying wooden planks along coal mine tunnels as two parallel tracks upon which wagons could be drawn. These tracks soon were seen to have use above ground, too, as a transport highway from mine to sea and waterway. A century later, just after the moment some former British colonies in North America became the United States, a coal operator married the steam engine of Watt with the task of moving coal from the seam face and, other men associated with large collieries produced the first railroad expressly for the purpose of hauling coal.

It couldn't have run very long before other uses suggested themselves. Passenger travel followed almost immediately—the world's first reliable transportation system. Once unleashed on an idea this powerful, the globally successful British engineering community had a field day extending it. By 1838, the first steamship had crossed the Atlantic; a short while later transatlantic travel was on a *timetable*, just as classrooms in factory schools would come to be.

The abundance of wood in the U.S. slowed the development of efficient railroads for an interval, as after all wood was free. But as trains improved with dazzling speed, the economy wood offered was seen as a counterfeit—wood has only half the punch of coal. By 1836, coal had driven wood from the infant railroads. Explosive growth followed at once. Trackage grew from 1,100 miles in 1836 to 2,800 miles in 1841 to 5,600 miles in 1845, to 11,000 miles in 1850, to 22,000 miles in 1855, to 44,000 miles in 1860 on the eve of the Civil War.

Could the North have overwhelmed the South so handily without railroads? Would the West have developed the same way? The railroad, byproduct of the desire to gouge coal out of the earth, was a general's best friend. And America's first working compulsion schools were given to the nation by the Boston School Committee, an elite assembly importantly underwritten by money and influence from Peabody coal and railroading interests the year after Andrew Jackson left office. Far-sighted businessmen had seen the future before anyone else.

Coal Gives The Coup De Grâce

The democracy which unprompted arises when people are on the same footing was finished with the coming of coal-fired steam locomotives. Before railroads, production was decentralized and dispersed among a myriad of local crafts people. It was production on a small scale, mostly with local raw materials, by and for local people. Since horse drawn vehicles couldn't reliably expect to make 30 miles a day, weather was always a vital reality in that kind of transport. Mud, snow, flooded creeks, dried up watercourses in summer—all were forces turning people inward where they created lives of profound localness.

On the seacoast it was different. There trading was international, and great trading families accumulated large stocks of capital, but still production wasn't centralized in factories. The pressure of idle capital, however, increasingly portended that something would come along to set this money in motion eventually. Meanwhile, it was a world in which everyone was a producer of some kind or a trader, entertainer, schoolteacher, logger, fisherman, butcher, baker, blacksmith, minister. Little producers made the economic decisions and determined the pace of work. The ultimate customers were friends and neighbors.

As mass production evolved, the job of production was broken into small parts. Instead of finishing things, a worker would do the same task over and over. Fragmenting work this way allowed it to be mechanized, which involved an astonishing and unfamiliar control of time. Human beings now worked at the machine's pace, not the reverse, and the machine's pace was regulated by a manager who no longer shared the physical task. Could learning in school be regulated the same way? The idea was too promising not to have its trial.

Workers in mass production work space are jammed closely together in a mockery of sociability, just as school kids were to be. Division of labor sharply reduced the *meaning* of work to employees. Only managers understood completely what was going on. Close supervision meant radical loss of freedom from what had been known before. Now knowledge of how to do important work passed out of local possession into the hands of a few owners and managers.

Cheap manufactured goods ruined artisans. And as if in answer to a capitalist's prayers, population exploded in the coal-producing countries, guaranteeing cheaper and cheaper labor as the coal age progressed. The population of Britain had increased only 15 percent from 1651 to 1800, but it grew thirteen times faster in the next coal century. The population of Germany rose 300 percent, the United States 1,700 percent. It was as if having other forms of personal significance stripped from them, people turned to family-building for solace, evidence they were really alive. By 1913, coal mining afforded employment to one in every ten wage-earners in the United States.

Completion of the nation's railroad network allowed the rise of business and banking communities with ties to every whistle-stop and area of opportunity, increasing concentration of capital into pools and trusts. "The whole country has become a close neighborhood," said one businessman in 1888. Invention and harnessing of steam power precipitated the greatest economic revolution of modern times. New forms of power required large-scale organization and a degree of social coordination and centralized planning undreamed of in Western societies since the Egypt of Rameses.

As the implications of coal penetrated the national imagination, it was seen more and more by employers that the English class system provided just the efficiency demanded by the logic of mechanization—everyone to his or her place in the order. The madness of Jacksonian democracy on the other hand, the irrationality of Southern sectionalism, the tradition of small entrepreneurialism, all these would have to be overcome.

The end product of a managerial mass production economic system and an orderly social system seemed worth any grief to bring about. In the 1840s, British capitalists, pockets jingling with the royal profits of earlier industrial decades and reacting against social unrest in Britain and the Continent, escalated their investments in the United States, bringing with their crowns, pounds and shillings, a political consciousness and social philosophy some Americans thought had been banished forever from these shores.

These new colonizers carried a message that there had to be social solidarity among the upper classes for capital to work. Financial capital was the master machine that activated all other machinery. Capital had to be massed in a few hands to be used well, and massing wasn't possible unless a great degree of trust permeated the society of capitalists. That meant living together, sharing the same philosophical beliefs on big questions, marrying into each other's families, maintaining a distance from ordinary people who would certainly have to be ill-treated from time to time out of the exigencies of liberal economics. The greatest service that Edith Wharton and Henry James, William Dean Howells and a few other writers did for history was to chronicle this withdrawal of capital into a private world as the linchpin of the new system.

For the moment, however, it's only important to see how reciprocal the demands of industrialization and the demands of class snobbishness really are. It isn't so much that people gaining wealth began to disdain their ordinary neighbors as it is that such disdain is an integral part of the wealth-building process. Doing so builds team spirit among various wealth seekers. Without such spirit, capital could hardly exist in a stable form because great centralized businesses and bureaus couldn't survive without a mutual aid society of interlocking directorates which act effectively to restrain competition.

Whether this process of separation and refinement of human raw material had any important influence on the shape and purpose of forced schooling, I leave to your own judgment. It's for you to decide if what Engels termed the contradiction between the social character of production and its control by a few individuals was magnified in the U.S. by the creation of a national managerial class. That happened in a very short span of time in the last quarter of the nineteenth century.

The Spectre Of Uncontrolled Breeding

School as we know it was the creation of four great coal powers whose ingenious employment of the coal-powered steam engine shrank distance and crippled local integrity and the credibility of local elites. But the U.S. produced almost as much coal as the other three school-bound nations put together, as you can see from figures for coal production in 1905: 1) United States—351 million tons; 2) United Kingdom—236 million tons; 3) Germany—121 million tons; 4) France—35 million tons.

Prior to the advent of coal-based economics, mass society was a phenomenon of the Orient, spoken of with contempt in the West. Even as late as 1941, I remember a barrage of adult discourse from press, screen, radio, and from conversations of elders that Japan and China had no regard for human life, by which I presume they meant individual human life. "*Banzai!*" was supposed to be the cry of fanatical Japanese infantrymen eager to die for the Emperor, but Western fighting men, in the words of H.G. Wells' wife, were "thinking bayonets." For that reason Germany was much more feared than Japan in WWII.

With the advent of coal and steam engines, modern civilization and modern schooling came about. One of the great original arguments for mass schooling was that it would tame and train children uprooted from families broken by mining and factory work. In sophisticated spots like Unitarian Boston and Quaker/Anglican Philadelphia, school was sold to the upper classes as a tool to keep children from rooting themselves in the culture of their own industrially-debased parents.

The full impact of coal-massified societies on human consciousness is caught inadvertently in Cal Tech nuclear scientist Harrison Brown's 1954, *The Challenge of Man's Future*, a book pronounced "great" by fellow Nobel Prize winning geneticist Hermann Müller. Brown examines carefully the probability that the human carrying capacity of the planet is between 50 and 200 billion people, before summarizing the reasons *this fact is best kept secret* [!]:

> If humanity had its way, it would not rest content until the earth is covered
> completely and to a considerable depth with a writhing mass of human
> beings, much as a dead cow is covered with a pulsating mass of maggots.

Brown's metaphors reveal something of the attitude that raised schooling in the first place on the industrial base of coal, steam, and steel. Among other things, the new institution would be an instrument to prevent mass humanity from "having its way."

This essay, characteristic of many such syntheses issuing from foundation, and corporate-sponsored university figures of reputation through the century, as well as from public intellectuals like H.G. Wells, was written on the island of Jamaica which to Brown "appears to be a tropical paradise," but his scientific eye sees it is actually "the world in miniature" where "the struggle for survival goes on" amidst "ugliness, starvation, and misery." In this deceptive utopia, the "comfortable and secure" 20 percent who live in a "machine civilization" made possible by coal and oil, are actually "in a very precarious position," threatened by the rapid multiplication of "the starving." Such paranoia runs like a backbone through Western history from Malthus to Carl Sagan.

Only the United States can stop the threat of overbreeding, says Nobel laureate Brown. "The destiny of humanity depends on our decisions and upon our actions." And what price should we pay for safety? Nothing less than "world authority with jurisdiction over population." The penalty for previous overproduction of the unfit had become by 1954 simply this, that "...thoughts and actions must be ever more strongly limited." [We must create a society] "where social organization is all-pervasive, complex and inflexible, and where the state completely dominates the individual." What is "inflexible" social organization but a class system? Remember your own school. Did a class system exist there? I can see you through my typewriter keys. You're nodding.

Global Associations Of Technique

In 1700 it took nineteen farmers to feed one non-farmer, a guarantee that people who minded other people's business would only be an accent note in general society. One hundred years later

England had driven its yeoman farmers almost out of existence, converting a few into an agricultural proletariat to take advantage of machine-age farming practices only sensible in large holdings. By 1900, one farmer could feed nineteen, releasing eighteen men and women for disposal otherwise. Schools during this period, however, remained trapped in the way things used to be, unable to deliver on their inherent potential as massifiers.

Between 1830 and 1840, the decade in which the Boston School Committee came into existence, a fantastic transformation built out of steam and coal became visible. When the decade began, the surface aspect of the nation was consistent with the familiar life of colonial times, the same relationships, the same values. By its end, modern American history begins. Chicago, a frontier fort in 1832, was by 1838 a flourishing city with eight daily steamboat connections to Buffalo, the Paris of Lake Erie.

But something to rival steam-driven transport in importance appeared at almost the same time: cheap steel. The embryonic steel industry which had come into existence in the eighteenth century revolutionized itself in the nineteenth when the secret of producing steel cheaply was revealed. Formerly steel had been bought dearly in small quantities by smelting iron ore with coke, converting the resulting iron pigs into wrought iron by puddling. This was followed by rolling and then by processing fine wrought iron through a further step called cementation. Steel made this way could only be used for high-grade articles like watch springs, knives, tools, and shoe buckles.

The first part of the new steel revolution followed from discovery of the Bessemer process in 1856. Now steel could be made directly from pig iron. In 1865 the Siemens-Martin open hearth technique gave a similar product of even more uniform quality than Bessemer steel. The next advance occurred in 1879 when Thomas and Gilchrist discovered how to use formerly unsuitable phosphoric iron ore (more common than non-phosphoric) in steelmaking, yielding as its byproduct valuable artificial fertilizer for agriculture. These two transformations made possible the substitution of steel for wrought-iron and opened hundreds of new uses. Steel rails gave a huge push to railway construction, and structural steelwork marked a stupendous advance in engineering possibilities, allowing a radical reconception of human society. Capital began to build for itself truly global associations which made national sovereignty irrelevant for a small class of leaders as long as a century ago.[3] And that fact alone had great relevance for the future of schooling. As steel articulated itself rationally, vertical integration became the order of the day. Iron and steel reached backwards to control coal mines and coking plants and forward to acquire rolling mills, plant mills, wire-drawing facilities, galvanized iron and tin plate establishments, rod mills, etc. Small under-takings were sucked inexorably into large trusts.

Every one of the most modern developments in technique and organization pioneered by steel was echoed in the new factory schools: increase in the size of the plant; integration of formerly

---

[3] This is the simplest explanation for events which would otherwise fall beyond the reach of the mind to understand—such as the well-documented fact, that legendary German armaments maker Krupp sold its cannon to France *during* World War I, shipping them to the enemy by a circuitous route clouded by clerical thaumaturgy, or that the Ford Motor Company built tanks and other armaments for the Nazi government *during* WWII, collecting its profits through middle men in neutral Spain. Ford petitioned the American government for compensation of damages suffered by its plants in wartime bombing raids, compensation it received by Act of Congress with hardly a dissenting vote. Nor were Krupp and Ford more than emblems of fairly common practice, even if one unknown to the common citizenry of combatant nations.

independent educational factors like family, church, library, and recreational facility into a coalition dominated by professional schooling; the specialization of all pedagogical labor; and the standardization of curriculum, testing, and acceptable educational behavior. What confused the issue for the participant population is that parents and students still believed that efficiency in the development of various literacies was the goal of the school exercise. Indeed, they still do. But that had ceased to be the purpose in big cities as early as 1905. Schooling was about efficiency. Social efficiency meant standardizing human units.

Surprisingly enough to those who expect institutional thinking will reflect their own thought only on a larger scale, what is an asset to a mass production economy is frequently a liability to an individual or a family. Creating value in children for a mass production workplace through schooling meant degrading their intellectual growth and discouraging any premature utility to the larger society. Ellwood P. Cubberley inadvertently spilled the beans in his classic *Public Education in the United States* when he admitted compulsion schooling would not work as long as children are allowed to be useful to the real world. To end that usefulness demanded legislation, inspectors, stiff penalties, and managed public opinion.

New York, Massachusetts, Connecticut, Ohio, Pennsylvania, Indiana, North Carolina, Michigan, Wisconsin, and Rhode Island led the charge to seal off the escape route of useful work for children just as they once led the drive for compulsion schooling in the first place. The child labor rhetoric of the day was impressively passionate, some of it genuinely felt and needed, but the cynical aspect can be detected in a loophole created for show business children—"professional children" as they are called in the argot. Whether the "work" of an acting child is less degrading than any other kind of work is a question not difficult for decent people to answer.

Labor Becomes Expendable

One dramatic illustration of the positive philosophy in action is written in coal dust. As a heat source coal seems a simple trade-off: we accept environmental degradation and the inevitable death and crippling of a number of coal miners (350,000 accidental deaths since 1800, 750,000 cases of black lung disease, and an unknown number of permanent and temporary injuries) in exchange for warmth in cold weather and for other good things. But all sorts of unpredictable benefits flowed from the struggle to make the business of keeping warm efficient, and the world of forced schooling was dictated by coal.

Consider the romantic gaslight era which by 1870, as far away as Denver and San Francisco, graced the nights of American villages and cities with magical illumination made possible by coal gas produced when coal is purified into coke. In addition to allowing the steel industry to replace the iron industry, this major unforeseen benefit turned night into day as settlements blazed with light. And with illumination, coal had only just begun to share its many secrets. It was also a storehouse of chemical wealth out of which the modern chemical industry was born. Coke ovens produced ammonia liquor as a byproduct from which agricultural fertilizer is easily prepared; it's also a basis for cheap, readily-available, medium-yield explosives.

Coal yields benzol and tars from which our dyes and many modern medicines are made; it yields gas which can be converted into electrical energy; it yields perfumes and dozens of other useful things. During the production of coal gas, sulphur—the source of sulfuric acid vital to many chemical processes—is collected. Coal tar can further be refined into kerosene. From 1850 to 1860, the German scientist August Wilhelm von Hoffmann working at the Royal College of Chemistry in England, made discoveries inspired by coal's extraordinary hidden potential which elevated chemistry into a national priority in those countries which maintained extra-territorial ambitions like the U.S. By 1896, heavier-than-air flight had been achieved long before the Wright brothers when a pilotless steam airplane *with a 40 foot wingspan* began making trips along the Potomac River near Washington in full view of many important spectators.

As great as coal and steam engines were at stimulating social ferment, they met their master in oil and the internal combustion engine. Coal is twice as efficient an energy source as wood; oil twice as efficient as coal. Oil made its debut just as the Civil War began. As with coal, there had been ancient references to this form of liquid coal in Strabo, Dioscorides, and Pliny. Records exist of its use in China and Japan in the Pre-Christian era (Marco Polo described the oil springs of Baku at the end of the thirteenth century). All that was needed was an engine adapted to its use.

The first patent for the use of gasoline motive power was issued in England in 1794. By 1820 at Cambridge University men knew how to use gas to move machinery. By 1860 gas engines were in limited use all over Europe, 400 in Paris alone. The first American exploitation of any importance occurred at Seneca Lake, New York, in 1859, not a long ride from the ancestral home of the Rockefeller family in the town of Bainbridge. Following the lead of coal, oil was soon producing a fossil fuel transformation of American society, even though irregular supply kept oil from achieving its dominant place in the energy pantheon quickly. But by 1898 the supply problem was solved. Twelve years later, oil replaced coal as the energy of choice, delivering advantages by weight, saving labor in transit, storage, and extraction, and just as with coal, undreamed of bonus benefits were harvested from oil. In 1910, a windfall of three million horsepower hours was generated from waste gas alone thrown off by oil used in blast furnace operation.

Burying Children Alive

Think of coal mines as vast experimental laboratories of human behavior testing the proposition that men, women and children will do virtually anything—even allow themselves to be consigned to damp dangerous tunnels under the ground for all the sunlight hours in order to have real work to do as part of the community of mankind. If the American Revolution could be said (as the *Declaration* held) to demonstrate a self-evident truth, that all were "endowed by a Creator with certain unalienable rights," the coal revolution tested the contrary proposition—just how far those rights could be taken away if exchanged for work. Work was shown by this unworldly occupation to be a value as necessary to human contentment as liberty and the pursuit of happiness. In lieu of alternatives, people would indeed bury themselves alive to get it.

And coal was a continuous, highly visible object lesson about just how thoroughly unseen outside interests could be imposed on childhood. For over a century in America, the best profit came from using young children as coal miners. By 1843, when Horace Mann visited coal-dependent Prussia to gather background for his *Seventh Report*, boys and girls between the ages of five and eight were at work in every coal mine in America. Fifty percent of all coal miners were children.

Children were employed as *trappers* to open and shut doors guiding air through the mine, as *fillers* to fill carriages as grown men knocked coal from the seams, and as *hurriers* to push trucks along to the workers at the foot of the shaft. In some places trucks were *pulled* instead of *pushed*, and little girls were employed as *pullers* because their small size was in harmony with the diminutive tunnels, and because they were more dependable than boys. An excerpt from a Pittsburgh newspaper of the day is instructive:

> A girdle is put round the naked waist, to which a chain from the carriage is hooked, and the girls crawl on their hands and knees, drawing the carriage after them.

One quiet stream in my own family background was the McManus family from West Elizabeth, Pennsylvania, Irish immigrants in the 1840s. Census records list some of them as coal miners. My grandmother was Moss McManus before she became Moss Zimmer. She never talked about the past or recalled a single ancestor except one, a McManus licensed as a Mississippi river pilot in a document signed by Abraham Lincoln which still floats around somewhere in the family. What of all those coal miners, Moss? No memories for your grandson? I suppose the answer is she was ashamed. Coal mining was something that ignorant, shanty-boat Irish did, not a fit occupation for lace-curtain Irish, as Moss tried so hard to be in the face of long odds.

Long after the owners of mines, mills, and factories had abandoned piety except on ceremonial occasions, miners would pray for the strength to endure what had to be endured. Their children would pray with them. Here are the words of a little eight-year-old girl—exactly the age of my own granddaughter Moss as I write this—who worked as a coal miner a hundred years ago. Worked, perhaps, for the famously civilized Dwights and Peabodys of New England:

> I'm a trapper in the Gamer Pit. I have to trap without a light and I'm scared.
> I go at four and sometimes half past three in the morning and come out at five
> and a half past. I never go to sleep. Sometimes I sing when I've light, but not
> in the dark, I dare not sing then.

Isn't the most incredible part of that the fact she could write so eloquently with no formal schooling at all? The year was 1867. A newspaper of that year observed:

> Chained, belted, harnessed like dogs in a go-cart, black, saturated with wet and
> more than half-naked—crawling upon their hands and feet and dragging their
> heavy loads behind them—they presented an appearance indescribably disgusting
> and unnatural.

The confinement of American children to warehouse schools less than a half-century later had been pioneered by the Massachusetts experiment we associate with Horace Mann in the decade just before the Civil War. No other state followed Massachusetts' lead, for a long time, but everywhere children were engaged in mining and factory work. The essential practice in confinement necessary to accept schooling as a natural burden of childhood was taking place there.

Schools were the anti-matter twins of mines and mills: the latter *added* children to the labor market, schools *subtracted* them. Both were important functions of a new, centralized command economy. By 1900, direct child labor had been rendered unnecessary by the swift onset of mechanization, except in those anomalous areas like theater, carnival, advertising and modeling where special pleading to keep children at work would succeed during the general campaign to insulate children from common life.

The End Of Competition

By 1905, industrial corporations employed 71 percent of all wage earners, mining enterprises 10 percent more. At exactly the moment forced-schooling legislation in America was being given its bite by the wholesale use of police, social service investigators, and public exhortation, corporate capitalism boiled up like sulphur in the Monongahela to color every aspect of national life. Corporate spokesmen and academic interpreters, often the same people, frequently explained what was happening as a stage in the evolution of the race. A Johns Hopkins professor writing in 1900 said that what was really happening behind the smokescreen of profit-making was "the sifting out of genius" and "the elimination of the weak."

The leading patent attorney in the nation speaking in the same year said nothing including the law could stem the new tide running, the only realistic course was "acquiescence and adjustment." Charles Willard of Sears & Roebuck was the speaker. Willard suggested the familiar American competitive system "is not necessarily meant for all eternity." Business was wisely overthrowing competitive wastefulness which produced only "panic, overproduction, bad distribution and uncertainty," in exchange for protected privilege on the part of producers.

The principles of the business revolution which gave us schooling are still virtually unknown to the public. Competition was effectively crippled nearly a century ago when, profoundly influenced by doctrines of Positivism and scientific Darwinism, corporate innovators like Carnegie and Morgan denounced competition's *evils,* urging the mogul class to reconstruct America and then the world, in the *cooperative* corporate image. "Nothing less than the supremacy of the world lies at our feet." said Carnegie prophetically. Adam Smith's competitive, self-regulating market would be the death of the new economy if not suppressed because it encouraged chronic overproduction.

Henry Holt, the publisher, speaking in 1908, said there was "too much enterprise." The only effective plan was to put whole industries under central control; the school industry was no exception. Excessive overproduction of brains is the root cause of the overproduction of everything else, he said.

James Livingston has written an excellent short account of this rapid social transformation, called *Origins of the Federal Reserve System*, from which I've taken some lessons. Livingston tells us that the very language of proponents of corporate America underwent a radical change at the start of the century. Business decisions began to be spoken of almost exclusively as courses of purposeful *social* action, not mere profit-seeking. Charles Phillips of the Delaware Trust wrote, for instance, "The banker, the merchant, the manufacturer, and the agent of transportation, *must unite* to create and maintain that reasonable distribution of opportunity, of advantage, and of profit, which alone can forestall revolution." It hardly requires genius to see how such a directive would play itself out in forced schooling.

In 1900, in his book *Corporations and the Public Welfare*, James Dill warned that the most critical social question of the day was figuring out how to get rid of the small entrepreneur, yet at the same time retain his loyalty "to a system based on private enterprise." The small entrepreneur had been the heart of the American republican ideal, the soul of its democratic strength. So the many school training habits which led directly to small entrepreneurship had to be eliminated.

Control of commodity *circulation* by a few demanded similar control in commodity *production*. To this end, immediate sanctions were leveled against older practices: first, destruction of skilled worker craft unions which, up to the Homestead steel strike in 1892, had regulated the terms of work in a factory. Inside a decade, all such unions were rendered ineffective with the single exception of the United Mine Workers. Second, professionalization of mental labor to place it under central control also was speedily accomplished through school requirements and licensing legislation.

In the emerging world of corporate Newspeak, education became schooling and schooling education. The positive philosophy freed business philosophers like Carnegie from the tyranny of feeling they had always to hire the best and brightest on their own independent terms for company operations. Let fools continue to walk that dead-end path. Science knew that obedient and faithful executives were superior to brilliant ones. Brains were needed, certainly, but like an excess of capsicum, too much of the mental stuff would ruin the national digestion. One of the main points of the dramatic shift to mass production and mass schooling was to turn Americans into a *mass* population.

America Is Massified

Older American forms of schooling would never have been equal to the responsibility coal, steam, steel and machinery laid upon them. As late as 1890, the duration of the average school year was 12 to 20 weeks. Even with that, school attendance hovered between 26 and 42 percent nationwide with the higher figure only in a few places like Salem, Massachusetts.

Yet America had to be massified, and quickly. Since the end of the nineteenth century, American government and big business had been fully committed, without public fanfare, to creating and maintaining a mass society. Mass society demands tight administration, close management to an extreme degree. Humanity becomes undependable, dangerous, childlike, and suicidal under such discipline. Holding this contradiction stable requires managers of systematic schooling to withdraw trust, to regard their clientele as hospital managers might think of potentially homicidal patients. Students, men under military discipline, and employees in post offices, hospitals, and other large systems are forced into a condition of less than complete sanity. They *are* dangerous[4] as history has shown again and again.

---

[4] As I write this, another of the long stream of post office massacres of recent years has just taken place in New Jersey. Vengeance by a disgruntled employee. In the same state a hospital attendant has been charged with murdering as many as a hundred of his patients by lethal injection, also a more common occurrence than we want to imagine, and two rich boys at Columbine High School in Littleton, Colorado, the site of a much-boasted-of scientific management revolution in 1994, have shot and killed thirteen of their classmates before taking their own lives. Human variation cannot be pent up for long in enormous synthetic systems without striving to somehow assert the "I" of things. Massified populations cannot exercise self-control very well since they depend on constant oversight to behave as required. When external controls are removed, anything becomes possible.

There are three indisputable triumphs of mass society we need to acknowledge to understand its strength: first, mass production offers *relative* physical comfort to almost all—even the poor have food, shelter, television as a story-teller to raise the illusion of community; second, as a byproduct of intense personal surveillance in mass society (to provide a steady stream of data to the producing and regulating classes) a large measure of personal security is available; third, mass society offers a predictable world, one with few surprises—anxieties of uncertainty are replaced in mass society with a rise in ennui and indifference.

German Mind Science

Back at the beginning of the nineteenth century, wise men and women, honorable individuals themselves, came with sadness to realize that for all the foreseeable future, more and more ordinary people would need to give their entire lives to a dark hole in the ground or in service to a mind-destroying machine if a coal-fired dream world was to happen. People who grew up in the clean air and the folk society of villages did not make good workers for the screaming factories or the tunnels underground, or the anthill offices.

What was needed was some kind of halfway house which would train individuals for the halfway lives ordinary people would be more and more called upon to lead. In a utopia of machinery and steam, there could be free lunch for unprecedented numbers—but only if there were chains, bread, and water for the rest, at least for some unknown while. Plans for such a halfway institution as forced schooling (think of it as a training factory or a training mine) came together in Boston, Philadelphia, and New York, drawn by the best minds, for the best motives. They inflicted stupendous damage on the libertarian rights and privileges bequeathed to Americans by the nation's founders.

Profits from the industrial engine signed the checks for many nineteenth century educational experiments like New Lanark in Scotland and New Harmony in Indiana. They bought Fanny Wright her school advocacy platform and helped her impose it on the Philadelphia Workingman's Party agenda in 1829. Many of the nineteenth century experimental social colonies looked upon themselves as early emanations of utopia, previews whispering to men and women what might be, if only they turned their backs on the past and schooled for a new day. The brevity of these experiments did nothing to discourage their successors.

The coal of Westphalia in association with the iron of Lorraine welded the scattered states of Germany into a ferocious utopian empire in the last half of the nineteenth century. That empire, birthplace of successful, mass forced-schooling, made war upon the world, spreading its conception of research universities and its Spartan state philosophy of universal indoctrination and subordination all over the planet. In 1868, Japan adopted large parts of the Prussian constitution together with the Prussian style of schooling. The garment that coal fashioned for Aryan children was worn enthusiastically by coal-free Nipponese as their own.

German mental science came to rule the classrooms of the world in the early twentieth century, nowhere more thoroughly than in coal-rich/oil-rich America. America provided a perch from which to study people closely and resources with which to find ways to bring them into compliance. Even without intense ideological motivation driving the project, the prospect of a reliable domestic market which could be milked in perpetuity would have been incentive enough to propel the school project, I believe.

These new studies growing out of the coal-swollen ranks of leisured academic lives suggested there should be radical changes in the mental diet of children. A plan emerged piecemeal in these years to be slowly inserted into national schooling. Seen from a distance a century later, it is possible to discern the still shimmering outline of a powerful strategy drawing together at least ten elements:

1) Removal of the active literacies of writing and speaking which enable individuals to link up with and to persuade others.

2) Destruction of the narrative of American history connecting the arguments of the founding fathers to historical events, defining what makes Americans different from others besides wealth.

3) Substitution of a historical "social studies" catalogue of facts in place of historical narrative.

4) Radical dilution of the academic content of formal curriculum which familiarized students with serious literature, philosophy, theology, etc. This has the effect of curtailing any serious inquiries into economics, politics, or religion.

5) Replacement of academics with a balanced-diet concept of "humanities," physical education, counseling, etc., as substance of the school day.

6) Obfuscation or outright denial of the simple, code-cracking drills which allow fluency in reading to anyone.

7) Forcing of willing and unwilling students together in a great leveling exercise which deliberately ignores traditional community canons of decency. An abstract justification of this on the grounds of psycho-social necessity is employed to undermine protests.

8) Enlargement of the school day and year to blot up outside opportunities to acquire useful knowledge leading to independent livelihoods; the insertion of misleading surrogates for this knowledge in the form of "shop" classes which actually teach little of skilled crafts.

9) Shifting of oversight from those who have the greatest personal stake in student development—parents, community leaders, and the students themselves—to a ladder of strangers progressively more remote from local reality. All school transactions to be

ultimately monitored by an absolute abstraction, the "standardized"
test, correlating with nothing real and very easily rigged to produce
whatever results are called for.

10)   Relentless low-level hostility against religious interpretations of meaning.

There you have the brilliant formula used to create a coal-fired mass mind.

Before his sudden death, I watched my beloved bachelor friend and long time fellow schoolteacher Martin Wallach slowly surrender to forces of massification he had long resisted. One day in his late 50s he said, "There isn't any reason to go out anymore. They send food in; I have 300 channels. Everything is on TV. I couldn't see it all if I had two lifetimes. With my telephone and modem I can get anything. Even girls. There's only trouble outside anyway." He fell dead a year later taking out his garbage.

Welcome to utopia. We don't pray or pledge allegiance to anything here, but condoms and Ritalin are free for the asking.

Rest in peace, Martin.

Mr. Martin Wallach stops to dream.

Parent's night conference with Martin Wallach under the big flag in 308.

CHAPTER NINE

The Cult Of

Scientific Management

On the night of June 9, 1834, a group of prominent men "chiefly engaged in commerce" gathered privately in a Boston drawing room to discuss a scheme of universal schooling. Secretary of this meeting was William Ellery Channing, Horace Mann's own minister as well as an international figure and the leading Unitarian of his day. The location of the meeting house is not entered in the minutes nor are the names of the assembly's participants apart from Channing. Even though the literacy rate in Massachusetts was 98 percent, and in neighboring Connecticut, 99.8 percent, the assembled businessmen agreed the present system of schooling allowed too much to depend upon chance. It encouraged more entrepreneurial exuberance than the social system could bear.

> — The minutes of this meeting are held today with the Appleton Papers, Massachusetts Historical Society.

Frederick W. Taylor

The first man on record to perceive how much additional production could be extracted from close regulation of labor was Frederick Winslow Taylor, son of a wealthy Philadelphia lawyer. "What I demand of the worker," Taylor said, "*is not to produce any longer by his own initiative*, but to execute punctiliously the orders given down to their minutest details."

The Taylors, a prominent Quaker family from Germantown, Pennsylvania, had taken Freddy to Europe for three years from 1869 to 1872, where he was attending an aristocratic German academy when von Moltke's Prussian *blitzkrieg* culminated in the French disaster at Sedan and a German Empire was finally proclaimed, ending a thousand years of disunion. Prussian schooling was the widely credited forge which made those miracles possible. The jubilation which spread through Germany underlined a presumably fatal difference between political systems which disciplined with ruthless efficiency, like Prussia's socialist paradise, and those devoted to whimsy and luxury, like France's. The lesson wasn't lost on little Fred.

Near the conclusion of his *Principles of Scientific Management* (1907), published 34 years later, Taylor summarized the new managerial discipline as follows:

1. A regimen of science, not rule of thumb.
2. An emphasis on harmony not the discord of competition.
3. An insistence on cooperation, not individualism.
4. A fixation on maximum output.
5. The development of each man to his greatest productivity.

Taylor's biographers, Wrege and Greenwood, wrote:

> He left us a great legacy. Frederick Taylor advanced a total system of management, one which he built from pieces taken from numerous others whom he rarely would credit.... His genius lies in being a missionary.

After Taylor's death in 1915, the *Frederick W. Taylor Cooperators* were formed to project his Scientific Management movement into the future. Frank Copley called Taylor "a man whose heart was aflame with missionary zeal."[1] Much about this Quaker-turned-Unitarian, who married into an *Arbella*-descended Puritan family before finally becoming an Episcopalian, bears decisively on the shape schooling in this country took. Wrege and Greenwood describe him as: "often arrogant, somewhat caustic, and inflexible in how his system should be implemented....Taylor was cerebral; like a machine he was polished and he was also intellectual....Taylor's brilliant reasoning was marred when he attempted to articulate it, for his delivery was often demeaning, even derogatory at times."

Frank Gilbreth's[2] *Motion Study* says:

> It is the never ceasing marvel concerning this man that age cannot wither nor custom stale his work. After many a weary day's study the investigator awakes from a dream of greatness to find he has only worked out a new proof for a problem Taylor has already solved. Time study, the instruction card, functional foremanship, the differential rate piece method of compensation, and numerous other scientifically derived methods of decreasing costs and increasing output and wages—these are by no means his only contributions to standardizing the trades.

---

[1] The similarity of this to the memorial tribute Mary Mann paid to her husband Horace is accidental, I presume.

[2] Gilbreth, the man who made the term "industrial engineering" familiar to the public, was a devotee of Taylorism. His daughter wrote a best-seller about the Gilbreth home, *Cheaper By The Dozen*, in which her father's penchant for refining work processes is recalled.

To fully grasp the effect of Taylor's industrial evangelism on American national schooling, you need to listen to him play teacher in his own words to Schmidt at Bethlehem Steel in the 1890s:

> Now Schmidt, you are a first-class pig-iron handler and know your business well. You have been handling at a rate of twelve and a half tons per day. I have given considerable study to handling pig-iron, and feel you could handle forty-seven tons of pig-iron per day if you really tried instead of twelve and a half tons.

> Skeptical but willing, Schmidt started to work, and all day long, and at regular intervals, was told by the men who stood over him with a watch, "now pick up a pig and walk. Now sit down and rest. Now walk—rest," etc. He worked when he was told to work, and rested when he was told to rest, and at half past five in the afternoon had his forty-seven tons loaded on the car.

Consider Taylor testifying before Congress in 1912 on the science of shoveling:

> There is a right way of forcing the shovel into materials and many wrong ways. Now, the way to shovel refractory stuff is to press the forearm hard against the upper part of the right leg just below the thigh, like this, take the end of the shovel in your right hand and when you push the shovel into the pile, instead of using the muscular effort of the arms, which is tiresome, throw the weight of your body on the shovel like this; that pushes your shovel in the pile with hardly any exertion and without tiring the arms in the least.

Harlow Pearson called Taylor's approach to the simplest tasks of working life "a meaningful and fundamental break with the past." Scientific management, or Taylorism, had four characteristics designed to make the worker "an interchangeable part of an interchangeable machine making interchangeable parts."

Since each quickly found its analogue in scientific schooling; let me show them to you:[3] 1) A mechanically controlled work pace; 2) The repetition of simple motions; 3) Tools and technique selected for the worker; 4) Only superficial attention is asked from the worker, just enough to keep up with the moving line. The connection of all to school procedure is apparent.

"In the past," Taylor wrote, "Man has been first. *In the future the system must be first.*" It was not sufficient to have physical movements standardized, the standardized worker "must be happy in his work," too, therefore his thought processes also must be standardized.[4] Scientific management was applied wholesale in American industry in the decade after 1910. It spread quickly to schools.

---

[3] List adapted from Melvin Kranzberg and Joseph Giles, *By the Sweat of Thy Brow.*

[4] Taylor was no garden-variety fanatic, he won the national doubles tennis title in 1881 with a racket of his own design, and pioneered slip-on shoes (to save time, of course). Being happy in your work was the demand of Bellamy and other leading socialist thinkers, otherwise you would have to be "adjusted" (hence the expression "well adjusted"). Taylor concurred.

In the preface to the classic study on the effects of scientific management on schooling in America, *Education and the Cult of Efficiency*[5], Raymond Callahan explains that when he set out to write, his intent was to explore the origin and development of business values in educational administration, an occurrence he tracks to about 1900. Callahan wanted to know *why* school administrators had adopted business practices and management parameters of assessment when "Education is not a business. The school is not a factory."

Could the inappropriate procedure be explained simply by a familiar process in which ideas and values flow from high-status groups to those of lesser distinction? As Callahan put it, "It does not take profound knowledge of American education to know that educators are, and have been, a relatively low-status, low-power group." But the degree of intellectual domination shocked him:

> *What was unexpected was the extent, not only of the power of business-industrial groups, but of the strength of the business ideology...and the extreme weakness and vulnerability of school administrators.* I had expected more professional autonomy and I was completely unprepared for the extent and degree of capitulation by administrators to whatever demands were made upon them. I was surprised and then dismayed to learn how many decisions they made or were forced to make, not on educational grounds, but as a means of appeasing their critics in order to maintain their positions in the school. [Emphasis added]

The Adoption Of Business Organization By Schools

In 1903, *The Atlantic Monthly* called for adoption of business organization by schools and William C. Bagley[6] was identifying the ideal teacher as one who would rigidly "hew to the line." Bagley's ideal school was a place strictly reduced to rigid routine; he repeatedly stressed in his writing a need for "unquestioned obedience."

Before 1900, school boards were large, clumsy organizations, with a seat available to represent every interest (they often had 30 to 50 members). A great transformation was engineered in the first decade of the twentieth century, however, and after 1910 they were dominated by businessmen, lawyers, real estate men, and politicians. Business pressure extended from the kindergarten rung of the new school ladder all the way into the German-inspired teacher training schools. *The Atlantic Monthly* approved what it had earlier asked for, saying in 1910, "Our universities are beginning to run as business colleges."

Successful industrial leaders were featured regularly in the press, holding forth on their success but seldom attributing it to book learning or scholarship. Carnegie, self-educated in libraries,

---

[5] Callahan's analysis why schoolmen are always vulnerable is somewhat innocent and ivory tower, and his recommendation for reform—to effectively protect their revenue stream from criticism on the part of the public—simply tragic; but his gathering of data is matchless and his judgment throughout in small matters and large is consistently illuminating.

[6] His jargon-enriched *Classroom Management* (1907) was reprinted 30 times in the next 20 years as a teacher training text. Bagley's metaphors drawn from big business can fairly be said to have controlled the pedagogical imagination for the entire twentieth century.

appears in his writings and public appearances as the leading school critic of the day; echoing Carnegie, the governor of Michigan welcomed an NEA convention to Detroit with his injunction: "The demand of the age is for practical education." The State Superintendent of Public Instruction in Michigan followed the governor:

> The character of our education must change with the oncoming of the years of this highly practical age. We have educated the mind to think and trained the vocal organs to express the thought, and we have forgotten the fact that in four times out of five the practical man expresses his thought by the hand rather than by mere words.

Something was cooking. The message was clear: academic education had become a strange kind of national emergency, just as had been prophesied by the Department of Education's *Circular of Information* in 1871.

Ten years earlier, Francis Parker had praised the elite *Committee of Ten* under Harvard president Charles Eliot for rejecting "tracking," the practice of school class assignment based upon future social destination. The committee had come down squarely for common schools, an ideal Parker said "worth all the pains necessary to produce the report. The conclusion is that there should be no such thing as class education." Parker had noticed the start of an attempt to provide common people with only partial education. He was relieved it had been turned back. Or so he thought.

The pronouncements of the Committee of Ten turned out to be the last gasp of the common school notion apart from Fourth of July rhetoric. The common school was being buried by the determination of new tycoon-class businessmen to see the demise of an older democratic-republican order and its dangerous libertarian ideals.

If "educators," as they were self-consciously beginning to refer to themselves, had any misunderstanding what was expected by 1910, NEA meetings of that year were specifically designed to clear them up. Attendees were told the business community had judged their work to date to be "theoretical, visionary, and impractical:"

> All over the country our courses are being attacked and the demand for revision is along the line of fitting mathematical teaching to the needs of the masses.

In 1909, Leonard Ayres charged in *Laggards in Our Schools* that although these institutions were filled with "retarded children," school programs were, alas, "fitted...to the unusually bright one." Ayres invented means for measuring the efficiency of school systems by computing the dropout/holdover rate—a game still in evidence today. This was begging the question with a vengeance but no challenge to this assessment was ever raised.

Taylor's system of management efficiency was being formally taught at Harvard and Darmouth by 1910. In the next year, 219 articles on the subject appeared in magazines, hundreds more followed: by 1917 a bibliography of 550 school management-science references was available from a Boston publisher. As the steel core of school reform, scientific management enjoyed national recognition. It was the main topic at the 1913 convention of the Department of Superintendence. Paul Hanus, professor of education at Harvard, launched a series of books for the World Book

Company under the title "School Efficiency Series," and famous muckraker, J.M. Rice, published his own *Scientific Management in Education* in 1934 showing local "ward" schooling an arena of low-lives and grifters.

Frederick Taylor's influence was not limited to America; it soon circled the globe. *Principles of Scientific Management* spread the efficiency mania over Europe, Japan, and China. A letter to the editor of *The Nation* in 1911 gives the flavor of what was happening:

> I am tired of scientific management, so-called. I have heard of it from scientific managers, from university presidents, from casual acquaintances in railway trains; I have read of it in the daily papers, the weekly paper, the ten-cent magazine, and in the *Outlook*. I have only missed its treatment by Theodore Roosevelt; but that is probably because I cannot keep up with his writings. For 15 years I have been a subscriber to a magazine dealing with engineering matters, feeling it incumbent on me to keep in touch but the touch has become a pressure, the pressure a crushing strain, until the mass of articles on shop practice and scientific management threatened to crush all thought out of my brain, and I stopped my subscription.

In an article from *Izvestia* dated April, 1918, Lenin urged the system upon Russians.

The Ford System And The Kronstadt Commune

"An anti-intellectual, a hater of individuals," is the way Richard Stites characterizes Taylor in his book on the utopian beginning of the Soviet Era, *Revolutionary Dreams*. "His system is the basis for virtually every twisted dystopia in our century, from death under the Gas Bell in Zamiatin's *We* for the unspeakable crime of deviance, to the maintenance of a fictitious state-operated underground in Orwell's *1984* in order to draw deviants into disclosing who they are."

Oddly enough, an actual scheme of dissident entrapment was the brainchild of J.P. Morgan, his unique contribution to the Cecil Rhodes-inspired "Round Table" group. Morgan contended that revolution could be subverted permanently by infiltrating the underground and subsidizing it; in this way the thinking of the opposition could be known as it developed and fatally compromised. Corporate, government, and foundation cash grants to subversives might be one way to derail the train of insurrection that Hegelian theory predicted would arise against every ruling class.

As this practice matured, the insights of Fabian socialism were stirred into the mix; gradually a socialist *leveling* through practices pioneered in Bismarck's Prussia came to be seen as the most efficient control system for the masses, the bottom 80 percent of the population in advanced industrial states. For the rest, an invigorating system of *laissez-faire* market competition would keep the advanced breeding stock on its toes.

A large fraction of the intellectual Left jumped on Taylor's bandwagon, even as labor universally opposed it. Lenin himself was an aggressive advocate:

> The war taught us much, not only that people suffered, but especially the fact that those who have the best technology, organization, discipline and the best machines emerge on top; it is this the war has taught us. It is essential to learn that without

machines, without discipline, it is impossible to live in modern society. It is necessary to master the highest technology or be crushed.

But even in Russia, workers resisted Taylorish methods. The rebellion of the Kronstadt Commune in 1921 charged that Bolsheviks were "planning to introduce the sweat labor system of Taylor." They were right.

Taylor distilled the essence of Bismarck's Prussian school training under whose regimen he had witnessed firsthand the defeat of France in 1871. His American syntheses of these disciplines made him the direct inspiration for Henry Ford and "Fordism." Between 1895 and 1915, Ford radically transformed factory procedure, relying on Taylorized management and a mass production assembly line marked by precision, continuity, coordination, speed, and standardization. Ford wrote two extraordinary essays in the 1920s, *The Meaning of Time*, and *Machinery: the New Messiah,* in which he equated planning, timing, precision, and the rest of the scientific management catalogue with the great moral meaning of life:

> A clean factory, clean tools, accurate gauges, and precise methods of manufacture produce a smooth working efficient machine [just as] clean thinking, clean living, and square dealing make for a decent home life.

By the 1920s, the reality of the Ford system paralleled the rules of a Prussian infantry regiment. Both were places where workers were held under close surveillance, kept silent, and punished for small infractions. Ford was unmoved by labor complaints. Men were disposable cogs in his machine: "A great business is really too big to be human," he commented in 1929. Fordism and Taylorism swept the Soviet Union as it had swept the U.S. and Western Europe. By the 1920s the words *fordizatsiya* and *teilorizatsiya,* both appellations describing good work habits, were common across Russia.

The National Press Attack On Academic Schooling

In May of 1911, the first salvo of a sustained national press attack on the academic ambitions of public schooling was fired. For the previous ten years the idea of school as an oasis of mental development built around a common, high-level curriculum had been steadily undermined by the rise of educational psychology and its empty child/elastic child hypotheses. Psychology was a business from the first, an aggressive business lobbying for jobs and school contracts. But resistance of parents, community groups, and students themselves to the new psychologized schooling was formidable.

As the summer of 1911 approached, the influential *Educational Review* gave educators something grim to muse on as they prepared to clean out their desks: "Must definite reforms with measurable results be foresworn," it asked, "that an antiquated school system may grind out useless produce?" The magazine demanded *quantifiable* proof of school's contributions to society—or education should have its budget cut. "The advocate of pure water or clean streets shows by how much the death rate will be altered with each proposed addition to his share of the budget—only a teacher is without such figures," the article, "An Economic Measure of School Efficiency," charged.

An editorial in *Ladies Home Journal* reported dissatisfaction with schools was increasing, claiming "On every hand signs are evident of a widely growing distrust of the effectiveness of the present education system." In Providence, the school board was criticized by the local press for declaring a holiday on the Monday preceding Decoration Day to allow a four-day vacation. "This cost the public $5,000 in loss of possible returns on the money invested," readers were informed.

Suddenly school critics were everywhere. A major assault was mounted in two popular journals, *Saturday Evening Post* and *Ladies Home Journal*, with millions each in circulation, both read by leaders of the middle classes. The *Post* sounded the anti-intellectual theme this way:

Miltonized, Chaucerized, Virgilized, Schillerized, physicked and chemicaled,
our high schools are giving an education that is of no use in the world—particularly
in the business world.

Three heavy punches in succession came from *Woman's* magazine: the first an article called "Our Public School System is an Utter Failure," a title which would seem to allow no further enhancement until the second part of the series topped it: "Public School: The Most Momentous Failure in American Life Today," and a third, written by James E. Russell, Dean of Columbia Teacher's College, went even further. Called "The Danger of Running a Fool Factory," it made this point: "If school cannot be made to drop its *mental development obsession* the whole system should be abolished on the grounds it squanders the resources of the country and wastes the lives of children."

The Fabian Spirit

To speak of scientific management in school and society without crediting the influence of the Fabians would do great disservice to truth, but the nature of Fabianism is so complex it raises questions this essay cannot answer. To deal with the Fabians in a brief compass as I'm going to do is to deal necessarily in simplifications in order to see a little how this charming group of scholars, writers, heirs, heiresses, scientists, philosophers, bombazines, gazebos, trust-fund babies, and successful men and women of affairs became the most potent force in the creation of the modern welfare state, distributors of its characteristically dumbed-down version of schooling. Yet pointing only to this often frivolous organization's eccentricity would be to disrespect the incredible accomplishments of Beatrice Webb and her associates, and their decisive effort on schooling. Mrs. Webb is the only woman ever deemed worthy of burial in Westminster Abbey.

What nineteenth-century Transcendentalists and Muggletonians hoped to be in reordering the triumvirate of society, school, and family, twentieth-century Fabians were. Although far from the only potent organization working behind the scenes to radically reshape domestic and international life, it would not be too far out of line to call the twentieth century the Fabian century. One thing is certain: the direction of modern schooling for the bottom 90 percent of our society has followed a largely Fabian design—and the puzzling security and prestige enjoyed at the moment by those who speak of "globalism" and "multiculturalism" is a direct result of heed paid earlier to Fabian prophecies that a welfare state, followed by an intense focus on internationalism, would be the mechanism elevating corporate society over political society, and a necessary precursor to utopia. Fabian theory is the *Das Kapital* of financial capitalism.

Fabianism always floated above simplistic politics, seeking to preempt both sides. The British Labour Party and its post-WWII welfare state are Fabianism made visible. This is well understood; not so easily comprehended are signs of an aristocratic temper—like this little anti-meritocractic Fabian gem found in a report of the British College of Surgeons:

> Medicine would lose immeasurably if the proportion of such students [from upper
> class and upper middle class homes] were to be reduced in favour of precocious
> children who qualify for subsidies [i.e., scholarship students].

Even though meritocracy is their reliable cover, social stratification was always the Fabian's real trump suit. Entitlements are another Fabian insertion into the social fabric, even though the idea antedates them, of course.

To realize the tremendous task Fabians originally assigned themselves (a significant part of which was given to schooling to perform) we need to reflect again on Darwin's shattering books, *Origin of Species* (1859) and *Descent of Man* (1871), each arguing in its own way that far from being blank slates, children are written upon indelibly by their *race* of origin, some "favored" in Darwin's language, some not. A powerful public relations initiative of recent years has attempted to separate Darwin from "social Darwinism," but it cannot be done because Darwin himself is the prototypical social Darwinist. Both books taken together issued a license for liberal upper classes to justify forced schooling. From an evolutionary perspective, schools are the indoctrination phase of a gigantic breeding experiment. Working class fantasies of "self-improvement" were dismissed from the start as sentimentality that evolutionary theory had no place for.

What Darwin accomplished with his books was a freeing of discussion from the narrow straitjacket it had worn when society was considered a matter of internal associations and relationships. Darwin made it possible to consider political affairs as a prime *instrument of social evolution*. Here was a pivotal moment in Western thought, a changing of the guard in which secular purpose replaced religious purpose, already long ago trashed by the Enlightenment.

For the poor, the working classes, and middle classes in the American sense,[7] this change in outlook, lauded by the most influential minds of the nineteenth century, was a catastrophe of titanic proportions, especially for government schoolchildren. Children could no longer simply be parents' darlings. Many were (biologically) a racial menace. The rest had to be thought of as soldiers in genetic combat, the moral equivalent of war. For all but a relative handful of favored families, aspiration was off the board as a scientific proposition.

For governments, children could no longer be considered individuals but were regarded as categories, rungs on a biological ladder. Evolutionary science pronounced the majority useless mouths waiting for nature to dispense with entirely. Nature (as expressed through her human agents) was to be understood not as cruel or oppressive but beautifully, functionally *purposeful*—a neo-pagan perspective to be reflected in the organization and administration of schools.

Three distinct and conflicting tendencies competed in the nineteenth century theory of society: first was the empirical tendency stemming from John Locke and David Hume which led to

---

[7] In the British sense, middle classes are a buffer protecting elites from the poor; our own statistical income-based designation leads to a more eclectic composition, and to somewhat less predictability of attitudes and values.

that outlook on the study of society we call pragmatism, and eventually to behavioristic psychology; the second line descended from Immanuel Kant, Hegel, Savigny, and others and led to the organic theory of the modern state, the preferred metaphor of Fabians (and many later systems theorists); the third outlook comes to us out of Rousseau, Diderot, d'Alembert, Bentham, the Mills, and leads almost directly to the utilitarian state of Marxian socialism. Each of these postures was savagely assailed over time by the development of academic Darwinism. After Darwin, utopia as a human-friendly place dies an agonizing death. The last conception of utopia, after Darwin which isn't some kind of hellish nightmare, is William Morris' *News from Nowhere*.

With only niggling reservations, the Fabian brain trust had no difficulty employing force to shape recalcitrant individuals, groups, and organizations. Force in the absence of divine injunctions is a tool to be employed unsentimentally. Fabian George Bernard Shaw established the principle wittily in 1920 when he said that under a Fabian future government:

> You would not be allowed to be poor. You would be forcibly fed, clothed, lodged, taught, and employed whether you like it or not. If it were discovered that you have not character and industry, you might possibly be executed in a kindly manner.
> — *Intelligent Woman's Guide to Socialism and Capitalism*

Fabianism came into existence around the year 1884, taking its name from Roman general Fabius Cunctator[8] who preserved the Roman state by defeating Hannibal, chipping away at Hannibal's patience and will to win by avoiding combat. Darwin was the weird holy man Fabians adored, he gave them their *principle*, a theory inspirationally equal to god-theory, around which a new organization of society could be justified.

Society, after Darwin, was incontrovertibly about good breeding. That was the only true goal it had, or scientifically *could* have. Before Darwin, the view of historical development which fits best with Anglo/American tradition was a conception of individual *rights* independent of any theory of reciprocal *obligations* to the State; the duty of leaders was to Society, not to Government, a crucial distinction in perfect harmony with the teachings of Reformation Christianity, which extended to all believers a conception of *individual* duty, *individual* responsibility, and a free will right to decide for oneself beyond any claims of states. John Calvin proclaimed in his *Institutes* that through natural law, the judgment of *conscience alone* was able to distinguish between justice and injustice. It's hard for secular minds to face, but the powerful freedoms of the West, unmatched by any other society at any other time, are rooted deeply in a religion so severe it revolts the modern temper.

For Protestant Christians, salvation was uniquely a matter between God and the individual. The mind of northern Europe had for centuries been fixed on the task of winning liberties for the

---

[8] The origins are disputed but it was an offshoot of Thomas Davidson's utopian group in New York, "The Fellowship of the New Life"—an American export to Britain, not the other way around. The reader should be warned I use the term "Fabian" more indiscriminately with less concern for actual affiliation through the rest of the book than I do here. Fabianism was a *zeitgeist* as well as a literal association, and thousands of twentieth-century influentials have been Fabians who might be uncomfortable around its flesh and blood adherents, or who would be puzzled at the label.

individual against the State.[9] Notable individual freedoms were taken from the State beginning symbolically at Runnemede in 1215. By 1859, six and a half centuries later in the Age of Darwin, individual rights were everywhere in the Anglo-Saxon world understood *to transcend theories of obligation to the state.* Herbert Spencer embodies this attitude unambiguously. The first and second amendments of our own constitution illustrate just how far this freedom process could carry. Say what you please before God and Man; protect yourself with a gun if need be from government interference.

Spencer as reigning British philosopher of the moment wrote in January, 1890, in the *Westminister Review*:

> The welfare of citizens cannot rightly be sacrificed to some supposed benefit of
> the State, the State is to be maintained solely for the benefit of citizens.[10] The
> corporate life in society must be subservient to the lives of its parts, instead of
> the lives of the parts being subservient to the corporate life.

This attitude constituted a violent contradiction of German strong-state, state-as-first-parent doctrine which held that interests of the individual as individual are without significance. But derogation of individual rights was entirely consistent with Darwinian science. The German authoritarian preference received an invigorating restorative with Darwin's advent. Natural selection, the operational principle of Darwinism, was held to reach individuals only indirectly—through the action of society. Hence society becomes a natural subject for regulation and intervention by the State.

To illustrate how reverberant a drum the innocent-sounding locution "natural selection"[11] can really be, translated into social practice, try to imagine how denial of black dignities and rights and the corresponding degradation of black family relationships in America because of this denial might well be reckoned an evolutionarily *positive* course, in Darwinian terms. By discouraging Negro breeding, eventually the numbers of this most disfavored race would diminish. The state not only had a vested interest in becoming an active agent of evolution, it could not help but become one, willy-nilly. Fabians set out to write a sensible evolutionary agenda when they entered the political arena. Once this bio-political connection is recognized, the past, present and future of this seemingly bumbling movement takes on a formidable coherence. Under the dottiness, lovability,

---

[9] The spelling preferred by baronial descendents of the actual event. See Chapter Twelve.

[10] Quite an antithesis from John F, Kennedy's "Ask not what your country can do for you but what you can do for your country" Inaugural of 1960 which measured the distance we had retreated since the Civil War.

[11] In 1900, Sidney Sherwood of Johns Hopkins University joined a host of prominent organizations and men like Andrew Carnegie in declaring the emergence of the corporate system as the highest stage in evolution. Sherwood suggested the modern corporation's historic task was to sort out "genius," to get rid of "the weak." This elimination is "the real function of the trust," and the formation of monopoly control is "natural selection of the highest order." Try to imagine how this outlook played out in corporate schooling.

intelligence, high social position, and genuine goodness of some of their works, the system held out as humanitarian by Fabians is grotesquely deceptive; in reality, Fabian compassion masks a real aloofness to humanity; it is purely an intellectual project in scientific management.

Thomas Davidson's *History of Education* seen through this lens transmutes in front of our eyes from the harmlessly addled excursion into romantic futurism it seems to be into a manual of frightening strategic goals and tactical methods. Fabians emerged in the first years of the twentieth century as great champions of social efficiency in the name of the evolutionary destiny of the race. This infused a powerful secular theology into the movement, allowing its members to revel privately in an ennobling destiny. The Fabian program spread quickly through the best colleges and universities under many different names, multiplying its de facto membership among young men and women blissfully unaware of their induction. They were only being modern. H.G. Wells called it "the open conspiracy" in an essay worth your time to hunt down bearing the same title.

As the movement developed, Fabians became aristocratic friends of other social-efficiency vanguards like Taylorism or allies of the Methodist social gospel crowd of liberal Christian religionists busy substituting Works for Faith in one of the most noteworthy religious reversals of all time. Especially, they became friends and advisors of industrialists and financiers, travelers in the same direction. This cross-fertilization occurred naturally, not out of petty motives of profit, but because by Fabian lights evolution had progressed furthest among the international business and banking classes!

These laughing gentry were impressively effective at whatever they turned their hands to because they understood principles of social leverage. Kitty Muggeridge writes:

> If you want to pinpoint the moment in time when the very first foundation of the Welfare State was laid, a reasonable date to choose would be the last fortnight of November in 1905 when Beatrice Webb was appointed to the Royal Commission on the Poor Law, and she convinced her protégé, Albert Beveridge, to join a committee for dealing with employment.

During Mrs. Webb's time on the Royal Commission, she laid down the first blueprint of cradle-to-grave social security to eradicate poverty "without toppling the whole social structure." She lived to see Beveridge promulgate her major ideas in the historic *Beveridge Report*, from which they were brought to life in post-WWII Britain and the United States.

Fabian practitioners developed Hegelian principles which they co-taught alongside Morgan bankers and other important financial allies over the first half of the twentieth century. One insightful Hegelianism was that to push ideas efficiently it was necessary first to co-opt both political Left *and* political Right. Adversarial politics—competition—was a loser's game.[12] By infiltrating all major media, by continual low intensity propaganda, by massive changes in group orientations

---

[12] The most dramatic example of abandoning competition and replacing it with cooperation was the breathtaking monopolization of first the nation's, then the world's oil supply by Standard Oil under the personal direction of John D. Rockefeller. Rockefeller despised the competitive marketplace, as did his fellow titans of finance and industry, J.P. Morgan and Andrew Carnegie. Rockefeller's negotiating team was instructed to accommodate any company willing to enter his cartel, to destroy any that resisted.

(accomplished through principles developed in the psychological-warfare bureaus of the military), and with the ability, using government intelligence agents and press contacts, to induce a succession of crises,[13] they accomplished that astonishing feat.

The Open Conspiracy

When I speak of Fabianism, or of any particular Fabians, actual or virtual like Kurt Lewin, once head of Britain's Psychological Warfare Bureau, or R.D. Laing, once staff psychologist at the Tavistock Institute, I have no interest in mounting a polemic against this particular conceit of the comfortable intelligentsia. Fabian strategy and tactics have been openly announced and discussed with clarity for nearly a century, whether identified as Fabian or not. Nothing illegal about it. I do think it a tragedy, however, that government school children are left in the dark about the existence of influential groups with complex social agendas aimed at their lives.

I've neglected to tell you so far about the role *stress* plays in Fabian evolutionary theory. Just as Hegel taught that history moves faster toward its conclusion by way of warfare, so evolutionary socialists were taught by Hegel to see *struggle* as the precipitant of evolutionary improvement for the species, a necessary purifier eliminating the weak from the breeding sweepstakes.[14] Society evolves slowly toward "social efficiency" all by itself; society under stress, however, evolves much faster! Thus the deliberate creation of crisis is an important tool of evolutionary socialists. Does that let you understand the government school *drama* a little better, or the well-publicized doomsday scenarios of environmentalists?

The London School of Economics is a Fabian creation. Mick Jagger attended; so did John F. Kennedy. The *Economist*, once elitist, now a worldwide pop-intellectual publication, is Fabian as is *The New Statesman* and Ruskin Labor College of Oxford. The legendary Royal Institute of International Affairs and the Tavistock Institute for Human Relations, premier mindbending institution of the world, are Fabian. Theodore Adorno, who (uncredited) wrote some of the early Beatles' lyrics (he was on the payroll of Tavistock at the time) traveled the Fabian road as well.

You needn't carry a card or even have heard the name Fabian to follow the wolf-in-sheep's-clothing flag. Fabianism is mainly a value-system with progressive objectives. Its social club aspect isn't for coal miners, farmers, or steam-fitters. We've all been exposed to many details of the Fabian program without realizing it: in the United States, some organizations heavily influenced by

---

[13] The government-created crisis, masquerading as an unexpected *external* provocation, is elementary Hegelian strategy. If you want to take Texas and California from Mexico, first shoot a few Americans while the press disinforms the nation that Mexican depredations against our nationals have to be stopped; if you want Cuba as a satrapy, blow up an American battleship and pin it on the Cubans. By this strategy, a nation which has decided to suspend its democratic traditions with a period of martial law (under which permanent social reordering would occur) might arrange a series of "terrorist" attacks upon itself which would justify the transformation as a defense of general public safety.

[14] In the "world peace" phenomenon so necessary to establish a unitary world order lies a real danger, according to evolutionists, of species deterioration caused by inadvertent preservation of inferior genes which would otherwise be killed or starved. Hence the *urgency* of insulating superior breeding stock from pollution through various strategies of social segregation. Among these, forced classification through schooling has been by far the most important.

Fabianism are the Ford Foundation, the Russell Sage Foundation, the Stanford Research Institute, the Carnegie endowments, the Aspen Institute, the Wharton School, and RAND. And this short list is illustrative, not complete. Tavistock underwrites or has intimate relations with 30 research institutions in the U.S., all which at one time or another have taken a player's hand in the shaping of American schooling.

Once again, you need to remember we aren't conspiracy hunting but tracking an idea, like micro-chipping an eel to see what holes it swims into in case we want to catch it later on. H.G. Wells, best known of all early Fabians, once wrote of the Fabian project:

> The political world of the Open Conspiracy must weaken, efface, incorporate and supersede existing governments....The character of the Open Conspiracy will then be plainly displayed. It will be a world religion. This large, loose assimilatory mass of groups and societies will definitely and obviously attempt to swallow up the entire population of the world and become a new human community....The immediate task before all people, a planned World State, *is appearing at a thousand points of light* [but]...generations of propaganda and education may have to precede it.

Zbigniew Brzezinski wrote his famous signature essay "The Technetronic Era" in 1981, a piece reeking with Fabianisms: dislike of direct popular power, relentless advocacy of the right and duty of evolutionarily advanced nations to administer less developed parts of the world, revulsion at populist demands for "selfish self-government" (home schooling would be a prime example), and stress on collectivism. Brzezinski said in the essay:

> It will soon be possible to assert almost continuous control over every citizen and to maintain up-to-date files containing even the most personal details about health and personal behavior of every citizen, in addition to the more customary data. These files will be subject to instantaneous retrieval by the authorities. Power will gravitate into the hands of those who control information.

In his essay, Brzezinski called common people, "an increasingly purposeless mass." And, of course, if the army of children collected in mass schooling is really "purposeless," what argument says it should exist at all?

An Everlasting Faith

Fabianism is a principal force and inspiration behind all major school legislation of the twentieth century. It will help us understand Fabian influence to look at the first Fabian-authored consideration of public schooling, the most talked-about education book of 1900, Thomas Davidson's *History of Education*.

My *Dictionary of American Biography* describes Davidson as a naturalized Scot, an American since 1867 and a follower of William Torrey Harris, federal Commissioner of Education—the most influential Hegelian in North America. Davidson was also first president of the Fabian Society in England, a fact not thought worthy of preservation in the biographical dictionary, but otherwise easy enough to confirm. This news is also absent from Pelling's *America and The British Left* although Davidson *is* credited there with "usurping" the Fabians.

In his important monograph "Education in the Forming of American Society," Bernard Bailyn, as you'll recall, said anyone bold enough to venture a history of American schooling would have to explain the sharp disjunction separating these local institutions as they existed from 1620 to1890 from the massification which followed afterwards. In presenting his case, Bailyn had cause to compare "two notable books" on the subject which both appeared in 1900. One was Davidson's, the other Edward Eggleston's.

Eggleston's *Transit of Civilization* Bailyn calls "a remarkably imaginative effort to analyze the original investment from which has developed Anglo-Saxon culture in America by probing the complex states of knowing and thinking, of feeling and passion of the seventeenth century colonists." The opening words of Eggleston's book, said Bailyn, make clear the central position of education in early America. Bailyn calls *Transit* "one of the subtlest and most original books ever written on the subject" and "a seminal work," but he notes how quickly it was "laid aside by American intelligentsia as an oddity, irrelevant to the interests of the group then firmly shaping the historical study of American education."

For that group, the book of books was Davidson's *History of Education*. William James called its author a "knight-errant of the intellectual life," an "exuberant polymath." Bailyn agrees that Davidson's "was a remarkable book":

> Davidson starts with "The Rise of Intelligence" when "man first rose above the
> brute." Then he trots briskly through "ancient Turanian," Semitic, and Aryan
> education, picks up speed on "civic education" in Judaea, Greece, and Rome,
> gallops swiftly across Hellenistic, Alexandrian, Patristic, and Muslim education;
> leaps magnificently over the thorny barriers of scholasticism, the mediaeval
> universities, Renaissance, Reformation, and Counter-Reformation, and then
> plunges wildly through the remaining five centuries in sixty-four pages flat.

It was less the frantic scope than the *purpose* of this strange philosophical essay that distinguished it in the eyes of an influential group of writers. Its purpose was to dignify a newly self-conscious profession called *Education*. Its argument, a heady distillation of conclusions from Social Darwinism, claimed that *modern education was a cosmic force leading mankind to full realization of itself*. Davidson's preface puts the intellectual core of Fabianism on center stage:

> My endeavor has been to present education as the last and highest form of
> evolution.... By placing education in relation to the whole process of evolution,
> as its highest form, I have hoped to impart to it a dignity which it could hardly
> otherwise receive or claim...when it is recognized to be the highest phase of
> the world-process. "World process" here is an echo of Kant and Hegel, and
> for the teacher to be the chief agent in that process, both it and he assumes a
> very different aspect.

Here is the intellectual and emotional antecedent of "creation spirituality," Pierre Teilhard de Chardin's assertion that evolution has become a *spiritual* inevitability in our time.

Suddenly mere schooling found itself elevated from its petty, despised position on the periphery of the known universe into an intimate involvement in the cosmic destiny of man, a master key too important to be left to parents. By 1906, Paul Monroe of Teachers College could write in his *Textbook in the History of Education* that knowledge of the "purpose of education" was to supply the teacher with "fundamentals of an everlasting faith as broad as human nature and as deep as the life of the race."

This *History of Education*, according to Bailyn, "came to be taught as an introductory course, a form of initiation, in every normal school, department of education, and teachers college in the country":

> The story had to be got straight. And so a few of the more imaginative of that
> energetic and able group of men concerned with mapping overall progress of
> "scientific" education, though not otherwise historians, took over the management
> of the historical work in education. With great virtuosity they drew up what
> became the patristic literature of a powerful academic ecclesia.

The official history of education

> grew in almost total isolation from the major influences and shaping minds of
> twentieth-century historiography; and its isolation proved to be self-intensifying:
> the more parochial the subject became, the less capable it was of attracting the
> kinds of scholars who could give it broad relevance and bring it back into the
> public domain. It soon displayed the exaggeration of weakness and extravagance
> of emphasis that are the typical results of sustained inbreeding.

These "educational missionaries" spoke of schools as if they were monasteries. By limiting the idea of education to formal school instruction, the public gradually lost sight of what the real thing was. The questions these specialists disputed were as irrelevant to real people as the disputes of medieval divines; there was about their writing a condescension for public concerns, for them "the whole range of education had become *an instrument of deliberate social purpose.*" After 1910, divergence between what various publics expected would happen in government schools and what the rapidly expanding school establishment intended to *make* happen opened a deep gulf between home and school, ordinary citizen and policymaker.

Regulating Lives Like Machinery

The real explanation for this sudden gulf between NEA policies in 1893 and 1911 had nothing to do with intervening feedback from teachers, principals, or superintendents about what schools needed; rather it signaled titanic forces gathering outside the closed universe of schooling with the intention of altering this nation's economy, politics, social relationships, future direction, eventually the terms of its national existence, using schools as instruments in the work.

Schoolmen were never invited to the policy table at which momentous decisions were made. When Ellwood P. Cubberley began tentatively to raise his voice in protest against radical changes being forced upon schools (in his history of education), particularly the sudden enforcement of compulsory attendance laws which brought amazing disruption into the heretofore well-mannered school world, he quickly pulled back without naming the community leaders—as he called them—who gave the actual orders. This evidence of impotence documents the pedagogue-status of even the most elevated titans of schooling like Cubberley. You can find this reference and others like it in *Public Education in the United States.*

Scientific management was about to merge with systematic schooling in the U.S.; it preferred to steal silently in on little cat's feet, but nobody ever questioned the right of a business philosophy to tamper with children's lives. On the cantilever principle of interlocking directorates pioneered by Morgan interests, scientific school management flowed into other institutional domains of American life, too. According to Taylor, application of mechanical power to production could be generalized into every arena of national life, even to the pulpit, certainly to schools. This would bring about a realization that people's lives could be regulated very like machinery, without sentiment. Any expenditure of time and energy demanded rationalization, whether first-grader or coalminer, behavior should be mathematically accounted for following the new statistical procedures of Galton and Pearson.

The scientific management movement was backed by many international bankers and industrialists. In 1905, the vice-president of the National City Bank of New York, Frank Vanderlip, made his way to the speaker's podium at the National Education Association's yearly convention to say:

> I am firmly convinced the economic success of Germany can be encompassed in a single word—*schoolmaster*. From the economic point of view the school system of Germany stands unparalleled.

German schools were psychologically managed, ours must be too. And so they would be. People of substance stood, they thought, on the verge of an ultimate secret. How to write upon the empty slates of empty children's minds in the dawning era of scientific management. What they would write there was a program to make dwarf and fractional human beings, people driven by implanted urges and habits beyond their control.

The Gary Plan

Frederick Taylor's gospel of efficiency demanded complete and intensive use of industrial plant facilities. From 1903 onwards, strenuous efforts were made to achieve full utilization of space by forcing year-round school on society. Callahan suggests it was "the children of America, who would have been unwilling victims of this scheme, who played a decisive role in beating the original effort to effect this back."

But east of Chicago, in the synthetic U.S. Steel company town of Gary, Indiana, Superintendent William A. Wirt, a former student of John Dewey's at the University of Chicago, was busy testing a radical school innovation soon to be sprung on the national scene called the Gary Plan.

Wirt had supposedly invented a new organizational scheme in which school subjects were *departmentalized*, this required movement of students from room to room on a regular basis so that all building spaces were in constant use. Bells would ring and just as with Pavlov's salivating dog, children would shift out of their seats and lurch toward yet another class.

In this way children could be exposed to many non-academic socialization experiences and much scientifically engineered physical activity, it would be a bonus value from the same investment, a curriculum apart from so-called basic subjects which by this time were being looked upon as an actual menace to long-range social goals. Wirt called his system the "work-study-play" school, but outside of Gary it was referred to simply as "the Gary Plan." Its noteworthy economical feature, rigorously scheduling a student body twice as large as before into the same space and time, earned it the informal name "platoon school."

While the prototype was being established and tested on children of the new industrial proletariat in Gary, the plan itself was merchandised from newsstand, pulpit, lecture circuit, lauded in administrative circles, soundly praised by first pedagogical couple John and Evelyn Dewey in their 1915 book, *Schools of Tomorrow*. The first inkling Gary might be a deliberate stepchild of the scientific management movement occurred in a February, 1911 article by Wirt for *The American School Board Journal*, "Scientific Management of School Plants." But a more thorough and forceful exposition of its provenance was presented in the *Elementary School Journal* by John Franklin Bobbit in a 1912 piece titled "Elimination of Waste in Education."

Bobbit said Gary schools were the work of businessmen who understood scientific management. Teaching was slated to become a specialized scientific calling conducted by pre-approved agents of the central business office. Classroom teachers would teach the same thing over and over to groups of traveling children; special subject teachers would deliver their special subjects to classes rotating through the building on a precision time schedule.[15]

Early in 1914, the Federal Bureau of Education, then located in the Interior Department, strongly endorsed Wirt's system. This led to one of the most dramatic and least-known events in twentieth century school history. In New York City, a spontaneous rebellion occurred on the part of the students and parents against extension of the Gary Plan to their own city. While the revolt had only short-lived effects, it highlights the demoralization of private life occasioned by passing methods of industry off as education.

The Jewish Student Riots

Less than three weeks before the mayoral election of 1917, rioting broke out at PS 171, an elementary school on Madison Avenue near 103rd Street in New York City which had adopted the Gary Plan. About a thousand demonstrators smashed windows, menaced passersby, shouted threats, and made school operation impossible. Over the next few days newspapers downplayed the riot,

---

[15] Bobbit was the influential schoolman who reorganized the Los Angeles school curriculum, replacing formal history with "Social Studies." Of the Bobbitized set of educational objectives, the five most important were 1) Social intercommunication 2) Maintenance of physical efficiency 3) Efficient citizenship 4) General social contacts and relationships 5) Leisure occupations. My own favorite is "efficient citizenship" which bears rolling around on the point of one's bayonet as the bill is presented for payment.

marginalizing the rioters as "street corner agitators" from Harlem and the Upper Eastside, but they were nothing of the sort, being mainly immigrant parents. Demonstrations and rioting spread to other Gary Plan schools, including high schools where student volunteers were available to join parents on the picket line.

At one place, 5,000 children marched. For ten days trouble continued, breaking out in first one place then another. Thousands of mothers milled around schools in Yorkville, a German immigrant section, and in East Harlem, complaining angrily their children had been put on "half-rations" of education. They meant that mental exercise had been removed from the center of things. Riots flared out into Williamsburg and Brownsville in the borough of Brooklyn; schools were stoned, police car tires slashed by demonstrators. Schools on the Lower Eastside and in the Bronx reported trouble also.

The most notable aspect of this rioting was its source in what today would be the bottom of the bellcurve-masses...and they were complaining that school was too easy! What could have possessed recently arrived immigrants to defy their betters? Whatever it was, it poisoned the promising political career of mayoral incumbent, John P. Mitchel, a well-connected, aristocratic young progressive who had been seriously mentioned as presidential timber. Although Teddy Roosevelt personally campaigned for him, Mitchel lost by a 2 to 1 margin when election day arrived shortly after the riots were over, the disruptions widely credited with bringing Mitchell down. In all, 300 students had to be arrested, almost all Jewish. I identify their ethnicity because today we don't usually expect Jewish kids to get arrested in bulk.

To understand what was happening requires us to meet an entity calling itself the Public Education Association. If we pierce its associational veil it is made up of bankers, society ladies, corporation lawyers, and in general, people with private fortunes or access to private fortunes. The PEA announced in 1911 an "*urgent need*" to transform public schools immediately into child welfare agencies. Shortly afterward, Mitchel, a member of the PEA, was elected mayor of New York. Superintendent Wirt in Gary was promptly contacted and offered the New York superintendency. He agreed, the first Gary schools opening in New York City in March 1915.

Bear in mind there was no public debate, no warning of this radical step. Just 75 days after the Gary trial began, the financial arm of New York City government declared it a total success, authorizing conversion of twelve more schools. (The original trial had only been for two.) This was done in June at the end of the school year when public attention was notoriously low. Then in September of 1915, after a net 100 days of trial, Comptroller Prendergast issued a formal report *recommending extension of the Gary plan into all schools of New York City!* He further recommended lengthening the school day and the school year.

At the very time this astonishing surprise was being prepared for the children of New York City in 1915, a series of highly laudatory articles sprouted like zits all over the periodical press calling the Gary Plan the answer to our nation's school prayers. One characteristic piece read, "*School must fill the vacuum of the home, school must be life itself as once the old household was a life itself.*" Like Rommel's Panzer columns, true believers were on the move. At the same time press agents were skillfully manipulating the press, officers of the Rockefeller Foundation, a body which supported the Gary plan wholeheartedly, were appointed without fanfare as members of the New York City Board of Education, compliments of Mayor Mitchel.

Immediately after Prendergast's report appeared calling for total Gary-ization of public schooling, a book written by a prominent young protégé of John Dewey's directed national attention to the Gary miracle "where children learn to play and prepare for vocations as well as to study abstractions." Titled *The Gary Schools*, its author, Randolph Bourne, was among the most beloved columnists for *The New Republic* in the days when that magazine, product of J.P. Morgan banker Willard Straight's personal patronage, took some of its editorial instruction directly from the tables of power in America.

In light of what happened in 1917, you might find it interesting to have your librarian scare up a copy of Bourne's *Gary Schools* so you can study how a well-orchestrated national propaganda campaign can colonize your mind. Even as Bourne's book was being read, determined opposition was forming.

In 1917, in spite of increasing grassroots protest, the elite Public Education Association urged the opening of 48 more Gary schools (there were by that time 32 in operation). Whoever was running the timetable on this thing had apparently tired of gradualism and was preparing to step from the shadows and open the engine full throttle. A letter from the PEA's director published in *The New York Times* warned "The situation is acute, no further delay." Here is a classic case study in Hegelian manufactured crisis used to unfreeze recalcitrant attitudes. Like magic, the Board of Estimate unfroze, voting sufficient funds to extend the Gary scheme to all New York City schools.

School riots followed hard on the heels of that vote. European immigrants, especially Jews from Germany (where collectivist thinking in the West had been perfected), knew exactly what the scientific Gary Plan would mean to their children. They weren't buying. In the fallout from these disturbances, socialite Mitchel was thrown out of office. The Gary schools themselves were dissolved by incoming Mayor Hylan who called them "a scheme" of the Rockefeller Foundation: "a system by which Rockefellers and their allies hope to educate coming generations in the 'doctrine of contentment,' another name for social serfdom."

The Rockefeller Report

The Gary tale is a model of how managed school machinery can be geared up in secret without public debate to deliver a product parents don't want. Part One of the Gary story is the lesson we learned from the impromptu opinion poll of Gary schooling taken by housewives and immigrant children, a poll whose results translated into riots. These immigrant parents concluded, having only their native wit and past experience to guide them, that Gary schools were caste schools. Not what they expected from America. They turned to the only weapon at their disposal— disruption—and it worked. They shrewdly recognized that boys in elite schools wouldn't tolerate the dumbing down their own were being asked to accept. They knew this would *close* doors of opportunity, not open them.

Some individual comments from parents and principals about Gary are worth preserving: "too much play and time-wasting," "they spend all day listening to the phonograph and dancing," "they change class every forty minutes, my daughter has to wear her coat constantly to keep it from being stolen," "the cult of the easy," "a step backwards in human development," "focusing on the group instead of the individual." One principal predicted if the plan were kept, retardation would multiply *as a result of minimal contact between teachers and students*. And so it has.

Part Two of the Gary story is the official Rockefeller report *condemning* Gary, circulated at Rockefeller headquarters in 1916, *but not issued until 1918*. Why this report was suppressed for two years we can only guess. You'll recall Mayor Hylan's charge that the Rockefeller Foundation moved heaven and earth to force its Gary plan on an unwitting and unwilling citizenry, using money, position, and influence to such an extent that a New York State Senate Resolution of 1916 accused the foundation of moving to gain complete control of the New York City Board of Education. Keep in mind that Rockefeller people were active in 1915, 1916, and 1917, lobbying to *impose* a Gary destiny on the public schools of New York City even after its own house analyst pointed to the intellectual damage these places caused.

The 1916 analytical report leapfrogged New York City to examine the original schools as they functioned back in Gary, Indiana. Written by Abraham Flexner,[16] it stated flatly that Gary schools were a total failure, "offering insubstantial programs and a general atmosphere which habituated students to inferior performance." Flexner's analysis was a massive repudiation of John Dewey's shallow *Schools of Tomorrow* hype for Gary.

Now we come to the mystery. *After* this bad idea crashed in New York City in 1917, the critical Rockefeller report held in house since 1916 was issued in 1918 to embarrass critics who had claimed the whole mess was the idea of the Rockefeller project officers. So we know in retrospect that the Rockefeller Foundation was aware of serious shortcomings *before* it used its political muscle to impose Gary on New York. Had the Flexner report been offered in a timely fashion before the riots, it would have spelled doom for the Gary Plan. Why it wasn't has never been explained.

The third and final part of the Gary story comes straight out of *Weird Tales*. In all existing accounts of the Gary drama, none mention the end of Superintendent Wirt's career after his New York defeat. Only Diane Ravitch (in *The Great School Wars*) even bothers to track Wirt back home to Gary, where he resumed the superintendency and became, she tells us, a "very conservative schoolman" in his later years. Ah, what Ravitch missed!

The full facts are engrossing: seventeen years after Wirt left New York City, a government publication printed the next significant chapter of the Wirt story. Its title: *Hearing, House Select Committee to Investigate Certain Statements of Dr. William Wirt, 73rd Congress, 2nd Session, April 10 and 17, 1934*. It seems that Dr. Wirt, while in Washington to attend a school administrators meeting in 1933, had been invited to an elite private dinner party at the home of a high Roosevelt administration official. The dinner was attended by well-placed members of the new government including A.A. Berle, a famous "inner circle" brain-truster. There, Wirt heard that the Depression was being artificially prolonged by credit rigging, until little people and businessmen were shaken enough to agree to a plan where Government must dominate business and commerce in the future!

All this he testified to before Congress. The transformation was to make *government* the source of long-term capital loans. Control of business would follow. Wirt testified he was told Roosevelt was only a puppet, that his hosts had made propaganda a science, that they could make newspapers and magazines beg for mercy by taking away much of their advertising, that leaders of

---

[16] A man considered the father of twentieth century American systematic medicine and a longtime employee of the Rockefeller Foundation.

business and labor would be silenced by offers of government contracts for materials and services provided they were subservient, that colleges and schools would be kept in line by promises of federal aid until such time as they were under safe control, and that farmers would be managed by letting key operators "get their hands in the public trough."

In the yellow journalism outburst following Wirt's disclosure, *Berle admitted everything*. But he said they were just pulling Wirt's leg! Pulling the leg of the one-time nationally acclaimed savior of public education. *Time Magazine, The New York Times*, and other major media ridiculed Wirt publicly, effectively silencing him. A few years later he died very horribly in an insane asylum,[17] claiming on his deathbed he had once been part of a well-organized, well-funded plot to deliberately destroy the American family through the Gary scheme.

How much of what poor, crazy Wirt said was true? Who knows? Of Wirt's earlier New York foray into the engineering of young people, New York City Mayor Hylan was once quoted in *The New York Times* (March 27, 1922):

> The real menace to our republic is this invisible government which like a giant octopus sprawls its slimy length over city, state and nation.... It has seized in its tentacles our executive officers, our legislative bodies, our schools, our courts, our newspapers, and every agency created for the public protection.... To depart from mere generalizations, let me say that at the head of this octopus are the Rockefeller Standard Oil interests.

During the crucial years of the school changeover from academic institution to behavioral modification instrument, the radical nature of the metamorphosis caught the attention of a few national politicians who spoke out, but could never muster enough strength for effective opposition. In the January 26, 1917, *Congressional Record*, for instance, Senator Chamberlain of Oregon entered these words:

> They are moving with military precision all along the line to get control of the education of the children of the land.

Senator Poindexter of Washington followed, saying:

> The cult of Rockefeller, the cult of Carnegie...as much to be guarded against in the educational system of this country as a particular religious sect.

And in the same issue, Senator Kenyon of Iowa related:

> There are certain colleges that have sought endowments, and the agent of the Rockefeller Foundation or the General Education Board had gone out and examined the curriculum of these colleges and compelled certain changes....

---

[17] St. Elizabeth's (where Ezra Pound was incarcerated after WWII) I am told his place of incarceration was a place often spoken of as one of America's political prisons.

It seems to me one of the most dangerous things that can go on in a republic is to have an institution of this power apparently trying to shape and mold the thought of the young people of this country.

Senator Works of California added:

These people...are attempting to get control of the whole educational work of the country.

It's all in the *Congressional Record*. Have a look if it interests you: 26 January,1917.

Obstacles On The Road To Centralization

Three major obstacles stood in the way of the great goal of using American schools to realize a scientifically programmed society. The first was the fact that American schooling was locally controlled. In 1930, when the massive socializing scheme was swinging into high gear, helped substantially by an attention-absorbing depression, this nation still had 144,102 local school boards.[18] At least one million, one hundred thousand *elected* citizens of local stature made decisions for this country's schools out of their wisdom and experience. Out of 70,000,000 adults between the ages of 30 and 65, one in every 40 was on a school board (30 years earlier than that the figure had been one in 20). Contrast either ratio with today's figure of one in 5,000.

The first task of scientifically managed schooling was to transfer management from a citizen yeomanry to a professional elite under the camouflage of consolidation for economy's sake. By 1932, the number of school districts was down to 127,300; by 1937 to 119,018; by 1950 to 83,719; by 1960 to 40,520; by 1970 to 18,000; by 1990 to 15,361. Citizen oversight was slowly squeezed out of the school institution, replaced by homogeneous managerial oversight, managers screened and trained, watched, loyalty-checked by Columbia, Stanford, Chicago, the Cleveland Conference, and similar organizations with private agendas for public schooling.

The second obstacle to an ideological takeover of schools was the historic influence of teachers as role models. Old-fashioned teachers had a disturbing proclivity to stress development of intellect through difficult reading, heavy writing assignments, and intense discussion. The problem of proud and independent teachers was harder to solve than the reading problem. As late as 1930 there were still 149,400 one room/one teacher schools in America, places not only cheap to operate but successful at developing tough-minded, independent thinkers. Most of the rest of our schools were small and administrator-free, too. The idea of principals who *did not teach* came very late in the school game in most places. The fantastic notion of a parasitic army of assistant principals, coordinators, and all the rest of the various familiar specialists of institutional schooling didn't exist at all until 1905, except in the speculations of teacher college dreamers.

---

[18] Down from 355,000 in 1900.

Two solutions were proposed about 1903 to suppress teacher influence and make instruction teacher-proof. The first was to grow a heretofore unknown administrative hierarchy of non-teaching principals, assistant principals, subject coordinators and the rest, to drop the teacher's status rank. And if degrading teacher status proved inadequate, another weapon, the standardized test, was soon to be available. By displacing the judgmental function from a visible teacher to a remote bastion of educational scientists somewhere, no mere classroom person could stray very far from approved texts without falling test scores among their students signaling the presence of such a deviant.[19] Both these initiatives were underway as World War I ended.

The third obstacle to effective centralization of management was the intimate *neighborhood* context of most American schools, one where school procedures could never escape organic oversight by parents and other local interests. Not a good venue from which to orchestrate the undermining of traditional society. James Bryant Conant, WWI poison gas specialist and by then chairman of a key Carnegie commission, reported in an ongoing national news story after the Sputnik moment that it was the small size of our schools causing the problem. Only large schools, said Conant, could have faculty and facilities large enough to cover the math and science we (presumably) lacked and Russia (presumably) had. The bigger the better.

In one bold stroke the American factory school of Lancaster days was reborn. Here a de-intellectualized Prussian-style curriculum could reign undetected. From 1960 to 1990, while student population was increasing 61 percent, the number of school administrators grew 342 percent. In constant dollars, costs shot up 331 percent, and teachers, who had fallen from 95 percent of all school personnel in 1915 to 70 percent in 1950—now fell still further, down and down until recently they comprised *less than 50 percent* of the jobs in the school game. School had become an employment project, the largest hiring hall in the world, bigger than agriculture, bigger than armies.

One other significant set of numbers parallels the absolute growth in the power and expense of government schooling, but inversely. In 1960, when these gigantic child welfare agencies called schools were just setting out on their enhanced mission, 85 percent of African-American children in New York were from intact, two-parent households. In 1990 in New York City, with the school budget drawing $9,300 a kid for its social welfare definition of education, that number dropped below 30 percent. School and the social work bureaucracies had done their work well, fashioning what looked to be a permanent underclass, one stripped of its possibility of escape, turned against itself. Scientific management had proven its value, although what that was obviously depended on one's perspective.

---

[19] None of this apparatus of checks and balances ever worked exactly as intended. A degraded, demoralized teaching staff, (and even many demoralized administrators) lacks interest or even energy to police the system effectively. Gross abuses are legion, the custom almost everywhere; records are changed, numbers regularly falsified. A common habit in my day was to fill out phony lunch forms *en masse* to make schools eligible for *Title I* monies. The chief legal officer for the state of California told me in Sacramento a few years ago that his state was unable to effectively monitor the compulsory attendance laws, a truth I can vouch for from firsthand experience.

PART THREE

A Personal
Interlude

And how can man die better
Than facing fearful odds,
For the ashes of his fathers
And the temples of his gods?
— Macauley, *Lays of Ancient Rome*

Mother, Sister, and Author, age 4. Swissvale (1940).

CHAPTER TEN

My Green River

Each person in a village has a face and a name, even a nickname.
Anonymity is impossible, for the villagers are not a mass...a village
has its own language, its customs, its rhythms...its life is interior....a
village cannot be global.

— Robert Vachon

The Character Of A Village

Before I went to first grade I could add, subtract, and multiply in my head. I knew my times tables not as work but as games Dad played on drives around Pittsburgh. Learning anything was easy when you felt like it. My father taught me that.

When I went to first grade I could read fluently. I loved to read grownup books I selected from the three-level glass-enclosed bookcase behind the front door in Swissvale. It held hundreds. I knew if I kept reading, things would eventually come. Mother taught me that and she was right. I remember taking down *The Decameron* time after time, only to find its deceptively simple language concealing meanings I couldn't fathom. Each time I put the book back I made a mental note to try again next month. And sure enough, one month it happened. I was ten.

My father was a cookie salesman. Mother called him that anyway when she was angry, which was often. He had gone to work as a teenager to help support my widowed grandmother and to help brother Frank, the smart one, through the University of Pittsburgh. Dad never got to college, but he was a genius just the same. Mother went for one year, she was a genius, too. They were the kind of people who expose the malice of bell curves and rankings for what it is. I miss them both and think of them often with love and gratitude.

Mother I called "Bootie" most of the time because that's what I heard her own mother say. Bootie read fairy tales to me in the cradle, she recited poems, she filled my ears and eyes with language even though she had little else in the way of things to give. One day she bought a set of encyclopedias from a door-to-door salesman that cost more than we could afford. I know because she and dad fought when he got home. From then on mother read from the encyclopedia every day. We read all the newspapers, too. In those days they only cost a couple of cents. I liked the Hearst *Sun-Telegraph* best because it used violent layout, and on the upper corner of the Sunday edition, a little boy dressed like a fop called "Puck" said in a speech balloon, "What fools these mortals be." I didn't know what that meant, but I said the words out loud often to punctuate adult conversation and always got a smile when I did.

As far as I can figure, any success I had as a schoolteacher came from what my mother, my father, my family, friends and town taught, not from a single thing I remember about Cornell and Columbia, my two colleges, not from any findings of institutes of child study or directives from departments of education. If I'm correct, then this insight is more significant than it may appear. The immense edifice of teacher instruction and schooling in general rests on the shaky hypothesis that expert intervention in childhood produces better people than might otherwise occur. I've come to doubt that.

A gigantic social investment rides on this hypothesis, one which might otherwise be spent on reducing stress on family life which interferes with happiness and the growth of intelligence. Had the small fortune spent on my own schooling been placed instead in my people and my place directly, I have a hunch I would have turned out better. Whatever the truth of this complex proposition, as long as you've paid your money and time to hear what I have to say, you have a right to know something about the fountainhead of my school-teaching practice, my growing up time on the green river Monongahela.

I feel grateful for the luck to be born in a tiny city with the character of a village on the river Monongahela in western Pennsylvania. People cared for each other there. Even the town wastrels had a history. But we minded our own business in Mon City, too. Both are important. Everyone seemed to understand that within broad limits there is no one best way to grow up. Rich or poor doesn't matter much if you know what's important. *Poverty can't make you miserable; only a bad character and a weak spirit can do that.*

In Monongahela, people seemed to know that children have a remarkable power to survive unfavorable environments as long as they have a part in a vital community. In the years I grew up, in the place I grew up, tales of social workers breaking up families "in the best interests of the child" weren't common, although on several occasions I heard uncle Bud threaten to punch out this man's lights or that one's if the person didn't start treating his wife better. Or his kids. Bud was always punching someone in the interest of justice.

Over the years any number of students found a way to tell me what they appreciated most about my classes was that I didn't waste their time. I think I learned how not to do that through a bit of good luck—being born in Monongahela during the Depression when money was tight and people were forced to continue older traditions of making their own meanings instead of buying them. And learning how many very different ways there were to grow strong. What the vast industry of professional child-rearing has told you about the right way to grow up matters less than you've been led to believe. Until you know that, you remain caught like a fly in the web of the great therapeutic community of modern life. That will make you sick quicker than anything.

Singing And Fishing Were Free

I went Christmas caroling long before I knew how to read or even what Christmas was about. I was three. The carolers stood on a corner diagonally across from my grandfather's printing office where their voices filled an informal amphitheater made by the slope of Second Street just before it met Main, the principal intersection of the town. If I had to guess where I learned to love rhythmical language it would be on that corner at the foot of Second Street hill.

In Monongahela I fished for carp and catfish made inedible by river acids leaching out of the mines and waste put there by the mills. I fished them out with homemade dough balls whipped together in grandmother Mossie's kitchen. In Monongahela I waited weekly for the changing of Binks McGregor's haberdashery window or Bill Pulaski's hardware display as eagerly as a theatregoer might wait to be refreshed by a new scenery change.

Mother's family, the Zimmers, and the branch of Gattos my father represented, were poor by modern big city standards, but not really poor for that time and place. It was only in late middle age I suddenly realized that sleeping three to a bed as mother, sister, and I did is almost an operational definition of poverty, or its close cousin. But it never occurred to me to think of myself as poor. Not once. Not ever. Even later on at Uniontown High School when we moved to a town with sharp social class gradations and a formal social calendar, I had little awareness of any unbridgeable gulf between myself and those people who invited me to country club parties and to homes grander than my own. Nor did they, I believe. A year at Cornell, however, made certain my innocence would come to an end.

Mother was not so lucky. Although she never spoke openly of it, I know now she was ashamed of having less than those she grew up with. Once she had had much more before Pappy, my grandad, was wiped out in the 1929 crash. She wasn't envious, mind you, she was ashamed, and this shame constrained her open nature. It made her sad and wistful when she was alone. It caused her to hide away from former friends and the world. She yearned for dignity, for the days when her clothes were made in Paris. So in the calculus of human misery she exercised her frustration on dad. Their many separations and his long absences from home on business even when they lived together are likely to have originated in this immaculate tension.

The great irony is that mother did beautifully well *without* money. She was resourceful, imaginative, generally optimistic, a woman with greater power to make something from nothing—totem poles from thread spools, an award-winning Halloween costume from scrap paper and cloth, to turn a walk through the hills into high quality adventure—than anyone. She had no extravagant appetites, didn't drink, didn't crave exotic food, glamorous places, or the latest gadgets. She set her own hair and it was always lovely. And she kept the cleanest house imaginable, full of pretty objects which she gathered watchfully and with superb taste on her journey through life. As if to compound the irony of her discontent, Mon City was hardly a place to be rich. There wasn't much to buy there.

The Greatest Fun Was Watching People Work

I shouldn't say nobody had money in Monongahela, but it's accurate to say nothing was expensive. Beer was the town passion, more a religion with the men, and a big glass only a nickel, the same price as twelve ounces of buttermilk or a candy bar three times heavier than the modern sort. Bones to make soup were free. Beyond movies—12 cents for kids—commercial entertainment hardly existed, a few bowling alleys at a nickel a frame, Redd's Beach (a pool at least ten miles away where swimming was a dime) and a roller-skating rink I never went to.

Where society thrived was in hundreds of ethnic social clubs and fraternal organizations up and down the Valley: the Moose, the Elks, the Oddfellows, Mystic Knights, Sons of Slovenia, the

Polish-American Society, the Russian-American Club. These were places for men to drink and talk cheaply except on Saturday night when ladies could drink and talk, too, alongside their men and have a dance. Sometimes with even a live band to give snap to the joint.

No kid in Mon City reached for the "Events and Activities" page of the papers because there wasn't one or any special kid places that people of all ages didn't frequent. When the men weren't playing *boccie* at the Italian Club, kids were allowed, passing first through a barroom reeking of unpasteurized stale beer. No special life was arranged for kids. Yet there was always a full menu; just spying on the adult world, watching people work, and setting out on expeditions to explore filled whatever time you wanted to spare. Until I got to Cornell, I can't recall anyone I ever knew saying, "I'm bored." And yet when I got to New York City, hardly a day passed without crying loud and long about ennui. Perhaps this indicates some important marker we've missed in our modern search to make private worlds for children—the constituents of meaning have been stripped away from these overspecialized places. Why a child would want to associate exclusively with children in a narrow age or social class range defies understanding. Why adults would impose such a fate on kids strikes me as an act of madness.

The greatest fun was watching work at construction sites, watching freight trains unload or coal up, studying lumberyards at work, seeing gas pumped, hoods lifted, metal welded, tires vulcanized, watching Johnny Nami cut hair, Vito fill chocolates. Best of all was trailing Charlie Bigerton, the cop, on his rounds without him catching on. When kids around town pooled data about Charlie we could recreate the police patrol schedule accurately enough that violating wartime curfew was like taking candy from a baby.

Sitting In The Dark

At 213 Second Street we lived over the printing office Grandad owned, the Zimmer Printing Company. "Since 1898," his swinging sign read. It was located only a block and a half from the green river west of the streetcar tracks on Main. In between river and streetcars was the Pennsylvania Railroad right of way and tracks which followed the river down to Pittsburgh. Our second floor bay window hung over the town's main intersection where trolleys from Charleroi and Donora passed constantly, clanging and hissing, all lit up in the dark night.

An incredible vision, these things, orange metal animals with people in their stomachs, throwing illuminated reflections in color onto the ceiling of our livingroom by an optical process I often thought to have explained to me but never did. Bright sparks flew from their wheels and fell from the air around the overhead power lines, burning sharp holes in dark places.

From our perch, we could also see long freight trains roaring along the river sending an orchestra of clanks and whistle shrieks into the sky. We could watch great paddle-wheel steamers plying the river in both directions, filling the air with columns of white steam.

From early till late, Grandmother Mossie sat rocking. She sat at the window facing the river, quietly observing this mechanical show of riverboat, train, and streetcar—four tiers of movement if you count the stream of auto traffic, five if you include the pedestrians, our neighbors, flowing north and south on Main far into the night hours. Though she seldom ventured to the street from our apartment after her great disgrace of fifteen years earlier when lack of money forced her to move abruptly one day from a large home with marble fireplaces. (She never spoke to my grandfather, not a word, after that, though they ate two meals a day at the same small table.) The telephone supplied sufficient new data about neighbors, enough so she could chart the transit of the civilization she had once known face to face.

Sitting with Moss in the darkness was always magic. Keeping track of the mechanisms out there, each with its own personality, rolling and gliding this way or that on mysterious errands, watching grandmother smoke Chesterfield after Chesterfield with which she would write glowing words in the air for me to read, beginning with my name, "Jackie." Words became something exciting seen that way. I couldn't get enough of them. Imagine the two of us sitting there year after year, never holding a recognizable conversation yet never tiring of each other's company. Sometimes Moss would ask me to find numbers in the inspired graphics of an eccentric comic strip, "Toonerville Trolley," so she could gamble two cents with the barber across the street who ran numbers between clipping hair.

Although we really didn't hold conversation in any customary fashion, Moss would comment out loud on a wide range of matters, often making allusions beyond my ken. Was she speaking to herself? I would react or not. Sometimes I asked a question. After a smoke-filled interval, she *might* answer. Sometimes she would teach me nonsense riddles like "A titimus, a tatimus, it took two "t"s to tie two "t"s to two small trees, How many "t"s are in all that?" Or tongue twisters like "rubber baby buggy bumpers" or "she sells sea shells by the sea shore," which I was supposed to say ten times in a row as fast as I could.

Sometimes the verses would sound ugly to modern ears as in "God made a nigger, He made him in the night; God made a nigger but forgot to make him white." Yet I have good reason to believe Moss never actually met or spoke with a black person in her entire life or harbored any ill-will towards them. It was just a word game.

On the subject of race, we all officially learned to sing about black people in third grade: "Darktown Strutters Ball," "Old Black Joe," and others. No discussion of race preceded or followed; they were just songs. Before you conclude Mon City must be a bigoted place, you need to know its tiny population contained the broadest diversity of ethnic groups living together in harmony. Ninety years earlier it had been a regular stop on the Underground Railroad. The barn of the Anawalt house was used for that purpose all through the 1850s.

If Vico's notion in *The New Science* is correct, we encounter the world in ways first implicit in ourselves. There can be no filling of blank slates in education, no pouring of wisdom into empty children; if Vico is correct, the Monongahela I bring dripping to you from the bottom of my river memory is a private city, revealing the interior of my own mind. Whether you believe the Fall is real or only a metaphor for the feeling we get when by losing our home, we find ourselves cut off from our creative source, who I am and why I taught the way I did is long ago and far away in that town, those people and that green river.

I Hung Around A Lot In Monongahela

The great destructive myth of the twentieth century was the aggressive contention that a child couldn't grow up correctly in the unique circumstances of his own family. In order to avoid having you finish this essay with the feeling it might have been all right for *my* family to influence my growth so intensely, but for many children with worse families that just wouldn't do, fix your attention a minute on the less savory aspects of my people, as they might be seen through social-service eyes. Both sets of grandparents and my mother and father were seriously alienated from one another, the men from the women and vice-versa.

On the Zimmer side, heavy drinking and German/Irish tempers led to one violent conflict after another, conflicts to which my sister and I were fully exposed. We grew like weeds as children, with full run of the town, including its most dangerous places, had no effective curfew, and tended to excess in everything. Did I forget to mention the constant profanity? By up-to-the-minute big-city standards my family skirted the boundary of court-ordered family dissolution more than once.

Since a substantial number of the families I worked with productively as a schoolteacher had similar rap sheets to my own by social hygiene standards, I want to offer you my Monongahela years as a case study of how a less than ideal family by social work standards can still teach courage, love, duty, self-reliance; can awaken curiosity and wonder; can be a laboratory for independent thought, well-rooted identity, and communitarian feelings; and can grow in memory as a beloved companion even when it is composed of ghosts.

The city of Monongahela itself is offered as a case study of a different sort, showing the power of common places to return loyalty by animating the tiniest details of existence. The town is a main character in my personal story, a *genius loci* interacting with my development as a schoolteacher. The extreme effort I invested in the physical presence of my classrooms when I taught was done, I think, because the physical presence of my town never left me even after I was far removed from it. I wanted that same sort of ally for my kids.

Gary Snyder once said, "Of all memberships we identify ourselves by, the one most forgotten that has greatest potential for healing is place." The quiet rage I felt at bearing the last name of a then socially disvalued minority, the multiple grievances I felt off and on against my parents for being a house divided, at my sister for making herself a stranger to me, at my dad for staying away so I grew up with only a distant acquaintanceship between us, the bewilderment I felt from having to sit nightly at dinner with grandparents who hadn't spoken to one another for 15 years and for whom I was required to act as go-between, the compounding of this bewilderment when I discovered my Italian grandfather had been buried in an unmarked grave, perhaps for taking a mistress, the utter divide geographically and culturally between mother's family and father's—the fantastic gulf between the expressive idiom of the Germans who treated rage and violence as if they were normal, and dad's people, the quintessence of decorous rationality, the absolute inability of mother to face the full demands of her maturity, yet her inspiring courage when her principles were challenged—all these made for an exciting, troubled, and even dangerous childhood. Would I have been better off in foster care do you think? Are others? Are you insane?

What allowed me to make sense of things against the kaleidoscope of these personal dynamics was that town and its river, two constants I depended upon. They were enough. I survived, even came to thrive because of my membership in Monongahela, the irreducible, unclassifiable, asystematic village of my boyhood. So different from the neo-villages of social work.

All the town's denizens played a part: the iridescent river dragonflies, the burbling streetcars, the prehistoric freight trains, the grandeur of the paddle-wheel boats, the unpackaged cookies and uncut-in-advance-of-purchase cheese and meat, women in faded cotton house-dresses who carried themselves with bearing and dignity in spite of everything, men who swore constantly and spit huge green and yellow globs of phlegm on the sidewalks, steelworkers who took every insult as mortal and mussed a little boy's hair because he was "Zim's nephew."

I hung around a lot in Monongahela looking at things and people, trying them on for size. Much is learned by being lazy. I learned to fish that way, to defend myself, to take risks by going down in the abandoned coal mine across the river full of strange machinery and black water—a primitive world with nobody around to tell me to be careful. I learned to take knocks without running away, to watch hard men and women reveal themselves through their choices. I cleaned Pappy's printing office after closing for a silver St. Gaudens walking Liberty 50-cent piece weekly, the most beautiful piece of American money ever made. I sold *Sun-Telegraphs* and *Post-Gazettes* on the corner of Second and Main for one cent a paper profit. I had a Kool-Aid stand on Main and Fourth on hot summer days.

Shouldn't you ask why your boy or girl needs to know anything about Iraq or about computer language before they can tell you the name of every tree, plant, and bird outside your window? What will happen to them with their high standardized test scores when they discover they can't fry an egg, sew a button, join things, build a house, sail a boat, ride a horse, gut a fish, pound a nail, or bring forth life and nurture it? Do you believe hiring those things done for you is the same? You fool, then. Why do you cooperate in the game of compulsion schooling when it makes children useless to themselves as adults, hardly able to tie their own shoes?

I learned to enjoy my own company in Monongahela, to feel at ease with anyone, to put my trust in personal qualities rather than statistical gradations. Anything else? Well, I learned to love there.

Just across the river bridge and over the river hill was open farm country, anyone could walk there in 30 minutes. Everyone was welcome, kids included. The farmers never complained. Mother would walk Joanie and I there in the early morning as mist was rising from the river. When she was 72, I wrote to her trying to explain what I'm trying to explain now, how her town had given me underpinnings to erect a life upon:

Dear Mom,

> I think what finally straightened me out was memory of those early morning walks you used to take with me up River Hill, with mist rising from the green river and trees, the open pits of abandoned coal mines producing their own kind of strange beauty in the soft silence of the new day. Coming out of the grit and rust of Monongahela, crossing the clean architecture of the old bridge with its dizzy view to the river below through the wide-set slats underfoot, that was a worthy introduction to the hills on the far shore. Going up those hills with you we startled many a rabbit to flight. I know you remember that, too. I was amazed that wild things lived so close to town. Then at the top we could see Monongahela in the valley the way birds must but when we turned away, everything was barns and cornland. You gave me our town. What a gift it was!

My best teachers in Monongahela were Frank Pizzica, the high-rolling car dealer; old Mr. Marcus, the druggist wiser than a doctor; Binks McGregor, psychological haberdasher; and Bill Pulaski, the fun-loving mayor. All would understand my belief that we need to be hiring different kinds of people to teach us, people who've proven themselves at life by bearing its pain like free spirits. *Nobody should be allowed to teach until they get to be 40.* No one who hasn't known grief, challenge, success, failure, or sadness should be allowed anywhere near kids.

We ought to be asking men and women who've raised families to teach, older men and women who know the way things are and why. Millions of retired people would make fine teachers; college degrees aren't a good way to hire anybody to do anything. Getting to teach should be a reward for proving over a long stretch of time that you understand and have command of your mind and heart.

And you should have to live near the school you teach at. I had some eccentric teachers in Monongahela, but not a single one didn't live close to me as a neighbor. All existed as characters with a history profiled in a hundred informal mental libraries, like the library of her neighbors my grandmother kept.

Shooting Birds

On the way up Third Street hill to Waverly school each morning to discover what song Miss Wible was going to have kids memorize that day, I would pass a shack made of age-blackened hemlock, the kind you see on old barns long gone in disrepair. This shack perched at the edge of an otherwise empty double lot grown wild in burdock, wild hollyhock, and briar. I knew the old woman who lived there as Moll Miner because boys tormented her by shouting that name as they passed in the daily processional headed for school. I never actually saw her until one Saturday morning when, for want of anything better to do, I went to shoot birds.

I had a Red Ryder BB rifle, Moll Miner's lot had birds, and so lying on my belly as if birds were wild Indians, I shot one. As it flopped around dying, the old woman ran shrieking from her shack to the fallen bird, raised it to her bosom and she fled shouting, "I know who you are. You're the printer's boy. Why did you kill it? What harm did it do to you?" Then overcome with sobs she disappeared into her shack.

Her wild white hair and old cotton housedress, light grey with faded pink roses, lingered in my vision after I went home. Who could answer such a question at eight or at 28? But being asked made me ask it of myself. I killed because I wanted to. I killed for fun. Who cared about birds? There were plenty of birds. But then, what did it mean, this crazy old lady taking the downed bird into her home? She said she knew me; how was that possible? It was all very puzzling. I found myself hoping the BB hadn't really killed the bird but only shocked it. I felt stupid and tried to put the incident out of my mind. A week or so later I got rid of my BB gun, trading it for an entrenching tool and some marbles. I told myself I was tired of it; it wasn't a real gun anyway. Around Halloween some kids were planning a prank on the old lady. I protested, saying we should pick on someone who could fight back and chase us. "We shouldn't pick on weak people," I said. "Anyway that lady's not crazy, she's very kind."

That winter, without asking, I shoveled the snow around her house. It was a business I usually did for pocket money, and I was good at it, but I didn't even ask permission. I just shoveled the sidewalk without asking for money. She watched me from her window without saying a word. Whether she recognized I was the boy who shot the bird, I wish I could tell you, but that's all there is. Not a sparrow falls, they say. That was the way I learned to care about moral values in Monongahela—by rubbing shoulders with men and women who cared about things other than what money bought, although they cared about money, too. I watched them. They talked to me. Have you noticed nobody talks to children in schools? I mean *nobody*. All verbal exchanges in school are instrumental. Person-to-person stuff is contrary to policy. That's why popular teachers are disliked and fired. They *talk* to kids. It's unacceptable.

On Punishment

There was a time when hamburger pretty much described Alpha and Omega in my limited food sensibility. My grandparents didn't much care, and in the realm of monitored eating, Bootie was a pushover, but not the new girl on Second Street, Bud's wife,—brought home from Cincinnati after WWII. Well I remember the evening Helen prepared Chinese food, hardly a daring thing anywhere now, but in those long gone days around Pittsburgh, radical cuisine. I shut my nine-year-old mouth and flatly refused to eat it.

"You will eat it," said Helen, "if you have to sit there all night." She was right. At midnight I did eat it. By then it tasted awful. But soon after the indignity, I discovered that miraculously I had developed a universal palate. I could eat and enjoy anything.

At ten and eleven, I still made occasional assaults on sister's sexual dignity. She was older, bigger, and stronger than me so there was little chance my vague tropisms could have caused any harm, but even that slight chance ended one afternoon, when on hearing one of these overtures, Pappy grabbed me abruptly behind the neck and back of a shoulder and proceeded to kick me like a football, painful step by painful step, up the staircase to our apartment.

On theft: having discovered where the printing office stock of petty cash was kept, I acquired a dollar without asking. How Pap knew it was me I never found out, but when he burst through the apartment calling my name in an angry bellow, I knew I had been nailed and fled to the bathroom, the only door inside the apartment with a lock. Ignoring his demands to come out, with the greatest relief I heard his footsteps grow faint and the front door slam. But no sooner had I relaxed than he was back, this time with a house-wrecking bar. He pried the bathroom door off, hinge by hinge. I still remember the ripping sound it made. But nothing else.

Almost every classroom in my junior high school and my high school had a wooden paddle hung prominently over the classroom door, nor were these merely decorative. I was personally struck about a dozen times in my school career; it always hurt. But it's also fair to say that unlike the assaults on my spirit I endured from time to time for bearing an Italian name at Cornell, none of these physical assaults caused any resentment to linger—in each instance, I deserved some sort of retribution for one malicious barbarism or another. I forgot the blows soon after they were administered. On the other hand, I harbor a significant amount of ill feeling for those teachers who humiliated me verbally; those I have no difficulty recalling.

It might seem from examples I've given that I believe some simple relation between pain and self-improvement exists. But it isn't simple—with the single exception of a teenage boy whose pleasure came from terrifying girls, I never struck a single kid in three decades in the classroom. What I'm really trying to call your attention to is that simplistic codebook of rules passed down to us from academic psychology and enshrined as sacred text. Punishment played an important and positive role in shaping me. It has in the shaping of everyone I've known as a friend. Punishment has also ruined its share of victims, I know. The difference may reside in whether it arises from legitimate human grievances or from the bloodless discipline of a bureaucracy. It's a question nobody should regard as closed.

Separations

For the first three years of my life I lived in Monongahela; then we moved to a tiny brick house in Swissvale, an urban village despite its bucolic name, a gritty part of industrial Pittsburgh.

We lived near Union Switch and Signal Corporation, a favorite goal of exploratory probes among the street urchins on Calumet to which I quickly pledged my loyalty.

On rainy days I would stand on the porch watching raindrops. It was next best to my lost river, I suppose. Sometimes on the porch of the next house, two enchanting little girls, Marilyn and Beverly, played. Because our porch was somewhat higher than theirs I could watch them unobserved (at least they pretended not to see me). Thus it was that I fell in love.

Marilyn was a year older than me, already in first grade. Even in 1939 that placed her impossibly beyond me in every regard. Still, as my next door neighbor, she spoke to me from time to time in that friendly but distant fashion grand ladies adopt with gardeners and chauffeurs. You would have to see how humble both our homes were to realize the peculiarity of my analogy.

Beverly, her sister, was a year younger. By the invisible code of the young in well-schooled areas she might well not have existed. Her presence on the social periphery merited the same attention you might give a barking puppy, but at the age of four I found myself helplessly in love with her older sister in the pure fashion the spiritual side of nature reserves as a sign, I think, that materiality isn't the whole or even the most important part.

The next year, when I matriculated at McElvy elementary, first graders and second were kept rigidly separated from each other even on the playground. The first heartbreak of my life, and the most profound, was the blinding epiphany I experienced as I hung on the heavy wire fence separating the first grade compound from the combined second/third grade play area. From the metal mesh I peered through astigmatically, I could see Marilyn laughing and playing with strange older boys, oblivious to my yearning. Each sound she made tore at my insides. The sobs I choked back were as deep at five as ever again I felt in grief, their traces etched in my mind six decades later.

So this was what being a year younger had to mean? My sister was two years older and she hardly ever spoke to me. Why should Marilyn? I slunk around to avoid being near her ever again after that horrible sight seared my little soul. I mention this epiphany of age-grading because of the striking contradiction to it Monongahela posed presenting a universe where all ages commingled, cross-fertilizing each other in a dynamic fashion I suddenly recognized one day was very like the colonial world described by Benjamin Franklin in his *Autobiography*.

Swissvale taught me also that mother and father were at war with each other—a sorry lesson to learn at five. That the battles were over differences of culture which have no rational solution I couldn't know. Each couple who tries to merge strong traditions as my parents did, must accept the challenge as vast, one not to be undertaken lightly or quit on easily. The voices of timeless generations are permanently merged in offspring; marriage is a legal fiction, but marriage in one's children is not. There is no way to divorce inside the kid's cells. When parents war on each other, they set the child to warring against himself, a contest which can never be won. It places an implacable enemy deep inside which can't be killed or exorcised, and from whose revenge there is no escape.

I thank God my parents chose the middle road, the endless dialectic. Dad, the liberal thinker (even though his party affiliation was Republican and his attitude conservative) always willing to concede the opposition some points; Mom, the arch conservative even though her voice was always liberal Democrats, full of prickly principles she was prepared to fight for, like Beau Geste, to the bitter end.

For all the hardly bearable stresses this endless combat generated, their choice to fight it out for 50 years saved me from even harsher grief. I love them both for struggling so hard without quitting. I know it was better for sister and me that way; it gave us a chance to understand both sides of our own nature, to make some accurate guesses about the gifts we possessed. It prepared us to be comfortable with ourselves. I think *they* were better for the 50-year war, too. Better than each would have been alone.

I remember FDR on the radio in our postage-stamp living room announcing Pearl Harbor, eight days before my sixth birthday. I remember the uneasy feeling I harbored for a long time at war reports from the Far East playing out of the old Philco, I thought the Japanese would cut off my hands because the war news said that's what Japs did to prisoners.

The high point of the Swissvale years for me wasn't the war or the phenomenal array of wax lips, sugar dot licorice, Fleers Dubble Bubble, and other penny candies which seemed to vanish all at once just a short time after the war ended, like dinosaurs. It wasn't leaping from a high wall with a Green Hornet cape streaming behind as I fell like a stone, scarring my knees for eternity. It wasn't even Marilyn herself. The hinge in all my years, separating what went before from all that followed, was the night sister and I awakened to the shrieking contralto of Mother's voice and the quieter second tenor of Father's, intermingling in the downstairs entrance hall.

I remember crawling to the upstairs landing bathed in shadows to find sister already there. The next five minutes was the closest we ever came to each other emotionally, the most important experience we ever shared. Bootie was threatening to leave Andy if something important wasn't done. She was so upset that efforts to calm her down (so the neighbors wouldn't hear) only fanned the flames higher. With the hindsight of better than a half century, I'm able to conclude now that they were arguing over an abortion for what would have been her third child, my never-to-be brother or sister.

Mother was tired of being poor and didn't want to be any poorer. She was tired of constant work when she had grown up with servants. She was overwhelmed by the unfairness of being confined with children, day in, day out, when her husband drove off to the outside world in a suit and tie, often to be gone for days at a time, living in hotels, seeing exciting things. She would have implied (because I was to hear the insinuation many times in their marriage) that he was living the life of Riley while she slaved.

Bootie wanted an abortion, and the angry words that went back and forth discussing what was then a crime wafted up the stairwell to where two little children sat huddled in uncomprehending disbelief. It was the end of our childhood. I was seven, Joan was nine. Finally Mother shouted, "I'm leaving!" and ran out the front door, slamming it so hard it made my ears hurt and the glass ring. "If that's the way you want it, I'm locking the door," my father said with a trace of humor in his voice, trying to defuse mother's anger, I think.

A few seconds of silence, then a pounding and pounding upon the locked door commenced. "Open the door! Open the door! Open the door or I'll break it down!" An instant later her fist and entire arm smashed through the glass panes in the front door. I saw bright arterial blood flying everywhere and bathing that disembodied hand and arm. I would rather be dead than see such a sight again. Indeed as I write I see Mother's bleeding arm in front of my eyes.

Do such things happen to nice people? Of course, and much more often than we acknowledge in our sanitized, wildly unrealistic human relations courses. It was the end of the world. Without waiting to see the next development, I ran back to bed and pulled the pillow tightly over my ears. If I had known what was coming next, I would have hid in the cellar and prayed.

A week later, Swissvale was gone for good. Just like that, without any warning, like the blinking light of fireflies in our long, narrow, weed-overgrown backyard, stopped abruptly on a secret firefly signal, on a secret tragic signal—Marilyn and Tinker, penny candy, McKelvy school and contact with my Italian relatives stopped for the next six years. With those familiar things gone, my parents went too. I never allowed myself to have parents again. Without any goodbyes they shipped us off to Catholic boarding school in the mountains near Latrobe, placed us in the hands of Ursaline nuns who accepted the old road to wisdom and maturity, a road reached through pain long and strong.

There was no explanation, none at least that I could understand for this catastrophe. In my fiftieth year Mother told me offhandedly in an unguarded moment about the abortion. She wasn't apologetic, only in a rare mood of candor glad to be unburdened of this weight on her spirit at last. "I couldn't take another child," she said. We stopped for a hamburger and the subject changed, but I knew a part of the mystery of my own spirit had been unlocked.

The contrast presented to my former life was stark and harsh. I had never made a bed in my life. Now I was forced to make one every morning, and the made bed was inspected! Used to the privacy of my own room, now I slept in a dormitory with fifteen other boys, some of whom would cry far into the night, every night. Sometimes I cried with them. Shortly after arrival, I was assigned a part in an assembly about roasting in Hell, complete with stage sets where we dressed up like flames. As the sinner unrepentant was tormented by devils, I jumped up and down to make it hot for the reprobate. I can hear my own reedy falsetto squeezing out these parentless verses:

Know ye not the burning anguish,
Of thee-eese souls, they-er heart's dee-zire?

I don't want to beat up on the sisters as if I were Fellini in *Juliet of the Spirits*. This was all kosher according to their lights, and it made a certain amount of sense to me, too. By that point in time, although nominally Roman Catholic, I probably hadn't been to church more than ten times counting Baptism and First Communion. Just walking around, though, is enough to make a kid conscious of good and evil, conscious, too, of the arbitrary nature of human justice. Even a little boy sees rottenness rewarded and good people smacked down. Unctuous rationalizations of this by otherwise sensible adults disgust little children. The sisters had a story that gave satisfying human sense to these matters. For all the things I hated about Xavier, I actually *liked* being a flame and many other aspects of the religious narrative. They felt right somehow in a way the dead universe of Newton, Darwin, or Marx never did.

I carried the status of exile around morning, noon, and night, the question never out of mind—what had I done to be sent here? Only a small part of me actually showed up in class or playground or dining hall each day, the rest of my being taking up residence in the lost Oz of Monongahela, even though Swissvale should have logically been the more proximate yearning since it was there we lived when I was sent away.

Joan was there, too, but we were in separate dormitories. In the year we spent at Xavier I can't remember holding a single conversation with my sister. Like soldiers whose unit has broken apart in dangerous terrain, we struggled alone looking for some personal way out of the homelessness. It couldn't have helped that sister was two years older than I. By that time she had been carefully indoctrinated, as I had been, that every age hangs separately. Sticks to its own class. You see how the trick is done?

At Xavier Academy, scarcely a week passed without a beating. I was publicly whipped for wetting the bed, whipped for mispronouncing French verbs, whipped for hiding beets inside my apple pie (hated beets, but the house rule was vegetables had to be eaten, dessert did not). Some telltale beet corner where a brown apple should have been must have given me away to a sharp-eyed stoolie—the kapo who bussed away dessert. I was nabbed at exactly the moment dining hall loudspeakers blared the wartime hit, "Coming in on a wing and a prayer. With one motor gone we can still carry on, coming in on a wing and a prayer." Most dramatic of all the beatings I endured, however, was the one following my apprehension by the Latrobe police.

The spirit that entered mother when she broke glass must have revived in me to set the stage for that whipping. One night after bed check, I set out to get home to my river. I felt sure my grandparents wouldn't turn me away. The break had been planned for weeks, nobody taken into my confidence. I had a dozen bags of salted peanuts from the commissary, a thin wool blanket and a pillow, and the leather football Uncle Bud gave me when he went away to war.

Most of the first night I walked, hiding in the tall grass away from the road all the next day eating peanuts. I had gotten away full of determination. I would make it home, I knew, if I could only figure out what direction Monongahela was in! But by mid-afternoon the following day, I made a fatal mistake. Tired of walking and hiding, I decided to hitch a ride as I had once seen Clark Gable do in a famous movie with Claudette Colbert. I was picked up by two matronly ladies whom I regaled deceitfully with a story of my falling out of the back of granddad's pickup truck where dog Nappy and I had been riding on the way back to Mon City. "He didn't notice I was gone and he probably thinks I jumped out when we got home and went to play."

I hadn't calculated the fatal football. As a precaution against theft (so they said) the Ursalines stamped "St. Xavier" many times on every possession. My football hadn't escaped the accusatory stencil. As we chatted like old comrades about how wonderful it was to be going to Monongahela, a town out of legend we all agreed, the nice ladies took me directly to the Latrobe police, who took me directly—heedless of my hot tears and promises to even let them have my football—back to the ladies in black.

The whole school assembled to see my disgrace. Boys and girls arranged in a long gauntlet through which I was forced on hands and knees to crawl the length of the administration building to where Mother Superior stood exhorting the throng to avoid my sorry example. When I arrived she slapped my face. I suppose my sister must have been there watching, too. Sister and I never discussed Xavier, not once, then or afterwards.

The intellectual program at Xavier, influenced heavily by a Jesuit college nearby, constituted a massive refutation of the watery brain diet of government schooling. I learned so much in a single year I was nearly in high school before I had to think very hard about any particular idea or procedure presented in public school. I learned how to separate pertinent stuff from dross, I learned what the difference between primary and secondary data was, and the significance of each, I learned how to evaluate separate witnesses of an event; I learned how to reach conclusions a half-dozen ways and what distortions the different dynamics of these methods threatened. I don't mean to imply at all that I became a professional thinker. I remained very much a seven and eight-year-old boy. But I moved far enough in that year to become comfortable with matters of mind and intellect.

Unlike the harsh treatment of our bodies at Xavier, even the worst boy there was assumed to have dignity, free will, and a power to choose right over wrong. Materialistic schooling, which is all public schooling, even at its best can ever hope to be, operates as if personality changes are ultimately caused externally, by applications of theory and by a skillful balancing of rewards and punishments. The idea that individuals have free will which supersedes any social programming is anathema to the very concept of forced schooling.[1] Was the Xavier year valuable or damaging? If the Ursalines and Jesuits hadn't forced me to see the gulf between intelligence and intellect, between thinking and disciplined thinking, who *would* have taken that responsibility?

The greatest intellectual event of my life occurred early in third grade before I was yanked out of Xavier and deposited back in Monongahela. From time to time a Jesuit brother from St. Vincent's College would cross the road to give a class at Xavier. The coming of a Jesuit to Xavier was always considered a big-time event even though there was constant tension between the Ursaline ladies and the Jesuit men. One lesson I received at the visiting brother's hands[2] altered my consciousness forever. By contemporary standards, the class might seem impossibly advanced in concept for third grade, but if you keep in mind the global war claiming major attention at the moment, then the fact that Brother Michael came to discuss causes of WWI as a prelude to its continuation in WWII is not so far-fetched.[3] After a brief lecture on each combatant and its cultural and historical characteristics, an outline of incitements to conflict was chalked on the board.

"Who will volunteer to face the back of the room and tell us the causes of World War One?"

"I will, Brother Michael," I said. And I did.

"Why did you say what you did?"

---

[1] In her bestseller of the 1990s, *It Takes a Village*, Hillary Clinton expressed puzzlement that Western conservative thought emphasizes *innate* qualities of individual children in contrast to Oriental concepts which stress the efficacy of correct *procedure*. There are a number of paths which led to this vital difference between West and East, but Western spiritual tradition, which insists that salvation is a personal matter and that personal responsibility must be accepted is the most important influence by far. See the Chapter, "Absolute Absolution."

[2] Traditions of intellectual refinement have long been associated with Jesuit orders. Jesuits were schoolmasters to the elites of Europe well before "school" was a common notion. Not long ago it was discovered that the rules of conduct George Washington carried with him were actually an English translation of a Jesuit manual, *Decency Among the Conversations of Men*, compiled by French Jesuits in 1595.

[3] It's almost impossible these days to chart the enormous gulf between schooling of the past, and that of the present, in intellectual terms, but a good way to get a quick measure of what might be missing is to read two autobiographies: the first that of John Stuart Mill covering a nineteenth century home education of a philosopher, the second by Norbert Wiener, father of cybernetics, dealing with the home education of a scientist. When you read what an eight-year-old's mind is capable of you will find my account pretty weak tea.

"Because that's what you wrote."

"Do you accept my explanation as correct?"

"Yes, sir." I expected a compliment would soon follow, as it did with our regular teacher.

"Then you must be a fool, Mr. Gatto. I lied to you. Those are not the causes at all." It was like being flattened by a steamroller. I had the sensation of being struck and losing the power of speech. Nothing remotely similar had ever happened to me.

"Listen carefully, Mr. Gatto, and I shall show you the true causes of the war which men of bad character try to hide," and so saying he rapidly erased the board and in swift fashion another list of reasons appeared. As each was written, a short, clear explanation followed in a scholarly tone of voice.

"Now do you see, Mr. Gatto, why you must be careful when you accept the explanation of another? Don't these new reasons make much more sense?"

"Yes, sir."

"And could you now face the back of the room and repeat what you just learned?"

"I could, sir." And I knew I could because I had a strong memory, but he never gave me that chance.

"Why are you so gullible? Why do you believe my lies? Is it because I wear clothing you associate with men of God? I despair you are so easy to fool. What will happen to you if you let others do your thinking for you?"

You see, like a great magician he had shifted that commonplace school lesson we would have forgotten by the next morning into a formidable challenge to the entire contents of our private minds, raising the important question, "Who can we believe?" At eight, while public school children were reading stories about talking animals, we had been escorted to the eggshell-thin foundation upon which authoritarian vanity rests and asked to inspect it.

There are many reasons to lie to children, the Jesuit said, and these seem good reasons to older men. Some truth you will know by divine intuition, he told us, but for the rest you must learn what tests to apply. Even then you should be cautious because it is not hard to fool even these tests.

Later I told the nun in charge of my dorm what had happened because my head was swimming and I needed a second opinion from someone older. "Jesuits!" she snapped, shaking her head, but would say no more.

Now that Xavier is reduced to a historical marker on Route 30 near Latrobe, I go back to it in imagination trying to determine how much of the panic I felt there was caused by the school itself, how much by the chemical fallout from my parents' troubled marriage, how much from the aftershock of exile. In wrestling with this, one thing comes clear: those nuns were the only people who ever tried to make me think seriously about questions of religion. Had it not been for Xavier, I might have passed my years as a kind of freethinker by default, vaguely aware an overwhelming percentage of the entire human race did and said things about a God I couldn't fathom. How can I reconcile that the worst year of my life left behind a dimension I should certainly have been poorer to have missed?

One day it was over. The night before it happened, Mother Superior told me to pack; I would be leaving the next morning. Strong, silent, unsentimental Pappy showed up the next day, threw my bag into the car, and drove me back to Monongahela. It was over, just like that.

Back home I went as if I'd never left. Mother was waiting, friendly and smiling as I had last seen her. We were installed, the three of us, in a double bed in a back room over the printing office.

Our room was reached through the kitchen and had another door opening onto an angled tarpaper roof from which on clear nights the stars could be seen, the green river scented. It was the happiest day of my life.

Where father was, nobody ever told me, and I never asked. This indifference wasn't entirely generated by anger but from a distinct sense that time was rapidly passing while I was still ignorant of important lessons I had to learn.

Principles

Five days a week the town turned its children out in the morning to march up the hill to Waverly or down to the end of town to high school. There was no school bus. Waverly was frozen midway between the one-room schoolhouse tradition of transferring responsibility to children—we fought to fill the inkwells, clean the pen nibs, sweep the floor, serve in the lunchroom, clean the erasers, help out our slower classmates in arithmetic and reading—and the specialized procedures and curriculum of the slowly dawning corporate age of schooling. While this latter style had been sold as more "socially efficient" ever since 1905, the realities of town life were such that nothing passed muster at Waverly which didn't first past muster with parents and the elders of the town.

School was something you took like medicine. You did it because your mother had done it and your grandmother. It was supposed to be good for you. Nobody believed it was decisively so. Looking back, I might agree this daily exercise with neighbors suddenly transformed into grammarians, historians, and mathematicians might well have been, as Mother said, "good for me." One thing is certain, these part-time specialists cared a great deal about mother's opinion of what they were doing, just as she cared about theirs in regard to her parenting.

The schoolteachers I remember are few but bear noting: Peg Hill who spoke to me exactly the way she did to the principal and won my heart for treating me as a peer; Miss Wible who taught me to sing and memorize song lyrics so ferociously my vocabulary of words and dramatic situations increased geometrically (even if we did whisper to each other that she was reading "love books" at her desk as we copied the day's words); old Miss McCullough who played "American Patrol" every single day for an entire school year on a *hand-cranked* phonograph: "You must be vigilant, you must be diligent, American Patrol!" Her expressionless face and brutally stark manner stifled any inclination to satire. If we have to have schoolteachers, let some be this kind.

At Waverly I learned about principle when Miss Hill read from Gibbon's *Decline and Fall of the Roman Empire*. She read of the courageous death of Blandina the slave, a teenage convert to Christianity who was offered her life to repudiate her faith and a cruel death if she refused. She refused. I learned that all the management savvy of the most powerful empire of history couldn't overwhelm the principles of a teenage slave.

Principles were a daily part of every study at Waverly. In latter days, schools replaced principles with an advanced form of pragmatism called "situational ethics" where principles were shown to be variable according to the demands of the moment. During the 1970s, forcing this study on children became an important part of the school religion. People with flexible principles reserve the right to betray their covenants. It's that simple. The misery of modern life can be graphed in the rising incidence of people who exercise the right to betray each other, whether business associates, friends, or even family. Pragmatists like to keep their options open. When you live by principles, whatever semantic ambiguity they involve you in, there are clear boundaries to what you will allow, even when nobody is watching.

Frances "Bootie" Zimmer was born on Halloween in 1911 at Monongahela General Hospital three years before the country had an income tax or a Federal Reserve Bank, in the first flush moments of scientific pedagogy practically realized. She was five years younger than dad, two inches taller, born in a country on the gold standard where common citizens carried precious metal in their pockets as money.

She was three when WWI began, six when the Gary Plan riots struck New York City schools. In the postwar years, her father, son of a German immigrant from the Palatinate, became prosperous by working around the clock as a print shop proprietor and sometimes investor in movies, carnivals, newspapers and real estate. His grandchildren are still in the printing business in Bethel Park near Pittsburgh 100 years later.

Bootie graduated from Monongahela High, where she was a cheerleader, in 1929 a few months before the market crash. Besides losing money, some other great catastrophe must have happened to the Zimmers then, but I've only been able to unearth a few shards of its nature. Whatever its full dimension, it included the sudden eviction of grandmother Moss from her home, the incarceration of great grandfather Frederick in an old-age institution far away, the flight of great grandmother Isabelle to Detroit at the age of 79, at a time when Detroit and the moon were equally distant, and the severing of ties between granddad and his brothers to the extent that though they lived cheek to jowl with us in the tiny city, I was neither aware of their existence nor did they once say hello. Ach!

In the great breakup, Bud ran to Chicago without a penny and without graduating from high school; mother, too, ran off in dramatic fashion, telling her best friend as she boarded a train for Pittsburgh that she would wave a handkerchief at the window if she intended to return. She didn't wave. And though she did return, she hid ever after, never speaking to any of her childhood friends again. I discovered all this when I advertised in the local paper after Bootie's death, asking to speak to anyone who had known her as a girl.

Mother was bone-thin with large blue eyes and hair gone white at 30, just as my own did. She lived on a razor's edge between a need to avoid shame and an almost equally desperate need to find a way to express her considerable talents, a goal conventional assessment would say eluded her forever. Yet everything she turned her hand to was marked by electrifying energy. Our Christmas trees were an art form. Our home was cleaner and neater than a hospital operating room. Beauty and good taste flowed out of her fingertips. But the shame, which she would rather have died than acknowledge, always defeated her in the end and made her melancholy when she thought no one was looking.

I think mother tried to force her fierce spirit into dad and live through him. When that failed, she pinned her hopes on me. This, I think, caused the original breach in the marriage. Compared to the driven Germans she knew best, dad must have provided a lifelong frustration. And though we never went hungry or lacked a roof, the absence of extra money represented decisive evidence to her of damnation, permanent exile from the fairyland of her youth.

And yet the exquisite irony bedevils me like a fury—never have I met anyone able to make such magic out of nothing. When, to her great surprise, she came into a considerable amount of money after father's death, like Midas' wish, it offered her nothing she really needed. Nor was she able to spend any of it to buy her heart's desire, an avenue for her talent and some dignity.

In 1932 Francis Zimmer went off alone on her frightening adventure, marrying into a magnificent Italian family which had pulled itself out of the immigrant stew while the patriarch was alive, only to plummet back into the soup after his death. She married all alone, without a father or mother there to give her away.

Giovanni Gatto, my grandfather, had been an enlightened *publicista* in Italy, an unheard of *Presbyterian* Italian who swept a contessa off her feet in Calabria in the elopement which resulted in her disinheritance. Together Giovanni and Lucrezia came to America with their young children and set up house in Pittsburgh.

Giovanni is another family ghost I worked to discover. After a short time in this country, he was hired (personally) by Andrew Mellon to be manager of the Foreign Exchange Department of Mellon Bank. He was a man for whom restaurants kept a personalized champagne bucket, a man who commissioned stone sculptures for his garden. Grandfather Gatto was also leader of the Freemasons of Pittsburgh, the Grand Venerable. An old news clipping I have reported his death in 35 column inches with three headlines and a dignified picture. The obituary called him "leader of the Italian colony of Pittsburgh," continuing, "fifty-eight cars, each carrying eight persons, were required to convey friends of the deceased to the cemetery and back home again."

His death produced a shock for the living. No assets survived Giovanni. Only a hasty sale of the home for much less than its value kept the family out of immediate poverty. The children scrambled to find a toehold in the working world and by a stoic acceptance of reduced circumstances managed to keep the family together and to support Lucrezia, who spoke little English. It was a pulling together the Zimmers had not been able to manage.

Ten years later, mother was drawn into this family orbit, she holding tight to her secrets, dad doing the same with his own. What the merger should have conferred on Joan and I was a striking band of distinctive individuals: big-hearted Laura, elegant Josephine, witty caustic Virginia, crotchety Achilles, (renamed Kelly), the humanist Nick, a genuine world-class intellect in Frank, the contessa Lucrezia. But instead our private hurts kept us separated as surely as the same force divided my sister and I.

Mother found subtle ways to discourage fraternization with the sociable Gattos, dad eventually taking the hint. Until I was fully grown and well into mid-life, the Gattos were a palimpsest for me; what cousins that family held, I was strictly partitioned from. When occasionally I was taken to visit Frank or Laura or Josephine, or all together, we were formal with each other, in Old World style. Each extended courtesy to me, complete with those little flourishes of etiquette which give significance to the best encounters of children with grownups—a quality once common and now rare which I transferred naturally into my schoolteaching.

Walking Around Monongahela

We're back in Monongahela now, a town of strong principles even if some are wacky or plain wrong. Pragmatism is a secondary theme here, scorned by most unless it keeps to its place, a bittersweet oddity because practicality is the town's lingua franca. The phenomenon of open scorn for the lower orders isn't seen in my Valley, never to the degree I experienced it later in Ithaca, Cambridge, and Manhattan. The oppressed are insufficiently docile in Monongahela to revile openly. So the Pinkerton detectives found out when they went to do Andrew Carnegie's dirty work at Homestead during the steel strike of 1893. There is only one restaurant in the town proper, "Peters." It's a place where the country club set drinks coffee alongside rubber jockeys from the tire vulcanizing shop across the street.

Several nights a week, long after dark when house lights were blazing, Mother would gather sister and me for long quiet walks up Second Street hill to the very top, then along the streets on the ridge line paralleling the river. From these and the morning walks on River Hill I learned to listen to my senses and see that town as a creature in itself instead of a background for my activity.

We would walk this way for hours, whispering to each other, looking in windows, and as we walked, Bootie would deliver an only partially intelligible stream of biographical lore about the families within; I realize now that she must have been talking to herself. It was like having a private Boswell to the Dr. Johnson of town society. When she had some money, which was now and then, we would buy candy at the little grocery at the top of the hill and share it together, sometimes two candy bars for the three of us or in flush times a whole bar each—and in the weeks following Christmas when there was holiday money, two each. On two-candy nights the atmosphere seemed so filled with chocolate perfume I could hardly sleep.

When my grandad was a boy in Monongahela he watched John Blythe, a planing mill operator, rebuild large sections of the town in the Italianate style. Blythe had no degree, and the religion of professional licensing was still in infancy, so he just did it without asking anyone's permission. Whole sections of the town are now handsome beyond any reasonable right to be because nobody stopped him. If you see a keystone over a window molding that's likely to be one of John's.

When my grandad was a boy in Monongahela he used to sit in Mounds Park, site of two ancient burial mounds left there by the Adena people three thousand years ago. In 1886, the Smithsonian robbed those graves and took the contents to Washington where they still sit in crates. The government built a baseball field where the mounds had been to compensate the town. When my grandad was a boy, school was voluntary. Some went, but most not for long; it was a free will choice based on what you valued, not a government hustle to stabilize social classes.

The College Of Zimmer And Hegel

The most important study I ever had wasn't at Cornell or Columbia, but in the windowless basement of the Zimmer Printing Company, a block and a half from the railroad tracks which paralleled the mysterious dark green river with its thick ice sheet near the banks in winter, its iridescent dragonflies in summer, and its always breathtaking sternwheelers pounding the river UP AND DOWN, BAM! BAM! BAM! going to places unknown on a river without beginning or end for me.

Before he went to Germany to beat up the Nazis, my warrior Uncle Bud worked on a riverboat that went down the Mississippi to New Orleans, on what mission I can't say, then on other boats that went up and down smaller local rivers. When I was five, he once threw an orange to me from a riverboat galley while it passed through a lock. A right fielder's strong throwing arm sent that orange 200 feet out of the watery trench straight into my hands, I didn't even have to move.

In the basement of the printing office, Bud's father ("the General" as Moss called him behind his back) moved strong hands in and out of a printing press. Those presses are gone, but my grandfather's hands will never be gone; they remain on my shoulder as I write this. I would sit on the steps into his subterranean world, watching closely hour after hour as those rough hands fed sheets of paper into the steam-driven clamshell press. It went BAM! (feed) BAM! (feed) BAM! (feed) like the riverboats and bit by bit the job piled up on the table next to the press.

It was a classroom without bells or tests. I never got bored, never got out of line. In school I was thrown out of class frequently for troublemaking, but Pappy wouldn't stand for nonsense. Not a scrap of it. He was all purpose. I never saw a man concentrate as he did, as long as it took, whatever was called for. I transferred that model unconsciously to my teaching. While my colleagues were ruled by start-up times, bell schedules, lunch hour, loud-speaker announcements, and dismissal, I was oblivious to those. I was ruled by the job to be done, kid by kid, until it was over, whatever that meant, kid by kid.

No baseball or football, no fishing, no shopping, no romantic adventure could possibly match the fascination I felt watching that tough old man in his tough old town work his hand-fed press in a naked light bulb lit cellar without any supervisor to tell him what to do or how to feel about it. He knew how to design, to do layout, set type, buy paper, ink presses and repair them, clean up, negotiate with customers, price jobs, and keep the whole ensemble interacting. How did he learn this without school?

He worked as naturally as he breathed, a perfect hero to me—I wonder if he understood that. On some secret level it was Pappy who held our family together, regardless of his position as pariah to his wife and his estranged brothers, regardless of an ambivalent relationship of few words with his daughter and son, granddaughter and grandson, and with his remaining brother, Will, the one who still spoke to him and worked alongside him at the presses. I say "spoke" when the best I can personally attest to is only association. They worked side by side but I never actually heard a single conversation between them. Will never entered our apartment above the shop. He slept on the press table in the basement. Yet Pappy kept the family faith. He knew his duty. When Bud brought his elegant wife home from the war, she would sit in Pappy's room talking to him hour after hour, the two snorting and laughing thick as thieves. It was only his own bloodline he had lost the key of conversation with.

I realize today that if Pappy couldn't count on himself he was out of business and the rest of us in the poorhouse. If he didn't like himself he would have gone crazy alone with those heavy metal rhythms in the eternal gloom of the printing office basement. As I watched him he never said a word, didn't throw a glance in my direction. I had to supply my own incentive, welcome to stay or go, yet I sense he appreciated my presence. Perhaps he did understand how I loved him. Sometimes when the job was finished he would lecture me a little about politics I didn't understand.

In the craft tradition, printers are independent, even dangerous men. Ben Franklin was a printer like my German grandfather, himself preoccupied with things German at times. Movable type itself is German. Pappy was a serious student of the Prussian philosopher Hegel. I would hear Hegel's name in his conversations with Bud's wife, Helen. Late in his own life he began to speak to my father again. And sometimes even to me in my middle teens. I remember references to Hegel from those times, too.

Hegel was philosopher in residence at the University of Berlin during the years Prussia was committing itself to forced schooling. It's not farfetched to regard Hegel as the most influential thinker in modern history. Virtually everyone who made political footprints in the past two centuries, school people included, was Hegelian, or anti-Hegelian. Even today many knowledgeable people have no idea how important Hegel has been to deliberations of important men as they debated our common future.

Hegel was important wherever strict social control was an issue. Ambitious states couldn't let a single child escape, said Hegel. Hegel believed nothing happened by accident; he thought history was headed somewhere and that its direction could be controlled. "Men as gods" is Hegel's theme before H.G. Wells'. Hegel believed when battle cannon roared, it was God talking to himself, working out his own nature dialectically. It's a formidable concept. No wonder it appealed to men who didn't labor, yet disdained easeful luxury. It engaged a printer's attention, and a little boy's, too.

When I began to teach, I took the lessons of Monongahela and my two families to heart. The harder I struggled to understand myself, the better luck I had with other people's kids. A person has to know where his dead are buried and what his duty is before you can trust him. Whatever I had to teach children is locked up in the words you just read, as is the genesis of my critique of forced schooling.

My father at 34 (1940). As a young man he took out bank loans he didn't need in order to establish credit worthiness.

I AM 5 YEARS OLD HERE AT 7541 CALUMET STREET, SWISSVALE, PENNA. (1941) AND THIS IS MY FIRST GIRLFRIEND MARILYN WALLACE WHO I REMEMBER LOVING PURELY

PART FOUR

Metamorphosis

Ignorance was widespread and formal education did not flourish in the Chesapeake. This condition was not an accident. It was deliberately contrived by Virginia's elite, who positively feared learning among the general population.
— David Hackett Fischer, *Albion's Seed*

Poor people, abject people, dirty people, ill-fed, ill-clothed people poison us, morally and physically; they kill the happiness of society, they force us to do away with our own liberties and organize unnatural cruelties for fear they should rise against us and drag us down into the abyss.
— George Bernard Shaw, *Major Barbara*

CHAPTER ELEVEN

The Crunch

*The thesis I venture to submit to you is as follows: That during the
past forty or fifty years those who are responsible for education have
progressively removed from the curriculum of studies the Western
culture which produced the modern democratic state; That the schools
and colleges have, therefore, been sending out into the world men who
no longer understand the creative principle of the society in which they
must live; That deprived of their cultural tradition, the newly educated
Western men no longer possess in the form and substance of their own
minds and spirits and ideas, the premises, the rationale, the logic, the
method, the values of the deposited wisdom which are the genius of the
development of Western civilization; That the prevailing education is
destined, if it continues, to destroy Western civilization and is in fact
destroying it.*

*I realize quite well that this thesis constitutes a sweeping indictment
of modern education. But I believe the indictment is justified and
there is a prima facie case for entering this indictment.*
> — Walter Lippmann, speaking before the Association for
> the Advancement of Science, December 29, 1940

The Struggle For Homogeneity

In 1882, an *Atlantic Monthly* writer predicted a coming struggle for preservation of the
American social order. European immigrants were polarizing the country, upsetting the
"homogeneity on which free government must rest." That idea of a necessary homogeneity made
it certain that all lanes out of the 1880s led to orthodoxy on a national scale. There was to be an
official American highway, its roadbed built from police manuals and schoolteacher training texts.

Citizens would now be *graded* against the official standard, up to the highest mark, "100 percent American."

In the 30 years between 1890 and 1920, the original idea of America as a cosmopolitan association of peoples, each with its own integrity, disintegrated to be replaced by urgent calls for national unity. Even before WWI added its own shrill hysterics to the national project of regimentation, new social agencies were in full cry on every front, aggressively taking the battle of Americanization to millions of bewildered immigrants and their children.

The elite-managed "birth-control" movement, which culminated 100 years later in legal abortion, became visible and active during this period, distributing millions of pieces of literature yearly aimed at controlling lower-class breeding instincts, an urgent priority in the national elite agenda. Malthus, Darwin, Galton, and Pearson became secular saints at the Lawrence and Sheffield Scientific Schools at Harvard and Yale. Judge Ben Lindsay of the Denver Children's Court, flogging easy access to pornography as an indirect form of sterilization for underclass men, was a different tile in the same mosaic, as was institutional adoption. The planned parenthood movement, in our day swollen to billion dollar corporate status, was one side of a coin whose obverse was the prospering abortion, birth control and adoption industries of mid to late twentieth century America. In those crucial years, a sudden host of licensing acts closed down employment in a wide range of lucrative work—rationing the right to practice trades much as kings and queens of England had done, distributing the work to favored groups and individuals willing to satisfy screening commissions that they met qualifications often unrelated to the actual work. Licensing suddenly became an important factor in economic life as it had been in royal England. Unseen hands supervised this professionalization movement which endowed favored colleges and institutes, text producers, testing agencies, clothing manufacturers, and other allies with virtual sinecures.

Professional schools—even for bus drivers and detectives—imposed the chastening discipline of elaborate formal procedures, expensive and time-consuming "training," on what had once been areas of relatively free-form career design. And medicine, law, architecture, engineering, pharmacology—the blue-ribbon work licenses—were suddenly rigorously monitored, rationed by political fortune. Immigrants were often excluded from meeting these qualification demands, many middle-class immigrants with a successful history of professional practice back in Europe were plunged into destitution, their families disintegrating under the artificial stresses. Others, like my own family, scrambled to abandon their home culture as far as possible in a go-along-with-the-crowd response to danger.

One of the hardest things for any present-day reader to grasp about this era was the brazenness of the regimentation. Scientific management was in its most enthusiastic public phase then, monumentally zealous, maddingly smug. The state lay under effective control of a relatively small number of powerful families freed by the Darwinian religion from ethical obligation to a democratic national agenda, or even to its familiar republican/libertarian antithesis. Yet those antagonists comprised the bedrock antinomies of our once revolutionary public order, and without the eternal argument they provoked there was no recognizable America.

Eugenics Arrives

Between 1890 and 1920, the percentage of our population adjudged "feebleminded" and condemned to institutional confinement more than doubled. The long-contemplated hygienic form of social control of eighteenth century German social thinker Johann Frank, "complete medical policing," was launched with a vengeance. Few intimidations are more effective than the threat of a stay in an insane asylum. Did the fraction of crazies really double in those three decades? The answer given by one contemporary was elliptically Darwinian: "Marriage of these inferiors is a veritable manufactory of degenerates." It could no longer go unchecked.

American Birth Control League[1] thinking as expressed by Yale psychologist Arnold L. Gesell, said, "*society need not wait for perfection of the infant science of eugenics before proceeding upon a course which will prevent renewal of defective protoplasm contaminating the stream of life.*" Gesell's *The Family and the Nation* (1909), a thorough product of the new zeitgeist, advocated "*eugenic violence*" in dealing with inferiors: "We must do as with the feebleminded, organize the extinction of the tribe." [Emphasis added]

Here was a far different promise of American life, a Connecticut Valley Yale-style pledge; yet governors of the Birth Control League were acclaimed heroes in every progressive assembly. With this thrust, old-line Calvinism converted its theological elements into scientific truth, supported mathematically by the new Galtonian discipline of statistics. Yale was the most important command center for the re-emergence of old-time Puritan religion, now thoroughly disguised behind the language of research methodology.

The eugenics movement begun by Galton in England was energetically spread to the United States by his followers. Besides destroying lesser breeds (as they were routinely called) by abortion, sterilization, adoption, celibacy, two-job family separations, low-wage rates to dull the zest for living, and, above all, schooling to dull the mind and debase the character, other methods were clinically discussed in journals including a childlessness which could be induced through easy availability of pornography.[2] Galtonians advocated the notion of breeding a super race.

Humanist Scott Nearing wrote his masterpiece, *The Super Race: An American Problem*, in 1912 just as the drive to destroy an academic curriculum in public schools was reaching its first crescendo. By "problem" Nearing wasn't indicating a moral dilemma, simply arguing that to solve the engineering challenge posed in creating supermen out of genetic raw stock, only America had the resources to take up the challenge.

Mr. Hitler Reads Mr. Ford

The problem of the moment during the first mass immigration period, 1848 to 1860, and also during the second, 1871 to 1914, was that the unique national experience creating a particular American culture was still too green, too historically recent to be able to tolerate the sophisticated competition pluralism brings. A cosmopolitan society like that of Roman England in the fifth century wasn't possible for America to accept without damages to the natural development, already underway.

---

[1] The early manifestation under Margaret Sanger's influence of the organization which later changed its name to Planned Parenthood.

[2] As mentioned previously, this was Judge Ben Lindsay's idea, Lindsay was the man often credited with perfecting Children's Court procedures, particularity its suspension of dependents' customary legal rights.

The possibility inherent in a bazaar society excited Americans, but like Horace Mann, it made them uneasy, too. Unsure of their own identity, how could they allow foreign ways to flow freely in and around their own? Under the masks of sophistication and civility there was only one realistic solution to human variability, the solution of the Order of the Star-Spangled Banner (popularly called "The Know Nothing Party"), "You must be as we are." Those who surrendered to such pressure, as many newcomers did, were ultimately worse off than those who insulated themselves in ghettos.[3]

Some pages back I referred to the brazenness of our new social arrangements, a sense of vulgar pushiness the student feels radiating from various temples of reform. In some crazy way the ornamentation of the period carries the flavor of its arrogance; it prepares us to understand the future—that time in which we now live, our own age where "home cooking" means commercially homogenized food *product* defrosted, where an entire nation sits down each evening to commercial entertainment, hears the same processed news, wears the same clothing, takes direction from the same green road signs, thinks the same pre-framed thoughts, and relegates its children and old people to the same scientific care of strangers in "nursing" homes and schools.

A signpost of the times: in 1920, the Henry Ford Publishing Company distributed two million copies of its recent best-seller to all libraries and all schools in the nation, free. The book: *The International Jew: World's Foremost Problem*. Adolf Hitler was still a poor war hero, living in Munich with Ernst Hanfstaengel, the half-American Harvard graduate whose mother was one of the legendary Sedgwicks. Hitler had Ford's book read to him by Hanfstaengel. In the pages of *Mein Kampf*, Ford is lavishly praised. Of Ford's other efforts to define the 100 percent American, at least one more deserves special mention. Speaking and writing English had very little to do with work on a Ford assembly line, but Ford decided to make English-language classes compulsory. The first thing foreign-speaking Ford employees learned to say: "I am a good American."

Ford students were graduated in a musical extravaganza that bears close attention as an indicator of the American spiritual climate after WWI. A huge black pot took up the middle of a stage, from which hung a large sign, "MELTING POT." From backstage an endless procession of costumed immigrants descended into the pot on a ladder reaching into its bowels. Each wore a sign identifying his former homeland. Simultaneously, from either side of the pot two other streams of men emerged converted into real Americans, dressed in identical clothing. Each waved a small American flag while a brass band played "America the Beautiful" *fortissimo*. Wives and children cheered wildly when cue cards were flashed.

It was nothing short of marvelous that world champion Jew-baiter Henry Ford, architect of the most opulent and sinister foundation of them all,[4] major player in the psychologization of

---

[3] This process of very slow assimilation into settled groups is a pattern everywhere, particularly noticeable in smaller communities where it may take two or three *generations* or even longer for a new family to be incorporated into the most intimate society. Ghettos often serve well as mediators of transition while the record of professional social agencies in this regard is disastrous.

[4] Many people I meet consider the Ford Foundation a model of enlightened corporate beneficence, and although Jesse Jackson's "Hymietown" remark ended his serious political prospects in America, Ford's much richer and more relentless scorn for those he considered mongrel races and religions, particularly the Jews, has long been forgiven and forgotten. On July 30, 1938, the Hitler government presented Henry Ford the Grand Cross of the German Eagle, the highest award possible to a foreigner.

American schooling, was a closet impresario in the bargain! Ford completed the circle: three great private fortunes which were to dominate early twentieth century public schooling—Carnegie's, Rockefeller's and Ford's—each with a stupendous megalomaniac in charge of the checkbook, each dedicating the power of great wealth not to conspicuous consumption but to radical experiments in changing human nature. The hardest lesson to master is that they weren't doing this for profit or fame—but out of a quality of conviction reserved only for true believers.

There was no room in America for the faint-hearted. If a man wanted to be 100 percent American, he had to reject his original homeland. Other Americanizing themes were heard, too, General Leonard Wood growled that the Prussian practice of "Universal Military Service" was the best means to make the unassimilated "understand they are American." By the time I graduated from high school in 1953, universal military training took me away to Kentucky and Texas, to become an American, I suppose. After government school, government army, and Anglican Columbia were through with me, I had lost the map to get back home.

All over the American Midwest, "Fitter Families Competitions" were held at state fairs and expositions, ranking American families by objective criteria, much as hogs or cattle are ranked. Winners got wide play in the press, ramming the point home to immigrant families that the mustard would be cut in the land of the star-spangled banner by mathematical checklist attention to recipes and rules. After all, God himself had probably been a research scientist, or so President William Rainey Harper of the University of Chicago declared to the nation.

Racial Suicide

President Francis Amasa Walker of M.I.T. first declared in 1891 what was soon to become an upper class mantra: Anglo-Saxons were quietly committing "racial suicide." The insult of competing with Latin/Slav/Celtic folkways seemingly discouraged reproduction among families of the old stock. After that bombshell, an orchestrated campaign of scientific racism swept the United States and didn't flag in public energy for 40 long years.

Racial suicide was the Red Scare, Fifth Column, and AIDS epidemic of its day all rolled into one. In the long history of manufactured crises, it ranks up there with the Reichstag fire, Pearl Harbor, the Gulf of Tonkin, the gasoline shortage of 1973, the Asian economic miracle, and corporate downsizing as a prime example of modern psychological management of public opinion. The racial suicide theme sounded at exactly the moment public schooling was transforming itself into forced government schooling.

The American campaign against racial suicide enlisted great scientists of the day to produce a full library of books, scientific journal articles, popular magazine pieces, legislation, lectures, and indirect school curriculum. It caught the attention of the entire civilized world, including Imperial Germany and Imperial Japan. Both sent official study delegations to America to observe the resourcefulness of this new industrial utopia in purging itself of its original democratic character. It is as if there exists some tacit understanding on the part of mainline scholarship and journalism to steer clear of the shoals of this period, but even an amateur like myself finds enough to indicate that racial suicide provided a leading motive to justify the radical shift of American society toward well-schooled orthodoxy. What is intriguing in light of the relative amnesia concerning these connections is the sheer quantity of the damning data. Genetic experimentation, once teased from its hiding holes, is revealed as a master political project of the twentieth century with the U.S., Germany, and England its enthusiastic sponsors. Data gathered in school surveys and social experimentation with children has been an important source of grist for this initiative.

M.I.T.'s Walker got an intellectual boost from activities of the influential American sociologist Edward A. Ross, who explained to the American Academy of Political and Social Science exactly how unchecked Asiatic immigration would lead to the extinction of the American people. Higher races, he said, will not endure competition from lower ones. After that, even Teddy Roosevelt was issuing marching orders to Anglo-Saxon mothers, asking well-bred ladies to mobilize their loins in an effort to arrest the suicidal decline. Breed as if the race depended on it, said Roosevelt. Eugenics had openly become national politics for the first time in America, but hardly the last.

Harper's Weekly chastised Roosevelt, saying mere exhortation would have no effect *as long as immigration continued to reduce the native birthrate* by insulting our best breeders. From 1905 to 1909 at least one major popular magazine article on the subject appeared *every single month* to keep the race pot boiling. Books appearing to respectful reviews warned that *race-suicide* would "toll the passing of this great Anglo-Teuton people" giving the nation over to Latins, Slavs, or worse, Jews and other Asiatics.

Meanwhile the long-ignored genetic work of monk Gregor Mendel was conveniently rediscovered, adding more fuel to the fires of racial thinking. Here, presumably, was a humble but observant man of God showing *mathematically* that something was at work causing transmission of behaviors and characteristics from generation to generation, independent of any effect of nurture or education. Horse, dog, and rose breeders had empirically derived these principles a thousand years and more before Mendel, but credit passed to university science for the "discovery."

Into the center of this racial excitement strode the formidable figure of Sir Francis Galton, first cousin of Charles Darwin, in line of descent from Malthus, possessor of incredible intellectual ability and indefatigable energy, a man of great personal wealth, a knight of the realm. Galton preached improvement of the human breed with evangelical fervor, demanding a policy of biological positivism which would produce the same genetic dividends positivism in the hard sciences of chemistry and physics was doing. The "eugenics movement" as it was now called, would save us socially by manipulating the best to breed and encouraging the worst to die out. School would have a major role to play in this. Race-improvement was in the air, its method compounded out of state action and forced schooling.

Galton's inspiration and abundant American money—much of it Andrew Carnegie's and Mrs. Averill Harriman's—opened the first racial science laboratory in the world at Cold Spring Harbor, Long Island, in 1904. And kept it open for 35 years until Hitler's invasion of Poland made discretion seem the wiser part of zealotry for the moment at the Carnegie Corporation, and it was quietly shut down. The last president at the Cold Spring facility was M.I.T. president Vannevar Bush, often called "The Father of the Atomic Bomb." Eugenic thinking injected energy into the exploding "mental hygiene" movement, too. Word went out to the recently erected national network of hospitals that it was okay to begin sterilizing mental defectives. This green light came complete with legislative licenses to decide *who* those defectives were—and freedom from legal jeopardy.

A scholarly book from M.I.T. created intellectual havoc in the year 1899 and long afterwards, lending maximum credibility to the eugenicist agenda. *The Races of Europe* was written by brilliant economist William Z. Ripley; it armed the racial-suicide crowd and its companion group of enthusiasts, the racial-science crowd, with information that Europe was divided into three races, *easily discernible from one another by physical measurements*. First, a race of blond long heads (the Teutons); second, a central race of stocky round heads (the Alpines); and third, a southern race of slender, dark long heads (the Mediterraneans). Here, finally was a way to distinguish reliably among the qualities of old immigration and new! Ripley was a 100 percent American scholar who took the 28-year-old Darwinian concept of "reversion" and charged it with new energy.

Was it possible, Ripley asked, that promiscuous breeding of Nordic peoples with Southern Europeans could doom the New England Anglo-Nordic stock? Incipient race suicide could only be dealt with by legislation. *Education* should be employed to raise the current immigrant's "standard of morality," making him more tolerable to society. That would help. But *nothing* could be done about *reversion*. Sub-men could not be allowed to couple with 100 percent American female breeding stock.

All the pieces were now in position for full-scale national hysteria to commence, an era of sanctions buttressed by the authority of peerless scientific experts. American society would require harsh discipline after the Prussian fashion in order to meet this challenge. Thanks to men like Ripley, it could do so with an exalted sense of mathematical righteousness. The first requirement would be to force the dangerous classes into schools. Laws were on the books, time to enforce them.

A covert American sterilization program managed by trusted administrators in the brand new hospital network went on in the same years forced schooling was being brought along. This sterilization initiative occasionally broke silence in highly specialized journals whose reader discretion was taken for granted. Thus Charles V. Carrington, writing in the *Journal of Criminal Law, Criminology, and Police Science* (July, 1910), reported on two interesting cases of successful involuntary sterilization. One involved an "epileptic masturbator" who after vasectomy, "ceased masturbating altogether." The other was a black man given also to masturbation and general devilry. After sterilization, he became "a strong, well-developed young Negro, *nicely behaved*, and not a masturbatory sodomist," Carrington reported. Surgical intervention as social policy was given its precedents in America long before the Nazi era.

Advocates for Yaleman Gesell's "eugenic violence" offensive against the underclasses swung from every point on the scientific compass. William McDougall, the eminent social psychologist, announced himself a champion of Nordic superiority; Ellsworth Huntington, prominent Yale geographer, wrote *The Character of Races*, showing that only one race had any real moral character. Henry Fairfield Osborn, president and founder of the American Museum of Natural History, gave the "Address of Welcome" to the Second International Congress of Eugenics; Osborn's close friend Lothrop Stoddard wrote *The Revolt Against Civilization: Menace of the Underman*; and psychologist James McKeen Cattell, a force in the rise of standardized testing, wrote to Galton, "We are following in America your advice and example."

The famous humanitarian anthropologist Alfred L. Kroeber remarked acidly to a newsman that *anti-eugenic* protests came only from the "orthodoxly religious," rarely from the enlightened camp of science. So there it was. Keep them all in mind: Kroeber, Gesell, Ripley, McDougall,

Huntington, Osborn, great scientific humanist names whose work underscored how important a role forced schooling was designed to play. Scientific studies had shown conclusively that extending the period and intensity of schooling caused sharp declines in fertility and sterility in many. Part of school's stealth curriculum would be a steady enlargement of its reach over the century.

Two more examples will drive home the relentlessness of this long scientific campaign against American tradition. J.B.S. Haldane, a distinguished Fabian geneticist from England, issued a lurid warning about what might happen if blonde women bred with human demi-apes like Italians, Jews, and other kinds of retrograde biology: "A new type of submen, abhorred by nature, ugly as no natural product is ugly" would emerge. The new hypothesis held that female offspring of such unions would be too repulsive to look upon.

In *Daedalus, or Science and the Future*, Haldane said there were really only four fundamental biological innovations of prehistory: 1) Domestication of animals; 2) Domestication of plants; 3) The use of fungi for the production of alcohol; 4) The invention of frontal copulation "which altered the path of sexual selection, focused the attention of man as a lover upon woman's face and breasts, and changed our ideal of beauty from the steatopygous Hottentot to the modern European, from the Venus of Brassenpouy to the Venus of Milo."

All evolution might be in jeopardy if there were no more pretty faces to look at, this was the thesis. There is an aura of the absurd about these assertions today, but it would be well to reflect on the institutional world that emerged from the other end of this same forge, for it is the new moral world you and I live in, a fully scientized and organized society, managed by the best people—people who prefer to remain out of sight of the *hoi polloi*, in walled villages and other redoubts.

The Passing Of The Great Race

No discussion of the dreamlike years of overt American scientific racism and schooling would be complete without a nod to the ghost of Madison Grant, who has mysteriously vanished from the pages of some standard biographical references though they still carry his cousins, Grant the portrait painter and Grant the educator. No matter, I shall tell you about him. If you have ever been to the Bronx Zoo[5] you have been a guest of Mr. Grant's beneficent imagination, for he was its founder and the founder of its parent, the New York Zoological Society. The Bronx Zoo,its fame and good works inspire worldwide graditude. Grant's legacy to us, as free libraries were Carnegie's.

Grant was a lifelong bachelor, a childless man. Like many people associated with public schooling on a policy level, Grant came from a patrician family which had graced society from colonial days. No Grant ever held a menial job. Madison Grant was considered to be a leading scientific naturalist of his time. His monographs on the Rocky Mountain goat, the moose, and the caribou are little classics of their kind, still consulted. Men and women related to Grant have been directors of American society since the Age of the Mathers.

Grant was deeply disgusted by the mixing of European races underway here; he believed the foundation of our national and cultural life lay in racial purity and backed this opinion with action. It is hardly possible to believe some of this attitude didn't enter into the museum's presentation of

---

[5] As 500,000 school trips to date have been.

data and even into those hundreds of thousands of school field trips. In Grant's competent hands, the boldness and sweep of old Anglo-Saxon tradition was fused into a systematic world view, then broadcast through books and lectures to the entire planet. His *magnum opus* appeared in 1916 bearing the epic title, *The Passing of the Great Race*, introduction by Museum of Natural History luminary Henry Fairfield Osborn—a man who wrote one of the texts I used myself as a junior high school student.

The Passing of the Great Race warns that the ruling race of the Western world is beginning to wane because of a "fatuous belief" that environment can alter heredity.[6] The clear connection to the predestination canon of Calvin and to the great Norse tradition of implacable Fate is too unmistakable to miss. Grant's own genealogy came from both these strains in European history. Whatever else he was, Grant was neither dull nor commonplace. Using Darwin and Mendelian genetics to support his argument, Grant said flatly that different races do not blend, that mixing "gives us a race reverting to the more ancient and lower type." A "cross between any of the three European races and a Jew is a Jew."

Grant argued that culture is racially determined. Alpines have always been peasants, Mediterraneans, artists and intellectuals; but "the white man par excellence" was the Nordic blond conqueror of the North: explorers, fighters, rulers, aristocrats, organizers of the world. In early America the stock was purely Nordic, now swarming hybrids threatened it with destruction except in a few zones of racial purity like Minnesota.

Madison Grant felt democracy as a political system violated scientific facts of heredity the same way Christianity did, by favoring the weak. This led inexorably to biological decadence. Even *national* consciousness might confuse one's rational *first* loyalty, which had to be race. This was the codex of the Bronx Zoo's founder. Six years after its publication, *The Passing of the Great Race* was still in print and Grant's New York Zoological Society more respectable than ever. Eventually Margaret Mead was beneficiary of considerable patronage from Grant's Museum of Natural History, as indeed the whole shaky new community of anthropological thought became. Although Mead's work appears to contradict Grant's, by the time the academic world began to push the relativism of Mead, Benedict, and other interpreters of primitive culture, a double standard had settled in on intellectual life in the U.S. and Europe.

For those whose status was secure by birth, theories of inherited quality were available. For the great mass of others, however, the body of theory which paid off in foundation grants, the one driving modern political and economic development, was that corpus of studies exploring the notion of *extreme plasticity* in human nature, a pliability grading into shapelessness. If mankind were seen to be clay, radical social action justifying continuous intervention could surely bring utopia within reach while providing expanding opportunities to academics. The academic marketplace eagerly supplied evidence that quality was innate to the powerful, *and* evidence that human nature was empty to the rest of us.

---

[6] Simplified, the belief that human nature could be changed, complicated enormously by a collateral belief that there are a variety of such natures, correlated with race and other variables. As I warn elsewhere, these men used the concept "race" in a more intimate way than contemporary ears are used to. As Grant would have viewed things, "white" or "Caucasian" is subject to many subdivisions each of which has a value rank. The "great race" in America is Aryan.

The Poison Of Democracy

WWI provided the spring for the United States to devise the most extensive national classification program in history. Prior to the war, eugenicists evaluated racial and national groups by comparing numbers of one group or another on "lists of distinction,"[7] but they had no way of penetrating the secret inner spaces of consciousness. On the verge of the world war the new social discipline of psychology, struggling to attain a status of hard science, claimed to be able to change all that. It boasted of a power to go deep into the hidden regions of the brain. The new techno-miracle of the day was the invention of a mysterious "intelligence test," an "IQ" score which allegedly could place secrets of intellectual power at the disposal of managerial science.

The just assembled American army of WWI was soon subject to mass intelligence measurement under the direction of Robert M. Yerkes, president of the American Physiological Association, an organization recently invented by Wundtian protégé G. Stanley Hall. Results published after the war showed remarkable correlation with similar tests on American school children. While Yerkes was reporting these findings to the National Academy of Sciences, famous psychologist Dr. William McDougall was summarizing the civilian studies for the general public in his book, *Is America Safe for Democracy?* Latins and Slavs in fair mental competition scored significantly lower than native whites, he said. How then could they be given a vote *equal* to white men?

McDougall claimed that hard data unmistakably revealed that a racial interpretation of history was the correct one. In his book, *A Study of American Intelligence*, psychologist Carl Brigham concluded in 1923 that "the intellectual superiority of our Nordic group over Alpine, Mediterranean and Negro groups has been demonstrated."

After 1923, racism was a truth of science. Word quickly spread into every corner of Europe; but particularly in defeated Germany, ancient Teutonic barrier against Slavic incursion, these new truths were enthusiastically discussed. General agreement confirmed Nordic superiority. The popular writer Kenneth Roberts (*Northwest Passage*) took up the cry. One of America's foremost novelists, he lectured American book dealers from the pages of the specialist journal *Bookman* that "the Alpine school of fiction" spread *the poison of democracy* through the whole culture. School texts were appropriately adjusted. Roberts identified himself, as you may already have guessed, as 100 percent Nordic.

Now intelligence tests were huckstered in school district after school district; fortunes accrued to well-placed pedagogical leaders and their political allies. Every child would now be given a magical number ranking it scientifically in the great race of life. School grades might vary according to the whim of teachers, but IQ scores were unvarying, an emotionless badge of biological honor or shame, marking innate, almost unchanging ability. Millions of tests administered annually to primary and secondary students would prove the "value rank" of the American peoples. Mental ages were dutifully entered on permanent record cards with as much assurance as Horace Mann, Barnas Sears, Torrey Harris, John Dewey, and G. Stanley Hall had accepted skull maps drawn by their favorite phrenologists.

---

[7] An invention of Galton.

Every day science seemed to make it clearer and clearer that forcing everyone to fit the Anglo-Saxon mold was indeed doing humanity a mighty favor. If children couldn't biologically be Anglo/Nordic, they could be so acculturated, at least a portion of that way, through regular drill. After all, hadn't psychology proven how malleable human nature was? Henry Fairfield Osborn stepped forward from his duties at the American Museum of Natural History to announce portentously that Christopher Columbus—always a choking point (as a Latin) for America's cultural leadership—was actually Nordic.

The American Protective League

By the First World War, political leadership was ferreting out disloyalty and enforcing scientific conformity. Any number of private and secret societies appeared to forward this cause. The "Anti-Yellow Dog League" was one of these, composed of schoolboys above the age of 10, who searched out disloyalty each day from one of its thousand branches nationwide, barking like German shepherds when a disloyal yellow dog, otherwise someone looking like you or me, was flushed from cover and branded. Schools enthusiastically cooperated in "Dog Hunts" as they were called.

The U.S. Justice Department secretly empowered private associations as volunteer spy-hunters. One, the American Protective League (APL), earned semi-official status in the national surveillance game, in time growing to enormous size. Founded by a Chicago advertising man, the APL had 1,200 units functioning across America, all staffed by business and professional people. It was a genuine secret society replete with oath and rituals. Membership gave every operative the authority to be a national policeman. The first location placed under surveillance in every neighborhood was the local public school. Assignments were given by the old (Federal) Bureau of Investigation and by the War Department's Intelligence Division to report on "seditious and disloyal" conversation. From the *authorized* history of the APL comes this specimen case:

> *Powers County, Colorado: investigated fifty cases of mouth-to-mouth propaganda,*
> *a notable cause being that of a German Lutheran minister who refused to answer the*
> *questions as to which side he wished to win the war. He asked for time. The next day*
> *he declared very promptly that he wanted the United States to win. He was instructed*
> *to prove this by preaching and praying it in private as well as in public, which he*
> *agreed to do.*

The APL checked up on people who failed to buy Liberty Bonds. It spotted violators of food and gasoline regulations, rounded up draft evaders in New York, disrupted Socialist meetings in Cleveland, broke strikes, threatened union men with immediate induction into the army. The attorney general of the United States reported to Congress, "*It is safe to say never in history has this country been so thoroughly policed.*" Nor the training of the young so well regulated, he might have added.

Guaranteed Customers

Prior to 1860 Americans didn't demand a high level of national solidarity—a loose sort of catch-as-catch-can unity satisfied the nation in spite of the existence even then of patriotic special interest groups like Know-Nothings. Neither by geography, culture, common experience, or preference was the United States naturally a single country although it did possess a common language. But conformity had been ordered by corporate and banking interests from the Northeast, so one country it would become.

Stupendous profits accrued to these interests from the Civil War, and its great lesson of national regimentation into squads, platoons, brigades, companies, regiments, and army corps was not lost on the winners. Warfare in its nature forces men to wear "value-ranks" openly for all to see, forces everyone to subordinate themselves to higher ranks, higher ranks to subordinate themselves to invisible orders. War conditions men to rule and to be ruled. Modern war creates a society far different in type and scale from the ragged and bizarre individuality which emerged out of the American Revolution. With everyone dressing alike, eating alike, and doing everything else alike, maximum profit can be derived from the use of mass-production machinery in an ideal environment where the goods of production are swiftly wasted, and military "consumers" are literally forbidden the right to refuse to consume! A soldier *must* wear his uniform, eat his food, fire his rifle. Guaranteed customers is a benchmark of the commercial millennium.

Industrial Efficiency

After the Civil War, the guaranteed customer was not a thing prudent businessmen were willing to surrender. Could there be some different way to bring about uniformity again without another conflict? Vast fortunes awaited those who would hasten such a jubilee. Consolidation. Specialization. These were the magical principles President Harper was to preach 40 years later at the University of Chicago. Whatever sustained national unity was good, including war, whatever retarded it was bad. School was an answer, but it seemed hopelessly far away in 1865.

Things were moving slowly on these appointed tracks when a gigantic mass of Latin, and then Slavic, immigration was summoned to the U.S. to labor, in the 1870s and afterwards. It came colorfully dressed, swilling wine, hugging and kissing children, eyes full of hope. Latin immigration would seem to represent a major setback for the realization of any systematic utopia and its schools. But a president had been shot dead in 1865. Soon another was shot dead by a presumed (though not actual) immigrant barely 15 years later. Rioting followed, bloody strikes, national dissension. It was a time tailor-made for schoolmen, an opportunity to manage history.

The Americanization movement, which guaranteed forced schooling to its first mass clientele, was managed from several bases; three important ones were social settlement houses, newly minted patriotic hereditary societies, and elite private schools (which had sprung up in profusion after 1880). Madison Grant was a charter member of one of the patriotic groups, "The Society of Colonial Wars." All compartments of the Americanization machine cooperated to wrack the immigrant family to its breaking point. But some, like settlement houses, were relatively subtle in their effects. In these, the home culture was inadvertently denigrated by automatic daily comparison with the settlement culture, a genteel world constructed by society ladies dedicated to serving the poor.

Hereditary societies worked a different way: Through educational channels, lectures, rallies, literature they broadcast a code of attitudes directed at the top of society. Mainline Protestant churches were next to climb on the Americanization bandwagon, the "home-missions" program became a principal gathering station for adoptable foreign children. By 1907 the YMCA was heavily into this work, but the still embryonic undertaking of leveling the masses lacked leadership and direction.

Such would eventually be supplied by Frances Kellor, a muckraker and a tremendous force for conformity in government schooling. Kellor, the official presiding genius of the Americanization movement, came out of an unlikely quarter, yet in retrospect an entirely natural one. She was the daughter of a washerwoman, informally adopted out of poverty by two wealthy local spinsters, eventually sent to Cornell for a law degree through their generosity. After a turn toward sociology at the University of Chicago, Kellor mastered Harper's twin lessons of specialization and consolidation and set out boldly to *reform* Americas immigrant families.

Her first muckraking book, *Out of Work*, was published in 1904. For the next two years she drafted remedial legislation and earned her spurs lobbying. By 1906, she had Teddy Roosevelt's personal ear. Six years later, she was head of the Progressive Party's publicity department and research arm. Kellor, under William Rainey Harper's inspiration, became an advocate of *industrial efficiency*. She despised waste and disorder, urging that "opportunity" be rationalized and put under control—the first hint of school-to-work legislation to follow far ahead in the waning decades of the century. Work and licenses should be used as incentives to build national unity. Discipline was the ticket, and for discipline, carrots were required as well as sticks.

Charles Evans Hughes, then Governor, made Kellor the first woman ever to head a state agency, appointing her director of the Bureau of Industries and Immigration in New York. By 1909, supported by prominent allies, she organized a New York Branch of the North American Civic League, a Boston-based, business-rostered outfit intended to protect the national status quo from various foreign menaces. Under her direction, the New York branch developed its own program. It isn't clear how much of the Boston agenda they carried on—it had mainly involved sending agents into foreign communities to act as industrial spies and to lead anti-strike movements—but in any case, by 1914 Kellor's group was writing its own menu.

It opened by demanding centralized federal action: Americanization was failing "without a national goal." Her new "Committee for Immigrants in America" thereafter proclaimed itself the central clearinghouse to unify all public and private agencies in a national spearhead to "make all these people one nation." When government failed to come up with money for a bureau, Miss Kellor's own backers—who included Mrs. Averill Harriman and Felix Warburg, the Rothschild banker—did just that, and this private entity was duly incorporated into the government of the United States! "The Division of Immigrant Education," while officially federal, was in fact the subsidized creation of Frances Kellor's private lobby. Immigrant education meant public school education, for it was to compulsion schooling the children of immigration were consigned, and immigrant children, in a reversal of traditional roles, became the teachers of their immigrant parents, thus ruining their families.

When World War I began, Americanization took over as the great national popular crusade. A drive for national conformity pushed itself dramatically to the forefront of the public agenda. Kellor and her colleagues swiftly enlisted cooperation from mayors, school authorities, churches, and civic groups; prepared data for speakers; distributed suggested agenda and programs, buttons, and posters; and lectured in schools. When Fourth of July 1915 arrived, 107 cities celebrated it as

"Americanization Day," and the country resounded with the committee's slogan "Many Peoples, but One Nation."[8]

Now Kellor's organization transmuted itself into "The National Americanization Committee," shifting its emphasis from education to the breaking of immigrant ties to the Old World. Its former slogan, "Many Peoples, But One Nation," was replaced with a blunt "America First." In this transformation, children became the sharpest weapon directed at their parents' home culture. Kellor called Americanization "the civilian side of national defense." She appeared before a group of industrialists and bankers calling itself the National Security League to warn of coming peril from subversion on the part of immigrants. One of the most distressing anomalies confronting Kellor and the NSL was an almost total lack of publicizable sabotage incidents on the domestic front in WWI which made it difficult to maintain the desired national mood of fear and anger.

High-Pressure Salesmanship

In 1916, the year of Madison Grant's *Passing of the Great Race*, Kellor published *Straight America*. In it she called for universal military service, industrial mobilization, a continuing military build-up, precisely engineered school curricula, and total Americanization, an urgent package to revitalize nationalism. America was not yet at war.

President Wilson was at that time reading secret surveys which told him Americans had no interest in becoming involved in the European conflict. Furthermore, national sympathy was swinging away from the English and actually favored German victory against Britain. There was no time to waste; the war had to be joined at once. John Higham called it "an adventure in high pressure salesmanship."

> Thousands of agencies were in some measure engaged: schools, churches, fraternal orders, patriotic societies, civic organizations, chambers of commerce, philanthrophies, railroads, and industries, and—to a limited degree—trade unions. There was much duplication, overlapping, and pawing of the air. Many harassed their local school superintendents....

At the end of 1917, Minnesota's legislature approved the world's first secret adoption law, sealing original birth records forever so that worthy families who received a child for adoption—almost always children transferred from an immigrant family of Latin/Slav/Alpine peasant stripe to a family of northern European origins—would not have to fear the original parents demanding their child back. The original Boston adoption law of 1848 had been given horrendous loopholes. Now these were sealed 69 years later.

Toward the end of the war, a striking event much feared since the Communist revolutions of 1848 came to pass. The huge European state of Russia fell to a socialist revolution. It was as if

---

[8] There is some evidence American social engineering was being studied abroad. Zamiatin's *We*, the horrifying scientific dystopia of a world government bearing the name "The United State" was published in Russia a few years later as if in anticipation of an American future for everyone.

Russian immigrants in our midst had driven a knife into our national heart and, by extension, that all immigrants had conspired in the crime. Had all our civilizing efforts been wasted? Now Americanization moved into a terrifying phase in response to this perceived threat from outside. The nation was to be purified before a red shadow arose here, too. Frances Kellor began to actively seek assistance from business groups to build what she called "the new *interventionist* republic of America."

At an unpublicized dinner meeting at Sherry's Restaurant near Wall Street in November of 1918, Frances Kellor addressed the 50 largest employers of foreign labor, warning them Americanization had been a failure—that really dangerous times were ahead with Bolshevik menace concealed in every workplace. *Kellor proposed a partnership of business and social work* to "break up the nationalistic, racial groups." The easiest way to do that was to weaken close family life. Miss Kellor, who had never enjoyed a family life herself, was the perfect person to lead such a charge.

At the Wall Street meeting, plans were laid for a semi-secret organization of Americanizers to be formed out of interested volunteers from major industrial corporations. An impressive amount of money was pledged at the initial meeting, the story of which you can follow in John Higham's classic account of our immigration years, *Strangers in the Land*. "The Inter-Racial Council" presented the external aspect of an eclectic public-spirited enterprise—it even recruited some conservative immigrant representatives as members—but, in fact, it was controlled by Kellor's backers.

The IRC acted both as intelligence gathering office and propaganda agency. In its first year of existence, Kellor put together an association of advertisers to strong-arm the immigrant press into running anti-radical propaganda. Using this muscle, immigrants could be instructed from far away how to think and what to think about, while remaining unaware of the source of instruction because immediate pressure came from a familiar editor. Advertising revenue could be advanced, as well as withdrawn, providing both carrot and stick, the complete behavioral formula.

A New Collectivism

By 1919 a deluge of state legislation appeared, specifically designed to counteract rampant Bolshevism. Idaho and Utah established criminal penalties for not attending Americanization classes. Fifteen states ordered English to be the only language of instruction in all schools, public and private. Nebraska demanded that all meetings be conducted in English. Oregon required every foreign language publication to display prominently a literal English translation of its entire contents. In 1922, Oregon *outlawed* private schools for elementary children, a decision reversed by the Supreme Court later in the *Pierce vs Society of Sisters* case (1925).

The experience of these times gave reformers a grand taste for blood. Government intervention everywhere was proclaimed the antidote for dissent. Intervention took many unexpected shapes. For instance, the "Athlete's Americanization League" agitated intensely to provide free sports equipment for every public school with its battle cry: "Sports are the logical antidote for unrest." By the time national passion cooled, in every nook and cranny of American life new social organizations with powerful government or private sponsorship flourished. All fed on intervention into families for their nourishment; all clamored to grow larger, all schemed to produce political testimony of their value. A new republic was here at last, just as Herbert Croly had announced, and government school was to be its church.

CHAPTER TWELVE

Daughters Of The

Barons Of Runnemede

Membership Requirements

*Membership in the Society is composed of women who are of legal
age and the lineal descendant of one or more of the twenty-five Barons,
selected to enforce the Magna Carta, those Barons in arms from the
date of King John's Coronation until June 15, 1215. Membership is by
invitation only. Within the Society there is an Order of Distinction
Committee composed of members who trace their ancestry to Knights
of the Garter, Ladies of the Garter and Knights of the Bath.*

> — Charter, The Daughters of the Barons
> of Runnemede [who prefer this variant
> spelling]

A Scientifically Humane Future

In the founding decades of American forced schooling, Rockefeller's General Education
Board and Carnegie's foundation spent more money on schools than the national government did.
What can a fact like that *mean*? Because they possessed a coherent perspective, had funds to apply
to command the energies of the ambitious, possessed a national network of practical men of affairs,
and at the same time could tap a pool of academic knowledge about the management of populations
held in the universities they endowed, these and a small handful of men like them commanded
decisive influence on forced schooling. Other influences had importance, too, but none more than
this commitment of a scientifically benevolent American ruling class whose oversight of the

economy and other aspects of living was deemed proper because of its evolutionary merit by the findings of modern science. The burden of this chapter will be to show how a national upper class came about, what was on its mind, and how schools were the natural vehicle it mounted to ride into a scientifically humane, thoroughly utopian future.

Exclusive Heredity

At the end of the nineteenth century, an explosion in the creation of exclusive hereditary societies took place which couldn't have been predicted from the course of the American past. These peculiar clubs constituted the most flagrant leading edge of a broad-based movement to erect nothing less than a coherent national upper class whose boundary was drawn in bloodlines. This might be better understood as an early manifestation of the genetically charged environment of American life at the advent of the twenty-first century. This social enclosure movement produced orthodox factory schooling for the masses as one of its very first policy thrusts. It produced the licensing phenomenon which echoed the traditional right of English kings to confer a living on some loyal subjects by reserving good things for them which are denied to others. Many other aspects of class/caste-based government and society we have been wrestling with ever since we came out of this period.

Evidence that this movement was organized to concentrate power within a Brahmin caste stratum is caught by the sudden ostracism of Jews from the ranks of America's leading social clubs in the decade and a half directly following Herbert Spencer's visit to America. This was far from business as usual. Jesse Seligman, a *founder* of New York's Union League Club, was forced to resign in 1893 when his son was blackballed by the membership committee. Joseph Gratz, *president* of the exclusive Philadelphia Club during the Civil War, lived to see the rest of his own family later shunned from the same place. The Westmoreland in Richmond boasted a Jewish president in the 1870s, but soon afterwards began a policy of rigid exclusion; The University Club of Cincinnati broke up in 1896 over admission of a Jewish member. The point is whatever was wrong with Jews now hadn't been wrong earlier. Who was giving the orders to freeze out the Jews? And why?

The striking change of attitude toward Jews displayed by Bostonian blue blood and author, Henry Adams, is a clue to where the commands might have originated, since the Adams family can be presumed beyond easy intimidation or facile persuasion. Adams'1890 novel *Democracy* illustrated the author's lifelong acceptance of Jews. *Democracy* featured Jewish characters as members of Washington society with no ethnic stigma even hinted at. In 750 intimate letters of Adams from 1858 through 1896, the designation "Jew" never even occurs. *Suddenly it shows up in 1896.* Thirty-eight years of correspondence without one invidious reference to Jews was followed by 22 years with many. After 1896 Adams seemed to lose his faith entirely in the Unitarian tradition, becoming, after 1896, a follower of Darwin and Spencer, a believer in privileged heredities and races. H.G. Wells' *The Future in America* (1906) called attention to the transformation the English writer witnessed on a visit to this country: "The older American population," said Wells, "is being floated up on the top of this immigrant influx, a sterile aristocracy above a racially different and astonishingly fecund proletariat...." That fecundity and that racial difference dictated a second American Revolution would be fought silently from the Atlantic to the Pacific about a century ago, this time a revolution in which British class-based episcopal politics emerged victorious after a century and a quarter of rejection.

Divinely Appointed Intelligence

All through the British colonial history of America, the managerial class of these colonies was drawn from Church of England gentry and aristocrats. As you might expect, this leadership shared the British state church's creative distaste toward education for the underclasses. And underclass then was a term for which the customary narrow modern usage is quite unsuitable. Every class not included in the leadership cadre was an underclass. The eye-topped pyramid on the back of our one-dollar bill catches the idea of such an episcopate beautifully: divinely appointed intelligence ruling the blind stones beneath.

The episcopal rule of British America is well enough documented, yet still it remains largely unremarked how many revolutionary leaders were still communicants of the Church of England—Russell Kirk estimated 29 of the 55 delegates attending the Constitutional Convention of 1787. They may have been willing to push the mother country away, but their own attitude toward popular sovereignty was ambivalent. Little-known even today is the long private effort of Ben Franklin to induce British royal government to displace the Quaker Penns of Pennsylvania and take command of the state. Between 1755 and 1768, Franklin labored mightily at this, reluctantly abandoning his dream and jumping ship to the revolutionary conspirators just in time to save his own position.[1] After Braddock's defeat, Franklin joined forces with the influential Anglican priest William Smith in a venture they called "The Society for Propagating Christian Knowledge among Germans settled in Pennsylvania." This association, a harbinger of government schools to come, had nothing much to do with reading and counting, but everything to do with socializing German children as English.

Braddock's defeat on the Monongahela was the straw that tipped America's influential Quakers into the Anglican camp; it joined two influential, socially-exclusionary sects in bonds of mutual assistance. When the great explosion of elite private boarding academies took place in the late nineteenth century period when hereditarian societies were also forming (and for the same purpose), Episcopalian schools made up *half* the total of such schools, a fraction 1,650 percent greater than their denominational share of population would have warranted. They still do. And Quakers, at present just 1/2600 of the American population (.04 percent), control five percent of the inner circle of elite private boarding schools (many elite day schools, as well). This constitutes *52,000 percent* more participation than bare Quaker numbers would seem to warrant! A managerial class was circling the wagons, protecting its own children from the epic social conditioning yet to come, and perhaps from the biological menace Darwin and Galton had warned about.

---

[1] As little known as Ben's skullduggery is the fact that his only son was the Royal Governor of New Jersey, a loyal Church of England man who fled to England during the war and never spoke to his father again (until Franklin's life was nearly over) because of gentle Ben's treachery. Even then the breach between father and son could not be healed.

The Paxton Boys

How the decisive collaboration in which Quaker men of wealth felt driven by circumstance to seek protection from the Established Church of England happened in the months after Braddock's army was cut to pieces on October 16, 1755, is a fascinating story. The Western frontier of colonial America promptly exploded, after the British defeat. Delawares and Shawnees attacked across Western Pennsylvania, burning all forts except Pitt. By November they were across the mountains and the Susquehanna, and in January the whole frontier collapsed. Settlers fled, many running on until they reached Philadelphia, "almost crazy with anxiety." Scotch-Irish Presbyterians on the Monongahela blamed their trouble on rich Philadelphia Quakers controlling the legislature who had prevented levies for frontier defense.

An unauthorized Presbyterian militia hastily assembled, the notorious Paxton Boys, whose columns proceeded to march on Philadelphia! I can hardly do justice here to that lively time besides reminding you that Pennsylvania to this day is divided East/West. The net upshot of Braddock's fatal *hauteur* was to send Scotch-Irish Presbyterians on the warpath against Quakers and to drive important Quaker interests into Tory arms for protection from their fellow Pennsylvanians.

Thus at the very moment British authority and rigid class attitudes came into question for many Americans, conservative Quakers, conspicuously wealthy and in control of the mainstream press, became quiet proponents of it. "I could wish," said Thomas Wharton (for whose Quaker family the business school is named at Penn), "to see that Religion [Anglicanism] bear the Reins of Government throughout the Continent." In the exact decade when Americans were growing most fearful of the rise of an American civil episcopate, these Friends "cheered the news of the growth of Anglicanism," according to Jack Marietta, the Quaker historian. So the dormant seeds for a delayed Anglican revival were buried in Pennsylvania/New Jersey/Delaware soil right from our national beginnings. And Philadelphia remained Tory to its heart as the long Revolution unfolded.

Soldiers For Their Class

These buried seeds sent up no more than stunted shoots until the late nineteenth century when skillfully induced mass immigration—cheap Catholic labor by the boatload—triggered a perceived need for emergency social action on an Anglican model. At that moment, casting about for a blueprint of order in the disturbing period of mass immigration, the new industrial and commercial elites discarded existing American models: the tentative intellectual meritocracy of the Unitarians, the rude familism of the Presbyterians, the libertarian democracy of the General Baptists, the proud communitarianism of Congregationalists and Quakers, the religiously centered communities of the pietists; all had to give way since all were both *local* and *particular* forms. None could accommodate a general habit of rule from afar very well. None was able to maintain tight enough class discipline. Congregationalists were closest to this ideal, but even they had radically weakened their own theological discipline with the Half-Way Covenant and then thoroughly liberalized themselves in the Second Great Awakening after 1795. None of these forms would do as a universal blueprint of stable government.

Only one acceptable discipline had for centuries proven itself under fire, able to bend diverse, distant, and hostile peoples to its organization, and that was the Anglican Communion. In India, Africa, Asia, Canada, wherever the British flag flew, it had been capable of the hard decisions necessary to maintain a subordinated order and protect the privileges which accrue to those who subordinate that order.

Peter Cookson and Caroline Persell cast a great deal of light on the Anglican temper in their book, *Preparing For Power: America's Elite Boarding Schools*, particularly the turn of the century period when almost all the 289 boarding schools which matter were created:[2]

> The difference between a public school and an elite private school is, in one
> sense, the difference between factory and club. Public schools are evaluated
> on how good a *product* they turn out, and the measure of quality control is
> inevitably an achievement score of some kind....[but] to compare public and
> private schools in terms of output really misses the point.

Cookson and Persell, searching for reasons to explain the need for total institutions to train the young, concluded: "The *shared ordeal* of the prep rites of passage create bonds of loyalty that differences in background cannot unravel."

Collective identity forged in prep schools becomes the basis of upper-class solidarity and consciousness, but sharing alone will not preserve or enhance a class's interest; as a group, members must be willing to exercise their power:

> The preservation of privilege requires the exercise of power, and those who
> exercise it cannot be too squeamish about the injuries that any ensuing conflict
> imposes on the losers....The founders of the schools recognized that unless
> their sons and grandsons were willing to take up the struggle for the preservation
> of their class interests, privilege would slip from the hands of the elite and
> eventually power would pass to either a competing elite or to a rising underclass.

Private school students are enlisted as soldiers for their class, like Viking rowers, tough, loyal to each other, "ready to take command without self-doubt." Cookson and Persell say currently, "Boarding schools were not founded to produce Hamlets, but Dukes of Wellington. The whole point of status seminaries is *the destruction* of innocence...not its preservation."

I hope this illuminates those esoteric membership requirements of the Daughters a bit. Whatever your personal outlook on such matters, you need to take seriously the creation of over a hundred new hereditary associations, associations with all the birthmarks of secret societies, which were gestated and came to term in the decades 1870 to 1900 (or just outside that narrow compass),

---

[2] The inner ring of these schools, which sets the standard for the rest, includes these sixteen: Groton, St. Paul's, Deerfield, Gunnery, Choate, Middlesex, Lawrenceville, Hotchkiss, St George's, Kent, Hill, Episcopal High (not Episcopal Prep!), Andover, Exeter, Culver Military, St. Marks, and perhaps three or four others. About 52 percent of the elite boarding schools are connected with the Episcopal Church and 5 percent with the Quaker faith.

each designed that it might in a perfectly orderly, fair way, free of any emotional bias, exclude all unwanted breeding stock by the application of hereditary screening and at the same time concentrate biological and social excellence. In the same time frame, five of the Seven Sisters—the female Ivy League—opened their doors for the first time, concentrating the future motherhood of a new race for its class inoculation.

Organizing Caste

In Darwin's second important book, *Descent of Man*, the fate in store for those liberal societies which allow mongrelization of the racial stock was made clear. They would fall prey to the ruthlessly evenhanded workings of evolution and devolve through reversion. The lesson of *Descent* was not lost on Boston, New York, Philadelphia, Chicago, or San Francisco. In one brief instant the rationale for a caste system was born and accepted. No merit system ever after could seriously breach the hereditarian barrier any more than it could budge the "scientific" bell-curve barrier. A *biological* basis for morality had been established.

One of the hundred new hereditarian societies (all survive, by the way) was "The Aztec Club of 1847" cherishing those who participated in the Mexican War as commissioned officers, and their descendants. The Aztec Club actually anticipated the intense, hereditarian period by a few years and so may be considered a pioneer. Had you been an Aztec at the founding dinner in 1880, you would have been at a table with Presidents Grant and Jefferson Davis, as well as, a fraternity of names engraved in legend. Presidents Taylor and Pierce, and Generals Lee and Pickett were dead, or they would have been there, too. The Aztec Club of 1847. Not a single public school teacher of the nearly three million in the U.S. has ever been on its rolls, I'm told. Are we in the presence here of some higher truth?

The Society of California Pioneers was another of these new hereditarian bodies which came to exist in the narrow zone of time just before effective mass compulsion schooling. This particular society celebrates "those memorable pioneers whose enterprise induced them to become the founders of a new State." I don't think you ought to summon up a mental picture of some grizzled prospector to fit that enterprise. Leland Stanford's family better fits the bill.

Here is a baker's dozen of other outfits to allow you to see more clearly the outlines of the new society emerging like an English phoenix out of the ashes of our democratic republic:

The Order of Americans of Armorial Ancestry
The Society of Mayflower Descendants
The Society of Americans of Royal Descent
The Daughters of the Utah Pioneers
The Women Descendants of the Ancient and Honorable Artillery
The Order of the First Families of Virginia
The Order of the Crown of Charlemagne
The Order of the Three Crusades, 1096-1192
The Descendants of Colonial Governors
The Society of Cincinnati
The Society of Founders of Norwich, Connecticut
The Swedish American Colonial Society
The Descendants of Colonial Clergy

The popular leviathans of this confederation of special blood were the National Society of the Sons of the American Revolution, which enrolled eleven of the next twelve Presidents as members (Nixon was eligible but declined), and its sister society, the D.A.R.

The yeast of Latin, Slavic, and Celtic immigration falling on the dough of Darwinism provoked the great families of the United States into building a ruling caste with a shared common agenda, a program for national and international development, and a schedule of social regulations to be imposed gradually on the future. If you can't deduce that program for yourself as it employs mass schooling you might wish to write the Society of Cincinnati for enlightenment. The sudden appearance of these associations, excluding from membership all non-Aryan immigrants, provides us with a sign this new caste had consciousness of itself as a caste. Otherwise, development would have been more gradual. It marks a great dividing line in American history. As the hereditarian wave rolled up the beach, even you could have designed the schools it was going to need.

One thing missing from the utopia of diverse hereditarian groups which were gathering—the scientific racists, the private clubs, schools, churches, neighborhoods, secret societies like Bones at Yale or Ivy at Princeton, special universities which served as a later stage in the elite recruitment and production cycle,[3] etc.—was a grand secular myth. Something less creepy than a naked assertion of successful protoplasm climbing up biological ladders out of the primordial slime was necessary to inspire the exclusive new establishment forming. Some stirring transcendental story to complete the capture and inspiration of the ruling class mind.

Such a thing had to be found and it was. The creation myth of American caste would appear unexpectedly in the form of an ancient language uniting the powerful classes of the United States into a romantic band of spiritual brothers, a story to which we turn next.

Your Family Tree

In 1896, Latin and Slavic immigration exceeded in body count for the first time the numbers arriving from the ancient lands of the Anglo-Saxons. In certain circles that was deemed a catastrophe second only to the Deluge. This moment had been anticipated for years, of course, and protections for good blood, or "the gene pool" as some preferred to call it, were popping like corn in the form of exclusionary associations you've seen and others like them. This was defensive. But other implements of war were being fashioned, weapons of *offensive* capability, social engines like modern factory schools, standing armies, social work empires designed to remake incoming aliens into shapes more agreeable to the spirit of the "Great Race," a term I'll explain in a moment. This machinery was grinding out "Americanized" Americans by 1913, just 62 years after the Know-Nothing Party of Massachusetts invented the term.

---

[3] Earlier I gave you a list of the inner-circle private boarding schools, the central ones of the 289 that matter most in the calculus of class. This seems as good a time as any to give you an inner circle of American colleges and universities. The sanctum of *social* power is found at these schools: Princeton, Brown, Harvard, Yale, Dartmouth, Georgetown, Duke, Cornell, Stanford, University of Virginia, University of Michigan, University of California (Berkeley), University of North Carolina (Chapel Hill), Columbia, University of Pennsylvania, Vanderbilt, Williams, Amherst, Colgate, and a tie between Boston College and Boston University. There are other knots of power, but if training of national leadership is the relevant issue, not the training of minds willing to serve as *instruments* of a national leadership, then the 20 I've taken are the heart of the heart of caste in America, much as the Monongahela Valley was the heart of the heart of libertarian America.

New hereditary societies took a leading hand in Americanization. So did important monied interests. Chicago financial power got the Children's Court idea rolling at the beginning of the twentieth century just as Boston railroad, mining, and real estate interests had initiated the compulsion school idea in the nineteenth. The Children's Court institution was nationalized rapidly, a most effective intimidation to use against uncooperative immigrants. Such courts soon displayed a valuable second side, supplying children to the childless of the politically better-connected sort with few questions asked. The similarity of this transfer function to the historic "Baby Trains" of Charles Loring Brace's "Children's Aid Society" 50 years earlier wasn't lost on the new breed of social engineer graduating from the right colleges in 1900.

These new activist graduates, trained in the Chicago school of sociology and its anthropological variants by Ross, Cooley, Boas, and other seminal figures, had little sentimentality about individual destinies or family sovereignty either. All thought in terms of the collective improvement of society by long-range evolution. In the short run all were environmental determinists who believed protoplasm was wonderfully malleable, if not entirely empty.

In 1898 the D.A.R., best known of all hereditarian societies, began issuing scientifically designed propaganda lectures on American history and government. By 1904, the Society of Colonial Dames was preparing school curriculum. In the same year the Sons of the American Revolution distributed millions of pieces of historical interpretation to schools, all paid for by the U.S. Department of Commerce. The *Social Register*, founded 1887, quickly became a useful index for the new associational aristocracy, bearing witness to those who could be trusted with the exciting work underway. Tiffany's started a genealogy department in 1875 to catch the first business from elites made edgy by *Descent of Man*, and as the century ended, genealogical reference books came tumbling from the assembly line to assist Anglo-Saxons in finding each other: the *Gore Roll*, Boston's *American Armoury and Blue Book*, and more like those.

As late as 1929, even with *Mein Kampf* in bookstalls telling the story of Aryans past and present, Stanford president David Starr Jordan published his own guide to good blood, *Your Family Tree*. It provided in painstaking detail the descent of America's new industrial aristocracy from monarchs of great Aryan houses. Abe Lincoln, Grover Cleveland, and John D. Rockefeller, said Jordan, came out of the house of Henry I of France; Ulysses S. Grant was in a line from William the Conqueror; Coolidge and Shakespeare descended from Charlemagne. William Howard Taft, J.P. Morgan, and Jordan himself from King David of Scotland! So it went.[4] Was this all just simple amusement or did the game have some implications for the rest of us not so blue-blooded? Who were these Aryans scholars talking about; what was this "Great Race?" The answers were to prove both fabulous and chilling.

The Fatal Sound Shift

During the sixteenth century, a studious Italian merchant living in India pointed out to his wealthy friends some striking similarities between ancient Sanskrit and Italian: *deva/dio* for God,

---

[4] The Crane plumbing family rejected the coat of arms suggested for them, a hand gripping the handle of a toilet chain with the motto "*Apres moi le deluge.*"

sarpa/serpe for snake, etc. All the Sanskrit numbers seemed related to the numbers of Italian. What could this mean? This early intuition came and went without much of a stir.

Then in 1786, during the early British occupation of India, the subject was addressed anew. In his speech to the Bengal-Oriental Society that year, Sir William Jones announced he believed a family connection existed between Sanskrit and English. It was tantamount to the University of Rome splitting the atom. Sir William declared Latin, Greek, and Sanskrit sprang "from some common source which perhaps no longer exists." Among English and Sanskrit he showed evidence for "a stronger affinity than could possibly have been produced by accident."

What common source might be the parent of Western civilization? Jones could not say, but only thirteen years later Sharon Turner's two-volume work, *The History of the Anglo-Saxons,* claimed to provide clues. There, replete with thousands of illustrations, was a record of Angles, Saxons, and Jutes out of ancient Germania as it had been preserved in song and story, *Beowulf* raised to a haunting power. Hundreds of cognates between modern English custom and ancient prototypes had been tracked by Turner; there seemed to be a stirring continuity between what Tacitus said about Germania and what upper-class English/American eyes saw when they looked into their modern mirrors.

The favorite occupations in antiquity were war, the chase, rough and tumble sports, wenching, and drinking, not unlike the preferences of contemporary Englishmen. When not thus engaged, men often lay idly about leaving all work for women to do. Gambling was common and every free man was expected to bear arms. Could the English be the mighty Aryans of prehistory?

In 1808, Karl Wilhelm Frederick von Schlegel, founder and editor of the *Athenaeum*, chief voice of German romanticism, wrote a scientific study of Sanskrit which maintained that the languages of India, Persia, Greece, Germany, Italy, and England were connected by common descent from an extinct tongue. Schlegel proposed the name *Indo-Germanic* for the vanished dialect. We are forced, he said, to believe all these widely separate nations are descendents of a single primitive people's influence. Oddly enough, Schlegel learned Sanskrit himself at the hands of Alexander Hamilton, his close friend and a close friend to the Prussian government. Both Hamilton and Prussia esteemed Schlegel highly.

To put yourself in touch with this exciting moment in recent history requires only a visit to a neighborhood library. The language and customs of this ancient Aryan people are caught in Vedic literature—the story of an invading people who forced themselves on the Indian subcontinent. As Americans had forced themselves on North American natives, a resonant parallel. Aryan literature was exclusively a literature of battle and unyielding hostility, the Vedas stirring hymns of a people surrounded by strangers alien in race and religion.

There could be no peace with such strangers; their destruction was a duty owed to God. Full of vigor, the Vedas breathe the attitudes of an invading race bent on conquest, a cultural prescription with which to meet the challenges of modern times. If only a way could be found to link this warrior people with the elites of England and America.

In 1816, the brilliant young Danish scholar Rasmus Rask not only accepted the relationship of Germanic, Hellenic, Italic, Baltic, and Indo-Iranian, but went further and found the missing connection. Rask had seen something no one else had noticed: between some Germanic streams of language and the others a regular sound-shift had occurred transforming the sounds of B, D, and G into those of P, T, and K. It meant an absolute identification could be established between England and ancient Germania. Rask wasn't prominent enough to promote this theory very far, but the man who stole it from him was—Jacob Grimm of fairy-tale fame. In the second edition of *Deutsche Grammatik* (1822) Grimm claimed the sound shift discovery which to this day is called "Grimm's Law." Salons on both sides of the Atlantic buzzed with the exciting news.

Our Manifest Destiny

Now the Aryans became the Anglo-Saxons. Endings in Sanskrit, Persian, Greek, Latin, and Germanic showed how they had moved across the world, said another German researcher Franz Bopp. By 1820, a Gothic vogue was afoot. Even the bare possibility that some of us were offspring of a powerful race out of time inspired enthusiasm, giving credence to the old Puritan notion of "Election," that America had a divine destiny as a people. This incredible Aryan drama, like the notion of evolution a few decades later with which it should be seen in collegial relation, almost instantly began to embody itself in more practical affairs of life.

To New York State University regent John O'Sullivan, Grimm's tale was the long-awaited scientific proof of an American destiny, a Manifest Destiny as he and innumerable voices that followed were to call it:

The right of our manifest destiny is to overspread and to possess the whole of the continent which Providence has given up for the great experiment.

In 1851, as *Moby Dick* was coming off the press with its parable of Ahab, a year after *Scarlet Letter* had plumbed the secrets of Puritan society, regent O'Sullivan personally equipped a war vessel for an attack on Cuba. O'Sullivan's *Cleopatra* was seized in New York harbor as she weighed anchor, disgorging several hundred armed Hungarian and German cutthroats, "Kossuth sympathizers" as the press mistakenly called them. Indeed, the scheme to "liberate" Hungary, nominally under Hungarian aristocrat Lajos Kossuth, had been hatched by the same *zeitgeist* and in the same place, New York City. Charged with violating the Neutrality Act of 1818, O'Sullivan beat the rap. Cuba was safe for another 47 years until the battleship *Maine* blew up mysteriously in Havana harbor.

Buried in the indestructible heart of this imported Aryan linguistic romance was ample justification for a national charter of bold expansionism. In spite of the fact much of the American nation was empty still, it provided an inspiration to empire as O'Sullivan's abortive sortie demonstrated, a racial mandate to enlarge areas of American influence as Aryans once had conquered as far as ambition could carry them. Race was the font of our national greatness. But how to preserve the Great Race from miscegenation? It was a question asked long before Darwin lent the query the authority of official science.

The Lost Tribes

As the exciting intelligence from Germany traveled through America, it encountered resistance, for America was a region where class lines were still elastic, based on accomplishment and worldly success, not upon guarantees cemented in blood. Yet the tide was running toward a different form of reckoning. Horace Bushnell, famous Congregationalist pastor of Hartford (where the city park is named for him) thundered from his pulpit in 1837 that noble Anglo-Saxon blood must be preserved against pollution. By 1843, the big book in Unitarian Boston was *The Goths of New England*. German schooling seemed right for us because we *were* Germans! Germany held answers for the grandchildren of Englishmen, who had been Germans long ago.

In 1848, at the height of the Irish Catholic menace, *The American Whig Review* published "The Anglo-Saxon Race." That same year *The North American Review* responded with, "The Anglo-Saxon Race." Now the *Whig Review* stirred the pot with its own spoon, "The Anglo-Saxons and the Americans." Interest in the topic wouldn't quit, perhaps because *Origin of Species* finally placed consideration of racial matters in public attention. Racial fervor was still at white heat in 1875 when a popular book, *The Anglo-Saxon Race: Its History, Character and Destiny*, traveled with Chautauqua to every corner of the nation.

The writings of William Henry Poole showed the Saxon race to be *the lost tribes of Israel!* To this day, most American Jews are unaware that a substantial number of old-family Anglo-Saxons consider *themselves* to be the real Jews—and the nominal Jews imposters! Between 1833 and 1852 Franz Bopp published book after book of his spectacular multi-volume work, *Comparative Grammar,* which drove any lingering skeptics to cover. The Aryans were real. Case closed.

Whatever guardian spirit watches over such things assigned the task of presenting Aryan tribal character and tying it to contemporary Anglo-Saxons to Sir Henry James Sumner Maine, English comparative jurist and historian. Maine graduated from Cambridge in 1844 with the reputation of being the most brilliant classical scholar of all time. Maine was the Michael Jordan of legal history. His *Ancient Law* (1861) earned him a world-class reputation in one stroke. In a series of magnificent literary studies which followed, he brought to life the ancient world of Germania with singular felicity and power. Anglo-Saxons and Aryans lived again as one people.

In the crucial year which saw Darwin's *Descent of Man* published, Maine's spectacular *Village Communities in the East and West* showed the world the rough-hewn genius of the primitive Anglo-Saxon world. Maine reiterated his contention that stranger-adoption was among the critical discoveries which led to Anglo-Saxon greatness. This message fell on particularly fertile ground in a New England whose soil had been prepared for this exact message by centuries of reading *The New England Primer*, with its grim warning that children are only *loaned* to their parents.

And what a message Maine carried—society *thrived* when children were detached from their own parents and cultures! It was a potent foundation on which to set the institution of forced schooling. Appearing shortly after the radical Massachusetts adoption law intended to disassemble Irish immigrant families, Maine silenced the new institution's critics, paving the way for eventual resignation to long-term school incarceration, too:

> The part played by the legal fiction of adoption in the constitution of primitive society and the civilization of the race is so important that Sir Henry Sumner Maine, in his *Ancient Law*, expresses the opinion that, had it never existed, the primitive groups of mankind could not have coalesced except on terms of absolute superiority on the one side, and absolute subjection on the other. With the institution of adoption, however, one people might *feign itself* as descended from the same stock as the people to whose *sacra gentilica* it was admitted....
> — Encyclopedia Britannica, 11th edition, "Adoption"

In a grand stroke, Sir Henry provided enlightened justification for *every* form of synthetic parenting social engineers could concoct, including the most important, mass forced schooling.

Unpopular Government

Each successive book by Maine built his case more strongly: *Early Law and Custom* (1883), *Early History of Institutions* (1875). His magnificent *tour de force, Popular Government* (1885), smashed the very basis for popular democracy. After Maine, only a fool could believe *non*-Anglo-Saxon groups should participate as equals in important decision making. At the same time, Maine's forceful dismissal of the fundamental equality of ordinary or different peoples was confirmed by the academic science of evolution and by commercial and manufacturing interests eager to collapse smaller enterprises into large ones. Maine's regal pronouncements were supported by mainstream urban Protestant churches and by established middle classes. Democratic America had been given its death sentence.

Sir Henry's work became a favorite text for sermons, lectures, Chautauqua magazine journalism and for the conversation of the best people; his effect is reflected symbolically in a resolution from the Scranton Board of Trade of all places, which characterized immigrants as:

> The most ignorant and vicious of European population, including necessarily a vast number of the criminal class; people who come here not to become good citizens, but to prey upon our people and our industries; a class utterly without character and incapable of understanding or appreciating our institutions, and therefore a menace to our commonwealth.

Popular Government was deliberately unpopular in tone. There was no connection between democracy and progress; the reverse was true. Maine's account of racial history was accepted widely by the prosperous. It admirably complemented the torrent of scientifically mathematicized racism pouring out of M.I.T., Harvard, Stanford, Yale, and virtually every bastion of high academia right through the WWI period and even beyond scientific racism, which determined the shape of government schooling in large measure, and still does.

Kinship Is Mythical

Aryans, said Maine, were not overly sentimental about children. They maintained the right to kill or sell their children and carried this custom with them as they spread over the earth, almost up to the outskirts of modern Beijing. These Great Ones had an intensely practical streak, tending to extract from every association its maximum payoff.

This pragmatism led them to extend privileges of kinship to every association in which a good chance of profit might lurk. This casual disregard of blood ties led to powerful alliances much more adaptable to local circumstance than any pure blood-allegiance system could be, such as the one the Japanese practice. In other words, Anglo-Saxons were prepared to call anyone "family" for a price. Similarly, Anglo-Saxon ties to priests and gods were mostly ceremonial. All rules, ethics, and morals were kept flexible, relative to the needs of the moment. This lack of commitment to much of anything except possessions allowed Aryans to overturn local ways in which people held to principles and to local faith.

Pragmatism was an impressive and effective technological advance in politics, if not in morality. In the science of society, the leadership reserved the right to lie, cheat, deceive, be generally faithless wherever advantage presented itself, and not only to do these things to the enemy but to one's own people if need be—a moral code well suited to a fast-moving warrior people. But a price had to be paid. Over time, the idea of real kinship became more and more fictitious, family life characterized as much by ritual and ceremony as love. And in many places, said Maine, kinship, owing to mass adoption of children from conquered peoples, *became mythical for whole clans.* Nobody was who they said they were or thought themselves to be.

It is surely one of the grim jokes of history that the root identity of American elites was crystalizing at the turn of the century around blood relationships to a warrior people so indifferent to blood relationships, they often had no idea who they really were. With Anglo-Saxons, the abstract principle always counted for more than flesh and blood.

Once the character of the Aryans was known, there remained only the exciting task of establishing the homeland, the ancient forge of these virile conquerors. The behavioral ideals they willed their descendants—to impose upon lesser peoples—were written clearly enough on the chalkboards of the new schooling. Total submission led the list. But giving the Aryans a birthplace (assuming it was the right one) would complete the circle of triumph. To the elite mind that job was over by 1880. The ancient ancestor could now be fixed by common agreement somewhere in the cold North around the Baltic Sea. Some said Scandinavia. Some said North-Central Germany. But the chief detectives holding the Anglo/American franchise on truth homed in on that zone between the Elbe and the Oder Rivers, to the lands comprising the regions of modern Prussia!

The Machine Gun Builds Hotchkiss

The widow of the man who perfected the machine gun founded the Hotchkiss School; a Lowell and a Forbes funded Middlesex; the DuPonts were the patrons of Kent; St. George's was underwritten by the Brown family whose name graces Brown University; Choate looked to the Mellon family for generous checks; J.P. Morgan was behind Groton. Over 90 percent of the great American private boarding schools issued from that short period just after Herbert Spencer's American visit and just before the indirect edict to the National Education Association, that it must play ball with the de-intellectualization of public schooling or it would be abandoned by America's business leadership.

Elite private boarding schools were an important cornerstone in the foundation of a permanent American upper class whose children were to be socialized for power. They were great schools for the Great Race, intended to forge a collective identity among children of privilege, training them to be bankers, financiers, partners in law firms, corporate directors, negotiators of international treaties and contracts, patrons of the arts, philanthropists, directors of welfare organizations, members of advisory panels, government elites, and business elites.

Michael Useem's post-WWII study showed that just 13 elite boarding schools educated 10 percent of all the directors of large American business corporations, and 15 percent of all the directors who held three or more directorships. These schools collectively graduated less than 1,000 students a year. More spectacular pedagogy than that is hard to imagine.

In England, the pioneer feminist Victoria Woodhull published *The Rapid Multiplication of The Unfit*. And in the States Edward A. Ross, trained in Germany—University of Wisconsin pioneer of American sociology—was writing *The Old World in the New*, saying that "beaten members of beaten breeds" would destroy us unless placed under control. They were "subhuman." Ross was joined by virtually every leading social scientist of his generation in warning about the ill effects of blood pollution: Richard Ely, William Z. Ripley, Richard Mayo Smith, John R. Commons, Davis Dewey, Franklin Giddings, and many more. None disagreed with Ross. Morons were multiplying. The government had to be made aware of *the biological consequences of social policy*.

But while beaten members of beaten breeds had to be zipped up tight in isolation, ward schools and neighborhoods of their own, watched over by social gospelers, settlement houses, and social workers trained in the new social science, a new American social dimension was being created from scratch in which the best people could associate freely, could rear children properly, could reap rewards they deserved as the most advanced class on the evolutionary tree. That was not only justice, it was prudent preparation for an even better biological future.

The way the new shadow society, a universe parallel to the one everyone else could see, had to operate after it had first constructed for itself *a theory of establishment* and *a theology of caste* was by creating a new social structure, corporate in nature, in which man was progressively defined by who he affiliated with, his synthetic, associational tribe—not by his independent talents and accomplishments. If these affiliations were only local, then status was correspondingly diminished; the trick was to progressively graduate to memberships which had regional, national, or even international status, and this associational prestige would then be transferred to the individual. What a perfect way to keep out the riffraff and porch monkeys this would prove to be!

When John Lupton, Director of Development at the Choate School in Wallingford, Connecticut said, "There is no door in this entire country that cannot be opened by a Choate graduate. I can go anywhere in this country and anywhere there's a man I want to see... I can find a Choate man to open that door for me," it was no idle boast, nor was the statement a simple expression of snobbery. The crucial variables in identifying the right people in the new exclusionary America no longer included high profile expressions of superiority. What they did include were: 1) Membership in the right metropolitan clubs. 2) An address in the right neighborhoods. 3) A degree from the right college. 4) A membership in the right country club. 5) Attendance at the right summer resorts. 6) Attendance at the right churches. 7) Passage through the right private schools. 8) An invitation to the right hereditary association. 9) Involvement in the right charities. 10) Trusteeships, boards, advisory councils. 11) The right marriages, alliances, a Social register listing. 12) Money, manners, style, physical beauty, health, conversation.

I've made no attempt to enter subtleties of gradation, only to indicate how the ephors behind public schooling and virtually all significant decision-making in modern American society created, quite self-consciously, a well-regulated world within a world for themselves. Provision was made to allow some movement up from other classes. Clubs for instance were also agencies for assimilating men of talent and their families into an upperclass way of life and social organization.

If we are unwilling to face how very far-reaching the effects of this American establishment are to schoolchildren, there is just no good way to think about school reform.[5] Darwin's evolutionary racism, Galton's mathematical racism, Maine's anthropological racism, Anglican theological racism/classism, all are deeply embedded in the structure of mass schooling and the economy it serves. They *cannot* be extirpated by rational discussion; these viruses are carried by institutional structures not amenable to social discussion.

Fountains Of Business Wealth

The new American establishment of the twentieth century was organized around the fountains of wealth international corporate business provides. By 1900 huge businesses had begun already to dominate American schooling, and the metropolitan clubs where business was transacted lay at the core of upper class authority in every major city in the nation. The men's club emerged as the principal agency where business agreements were struck and, indirectly, where school policy was forged.

In 1959, *Fortune* magazine shocked a portion of our still innocent nation by announcing where national policy and important deals really were made in New York City. If the matter was relatively minor, the venue would be *the Metropolitan, the Union League,* or *the University*; if it were a middling matter it would be determined at *the Knickerbocker* or *the Racquet*; and if it required the utmost attention of powerful men, *Brook* or *Links*. Nothing happened in boardrooms or executive suites where it could be overheard by outlanders. Each city had this private ground where aristocracy met quietly out of the reach of prying eyes or unwelcome attendants. In San Francisco, the Pacific Union; in Washington, Cosmos or the Chevy Chase Club; the Somerset in Boston; Duquesne in Pittsburgh; the Philadelphia Club in Philadelphia; the Chicago Club in Chicago. Once hands were shaken in these places, the process of public debate and certification was choreographed elsewhere for public and press. Government business came to be done this way, too.

The entire web of affiliations among insiders in business, government, and the nonprofit sector operates through interpersonal and institutional ties which interconnect at the highest levels of finance, politics, commerce, school affairs, social work, the arts, and the media. Continuing conflicts of value within the leadership community give an appearance of adversarial proceedings, but each passing decade brings more and more harmony to the unseen community which plans the fate of schools and work.

The General Education Board And Friends

Reading though the "Occasional Letters" of the Rockefeller Foundation's General Education Board, an endowment unrivaled in school policy influence in the first half of the twentieth century

---

[5] Nelson W. Aldrich, grandson of Senator Aldrich of Rhode Island, who was one of the principal architects of the Federal Reserve system, put it this way in his book, *Old Money*: "Membership in this patriciate brought with it much besides wealth, of course: complete domination of all educational and cultural institutions, ownership and control of the news media [and a variety of other assets]." Direct and indirect domination of the forced schooling mechanism by the patriciate has never been adequately explored, perhaps owing to its owners of both the tools of research (in the colleges) and the tools of dissemination (in the media).

except by Andrew Carnegie's various philanthropies, seven curious elements force themselves on the careful reader:

1) There appears a clear intention to mold people through schooling, 2) There is a clear intention to eliminate tradition and scholarship, 3) The net effect of various projects is to create a strong class system verging on caste, 4) There is a clear intent to reduce mass critical intelligence while supporting infinite specialization, 5) There is clear intent to weaken parental influence, 6) There is clear intent to overthrow accepted custom, 7) There is striking congruency between the cumulative purposes of GEB projects and the utopian precepts of the oddball religious sect, once known as Perfectionism, a secular religion aimed at making the perfection of human nature the purpose of existence. The agenda of philanthropy, which had so much to do with the schools we got, turns out to contain an intensely political component.

This is not to deny that genuine altruistic interests aren't also a part of philanthropy, but as Ellen Lagemann correctly reflects in her interesting history of the Carnegie Foundation for the Advancement of Teaching, *Private Power for the Public Good*, "In advancing some interests, foundations have inevitably *not* advanced others. Hence their actions must have political consequences, even when political purposes are not avowed or even intended. To avoid politics in dealing with foundation history is to miss a crucial part of the story."

Edward Berman in *Harvard Education Review*, 49 (1979), puts it more brusquely. Focusing on Rockefeller, Carnegie, and Ford philanthropies, he concludes that the "public rhetoric of disinterested humanitarianism was little more than a facade" behind which the interests of the political state (not necessarily those of society) "have been actively furthered." The rise of foundations to key positions in educational policy formation amounted to what Clarence Karier called "the development of a fourth branch of government, one that effectively represented the interests of American corporate wealth."

The corporate foundation is mainly a twentieth century phenomenon, growing from 21 specimens of the breed in 1900 to approximately 50,000 by 1990. From the beginning, foundations aimed squarely at educational policy formation. Rockefeller's General Education Board obtained an incorporating act from Congress in 1903 and immediately began to organize schooling in the South, joining the older Slater cotton/woolen manufacturing interests and Peabody banking interests in a coalition in which Rockefeller picked up many of the bills.

From the start, the GEB had a mission. A letter from John D. Rockefeller specified that his gifts were to be used "to promote a comprehensive system." You might well ask what interests the system was designed to promote but you would be asking the wrong question. "The key word is system," the Baptist minister Frederick Gates, hired to disburse Rockefeller largesse, said tersely. American life was too unsystematic to suit corporate genius. Rockefeller's foundation was about systematizing us.

In 1913, the Sixty-Second Congress created a commission to investigate the role of these new foundations of Carnegie, Rockefeller, and of other corporate families. After a year of testimony it concluded:

> The domination of men in whose hands the final control of a large part of
> American industry rests is not limited to their employees, but is being rapidly
> extended to control the education and social services of the nation.

Foundation grants directly enhance the interests of the corporations sponsoring them. The conclusion of this congressional commission:

> The giant foundation exercises enormous power through direct use of its funds, free of any statutory entanglements so they can be directed precisely to the levers of a situation; this power, however, is substantially increased by building collateral alliances which insulate it from criticism and scrutiny.

Foundations automatically make friends among banks which hold their large deposits, in investment houses which multiply their monies, in law firms which act as their counsels, and inside the many firms, institutions, and individuals with which they deal and whom they benefit. By careful selection of trustees from the ranks of high editorial personnel and other media executives and proprietors, they can assure themselves press support, and by engaging public relations counselors can further create good publicity. As René Wormser, chief counsel for the second congressional inquiry into foundation life (1953), put it:

> All its connections and associations, plus the often sycophantic adulation of the many institutions and individuals who receive largesse from the foundation, give it an enormous aggregate of power and influence. This power extends beyond its immediate circle of associations, to those who hope to benefit from its bounty.

In 1919, using Rockefeller money, John Dewey, by now a professor at Columbia Teachers College, an institution heavily endowed by Rockefeller, founded the Progressive Education Association. Through its existence it spread the philosophy which undergirds welfare capitalism—that the bulk of the population is biologically childlike, requiring lifelong care.

From the start, Dewey was joined by other Columbia professors who made no secret that the objective of the PEA project was to use the educational system as a tool to accomplish political goals:

> A new public mind is to be created. How? Only by creating tens of millions of individual minds and welding them into a new social mind. Old stereotypes must be broken up and "new climates of opinion" formed in the neighborhoods of America.

> Through the schools of the world we shall disseminate a *new conception of government*—one that will embrace all the activities of men, one that will postulate *the need of scientific control*...in the interest of all people.
> — Harold Rugg, *The Great Technology* (1933)

In similar fashion, the work of the Social Science Research Council culminated in a statement of *Conclusions and Recommendations* on its Carnegie Foundation-funded operations which had enormous and lasting impact upon education in the United States. *Conclusions* (1934) heralded the decline of the old order, stating aggressively that "*a new age* of collectivism is emerging" which will involve the supplanting of private property by public property" and will require "experimentation" and "almost certainly...a larger measure of *compulsory cooperation* of citizens...a corresponding enlargement of the functions of government, and an increasing state intervention... Rights will be altered and abridged."

Conclusions was a call to the teacher colleges to instruct their students to "condition" children into an acceptance of the new order in progress. Reading, writing, and arithmetic were to be marginalized as irrelevant, even counterproductive. "As often repeated, the first step is to consolidate leadership around the philosophy and purpose of education *herein expounded*." The difficulties in trying to understand what such an odd locution as "compulsory cooperation" might really mean, or even trying to determine what historic definition of "education" would fit such a usage were ignored. Those who wrote this report, and some of those who read it, were the only ones who held the Rosetta Stone to decipher it.

In an article in *Progressive Education Magazine*, Professor Norman Woelfel wrote in response to the Carnegie report: "It might be necessary paradoxically for us to control our press as the Russian press is controlled and as the Nazi press is controlled.... In the minds of men who think experimentally, America is conceived as having a destiny which bursts the all too obvious limitations of Christian religious sanctions."

The Rockefeller-endowed Lincoln Experimental School at Columbia Teachers College was the testing ground for Harold Rugg's series of textbooks which moved five million copies by 1940 and millions more after that. In these books Rugg advanced this theory: "Education must be used to condition the people to accept social change....The chief function of schools is to plan the future of society."

In *Social Chaos and the Public Mind* (1933), a book which, like many of his activities over three vital decades on the school front, was eventually translated into practice in urban centers. Rugg advocated that the major task of schools be seen as "indoctrinating" youth, using social "science" as the "core of the school curriculum" to bring about the desired climate of public opinion.

Some attitudes Rugg advocated teaching were reconstruction of the national economic system to provide for central controls and an implantation of the attitude that educators as a group were "vastly superior to a priesthood:"

> Our task is to create swiftly a compact body of minority opinion for the
> scientific reconstruction of our social order.

Money for Rugg's six textbooks came from Rockefeller foundation grants to the Lincoln School. He was paid two salaries by the foundation, one as an educational psychologist for Lincoln, the other as a professor of education at Teachers College, in addition to salaries for secretarial and research services. The General Education Board provided a sum (equivalent to $500,000 in year 2000 purchasing power) to produce three books which were then distributed by the National Education Association.

In 1954, a second congressional investigation of foundation tampering (with schools and American social life) was attempted, headed by Carroll Reece of Tennessee. The Reece Commission quickly ran into a buzzsaw of opposition directed at it out of influential centers of American corporate life. Major national newspapers hurled scathing criticisms, which, together with pressure from other potent political adversaries, forced the committee to disband prematurely, but before there were some tentative findings:

> The power of the individual large foundation is enormous. Its various forms of patronage carry with them elements of thought control. It exerts immense influence on educator, educational processes, and educational institutions. It is capable of invisible coercion. It can materially predetermine the development of social and political concepts, academic opinion, thought leadership, public opinion.

> The power to influence national policy is amplified tremendously when foundations act in concert. There is such a concentration of foundation power in the United States, operating in education and the social sciences, with a gigantic aggregate of capital and income. This *Interlock* has some of the characteristics of an intellectual cartel. It operates in part through certain intermediary organizations supported by the foundations. It has ramifications in almost every phase of education.

> It has come to exercise very extensive practical control over social science and education. A system has arisen which gives enormous power to a relatively small group of individuals, having at their virtual command huge sums in public trust funds.

> The power of the large foundations and The Interlock has so influenced press, radio, television, and even government that it has become extremely difficult for objective criticism of anything the Interlock approves to get into news channels—without having first been ridiculed, slanted and discredited.

> Research in the social sciences plays a key part in the evolution of our society. Such research is now almost wholly in the control of professional employees of the large foundations. Even the great sums allotted by federal government to social science research have come into the virtual control of this professional group.

> Foundations have promoted a great excess of empirical research as contrasted with theoretical research, promoting an irresponsible "fact-finding mania" leading all too frequently to "scientism" or fake science.

> Associated with the excessive support of empirical method, the concentration of foundation power has tended to promote "moral relativity" to the detriment of our basic moral, religious, and governmental principles. It has tended to promote the concept of "social engineering," that foundation-approved "social scientists" alone are capable of guiding us into better ways of living, substituting synthetic principles for fundamental principles of action.

> These foundations and their intermediaries engage extensively in political activity, not in the form of direct support of candidates or parties, but in the conscious promotion of carefully calculated political concepts.

The impact of foundation money upon education has been very heavy, tending to promote uniformity in approach and method, tending to induce the educator to become an agent for social change and a propagandist for the development of our society in the direction of some form of collectivism. In the international field, foundations and the Interlock, together with certain intermediary organizations, have exercised a strong effect upon foreign policy and *upon public education in things international*. This has been accomplished by vast propaganda, by supplying executives and advisers to government, and by controlling research through the power of the purse. The net result has been to promote "internationalism" in a particular sense—a form directed toward "world government" and a derogation of American nationalism.

Here we find ourselves confronted with the puzzling duty of interpreting why two separate congressional committees convened 50 years apart to study the workings of the new foundation institutions, one under a Democratic Congress, one under a Republican Congress, both reached essentially the same conclusions. Both adjudged foundations a clear and present danger to the traditional liberties of American national life. Both pointed to the use of foundation influence to create the blueprint of American school life. Both saw that class system in America had emerged and was being supported by the class system in schooling. Both called for drastic action. And both were totally ignored.

Actually the word "ignored" doesn't begin to do justice to what really occurred. These congressional investigations—like Sir Walter Scott's missing *Life of Napoleon Bonaparte*—have not only vanished from public imagination, they aren't even alluded to in press discussions of schooling. Exactly as if they had never happened. Now this would be more understandable if their specific philanthropies were dull, pedestrian giveaways designed to distribute largesse and to build up good feeling toward the benevolence of colossal wealth and power. But the reality is strikingly different—corporate wealth through the foundations has advanced importantly the dumbing down of America's schools, the creation of a scientific class system, and important attacks on family integrity, national identification, religious rights, and national sovereignty.

"School is the cheapest police," Horace Mann once said. It was a sentiment publicly spoken by every name—Sears, Pierce, Harris, Stowe, Lancaster, and the rest—prominently involved in creating universal school systems for the coal powers. One has only to browse Merle Curti's *Social Ideas of the Great Educators* to discover that the greatest social idea educators had to sell the rich, and which they lost no opportunity to sell, was the police function of schooling. Although a pedagogical turn in the Quaker imagination is the reason schools came to look like penitentiaries, Quakers are not the principal reason they came to behave like maximum security institutions. The reason they came to exist at all was to stabilize the social order and train the ranks. In a scientific, industrialized, corporate age, "stability" was much more exquisitely defined than ordinary people could imagine. To realize the new stability, the best breeding stock had to be drawn up into reservations, likewise the ordinary. "The Daughters of the Barons of Runnemede" is only a small piece of the puzzle; many more efficient and subtler quarantines were essayed.

Perhaps subtlest of all was the welfare state, a welfare program for everybody including the lowest in which the political state bestowed alms the way the corporate Church used to do. Although the most visible beneficiaries of this gigantic project were those groups increasingly referred to as "masses," the poor were actually people most poorly served by this latter-day Hindu creation of Fabian socialism and the corporate brain trust. Subsidizing the excluded of the new society and economy was, it was believed, a humanitarian way to calm these troubled waters until the Darwinian storm had run its inevitable course into a new, genetically-arranged utopia.

In a report from the Carnegie endowment, issued in 1984 and widely publicized, the connection between corporate capitalism and the welfare state becomes manifest in a public document bearing the name Alan Pifer, then president of the Carnegie Corporation. Apparently fearing that the Reagan administration would alter the design of the Fabian project beyond its ability to survive, Pifer warned:

> A mounting possibility of severe social unrest, and the consequent development
> among the upper classes and the business community of sufficient fear for the
> survival of our capitalist economic system to bring about an abrupt change of
> course. Just as we built the general welfare state...and expanded it in the 1960s
> as a safety valve for the easing of social tension, so will we do it again in the
> 1980s. Any other path is too risky.

In the report quoted from, new conceptions of pedagogy were introduced which we now see struggling to be born: national certification for school teachers, bypassing the last vestige of local control in states, cities, and villages; a hierarchy of teacher positions; a project to bring to an end the hierarchy of school administrators—now adjudged largely an expenditure counter-productive to good social order, a failed experiment.

In the new form, lead teachers manage schools after the British fashion and hire business administrators. The first expressions of this new initiative included the "mini-school" movement, now evolved into the charter school movement. Without denying these ideas a measure of merit, understanding that their source is the same institutional consciousness which once sent river ironclads full of armed detectives to break the steel union at Homestead, machine-gunned the strikers at River Rouge, and burned to death women and children in Ludlow, should inspire some emotions more pensive than starry-eyed enthusiasm.

The actual corridor on which the author spent much of his adult life.

CHAPTER THIRTEEN

The Empty Child

Walden Two (1948) B.F. Skinner.   This utopist is a psychologist, inventor of a mechanical baby-tender, presently engaged on experiments testing the habit capacities of pigeons. Halfway through this contemporary utopia, the reader may feel sure, as we did, that this is a beautifully ironic satire on what has been called "behavioral engineering".... Of all the dictatorships espoused by utopists, this is the most profound....The citizen of this ideal society is placed during his first year in a sterile cubicle, wherein the conditioning begins.... In conclusion, the perpetrator of this "modern" utopia looks down from a nearby hill of the community which is his handiwork and proclaims: "I like to play God!"

— Negley and Patrick, *The Quest For Utopia*

Miss Skinner Commits Self-Slaughter

At the university people used to call Kings College before the American Revolution, I lived for a time under a psychological regime called Behaviorism, in the last golden moments before Mind Science took over American schooling. At Columbia, I was in on the transformation without ever knowing it. By the time it happened, I had shape-shifted into a schoolteacher, assigned to spend my adult life as a technician in the human rat cage we call public education.

Although I may flatter myself, for one brief instant I think I was the summer favorite of Dr. Fred S. Keller at Columbia, a leading behaviorist of the late 1950s whose own college textbook was dedicated to his mentor, B.F. Skinner, that most famous of all behaviorists from Harvard. Skinner was then rearing his own infant daughter in a closed container with a window, rigged with signaling levers and a food chute, called a Skinner Box.

Italian parents giving their own children a glass of wine in those days might have ended up in jail and their children in foster care, but what Skinner did was perfectly legal. For all I know, it still is. What happened to Miss Skinner? She killed herself at 21. You win some, you lose some when you're a big-time rat psychologist raising your daughter in a cage.

Speaking of boxes, Skinner commanded boxes of legal tender lecturing and consulting with business executives on the secrets of mass behavior he had presumably learned by watching trapped rats. From a marketing standpoint, the hardest task the rising stock of behavioral psychology had in peddling its wares was masking its basic stimulus-response message (albeit one with a tiny twist) in enough different ways to justify calling Behaviorism "a school." Fat consultancies were beginning to be available in the postwar years, but the total lore of Behaviorism could be learned in about a day, so its embarrassing thinness required fast footwork to conceal. Being a behaviorist then would hardly have taxed the intellect of a parking lot attendant; it still doesn't.

In those days, the U.S. Government was buying heavily into these not-so-secret secrets, as if anticipating that needy moment scheduled to arrive at the end of the twentieth century when Richard Barnet of the Institute for Policy Studies would write for *Harper's* in a voice freighted with doom:

> The problem is starkly simple. An astonishingly large and increasing
> number of human beings are not needed or wanted to make the goods
> or provide the services that the paying customers of the world can afford.

In the decades prior to this Malthusian assessment, a whole psychological Institute for Social Cookery sprang up like a toadstool in the U.S. to offer recipe books for America's future. Even then they knew that 80 percent of the next generation was neither needed nor wanted. Remedies had to be found to dispose of the menace psychologically.

Skinner had wonderful recipes, better than anyone's. Not surprisingly, his procedures possessed a vague familiarity to readers listed in the *Blue Book* or the *Social Register*, people whose culture made them familiar with the training of dogs and falcons. Skinner had recipes for bed wetting, for interpersonal success, for management of labor, for hugging, for decision-making. His industrial group prepackaged hypotheses to train anyone for any situation. By 1957, his machines constituted the psychological technology of choice in institutions with helpless populations: juvenile detention centers, homes for the retarded, homes for wayward mothers, adoption agencies, orphan asylums—everywhere the image of childhood was most debased. The pot of gold at the end of Skinner's rainbow was School.

Behaviorism's main psychological rival in 1957 was psychoanalysis, but this rival had lost momentum by the time big government checks were available to buy psychological services. There were many demerits against psychoanalysis: its primitive narrative theory, besides sounding weird, had a desperate time *proving* anything statistically. Its basic technique required simple data to be elaborated beyond the bounds of credibility. Even where that was tolerable, it was useless in a modern school setting built around a simulacrum of precision in labeling.

Social learning theorists, many academic psychiatrists, anthropologists, or other specialists identified with a university or famous institution like the Mayo Clinic, were Behaviorism's closest cash competition. But behind the complex exterior webs they wove about social behavior, all were really behaviorists at heart. Though they spun theory in the mood of Rousseau, the payoff in each case came down to selling behavioral prescriptions to the policy classes. Their instincts might lead them into lyrical flights that could link rock falls in the Crab Nebula to the fall of sparrows in Monongahela, but the bread and butter argument was that mass populations could be and should be controlled by the proper use of carrots and sticks.

Another respectable rival for the crown Behaviorism found itself holding after WWII was stage theory, which could vary from the poetic grammar of Erik Eriksson to the impenetrable mathematical tapestry of Jean Piaget, an exercise in *chutzpah* weaving the psychological destiny of mankind out of the testimony of less than two dozen bourgeois Swiss kids. Modest academic empires could be erected on allegiance to one stage theory or another, but there were so many they tended to get in each other's way. Like seven-step programs to lose weight and keep it off, stage theory provided friendly alternatives to training children like rats—but the more it came into direct competition with the misleading precision of Skinnerian psychology, the sillier its clay feet looked.

All stage theory is embarrassingly culture-bound. Talk about the attention span of kids and suddenly you are forced to confront the fact that while 18-month-old Americans become restless after 30 seconds, Chinese of that age can closely watch a demonstration for five minutes. And while eight-year-old New Yorkers can barely tie their shoes, eight-year-old Amish put in a full work day on the family homestead. Even in a population apparently homogenous, stage theory can neither predict nor prescribe for individual cases. Stage theories sound right for the same reason astrological predictions do, but the disconnect between ideal narratives and reality becomes all too clear when you try to act on them.

When stage theory was entering its own golden age in the late 1960s, Behaviorism was already entrenched as the psychology of choice. The federal government's BSTEP document and many similar initiatives to control teacher preparation had won the field for the stimulus-response business. So much money was pouring into psychological schooling from government/corporate sources, however, that rat psychologists couldn't absorb it all. A-foot-in-the-door opportunity presented itself, which stage theorists scrambled to seize.

The controlling metaphor of all scientific stage theories is not, like Behaviorism's, that people are built like machinery, but that they grow like vegetables. *Kinder* requires *garten*, an easy sell to people sick of being treated like machinery. *For all its seeming humanitarianism, stage theory is just another way to look beyond individuals to social class abstractions. If nobody possesses a singular spirit, then nobody has a sovereign personal destiny.* Mother Theresa, Tolstoy, Hitler—they don't signify for stage theory, though from time to time they are asked to stand as representatives of types.

Behaviorists

To understand empty child theory best, you have to visit with behaviorists. Their meal ticket was hastily jerry-built during the 1920s by the advertising agency guru John Watson and by Edward Lee Thorndike, founder of educational psychology. Watson and Thorndike are two of the great academic fast-buck artists of modern history. Like much that passes for wisdom on the collegiate circuit, their baby was stitched together from the carcasses of older ideas. Behaviorism (Thorndike's version, stillborn, was called "Connectionism") was a purified hybrid of Wilhelm Wundt's laboratory at Leipzig and Comte's Positivism broadcast in the pragmatic idiom of the Scottish common-sense philosophers. We needn't trace all the dead body parts pasted together to sigh at the claim of an originality which isn't there—reminiscent of Howard Gardner's present fashion as seer of multiple intelligence theory—which is an idea as ancient as the pyramids.

Behaviorists read entrails; they spy on the movements of trapped and hopeless animals, usually rats or pigeons, which gives them the advantage over other psychologists of standing on a pile of animal corpses as the emblem of their science. The study of learning is their chief occupation, how flexibly rats can be driven to run a maze or press a bar with the proper schedule of reward and punishment. Almost from the start they abjured the use of the terms *reward* and *punishment*, correctly concluding that these beg the question. Who is to say what is rewarding except the subject? And the subject tells us more credibly with his future behavior than with his testimony. You can only tell whether a reward is truly rewarding from watching future behavior. This accurate little semantic curve ball allows a new discipline to grow around the terms "positive reinforcement" (reward) and "negative reinforcement" (punishment).

Behavior to behaviorists is only what can be seen and measured; there is no inner life. Skinner added a wrinkle to the simpler idea of Pavlovian conditioning from which subsequent libraries of learned essays have been written—when he stated that the stimulus for behavior is usually generated internally. In his so-called "operant" conditioning, the stimulus is thus written with a small "s" rather than with a Pavlovian capital "S." So what? Just this: Skinner's lower-case, internal "s" leaves a tiny hole for the ghost of free will to sneak through!

Despite the furor this created in the world of academic psychology, the tempest-in-a-teapot nature of lower-case/upper-case stimuli is revealed from Skinner's further assertion these mysterious internal stimuli of his can be perfectly controlled by manipulating exterior reinforcements according to proper schedules. In other words, even if you do have a will (not certain), your will is still perfectly programmable. You can be brought to love Big Brother all the same.

The way I came to the attention of Dr. Keller's teaching assistants was by writing a program to cause coeds to surrender their virginity behaviorally without realizing they had been scored with an operant conditioning program. My blueprint delighted the assistants. Copies were prepared and sent informally to other colleges; one went, I believe, to Skinner himself. When I look back on my well-schooled self who played this stupid prank I'm disgusted, but it should serve as a warning how an army of grown-up children was and still is encouraged to experiment on each other as a form of higher-level modern thinking. An entire echelon of management has been trained in the habit of scientific pornography caught by the title of the Cole Porter song, "Anything Goes."

Behaviorism has no built-in moral brakes to restrain it other than legal jeopardy. You hardly have to guess how irresistible this outlook was to cigarette companies, proprietary drug purveyors, market researches, hustlers of white bread, bankers, stock salesmen, makers of extruded plastic knick-knacks, sugar brokers, and, of course, to men on horseback and heads of state. A short time after I began as a behaviorist, I quit, having seen enough of the ragged Eichmannesque crew at Columbia drawn like iron fillings to this magnetic program which promised to simplify all the confusion of life into underlying schemes of reinforcement.

Plasticity

The worm lives in our initial conception of human nature. Are human beings to be trusted? With what reservations? To what degree? The official answer has lately been "not much," at least since the end of WWII. Christopher Lasch was able to locate some form of surveillance, apprehension, confinement, or other security procedure at the bottom of more than a fifth of the jobs in the U.S. Presumably that's because we don't trust each other. Where could that mistrust have been learned?

As we measure each other, we select a course to follow. A curriculum is a racecourse. How we lay it out is contingent on assumptions we make about the horses and spectators. So it is with school. Are children empty vessels? What do you think? I suspect not many parents look at their offspring as empty vessels because contradictory evidence accumulates from birth, but the whole weight of our economy and its job prospects is built on the outlook that people are empty, or so plastic it's the same thing.

The commodification of childhood—making it a product which can be sold—demands a psychological frame in which kids can be molded. A handful of philosophers dominate modern thinking because they argue this idea, and in arguing it they open up possibilities to guide history to a conclusion in some perfected society. Are children empty? John Locke said they were in his *Essay Concerning Human Understanding:*

> Let us suppose the mind to be, as we say, white paper, void of all
> characters, without any ideas; how comes it to be furnished? Whence
> comes it by that vast store...? To this I answer in one word, from
> Experience; in that all our knowledge is founded, and from that it
> ultimately derives itself.

Are there no innate ideas? Does the mind lack capacities and powers of its own, being etched exclusively by sensory inputs? Locke apparently thought so, with only a few disclaimers so wispy they were abandoned by his standard bearers almost at once. Are minds blank like white paper, capable of accepting writing from whoever possesses the paper; empty like a gas tank or a sugar bowl to be filled by anyone who can locate the filler-hole? Was Fred Watson right when he said in 1930:

> Give me a dozen healthy infants, well-formed, and my own specified world
> to bring them up in and I'll guarantee to take any one at random and train
> him to become any type of specialist I might select—doctor, lawyer, artist,
> merchant-chief, and yes, even beggar-man and thief, regardless of his talents,
> his penchants, tendencies, abilities, vocations, and race of his ancestors.

Do you find something attractive in that presumption of plasticity in human nature? So did Joseph Stalin and Chairman Mao, two of the century's foremost applied behaviorists on the grand scale. So did Marshall Tito, a bargain-basement behaviorist in what used to be called Yugoslavia. A great many reflective analyses have placed our own two Roosevelt presidencies in the same broad category.

The trouble in school arises from disagreement about what life is *for*. If we believe human beings have no unique personal essence, this question is meaningless, but even then you can't get rid of the idea easily. Life commands your answer. You cannot refuse because your actions write your answer large for everyone to see, even if you don't see it yourself. As you regard human nature, you will teach. Or as someone else regards it, you will teach. There aren't any third ways.

Is human nature empty? If it is, who claims a right to fill it? In such circumstances, what can "school" mean?

If ever a situation was capable of revealing the exquisite power of metaphor to control our lives, this must be it. Are children empty? As helpless infants and dependent youth we lay exposed to the metaphors of our guardians; they colonize our spirit.

Elasticity

Among structural engineers, the terms *plastic* and *elastic* describe propensities of material; these are concepts which can also be brought to bear on the question whether human nature is built out of accidents of experience or whether there is some divine inner spark in all of us that makes each person unique and self-determining. As you decide, the schools which march forward from your decision are predestinated. Immanuel Kant thought both conditions possible, a strong, continuous effort of will tipping the balance.

In structural engineering, implications of the original builder/creator's decision are inescapable; constructions like bridges and skyscrapers do have an inner nature given them by the materials chosen and the shapes imposed, an integrity long experience has allowed us to profile. The structure will defend this integrity, resisting wind stress, for example, which threatens to change its shape permanently. Here's how the defense works:

When stress increases dangerously as it would in a hurricane, the building material becomes elastic, surrendering part of its integrity temporarily to protect the rest, compromising to save its total character in the long run. When the wind abates the urge to resume the original shape becomes dominant and the bridge or whatever relaxes back to normal. A human analogy is that we remember who we are in school even when coerced to act like somebody else. In engineering, this integrity of memory is called elastic behavior. Actors practice deliberate elasticity and the Chechens or the Hmong express remarkable group elasticity. After violent stresses abate, they remember who they are.

But another road exists. To end unbearable stress, material has a choice of surrendering its memory. Under continued stress, material can become plastic, losing its elasticity and changing its shape permanently. Watch your own kids as their schooling progresses. Are they like Chechens with a fierce personal integrity and an inner resilience? Or under the stress of the social laboratory of schooling, have they become plastic over time, kids you hardly recognize, kids who've lost their original integrity?

In the collapse of a bridge or building in high wind, a decisive turning point is reached when the structure abandons its nature and becomes plastic. Trained observers can tell when elasticity is fading because prior to the moment of collapse the structure cannot regain its original shape, it loses its spirit, taking on new and unexpected shapes in a struggle to resist further change. When this happens it is wordlessly crying HELP ME! HELP ME! just as so many kids in all the schools in which I ever taught did.

The most important task I assigned myself as a schoolteacher was helping kids regain their integrity, but I lost many, their desperate, last-ditch resistance giving way, their integrity shattering before my horrified eyes. Look back in memory at your kids before first grade, then fast forward to seventh. Have they disintegrated into warring fragments divided against themselves? Don't believe anyone who tells you that's natural human development.

If there are no absolutes, as pragmatists like Dewey assert, then human nature must be plastic. Then the spirit can be successfully deformed from its original shape and will have no sanctuary in which to resist institutional stamping. The Deweys further assert that human nature processed this way is able to perform efficiently what is asked of it later on by society. Escaping our original identity will actually improve most of us, they say. *This is the basic hypothesis of utopia-building, that the structure of personhood can be broken and reformed again and again for the better.*

Plasticity is the base on which scientific psychology must stand if it is to be prescriptive, and if not prescriptive, who needs it? Finding an aggressive, instrumental psychology associated with schooling is a sure sign empty-child attitudes aren't far away. The notion of empty children has origins predating psychology, of course, but the most important engine reshaping American schools into socialization laboratories,[1] after Wundt, was the widely publicized work of Russian physiologist Ivan Pavlov (1849-1936) who had been a student of Wundt at Leipzig. Pavlov won the Nobel in 1904, credited with discovering the conditioned reflex whereby systems of physical function *thought to be fixed biologically*, like the salivation of dogs, could be rewired to irrelevant outside stimuli, like bells ringing.

This had immense influence on the spread of behavioral psychology into government agencies and corporate boardrooms, for it seemed to herald the discovery of master wiring diagrams which could eventually bring the entire population under control of physiological psychology.

Pavlov became the most prestigious ally of the behavioral enterprise with his Nobel. His text *The Conditioned Reflex* (1926) provided a sacred document to be waved at skeptics, and his Russian nationality aided immeasurably, harmonizing well with the long romance American intellectuals had

---

[1] The whole concept of "socialization" has been the subject of a large library of books and may be considered to occupy an honored role as one of the most important ongoing studies (and debates) in modern history. In shorthand, what socialization is concerned with from a political standpoint is the discovery and application of a system of domination which does not involve physical coercion. Which (as Hegel is thought to have proven) will inevitably provoke the formation of a formidable counter-force, in time overthrowing the coercive force. The recent fall of the Soviet Union might be taken as an object lesson.

Before Hegel, the state church of England was a diligent student of socialization for 250 years along with other institutions of that society. The British landowning class was a great university of understanding how to proceed adversarially against restive groups without overt signs of intimidation, and the learnings of this class were transmitted to America. For example, during the second great enclosure movement which ended in 1875, with half of all British agricultural land in the hands of just 2,000 people, owners maintained social and political control over even the smallest everyday affairs of the countryside and village. Village halls were usually under control of the Church of England whose clergy were certifiably safe, its officials doubling as listening posts among the population. All accommodations suitable for meetings were under direct or indirect control of the landed interests. It was almost impossible for any sort of activity to take place unless it met with the approval of owners.

Lacking a long tradition of upperclass solidarity, the United States had to distill lessons from England and elsewhere with a science of public opinion control whose ultimate base was the new schools. Still, before schooling could be brought efficiently to that purpose, much time had to pass during which other initiatives in socialization were tried. One of these, the control of print sources of information, is particularly instructive.

After the Rockefeller disaster in the coal fields of southeastern Colorado in April of 1914, ordinary counter-publicity was insufficient to stem the tide of attacks on corporate America coming from mass circulation magazines such as *Leslie's Illustrated Weekly, McClures's, Everybody's, Success, Hampton's, Collier's, The Arena, The Masses,* and others. A counterattack was launched to destroy the effectiveness of the magazines employing a variety of methods: West Virginia Pulp and Paper bought *McClure's, Butterick Patterns* bought *Everybody's,* bankers folded *Success* by calling in its loans and ordered the editors of *Collier's* to change its editorial policies, the distributor of *Arena* informed the publisher that unsold copies would no longer be returned, and Max Eastman's *Masses* was doomed by the passage of legislation enabling the postmaster to remove any publication from the mails at his own discretion. Through these and similar measures, the press and magazines of the United States had been fairly effectively muzzled by 1915 with not a single printing press broken by labor goons. These mid-range steps in the socialization of American society can best be seen as exposing the will to homogenize at work in this country once the entire economy has been corporatized.

with the Soviet Union. Even today Pavlov is a name to conjure with. Russian revolutionary experimentation allowed the testing of what was possible to go much further and faster than could have happened in America and western Europe.

Notions of emptiness turn the pedestrian problem of basic skills schooling into the complex political question of which outside agencies with particular agendas to impose will be allowed to write the curriculum. And there are nuances. For instance, the old-fashioned idea of an empty container suggests a hollow to be filled, an approach not unfamiliar to people who went to school before 1960. But *plastic emptiness* is a different matter. It might lead to an armory of tricks designed to fix, distract, and motivate the subject to cooperate in its own transformation—the new style commonly found in public schools after 1960. The newer style has given rise to an intricately elaborated *theory of incentives* capable of assisting managers to work their agenda on the managed. Only a few years ago, almost every public-school teacher in the country had to submit a list of classroom motivations used for inspection by school managers.

Emptiness: The Master Theory

Conceptions of emptiness to be filled as the foundation metaphor of schooling are not confined to hollowness and plasticity, but also include theories of mechanism. La Mettrie's[2] *Man, The Machine* vision from the Enlightenment, for instance is evidence an idea regularly recurring for millennia. If we are mechanisms, we must be predetermined, as Calvin said. Then the whole notion of "Education" is nonsensical. There is no independent inner essence to be drawn forth and developed. Only *adjustments* are possible, and if the contraption doesn't work right it should be junked. Everything important about machinery is superficial.

This notion of *machine emptiness* has been the master theory of human nature since the beginning of the nineteenth century. It still takes turns in curriculum formation with theories of vegetable emptiness, plastic emptiness, systems emptiness, and from time to time, some good old-fashioned Lockean blank sheet emptiness. Nobody writes curriculum for self-determined spiritual individuals and expects to sell it in the public school market.

This hardline empiricism descends to us most directly from Locke and Hume, who both said mind lacks capacities and powers of its own. It has no innate contents. Everything etched there comes from simple sense impressions mixed and compounded. This chilly notion was greatly refined by the French *ideologues*[3] who thought the world so orderly and mechanical, the future

---

[2] Julien Offray DeLaMettrie (1709-1751) was earliest of the materialistic writers of the Enlightenment. His conclusion that religious thought was a physical disorder akin to fever forced him to flee France. In the middle of the eighteenth century his two master works, *Man, The Machine* and *Man, The Plant*, stated principles which are self-evident from the titles. The ethics of these principles are worked out in later essays. The purpose of life is to pleasure the senses, virtue is measured by self-love, the hope of the world lies in the spread of atheism. LaMettrie was compelled to flee Holland and accept the protection of Frederick of Prussia in 1748. The chief authority for his life is an essay "The Elegy," written by Frederick II himself.

[3] Ideologue is a term coined by Antoine Destuit de Tracy around 1790 to describe those empiricists and rationalists concerned to establish a new order in the intellectual realm, eradicating the influence of religion, replacing it with universal education as the premier solution to the reform of human shortcomings. They believed Hume's rationalized morality (after the methods of chemistry, physics, mathematics, and astronomy) was the best way to accomplish this.

course of history could be predicted on the basis of the position and velocity of molecules. For these men, the importance of human agency vanished entirely. With Napoleon, these ideas were given global reach a few years later. So seductive is this mechanical world view it has proven itself immune to damage by facts which contradict it.[4]

A Metaphysical Commitment

At the core of every scientific research program (and forced schooling is the largest such program in history) lies a metaphysical commitment on which all decision-making rests. For instance, the perspective of which pedagogy and behavioral science are both latter-day extensions rests on six pillars:

1) The world is independent of thought. It is atomic in its basic constituents.
2) The real properties of bodies are bulk, figure, texture, and motion.
3) Time and Space are real entities; the latter is Euclidean in its properties.
4) Mass is inert. Rest or uniform motion are equally "natural" conditions involving no consciousness.
5) Gravitational attraction exists between all masses.
6) Energy is conserved in interactions.

There is no obvious procedure for establishing any of these principles as true. There is no obvious experimental *disproof* of them either, or any way to meet Karl Popper's falsification requirement or Quine's modification of it. Yet these religious principles, as much metaphysics as physics, constitute the backbone of the most powerful research program in modern history: Newtonian physics and its modern fellow travelers.[5]

The psychology which most naturally emerges from a mechanical world view is Behaviorism, an outlook which dominates American school thinking. When you hear that classrooms have been *psychologized*, what the speaker usually means is that under the surface appearance of old-fashioned lessons what actually is underway is an experiment with human machines in a controlled setting. These experiments follow some predetermined program during which various "adjustments" are made as data feeds back to the design engineers. In a psychologized classroom, teachers and common administrators are pedagogues, kept unaware of the significance of the processes they superintend. After a century of being on the outside, there is a strong tradition of indifference or outright cynicism about ultimate purpose among both groups.

---

[4] For instance, the serious problems encountered by mechanists in the nineteenth century when developments in electricity revealed a cornucopia of nonmechanical, non-gravitational forces and entities which eroded the classical conception of matter. In optics, the work of Young and Fresnel on diffraction and refraction made Newton's particle theory of light untenable, yet it was still being taught in senior physics at Uniontown High School when I got there in the 1950s. The earth might move but human nature only accepts the move when it suits *human* purposes.

[5] My discussion here is instructed by the lectures of Michael Matthews, the scientific philosopher.

Behaviorism holds a *fictionalist* attitude toward intelligence: mind simply doesn't exist. "Intelligence" is only behavioral shorthand for, "In condition A, player B will act in range C, D, and E rather than A, B and C." There is no substantive intelligence, *only dynamic relationships* with different settings and different dramatic ceremonies.

The classic statement of behavioristic intelligence is E.G. Boring's 1923 definition, "Intelligence is what an intelligence test measures." Echoes of Boring reverberate in Conant's sterile definition of education as "what goes on in schools." Education is whatever schools say it is. This is a carry-over of Percy Bridgman's[6] recommendation for an ultimate kind of simplification in physics sometimes known as *operationalism* (which gives us the familiar "operational definition"), e.g. Boring's definition of intelligence. This project in science grew out of the positivistic project in philosophy which contends that all significant meaning lies on the surface of things. Positivism spurns any analysis of the deep structure underlying appearances. Psychological Behaviorism is positivism applied to the conjecture that a science of behavior *might* be established. It's a guess how things *ought* to work, not a science of how they do.

B.F. Skinner's entire strategy of behavioral trickery designed to create beliefs, attitudes, and behavior patterns in whole societies is set down in *Walden Two*, a bizarre illustration of some presumed uses of emptiness, but also a summary of observations (all uncredited by Skinner) of earlier undertakings in psychological warfare, propaganda, advertising research, etc., including contributions from public relations, marketing, schooling, military experience, and animal training. Much that Skinner claimed as his own wasn't even secondhand—it had been commonplace for centuries among philosophers. Perhaps all of it is no more than that.

The Limits Of Behavioral Theory

The multibillion dollar school-materials industry is stuffed with curriculum psychologized through application of behaviorist theory in its design and operation. What these kits are about is introducing various forms of external reinforcement into learning, based on the hypothesis the student is a stimulus-response machine. This surrender to questionable science fails its own test of rationality in these regards:

First and foremost, the materials don't *work* dependably. Behavior *can* be affected, but fallout is often negative and daunting. The insubstantial metaphysics of Behaviorism leads it to radically simplify reality; the content of this psychology is then always being undermined by experience.

Even some presumed core truths, e.g., "simple to complex, we learn to walk before we can run" (I've humanized the barbaric jargon of the field), are only half-truths whose application in a classroom provoke trouble. In suburban schools a slow chaos of *boredom* ensues from every behavioral program;[7] in ghetto schools the boredom turns to violence. Even in better neighborhoods,

---

[6] Physics professor, Harvard. He won the 1946 Nobel Prize. Perhaps the most influential American writer on the philosophy of science in the twentieth century.

[7] Simulation games are a notorious example because they suggest through their operations that human affairs are only simple games, less complicated than chess, in which mathematical strategies always prevail. The destructive effect of simulations appears to be cumulative. As a teacher I stayed away from them as if they were toadstools.

the result of psychological manipulation is indifference, cynicism, and overall loss of respect for the pedagogical enterprise. Behavioral theory demands endless recorded observations and assessments in the face of mountainous evidence that interruption and delay caused by "assessments" makes trouble.

By stressing *the importance of controlled experience and sensation* as the building blocks of training, Behaviorism reveals its inability to deal with the inconvenient truth that a huge fraction of experience is conceptualized in language. Without mastery of language and metaphor, we are condemned to mystification. The inescapable reality is that behind the universality of abstraction, we have a particular language with a particular personality. It takes hard work to learn how to use it, harder work to learn how to protect yourself from the deceptive language of strangers. Even our earliest experience is mediated through language since the birth vault itself is not soundproof.

Reality Engages The Banana

Michael Matthews' analysis of language as a primary behavior in itself will serve as an illustration of the holes in rat psychology. His subject is the simple banana. Contrary to the religion of Behaviorism, we don't experience bananas as soft, yellowish, mildly fibrous sense impressions. Instead reality engages the banana in drama: "Food!", "Good for you!", "Swallow it down or I'll beat you into jelly!" We learn rules about bananas (Don't rub them in the carpet), futurity (Let's have bananas again tomorrow), and value (These damn bananas cost an arm and a leg!). And we learn these things through words.

When Behaviorism pontificates that children should all "learn from experience," with the implication that books and intellectual concepts count for little, it exposes its own poverty. Behaviorism provides no way to quantify the overwhelming presence of language as *the* major experience of modern life for everyone, rich and poor. Behaviorism has to pretend words don't really matter, only "behavior" (as it defines the term).

To maintain that all knowledge is exclusively sense experience is actually not to say much at all since sense experience is continuous and unstoppable as long as we are alive. That is like saying you need to breathe to stay alive or eat to prevent hunger. Who disagrees? The fascinating aspect of this psychological shell game lies in the self-understanding of behavioral experts that they have nothing much to sell their clientele that a dog trainer wouldn't peddle for pennies. The low instinct of this poor relative of philosophy has always been to preempt common knowledge and learning ways, translate the operations into argot, process them into an institutional form, then find customers to buy the result.

There is no *purpose* down deep in any of these empty-child systems except the jigsaw puzzle addict's purpose of making every piece FIT. Why don't children learn to read in schools? *Because it doesn't matter* in a behavioral universe. This goes far beyond a contest of many methods, it's a contest of perspectives. Why *should* they read? We have too many smart people as it is; only a few have any work worth doing. Only the logic of machinery and systems protects your girl and boy when you send them off to behavioral laboratories on the yellow behaviorist bus. *Should* systems care? They aren't mom and dad, you know.

Programming The Empty Child

To get an act of faith this unlikely off the ground there had to be some more potent vision than Skinner could provide, some evidence more compelling than reinforcement schedule data to inspire men of affairs to back the project. There had to be foundational visions for the scientific quest. One will have to stand for all, and the one I've selected for examination is among the most horrifyingly influential books ever to issue from a human pen, a rival in every way to Frederick Taylor's *Scientific Management*. The author was Jean Jacques Rousseau. The book, *Emile*, published in 1762. Whether Rousseau had given his own five children away to the foundling home before or after he wrote it, I can't say for sure. Before, I'm told.

Emile is a detailed account of the total transformation of a boy of ten under the precisely calculated behavioral ministrations of a psychological schoolmaster. *Rousseau showed the world how to write on the empty child Locke had fathered*; he supplied means by which Locke's potent image could be converted to methodology. It took only a quarter century for Germans to catch on to the pick-and-shovel utility of dreamy Rousseau, only a little longer for Americans and English to do the same. Once Rousseau was fully digested, the temptation to see society's children as *human resources* proved irresistible to those nations which had gone furthest in developing the mineral resource, coal, and its useful spirits, heat and steam.

Rousseau's influence over pedagogy began when empty child explanations of human nature came to dominate. With emotional religion, village life, local elites, and American tradition reeling from hammer blows of mass immigration, the nation was broadly transformed at the beginning of the twentieth century without much conscious public awareness of what was happening.

One blueprint for the great transformation was *Emile*, an attempt to reestablish Eden using a procedure Rousseau called "negative education." Before the book gets to protagonist Emile, we are treated to this instructive vignette of an anonymous student:

> The poor child lets himself be taken away, he turned to look backward
> with regret, fell silent, and departed, his eyes swollen with tears he
> dared not shed and his heavy heart with the sigh he dared not exhale.

Thus is the student victim led to the schoolmaster. What happens next is reassurance that such a scene will never claim Emile:

> Oh you [spoken to Emile] who have nothing similar to fear; you, for whom
> no time of life is a time of constraint or boredom; you, who look forward to
> the day without disquiet and to the night without impatience—come, my
> happy and good natured pupil, come and console us.[8]

---

[8] The creepy tone of this authorial voice reminded me of a similar modern voice used by a district school psychologist for the Londonderry, New Hampshire, public schools writing in an *Education Week* article, "Teacher as Therapist:" (October, 1995):

Look at Rousseau's scene closely. Overlook its sexual innuendo and you notice the effusion is couched entirely in negatives. The teacher has no positive expectations at all, he promises an absence of pain, boredom, and ill-temper, just what Prozac delivers. Emile's instructor says the boy likes him because he knows "he will never be a long time without distraction" and because "we never depend on each other."

This idea of negation is striking. Nobody owes anybody anything; obligation and duty are illusions. Emile isn't happy; he's "the opposite of the unhappy child." Emile will learn "to commit himself to the habit of not contracting any habits." He will have no passionately held commitments, no outside interests, no enthusiasms, and no significant relationships other than with the tutor. He must void his memory of everything but the immediate moment, as children raised in adoption and foster care are prone to do. He is to feel, not think. He is to be emptied in preparation for his initiation as a mindless article of nature.

The similarity of all this to a drugged state dawns on the critical reader. Emile is to find negative freedom—freedom from attachment, freedom from danger, freedom from duty and responsibility, etc. But Rousseau scrupulously avoids a question anybody might ask: What is this freedom for? What is its point?

Dr. Watson Presumes

Leapfrogging several centuries, Dr. John B. Watson, modern father of Behaviorism, answered that question this way in the closing paragraphs of his *Behaviorism* (1925), when he appealed to parents to surrender quietly:

> I am trying to dangle a stimulus in front of you which if acted upon will gradually change this universe. For the universe will change if you bring your children up not in the freedom of the libertine, but in behavioristic freedom.... Will not these children in turn with their better ways of living and thinking replace us as society, and in turn bring up their children in a still more scientific way, until the world finally becomes a place fit for human habitation?

It was an offer School wasn't about to let your kid refuse. Edna Heidbredder, in a wonderful little book, *Seven Psychologies* (1933), was the first insider to put the bell on this cat. A psychology professor from Minnesota, she described the advent of Behaviorism this way seven decades ago:

> The simple fact is that American psychologists had grown restive under conventional restraints. They were finding the old problems lifeless and thin,

---

"Welcome"....We get a good feeling on entering this classroom.... M&M's for every correct math problem [aren't necessary]. A smile, on the other hand, a "Good Job!" or a pat on the back may be effective and all that is necessary. Smiling faces on papers (even at the high-level) with special recognition at the end of the week for the students with the most faces...can be powerful.... By setting appropriate expectations within a system of positive recognition and negative consequences, teachers become therapists.

they were "half sick of shadows" and...welcomed a plain, downright revolt. [Behaviorism] called upon its followers to fight an enemy who must be utterly destroyed, not merely to parley with one who might be induced to modify his ways.

John B. Watson, a fast-buck adman turned psychologist, issued this warning in 1919: *The human creature is purely a stimulus-response machine*. The notion of consciousness is a "useless and vicious" survival of medieval religious "superstition." Behaviorism does not "pretend to be disinterested psychology," it is "frankly" an applied science. Miss Heidbredder continues: "Behaviorism is distinctly interested in the welfare and salvation—the strictly secular salvation—of the human race."

She saw Behaviorism making "enormous conquests" of other psychologies through its "violence" and "steady infiltration" of the marketplace, figuring " in editorials, literary criticism, social and political discussions, and sermons.... Its program for bettering humanity by the most efficient methods of science has made an all but irresistible appeal to the attention of the American public."

"It has become a crusade," she said, "against the enemies of science, much more than a mere school of psychology." It has "something of the character of a cult." Its adherents "are devoted to a cause; they are in possession of a truth." And the heart of that truth is "if human beings are to be *improved* "we must recognize" the importance of infancy," for in infancy "the student may see behavior in the making, may note the repertoire of reactions a human being has...and discover the ways in which they are modified...." During the early years a child may be taught "fear," "defeat," and "surrender"—or of course their opposites. From "the standpoint of practical control" youth was the name of the game for this aggressive cult; it flowed like poisoned syrup into every nook and cranny of the economy, into advertising, public relations, packaging, radio, press, television in its dramatic programming, news programming, and public affairs shows, into military training, "psychological" warfare, and intelligence operations, but while all this was going on, selected tendrils from the same behavioral crusade snaked into the Federal Bureau of Education, state education departments, teacher training institutions, think tanks, and foundations. The movement was leveraged with astonishing amounts of business and government cash and other resources from the late 1950s onwards because the payoff it promised to deliver was vast. The prize: the colonization of the young before they had an opportunity to develop resistance. The holy grail of market research.

Back to Rousseau's *Emile*. When I left you hanging, you had just learned that Emile's "liberty" was a well-regulated one. Rousseau hastens to warn us the teacher must take great pains to "hide from his student the laws that limit his freedom." It will not do for the subject to see the walls of his jail. Emile is happy because he thinks no chains are held on him by his teacher/facilitator. But he is wrong. In fact the tutor makes Emile entirely dependent on minuscule rewards and microscopic punishments, like changes in vocal tone. He programs Emile without the boy's knowledge, boasting of this in asides to the reader. Emile is conditioned according to predetermined plan every minute, his instruction is an ultimate form of invisible mind control. The goals of Rousseau's educational plan are resignation, passivity, patience, and, joker-in-the-deck, levelheadedness.

This treating of pupils as guinea pigs became B.F. Skinner's stock in trade. In a moment of candor he once claimed, "We can achieve a sort of control under which the controlled nevertheless feel free, though they are following a code much more scrupulously than was ever the case under the old system." Rousseau was Skinner's tutor.

Cleaning The Canvas

Traditional education can be seen as sculptural in nature, individual destiny is written somewhere within the human being, awaiting dross to be removed before a true image shines forth. Schooling, on the other hand, seeks a way to make mind and character blank, so others may chisel the destiny thereon.

Karl Popper's book *The Open Society and Its Enemies* reveals with great clarity how old the idea of *tabula rasa* (erroneously attributed to John Locke) actually is. In writing of Plato's great utopia, *The Republic*, Popper shows Socrates telling auditors: "They will take as their canvas a city and the characters of men, and they will, first of all, *make their canvas clean*—by no means an easy matter....They will not start work on a city nor on an individual unless they are given a clean canvas, or have cleaned it themselves:"

> In the same spirit, Plato says in *The Statesman* of the royal rulers who rule in accordance with the royal science of statesmanship: "Whether they happen to rule by law or without law, over willing or unwilling subjects;...whether they purge the state for its good by killing or banishing some of its citizens—as long as they proceed according to science...this form of government must be declared the only one that is right." This is what canvas-cleaning means. He must eradicate existing institutions and traditions. He must purify, purge, expel, banish and kill.

Canvas-cleaning frees the individual of all responsibility. Morality is voided, replaced by reinforcement schedules. In their most enlightened form, theories of a therapeutic community are those in which *only* positive reinforcements are prescribed.

The therapeutic community is as close as your nearest public school. In the article "Teacher as Therapist," (footnote, page 270-271), a glimpse of Emile programmed on a national scale is available. Its innocently garrulous author paints a landscape of therapy, openly identifying schools as behavioral training centers whose positive and negative reinforcement schedules are planned cooperatively in advance, and each teacher is a therapist. Here everything is planned; down to the smallest "minimal recognition," nothing is accidental. Planned smiles or "stern looks," spontaneity is a weed to be exterminated—you will remember the injunction to draw smiling faces on every paper, "even at the high school level."

An important support girder of therapeutic community is a conviction that social order can be maintained by inducing students to *depend emotionally on the approval of teachers*. Horace Mann was thoroughly familiar with this principle. Here are Mann's words on the matter:

When a difficult question has been put to a child, the Teacher approaches with a mingled look of concern and encouragement [even minimal recognition requires planning, here you have a primer of instructional text]; he stands before him, the light and shade of hope and fear alternately crossing his countenance. If the little wrestler triumphs, the Teacher felicitates him upon his success; perhaps seizes and shakes him by the hand *in token congratulation*; and when the difficulty has been formidable and the effort triumphant, I have seen Teacher catch up the child and embrace him, as though he were not able to contain his joy...and all this done *so naturally and so unaffectedly* as to excite no other feeling in the residue of the children than a desire, by the same means, *to win the same caresses....*

Children were to be "loved into submission; controlled with gestures, glances, tones of voice as if they were sensitive machinery." What this passes for today is humanistic education, but the term has virtually the same magnitude of disconnect from the historical humanism of the Erasmus/DeFeltre stripe (which honored the mind and truly free choice) as modern schooling is disconnected from any common understanding of the word education.

Therapy As Curriculum

To say that various psychologies dominate modern schooling is hardly to plow new ground. The tough thing to do is to show how that happened and why—and how the project progresses to its unseen goals. The *Atlantic Monthly* had this to say in April, 1993:

Schools have turned to therapeutic remediation. A growing proportion of many school budgets is devoted to counseling and other psychological services. The curriculum is becoming more therapeutic: children are taking courses in self-esteem, conflict resolution, and aggression management. Parental advisory groups are conscientiously debating alternative approaches to traditional school discipline, ranging from teacher training in mediation to the introduction of metal detectors and security guards in the schools. Schools are increasingly becoming emergency rooms of the emotions devoted...to repairing hearts. As a result, the mission is the psychologizing of American education.

Five years before I ran across that *Atlantic* broadside, I encountered a different analysis in the financial magazine *Forbes*. I was surprised to discover *Forbes* had correctly tracked the closest inspiration for school psychologizing, both its aims and its techniques, to the pedagogy of China and the Soviet Union. Not similar practices and programs, mind you, identical ones. The great initial link with Russia, I knew, had been from the Wundtian Ivan Pavlov, but the Chinese connection was news to me. I was unaware then of John Dewey's tenure there in the 1920s, and had given no thought, for that reason, to its possible significance:

The techniques of brainwashing developed in totalitarian countries are routinely used in psychological conditioning programs imposed on school children. These include emotional shock and desensitization, psychological isolation from sources of support, stripping away defenses, manipulative cross-examination of the individual's underlying moral values by psychological rather than rational means. These techniques are not confined to separate courses or programs...they are not isolated idiosyncracies of particular teachers. They are products of numerous books and other educational materials in programs packaged by organizations that sell such curricula to administrators and teach the techniques to teachers. Some packages even include instructions on how to deal with parents and others who object. Stripping away psychological defenses can be done through assignments to keep diaries to be discussed in group sessions, and through role-playing assignments, both techniques used in the original brainwashing programs in China under Mao.

The *Forbes* writer, Thomas Sowell, perhaps invoking the slave states in part to rouse the reader's capitalist dander, could hardly have been aware himself how carefully industrial and institutional interest has seeded Russia, China, Japan, and the Pacific Islands with the doctrine of psychological schooling long ago, nearly at the beginning of the century, and in Japan's case even before that. All along we have harvested these experimental growths in foreign soil for what they seem to prove about people-shaping.

For example, the current push for *School-to-Work* deep mines specific practices of the former Soviet Union, even to the point of using identical language from Soviet texts. School-to-Work was a project installed in Russia by Americans in the 1920s to test the advice of the nineteenth century Swiss aristocrat, von Fellenberg, that manual labor should be combined with academic schooling. Fellenberg's doctrine was a short-lived fad in this country in the 1830s, but ever after it had a place in the mind of certain men of affairs and social theorists. The opportunity afforded by Russia's chaos after WWI seemed too promising to pass up.

The New Thought Tide

The great forced schooling plan even long ago was a global movement. Anatomizing its full scope is well beyond my power, but I can open your eyes partway to this poorly understood dimension of our pedagogy. Think of China, the Asian giant so prominently fixed now in headline news. Its revolution which ended the rule of emperors and empresses was conceived, planned, and paid for by Western money and intellectuals and by representatives of prominent families of business, media, and finance who followed the green flag of commerce there.

This is a story abundantly related by others, but less well known is the role of ambitious Western ideologues like Bertrand Russell, who assumed a professorship at the University of Peking in 1920 and John Dewey, who lived there for two years in the 1920s. Men like this saw a unique chance to paint on a vast blank canvas as Cecil Rhodes had shown somewhat earlier in Africa could be done by only a bare handful of men.

Listen to an early stage of the plan taken from a Columbia Teachers College text written in 1931. The author is John Childs, rising academic star, friend of Dewey. The book, *Education and the Philosophy of Experimentalism*:

During the World War, a brilliant group of young Chinese thinkers launched a movement which soon became nationwide in its influence. This movement was called in Chinese the "Hsin Szu Ch'au" which literally translated means the "New Thought Tide." Because many features of New Thought Tide were similar to those of the earlier European awakening, it became popularly known in English as "The Chinese Renaissance."

While the sources of this intellectual and social movement were various, it is undoubtedly true that some of its most able leaders had been influenced profoundly by the ideas of John Dewey....They found intellectual tools almost ideally suited to their purposes in Dewey's philosophy.... Among these tools...his view of the instrumental character of thought, his demand that all tradition, beliefs and institutions be tested continuously by their capacity to meet contemporary human needs, and his faith that the wholehearted use of the experimental attitude and method would achieve results in the social field similar to those already secured in the field of the natural sciences.

At about the time of the close of the World War, Dewey visited China. For two years, through lectures, writing, and teaching, he gave in-person powerful reinforcement to the work of the Chinese Renaissance leaders.

It's sobering to think of sad-eyed John Dewey as a godfather of Maoist China, but that he certainly was.

To Abolish Thinking

Dewey's Experimentalism[9] represented a new faith which was swallowed whole in Watson's Behaviorism. According to Childs, the unavowed aim of the triumphant psychology was "*to abolish thinking, at least for the many; for if thinking were possible the few could do it for the rest.*" For Dewey as for the behaviorists, the notion of *purpose* was peculiarly suspect since the concept of *conditioning* seemed to obsolete the more romantic term. A psychological science born of physics was sufficient to explain everything. The only utopia Behaviorism allowed was one in which the gathering of facts, statistical processing, and action based on research was allowed.

---

[9] The best evidence of how intensely the *zeitgeist* worked on Dewey is found in the many mutations his philosophy underwent. After an early flirtation with phrenology, Dewey became a leader of the Young Hegelians while William Torrey Harris, the Hegelian, presided over the Federal Department of Education, then for a brief time was a fellow traveler with the Young Herbartians when that was voguish at Columbia Teachers. Soon, however, we find him standing in line of descent from Pierce and James as a pragmatist. Thereafter he launched Instrumentalism (crashed) and Experimentalism (crashed). And there were other attempts to build a movement.

His long career is marked by confusion, vaunting ambition, and suspicious alliances with industrialists which earned him bitter enmity from his one-time acolyte, the brilliant radical Randolph Bourne. In retaliation against Bourne's criticism, Dewey destroyed Bourne's writing career by foreclosing his access to publication under threat that Dewey himself would not write for any magazine that carried Bourne's work!

It is tempting to bash (or worship) Dewey for high crimes (or high saintliness), depending on one's politics, but a greater insight into the larger social process at work can be gained by considering him as an emblem of a new class of hired gun in America, the university intellectual whose prominence comes from a supposed independence and purity of motives but who simultaneously exists (most often unwittingly) as protégé, mouthpiece, and disguise for more powerful wills than his own. Henry Kissinger or Zbigniew Brzezinski are prime examples of the type in our own day.

Dewey was determined his experimental subjects would be brought to actively participate in the ongoing experiments, not necessarily with their knowledge. All education was aimed at directing the responses of children. Orwell is really satirizing Deweyists and Fabians in his post-WWII dystopian nightmare, *1984*, when Winston Smith's execution is delayed until he can be brought to denounce the people he loves and to transfer his love to Big Brother. In Dewey's world this is only bringing Smith into active participation. That it is in his own degradation is final proof private purposes have been surrendered and the conditioning is complete.

"[We] reject completely the hypothesis of choice. We consider the traditional doctrine of 'free-will' to be both intellectually untenable and practically undesirable," is the way Childs translates Dewey. The new systems theorists, experimentalists, and behaviorists are all Wundt's children in regarding human life as a mechanical phenomenon.[10] But they are polemicists, too.

---

[10] The bleak notion of mechanism first appears unmistakably in recorded Western history in the Old Norse Religion as the theology of ancient Scandinavia is sometimes called. It is the only known major religion to have no ethical code other than pragmatism. What works is right. In Old Norse thinking, nothing was immortal, neither man nor gods; both were mere accidental conjunctions of heat and cold at the beginning of time—and they are destined to pass back into that state in an endless round.

Old Norse establishes itself in England after the Norman Conquest, locating its brain center at Cambridge, particularly at College Emmanuel from which the Puritan colonization of New England was conceived, launched, and sustained. Old Norse was slowly scientized into rational religion (various unitarian colorations) over centuries. It transmuted into politics as well, particularly the form known in England and America as Whig. An amusing clue to that is found in the history of the brilliant Whig family of Russell which produced Bertrand and many more prominent names— the Russells trace their ancestry back to Thor.

Understanding the characteristics of the Old Norse outlook in its rampant experimentalism and pragmatic nature allows us to see the road the 5,000-year civilization of China was put upon by its "New Thought Tide," and to understand how the relentlessly unsentimental caste system of Old Norse history could lead to this astonishing admission in 1908 at a National Education Association national convention:

> How can a nation endure that deliberately seeks to rouse ambitions and
> aspirations in the oncoming generations which...cannot possibly be
> fulfilled?....How can we justify our practice in schooling the masses in
> precisely the same manner as we do those who are to be leaders? Is
> human nature so constituted that those who fail will readily acquiesce in
> the success of their rivals?

The speaker was a Russell, James Russell, Dean of Columbia Teachers College. No pussy-footing there.

The Old Norse character, despising the poor and the common, passes undiluted through Malthus' famous 1798 essay in which he argues that famine, plague, and "other forms of destruction" should be visited on the poor. "We should encourage habits of filth...make the streets narrower...crowd more people into the houses and court the return

Notice Childs' hint that even if free will were intellectually tenable, it would only cause trouble.

Wundt!

The great energy that drives modern schooling owes much to a current of influence arising out of the psychology laboratory of Wilhelm Wundt at the University of Leipzig in Saxony. With a stream of international assistants, Wundt set out to examine how the human machine was best adjusted. By 1880, he laid the basis for Pavlov's work and the work of Watson in America, for the medical procedure of lobotomy, for electroshock therapy, and for the scientific view that school was a ground for social training, "socialization" in John Dewey's terminology.

Among Wundt's principal assistants was the flamboyant American, G. Stanley Hall, who organized the psychology lab at John Hopkins in 1887, established the *American Journal of Psychology*, and saw to it that Sigmund Freud was brought to America for a debut here. Stanley Hall's own star pupil at Hopkins was the Vermonter, John Dewey. Wundt's first assistant, James McKeen Cattell, was also an American, eventually the patron saint of psychological testing here. He was also the chief promoter of something called "the sight reading method," the havoc from which helped change the direction of American society. Cattell was the first "Professor of Psychology" so titled in all the world, reigning at the University of Pennsylvania. In 1894, he founded *The Psychological Review*. Over the next 25 years, he trained 344 doctoral candidates. In these stories and many others like them, the influence of Wundt and Prussia multiplied. Cattell later created the reference books *Leaders in Education, American Men of Science*, and *The Directory of American Scholars*, and for good measure, founded *Popular Science,* all of which boosted the stock of the infant discipline.

Other Wundtian Ph.D.s in the U.S. included James Baldwin who set up the psych lab at Princeton, Andrew Armstrong who did the same at Wesleyan, Charles Judd who became Director of Education at the University of Chicago, and James Earl Russell, president of Teachers College at Columbia. There were many others.

Russell's Teachers College, the Rockefeller-sponsored, Prussian-inspired seminary on 120th Street in New York City, had a long reign dominating American pedagogy. By 1950, it had processed an unbelievable one-third of all presidents of teacher-training institutions, one-fifth of all American public schoolteachers, one-quarter of all superintendents. Thus the influence of Prussian thought dominated American school policy at a high level by 1914, and the Prussian tincture was virtually universal by 1930.

---

of the plague." No pussy-footing there, either. Over a century later in *Women and the New Race* (1920), Margaret Sanger wrote, "the most merciful things a large family can do to one of its infant members is to kill it." Great Britain's Prince Philip said that if he were reincarnated he would wish to return as "a killer virus to lower human population levels." And in the November 1991 UNESCO *Courier*, Jacques Cousteau writes to demand "we must eliminate 350,000 people per day. It is a horrible thing to say, but it's just as bad not to say it."

Suppose you were among the inner circle of global policymakers and you shared these attitudes? Might you not work to realize them in the long-range management of children through curriculum, testing, and the procedural architectonics of schooling?

Some parts of the country were more resistant to the dumbing down of curriculum and the psycho-socializing of the classroom than others, but by a process of attrition Prussianization gained important beachheads year by year—through private foundation projects, textbook publishing, supervisory associations, and on through every aspect of school. The psychological manipulation of the child suggested by Plato had been investigated by Locke, raised to clinical status by Rousseau, refined into method by Helvetius and Herbart, justified philosophically as the essential religion by Comte, and scientized by Wundt. One does not educate machines, one adjusts them.

The peculiar undertaking of educational psychology was begun by Edward Thorndike of Teachers College in 1903. Thorndike, whose once famous puzzle box became the Skinner box of later behavioral psychology after minor modifications, was the protégé of Wundtians Judd and Armstrong at Wesleyan, taking his Ph.D. under Wundtian Cattell before being offered a post by Wundtian Russell at Teachers College.

According to Thorndike, the aim of a teacher is to "produce and prevent certain responses," and the purpose of education is to promote "adjustment." In *Elementary Principles of Education* (1929), he urged the deconstruction of emphasis on "intellectual resources" for the young, advice that was largely taken. It was bad advice in light of modern brain research suggesting direct ties between the size and complexity of the brain and strenuous thought grappled with early on.

Thorndike said intelligence was virtually set at birth—real change was impossible—a scientific pronouncement which helped to justify putting the brakes on ambitious curriculum. But in the vitally important behavioral area—in beliefs, attitudes, and loyalties—Thorndike did not disappoint the empty child crowd. In those areas so important to corporate and government health, children were to be as malleable as anyone could want them. An early ranking of school kids by intelligence would allow them to be separated into tracks for behavioral processing. Thorndike soon became a driving force in the growth of national testing, a new institution which would have consigned Benjamin Franklin and Andrew Carnegie to reform school and Edison to Special Education. Even before we got the actual test, Thorndike became a significant political ally of the semi-covert sterilization campaign taking place in America.

That pioneering eugenic program seemed socially beneficial to those casually aware of it, and it was enthusiastically championed by some genuine American legends like Oliver Wendell Holmes. But if you find yourself nodding in agreement that morons have no business with babies, you might want to consider that according to Thorndike's fellow psychologist H.H. Goddard at Princeton, 83 percent of all Jews and 79 percent of all Italians were in the mental defective class. The real difficulty with scientific psychology or other scientific social science is that it seems to be able to produce proof of anything on command, convincing proof, too, delivered by sincere men and women just trying to get along by going along.

Napoleon Of Mind Science

William James wrote in 1879:

> [Wundt] aims on being a Napoleon....Unfortunately he will never have a Waterloo....cut him up like a worm and each fragment crawls....you can't kill him.

From his laboratory in upper Saxony near the Prussian border, Wundt wrote 53,735 published pages in the 68 years between 1853 and 1920, words which sculpted modern schooling, from a disorderly attempt to heighten human promise in individuals or to glorify God's creation, into mandated psychological indoctrination.

Wundt's childhood was unrelieved by fun. He never played. He had no friends. He failed to find love in his family. From this austere forge, a Ph.D. emerged humorless, indefatigable, and aggressive. At his end he returned to the earth childless. Wundt is the senior psychologist in the history of psychology, says Boring: "Before him there was psychology but no psychologists, only philosophers."

Coming out of the physiological tradition of psychophysics in Germany, Wundt followed the path of LeMettrie, Condillac, and Descartes in France who argued, each in his own way, that what we think of as personality is only a collection of physiological facts. Humanity is an illusion.

Wundt had a huge advantage over the mechanists before him. For him the time was right, all religious and romantic opposition in disarray, bewildered by the rapid onset of machinery into society. Over in England, Darwin's brilliant cousin Francis Galton was vigorously promoting mathematical prediction into the status of a successful cult. In one short decade, bastions of a more ancient scholarly edifice were overrun by number crunchers. A bleak future suddenly loomed for men who remained unconvinced that any transcendental power was locked up in quantification of nature and humankind.

The Pythagorean brotherhood was reseating itself inexorably in this great age of Wundt, the two in harmony as both contributed heavily to the centralization of things and to the tidal wave of scientific racism which drowned the university world for decades, culminating in the racial science station maintained on the old Astor estate in Cold Spring Harbor, Long Island, by Carnegie interests until the events of September, 1939, caused it to quietly close its doors.[11] Even at the beginning of the marriage of scholarship and statistics, its principals saw little need to broaden their investigations into real life, an ominous foreshadowing of the eugenical outlook that followed.

A friendless, loveless, childless male German calling himself a psychologist set out, I think, to prove his human condition didn't matter because feelings were only an aberration. His premises and methodology were imported into an expanding American system of child confinement and through that system disseminated to administrators, teachers, counselors, collegians, and the national consciousness.

---

[11] America's academic romance with scientific racism, which led directly to mass sterilization experiments in this country, has been widely studied in Europe but is still little known even among the college-trained population here. An entire study can be made of the penetration of this notion—that the makeup of the species is and ought to be controllable by an elite—into every aspect of American school where it remains to this day. I would urge any reader with time and inclination to explore this matter to get Daniel J. Kevles' *In The Name of Eugenics* where a thorough account and a thorough source bibliography are set down. This essay offers a disturbing discussion which should open your eyes to how ideas flow through modern society and inevitably are translated into schooling. Dr. Kevles is on the history faculty at California Institute of Technology.

Oddly enough, on December 11, 1998, the *New York Times* front page carried news that an organization in Cold Spring Harbor, Long Island, had deciphered the full genetic code of a microscopic round worm, a landmark achievement. The president of the National Academy of Sciences is quoted as saying, "In the last 10 years we have come to realize humans are more like worms than we ever imagined." Whether the Cold Spring facility which announced this has any connection with the former racial science station, I do not know.

As Germany became the intellectual's darling of the moment at the end of the nineteenth century, a long-dead German philosopher, Kant's successor at the University of Berlin, Johann Herbart, enjoyed a vogue in school-intoxicated America. "Herbartianism" is probably the first of a long line of pseudoscientific enthusiasms to sweep the halls of pedagogy. A good German, Herbart laid out with precision the famous Herbartian Five-Step Program, not a dance but a psychologized teacher training program. By 1895, there was a National Herbartian Society to spread the good news, enrolling the likes of Nicholas Murray Butler of Columbia and John Dewey. Herbart was finally laid to rest sometime before WWI when Dewey's interest cooled, but his passage was a harbinger of many Herbart-oid enthusiasms to follow as a regular procession of educational gurus rose and fell with the fashion of the moment. The Moorish dance of scientific pedagogy accelerated its tempo relentlessly, and arms, legs, heads, perspiration, cries of venereal delight, and some anguish, too, mingled in the hypnotic whirl of laboratory dervishes. By 1910, Dewey was substituting his own five steps for Herbart's in a book called *How We Think*. Few who read it noticed that a case was being made that we don't actually think at all. Thinking was only an elusive kind of problem-solving behavior, called into being by dedicated activity; otherwise we are mindless.

What Is Sanity?

What we today call the science of child development grew out of the ambition of G. Stanley Hall, Wundt's first assistant at Leipzig, Dewey's mentor at Hopkins, and a man with a titanic ego. Hall inserted the word "adolescence" into the American vocabulary in 1904. If you wonder what happened to this class before they were so labeled, you can reflect on the experience of Washington, Franklin, Farragut, and Carnegie, who couldn't spare the time to be children any longer than necessary. Hall, a fantastic pitchman, laid the groundwork for a host of special disciplines from child development to mental testing.

Hall told all who listened that the education of the child was the most important task of the race, our primary mission, and the new science of psychology could swiftly transform the race into what it should be. Hall may never have done a single worthwhile scientific experiment in his life but he understood that Americans could be sold a sizzle without the steak. Thanks in large measure to Hall's trumpet, an edifice of child development rose out of the funding of psychological laboratories in the early 1900s during the famous Red Scare period.

In 1924, the Child Welfare Institute opened at Teachers College, underwritten by the Rockefeller foundation. Another was opened in 1927 at the University of California. Generous donations for the study of all phases of child growth and development poured into the hands of researchers from the largest foundations. Thirty-five years later, during what might be thought of as the nation's fourth Red Scare, the moment the Soviets beat America into space, the U.S. Education Office presided over a comprehensive infiltration of teacher training and schools.[12] Judiciously applied funds and arm-twisting made certain these staging areas would pay proper attention to the psychological aspect of schooling.

---

[12] The story of the BSTEP document and the Delphi Technique, two elements in this initiative, is told in Beverly Eakman's *Education For the New World Order*, a book by a Department of Justice employee which offers an interesting and accessible way to dip your toe in the shadow world of intrigue and marketing behind the scenes of schooling. Also interesting (and much better edited) is Eakman's *Cloning of the American Mind*.

Dewey, Hall, Thorndike, Cattell, Goddard, Russell, and all the other intellectual step-children of Wundt and the homeless mind he stood for, set out to change the conception of what constitutes education. They got powerful assistance from great industrial foundations and their house universities like Teachers College. Under the direction of James Earl Russell, president (and head of the psychology department), Teachers College came to boast training where "psychology stands first." Wherever Columbia graduates went this view went with them.

Harold Rugg, Teachers College professor and author of many national texts, defined the revolution this way:

> Through schools of the world we shall disseminate a new conception of
> government—one that will embrace all the collective activities of men;
> one that will postulate the need for scientific control and operation of
> economic activities....

The brand-new profession of psychiatry flocked to the banner of this new philosophy of psychological indoctrination as a proper government activity, perhaps sensing that business and status could flow from the connection if it were authoritatively established. Ralph Truitt, head of the then embryonic Division of Child Guidance Clinics for the Psychiatric Association, wrote in 1927, "the school should be the focus of the attack."

The White House appeared in the picture like a guardian angel watching over the efforts this frail infant was making to stand. In 1930, 1,200 child development "experts" were invited to the White House Conference on Child Health and Protection, an event with no precedent. One primary focus of attendees was the role "failure" played as a principal source of children's problems. The echo of Rousseau was unmistakable. No attempt was made to examine how regularly prominent Americans like Washington or successful businessmen like Carnegie had surmounted early failure. Instead, a plan to eliminate failure structurally from formal schooling was considered and endorsed—failure could be eliminated if schools were converted into laboratories of life adjustment and intellectual standards were muted.

By 1948, the concept of collective (as opposed to individual) mental health was introduced at an international meeting in Britain to discuss the use of schools as an instrument to promote mental health. But what *was* mental health? What did a fully sane man or woman look like? Out of this conference in the U.K. two psychiatrists, J.R. Rees and G. Brock Chisholm, leveraged a profitable new organization for themselves—the World Federation for Mental Health. It claimed expertise in preventative measures and pinpointed the training of children as the proper point of attack:

> The training of children is making a thousand neurotics for every one
> psychiatrists can hope to help with psychotherapy.

Chisholm *knew* what caused the problem in childhood; he knew how to fix it, too:

> The only lowest common denominator of all civilizations and the only
> psychological force capable of producing these perversions is morality,
> the concept of right and wrong.

Shakespeare and the Vikings had been right; there's nothing good or bad but thinking makes it so. Morality was the problem. With WWII behind us and everything adrift, a perfect opportunity to rebuild social life in school and elsewhere—on a new amoral, scientific logic—was presenting itself:

> We have swallowed all manner of poisonous certainties fed us by our
> parents, our Sunday and day school teachers, our politician, our priests,
> our newspapers....The results, the inevitable results, are frustration,
> inferiority, neurosis and inability to enjoy living.... If the race is to be
> freed from its crippling burden of good and evil it must be psychiatrists
> who take the original responsibility.

Old Norse pragmatism, the philosophy most likely to succeed among upper-crust thinkers in the Northeastern United States was reasserting itself as global psychiatry.

The next great advance in pedagogy was the initiative of a newly formed governmental body, the National Institute of Mental Health. In 1950, it arranged the White House Conference on Education to warn that a psychological time-bomb was ticking inside the schools. An epidemic of mental *insufficiency* was said to be loose among ordinary Americans, imperiling the advances industry and the arts had given America. Barbarians were already through the gates and among us!

Bending The Student To Reality

Twice before, attempts had been made to tell the story of an Armageddon ahead if the government penny-pinched on the funding of psychological services. First was the great feeble-mindedness panic which preceded and spanned the First World War when word was spread from academic centers that feeble-mindedness was rampant among Americans.

The "moron!" "imbecile!" and "idiot!" insults which ricocheted around my elementary school in the early 1940s were one legacy of this premature marketing campaign. During WWII, this drive to convince keepers of the purse that the general population was a body needing permanent care was helped powerfully by a diffusion of British psychological warfare bureau reports stating that the majority of common British soldiers were mentally deficient. Now that notion (and its implied corrective, buying protection from psychologists) made inroads on American managerial consciousness, producing monies to further study the retarded contingent among us.

Reading the text "Proceedings of the Mid-Century White House Conference on Children and Youth," we learn that school has "responsibility to detect mental disabilities which have escaped parental or pre-school observation." Another huge duty it had was the need to "initiate all necessary health services through various agencies." Still another, to provide "counseling services for all individuals at all age levels."

The classic line in the entire massive document is, "Not only does the child need to be treated but those around him also need help." A hospital society was needed to care for all the morons, idiots, and mental defectives science had discovered lurking among the sane. It would need school as its diagnostic clinic and principal referral service. Western religious teaching—that nobody can escape personal responsibility—was chased from the field by Wundt's minimalist outlook on human nature as mechanism. A complex process was then set in motion which could not fail to need forced instruction to complete itself.

NIMH used the deliberations of the 1950 conference to secure government funding for an enormous five-year study of the mental health of the nation, a study conducted by the very people whose careers would be enhanced by any official determination that the nation faced grave problems from its morons and other defectives. Can you guess what the final document said?

"Action for Mental Health" proposed that school curriculum "be designed to bend the student to the realities of society." It should be "designed to promote mental health as an instrument for social progress," and as a means of "altering culture."

What factors inhibit mental health that are directly in the hands of school authorities to change? Just these: expectations that children should be held responsible for their actions, expectations that it is important for all children to develop intelligence, the misperceived need to assign some public stigma when children lagged behind a common standard. New protocols were issued, sanctions followed. The network of teacher colleges, state education departments, supervisory associations, grant-making bodies, and national media inoculated the learning system with these ideas, and local managers grew fearful of punishment for opposition.

In 1962, a NIMH-sponsored report, "The Role of Schools in Mental Health," stated unambiguously, "*Education does not mean teaching people to know.*" What then? "It means teaching them to behave as they do not behave," a clear echo of the General Education Board's "Occasional Letter Number One" of 1906. Schools were behavioral engineering plants, what remained was to convince kids and parents there was no place to hide.

The report was featured at the 1962 Governor's Conference, appearing along with a proclamation calling on all states to fund these new school programs and use every state agency to further the work. Provisions were discussed to overturn resistance on the part of parents; tough cases, it was advised, could be subjected to multiple pressures around the clock until they stopped resisting. Meanwhile, alarming statistics were circulated about the rapid growth of mental illness within society.

The watershed moment when modern schooling swept all competition from the field was the passage of the Elementary and Secondary Education Act in 1965 (ESEA). The Act allocated substantial federal funds to psychological and psychiatric programs in school, opening the door to a full palette of "interventions" by psychologists, psychiatrists, social workers, agencies, and various specialists. All were invited to use the schoolhouse as a satellite office, in urban ghettos, as a primary office. Now it was the law.

Along the way to this milestone, important way stations were reached beyond the scope of this book to list. The strand I've shown is only one of many in the tapestry. The psychological goals of this project and the quality of mind in back of them are caught fairly in the keynote address to the 1973 Childhood International Education Seminar in Boulder, Colorado, delivered by Harvard psychiatrist, Chester M. Pierce. This quote appears to have been edited out of printed transcripts of the talk, but was reported by newspapers in actual attendance:

> Every child in America entering school at the age of five is mentally ill
> because he comes to school with certain allegiances to our founding
> fathers, toward our elected officials, toward his parents, toward a belief
> in a supernatural being, and toward the sovereignty of this nation as a
> separate entity. It's up to you as teachers to make all these sick children
> well—by creating the international child of the future.

Perhaps it's only a fortuitous coincidence that in the ongoing psychologization of schools from 1903 onwards, the single most prominent thread—the nearly universal prescription for betterment offered by every agency, analyst, and spokesperson for mental health—has been the end of competition in every aspect of training and the substitution of cooperation and intergroup, interpersonal harmony. In utopia, everyone has a fixed place. Envy and ambition are unwelcome, at least among the common classes. The prescription should sound familiar, we've encountered it before as the marching orders of the Prussian *volksschulen*. Unfortunately we know only too well how *that* Pestalozzian story ended.

Paying Children To Learn

As it turned out, my own period of behaviorist training came back to haunt me 30 years later as garlic sausage eaten after midnight returns the next afternoon to avenge being chewed. In 1989, to my delight, I secured a substantial cash grant from a small foundation to pay kids for what heretofore they had been doing in my class for free. Does that sound like a good idea to you? I guess it did to me, I'm ashamed to say.

Wouldn't you imagine that after 28 years of increasingly successful classroom practice I might have known better? But then if we were perfect, who would eat garlic sausage after midnight? The great irony is that after a long teaching career, I always made it a *major* point of instruction to actively teach disrespect for bribes and grades. I never gave gold stars. I never gave overt praise, because I believe without question that learning *is* its own reward. Nothing ever happened in my experience with kids to change my mind about that. Soaping kids, as street children called it then, always struck me as a nasty, self-serving tactic. Addicting people to praise as a motivator puts them on a slippery slope toward a lifetime of fear and exploitation, always looking for some expert to approve of them.

Let me set the stage for the abandonment of my own principles. Take a large sum of money, which for dramatic purposes, I converted into 50 and 100 dollar bills. Add the money to a limited number of kids, many of them dirt poor, some having never eaten off a tablecloth, one who was living on the street in an abandoned car. None of the victims had much experience with pocket money beyond a dollar or two. Is this the classic capitalist tension out of which a sawbuck or a C-note should produce beautiful music?

Now overlook my supercilious characterization. See the kids beneath their shabby clothing and rude manners as quick, intelligent beings, more aware of connections than any child development theory knows how to explain. Here were kids already doing prodigies of real intellectual work, not what the curriculum manual called for, of course, but what I, in my willful, outlaw way had set out for them. The board of education saw a roomful of ghetto kids, but I knew better, having decided years before that the bell curve was an instrument of deceit, one rich with subleties, some of them unfathomable, but propaganda all the same.

So there I was with all this money, accountable to nobody for its use but myself. Plenty for everyone. How to spend it? Using all the lore acquired long ago at Columbia's Psychology Department, I set up reinforcement schedules to hook the kids to cash, beginning continuously—paying off at every try—then changing to periodic schedules after the victim was in the net, and finally shifting to aperiodic reinforcements so the learning would dig deep and last.

From thorough personal familiarity with each kid and a data bank to boot, I had no doubt that the activities I selected would be intrinsically interesting anyway, so the financial incentives would only intensify student interest. What a surprise I got!

Instead of becoming a model experiment proving the power of market incentives, disaster occurred. Quality in work dropped noticeably, interest lessened markedly. In everything but the money, that is. And yet even enthusiasm for that tailed off after the first few payments; greed remained but delight disappeared.

All this performance loss was accompanied by the growth of disturbing personal behavior—kids who once liked each other now tried to sabotage each other's work. The only rational reason I could conceive for this was an unconscious attempt to keep the pool of available cash as large as possible. Nor was that the end of the strange behavior the addition of cash incentives caused in my classes. Now kids began to do as little as possible to achieve a payout where once they had striven for a standard of excellence. Large zones of deceptive practice appeared, to the degree I could no longer trust data presented, because it so frequently was made out of whole cloth.

Like Margaret Mead's South Sea sexual fantasies, E.L. Burtt's fabulous imaginary twin data, Dr. Kinsey's bogus sexual statistics, or Sigmund Freud's counterfeit narratives of hysteria and dream, like the amazing discovery of the mysterious bone which led to the "proof" of Piltdown Man having been discovered by none other than Pierre Teilhard de Chardin (who after the fraud was exploded refused to discuss his lucky find ever again), my children it seemed were able to discern how the academic game is played, or perhaps more accurately, they figured out the professional game which is about fame and fortune much more than any service to mankind. The little entrepreneurs were telling me what they thought I wanted to hear!

In other unnerving trends, losers began to peach on winners, reporting their friends had cheated through falsification of data or otherwise had unfairly acquired prizes. Suddenly I was faced with an epidemic of kids ratting on each other. One day I just got sick of it. I confessed to following an animal-training program in launching the incentives. Then I inventoried the remaining money, still thousands of dollars, and passed it out in equal shares at the top of the second floor stairs facing Amsterdam Avenue. I instructed the kids to sneak out the back door one at a time to avoid detection, then run like the wind with their loot until they got home.

How they spent their unearned money was no business of mine, I told them, but from that day forward there would be no rewards as long as I was their teacher. And so ended my own brief romance with empty child pedagogy.

CHAPTER FOURTEEN

Absolute Absolution

The leading principle of Utopian religion is the repudiation of the doctrine of Original Sin.
— H.G. Wells, *A Modern Utopia* (1915)

Everything functions as if death did not exist. Nobody takes it into account; it is suppressed everywhere....We now seem possessed by the Promethean desire to cure death.
— Octavio Paz, *The Labyrinth of Solitude* (1950)

Education is the modern world's temporal religion...
— Bob Chase, president, National Education Association, *NEA TODAY*, April 1997

The Problem Of God

The problem of God has always been a central question of Western intellectual life; the flight from this heritage is best evidence that school is a project having little to do with education as the West defined it for thousands of years. It's difficult to imagine anyone who lacks an understanding of Western spirituality regarding themselves as educated. And yet, American schools have been forbidden to enter this arena even in a token way since 1947.

In spite of the irony that mainstream Protestant church support at the beginning is the only reason we have American compulsion schools at all, the rug was pulled out under the feet of the churches quite suddenly at the end of the nineteenth century. The pretext: that was the only way to keep Catholicism out of the schools. When the second shoe fell with the *Everson* decision by the U.S. Supreme Court in 1947, God was pitched out on His ear entirely.

Before we go forward we need to go back. The transformation businessmen wrought in the idea of education at the end of the nineteenth century and the early decades of the twentieth is the familiar system we have today. Max Otto argued in his intriguing essay *Science and the Moral Life* (1949) that a philosophical revolution had been pulled off by businessmen under everybody's nose. Otto described what most college graduates still don't know—that the traditional economy, where wants regulate what is produced, is dead. The new economy depends upon *creating* demand for whatever stuff machinery, fossil fuel, and industrialized imagination can produce. When this reversal was concluded, *consumption*, once only one detail among many in people's lives, now became the most important end. Great consumers are heroes to a machine society; the frugal, villains.

In such a universe, schools have no choice but to participate. Supporting the economic system became the second important mission of mass schooling's existence, but in doing so, *materiality* found itself at war with an older family of spiritual interests. In the general society going about its business, it wasn't easy to see this contest clearly, to recognize that great corporations which provided employment, endowed universities, museums, schools and churches, and which spoke powerfully on important issues of the day, actually had a life-and-death stake in the formation of correct psychological attitudes among children toward production and consumption.

It was nature, not conspiracy, Otto wrote, that drove businessmen "to devote themselves to something besides business." It was only natural "they should try to control education and to supplant religion as a definer of ideals." The class of businessmen who operated on a national and international basis, having estranged themselves from considerations of nation, culture, and tradition, having virtually freed themselves from competitive risk because they owned the legislative and judicial processes, now turned their attention to cosmic themes of social management.

In this fashion, minister gave way to schoolteacher, schoolteacher became *pedagogus* under direction of the controllers of work.

Spirits Are Dangerous

The net effect of holding children in confinement for twelve years without honor paid to the spirit is a compelling demonstration that the State considers the Western spiritual tradition dangerous. And of course it is. School is about creating loyalty to certain goals and habits, a vision of life, support for a class structure, an intricate system of human relationships cleverly designed to manufacture the continuous low level of discontent upon which mass production and finance rely.

Once the mechanism is identified, its dynamics aren't hard to understand. Spiritually contented people are dangerous for a variety of reasons. They don't make reliable servants because they won't jump at every command. They test what is requested against a code of moral principle. Those who are spiritually secure can't easily be driven to sacrifice family relations. Corporate and financial capitalism are hardly possible on any massive scale once a population finds its spiritual center.

For a society like ours to work, we need to feel something is fundamentally wrong when we can't continually do better—expand our farms and businesses, win a raise, take exotic vacations. This is the way our loan/repayment cycle—the credit economy—is sustained. The human tendency to simply enjoy work, and the companionship of other workers is turned into a race to *outdo* colleagues, to climb employment ladders. Ambition is a trigger of corporate life and at the same time an acid dissolving communities. By spreading contentment on the cheap, spirituality was a danger to the new economy's natural growth principle. So in a sense it was rational self-interest, not conspiracy, that drove enlightened men to agree in their sporting places, drawing rooms and clubs that religious activity would have to be dampened down.

What they couldn't see is that through substitution of schooling for Bible religion, they were sawing through two of the four main social supports of Western civilization. Think of your dining room table; it was like breaking two of its legs off, replacing one with a tall stack of dishes and one with a large dog. The top of the table would look the same covered in cloth but it wouldn't be a good bet to get you through dinner. A century earlier, Hamilton and Jefferson had speculated whether it might be possible to replace religion with a civil substitute. The heady ideas of the French Revolution were on everybody's lips. A civil substitute built on expanding the humble grassroots institution of schooling might well free leaders from the divided loyalty religion imposes. Could an ethical system based on law produce the same quality of human society as a moral system based on divine inspiration? Jefferson was skeptical. Despite his fears, the experiment was soon to be tried.

Foundations Of The Western Outlook

We will never fully understand American schools until we think long and hard about religion. Whether you are Buddhist, Jew, Moslem, Hindu, Baptist, Confucian, Catholic, Protestant, agnostic, or atheist, this is a hunt for important threads in the tapestry overlooked by secular academic exegesis. More specifically, our quest is for insights of Protestant Christian dissent which have been buried at least a century, insights which I hope will cause you to look at schools a different way.

To find out what School seeks to replace, we have to uncover the four pillars which hold up Western society. Two come from the Nordic rim of Europe: the first, a unique belief in the sovereign rights of the individual; the second, what we have come to call scientific vision. Everywhere else but in the West individual and family were submerged in one or another collective system. Only here were the chips bet on liberty of individual conscience.

The ambition to know everything appears in history in the stories of the Old Norse god, Odin, god of Mind and god of Family Destruction, too. No other mythology than the Norse puts pride of intellect together with a license to pry so at the center of things. Science presumes absolute license. Nothing can be forbidden. *Science and individualism are the two secular foundations of Western outlook.*

Our other two supports for social meaning are religious and moral. Both originate in the South of Europe. From this graft of North and South comes the most important intellectual synthesis so far seen on this planet, Western civilization. One of these Mediterranean legs is a specific moral code coming out of the Decalogue, of Judaism working through the Gospels of Christianity. The rules are these:

1. Love, care for, and help others.
2. Bear witness to the good.
3. Respect your parents and ancestors.
4. Respect the mysteries; know your place in them.
5. Don't envy.

6.   Don't lie or bear false witness.
7.   Don't steal.
8.   Don't kill.
9.   Don't betray your mate.

The fourth and most difficult leg comes from a Christian interpretation of *Genesis*. It is constituted out of a willing acceptance of certain penalties incurred by eating from the Tree of Knowledge against God's command. The Original Sin. For disobedience, Adam, Eve, and their descendants were sentenced to four punishments.

The first was *labor*. There was no need to work in Eden, but after the Expulsion, we had to care for ourselves. The second penalty was *pain*. There was no pain in Eden; but now our weak nature was subject to being led astray, to feeling pain, even from natural acts like childbirth, whether we were good people or bad people. Third was the two-edged *free will* penalty, including the right to choose Evil which would now lurk everywhere. Recall that in Eden there was exactly one wrong thing to do, eating the fruit of a particular tree. Now we would have to endure the stress of constant moral armament against a thousand temptations or of surrendering to sin. Last and most important, the term of human life would be strictly limited. Nobody would escape death. The more you have in wealth, family, community, and friends, the more you are tempted to curse God as you witness yourself day by day losing physical strength, beauty, energy—eventually losing everything.

Before the sixteenth century, the orthodox Christian view was that human nature was equal to carrying this burden. It was weak, but capable of finding strength through faith. This doctrine of inescapable sin, and redemption through personal choice, carries a map of meaning through which to organize one's entire life. Face the inevitable in a spirit of humility and you are saved. This lesser-known side of the Christian curriculum, the one generated out of Original Sin, lacked a Cecil B. DeMille to illustrate its value, but once aware, a life could draw strength and purpose from it.

What I'm calling the Christian curriculum assigns specific duties to men and women. No other system of meaning anywhere, at any time in history, has shown a record of power and endurance like this one, continuously enlarging its influence over all mankind (not just Christians) because it speaks directly to ordinary people without the mediation of elites or priesthoods.

Superficially, you might argue that the success of the West is the result of its guns being better, but really it's that the story of *hope* we have to relate is superior to any other.

Codes Of Meaning

This unique moral chronicle led to an everyday behavioral code which worked so well that in a matter of centuries it became the dominant perspective of Europe, and soon it made inroads into every belief system across the planet. But the sheer extent of its success caused it to run afoul of three other competing systems for producing meaning, each holding common people in contempt or worse. These competing codes viewed Christianity antagonistically because of its power to liberate ordinary people from the bondage of fear and envy.

Those competing codes of meaning gave us formal schooling, public and private. The first competitor, the aristocratic code, comes out of pagan traditions. It is still the philosophy taught in upper-class boarding schools like Middlesex and Gunnery, and through home training and particular class institutions. Its operating principles are leadership, sportsmanship, courage, disdain for hardship, team play, self-sacrifice (for the team), and devotion to duty—as noble traditions define duty. The boardrooms of certain global corporations are one of the great preserves of this exclusive but universally attractive pagan attitude.

The second code in competition with Christianity was taken from the practice of great *commercial* civilizations like the Hanseatic League of medieval times or the society of Holland in the seventeenth century. This behavioral code makes security, comfort, health and wealth the central purpose of life. The main thrust of this kind of seeking is radically anti-Christian, but the contradiction isn't obvious when the two come into contact because commercial cultures emphasize peaceful coexistence, tolerance, cooperation, and pragmatism. They reject the value of pain, and take principled behavior with a grain of salt, everything being *relative* to security and prosperity. Pragmatism is the watchword.

The wealth a commercial perspective delivers provided a dilemma for Puritan society to wrestle with since the intense neo-Christianity of Puritanism was yoked to an intense talent for commercial transaction. This contradiction was resolved by declaring wealth a reliable sign of God's favor as poverty was a sign of His condemnation. Both pagan and mercantile ethical codes operated behind a facade of Christianity during the Christian era, weakening the gospel religion, while at the same time, profiting from it and paying lip service to it. Proponents of these different frames called themselves Christians but did not live like Christians, rejecting certain tenets of Christianity we've just examined, those which interfered with personal gain. Yet in both cases, the life maps these competing theories tried to substitute were not, ultimately, satisfying enough to stop the spreading influence of Christian vision.

Stated more directly, these competing moral codes were unable to deliver sufficient tangible day-to-day meaning to compete against the religious prescription of a simple life resigned with dignity and joy to work, pain, self-control, moral choice, aging, and death. Neither the pagan outlook nor the commercial philosophy was equal to overthrowing their unworldly rival. Because the commercial code lacked sufficient magic and mystery, and the aristocratic code, which had those things, froze out the majority from enjoying them, it fell to yet a third scheme for organizing meaning to eventually cause the major sabotage of spiritual life.

I refer to the form of practical magic we call Science. Kept rigorously and strictly subordinate to human needs, science is an undeniably valuable way to negotiate the physical world. But its tendency has always been to break loose from these constraints and try to explain the *purpose* of life. Instead of remaining merely a useful description of how things work, great synthesizing theories like Big Bang or Natural Selection purport to explain the origin of the universe or how life best progresses. Yet these things, by their nature, are beyond proof or disproof. Few laymen understand that the synthesizing theories of Science are religious revelations in disguise.

In the years around the beginning of the twentieth century, the scientific outlook as a substitute religion took command of compulsion schools and began to work to eradicate any transcendental curriculum in them. This happened in stages. First was the passage of compulsion school legislation and invention of the factory school (isolated from family and community), appearing in conjunction with the extermination of the one-room school. That job was largely done by 1900. The second stage was introduction of hierarchical layers of school management and government selected and regulated teaching staff. That job was complete by 1930. The third stage comprised socialization of the school into a world of "classes" and de-individualized individuals who looked to school authorities for leadership instead of their own parents and churches. This was accomplished by 1960. The fourth and last stage (so far) was the psychologizing of the classroom, a process begun full scale in 1960, which, with the advent of national standardized testing, outcomes-based education, Title I legislation, school-to-work legislation, et.al., was accelerating as the last century ended.

All these are ambitious designs to control how children think, feel, and behave. There had been signs of this intention two centuries before, but without long-term confinement of children to great warehouses, the amount of isolation and mind-control needed to successfully introduce civil religion through schooling just wasn't available.

The Scientific Curriculum

The particulars of the scientific curriculum designed to replace the Christian curriculum look like this:

First, it asked for a sharply critical attitude toward parental, community, and traditional values. Nothing familiar, the children were told, should remain unexamined or go unchallenged. The old-fashioned was to be discarded. Indeed, the study of history itself was stopped. Respect for tradition was held sentimental and counterproductive. Only one thing could *not* be challenged, and that was the school religion itself where even minor rebellion was dealt with harshly.

Second, the scientific curriculum asked for objectivity, for the suppression of human feelings which stand in the way of pursuing *knowledge* as the ultimate good. Thinking works best when everything is considered an equally lifeless object. Then things can be regarded with objectivity. Of course kids resist this deadening of nature and so have to be trained to see nature as mechanical. Have no feeling for the frog you are dissecting or the butterfly you kill for a school project—soon you may have no feeling for the humiliation of your classmates or the enfeeblement of your own parents. After all, humiliation constitutes the major tool of behavior control in schools, a tool used alike to control students, teachers, and administrators.

Third, the scientific curriculum advises neutrality. Make no lasting commitments to anything because loyalty and sentiment spell the end of flexibility; they close off options.

Last, the new scheme demanded that visible things which could be numbered and counted be acknowledged as the only reality. God could not exist; He could not be seen.

The religion of science says there is no good or evil. Experts will tell you what to feel based on pragmatic considerations. Since there is no free will nor any divine morality, there is no such thing as individual responsibility, no sin, no redemption. Just mathematical decision-making; grounded in utilitarianism or the *lex talonis*, it makes little difference which. The religion of Science says that work is for fools. Machines can be built to do hard work, and what machines don't do, servants and wage slaves can. Work as little as you can get away with—that's how the *new* success is measured. The religion of Science says good feelings and physical sensations are what life is all about.

Drugs are such an important part of feeling good we began to need drugstores to sell the many varieties available. People should try virtually everything; that is the message of the drug-store and all advertising. Leave no stone unturned in the search for sensual pleasure. With science-magic you don't even have to worry about a hangover. Simply take vitamin B and keep on drinking—nor need you worry about incurring the responsibility of a family with the advent of cheap contraceptives and risk-free legal abortion. Lastly, the religion of Science teaches that death, aging, and sickness are ultimate evils. With pills, potions, lotions, aerobics, and surgery you can stave off death and aging, eventually the magical medical industry will erase those scourges from human affairs.

There. It is done. See how point for point the curriculum of science, upgraded from an instrument to a religion, revokes each of the penalties Christianity urged we accept gladly? See how Science can be sold as the nostrum to grant absolute absolution from these?

Everson v. Board Of Education (1947)

The Supreme Court decision *Everson v. Board of Education 330 U.S. 18. (1947)* prepared the dismissal of religion from American public schools. We are hidden by more than a half-century from the shock and numbness this new doctrine of "separation of church and state" occasioned, a great bewilderment caused in part by the absence of any hint of such a separation doctrine in the Declaration, Constitution, or the Bill of Rights.

The Courts, which erected the wall of separation, went on to radically change the entire face of American jurisprudence, establishing firmly a principle which had only operated spottily in the past, the "judicial review" power which made the judiciary final arbiter of which laws were legal. No longer could the people's representatives expect that by working for legislation, their will would be honored by the courts. A new and higher power had spoken, a power with the ability to dispense with religion in government facilities, including schools and the towns and villages of America where public property was concerned.

Everson was no simple *coup d'etat*, but an act of Counter-Reformation warfare aimed at the independent and dissenting Protestant-Christian traditions of America. To understand the scope of this campaign, you have to look at a selection of court decisions to appreciate the range of targets *Everson* was intended to hit:

Item: A verbal prayer offered in a school is unconstitutional, even if it is both denominationally neutral and voluntarily participated in. *Engle v. Vitale*, 1962; *Abington v. Schempp*, 1963; *Commissioner of Ed. v. School Committee of Leyden*, 1971.

Item: Freedom of speech and press is guaranteed to students unless the topic is religious, at which time such speech becomes unconstitutional. *Stein v. Oshinsky*, 1965; *Collins v. Chandler Unified School District*, 1981.

Item: If a student prays over lunch, it is unconstitutional for him to pray aloud. *Reed v. van Hoven*, 1965.

Item: It is unconstitutional for kindergarten students to recite: "We thank you for the birds that sing; We thank you [God] for everything," even though the word "God" is not uttered. *DeSpain v. Dekalb County Community School District*, 1967.

Item: It is unconstitutional for a war memorial to be erected in the shape of a cross. *Lowe v. City of Eugene*, 1969.

Item: It is unconstitutional for students to arrive at school early to hear a student volunteer read prayers. *State Board of Ed. v. Board of Ed. of Netcong*, 1970.

Item: It is unconstitutional for a Board of Education to use or refer to the word "God" in any of its official writings. *State v. Whisner*, 1976.

Item: It is unconstitutional for a kindergarten class to ask during a school assembly whose birthday is celebrated by Christmas. *Florey v. Sioux Falls School District*, 1979.

Item: It is unconstitutional for the Ten Commandments to hang on the walls of a classroom. *Stone v. Graham*, 1980; *Ring v. Grand Forks Public School District*, 1980; *Lanner v. Wimmer*, 1981.

Item: A bill becomes unconstitutional even though the wording may be constitutionally acceptable, if the legislator who introduced the bill had a religious activity in his mind when he authored it. *Wallace v. Jaffree*, 1984.

Item: It is unconstitutional for a kindergarten class to recite: "God is great, God is good, let us thank Him for our food." *Wallace v. Jaffree*, 1984.

Item: It is unconstitutional for a school graduation ceremony to contain an opening or closing prayer. *Graham v. Central Community School District*, 1985; *Disselbrett v. Douglas School District*, 1986.

Item: In the Alaska public schools in 1987, students were told that they could not use the word "Christmas" in school because it had the word "Christ" in it.

Item: In Virginia, a federal court ruled in 1987 that homosexual newspapers may be distributed on a high school campus, but religious newspapers may not be.

Item: In 1987, a 185-year-old symbol of a Nevada city had to be changed because of its "religious significance."

Item: In 1988, an elementary school principal in Denver removed the Bible from the school library.

Item: In Colorado Springs, 1993, an elementary school music teacher was prevented from teaching Christmas carols because of alleged violations of the separation of church and state.

Item: In 1996, 10-year-old James Gierke of Omaha was prohibited from reading his Bible silently during free time in the Omaha schools.

Item: In 1996, the chief administrative judge of Passaic County, N.J., ruled juries could no longer be sworn in using the Bible.

Judaism

Religion is a school of its own, teaching what it values and disvalues, and why. Judaism, for instance, the older brother of Christianity, has norms which have had important influence on the formation of American character. Although very few Jews lived here until the late nineteenth century, the holy books of Christianity had been conceived by people reared culturally and religiously as Jews, and the elders of the New England colony actually looked upon themselves from time to time as the lost tribes of Israel.

What can be extracted as living wisdom from these Jewish religious thinkers when sieved through many centuries of Christian cloth? The following at a bedrock minimum:

1) As a condition of creation, humans are called upon to honor their origins in flesh through honoring the father and mother and in the spirit by closely studying the first five books of the Old Testament (known as Torah), to dwell upon divine origins and a time when God directly interceded in the affairs of mankind.

2) The acceptance that authority is morally *grounded in divine authority*. The Commandments must be kept; God will not allow compromise. From this comes respect for law and further organization of Jewish culture around the belief that there is a right way to do everything, discernible to intellect, revealed by wise scholars to ordinary people. Close reading and subtly layered exegesis are Jewish values which became benchmarks of Western intellect.

3) The Law of Hospitality to Strangers—in the tradition of Abraham and the angels, the Jewish Talmud teaches that strangers are to be treated with respect and affection. This *openness to experience* led to great advantages for Jews as they traveled everywhere. It encouraged them to be curious, not always to remain self-ghettoized, but to take risks in mingling.

4) A tradition of prayer, and respect for prayer, as a way to know "before whom you stand," the legend written above the ark containing the Torah scrolls.

Judaism teaches that God wants our love and loves us in return. The first five books of the Bible are His gift to purify our hearts with the story of a pilgrim people making its way through the desert to God. Judaism teaches a way of life that sanctifies the everyday, an outlook that sees no accidents—not a sparrow falling—without its moral charge to select a course carefully, since God always offers a road to the good as well as a road to trouble as his way of honoring free will. Christianity has to some extent incorporated these precepts, but it also has a unique doctrine of its own. I'll turn to that now.

The Dalai Lama And The Genius Of The West

Sometime ago, I found myself on a warm evening in June in Boulder, Colorado, sitting in a big white tent on a camp chair directly in front of the Dalai Lama about fourteen feet away with nobody between us.[1] As he spoke, our eyes met now and then, as I listened with growing delight to this eloquent, humorous, plain-spoken man talk about wisdom and the world. Most of the things he said were familiar: that love and compassion are human necessities, that forgiveness is essential, that Western education lacks a dimension of heart, that Americans need to rely more on inner resources; but some of his presentation was surprising—that it is better to stick with the wisdom traditions of one's own land than to run from them pursuing in exotica what was under your nose all the time.

---

[1] The occasion was a Spirituality in Education conference at the Naropa Institute, non-sectarian in nature, at which I was asked to speak.

At one point, with what looked to me like a mischievous gleam in his eye, he offered that he had always been made to feel welcome in Christian countries, but Christians were not so welcome in his own country. I suspect that many who were there primarily to add to their Buddhist understanding missed this pointed aside.

It was only when Tenzin Gyatso, fourteenth Dalai Lama, spiritual and temporal leader of the Tibetan people, came briefly to the structure, goal, and utility of Buddhism—a location he spent no more than five minutes visiting—that I was able to see in somewhat sharp perspective where Christianity had taken a different path, and American Christianity a very different one. The goal of Buddhism was "happiness," he said, happiness was the key. The Dalai Lama divided major world religions into "God-religions" and "God-less" religions, with Buddhism in the latter category.

His Holiness seemed to focus marvelously when in response to a question from the audience about how wealthy people and countries could find spirituality, he replied (again I think with a mischievous smile) that Buddhism, with its orientation toward comfortable situations, found it easier for rich people to be spiritual than poor ones! Tenzin Gyatso also tossed another bitter herb into the pot for those romantic souls who expect a continuous sweet presence in their lives from imported religious teaching which they feel lacking in their own. The Dalai Lama said at another juncture, as if talking to himself, that religion was not for every day; religion was for times of pain. To quote from memory with confidence I'm being accurate, his exact words were, "Religion something like medicine, when no pain no need medicine; same thing religion."

The next morning, it was my turn to speak, and with the Dalai Lama's words fresh in mind, I was able to frame the Christian road as one whose goal wasn't "happiness" in the usual sense. It was a road where wealth can be an obstacle to the ends of obedience to God, to loving neighbors as you love yourself, and to redemption through self-transcendence. Unlike Tibetan Buddhism, Western religion has no ultra-specific application, so it can't be compared with medicine. According to Christianity, religion is not a sometimes thing when you need it but a medium in which we act out our lives. Nothing has any meaning without religion. Remember, even if you violently disagree with what I just said here, it isn't relevant to this discussion. I feel no urgency to convert you to anything. My purpose is only to show that the wisdom tradition of American Christianity has something huge to say about where we've misstepped in mass compulsion schooling.

The neglected genius of American Christianity has taken on greater urgency for me—a lapsed Roman Catholic—as I enter old age because it doesn't take much wisdom to see that Americans have been substantially broken away from their own wisdom tradition by forces hostile to its continuance. No mechanism employed to do this has been more important than the agency we call public schooling. In neglecting this wisdom tie we have gradually forgotten a powerful doctrine assembled over thousands of years by countless millions of minds, hearts, and spirits, which addresses the important common problems of life which experience has shown to be impervious to riches, intellect, charm, science, or powerful connections.

Wherever I go in the United States these days I hear of something called the crisis of discipline, how children are not motivated, how they resist learning. That is nonsense, of course. Children resist teaching, as they should, but nobody resists learning. However, I won't dispute that schools are often in chaos. Even ones that *seem* quiet and orderly are in moral chaos beyond the power of investigative journalism so far to penetrate. Disconnected children underline school's failure as they come to public attention, so they must be explained some way by authorities.

I don't think it's off the mark to say that all of us, whatever else we disagree upon, want kids to have discipline in the sense of self-control. That goes for black mothers in Harlem, too, despite the scientific religion of schooling which believes those mothers to be genetically challenged. But we all want something besides just good behavior. We pray for discipline in the more specialized sense of intellectual interests and skills well enough mastered to provide joy and consolation to all our lives—and maybe even a buck, too.

A discipline is what people who drink vermouth cassis instead of red whiskey call a field of learning like chemistry, history, philosophy, etc., and its lore. The good student is literally a disciple of a discipline. The words are from the Latin *disciplinare* and *discipulus*. By the way, I learned this all from a schoolteacher in Utica, New York, named Orin Domenico, who writes me, and I pay attention. In this discipline matter, I'm Orin's disciple.

The most famous discipline in Western tradition is that of Jesus Christ. That's true today and it was true 1,500 years ago. And the most famous disciples are Jesus' twelve apostles. What did Christ's model of educational discipline look like? Attendance wasn't mandatory, for one thing. Christ didn't set up the Judea compulsory school system. He issued an invitation, "Follow me," and some did and some didn't. Christ didn't send the truant officer after those who didn't.

Orin tells me the first characteristic of this model is a *calling*. Those who pursued Christ's discipline did so out of desire. It was their own choice. They were called to it by an inner voice, a voice we never give students enough time alone to possibly hear, and that's more true of the good schools than it is of the bad ones. Our present system of schooling alienates us so sharply from inner genius, most of us are barred from being able ever to hear our calling. Calling in most of us shrivels to fantasy and daydreams as a remnant of what might have been.

The second characteristic of Christ's discipline was *commitment*. Following Jesus wasn't easy. You had to drop everything else and there was zero chance you could get rich. You had to love what you were doing; only love could induce you to walk across deserts, sleep in the wilderness, hang out with shady characters, and suffer scorn from all the established folks.

The third characteristic of Christ's model of discipleship was *self-awareness and independence*. Christ's disciples weren't stooges. They had to think for themselves and draw their own conclusions from the shared experience. Christ didn't give many lectures or handouts. He mostly taught by his own practice, and through parables open to interpretation. Orin, my coach, personally doubts Christ ever intended to start an institutional religion because institutions invariably corrupt ideas unless kept small. They regiment thinking and tend toward military forms of discipline. I don't think he's right about Christ's intention, but it's hard to disagree about institutional pathology.

Finally, Christ's model of discipline requires a *master* to follow—one who has himself or herself submitted to discipline and still practices it. The way Orin puts it is this: Christ didn't say, "You guys stay here in the desert and fast for a month. I'll be over at the Ramada. You can find me in the bar if you need help." He didn't begin his own public life until he was almost a rabbi, one fully versed in his tradition.

One way out of the fix we're in with schools would be a return to discipleship in education. During early adolescence, students without a clear sense of calling might have a series of apprenticeships and mentorships which mostly involve self-education. Our students have pressing needs to be alone with themselves, wrestling against obstacles, both internal demons and external barricades to self-direction.

As it is, we currently drown students in low-level busy work, shoving them together in forced associations which teach them to hate other people, not love them. We subject them to the filthiest, most pornographic regimens of constant surveillance and ranking so they never experience the solitude and reflection necessary to become a whole man or woman. You are perfectly at liberty to believe these foolish practices evolved accidentally or through bad judgment, and I will defend your right to believe that right up to the minute the men with nets come to take you away.

Religion And Rationality

The Supreme Court *Everson* ruling of 1947 established the principle that America would have no truck with spirits. There was no mention that the previous 150 years of American judicial history passed without any other court finding this well-hidden meaning in the Constitution. But even if we grant the ruling is sincere, an expression of the rational principle behind modern leadership, we would be justified in challenging *Everson* because of the grotesque record laid down over the past fifty years of spiritless schooling. Dis-spirited schooling has been tested and found fully wanting. I think that's partially because it denies the metaphysical reality recognized by men and women worldwide, today and in every age.

It is ironic from a contrarian viewpoint that the most prestigious scientific position in the world today is surely heading up the human genome project, and that project, as I write, is in the hands of a born-again Christian. Corporations are lined up all the way to China to make fortunes out of genetic manipulation. The director of that project is a man named Dr. Francis X. Collins, who, according to *The New York Times*, personally recognizes religion as the most important reality in his life. Collins was reared in an agnostic home in western Virginia where he was home schooled by his outspoken, radical mother who stretched the school law in a number of ways to give him an education. While in medical school, he came to the conclusion that he would become a born-again Christian because the decision was "intellectually inescapable." And he has maintained that faith energetically ever since, a decision that makes his professional colleagues very uncomfortable.

The difficulty with rational thought, however valuable a tool it certainly is, is that it misses the deepest properties of human nature: our feelings of loneliness and incompletion, our sense of sin, our need to love, our longing after immortality. Let me illustrate how rational thinking preempts terrain where it has no business and makes a wretched mess of human affairs. After this, you can tell your grandchildren that you actually heard someone at the onset of the twenty-first century challenging Galileo's heliocentric theory.

In materially evidentiary terms, the sun is at the center of the solar system, not the Earth, and the solar system itself is lost in the endless immensity of space. I suppose most of you believe that; how could you not? And yet, as far as we scientifically know to date, only planet Earth looks as if it were designed with people in mind. I know that Carl Sagan said we'll find millions of populated planets eventually, but right now there's only hard evidence of one. As far as we know, you can't go anyplace but Earth and stay alive for long. So as of 2000, Earth is clearly the whole of the human universe. I want to push this a little farther, however, so stick with me.

Planet Earth is most definitely not the center of your personal life; it's merely a background which floats in and out of conscious thought. The truth is that both psychologically and spiritually *you* are the center of the solar system and the universe. Don't be modest or try to hide the fact. The minute you deny what I just said, you're in full flight from the responsibility this personal centrality entails: to make things better for the rest of us who are on the periphery of your consciousness.

When you deny your own centrality, you necessarily lose some trust in yourself to move mountains. As your self-trust wanes—and school is there to drill you in distrusting yourself (what else do you think it means to wait for teacher to tell you what to do?)—you lose some self-respect. Without full self-respect, you can hardly love yourself very much because we can't really love those we don't respect (except, curiously enough, by an act of faith). When you can't trust or even like yourself very much, you're in a much worse predicament than you may realize because those things are a preamble to sustaining loving relationships with other people and with the world outside.

Think of it this way: you must be convinced of your own worth before you ask for the love of another or else the bargain will be unsound. You'll be trading discounted merchandise unless both of you are similarly disadvantaged and perhaps even then your relationship will disintegrate.

The trouble with Galileo's way is that it's a partial truth. It's right about the relations of dead matter; it's wrong about the geography of the spirit. Schools can only teach Galileo's victory over the Church; they can't afford to harbor children who command personal power. So the subtlety of the analysis that you and I just went through about the way religion confers power has to be foregone. Galileo's rightness is only a tiny part of a real education; his blindness is much more to the point. The goal of real education is to bring us to a place where we take full responsibility for our own lives; in that quest, Galileo is only one more fact of limited human consequence.

The ancient religious question of free will marks the real difference between schooling and education. *Education is conceived in Western history as a road to knowing yourself, and through that knowledge, arriving at a further understanding of community, relationships, jeopardy, living nature, and inanimate matter.* But none of those things has any particular meaning until you see what they *lead up to, finally being in full command of the spectacular gift of free will*: a force completely beyond the power of science to understand.

With the tool of free will, anyone can forge a personal purpose. Free will allows infinite numbers of human stories to be written in which a personal *you* is the main character. The sciences, on the other hand, hard or soft, assume that purpose and free will are hogwash, given enough data, everything will be seen as explainable predetermined, and hence predictable.

Schooling is an instrument to disseminate this bleak and sterile vision of a blind-chance universe. When schooling displaced education in the U.S. just about a century ago, a deterministic world could be imposed by discipline. We entrap children simply by ignoring the universal human awareness that there is something dreadfully important beyond the rational. We cause children to mistrust themselves so severely they come to depend on cost-benefit analyses for everything. *We teach them to scorn faith so comprehensively that buying things and feeling good becomes the point of their lives.*

The Soviet empire did this brilliantly for a little over 70 years. Its surveillance capability was total. It maintained dossiers on each human unit, logged every deviation, and assigned a mathematical value so that citizens could be ranked against each other. Does that sound familiar? It schooled every child in a fashion prescribed by the best psychological experts. It strictly controlled the rewards of work to ensure compliance, and it developed a punishment system unheard of in its comprehensiveness.

The Soviet Union lasted one lifetime. Our softer form of spiritual suffocation has already been in place for two. The neglected genius of the West, neglected by the forced schooling institution as deliberate policy, resides in its historical collection of spiritual doctrines which grant dignity and responsibility to ordinary individuals, not elites.

I have the greatest respect for every other religious tradition in the world, but not one of them has ever done this or attempted to do this. Western religion correctly identified problems no one can escape, problems for which there are no material solutions, problems you can't elude with money, intellect, charm, politics, or powerful connections. It said also that these problems were, paradoxically, fundamental to human happiness. Serious problems *necessary* to our happiness? That's some perverse doom, I know you'll agree. The question is what to do about it?

The Illusion Of Punishment

What Western spirituality says is paradoxical—rather than avoiding these punishments, it asks you to embrace them. It taught the counter-intuitive response that willing acceptance of these burdens was the only way to a good, full life, the only way to inner peace. Bending your head in obedience, it will be raised up strong, brave, indomitable, and wise. Now let me go through the list of penalties from this perspective:

About labor, the religious voice says that work is the only avenue to genuine self-respect. Work develops independence, self-reliance, resourcefulness. Work itself is a value, above a paycheck, above praise, above accomplishment. Work produces a spiritual reward unknown to the reinforcement schedules of behavioral psychologists like B.F. Skinner, but if you tackle it gladly, without resentment or avoidance, whether you're digging a ditch or building a skyscraper, you'll find the key to yourself in work. If the secular aversion to work is a thing to be rationalized as schools do, requiring only minimal effort from children, a horrifying problem is created for our entire society, one which has proven so far incurable: I refer to the psychological, social, and spiritual anxieties that arise when people have no useful work to do. Phony work, no matter how well paid or praised, causes such great emotional distortions that the major efforts of our civilization will soon go into solving them, with no hint of any answer in sight.

In the economy we have allowed to evolve, the real political dilemma everywhere is keeping people occupied; jobs have to be invented by government agencies and corporations; both employ millions and millions of people for which they have no real use. It's an inside secret among top-echelon management that should you need to cause a rise in stock value this can be engineered by eliminating thousands of "useless" jobs; that is done regularly and, I would presume, cynically.

Young men and women during their brightest, most energetic years are kept from working or from being a part of the general society. This is done to keep them from aggravating this delicate work situation, either by working too eagerly, as kids are prone to do, or by inventing their own work, which could cause shocks throughout the economy. This violation of the injunction to work, which Western spirituality imposed, has backed us into a corner from which no authority has any idea how to extricate us. We cannot afford to let too many children really learn to work as Amish children do, for fear they will discover its great secret: work isn't a curse, but a salvation.

About the second penalty, *pain*, Western spirituality has regarded pain as a friend because it forces attention off things of this world and puts it squarely back on the center of the universe, yourself. Pain and distress in all forms are ways we learn self-control (among other valuable lessons), but the siren call of sensuality lures us to court physical satisfactions and to despise pain as a spoiler of pleasure. Western spirituality teaches that pain is a road to self-knowledge, self-knowledge a road to trusting yourself. Without trust, you can't like yourself; without liking yourself, how can you feel capable of giving love?

About the third penalty, *good and evil*, Western spirituality demands you write your own script through the world. In a spiritual being, everything is morally charged, nothing neutral. Choosing is a daily burden, but one which makes literally everything into a big deal.

I heard second hand, recently, about a woman who said to her mother about an affair she was conducting openly, despite the protest of her husband and in full knowledge of her six-year-old daughter, "It's no big deal." That's what she said to her mother. But if infidelity, divorce, and the shattering of innocence in a child isn't a big deal, then what could ever be? By intensifying our moral sense, we constantly feel the exhilaration of being alive in a universe where everything is a big deal.

To have much of a life, you must bring as many choices as you can out of preprogrammed mode and under the conscious command of your will. The bigger the life you seek, the less anything can be made automatic, as if you were only a piece of machinery. And because every choice has moral dimension, it will incline toward one or the other pole of that classic dichotomy: good and evil.

Despite extenuating circumstances—and they are legion—the accumulating record of our choices marks us as worthy or unworthy people. Even if nobody else is aware how accounts stand, deep inside yourself the running balance will vitally affect your ability to trust, to love, to gain peace and wisdom from relationships and community.

And finally, *aging and death*. In the Western spiritual tradition, which grew out of a belief in Original Sin, the focus was primarily on the lesson that nothing in this world is more than illusion. This is only a stage on some longer journey we do not fully understand. To fall in love with your physical beauty or your wealth, your health, or your power to experience good feelings is to kid yourself because they will be taken away. A 94-year-old aunt of mine with a Ph.D. from the University of Chicago and a woman I love dearly, said to me tearfully after the death of her husband, who had left her in comfortable circumstances, "They don't let you win. There is no way to win."

She had lived her life in the camp of science, honorably observing all its rules of rationality, but at his passing, science was useless to her. The Western spiritual tradition would reply, "Of course you can win. Everyone can win. And if you think you can't, then you're playing the wrong game." The only thing that gives our time on Earth any deep significance is that none of this will last. Only that temporality gives our relationships any urgency. If you were indestructible, what a curse! How could it possibly matter whether you did anything today or next year or in the next 100 years, learned anything, loved anybody? There would always be time for anything and everything. What would be the big deal about anything?

Everyone has known the experience of having too much candy, too much company, or even too much money, so that no individual purchase involves real choice because real choice always closes the door on other choices. I know that we would all like to have endless amounts of money, but the truth is too much money wipes out our pleasure in choosing since we can now choose everything. That's what Roman emperor Marcus Aurelius discovered for himself in his reflections about what really matters—the *Meditations*, one of the great classics in Western history. He discovered none of the important things were for sale. If you don't believe an emperor would feel this way, read the *Meditations*.

Too much time, like too much money, can hang heavily on our hands as well. Look at the millions of bored schoolchildren. They know what I mean. The corrective for this boredom is a full spiritual awareness that time is finite. As you spend time on one thing, you lose forever the chance to spend it on something else. Time is always a big deal.

Science can't help with time. In fact, living scientifically so as not to waste time, becoming one of those poor souls who never goes anywhere without a list, is the best guarantee your life will be eaten up by errands and that none of those errands will ever become the big deal you desperately need to finally love yourself. The list of things to do will go ever onward and onward. The best lives are full of contemplation, full of solitude, full of self-examination, full of private, personal attempts to engage the metaphysical mystery of existence, to create an inner life.

We make the best of our limited time by alternating effort with reflection, and I mean reflection completely free of the get-something motive. Whenever I see a kid daydreaming in school, I'm careful never to shock the reverie out of existence.

Buddha is reputed to have said, "Do nothing. Time is too precious to waste." If that advice seems impossible in the world described on the evening news, reflect on the awesome fact that in spite of hype, you still live on a planet where 67 percent of the world's entire population has never made or received a single phone call and where the Old Order Amish of Lancaster County live prosperous lives virtually free of crime, of divorce, or of children who go beyond the eighth grade in school. Yet not a single one has a college degree, a tractor to plow with, a telephone in the house, or is on welfare.

If I seem to have stepped away from original sin with these facts, it is not so. Until you acknowledge that the factual contents of your mind upon which you base decisions have been inserted there by others whose motives you cannot fully understand, you will never come to appreciate the neglected genius of Western spirituality which teaches that you are the center of the universe. And that the most important things worth knowing are innate in you already. They cannot be learned through schooling. They are self-taught through the burdens of having to work, having to sort out right from wrong, having to check your appetites, and having to age and die.

The effect of this formula on world history has been titanic. It brought every citizen in the West a mandate to be sovereign, which we still have not learned to use wisely, but which offers the potential for such wisdom. Western spirituality granted every single individual a purpose for being alive, a purpose independent of mass behavioral prescriptions, money, experts, schools, and governments. It conferred significance on every aspect of relationship and community. It carried inside its ideas the seeds of a self-activating curriculum which gives meaning to time.

In Western spirituality, everyone counts. It offers a basic, matter-of-fact set of practical guidelines, street lamps for the village of your life. Nobody has to wander aimlessly in the universe of Western spirituality. What constitutes a meaningful life is clearly spelled out: self-knowledge, duty, responsibility, acceptance of aging and loss, preparation for death. In this neglected genius of the West, no teacher or guru does the work for you; you do it for yourself. It's time to teach these things to our children once again.

CHAPTER FIFTEEN

The Psychopathology Of

Everyday Schooling

In 1909 a factory inspector did an informal survey of 500 working children in 20 factories. She found that 412 of them would rather work in the terrible conditions of the factories than return to school.
— Helen Todd, "Why Children Work,"
McClure's Magazine (April, 1913)

In one experiment in Milwaukee, for example, 8,000 youth...were asked if they would return full-time to school if they were paid about the same wages as they earned at work; only 16 said they would.
— David Tyack, *Managers of Virtue*

An Arena Of Dishonesty

I remember clearly the last school where I worked, on the wealthy Upper Westside of Manhattan. An attractive atmosphere of good-natured dishonesty was the lingua franca of hallway and classroom, a grace caused oddly enough by the school's unwritten policy of cutting unruly children all the slack they could use.

Student terrorists, muggers, sexual predators, and thieves, including two of my own pupils who had just robbed a neighborhood grocery of $300 and had been apprehended coming back to class, were regularly returned to their lessons after a brief lecture from the principal. All received the same mercy. There was no such thing as being held to account at my school. This behavioral strategy—leveling good, bad, ugly into one undifferentiated lumpenproletariat[1]—may seem odd or morally repugnant in conventional terms, but it constituted masterful psychological management

---

[1] Except for a small fraction of Gifted and Talented Honors kids sequestered in a remote corner of the third floor who followed different protocols.

from the perspective of enlightened pedagogy. What this policy served and served well was to prioritize order and harmony above justice or academic development.

Once you know the code, the procedure is an old one. It can hardly be called radical politics except by the terminally innocent. If you spend a few hours with Erving Goffman's work on the management of institutions, you discover that the strongest inmates in an asylum and the asylum's management have a bond; they need each other. This isn't cynical. It's a price that must be paid for the benefits of mega-institutions. The vast Civil War prison camp of Andersonville couldn't have operated without active cooperation from its more dangerous inmates; so too, Dachau; so it is in school.

A tacit hands-off policy pays impressive dividends. In the case of my school, those dividends were reflected in the neighborhood newspaper's customary reference to the place as "The Westside's Best-Kept Secret." This was supposed to mean that private school conditions obtained inside the building, civility was honored, the battlefield aspect of other schools with large minority populations was missing. And it was true. The tone of the place was as good as could be found in Community School District 3. It was as if by withdrawing every expectation from the rowdy, their affability rose in inverse proportion.

Not long after my transfer into this school I came into home room one morning to discover Jack, a handsome young fellow of thirteen, running a crap game in the back of the room, a funny looking cigarette in his mouth. "Hey, Jack, knock it off," I snapped, and like the surprisingly courteous boy he was, he did. But a little while later there was Jack undressing a girl fairly conspicuously in the same corner, and this time when I intervened harshly he was slow to comply. A second order got no better results. "If I have to waste time on this junk again, Jack, you can cool your heels in the principal's office," I said.

Jack looked disappointed in me. He spoke frankly as if we were both men of the same world: "Look, Gatto," he told me in a low, pleasant voice so as not to embarrass me, "it won't do any good. Save yourself the trouble. That lady will wink at me, hold me there for eight minutes—I've timed her before—and dump me back here. Why make trouble for yourself?" He was right. Eight minutes.

How could such a policy produce hallway decorum and relative quiet in classrooms, you may ask? Well, look at it this way: it's tailor-made to be non-confrontational with dangerous kids. True, it spreads terror and bewilderment among their victims, but happy or unhappy, the weak are no problem for school managers; long experience with natural selection at my school had caused unfortunates to adapt, in Darwinian fashion, to their role as prey. Like edible animals they continued to the water hole in spite of every indignity awaiting. That hands-off modus vivendi extended to every operation. Only once in four years did I hear any teacher make an indirect reference to what was happening. One day I heard a lady remark offhandedly to a friend, "It's like we signed the last Indian treaty here: you leave us alone; we leave you alone."

It's not hard to see that, besides its beneficial immediate effect, this pragmatic policy has a powerful training function, too. Through it an army of young witnesses to officially sanctioned bad conduct learn how little value good conduct has. They learn pragmatism. Part of its silent testimony is that the strong will always successfully suppress the weak, so the weak learn to endure. They learn that appeals to authority are full of risk, so they don't make them often. They learn what they need in order to be foot soldiers in a mass army.

Psychopathic. An overheated word to characterize *successful, pragmatic solutions to the control of institutional chaos.* Isn't this process a cheap and effective way to keep student entropy in check at the cost of no more than a little grief on the part of some dumb animals? Is it really psychopathic or only strategic sophistication? My principal, let's call her Lulu to protect the guilty, once explained at a public meeting there was little she could do about the unfortunate past and present of these kids, and she acknowledged they probably didn't have bright prospects for the future—but while they were here they would know *she* cared about them, no one would be unduly hassled. Nobody in the audience took what she said as insincere, nor do I think it was. She believed what she said.

Psychopathic. The word summons up flashing eyes and floating hair, men hiding gasoline bombs under their coats in crowded subway cars on the way to Merrill Lynch for revenge. But set aside any lurid associations you may have with the term; I'm using it as a label to describe people without consciences, nothing more. Psychopaths and sociopaths are often our charming and intelligent roommates in corporations and institutions. They mimic perfectly the necessary protective coloration of compassion and concern, they mimic human discourse. Yet underneath that surface disguise they are circuit boards of scientific *rationality*, pure expressions of pragmatism.

All large bureaucracies, public or private, are psychopathic to the degree they are well-managed. It's a genuine paradox, but time to face the truth of it. Corporate policies like downsizing and environmental degradation, which reduce the quality of life for enormous numbers of people, make perfectly rational sense as devices to reach profitability. Even could it be proven that the theory of *homo economicus* has a long-range moral component in which, as is sometimes argued in policy circles, the pain of the moment leads inevitably to a better tomorrow for those who survive—the thing would still be psychopathic. An older America would have little hesitation labeling it as Evil. I've reached for the term psychopathic in place of Evil in deference to modern antipathies. The whole matter is in harmony with classic evolutionary theory and theological notions of limited salvation. I find that congruence interesting.

The sensationalistic charge that all large corporations, including school corporations, are psychopathic becomes less inflammatory if you admit the obvious first, that all such entities are *non-human*. Forget the human beings who populate corporate structures. Sure, some of them sabotage corporate integrity from time to time and behave like human beings, but never consistently, or ever for long, for if that were the story, corporate *coherence* would be impossible, as it often is in Third World countries. Now at least you see where I'm coming from in categorizing the institutional corporation of school as psychopathic. Moral codes don't drive school decision-making. That means School sometimes decides to ignore your wimpy kid being beaten up for his lunch money in order to oil some greater wheels. School has no tear ducts with which to weep.

The Game Is Crooked

Hannah Arendt's analysis of the remarkable *banality* of Nazi-era organizational character calls attention to its excessive orderliness, unfailing courtesy, neat files, schedules for everything, efficient supply procedures, and the dullness and emotional poverty of Adolf Eichmann, who supervised the destruction of many lives without any particular malice. He even *liked* Jews. That he was part of a company dedicated to the conversion of animate into inanimate on a wholesale basis wasn't his fault. It was just a job. His rational duty was to do his best at it. Unless mankind is allowed to possess some peculiar godlike dignity, a soul perhaps, Eichmann had a right to say to his critics—what difference between what I do and the slaughter of British beef to prevent mad cow disease? Nothing personal. Is it a shortage of people that makes you so angry?

That's the real point, isn't it? Once a mission is defined with pure objectivity, psychopathic procedure makes perfect sense. If men and women can think about *genocide* that way, you can understand why merely screwing up children wouldn't trouble the sleep of school administrators. *Their job isn't about children; it's about systems maintenance.* The school institution has always had a strong shadow mission to refute the irrefutable fact that all kids want to learn to be their best and strongest selves. They don't need to be forced to do this.

School is a *tour de force* designed to recreate human nature around a different premise, constructing proof that most kids don't want to learn because they are biologically defective. School succeeds in this private aim *only* by failing in its public mission; that's the knuckle-ball school critics always miss. Only a delicate blend of abject failures, mid-range failures, and minor failures mixed together with a topping of successes, guarantees the ongoing health of the school enterprise. School is as good an illustration of the work of natural selection in institutional life as we have. The only drawback is, the game is crooked. Like an undertaker who murders to boost business or a glazier who breaks glass in the stillness of the night[2] to stimulate trade, schools *create* the problems they seem to exist to solve.

Psychopathic Programming

I could regale you with mountains of statistics to illustrate the damage schools cause. I could bring before your attention a line of case studies to illustrate the mutilation of specific individuals—even those who have been apparently privileged as its "gifted and talented."[3] What would that prove? You've heard those stories, read these figures before until you went numb from the assault on common sense. School can't be that bad, you say. *You* survived, didn't you? Or did you? Review what you learned there. Has it made a crucial difference for good in your life? Don't answer. I know it hasn't. You surrendered twelve years of your life because you had no choice. You paid your dues, I paid mine. But who collected those dues?

In 1911, a prominent German sociologist, Robert Michels, warned in his book *Political Parties* that the size and prosperity of modern bureaucracies had given them unprecedented ability to buy friends. In this way they armor themselves against internal reform and make themselves

---

[2] This particular form of rational psychopathy has been an epidemic in Manhattan for decades, and it has struck my own life more than once. Auto-glass installers send agents through lines of parked cars late at night to crack their windshields on the sensible supposition that in a trade without many practitioners, a decent proportion of new work will go to the creators of the need.

[3] What I would never do is to argue that the damage to human potential is adequately caught in the rise or fall of SAT scores or any other standardized measure because these markers are too unreliable—besides being far too prone to strategic manipulation.

impregnable to outside reform. Across this great epoch of bureaucracy, Michel's warning has been strikingly borne out. Where school is concerned we have lived through six major periods of crisis since its beginning, zones of social turmoil where outsiders have demanded the state change the way it provides for the schooling of children.[4] Each crisis can be used as a stepping stone leading us back to the original wrong path we took at the beginnings.

All alleged reforms have left schooling exactly in the shape they found it, except bigger, richer, politically stronger. And morally and intellectually worse by the standards of the common American village of yesteryear which still lives in our hearts. Many people of conscience only defend institutional schooling because they can't imagine what would happen without any schools, especially what might happen to the poor. This compassionate and articulate contingent has consistently been fronted by the real engineers of schooling, skillfully used as shock troops to support the cumulative destruction of American working class and peasant culture, a destruction largely effected through schooling.

Psychopathic programming is incapable of change. It lacks moral dimension or ethical mind beyond the pragmatic. Institutional morality is always public relations; once institutional machinery of sufficient size and complexity is built, a logical movement commences internally aimed toward subordination of all ethical mandates and eventual elimination of them. Even if quality personnel are stationed on the parapets in the *first* generation of new institutional existence, that original vigilance will flag as pioneers give way to time-servers. The only reliable defense against this is to keep institutions weak and dispersed, even if that means sacrificing efficiency and holding them on a very short leash.

Michel wrote in *Political Parties* that the primary mission of all institutional managers (including school managers) is to cause their institution to grow in power, in number of employees, in autonomy from public oversight, and in rewards for key personnel. The primary mission is never, of course, the publicly announced one. Whether we are talking about bureaucracies assigned to wage war, deliver mail, or educate children, there is no difference.

In the course of things, this rationalization isn't a straight line matter. There *can* be pullbacks in the face of criticism, for example. But examined over time, movement toward rationalizing operations is always unidirectional, public outrage against the immoral effects of this is buffered by purchased political friendships, by seemingly neutral public authorities who always find it prudent to argue for delay, in confidence the heat will cool. In this way momentum is spent, public attention diverted, until the next upwelling of outrage. These strategies of opinion management are taught calmly through elite graduate university training in the best schools, here as was true in Prussia. Corporate bureaucracies, including those in the so-called public sphere, know how to wear out critics. There is no malicious intent, only a striving for efficiency.

Something has been happening in America since the end of WWII, accelerating since the flight of Sputnik and the invasion of Vietnam. A massive effort is underway to link centrally

---

[4] Different addictive readers of school histories might tally eight crises or five, so the stab at specificity shouldn't be taken too seriously by any reader. What it *is* meant to indicate is that careful immersion in pedagogical history will reveal, even to the most skeptical, that mass schooling has been in nearly constant crisis since its inception. There never was a golden age of mass schooling, nor can there ever be.

organized control of jobs with centrally organized administration of schooling. This would be an American equivalent of the Chinese "Dangan"—linking a personal file begun in kindergarten (recording academic performance, attitudes, behavioral characteristics, medical records, and other personal data) with all work opportunities. In China the Dangan can't be escaped. It is part of a web of social controls which ensure stable social order; justice has nothing to do with it. The Dangan is coming to the United States under cover of skillfully engineered changes in medicine, employment, education, social service, etc., seemingly remote from one another. In fact, the pieces are being coordinated through an interlink between foundations, grant-making government departments, corporate public relations, key universities, and similar agencies out of public view.

This American Dangan will begin with longer school days and years, with more public resources devoted to institutional schooling, with more job opportunities in the school field, more emphasis on standardized testing, more national examinations, plus hitherto unheard of developments like national teaching licenses, national curricula, national goals, national standards, and with the great dream of corporate America since 1900, School-to-Work legislation organizing the youth of America into precocious work battalions. *A Dangan in its nature is always psychopathic. It buries its mistakes.*

What Really Goes On

School wreaks havoc on human foundations in at least eight substantive ways so deeply buried few notice them, and fewer still can imagine any other way for children to grow up:

1) The first lesson schools teach is *forgetfulness*; forcing children to forget how they taught themselves important things like walking and talking. This is done so pleasantly and painlessly that the *one* area of schooling most of us would agree has few problems is elementary school—even through it is there that the massive damage to language-making occurs. Jerry Farber captured the truth over 30 years ago in his lapidary metaphor "Student as Nigger" and developed it in the beautiful essay of the same name. If we forced children to learn to walk with the same methods we use to force them to read, a few would learn to walk well in spite of us, most would walk indifferently, without pleasure, and a portion of the remainder would not become ambulatory at all. The push to extend "day care" further and further into currently unschooled time importantly assists the formal twelve-year sequence, assuring utmost tractability among first graders.

2) The second lesson schools teach is *bewilderment and confusion*. Virtually nothing selected by schools as basic *is* basic, all curriculum is subordinate to standards imposed by behavioral psychology, and to a lesser extent Freudian precepts compounded into a hash with "third force" psychology (centering on the writings of Carl Rogers and Abraham Maslow). None of these systems accurately describes human reality, but their lodgement in university/business seven-step mythologies makes them dangerously invulnerable to common-sense criticism.

None of the allegedly scientific school sequences is empirically defensible. All lack evidence of being much more than superstition cleverly hybridized with a body of borrowed fact. Pestalozzi's basic "simple to complex" formulation, for instance, is a prescription for disaster in the classroom since no two minds have the same "simple" starting point, and in the more advanced schedules, children are frequently more knowledgeable than their overseers—witness the wretched record of public school computer instruction when compared to self-discovery programs undertaken informally.

Similarly, endless rounds of shallow "subjects" mediated by well-meaning men and women who have only the most superficial knowledge of what they speak is the correct introduction of children to the liar's world of institutional life which promises what it has no intention of delivering. Sane people seek meaning, not disconnected facts, but schools teach the unrelating of everything.

3) The third lesson schools teach is that *children are assigned* by experts to a social class and must stay in the class to which they have been assigned. This is an Egyptian outlook, but its Oriental message only begins to suggest the bad fit it produces in America. The natural genius of the United States as explored and set down in covenants over the first two-thirds of our history has now been radically degraded and overthrown. The class system is reawakened through schooling. So rigid have American classifications become that our society has taken on the aspect of caste, which teaches unwarranted self-esteem and its converse—envy, self-hatred, and surrender. In class systems, the state assigns your place in class, and if you know what's good for you you come to know it, too.

4) The fourth lesson schools teach is *indifference*. By bells and other concentration-destroying technology, schools teach that nothing is worth finishing because some arbitrary power intervenes both periodically and aperiodically. If nothing is worth finishing, nothing is worth starting. Don't you see how one follows the other? Love of learning can't survive this steady drill. Students are taught to work for little favors and ceremonial grades which correlate poorly with their actual ability. By addicting children to outside approval and nonsense rewards, schools make them indifferent to the real power and potential that self-discovery contains. Schools alienate the winners as well as the losers.

5) The fifth lesson schools teach is *emotional dependency*. By stars, checks, smiles, frowns, prizes, honors, and disgraces, schools condition children to lifelong emotional dependency. It's like training a dog. The reward/punishment cycle, known to animal trainers from antiquity, is the heart of a human psychology distilled in nineteenth century Leipzig and incorporated thoroughly into the scientific management revolution of the early twentieth century. Half a decade later it had infected every school system, so all-pervasive at century's end few people can imagine a different way to go about management. And indeed there isn't a better one if the goal of managed lives in a managed economy and a managed social order is what you're after.

Each day, schools reinforce how absolute and arbitrary power really is by granting and denying access to fundamental needs for toilets, water, privacy, and movement. In this way, basic human rights which usually require only individual volition, are transformed into privileges not to be taken for granted.

6) The sixth lesson schools teach is *intellectual dependency*. Good people wait for a teacher to tell them what to do. Good people do it the way the teacher wants it done. Good teachers in their turn wait for the curriculum supervisor or textbook to tell *them* what to do. Principals are evaluated according to an ability to make these groups conform to expectations; superintendents upon their ability to make principals conform; state education departments on their ability to efficiently direct and control the thinking of superintendents according to instructions which originate with foundations, universities, and politicians sensitive to the quietly expressed wishes of powerful corporations, and other interests.

For all its clumsy execution, school is a textbook illustration of how the bureaucratic chain of command is supposed to work. Once the thing is running, virtually nobody can alter its direction who doesn't understand the complex code for making it work, a code that never stops trying to complicate itself further so that human control is made impossible. The sixth lesson of schooling teaches that experts make all important choices, but it is useless to remonstrate with the expert nearest you because he is as helpless as you are to change the system.

7) The seventh lesson schools teach is *provisional self-esteem*. Self-respect in children must be made contingent on the certification of experts through rituals of number magic. It must not be self-generated as it was for Benjamin Franklin, the Wright brothers, Thomas Edison, or Henry Ford. The role of grades, report cards, standardized tests, prizes, scholarships, and other awards in effecting this process is too obvious to belabor, but it's the daily encounter with hundreds of verbal and nonverbal cues sent by teachers that shapes the quality of self-doubt most effectively.

8) The last lesson school teaches I'll call *the glass house effect*: It teaches how hopeless it is to resist because you are always watched. There is no place to hide. Nor should you want to. Your avoidance behavior is actually a signal you *should* be watched even more closely than the others. Privacy is a thought crime. School sees to it that there is no private time, no private space, no minute uncommanded, no desk free from search, no bruise not inspected by medical policing or the counseling arm of thought patrols.

The most sensitive children I had each year knew on some level what was really going on. But we choked the treacherous breath out of them until they acknowledged they depended on us for their futures. Hard-core cases were remaindered to adjustment agencies where they converted themselves into manageable cynics.

Pathology As A Natural Byproduct

With these eight lessons in hand you should have less trouble seeing that the social pathologies we associate with modern children are natural byproducts of our modern system of schooling which produces:

• Children indifferent to the adult world of values and accomplishment, defying the universal human experience laid down over thousands of years that a close study of grownups is always the most exciting and one of the most necessary occupations of youth. Have you noticed how very few people, adults included, want to grow up anymore? Toys are the lingua franca of American society for the masses *and* the classes.

• Children with almost no curiosity. Children who can't even concentrate for long on things they themselves choose to do. Children taught to channel-change by a pedagogy employing the strategy, "and now for something different," but kids who also realize dimly that the same damn show is on every channel.

• Children with a poor sense of the future, of how tomorrow is linked to today. Children who live in a continuous present. Conversely, children with no sense of the past and of how the past has shaped and limited the present, shaped and limited their own choices, predetermined their values and destinies to an overwhelming degree.

• Children who lack compassion for misfortune, who laugh at weakness, who betray their friends and families, who show contempt for people whose need for help shows too plainly. Children condemned to be alone, to age with bitterness, to die in fear.

• Children who can't stand intimacy or frankness. Children who masquerade behind personalities hastily fabricated from watching television and from other distorted gauges of human nature. Behind the masks lurk crippled souls. Aware of this, they avoid the close scrutiny intimate relationships demand because it will expose their shallowness of which they have some awareness.

• Materialistic children who assign a price to everything and who avoid spending too much time with people who promise no immediate payback—a group which often includes their own parents. Children who follow the lead of schoolteachers, grading and ranking everything: "the best," "the biggest," "the finest," "the worst." Everything simplified into simple-minded categories by the implied judgment of a cash price, deemed an infallible guide to value.

• Dependent children who grow up to be whining, treacherous, terrified, dependent adults, passive and timid in the face of new challenges. And yet this crippling condition is often hidden under a patina of bravado, anger, aggressiveness.

A Critical Appraisal

In the latter half of the nineteenth century, as the new school institution slowly took root after the Civil War in big cities and the defeated South, some of the best minds in the land, people fit by their social rank to comment publicly, spoke out as they watched its first phalanx of graduates take their place in the traditional American world. All these speakers had been trained themselves in the older, a-systematic, non-institutional schools. At the beginning of another new century, it is eerie to hear what these great-grandfathers of ours had to say about the mass schooling phenomenon as they approached their own fateful new century:

In 1867, world-famous American physician and academic, Vincent Youmans, lectured the London College of Preceptors about the school institution just coming into being:

> School produces mental perversion and absolute stupidity. It produces bodily
> disease. It produces these things by measures which operate to the prejudice
> of the growing brain. It is not to be doubted that dullness, indocility, and
> viciousness are frequently aggravated by the lessons of school.

Thirteen years later, Francis Parkman (*of Parkman's Oregon Trail* fame) delivered a similar judgment. The year was 1880, at the very moment Wundt was founding his laboratory of scientific psychology in Germany:

> Many had hoped that by giving *a partial teaching* to great numbers of persons,
> a thirst for knowledge might be awakened. Thus far, the results have not equaled
> expectations. Schools have not borne any fruit on which we have cause to
> congratulate ourselves.

In 1885, the president of Columbia University said:

> The result actually attained under our present system of instruction are neither
> very flattering nor very encouraging.

In 1895, the president of Harvard said:

> Ordinary schooling produces dullness. A young man whose intellectual powers
> are worth cultivating cannot be willing to cultivate them by pursuing phantoms
> as the schools now insist upon.

When he said this, compulsion schooling in its first manifestation was approaching its forty-third year of operations in Massachusetts, and running at high efficiency in Cambridge where Harvard is located.

Then the great metamorphosis to an even more efficient scientific form of pedagogy took place, in the early years of the twentieth century. Four years before WWI broke out, a well-known European thinker and schoolman, Paul Geheeb, whom Einstein, Herman Hesse, and Albert Schweitzer all were to claim as a friend, made this commentary on English and German types of forced schooling:

> The dissatisfaction with public schools is widely felt. Countless attempts to
> reform them have failed. People complain about the 'overburdening' of
> schools; educators argue about which parts of curriculum should be cut; but
> school cannot be reformed with a pair of scissors. *The solution is not to be
> found in educational institutions.*

In 1930, the yearly Inglis Lecture at Harvard made the same case:

> We have absolutely nothing to show for our colossal investment in common
> schooling after 80 years of trying.

Thirty years passed before John Gardner's "Annual Report to the Carnegie Corporation" in 1960 added this:

> Too many young people gain nothing [from school] except the conviction
> they are misfits.

The record after 1960 is no different. It is hardly unfair to say that the *stupidity* of 1867, the *fruitlessness* of 1880, the *dullness* of 1895, the *cannot be reformed* of 1910, the *absolutely nothing* of 1930, and the *nothing* of 1960 has been continued into the schools of 2000. We pay four times more in real dollars than we did in 1930 and thus we buy even more of what mass schooling dollars always bought.

Vox Populi

Just under 1,800 people wrote letters to me in the year I was New York State Teacher of the Year, responding to a series of essays I wrote about what I had witnessed as a schoolteacher, essays which have now become part of this book. In a strange way, those different letters were 1,800 versions of the same letter, a spontaneous outcry against the violation so many feel being compelled to be a character in someone else's fantasy of how to grow up. Listen to a few of these voices:

Huntington, West Virginia "Home schooling may be stressful but it's nothing compared to the stress I experienced watching my daughter's self-respect and creative energy drain away within the first few weeks of third grade."

Toronto, Canada "Little has changed since I was asked to sit in straight rows and memorize an irrelevant curriculum. Recently my wife quit her job because we fear losing contact with our children as they enter a school system we cannot understand and are unable to change."

Frankfurt, Illinois "I had a rich personal inquiry going on in many things. School was for me a tedious interruption of my otherwise interesting life."

Yelm, Washington "My passion is that my daughter be allowed to grow up being completely who she is. Right now she is a happy, enthusiastic, self-taught child of eight and a half. She taught herself to read at four, reads everything. School to me has always felt sick at the core of its concept."

Madison, Wisconsin "I'm desperate what to do. Three bright and lively children but everyday I see a closing down of enthusiasm as they grind their way through a predetermined school program."

Reno, Nevada "My wife and I came to the end of the rope with public education four years ago. I was tired of seeing my once happy child constantly in tears."

Santa Barbara, California "I just took my 8-year-old daughter from school. Bit by bit she was becoming silent, even fearful. From her anxiety to reach the school bus on time to the times she was visibly shaken from criticism of her homework. Day by day she was changing for the worse. But the absolute end was the destructive effect the culture of schoolchildren's values had on her behavior. Now she laughs again. I have my laughing girl back."

Pittsburgh, Pennsylvania "School started to destroy my family by dividing us from one another instead of joining us. It created separatism among the kids, among the classes, among ages, among parents and children. After I took my second grader from school she began to blossom. She loves her time now, the time is the gift."

Huntersville, North Carolina "I defined myself as a child by my accomplishments at school just as I had been taught to. I was a National Merit Scholar and a Presidential Scholar but I couldn't even make it through two years of college because my own authoritarian schooling had left me completely unprepared to make my own decisions."

St. Louis, Missouri "Mr. Gatto, you are describing my daughter when you name the pathological symptoms our children display as a result of their schooling. And you are describing *me*—which pains me almost unbearably to recognize and admit."

Haverhill, Massachusetts "I have no certificates of great accomplishment, no titles, no diploma except a high school one, no degree except when I have a fever. Yet I do have experience gained while raising three daughters. I'd like to paint a picture for you. I had to take my daughter out of kindergarten after five weeks. This happy, self-regulating child I was raising showed great signs of stress in that short of a time. I remembered the rebellion of my two angry teenagers, suddenly made the connection, and took her from school. And so the last girl I raised as a free child. There have been no signs of anger or rebellion since then. That was 17 years ago.

The Systems Idea In Action

Society is composed of persons who cannot design, build, repair, or even operate most of the devices upon which their lives depend.... In the complexity of this world people are confronted with extraordinary events and functions that are literally unintelligible to them. They are unable to give an adequate explanation of man-made phenomena in their immediate experience. They are unable to form a coherent, rational picture of the whole. Under the circumstances, all persons do, and indeed must, accept a great number of things on faith....Their way of understanding is basically religious, rather than scientific; only a small portion of one's everyday experience in the technological society can be made scientific....The plight of members of the technological society can be compared to that of a newborn child. Much of the data that enters its sense does not form coherent wholes. There are many things the child cannot understand or, after it has learned to speak, cannot successfully explain to anyone.... Citizens of the modern age in this respect are less fortunate than children. They never escape a fundamental bewilderment in the face of the complex world that their senses report. They are not able to organize all or even very much of this into sensible wholes.... An objection might be raised that difficulties of the sort I have mentioned soon will have remedies. Systems theory, artificial intelligence, or some new modern way of knowing will alleviate the burdens.... Soon there will exist tools of intellectual synthesis. I must report I found no such tools in practice. I have surveyed the various candidates for this honor—systems theory and systems analysis, computer sciences and artificial intelligence, new methods of coding great masses of information, the strategy of disjointed incrementalism and so forth. As relief for the difficulties raised here none of these offers much help.... The systems idea is another—and indeed the ultimate—technique to shape man and society....

— Langdon Winner, *Autonomous Technology: Technics-Out-Of-Control* (MIT Press, 1989)

By allowing the existence of large bureaucratic systems under centralized control, whether corporate, governmental, or institutional, we unwittingly enter into a hideous conspiracy against ourselves, one in which we resolutely work to limit the growth of our minds and spirits. The only conceivable answer is to break the power of these things, through grit, courage, indomitability and resolution if possible, through acts of personal sabotage and disloyalty if not.

PART FIVE

The Problem Of
Modern Schooling

*Moses wanted to turn a tribe of enslaved Hebrews into free men.
You would think that all he had to do was to gather the slaves
and tell them that they were free. But Moses knew better. He knew
that the transformation of slaves into free men was more difficult
and painful than the transformation of free men into slaves.... Moses
discovered that no spectacle, no myth, no miracles could turn slaves
into free men. It cannot be done. So he led the slaves back into the
desert, and waited forty years until the slave generation died, and a
new generation, desert born and bred, was ready to enter the
promised land.*

> — Eric Hoffer, diary entry, May 20, 1959, while unloading
> the *Harunassan Maru* at Pier 26, San Francisco

The Odysseus Group presents:

An Evening With
NEW YORK STATE TEACHER OF THE YEAR
JOHN TAYLOR GATTO
AND SEVEN OTHER VOICES OF SCHOOL REFORM
At
CARNEGIE HALL
WEDNESDAY, NOVEMBER 13TH, 7:30 P.M. *SHARP*
IN A DISCUSSION OF

THE EXHAUSTED SCHOOL

A SPEAKOUT ON PARENT-CHOICE SCHOOLS...AND MUCH MORE. • *FIND OUT WHY OUR SCHOOLS ARE DYING*

Your ideas are splendid. I just hope someone is listening.
-Christopher Lasch

...Gatto is the most important school reformer in years, a broad-ranging intellect.
-John Holt, Inc. Cambridge Mass.

YOU WILL LEARN:

☛ *How to Bend the Bars of Our Traditional Factory Schools!*

☛ *What real Public School Alternatives Can Do!*

☛ *Exciting Private School Choices at Bargain Prices!*

☛ *How to Get an Education at Home!*

☛ *Why You Should Listen to the Voices of Self-Schooling!*

☛ *How Free-Market Choices can Revive American Education!*

John Taylor Gatto

Featuring:

JOHN TAYLOR GATTO: New York State Teacher of the Year, 1991; author, "Dumbing Us Down"; creator of "The Guerrilla Curriculum". **DAN GREENBERG:** Founder of the astonishing Sudbury Valley School near Boston, located on a beautiful estate where for 1/3 the cost of government schooling children teach themselves to read, write and do arithmetic. **PATRICK FARENGA:** President, John Holt Associates of Cambridge; publisher, "Growing Without Schooling" magazine, the nationally recognized leader of the American homeschooling movement. **MARY LEUE:** SUNY Senior Fellow in Humanities and founder of The Albany Free School, a continuously successful alternative school for 22 years, owning 10 buildings earned by school community efforts, operating 6 businesses as part of the "community" curriculum. **DAVID LEHMAN:** Principal of a nationally famous public school operated on democratic principles, The Ithaca Public Alternative Community School in Ithaca, New York.

And 4 former students of Mr. Gatto's:

ROLAND LEGIARDI-LAURA: Major projects structural engineer, self-taught; director, "Azul" (9 international film awards) self-taught; co-director of "The Nuyorican Poet's Cafe", world famous poetry nightclub. **BARBARA JILL CUMMINGS:** 24 year old author, "Dam the Rivers, Damn the People" (World Wildlife Fund); lecturer; UCLA student. **JAMAAL WATSON & VICTOR GONZALEZ:** 14 year old creators of "Elvis Impersonator"; winners 3 citywide essay contests; consultants to Senator Bob Kerrey on educational matters; students at Art & Design High School

Dedicated to the memory of JUDITH KIRSH KOVACH,   a shining example of courage in the Face of Adversity.

☛ Tickets;
Box, $30; Parquet, $15; Dress Circle, $12; Balcony,$10 front, $5 rear. Patron's boxes in the first and second tiers are also available by contacting The Odysseus Group directly. Tickets are available through **CARNEGIE CHARGE: (212) 247-7800**. 7 days a week from 11-8, or Carnegie Box Office. The Odysseus Group may be reached for information or exclusive boxes by calling (212) 529-9327 or (212) 874-3631 or by writing to John Taylor, 235 West 76th Street, New York, New York 10023.

CHAPTER SIXTEEN

A Conspiracy

Against Ourselves

A lower middle class which has received secondary or even university education without being given any corresponding outlet for its trained abilities was the backbone of the twentieth century Fascist Party in Italy and the National Socialist Party in Germany. The demoniac driving force which carried Mussolini and Hitler to power was generated out of this intellectual proletariat's exasperation at finding its painful efforts at self-improvement were not sufficient.

— Arnold Toynbee, *A Study of History*

Two Social Revolutions Become One

Solve this problem and school will heal itself: children know that schooling is not fair, not honest, not driven by integrity. They know they are devalued in classes and grades,[1] that the institution is indifferent to them as individuals. The rhetoric of caring contradicts what school procedure and content says, that many children have no tolerable future and most have a sharply proscribed one. The problem is structural. School has been built to serve a society of associations: corporations, institutions, and agencies. Kids know this instinctively. How should they feel about it? How should we?

As soon as you break free of the orbit of received wisdom you have little trouble figuring out why, in the nature of things, government schools and those private schools which imitate the government model have to make most children dumb, allowing only a few to escape the trap. The

---

[1] The labels, themselves, are an affront to decency. Who besides a degraded rabble would voluntarily present itself to be graded and classified like meat? No wonder school is compulsory.

problem stems from the structure of our economy and social organization. When you start with such pyramid-shaped givens and then ask yourself what kind of schooling they would require to maintain themselves any mystery dissipates—these things are inhuman conspiracies all right, but not conspiracies of people against people, although circumstances make them appear so. School is a conflict pitting the needs of social machinery against the needs of the human spirit. It is a war of mechanism against flesh and blood, self-maintaining social mechanisms that only require human architects to get launched.

I'll bring this down to Earth. Try to see that an intricately subordinated industrial/commercial system has only limited use for hundreds of millions of self-reliant, resourceful readers and critical thinkers. In an egalitarian, entrepreneurially-based economy of confederated families like the one the Amish have or the Mondragon folk in the Basque region of Spain, any number of self-reliant people can be accommodated usefully, but not in a concentrated command-type economy like our own. Where on earth would they fit? In a great fanfare of moral fervor some years back, the Ford Motor Company opened the world's most productive auto engine plant in Chihuahua, Mexico. It insisted on hiring employees with 50 percent more school training than the Mexican norm of six years, but as time passed Ford removed its requirements and began to hire school dropouts, training them quite well in four to twelve weeks. The hype that education is essential to robot-like work was quietly abandoned.

Our economy has no adequate outlet of expression for its artists, dancers, poets, painters, farmers, film makers, wildcat business people, handcraft workers, whiskey makers, intellectuals, or a thousand other useful human enterprises—no outlet except corporate work or fringe slots on the periphery of things. Unless you do "creative" work the company way, you run afoul of a host of laws and regulations put on the books to control the dangerous products of imagination which can never be safely tolerated by a centralized command system.

Before you can reach a point of effectiveness in defending your own children or your principles against the assault of blind social machinery, you have to stop conspiring against yourself by attempting to negotiate with a set of abstract principles and rules which, by its nature, cannot respond. Under all its disguises, that is what institutional schooling is, an abstraction which has escaped its handlers. *Nobody can reform it. First you have to realize that human values are the stuff of madness to a system; in systems-logic the schools we have are already the schools the system needs; the only way they could be much improved is to have kids eat, sleep, live and die there.*

Schools got the way they were at the start of the twentieth century as part of a vast, intensely engineered social revolution in which all major institutions were overhauled to work together in harmonious managerial efficiency. Ours was to be an improvement on the English system, which once depended on a shared upper-class culture for its coherence. Ours would be subject to a rational framework of science, law, instruction, and mathematically derived merit.

When J.P. Morgan reorganized the American marketplace into a cooperating world of trusts at the end of the nineteenth century, he was creating a business and financial subsystem to interlink with the subsystem of government, the subsystem of schooling, and other subsystems to regulate every other aspect of national life. None of this was conspiratorial. Each step of it was purchased with coin and a keen understanding of human nature. Each increment was rationally defensible. But the net effect was the destruction of small-town, small-government America, strong families, individual liberty, and a lot of other things people weren't aware they were trading for a regular corporate paycheck.

A huge price had to be paid for business and government efficiency, a price we still pay in the quality of our existence. Part of what kids gave up was the prospect of being able to read very well, an historic part of the American genius. School had instead to train them for their role in the new over-arching social system. But spare yourself the agony of thinking of this as a conspiracy. It was and is a fully rational transaction, the very epitome of rationalization engendered by a group of honorable men, all honorable men. *The real conspirators were ourselves. When we sold our liberty for the promise of security, we became like children in a conspiracy against growing up, sad children who conspire against their own children, consigning them over and over to the denaturing vats of compulsory state factory-schooling.*

The Fear Of Common Intelligence

The fear of common people learning too much is a recurrent theme in state records around the world. The founder of the Chinese state, the Emperor Ts'in She Hwang-ti, burned the work of the philosophers for fear their ideas would poison his own plans. The Caliph Ùmar of Syria wrote instructions to destroy the perhaps apocryphal library at Alexandria, using this airtight syllogism:

> If these writings of the Greeks agree with the Book of God they are useless
> and need not be preserved; if they disagree they are pernicious and ought to
> be destroyed.

Literary bonfires in Nazi Germany are often invoked as a vivid symbol of the deepest barbarism of the twentieth century, but extensive public reporting of those actions forced them to stop by causing worldwide unease. Much more effective have been those silent blast furnaces used by public library systems and great American universities to dispose of three million excess books yearly because of a shortage of shelf space. Why aren't they given to schools?

There are other ways to burn books without matches. Consider the great leap forward undertaken in the modern Turkish state under Kemal Ataturk. Unlike Hitler, who burned only some of the past, Ataturk burned it all without fire by radically changing the Turkish national alphabet so that all the vital writings of the past were entombed in an obsolete symbol system. Not a single Turk voted to have this done, yet all accepted it.

From 1929 on, all books and newspapers were printed in the new alphabet. All documents were composed in it. All schoolchildren were instructed in it and no other. The classics of Persia, Arabia, and Turkey vanished without a trace for the next generation. Obliterate the national memory bound up in history and literature, sift carefully what can be translated, and you open a gulf between old and young, past and present, which can't be crossed, rendering children vulnerable to any form of synthetic lore authorities deem advisable.

Turkish experimentation is echoed today in mainland China where a fifth of the population of the planet is cut off from the long past of Chinese literature and philosophy, one of the very few significant bodies of thought on the human record. The method being used is a radical simplification of the characters of the language which will have, in the fullness of time, the same result as burning books, putting them effectively out of reach. Lord Lindsay of Birker, a professor at Yenching University outside Beijing where I went recently to see for myself the effects of Westernization on the young Chinese elite, says the generation educated entirely in simplified characters will have difficulty reading anything published in China before the late 1950s.

First, said Plato, wipe the slate clean.

There are many ways to burn books without a match. You can order the reading of childish books to be substituted for serious ones, as we have done. You can simplify the language you allow in school books to the point that students become disgusted with reading because it demeans them, being thinner gruel than their spoken speech. We have done that, too. One subtle and very effective strategy is to fill books with pictures and lively graphics so they trivialize words in the same fashion the worst tabloid newspapers do—forcing pictures and graphs into space where readers should be building pictures of their own, preempting room into which personal intellect should be expanding. In this we are the world's master.

Samuel Johnson entered a note into his diary several hundred years ago about the powerful effect reading *Hamlet* was having upon him. He was nine at the time. Abraham Cowley wrote of his "infinite delight" with *Spenser's Faerie Queen*—an epic poem that treats moral values allegorically in nine-line stanzas that never existed before Spenser (and hardly since). He spoke of his pleasure with its "Stories of Knights and Giants and Monsters and Brave Houses." Cowley was twelve at the time. It couldn't have been an easy read in 1630 for anyone, and it's beyond the reach of many elite college graduates today. What happened? The answer is that *Dick and Jane* happened. "Frank had a dog. His name was Spot." That happened.

The Cult Of Forced Schooling

The most candid account of the changeover from old-style American free market schooling to the laboratory variety we have under the close eye of society's managers is a book long out of print. But the author was famous enough in his day that a yearly lecture at Harvard is named after him, so with a bit of effort on your part, and perhaps a kind word to your local librarian, in due time you should be able to find a hair-raising account of the school transformation written by one of the insiders.

The book in question bears the soporific title *Principles of Secondary Education*. Published in 1918 near the end of the great school revolution, *Principles* offers a unique account of the project written through the eyes of an important revolutionary. Any lingering doubts you may have about the purposes of government schooling should be put to rest by Alexander Inglis. The principal purpose of the vast enterprise was to place control of the new social and economic machinery out of reach of the mob.

The great social engineers were confronted by the formidable challenge of working their magic in a democracy, least efficient and most unpredictable of political forms. School was designed to neutralize as much as possible any risk of being blind-sided by the democratic will. Nelson W. Aldrich Jr., writing of his grandfather Senator Aldrich, one of the principal architects of the Federal Reserve System which had come into being while Inglis' cohort built the schools—and whose intent was much the same, to remove economic machinery from public interference—caught the attitude of the builders perfectly in his book *Old Money*. Grandfather, he writes, believed that history, evolution, and a saving grace found their best advocates in him and in men like him, in his family and in families like his, down to the close of time. But the price of his privilege, the senator knew, "was vigilance—vigilance, above all, against the resentment of those who never could emerge." Once in Paris, Senator Aldrich saw two men "of the middle or lower class," as he described them, drinking absinthe in a café. That evening back at his hotel he wrote these words:

> As I looked upon their dull wild stupor I wondered what dreams were
> evolved from the depths of the bitter glass. Multiply that scene and you
> have the possibility of the wildest revolution or the most terrible outrages.

Alexander Inglis, author of *Principles of Secondary Education*, was of this class. He wrote that the new schools were being expressly created to serve a command economy and command society, one in which the controlling coalition would be drawn from important institutional stakeholders in the future. According to James Bryant Conant, another progressive aristocrat from whom I first learned of Inglis in a perfectly frightening book called *The Child, The Parent, and the State* (1959), the school transformation had been ordered by "certain industrialists and the innovative who were altering the nature of the industrial process."

Conant himself is a school name that resonates through the central third of the twentieth century, president of Harvard from 1933 to 1953. His book, *The American High School Today* (1959), was one of the important springs that pushed secondary schools to gigantic size in the 1960s and forced consolidation of many small school districts into larger ones. His career began as a poison gas specialist in WWI, a task assigned only to young men whose family lineage could be trusted, with other notable way stations on his path being service in the secret atomic bomb project during WWII and a stint as U.S. High Commissioner for Germany during the military occupation after 1945.

In his book Conant brusquely acknowledges that conversion of old-style American education into Prussian-style schooling was done as a *coup de main,* but his greater motive in 1959 was to speak directly to men and women of his own class who were beginning to believe the new school procedure might be unsuited to human needs, that experience dictated a return to older institutional pluralistic ways.

No, Conant fairly shouts, the clock cannot be turned back! "Clearly, the total process is irreversible." Severe consequences would certainly follow the break-up of this carefully contrived behavioral-training machine:

> A successful counterrevolution...would require reorientation of a complex
> social pattern. Only a person bereft of reason would undertake [it].

Reading Conant is like overhearing a private conversation not meant for you yet fraught with the greatest personal significance. To Conant, school was a triumph of Anglo/Germanic pragmatism, a pinnacle of the social technocrat's problem-solving art. One task it performed with brilliance was to sharply curtail the American entrepreneurial spirit, a mission undertaken on perfectly sensible grounds, at least from a management perspective. As long as capital investments were at the mercy of millions of self-reliant, resourceful young entrepreneurs running about with a gleam in their eye, who would commit the huge flows of capital needed to continually tool and retool the commercial/industrial/financial machine? As long as the entire population could become producers, young people were loose cannon crashing around a storm-tossed deck threatening to destroy the corporate ship; confined, however, to employee status, they became suitable ballast upon which a dependable domestic market could be erected.

How to mute competition in the generation of tomorrow? That was the cutting-edge question. In his take-no-prisoners style acquired mixing poison gas and building atomic bombs, Conant tells us candidly the answer "was in the process of formulation" as early as the 1890s. By 1905 the nation obeyed this clarion call coast to coast: "Keep all youth in school full time through grade twelve." All youth, including those most unwilling to be there and those certain to take vengeance on their jailers.

President Conant was quick to acknowledge that "practical-minded" kids paid a heavy price from enforced confinement. But there it was—nothing could be done. It was a worthy trade-off. I suspect he was being disingenuous. Any mind sophisticated enough to calculate a way to short-circuit entrepreneurial energy, and ideology-driven enough to be willing to do that in service to a corporate takeover of the economy, is shrewd enough also to have foreseen the destructive side effects of having an angry and tough-minded band of prisoners forced against its will to remain in school with the docile. The net result on the intellectual possibilities of class instruction was near total wipe-out.

Did Conant understand the catastrophe he helped cause? I think he did. He would dispute my judgment, of course, that it was a catastrophe. One of his close friends was another highly placed schoolman, Ellwood P. Cubberley, the Stanford Education dean. Cubberley had himself written about the blow to serious classwork caused by early experiments in forcing universal school attendance. So it wasn't as if the destruction of academic integrity came as any surprise to insiders. Cubberley's house history of American education refers directly to this episode, although in somewhat elliptical prose. First published in 1919, it was republished in 1934, the same year Conant took office at Harvard. The two men talked and wrote to one another. Both knew the score. Yet for all his candor, it isn't hard to understand Conant's reticence about discussing this procedure. It's one thing to announce that children have to do involuntary duty for the state, quite another to describe the why and how of the matter in explicit detail.

Another prominent Harvard professor, Robert Ulich, wrote in his own book, *Philosophy of Education* (1961):

> [We are producing] more and more people who will be dissatisfied because
> the artificially prolonged time of formal schooling will arouse in them hopes
> which society cannot fulfill.... These men and women will form the avant-garde
> of the disgruntled. It is no exaggeration to say [people like these] were
> responsible for World War II.

Although Ulich is parroting Toynbee here, whose *Study of History* was a standard reference of speculative history for decades, the idea that serious intellectual schooling of a universal nature would be a sword pointed at the established order, has been an idea common in the West since at least the Tudors, and one openly discussed from 1890 onwards.

Thus I was less surprised than I might have been to open Walter Kotschnig's *Unemployment in the Learned Professions* (1937), which I purchased for 50 cents off a blanket on the street in front of Columbia University from a college graduate down on his luck, to find myself listening to an argument attributing the rise of Nazism directly to the expansion of German university enrollment after WWI. For Germany, this had been a short-term solution to postwar unemployment, like the G.I. Bill, but according to Kotschnig, the policy created a mob of well-educated people with a chip on their shoulder because there was no work—a situation which led swiftly downhill for the Weimar republic.

A whole new way to look at schooling from this management perspective emerges, a perspective which is the furthest thing from cynical. Of course there are implications for our contemporary situation. Much of our own 50 to 60 percent post-secondary college enrollment should be seen as a temporary solution to the otherwise awesome reality that two-thirds of all work in the U.S. is now part-time or short-term employment. In a highly centralized corporate workplace becoming ever more so with no end in sight, all jobs are sucked like debris in a tornado into four hierarchical funnels of vast proportions: corporate, governmental, institutional, and professional. Once work is preempted in this monopoly fashion, fear of too many smart people is legitimate, hard to exaggerate. If you let people learn too much they might kill you. Or so history and Senator Aldrich would have us believe.

Once privy to ideas like those entertained by Inglis, Conant, Ulich, and Kotschnig, most contemporary public school debate becomes nonsense. Without addressing philosophies and policies which sentence the largest part of our people to lives devoid of meaning, we might be better off not discussing school at all. A Trilateral Commission Report of 1974, *Crisis of Democracy*, offered with some urgency this advice: "*A program is necessary to lower the job expectations of those who receive a college education.*" Over the quarter-century separating this managerial proposition from the Millenium, such a program was launched—for reasons we now turn to the historian Toynbee to illuminate.

Disinherited Men And Women

In the chapter "Schism in the Body Social" from his monumental *Study of History*, Arnold Toynbee calls our attention to some dynamics of Western imperial success over the past four centuries which have important implications for the way state schooling is conducted. As major victories were registered, he tells us, "many diverse contingents of disinherited men and women" were subjected to "the ordeal of being enrolled in the Western internal proletariat." Between 1850 and 1950 "the manpower of no less than ten disintegrating civilizations [was] conscripted into the Western body social" and underwent "a process of standardization" which blurred or wiped out "the characteristic features by which these heterogeneous masses were once distinguished from one another."

Under his mannerly academic diction runs a river of insight explaining the paradox of forced schooling. It can allow no pilgrim way because it aims at leveling the turbulent singularity of youth, by a process of standardization, into featureless components of a universal mass mind and character. Nor, says Toynbee, has the victorious Western political state been content to prey upon its own kind:

> It has also rounded up almost all the surviving primitive societies; and while
> some of these, like the Tasmanians and most of the North American Indian

tribes have died of shock, others, like the Negroes of Tropical Africa, have managed to survive and set the Niger flowing into the Hudson and the Congo into the Mississippi—just as other activities of the same Western monster have set the Yangtse flowing into the Straits of Malaca.

Not only have Darwin's "disfavored" races been so manhandled, but the free domestic population of these countries has also been "uprooted from the countryside and chevied into the towns" in preparation for a strategic replacement of small-scale mixed farming by mass production specialized agriculture whose crops are produced by the modern analogue to "plantation slavery."

England was first to commodify agricultural products so intensely, "uprooting its own free peasantry for the economic profit of an oligarchy by turning plowland into pasture and common land into enclosures." This state-driven push away from the independent farms of yeomen reduced that class to "white trash" (in Toynbee's colorful idiom), and this disquieting social initiative was powerfully augmented by a pull from the urban industrial revolution also being engineered at the same time. Handicrafts were replaced by output from coal-driven machines. During the agonizing transition, owners of the new mechanical technology created another new technology of social control through abundant use of police, spies, sabotage, propaganda, and legislation to hasten the passing of the old ways of moral relationship.

Try hard to visualize through all this milling grief of "beaten peoples" and "disinherited men and women," not *their* agony but the perplexity of the corporate state. What is a modern scientific state, having transcended the principles of Christian life, to do with its masses once they have been "degraded to the ranks of a proletariat," and then further rendered superfluous by a stream of inventions? Even more today than yesterday, this is America's problem.

The question is all too real. It raises the grim spectre of revolution which public policy seeks to push away through schooling. What can anyone do with human flotsam in a crowded world that scorns their labor and scorns their companionship? Set them to watching television? From a scientific perspective, people management isn't all that different from dealing with industrial waste. At bottom, moral principle has little to do with it. Dispositions are mainly matters of possibility and *technique*. Here is the secret of scientific life which refuses to stay hidden amidst the hollow moral rhetoric of scientific schooling.

Toynbee's observation that most inhabitants of a modern state are in a condition of disinheritance and hence dangerous, calls for what he terms "creative solutions." One creative solution is to establish work for some of the dangerous classes by setting them to guard the rest. This guardian class is then privileged a little to compensate it for playing the dirty kapo role against the others.

Toynbee is eloquent about the function of bureaucrats in serving the creative minorities which manage society. Creative minorities always manage complex societies, according to Toynbee, but the dominant minorities which comprise modern social leadership are the degenerate descendants of this originally creative group. Dominant minorities manage the rest by conscription of all into a massive two-tier proletariat. The guiding protection is a mechanism to ensure these proletariats don't learn much lest they become "demoniac." This is the unsuspected function which school tolerance of bad behavior serves—in both school and society. The great majority of proles are kept away from what history refers to as education. This can be done inexpensively by leading children from ambitious exercises in reading, writing, declamation, self-discipline, and from significant practical experience in making things work. It really is that simple, and it needn't be done forever. Even a few years of control at the beginning of childhood will often suffice to set a lifetime stamp.

Toynbee, and by extension the entire cultivated leadership class he represented, was unable to see any other alternative to this stupefaction course because, as he hastened to assure us, "the religion of the masses" is violence. There is no other choice possible to responsible governors who accept the melancholy conclusion that peasants are indeed revolting. The only proles Toynbee could find in the historical record who managed to extricate themselves from a fatal coarseness did so by escaping their proletarian circumstances *first*. But if this were allowed for all, who would clean toilets?

You might expect such an observation would lead inevitably to some profound consideration of the astounding crimes of conquest and domination which create uprooted, landless classes in the first place—England's crimes against Ireland, India, China, and any number of other places being good examples. But a greater principle intervenes. According to certain sophisticated theory, you can't operate a modern economy without an underclass to control wage inflation; in spite of bell curve theory, a mass doesn't subordinate itself without some judicious assistance.

In his glorious *Republic*, which may have started it all, Plato causes Socrates to inform Glaucon and Adeimantus, 2,400 years ago, that they can't loll on couches eating grapes while others sweat to provide those grapes without first creating a fearsome security state to protect themselves from the commonality. It would appear that long ago some people realized that a substantial moral trade-off would be required to create ease for a fraction of the whole while the balance of the whole served that ease. Once that kind of privilege became the goal of Toynbee's creative minority, once high culture was defined as a sanctuary against evolutionary reversion, certain horrors institutionalized themselves.

The clearest escape route from tidal recurrence of caste madness is a society bred to argue, one trained to challenge. A mentally active people might be expected to recognize that the prizes of massification—freedom from labors like toilet cleaning, a life of endless consumption (and reflection upon future consumption)—aren't really worth very much. The fashioning of mass society isn't any chemical precondition of human progress. It's just as likely to be a signal that the last act of history is underway.

Serving The Imperial Virus

Toynbee thought he could calculate Britain's jeopardy if it allowed the masses dreams of independence by a comparison with Soviet Russia where revolutionary dreaming once dictated social arrangements:

> In Marxian Communism we have a notorious example in our midst of
> a modern Western philosophy which changed in a lifetime quite out of
> recognition into a proletarian religion, taking the path of violence and
> carving its New Jerusalem with the sword on the plains of Russia.

The working class proletariat conceived by Toynbee is in a permanent childlike state, one that requires constant management. Because of this ongoing necessity, a second proletariat must be created, "a special social class" which represents a professionalized proletariat, "often quite abruptly and artificially" gathered by the national leadership to aid in managing the lumpish mass of ordinary folk.

The size this bureaucratic cohort will reach depends upon the circumstances which call it into being. If the dominant minority decides to wage war, for instance, a vast enlargement of noncoms and line officers will occur; if it decides to concentrate public attention on charitable benevolence, a mushrooming of social work positions will ensue; if the public is to be kept fearfully amused and titillated by the spectacle of crime and law enforcement, a new horde of police and detectives will be trained and commissioned. *The social management of public attention is a vital aspect of modern states.* To the extent schools control an important share of the imagination of the young along with commercial entertainment, schools must be heavily involved in such a project. There is no possibility they can be allowed to opt out.

Social management of public attention through schooling can be seen as very similar to management of public attention by corporate advertising and by public relations initiatives. Mass production demands psychological interventions intended to create wants that otherwise wouldn't exist. School is an agency of this initiative among its other roles.

The professional proletariats created to do this important task and others like it can be seen, says Toynbee, to be "a special class of liaison officer" between the governing minorities and the masses. This English way of seeing middle classes clears some of the fog away. Consider the real-life effect of an abstract rule of first allegiance to management on those schoolteachers who work too intimately with parents, or struggle in children's interests too resolutely—inevitably they become marked for punishment. Good teachers from the human perspective are natural system-wreckers. They don't fit comfortably into a service class designed to assist governing elites to manage, their hearts aren't in it.

Toynbee is brutally candid about where loyal pedagogues fit: "As the [imperial] virus works deeper into the social life of the society which is in the process of being permeated and assimilated, the intelligentsia develops its most characteristic types: the schoolmaster... the civil servant... the lawyer...."

Quill-Driving *Babus*

A servant to the *imperial virus*! Here is a whole new take on what I was hired to do with my adult life. It helps to explain why I encountered such violent reactions from administrators as I innocently deviated further and further from my function in an effort to be useful to kids. While straining to find ways to be helpful, I constantly ran afoul of this hidden directive forced schooling was created to serve, about which I had not the tiniest clue previous except intuition.

Professional associations of proles expand or contract according to the schedule of the political state for absorbing fringe groups and outsiders for retraining in new habits and attitudes. If a great social project is underway, bureaucracy grows. When no compelling agenda is afoot it shrinks. As populations learn to discipline *themselves,* the need for expensive professional assistance to do it for them diminishes.

For instance, if the managerial promise of computer workstations is realized—hooking children into automatized learning systems which have been centrally engineered—then great numbers of schoolteachers and school administrators who were hired for a computerless moment now passed will melt away like ice in spring to be reabsorbed into the leveled and featureless common proletariat. My guess is that this process is already well underway. Low-level school administrators are a class facing imminent extinction if I read entrails correctly.

Indeed the bureaucratic giantism we have endured since the end of WWII has clearly lost momentum. Whether or not we should consider that a cause for celebration is problematical. A retreating bureaucracy is a sign the dominant minority considers the proletariat tamed, its own danger past; the bureaucratic buffer becomes superfluous. It marks a time when people can be trusted to control themselves. Woe to us all if that is so.

There is a catch, however, to the wonderful elasticity of bureaucracy. It is found in the degree of violent backlash occasioned by bureaucratic shrinkage, or down-sizing as it has come to be known. This dangerous reaction Toynbee refers to as "the bitterness of the intelligentsia."

Indeed, grounds for bitterness are formed in the very scheme for training civil servants. They surrender any prospect of developing full humanity in order to remain employed. Private judgment, for example, is an inevitable early casualty, personal courage is totally out of order. Bureaucrats often regard *themselves* privately as less than whole men and women, not totally insensitive to the devil's bargain aspect in what they do. For Toynbee:

> This liaison-class suffers from the congenital unhappiness of the hybrid
> who is an outcast from both the families that have combined to beget him.
> An intelligentsia is hated and despised by its own people.

He continues:

> And while the intelligentsia thus has no love lost on it at home, it also has
> no honor paid to it in the [workplace] whose manners and tricks it has so
> laboriously and ingeniously mastered. In the earlier days of the historic
> association between India and England, the Hindu intelligentsia which the
> British Raj had fostered for its own administrative convenience, was a
> common subject of English ridicule.

Servants of state and corporation, like schoolteachers, lawyers, and social workers, are inherently untrustworthy because of the stress and insult they constantly endure living and working suspended between two worlds. They must be carefully watched during training and subjected to spiritually deficient education to measure their dependability for the work ahead. If they swallow it, they get hired.

This hothouse situation creates fault lines deep in the breed which begin to crack open when employment is cut back. Because what these men and women do can, in fact, be done by almost anyone, they live in constant peril of being excessed even when a shrinkage isn't underway. Toynbee again:

> A Peter the Great wants so many Russian *chinovkniks* or an East India Company so many clerks, or a Mehmed Ali so many Egyptian shipwrights.... Potters in human clay set about to produce them, *but the process of manufacturing an intelligentsia is more difficult to stop than to start*; for the contempt in which the liaison class is held by those who profit by its services is offset by its prestige in the eyes of those eligible for enrollment in it.

The applicability of this principle to your own boy or girl in school, embedded painfully in one of the many bogus gifted and talented classes of recent years, or graduating from a watered-down college program set up to accommodate more than half of all young men and women, is this:

> Candidates increase out of all proportion to the opportunities for employing them and the original nucleus of the employed intelligentsia becomes swamped by an intellectual proletariat which is idle and destitute as well as outcast.

Now you have a proper frame in which to fit the armies of graduate students enduring a long extended childhood in prospect of a sinecure not likely to be there for most. In Toynbee's eye-opening language, this "handful of *chinovniks* is reenforced by a legion of nihilists, the handful of quill-driving *babus* by a legion of failed B.A.s." Be careful not to smirk; that quill-driving *babu* you see every morning in the shaving mirror is likely to be you.

Nor have you heard the worst: an intelligentsia's unhappiness builds geometrically—an underemployed *chinovnik* or *babu* becomes angrier and more cynical with the passage of years. Sometimes this rage discharges itself quickly, as when postal employees shoot up the joint; sometimes it takes centuries. For an example of the latter Toynbee offers us:

1)   The Russian intelligentsia, dating from the close of the seventeenth century, which "discharged its accumulated spite in the shattering Bolshevik Revolution of 1917,"

and

2)   The Bengali intelligentsia, dating from the latter part of the eighteenth century, which began in 1946 to display "a vein of revolutionary violence which is not yet seen in other parts of British India where local intelligentsia did not come into existence till fifty or a hundred years later." [Shortly after those lines were written, the intelligentsias brought British India down.]

I hope this helps you understand why, from a policymaker's standpoint, the decision to muzzle intellectual development through schooling has been in a bull market since the end of WWII despite the anomaly of the G.I. Bill. The larger the pool of educated but underemployed men and women, the louder the time-bomb ticks. It ought to be clear by now that the promises of schooling cannot be kept for a majority of Americans in an economy structured this way; only by plundering the planet can they be kept even temporarily for the critical majority necessary to keep the lid on things.

In the society just ahead, one profession has astonishingly good prospects. I'm referring to the various specialties associated with policing the angry, the disaffected, and the embittered. Because school promises are mathematically impossible to keep, they were, from the beginning, a Ponzi scheme like Social Security. The creative minority who unleashed this well-schooled whirlwind 100 years ago seems to have finally exhausted its imaginative power as it transmuted slowly into a dominant minority without much creative energy. Dr. Toynbee points to such a transition as an unmistakable sign of society in decline. Another ominous sign for Toynbee: the increasing use of police and armies to protect private interests.

In 1939, on the eve of war, the defense budget of the U.S. was $11 billion (translated into a constant dollar, year-2000 equivalent). We were at peace. Today, at peace again, without a visible enemy on the horizon *the defense budget is 24 times higher*. The appearance of a permanent military force in peacetime, which claims a huge share of society's total expenditure, can't be explained by saying we live in a dangerous time. When wasn't that true? It is our own leadership which lives dangerously, dwelling in a Darwinian world in which its own people are suspect, their danger so far contained by ensnaring the managed population through schooling into a conspiracy against themselves.

We meet everyday in school a reflection of the national leadership class displaying every indication it has abandoned its fundamental American obligation to raise ordinary people up, becoming instead an overseas transmitter of the original mother ideas of England.

The Release From Tutelage

What kind of schools do we need to extricate ourselves from the conspiracy to be much less than we really are? Why, *enlightened* schools, of course, in the sense Immanuel Kant wrote about them. "Man's release from a tutelage," said Kant, "is enlightenment. His tutelage is his inability to make use of his understanding without guidance from another." Tutelage is the oppressor we must overthrow, not conspiracy. Eva Brann of St. John's college saw the matter this way: the proper work of a real self, she said, is to be active in gathering and presenting, comparing and distinguishing, subjecting things to rules, judging. The very notion of America is a place where argument and self-reliance are demanded from all if we are to remain America. Annoying as it often is, our duty is to endure argument and encourage it. "Would the world be more beautiful were all our faces alike?" wrote Jefferson. "The Creator has made no two faces alike, so no two minds, and probably no two creeds."

The first Enlightenment was a false one. It merely transferred the right to direct our lives from a corporate Church and a hereditary nobility to a pack of experts whose minds were (and are) for sale to anyone with a checkbook. In the second Enlightenment we need to correct our mistakes, using what schools we decide to allow to help us strive for full consciousness, for self-assertion, mental independence, and personal sovereignty—for a release from tutelage for everybody. Only in this way can we make use of our understanding without guidance from strangers who work for a corporate state system, increasingly impatient with human beings.

MACADAM-GATTO #1

• COURAGE • IDEAS • HARD WORK •

IN 1980 YOU HELPED ME THROW THE RASCALS OUT OF OUR SCHOOLS. TOGETHER WE:

- COOKED THE BIG ENCHILADA'S GOOSE
- TURNED A COLD SHOULDER ON WASTE
- HAMMERED THE OLD BOY NETWORK
- PICKED UP READING/MATH SCORES
- PUT DOWN SCHOOL CRIME
- MADE IT HOT FOR THE POLITICIANS.

NOW I NEED YOUR HELP TO FINISH THE WORK, KEEP OUR SCHOOLS MARCHING AHEAD. I PUT 5000 HOURS ON THE JOB LAST TIME—NEXT TIME I'LL DO MORE! ELECTION DAY, MAY 3RD. VOTE EARLY AND OFTEN!

SCHOOL BOARD ELECTIONS, MAY 3RD   **1983**   • THE FIGHTING SCOT •

CHAPTER SEVENTEEN

The Politics

Of Schooling

*Each year the child is coming to belong more to the State and less
and less to the parent.*
— Ellwood P. Cubberley, Dean of the
School of Education, Stanford (1909)

*It was natural businessmen should devote themselves to something
besides business; that they should seek to influence the enactment
and administration of laws, national and international, and that
they should try to control education.*
— Max Otto, *Science and the Moral Life* (1949)

*Most people don't know who controls American education because
little attention has been given the question by either educators or the
public. Also because the question is not easily or neatly answered.*
— James D. Koerner, *Who Controls
American Education* (1968)

Three Holes In My Floor

In October 1990, three round holes the size of silver dollars appeared in the floor of my classroom at Booker T. Washington Junior High between West 107th and 108th streets in Spanish Harlem, about twelve blocks from Columbia Teachers College. My room was on the third floor and the holes went through to the second floor room beneath. In unguarded moments, those holes proved an irresistible lure to my students, who dropped spitballs, food, and ball bearings down on the heads of helpless children below without warning. The screams of outrage were appalling. So pragmatically, without thinking much about it, I closed off the holes with a large flat of plywood and dutifully sent a note to the school custodian asking for professional assistance.

The next day when I reported to work my makeshift closure was gone, the holes were open, and I found a warning against "unauthorized repairs" in my mailbox. That day three different teachers used the room with the holes. During each occupancy various objects plummeted through the floor to the consternation of occupants in the space below. In one particularly offensive assault, human waste was retrieved from the toilet, fashioned into a missile, and dropped on a shrieking victim. All the while, the attacking classroom exploded in cackles of laughter, I was later told.

On the third day of these aerial assaults, the building principal appeared at my door demanding the bombardment cease at once. I pointed out that I had been forbidden to close off the holes, that many other teachers used the room in my absence, that the school provided no sanctions for student aggressors, and that it was impossible to teach a class of 35 kids and still keep close watch on three well-dispersed holes in the floor. I offered to repair the holes again that very afternoon at my own expense, pointing out in a reasonable tone that this easy solution was *still* available and that, in my opinion, there were traces of insanity in allowing any protocol, however well meant, to delay solving the problem at once before another fecal bombardment was unleashed.

At the moment I had no idea that I was challenging an invisible legion of salarymen it had taken a century to evolve. I only wanted to spare myself those cries from below. My request was denied and I was reminded again not to take matters into my own hands. *Five months later a repair was effected* by a team of technicians. In the meantime, however, my classroom door lock had been broken and three panes of window glass facing Columbus Avenue shattered by vandals. The repair crew turned a deaf ear to what I felt was a pretty sensible request to do all the work at once, none of it complicated. The technicians were on a particular mission I was told. Only *it* had been duly authorized.

Commenting on the whole genus of such school turf wars, the *New York Observer's* Terry Golway said, "Critical decisions are made in a bureaucrat's office far from the site requiring repairs. One official's decision can be countermanded by another's, and layer upon layer of officialdom prolongs the process. A physical task that requires a couple of minutes work can take weeks, if not months, to snake through the bureaucracy. In the meantime the condition may worsen, causing inconvenience to children and teachers. In the end, no one is accountable." Thanks to Mr. Golway, I found out why the missile attack had been allowed to continue.

In my case, the problem lay in the journey of my original note to the custodian, where it was translated into form P.O. 18. P.O. 18 set out on a road which would terminate in an eventual repair but not before eight other stops were made along the way and 150 days had passed. A study of these eight stops will provide a scalpel to expose some of the gangrenous tissue of institutional schooling. Although this is New York City, something similar is found everywhere else the government school flag waves. I think we must finally grow up enough to realize that what follows is unavoidable, endemic to large systems:

Stop One: P.O. 18 was signed by the principal, who gave a copy to his secretary to file, returning the original to the custodian. This typically takes several days.

Stop Two: The custodian gave a copy of the form to his secretary to file, then sent the request on to a *District Plant Manager(DPM)*, one of 31 in New York City.

Stop Three: In an office far removed from my perforated floor, the DPM assigned the repair a *Priority Code*. Three or four weeks had now passed from the minute a ball bearing bounced off Paul Colon's head and a turd splattered in gooey fragments on Rosie Santiago's desk.[1] A copy of P.O. 18 was given to the DPM's secretary to file, and the form went to the Resource Planning Manager (RPM), based in Long Island City.

Stop Four: The RPM collects ALL the work orders in the city, sorting them according to priority codes and available resources, and selects a Resource Planning Team (RPT). This team then enters the P.O. 18 in its own computer. A repair sequence is arrested at Stop Four for a period of weeks.

Stop Five: The P.O. 18 is relayed to the Integrated Purchasing and Inventory System (IPIS), which spits out a Work Order and sends it to the *Supervising Supervisor*. Three months have passed, and used toilet paper is raining down into the airless cell beneath John Gatto's English class.

Stop Six: The *Supervising Supervisor* has one responsibility, to supervise the *Trade Supervisors* and decide which one will at some time not fix but *supervise* the fixing of my floor. Such a decision requires DUE TIME before an order is issued.

Stop Seven: The *Trade Supervisor* has responsibility for selecting service people of flesh and blood to actually do the work. Eventually the Trade Supervisor does this, dispatching a Work Crew to perform the repair. Time elapsed (in this case): five months. Some repairs take ten years. Some forever. I was lucky.

Stop Eight: Armed with bags and utility belts, tradespeople enter the school to *examine* the problem. If it can be repaired *with the tools they carry*, fine; if not they must fill out a P.O. 17 to requisition the needed materials and a new and different sequence begins. It's all very logical. Each step is justified. If you think this can be reformed you are indeed ignorant. Fire all these people and unless you are willing to kill them, they will just have to be employed in some other fashion equally useless.

---

[1] The actual names have been changed.

At the heart of the durability of mass schooling is a brilliantly designed power fragmentation system which distributes decision-making so widely among so many different warring interests that large scale change is impossible to those without a codebook. Even when a favorable chance alteration occurs, it has a short life span, usually exactly as long as the originator of the happy change has political protection. When the first boom of enthusiasm wanes or protection erodes, the innovation follows soon after.

No visible level of the system, top, middle or bottom, is allowed to institute any significant change without permission from many other layers. To secure this coalition of forces puts the supplicant in such a compromised position (and takes so long) that any possibility of very extensive alteration is foreclosed.

Structurally, control is divided among three categories of interdependent power: 1) government agencies, 2) the self-proclaimed knowledge industry, 3) various special interests, some permanent, some topical. Nominally children, teachers, and parents are included in this third group, but since all are kept virtually powerless, with rare exceptions they are looked upon only as nuisances to be gotten around. Parents are considered *the enemy* everywhere in the school establishment. An illustration of this awesome reality comes out of the catastrophe of New Math imposed on public schools during the 1960s and 1970s. In the training sessions, paid for by federal funds, school staff received *explicit instructions* to keep parents away.

In schoolteacher training classes for the New Math, prospective pedagogues were instructed to keep their hands off classroom instruction as much as possible. Student peer groups were to be considered by the teachers more important than parents in establishing motivation—more important than teachers, too. Kids were to learn "peer group control" of the operation by trial and error.

Nobody who understood the culture of kids in classrooms could have prescribed a more fatal medicine to law and order. But the experiment plunged recklessly ahead, this time on a national basis in the Vietnam-era United States. In the arithmetic of powerlessness that forced collectivism of this sort imposes, students, parents, and teachers are at the very bottom of the pecking order, but school administrators and local school boards are reduced by such politics to inconsequential mechanical functions, too.

Power ÷ 22

PLAYERS IN THE SCHOOL GAME

FIRST CATEGORY: Government Agencies

1)   State legislatures, particularly those politicians known in-house to specialize in educational matters

2)   Ambitious politicians with high public visibility

3)   Big-city school boards controlling lucrative contracts

4)   The courts

5)   Big-city departments of education

6)   State departments of education

7)   Federal Department of Education

8)   Other government agencies (National Science Foundation, National Training Laboratories, Defense Department, HUD, Labor Department, Health and Human Services, and many more)

SECOND CATEGORY: Active Special Interests

1)   Key private foundations.[2] About a dozen of these curious entities have been the most important shapers of national education policy in this century, particularly those of Carnegie, Ford, and Rockefeller.

2)   Giant corporations, acting through a private association called the Business Roundtable (BR), latest manifestation of a series of such associations dating back to the turn of the century. Some evidence of the centrality of business in the school mix was the composition of the New American Schools Development Corporation, its makeup of 18 members (which the uninitiated might assume would be drawn from a representative cross-section of parties interested in the shape of American schooling) was heavily weighted as follows: CEO, RJR Nabisco; CEO, Boeing; President, Exxon; CEO, AT&T; CEO, Ashland Oil; CEO, Martin Marietta; CEO, AMEX; CEO, Eastman Kodak; CEO, WARNACO; CEO, Honeywell; CEO, Ralston; CEO, Arvin; Chairman, BF Goodrich; two ex-governors, two publishers, a TV producer.

3)   The United Nations through UNESCO, the World Health Organization, UNICEF, etc.

---

[2] Ellen Condliffe Lagemann's *Private Power for the Public Good* (Wesleyan, 1986) is an excellent place to start to experience what Bernard Bailyn meant when he said that twentieth century schooling troubled many high-minded people. Miss Lagemann is a high-minded woman, obviously troubled by what she discovered poking around one of the Carnegie endowments.

The pages devoted to Rockefeller's General Education Board in Collier and Horowitz's *The Rockefellers: An American Dynasty* make a good simple introduction to another private endowment which ultimately will repay a deeper look; also, the pages on true believer Frederick T.Gates, the man who actually directed the spending of Rockefeller's money, bear close attention as well.

For a sharp look at how foundations shape our ideology, I recommend *Philanthropy and Cultural Imperialism: The Foundations at Home and Abroad*, and for a hair-raising finale René Wormser's *Foundations: Their Power and Influence* is *essential.* Wormser was a general counsel for the House Committee which set out to investigate tax-exempt organizations during the eighty-third Congress. Its stormy course and hair-raising disclosures are guaranteed to remove any lingering traces of innocence about the conduct of American education, international affairs, or what are called "the social sciences." Miss Lagemann's bibliography will lead you further, if needed.

4) Other private associations, National Association of Manufacturers, Council on Economic Development, The Advertising Council, Council on Foreign Relations, Foreign Policy Association, etc.

5) Professional unions, National Education Association, American Federation of Teachers, Council of Supervisory Associations, etc.

6) Private educational interest groups, Council on Basic Education, Progressive Education Association, etc.

7) Single-interest groups: abortion activists, pro and con; other advocates for specific interests.

THIRD CATEGORY: The "Knowledge" Industry

1) Colleges and universities

2) Teacher-training colleges

3) Researchers

4) Testing organizations

5) Materials producers (other than print)

6) Text publishers

7) "Knowledge" brokers, subsystem designers

Control of the educational enterprise is distributed among at least these 22 players, each of which can be subdivided into in-house warring factions which further remove the decision-making process from simple accessibility. The financial interests of these associational voices are served whether children learn to read or not.

There is little accountability. No matter how many assertions are made to the contrary, few penalties exist past a certain level on the organizational chart—unless a culprit runs afoul of the media—an explanation for the bitter truth whistle-blowers regularly discover when they tell all. Which explains why precious few experienced hands care to ruin themselves to act the hero. This is not to say sensitive, intelligent, moral and concerned individuals aren't distributed through each of the 22 categories, but the conflict of interest is so glaring between serving a system loyally and serving the public that it is finally overwhelming. Indeed, it isn't hard to see that in strictly economic terms this edifice of competing and conflicting interests *is better served by badly performing schools than by successful ones*. On economic grounds alone a *disincentive* exists to improve schools. When schools are bad, demands for increased funding and personnel, and professional control removed from public oversight, can be pressed by simply pointing to the perilous state of the enterprise. But when things go well, getting an extra buck is like pulling teeth.

Some of this political impasse grew naturally from a maze of competing interests, some grew from more cynical calculations with exactly the end in mind we see, but whatever the formative motives, the net result is virtually impervious to democratically generated change. No large change can occur in-system without a complicated coalition of separate interests backing it, not one of which can actually be a primary advocate for children and parents.

Valhalla

By the end of 1999, 75.5 million people out of a total population of 275 million were involved directly in providing and receiving what has come to be called education. And an unknown number of millions indirectly. About 67 million were enrolled in schools and colleges (38 million in K-8, 14 million in secondary schools), 15 million in colleges, four million employed as teachers or college faculty (two million elementary; two million secondary and college combined), and 4.5 million in some other school capacity. In other words, the primary organizing discipline of about 29 percent of the entire U.S. population consists of obedience to the routines and requests of an abstract social machine called School. And that's only so far. According to the U.S. Department of Education, these figures are expected to grow substantially through the first decade of the new century. Could Hegel himself have foreseen such an end to history, the planet as a universal schoolhouse *where nothing much is learned*?

At the top of this feeding chain are so-called public colleges. As Valhalla was the reward where Vikings killed in battle got to drink, fight, and fornicate in an endlessly regenerating loop, so public colleges are a lifetime of comfort and security for those systems people who play ball skillfully or belong to some political family with a record of playing ball.

If public colleges functioned in meritocractic ways as their supporters allege and as I suspect the general public believes they do, we would expect the economy of public schooling at this level to reflect with reasonable sensitivity what was happening in the total public economy. Spending on public colleges should be a litmus test how much respect is being accorded the democratic will at any given time. With that in mind try this garment on for size: *Tuition at public colleges over the last 14 years has increased three times as fast as household income, and more than three times faster than the rate of inflation, according to the General Accounting Office*. What pressure could possibly squeeze ordinary people to pay such outlandish costs, incurring debt burdens which enslave them and their children for many years to come?

How, you might ask, at the very instant the inherent *value* of these degrees is being challenged, at the very instant business magazines are predicting permanent radical downsizing of the middle-management force in private and public employment—the very slots public colleges license graduates to occupy, and at the very instant in time when the purchasing power of middle-class American incomes is worth less than it was 30 years ago and appears to be in a long-term continuing downtrend, how in light of these things have public college teachers been able to double their incomes (in real dollars) in the past 14 years and public college administrators raise their own share of the take 131 percent?

I'm asking how, not why. Greed is too common a characteristic of human nature to be very interesting. *How* was this done? Who *allowed* it? Not any "free market," I can tell you. We're talking about *several million* individuals who've managed to make their leisured and secure lives even more so at the same time their product is questioned and the work their attention supposedly qualifies students for is shipped overseas for labor cost advantages. It seems obvious to me that the whole lot of these collegiate time-servers lacks sufficient clout to treat *themselves* so well. Their favored treatment is then a *gift*. But from where, and why? Only from an investigation of the politics of schooling might come an adequate answer. So let's begin to look under a few rocks together.

I'm A Flunky, So's My Kid

On June 24, 1996, in Franklin County Ohio Common Pleas Court, the attorney for the American Federation of Teachers, speaking against Ohio's proposed parent-choice initiative, called parents "inconsequential conduits." The *Columbus Dispatch* quoted Dennis Widener, parent of three, as saying, "I can't believe we have to fight for an education. I'm a flunky and that's what they are trying to make my kid." Although his income was well below the poverty line, Mr. Widener was armed with comparative school information that convinced him his own children were being deliberately dumbed down. In public kindergarten his youngest daughter had only learned the alphabet, but he was fully aware that "at private school they were reading in kindergarten."

It's Not Your Money

Though it was twenty years and more ago, I remember well that day in 1979 when I loaded my old Ford station wagon with broken tape recorders, broken movie projectors, broken record players, broken tripods, broken typewriters, broken editing machines, etc., some nearly new and still under warranty, *and without notifying anyone* trucked it all over to the repair facility on Court Street in Brooklyn because the Bureau of Audio-Visual Instruction had failed to respond to three official requests for help from the school.

This was an errand of mercy for a new principal, a fine North Carolina lady serving her probationary period, a woman for whom I had high regard because she broke rules to do the things that mattered.[3] The executive on duty at BAVI had once been a "Coordinator" at the school I was coming from. Apart from his job title he was a likeable sort who reminded me of Arnold Stang on the old "Captain Video" show.

But when he saw my load of wreckage he exploded. "What are you trying to pull?" he said. "We don't have time to repair these things!" Official ladders of referral did in fact assign the repair function to BAVI; if not them, then who? Because I was there, the equipment was accepted, but shortly afterwards I heard on the grapevine it had been thrown out and my principal upbraided for her lack of decorum in trying to have it repaired. Broken machinery is a signal to buy new and may be reckoned among the lifeblood factors of school's partnership with the larger economy.

---

[3] She was denied tenure a few years later for failing to play ball with the district office and the teachers who mattered in the building. Although a *New York Times* editorial came to her defense (!), the superintendent was unrelenting. A year later *he* was expelled for crossing the local city councilwoman.

As long as I'm reminiscing, I remember also an earlier time when a different principal wanted to "make space" in the audio-visual vault. Some years earlier a one-time foundation windfall had been expended on 39 overhead projectors even though the school already had ten, and nobody but administrators and gym teachers used them anyway because they bored the life out of kids. "Could you help me out, John, and pitch those things somewhere after school when nobody is around to see? I'll owe you one." The reason I was asked, I think, besides the fact I always drove an old station wagon and had no reluctance about using it for school matters, was that I always insisted on talking as an equal to school people whatever their title or status. I saw them as colleagues, engaged in the same joint enterprise I was enrolled in myself.

This disrespect for the chain of command sometimes bred a kind of easy familiarity with administrators, denied more conventional teachers with an "us" and "them" outlook. In any case, I drove some of the junk to the dumpster at the entrance to the trail to Lake Rutherford in High Point State Park in New Jersey, the rest to a dump near my farm in Norwich, New York, where $10,000 or so in equipment was duly buried by the bulldozer. Incidentally, I recall being expressly forbidden to *give* these projectors away, because they might be "traced" back to Community School District 3.

Community School District 3, Manhattan, is the source of most of my school memories, the spot where I spent much of my adult working life. I remember a summer program there in 1971 where the administrator in charge ran frantically from room to room in the last week of the term asking that teachers "help him out" by spending some large amount of money ($30,000 is the figure that comes to mind) that he had squirreled away on the books. When we protested the school term was over, he explained he was fearful of being evaluated poorly on money management and that might cost him a chance to become a principal. Getting rid of money at the end of the term so it didn't have to be returned was a major recurring theme during my years in District 3.

Another District 3 story I'll not soon forget is the time the school board approved funds for the purchase of 5,000 Harbrace College Handbooks at $11 each *after it had been brought to their attention by my wife that the identical book was being remaindered in job lots at Barnes & Nobles's main store on Seventeenth Street for $1 a copy.* Not on the list of approved vendors, I might have been told, though it's too long ago to recall.

Why do these things happen? Any reasonable person might ask that question. And the answer is at one and the same time easy and not so easy to give. When we talk about politics in schooling we draw together as one what in reality are two quite different matters. It will clarify the discussion to divide school politics into a *macro* and a *micro* component. The *macro-politics* dictate that holes in floors cannot be fixed, or machinery repaired, or independent texts secured at the fair market rate. The macro-politics of schooling are deadly serious. They deal with policy issues unknown to the public, largely out of reach of elected representatives—senators and presidents included—and are almost impervious to public outrage and public morality. Hence the windfall for teachers and administrators at public colleges over the past decade and a half.

On the other hand, the *micro-politics* of schooling deal with the customary venality of little fish in their dealings with even littler fish. I speak of the invisible market in petty favors that school administrators run in virtually every public school in the land, a market that trades in after-school jobs, partial teaching programs, desirable rooms, desirable classes, schedules that enable certain teachers, but not others, to beat the Friday rush hour traffic to Long Island, all the contemptible non-cash currency without which the management of schooling would become very difficult. The micro-politics of schooling is degrading, disgusting, and demoralizing, but it pales in importance before macro-political decisions about time, sequencing, curriculum, personnel, ties of schooling to the economy, and matters of that magnitude, for which the opinions of school people are never significant.

What follows in this chapter will be mostly a consideration of the macro world, but if I had to sum up in one image how otherwise decent people conspire through schooling against hardworking ordinary people to waste their money, I would tell my auditors of the time I tried energetically to save a Social Studies chairman a substantial amount of money in purchasing supplies even though I wasn't in his department. I happened to know where he could buy what he wanted at about 50 percent less than he was prepared to pay. After tolerating my presentation and dismissing it, he became irritated when I pressed the case:

"What are you getting so agitated for, John? *Its not your money!*"

A Billion, Six For KC

What are the possibilities of reclaiming systematic schooling so it serves the general welfare? Surely the possibility of recharging the system when so many seem to desire such a course would be the best refutation of my buried thesis—that no trustworthy change is possible, that the school machine must be shattered into a hundred thousand parts before the pledges made in the founding documents of this country have a chance to be honored again. No one serves better as an emblem of the hopelessness of a gradual course of school reform or one that follows the dictates of conventional wisdom than Judge Russell G. Clark, of Kansas City, Missouri.

For more than 10 years Judge Clark oversaw the spending of a $1.6 billion windfall in an attempt to desegregate Kansas City schools and raise the reading and math scores of poor kids. I arbitrarily select his story from many which might be told to show how unlikely it is that the forces which gave us our present schools are likely to vanish, even in the face of outraged determination. Or that models of a better way to do things are likely to solve the problem, either.

Judge Russell G. Clark took over the Kansas City school district in 1984 after adjudicating a case in which the NAACP acted for plaintiffs in a suit against the school district. Although he began the long court proceedings as a former farm boy raised in the Ozarks without an activist judicial record, Clark's decision was favorable to the desegregationists beyond any reasonable expectation. *Clark invited those bringing the suit to dream up perfect schools and he would get money to pay for them!* Using the exceptional power granted federal judges, he unilaterally ordered the doubling of city property taxes.[4] When that provided inadequate revenue, he ordered the state to make up the difference. How's that for decisive, no-nonsense support for school reform as a social priority?

---

[4] They actually were raised 150 percent, from a base already not low. With what effect on homeowners just holding on was anyone's guess. Here, as in the case of Benson, Vermont, up ahead, the institution's aspect as predatory parasite appears in stark relief.

Suddenly the district was awash in money for TV studios, swimming pools, planetariums, zoos, computers, squadrons of teachers and specialists. "They had as much money as any school district will ever get," said Gary Orfield, a Harvard investigator who directed a post-mortem analysis. The result: "It didn't do very much." Actually the windfall accomplished this:

Average daily attendance went down, the dropout rate went up, the black-white achievement gap remained stationary, and the district was as segregated after 10 years of well-funded reform as it had been at the beginning. A former school board president whose children had been plaintiffs in the original suit leading to Judge Clark's takeover said she had "truly believed if we gave teachers and administrators everything they said they needed, that would make a huge difference. I knew it would take time, but I did believe by five years into this program we would see dramatic results educationally."

Who is the villain in this tale? I think Judge Clark. He just didn't get it. *The system isn't broken, so no amount of repair will fix it. What kids need isn't in any catalogue to buy, and giving schools more money just encourages them to do what they do best even more strenuously.*

Education's Most Powerful Voice

The 1996, National Education Association Convention had three times as many delegates attending as the Democratic National Convention; it offered a thousand dollar subsidy to any NEA member elected a delegate to the Democratic political gathering (but not to the Republican convention). More NEA members subsequently became delegates and claimed their $1,000 prizes than the entire representation of California, our most populous state. About one eighth of all the delegates who nominated Governor Bill Clinton for President were NEA members.

President Clinton had been the featured speaker at the NEA gathering. When he entered a convention hall hung with Clinton-Gore signs and crisscrossed with strobe lights, Clinton T-shirts and buttons were everywhere, the band blared out rock and roll, and Arkansas delegates pretended to play huge make-believe saxophones. The teacher crowd rocked the room. This was its moment to howl.

The NEA bills itself as "education's most powerful voice in Washington." It claims credit for creating the U.S. Department of Education, for passing Goals 2000, and for stopping the Senate from approving vouchers. Its platform resolutions and lobbying instructions to delegates include the following planks: "mandatory kindergarten with compulsory attendance"; opposition to "competency testing" as a condition of employment; "direct and confidential" child access to psychological, social, and health services without parental knowledge; "programs in the public schools for children from birth"; a resolution (B-67) criticizing home schooling as inadequate and calling for licenses issued by the state licensing agency for those who instruct in such schools; and a curriculum "approved by the state department of education."

The NEA also called for statehood for the District of Columbia, and announced its undying opposition to all voucher plans and tuition tax credit plans "or funding formulas that have the same effect." It threatened a boycott against Shell Oil for alleged environmental pollution in Nigeria. The NEA had a foreign policy as well as a pedagogical agenda.

For all this flash and filigree, while the NEA and other professional unions have had some effect on micro-politics in schooling, they have surprisingly little effect on public policy. For all the breast-beating, vilification and sanctimony which swirls about the union presence in schooling, where real power is concerned the professional organizations are not the movers and shakers they are reputed to be. Mostly unions are good copy for journalists and not much more.

Letter To The Editor

March 22, 1995
Letters to the Editor
The Education News

When I began teaching in 1961, the student population of School District 3 on the prosperous Upper Westside of Manhattan was over 20,000, and the cry was heard everywhere from the four district administrative employees (!) that schools were overcrowded.

But I was fresh from western Pennsylvania and saw something different, a small but significant fraction of the school's enrollment was made up of phantom kids in several categories: kids on the school register who had never shown up but were carried as if they had; kids who were absent but who for revenue purposes were entered as present; kids who were assigned to out-of-school programs of various sorts, some term-long, but who continued as phantoms to swell the apparent school rolls. Then there were the absentees, about 10 percent a day, who were actually marked absent, and the curious fact that after lunch attendance dipped precipitously sending that fraction soaring, although there seemed to be a gentleman's agreement not to document the fact.

So it was that when the press announced horrendous class sizes of 35 and 50, in my school, at least, the real number was about 28—still too many, of course, but manageable. Although everyone agreed there was absolutely no space available anywhere, by greasing the custodian's palm I was able to obtain a master key and a priceless document known as the "empty-room schedule." Would you believe there was *never* a time when multiple rooms in that building weren't empty? By training my kids in low-profile guerrilla tactics I was able to spread about half my class into different cubbyholes around the building where they worked happily and productively, in teams or alone.

Beginning in the 1980s this tactic became impossible because all the empty spaces did fill up—*even though the number of students District 3 was managing fell sharply from 20,000 to 10,000*, and with even more lax procedures to account for them than when I was originally hired. This latter development caused phantom children to multiply like rabbits. A simple act of long division will explain in outline what had happened: by dividing the number of students enrolled in my building by the number of teachers on the class register, I was able to discover that average class sizes should have been about 17.

And yet actual class sizes were about 28. The mystery of the now unavailable empty space vanishes in the ballooning numbers of "coordinators," "special supervisors," "community programs officers," and various other titular masks behind which deadwood was piling up. Each of these people required an "office" whether that be the former Nurse's Room, the dressing room behind the stage, or a conveniently large storage closet. It had happened to the Army and to IBM, why should schools be exempt?

John Taylor Gatto
New York, New York

Letter To The Principal

October 22, 1976
Principal
I.S. 44, Manhattan

Dear Walter:

A number of my colleagues have queried my participation in something called "The Urbania Complex" for which I only learned I had been forcibly recruited today from the large poster with my name on it (among others) mounted above the time clock.

My school within a school is called the "Lab School" because its design involves the formation and testing of hypotheses by students, their parents, and myself. What an "Urbania Complex" would be I have no idea, but long experience with the kind of mind that employs such mystical locutions suggests not much.

However, in a spirit of good fellowship, I read your "Memorandum 28" carefully and many things in it puzzled me, not least the apparent fact *you* have no idea what the Urbania Complex is yourself. How on earth, without the slightest word of advance notice or consultation, could you assign senior members of the professional staff to a program whose structure and intent you are ignorant of? You say we should trust the Department of Health, Education and Welfare to know what they are doing but on what grounds should such trust be based? Their ignorance of common civility? Not their track record certainly.

Your memo states that something called a "MiniMagnet" (?) "generated" (?) the Urbania Complex (?) which then generated my program and all the other ongoing programs which have been preempted like impressed sailors to man this ship. But that is wrong. All these "programs" would have operated exactly the same way without the intervention of HEW. I dislike having my name attached to false claims and I suspect other staff members do, too. I understand a spoonful of taxpayer sugar will be given to those teachers who swallow this medicine in the form of a $600 "expenses" voucher from HEW. District-wide that will amount to $60,000 in teacher bonuses, plus new "coordinator" jobs, office furniture, copy machines, and other free materials totaling, if your Memo 28 is accurate, *several millions of dollars* to the district.

Apart from the niggardly divvy to teachers who actually do the work, that's a lot of government money to be squandering—and I bet it will be carried on the books in disguise so that nobody looking at the district budget will be able to tell it's there.

I harbor no ill will against you because I'm certain you are doing what you have been asked to by the District, and they, ordered to do by the State, which in its turn has received orders from the federal government, the Carnegie Foundation, or some other strange player in this strange game of public schooling. But this letter is to tell you I decline that $600 along with the affiliation. If you need a further explanation it is that I would prefer not to.

Sincerely,

John Taylor Gatto
Head Teacher, The Lab School

Who Controls American Education?

James Koerner was a well-known national figure in the 1960s when he headed a presidential commission looking into the causes of civil unrest after Detroit's black riots. A former president of the Council for Basic Education, he had more than enough information and experience to write a public guide for laymen in which the players, policies, and processes of the system are laid bare.

The book, *Who Controls American Education?*, was published in 1968. The area even Koerner, with his gilt-edged résumé and contacts, hesitated to tread hard in was that region of philosophy, history, principles, and goals which might uncover the belief system that really drives mass schooling. While noting accurately the "missionary zeal" of those who sell ideas in the educational marketplace and deploring what he termed the "hideous coinages" of political palaver like "key influentials," "change agents," and "demand articulators," and while even noting that experts at the Educational Testing Service "tell us that schools should seek to build a new social order and that they, the experts, know what the new order should be," Koerner carefully avoided that sensitive zone of ultimate motives—except to caution laymen to "regard with great skepticism the solutions to educational problems that may be offered with great certitude by experts."

"It is not at all clear," continued the cautious Mr. Koerner, "that fundamental decisions are better made by people with postgraduate degrees than by those with undergraduate degrees, or with no degrees at all." Toward the end of his book, Koerner defined the upper echelons of school policy as "progressive, modern, life-adjustment" folk, but ducked away from explaining how people with these attitudes gained the driver's seat in a democracy from a body politic which largely rejects those perspectives.

Nor did he explain what keeps them there in the face of withering criticism. Koerner was impressed, however, with what he called "the staying power of the *ancien regime*" and challenged his readers to resign themselves to a long wait before they might expect the modern school establishment "to give all students a sound basic education":

> Anyone who thinks there [will be] a new establishment in charge of the vast industry
> of training and licensing teachers and administrators in this country has his head in
> the sand.

What we miss in Koerner's otherwise excellent manual on school politics is any speculation about its purpose. We are left to assume that a misguided affection for the underclasses—an excess of democracy, perhaps—caused this mess. That conclusion would be dead wrong. Such a madcap course could not have been pursued so long and hard without a clear *purpose* giving coherence to the melee, if only for the simple reason it costs so much. What Jaime Escalante and Marva Collins (and any number of teachers like them) demonstrate abundantly is that almost anyone can learn almost anything if a few rather fundamental preconditions are met, none of which costs much money. These teachers exploded the myth of the bell curve without ever setting out to do anything so adversarial.

The Logical Tragedy Of Benson, Vermont

In 1995, just about one hundred years after the inception of modern institutional schooling in America, the little town of Benson in Western Vermont set a national record by voting down its proposed school budget for the twelfth time.[5] Charlie Usher, assistant superintendent in Benson, declared his bewilderment at the town's irresponsibility. Said Usher, "We should all try to get at the root of why these people are willing to let their schools fall apart." I think Mr. Usher is right, so let's see what we can turn up by using common sense. But first, to show how united in outrage Benson school officials were, *Education Week*, the bible of the teaching business, quoted Theresa Mulholland, principal at the Benson school (more on this shortly) as saying nobody in town had a good explanation for what they were doing: "I think they just want to say 'No,' " she said, as if those townspeople were ornery kids or retarded children. Benson just didn't get it. Schools need lots of money, or, as Usher suggested, they fall apart.

The *Education Week* piece in which I read these things covered every single inch of a two-page tabloid spread, yet nowhere could I find a single word indicating the problem might just be that

---

[5] Shortly after this twelfth defeat at the hands of local citizens, the state stepped in to override the judgment of the voters. In January, 1996, the Vermont State Senate passed a bill to forcibly "lend" the Benson School District the full amount of its twelve-time citizen-rejected budget. Benson voters would now pay the full amount demanded by the school district *plus* interest!

its taxpayers and voters didn't regard the Benson system as their own. Nor is there even a hint Benson may have abandoned its belief that what goes on in school is an essential enterprise worth a substantial part of its income to promote.

So I read this newspaper account of a little town in Vermont and its defiance of the state school institution pretty carefully because I sensed some important message buried there. On the third run-through I discovered what I was looking for. Let's start with Assistant Superintendent Usher. His title implies that hidden somewhere out of sight there is a *Superintendent Somebody*, too. If you don't find that odd it's because I haven't told you that the entire school district of Benson *has exactly one school* with 137 kids in it. A brand-new school with a principal, too. Apparently you can't have a principal without an assistant superintendent giving orders to that lowly functionary and a superintendent giving orders to the assistant superintendent. Three high-ranking pedagogues whose collective cost for services is about $250,000—nearly $2,000 a kid. That's nice work if you can get it.

The new Benson school itself is worth a closer look. Its construction caused property taxes to go up 40 percent in one year, quite a shock to local homeowners just hanging on by their fingernails. This school would have been rejected outright by local taxpayers, who had (they thought) a perfectly good school already, but the state condemned the old school for not having wheelchair ramps and other features nobody ever considered an essential part of education before. Costs of reaching code compliance in the old structure were so close to the cost of a new school that taxpayers surrendered. The bond issue was finally voted. Even so, it passed only narrowly. What happened next will be no surprise. Benson School turned out to cost a lot more than voters expected. I am skeptical that it cost more than the State of Vermont expected, though.

I have some personal experience with Vermont's condemnation of sound school structures from the little town of Walden, hardly more than a speck on the map northeast of Benson in the most beautiful hill country you can imagine. A few years ago, four pretty one-room schools dating from the nineteenth century, schools still serving 120 kids with just *four* teachers and no administrators, were condemned by the same crew from Montpelier that gave Benson its current tax headache. I was asked by a citizen group in Walden to drive up and speak at a rally to save these remarkable community schools, beloved by their clientele. If I tell you when I woke in the morning in Walden a moose was rooting vegetables from the garden of my hostess' home you'll be able to imagine them better.

The group I came to speak for, "The Road Rats" as it called itself, had already defeated school consolidation the previous year. Montpelier's goal was to close the little schools and bus kids to a new central location miles from home. Now Montpelier took off the gloves. If persuasion and seduction wouldn't work, coercion would. Let's call what happened "The Benson Maneuver," passing building code provisions with no connection to normal reality. This accomplished, Vermont condemned the one-room schools for violation of these provisions. All official estimates to reach new code standards were very close to the price of consolidating the little schools into a big new one.

Road Rat resistance would be unlikely to mobilize a voting majority a second time; the publicists of mass-production economics have successfully altered public taste to believe it doesn't make sense to repair something old when for the same price you can have something new. Our only hope lay in getting a construction bid low enough that voters could see they had been flim-flammed.

It seemed worth a try. The Walden group had been unable to find a contractor willing to publicly oppose the will of Montpelier, but by a lucky accident I knew a Vermont master architect. I called his home in Montpelier. Two hours later he was in Walden touring the condemned buildings.

Vital to understanding why the state wanted these places closed so badly was that everything in such places worked against professionalization and standardization: parents were too close to the classroom to allow smooth "professional" governance to sneak by unnoticed. It wasn't possible in such schools to float a scientifically prepared curriculum initiative without having it come under close and critical scrutiny. That was intolerable to Montpelier, or rather to the larger octopus the Montpelier tentacle wiggled for.

After inspection, my architect pronounced the official estimates to reach code compliance cynical and dishonest. They were three times higher than the work would cost allowing for a normal profit. My architect knew the principals in the politically well-connected construction firms which had submitted the inflated bids. He knew the game they were playing, too. "The purpose of this is to kill one-room schools," he said. "All these guys will be paid off one way or another with state work for forwarding the agenda whether they get this state job or not." I asked if he would give us a counter-estimate we might use to wake up voters. "No," he said. "If I did I wouldn't get another building job in Vermont."

Let's get back to Benson, a classic illustration how the political state and its licensed allies feed like parasites on working men and women. Where *Education Week* saw deep mystery over citizen disaffection, the facts put a different spin on things. In a jurisdiction serving only 137 children, a number which would have been handled in the old and successful Walden schools with four teachers—and no supervisors other than the town's traditions and the willing oversight loving parents would provide because the students were, after all, their own kids—taxpayers were being forced to sustain the expense of:

1) A non-teaching superintendent
2) A non-teaching assistant superintendent
3) A non-teaching principal
4) A non-teaching assistant principal
5) A full-time nurse
6) A full-time guidance counselor
7) A full-time librarian
8) Eleven full-time schoolteachers
9) An unknown number of accessory personnel
10) Space, desks, supplies, technology for all of these

One hundred thirty-seven schoolchildren? Is there a soul who believes Benson's kids are better served in their new school with this mercenary army than Walden's 120 were in four rooms with four teachers? If so, the customary ways we measure educational success don't reflect this superiority. What happened at Benson—the use of forced schooling to impose career ladders of unnecessary work on a poor community—has happened all over North America. School is a jobs project for a large class of people it would be difficult to find employment for otherwise in a frightening job market, one in which the majority of all employment in the nation is either temporary or part-time.

Forcible redistribution of the income of others to provide work for pedagogues and for a support staff larger than the actual teaching corps is a pyramid scheme run at the expense of children. The more "make-work" which has to be found for school employees, the worse for kids because their own enterprise is stifled by constant professional tinkering in order to justify this employment. Suppose we eliminated the first seven positions from the list of functionaries paid in Benson: the superintendent, assistant superintendent, principal, assistant principal, nurse, guidance counselor, and librarian, plus three of the eleven teachers and all those accessory personnel. We'd have the work those folks do absorbed by the remaining eight teachers and whatever community volunteer assistance we could recruit. This would still allow a class size of only 17 kids per teacher, a ratio big-city teachers would kill to get, and hardly more than half the load one-room Walden teachers carried. Yet it would save this little community over half a million dollars yearly.

In our hypothetical example, we left Benson with eight teachers, twice the number Walden enjoyed in its 200-year experience with one-room schooling. Only a calculating machine could consider a large, consolidated school to which children must commute long distances as a real advance in human affairs. An advance in wasting time certainly. Consider this angle now: who in *your* judgment has a moral right to decide what size weight can be fastened on the backs of the working citizens of Benson? Whose decision *should* that be?

From a chart included in the *Education Week* article, I saw that Vermont school bureaucrats extracted $6,500 in 1995 for each student who sat in their spanking new schools. That computes at $162 a week per kid. Is it fair to ask how private schools provided satisfactory service for a national average of only $3,000 a kid, about $58 a week, the same year? Or how parochial schools did it for $2,300, $44 a week? Or home schools for a mere ten or $10 or $20? Do you believe public school kids were better served for the additional money spent?

Those other places could do it because they didn't support an anthill of political jobs, political purchases, and political routines. These other types of schooling understood—some through tradition, some through analysis, some through trusting inner voices—that transferring educational responsibility from children, parents, and communities to certified agents of the state erodes the value base of human life which is forever grounded in local and personal sovereignty.

Natural Selection

In 1895, the National Education Association announced that school science courses should be reorganized to teach evolution not as theory but as fact. Biology textbooks began to present evolution to secondary schools and colleges with an extraordinary aggressiveness:

> We do not know of any competent naturalist who has any hesitation in accepting the general doctrine.
> — Yale University Press (1895)

> There is no rival hypothesis to evolution, except the out-worn and completely
> refuted one of special creation, now retained only by the ignorant, dogmatic,
> and the prejudiced.
>
> — Macmillan Publishers (1895)

What evolution has to do with the macro-politics of schooling becomes clear if you consider that both are concerned with what should be encouraged to thrive; what assisted to perish. Evolutionary theory made all the difference in how systematic schooling was internally arranged. Too much effort wasn't wasted on hopeless trash, and the good stock was separated from the everyday. With justification.

Global entrepreneurs such as John D. Rockefeller and Andrew Carnegie found natural selection to be a perfect explanation for their laissez-faire economic principles. To Rockefeller, for instance, "the growth of large business is merely survival of the fittest;" *savage business practices aren't evil*, "merely the working out of a law of nature and a law of God." According to Herbert Spencer, nothing escaped evolution's power: "every single organism" or institution evolved, religions evolved, economies evolved; evolution exposed democratic theory for the childish fantasy it really was.

But among common men and women in America who still believed in special creation and democracy, the perception spread that a new political order was strip-mining their uniquely American common rights and liberties like so much coal. In the waning years of the nineteenth century, social unrest was the most crucial problem confronting the security of ambitious new industrial elites. When the myths of George Washington and Tom Paine were flushed down the memory hole of schooling, and the personal call to duty of Christianity was—to use Macmillan's word—"refuted," a long-range dilemma emerged with no easy solution: no attractive social narrative remained from which to draw meaning. Hedonism, so essential to business success, had a social downside whose dimensions were difficult to predict. And the scientific story, in spite of prodigious labor expended in its behalf, left the unfortunate impression that life was only a goofy accident devoid of any greater significance.

The Darwinian/Galtonian evolutionary script wrote the everyday citizen completely out of the story. It had to be faced that there was no room at the policy table for common citizens, yet thanks to the dangerous power vested in the American electorate through its national founding documents, the full bite of a democratic society stood as a latent threat to the would-be scientific ruling classes. Into this late nineteenth century industrializing, immigrant confusion of national strikes and violence, breakaway urbanization, proletarianized labor, and political corruption, two ideas surfaced to offer an apparently sensible path through the maze. Each was a highly sophisticated social technology.

One was the movement called Fabian socialism and its various fellow-traveling outriggers. The other was a kind of academic echo of Fabianism called "the theory of democratic elites"—offering a strange kind of democracy-lite which operated "democratically" without needing any direct popular authorization. Democratic elitism had, in fact, been the mock representational model of ancient Sparta. Its modern analogue retained the husk of democratic institutions while stifling the real voice of the people by depriving its elected spokesmen of any effective power, reducing the role of legislatures to a choice between competing expert conceptions.

In its modern form, the theory of democratic elitism comes partly from John Stuart Mill and partly from the work of Italian intellectual Gaetano Mosca, especially from a long essay written in 1896 translated into English as *The Ruling Class: Elements of a Science of Politics*,[6] a book vital to understanding twentieth century schooling. The way to make a political regime stable across the centuries had eluded every wise man of history, but Mosca found the key: elites must deliberately and selectively *feed* on the brains and vitality of the lesser classes.

Identified early enough inside the laboratory of government schooling, the best leadership of these classes could be uprooted and transplanted into ruling class society, reinvigorating the blood stock of the overclass: Count Dracula in education department drag. This genetic harvesting would deliver the best formula for social harmony. Potential future leaders among the underclasses would be targeted early in schooling, then weaned from any misguided loyalty to their own group, using incentives. Far from prying eyes, their minds would be conditioned in special "gifted" classes.

While this process of vetting went on, school would also be used to train most of us in our role in traditional status hierarchies. Class rankings, specialized tracking, daily habituation to payoffs and punishments, and other means would accomplish the trick. Those elected for advancement would be drawn bit by bit into identification with the upper crust and with its ways of dress, speech, expectation, etc. They would come in this fashion to look upon their group of origin as evolutionarily retarded—a brilliant imaginative coup.

It was profound advice, providing a social justification for the expense and trouble of the mass confinement schooling experiment, which had still not been fully launched when Mosca wrote. While it was one thing to suggest, as Darwin did, that natural selection would improve the breed, one thing to say with Sir Henry Maine that the destiny of the Great Race would be advanced, one thing to say with the episcopal religions that God's will would thereby be done, to an emerging super-class of industrialists and international bankers some more down-to-earth surety had to be offered. Now such a surety was at hand in Mosca's guarantee of social stability.

The theory of democratic elites, together with the promising new German mind sciences, provided all the tools needed to press ahead with the school experiment. Mosca's ideas were an academic hit across the recently Germanized university spectrum of America, a watchword in Germanized corporate boardrooms and private men's clubs. By the start of WWI, the familiar Common School idea survived only in the imagination of America's middle and working classes. In actual school practice it had given way to throughly regulated and tracked assemblages geared tightly to the clock, managed by layered hierarchies and all schematized into rigid class rankings. Class-reproduction was "scientifically" locked in place by standardized test scores, calibrated to the decimal. Objections were overridden by pointing to the "facts" of the matter. From its inception, evolutionary racism guided the forced-schooling car, test scores its communiques offered to the public as evidence that a higher law was being obeyed.

The theory of democratic elites provided a way to have plutocracy hide inside the skin of democracy, to have ordinary people represented by the best *selected by the best*. Here was Orwellian

---

[6] Mosca's answer to the problem of political stability can be read clearly in the blatantly anti-democratic first edition of this often revised and reprinted classic. (Later editions are subtler with the central message concealed somewhat in metaphor.) The rarely encountered 1923 edition had great influence on Walter Lippmann's post-WWI generation, the triumphant final version of 1939, which is easiest to locate, on Roosevelt's.

Newspeak of a very high order. Since the commons could not be trusted to select the best from amongst itself, the community of quality would have to do it for them, backstage, concealing (in the interests of social efficiency but also from humane motives) the full reality of the radical political transformation. America was whisked off stage and replaced by a political imposter, anglicized in its attitudes.

Walter Lippmann, among many, picked up these notes sounded by Mosca and augmented by the important American Fabian Herbert Croly in his book, *The Promise of American Life* (1909). Teddy Roosevelt's Progressive platform of 1912 was heavily larded with Croly/Mosca substance, *an outlook demanding the public step back* and let experts make the important decisions so the promise of American life could be realized. With these precepts in mind Lippmann, produced his own pair of influential books, *Public Opinion* (1922), followed by *The Phantom Public* (1925).

Public Opinion called for severe restrictions on public debate. The historic American argument was "a defect of democracy." It was impossible, said Lippmann, for the public even to *know* what its own best interests were. The public was hopelessly childish; it had to be cared for. Schools would have to teach children that the old ideal of active, participatory citizenship was biologically impossible. Decisions in complex industrial society had to be made by "invisible experts acting through government officials" for the good of all.

The proper thing to do, said Lippmann, was give the public a "fairy tale" explanation, something to sustain it emotionally, as we tell a bedtime story to infants. Later, as he saw the effects of his advice unfold, Lippmann would repudiate them, but that's another story. The common public would have to be neutralized *in the name of democracy* for this expert society, this new republic based on sciences of human behavior to work. In this new world it wouldn't do to have shoemakers and hairdressers mucking about while important people built the future. In the state institution of forced schooling it would be better in the long run if children learned little or nothing in the short run. America was coming full circle to its British/Germanic and episcopal beginnings.

In the Mosca/Croly/Lippmann redefinition of democracy, common people traded their right to be heard on policy matters in exchange for being taken care of. It was the mother's bargain with her infants. The enormous training project called School, proceeding in deliberate stages across the twentieth century as opportunity presented itself and traveling at the speed of electronics as the century ended, had as its purpose creation of an automatic social order which could be managed by unreachable national and international elites. It was a new type of flexible social organization capable of being driven in any direction at any time without the need to overcome interference.

By the end of WWI, the labor market and much state/municipal contracting in America was effectively controlled by Fabian-minded administrators, selected by Fabian-minded university placement rings, all nourished by rich contracts garnered with the assistance of political clubs. Whether any of these actually had any connection to the Fabian brain trust (few did) was irrelevant. The atmosphere of schooling was saturated with its disciplined notions of utopia.

Another natural force was at work as well. With each passing decade, there accumulated more reasons to defend schools exactly as they were, not on ideological grounds at all but as a jobs project and a contract-distribution station. Millions had a financial stake in keeping schools as they were. The true philosophical and economic focus of the thing needed only be known to a handful of well-positioned social engineers in universities, foundations, and private associations. The thing ran on momentum now. The reach of schooling grew longer without any special effort. Secondary school enrollment went from 15 percent of the population in 1910 to 40 percent in 1930, to 90 percent in 1960, and to blanket coverage by 1970. Almost every alternative to a well-schooled destiny was squeezed out, show business careers being a notable exception for the thoughtful to contemplate.

With this development, the job pool established by institutional schooling became the leading single source of work in the United States, the very heart of the economy in small cities, towns, and villages. In this way school became a major foundation for local elites, directly and indirectly, through contract and hiring powers. All over America school became the core of local economies while, ironically, at the same time local minds and local customs were being rigorously barred from the policy table of American life. The money served as an effective incentive to self-destruct.

Local schools and school boards began to behave as foreign intelligence bodies implanted in the cells of a host creature, parasitic growths on local life, remote-controlled from state and federal offices which dissolved local integrity by overriding its imperatives. Managers of this simulated "local" schooling descended on towns out of Stanford, Chicago, or Columbia Teachers almost on a status and income level with the ranking local leadership. As the century wore on, even the lowliest pedagogues were surprised to find themselves near the top of local wage scales.

By the 1970s, schools were plunged headlong into a political campaign to redefine *national* purpose as *international* purpose, and to formally redefine Democracy as the ritual democracy allowed by democratic elites. Control of schooling by then was so dispersed that power could hardly be located at all in the hands of local administrators and school boards. The world designed by Plato and Thomas Hobbes had become reality. If you could not locate power you could not tamper with it. Local control passed into the realm of fiction as distantly prepared instruction entered schooling from state and federal agencies; the inner reality was that it had not been prepared even there but in colleges, foundations, and corporations and also—a noteworthy new development—in the offices of various United Nations agencies.

The Great Transformation

One of the finest academic studies of the origins of our time and its economic antecedents is Karl Polanyi's *The Great Transformation*. Published in 1944, it has been kept in print ever since. Polanyi's explosive conclusion states unflinchingly that we must now become "resigned to the reality of the end of our liberty." How did he figure this out in 1944? By extrapolation from the track of modern history which he regarded as undirectional and which teaches us that the end of liberty is "a necessary evil." At the end of his book, Polanyi offers a perfect public relations solution to the anguish of losing freedom. By cleverly redefining the word to mean "a collective thing," the loss of liberty will not hurt so much, he says. This kind of therapeutic Newspeak has been a dominant element in national life for most of the twentieth century, infecting every schoolroom. Professional manipulation of attitudes by control of language and images, once the stock in trade of a few men of bad character like Edward L. Bernays, is a common tool of leadership. Polanyi's wish for us to be deluded (in our own best interests) has become the daily bread of everyone.

Walter Lippmann's disrespect for common citizens became the official government position during the administration of Franklin Roosevelt; it has remained so ever since. We can follow this development through the growth of the taxing power—less than five percent of an average income went to taxes in 1947, nearly half if all tax hits are tallied 50 years later. The trajectory inscribed mathematically is the removal of choice written in the language of the missing dollars. Someone, somewhere, decided to take care of us whether we wanted the help or not, schools were the hospitals where dependency implants were first installed.

The political basis for the schools we have and for the politics of schooling we struggle against was laid down just before the Wright brothers flew at Kitty Hawk. Where we are today is a kind of intertidal stage in which the last remnants of the historic American tradition are being set aside to make way for a thoroughly planned global economy and society, an economy apparently intended to be scientifically managed by a professional class of technicians at the bottom, a professional proletariat of rootless, well-paid men and women in the middle, and a small group, no more than one percent, of knowledgeable managers at the top.

Propaganda

To get where we got, public imagination had to be manufactured from command centers, but how was this managed? In 1914 Andrew Carnegie, spiritual leader of the original band of hard-nosed dreamers, gained influence over the Federal Council of Churches by extending heavy subsidies to its operations. And in 1918 Carnegie endowed a meeting in London of the American Historical Association where an agreement was made to rewrite American history in the interests of social efficiency. Not all leaders were of a single mind, of course. History isn't that simple. Beatrice Webb declined to accept financial aid from Carnegie on her visit, for instance, calling him "a little reptile" behind his back; the high-born Mrs. Webb saw through Carnegie's pretensions, right into the merchant-ledger of his tradesman soul. But enough were of a single mind it made no practical difference.

On July 4, 1919, the *London Times* carried a long account reporting favorably on the propaganda hydra being built by agents of Carnegie in the United States. According to the paper, men "trained in the arts of swaying public opinion" were broadcasting Carnegie's agenda, an agenda which aimed first at mobilizing world public opinion and then controlling it. The end of all this effort was already determined, said the *Times*—world government. As the newspaper set down the specifics in 1919, propaganda was the fuel to drive societies away from their past:

> Propaganda to mobilize the press, the church, the stage and cinema, the whole
> educational system, the universities, public and high schools, primary schools.
> Histories and textbooks will be revised. New books will be added, particularly
> in the primary school.

The same issue of the *London Times* carried a signed article by Owen Wister, famous author of the best-selling novel, *The Virginian*. Wister was then on the Carnegie payroll. He pulled no punches, informing the upscale British readership, "A movement to *correct* the schoolbooks of the United States has been started, and it will go on."

In March 1925, the *Saturday Evening Post* featured an article by a prominent Carnegie official who stated that to bring about the world Carnegie envisioned, "American labor will have to be reduced to the status of European labor."[7] Ten years later, on December 19, 1935, the *New York American* carried a long article about what it referred to as "a secret Carnegie Endowment conference" at the Westchester Country Club in Harrison, New York. Twenty-nine organizations attending each agreed to authorize a nationwide radio campaign managed and coordinated from behind the scenes, a campaign to commit the United States to a policy of internationalism. The group also agreed to present "vigorous counter-action" against those who opposed this country's entrance into the League of Nations. Pearl Harbor was only six years away, an international showcase for globalism without peer.

Soon after this conference, almost every school in the United States was provided with full-size color maps of the world and with League of Nations literature extolling the virtues of globalism. That's how it was done. That's how it still is done. Universal schooling is a permeable medium. There need not be conspiracy among its internal personnel to achieve astonishingly uniform results; multiply this tactical victory thousands of times and you get where we are. Today we call the continuation of this particular strand of leveling "multiculturalism"—even though every particular culture it touches is degraded and insulted by the shallow veneer of universalism which hides the politics of the thing.

Freud's Nephew

Early in the twentieth century, official language, including official school language, became a deliberate, systematic exercise in illusion. Governments have always lied, of course, but at the beginning of the twentieth century an accretion of psychological insights gathered from past epochs of magic, theology, philosophy, arts, warfare, rumor, and madness, were collected, codified, and the conclusions sold to the leaders of political states, global corporations, and other powerful interests, welded into a technology of professionalized dishonesty. Secrets of crowd behavior and the presumed instrumental wiring of human nature were made available to anyone with the price of admission. The newly official pragmatic philosophy became a kind of *anti-morality*, superior to any ethical code fashioned out of custom and philosophy.

Four hundred years after Niccolo Machiavelli wrote his treatise on scientific deceit, Edward L. Bernays began to practice the scientific art of public deception, trading heavily on his uncle Sigmund Freud's notoriety. A decade earlier, Ivy Lee's publicity savvy had rescued the Rockefellers from their Ludlow Massacre disgrace. Public Relations as political science was off and running on the fast track.

Bernays was only a solitary word magician at the time, of course, but he was in an ideal position to capitalize quickly upon his rhetorical talent and to set his stamp on the new science's future. In 1928, Bernays published two books in quick succession which planted his flag in the dream terrain of the "unconscious." The first, *Crystallizing Public Opinion*, the second, *Propaganda*. Adolf Hitler is said to have displayed both on a table in his office under a poster-sized picture of Henry Ford. The new world was blazing a trail into an even newer world than it imagined.

---

[7] If the article were written today, the magnitude of reduction would be to an Asian or "global" standard, I would imagine.

Both of Bernays' books argued that *language could be used successfully to create new realities*. Psychological science was so advanced, he claimed, it could substitute synthetic reality for natural reality, as urban society had successfully replaced our natural connection to birds, trees, and flowers with a substitute connection to billboards, cars, and bright lights.

Crystallizing Public Opinion and *Propaganda* had much to say to the newlyminted administrative classes burgeoning all over American schools and colleges. In *Propaganda*, Bernays redefined democratic society, in the interests of the mass-production economy. I've selected three short excerpts from Bernays' classic which enriched him with corporate work in the seven decades of life he had left after its publication (He died in 1995 at the age of 105.)

The first assertion of *Propaganda* was that common people had to be regimented *and governed from behind the scenes*. Here are Bernays' actual words:

> The need for invisible government has been increasingly demonstrated, the
> technical means have been invented and developed by which public opinion
> may be regimented.

The next important contention was that the critical pollution of language necessary to make this work was already in use:

> We are governed, our minds are molded, our tastes formed, our ideas suggested,
> largely by men we have never heard of. We are dominated by a relatively small
> number of persons who understand the mental processes and social patterns of
> the masses. It is they who pull the wires which control the public.

Finally, Bernays provides a moral justification for proceeding as the ephors had in Sparta:

> The conscious manipulation of organized habits and opinions of the masses is an
> important element in a democratic society. Those who manipulate this unseen
> mechanism constitute an invisible government which is the true ruling power in
> this country.

This attitude of manipulation as an important component of "democratic" management entered the urban factory-school classroom in a big way at a time when psychology was taking over from academics as the tool of choice in America's German-inspired teacher-training institutions.

Magic At Work

Magic in one form or another had always appealed to professional school authorities as the means to manage students. Horace Mann, as you know, dedicated his entire *Sixth Report* to a paean in praise of phrenology, the "science" of reading head bumps, and every major schoolman from Mann to G. Stanley Hall and John Dewey was a serious phrenologist—long after the craze had vanished from upper-class drawing rooms and salons. That should tell you something important about the inner itches of these men, I think. *The quest for certainty* in a confusing new land without rules was as much the religion of our founding schoolmen as searching one's family for signs of reprobation was for Puritans. But modern schoolmen needed a scientific cast over their religiosity, times having changed.

Early educational psychologists scientized the practice of manipulation behind a common expression of modern pedagogy—"motivation." Book after book advised pedagogues how to "motivate" charges with technical advice based on an underlying premise that young people did not want to learn and had to be tricked into it, a premise which on the face of common experience was absurd. As the significance of Bernays' arguments penetrated the high command of government and industry, so too did manipulation become *sine qua non* in classroom teaching, the standard by which teacher quality was measured.

But the *methods* of Bernays or of educational psychologists like Dewey, Munsterberg, Judd, Hall, Cattell, Terman, Thorndike, Goddard, and Watson which so radically transformed the shape of twentieth century schooling are about indoctrination strategies—building and using psychological tools to create compliant children. If nature hadn't cooperated by actually *making* empty children, then schooling would have to do the job. And yet, for what grand *purpose* children had to be emptied, not many knew; for those without religious training or ignorant of the evolutionary sciences, it made only the bleakest sort of sense.

The Culture Of Big Business

Between 1890 and 1930, the culture of big business took over the culture of public education, establishing scientific management and corporate style as the predominant imperative. Although linkages between business and education elites were complex, the goals and values of business established the rules by which both played. And while schools proved unwilling to dare influencing business, the reverse was far from true.

Businessmen dominated the political movement in schools to abolish the system of local control through wards nearly universal at the end of the nineteenth century. Along with professionals, businessmen served disproportionately on new streamlined school boards. Business language permeated the corridors of school management. Businessmen and their wives were the political force behind Froebelian kindergartens which removed young children from family influence, and they were behind vocational schooling, which left no romantic dreams for ordinary children.

The National Association of Manufacturers, the National Civic Foundation, the Ad Council, the Business Roundtable, and other business-relevant private associations publicized the need for school change, told the public how children should act, what they should honor, what behaviors would be rewarded. A steadily lengthening school year led to an extended career ladder, specialization, and a credential-oriented society. School people were assigned the role of bringing about a conflict-free world by teaching indirectly that the preemption of work by corporations and professions (later by government) was right, proper, and "scientific."

The Irish historian and philosopher W.E.H. Lecky, in his history of European rationalism published in 1883, predicted that temptations posed by a forced assemblage of children would prove in the end too strong to resist:

The opinions of ninety-nine persons out of every hundred are formed mainly by
education, and a Government can decide in whose hands the national education
is to be placed, what subjects it is to comprise, and what principles it is to convey.
                                                                    — *Rationalism in Europe*

"If all paths of honor and wealth" are monopolized, said Lecky, the powerful motive of self-
interest will be enough to bring most students to heel:

The simple fact of annexing certain penalties to the profession of particular
opinions, and rewards to the profession of opposite opinions, while it will
undoubtedly make many hypocrites, will also make many converts.

Once a system of reward and punishment is set up and broadcast by frequent public examples
of its power in action, the nature of argument is almost predetermined, although subjects of such a
regimen may be "entirely unconscious of the source of their opinions." Once the doctrine of
"exclusive salvation" for the cooperative (and damnation for the critic) is clearly established, rulers
will never be seriously questioned, thought Lecky.

By 1899 William H. Baldwin, president of the Long Island Railroad and the man for whom
the Baldwin locomotive was named, demonstrated how well the school lesson had been learned and
how forcible could be its application. Baldwin was a member of the Peabody/Rockefeller/Carnegie
"Southern Education Board," self-appointed to bring the benefits of Northern schooling to the war-
ravaged South. Although in the beginning of its career freed blacks were treated to the same type
of rigorous, classically oriented schooling we would call "liberal" today—meaning one designed to
liberate the judgment from prejudice and ignorance—as time passed it began to seem impolitic to
so treat blacks as equals. It alienated important elements in the Southern white community who were
more important fish for the Northern school net to land. Thus a decision was made to jettison
equality as a goal and make labor-value the most important determinant of which way each group
would be schooled.

There is perhaps no more naked statement of the political uses of schooling on record than
Baldwin's official word about "The Present Problem of Negro Education," delivered before the
Capon Springs Conference on Southern Education (1899):

Know that it is a crime for any teacher, white or black, to educate the Negro
for positions which are not open to him.

Important liberals like Edgar Gardner Murphy (whose descendants are still active in American
schooling) and other leading progressive humanists hastened to agree with Baldwin. In David
Tyack's analysis, these men sought to develop an applied technology of school decision-making
similar to technologies of production and management then transforming the bureaucratized
corporate economy. This technology reflected evolutionary presuppositions, rooting its values in
supposed evolutionary laws. Ideals could be hierarchically arranged and pinned down on a scale of
races, classes, sexes, and historical stages grounded allegedly in nature itself.

According to James Russell, for 30 years Dean of Teachers College, the purpose was to equip teachers and administrators for "missionary service." What we are looking to discover through building this new institution, said Russell, is *the modern significance of the old doctrines of original sin and salvation by grace—to bring forth works meet for repentance.*

Teachers College, Stanford, Chicago, Johns Hopkins, Wisconsin, Michigan, Yale, etc., were the West Points of the Educational Trust, men like Ellwood P. Cubberley its generals. Cubberley, also writer and editor of Houghton Mifflin's education series, the largest and most successful set of professional books published for school people in the first half of the twentieth century, legitimized by his influence the new reforms of vocational guidance, "junior" high schools, hygiene programs, and more. The book series gave him great power to shape the new science of education, making him a fortune. Its effects on school management were vast.

Cubberley wrote, "One bright child may easily be worth more to national life than thousands of low mentality." He taught influential schoolmen that genetic endowment explained success and failure in the social order and taught thousands of politicians the same lesson as well. Cubberley was one of a small band of leaders who invented professional school administration as an occupation, and professional school administration created the tracking system so that different grades of evolutionary raw material could be processed in different ways—one of many innovations science and business efficiency seemed to demand. In doing so, a strong class system possessing nearly the strength of a caste system was created, with important political implications for every American child.

Four Kinds Of Classroom

Jean Anyon, a professor at Rutgers, recently examined four major types of covert career preparation going on simultaneously in the school world, all traveling together under the label "public education." All use state-certified schoolteachers, all share roughly common budgets, all lead to intensely political outcomes.

In the first type of classroom, students are prepared for future wage labor that is mechanical and routine. Of course neither students nor parents are told this, and almost certainly teachers are not consciously aware of it themselves. The training regimen is this: all work is done in sequential fashion starting with simple tasks, working *very* slowly and progressing gradually to more difficult ones (but never to *very* difficult work). There is little decision-making or choice on the part of students, much rote behavior is practiced. Teachers hardly ever explain *why* any particular work is assigned or how one piece of work connects to other assignments. When explanations are undertaken they are shallow and platitudinous. "You'll need this later in life." Teachers spend most of their day at school controlling the time and space of children, and giving commands.

In the second type of classroom, students are prepared for low-level bureaucratic work, work with little creative element to it, work which does not reward critical appraisals of management. Directions are followed just as in the first type of classroom, but those directions often call for some deductive thinking, offer some selection, and leave a bit of room for student decision-making.

The third type of classroom finds students being trained for work that requires them to be producers of artistic, intellectual, scientific, and other kinds of productive enterprise. Often children work creatively and independently here. Through this experience, children learn how to interpret and evaluate reality, how to become their own best critics and supporters. They are trained to be alone with themselves without a need for constant authority intervention and approval. The teacher controls this class through endless negotiation. Anyon concludes: "In their schooling these children are acquiring symbolic capital, they are given opportunity to develop skills of linguistic, artistic, and scientific expression and creative elaboration of ideas in concrete form."

The fourth type of public school classroom trains students for ownership, leadership, and control. Every hot social issue is discussed, students are urged to look at a point from all sides. A leader, after all, has to understand every possible shade of human nature in order to effectively mobilize, organize, or defeat any possible opponent. In this kind of schoolroom bells are not used to begin and end periods. This classroom offers something none of the others do: "knowledge of and practice in manipulating socially legitimated tools of systems analysis."

It strikes me as curious how far Anyon's "elite" public school classroom number four still falls far short of the goals of elite private boarding schools, almost as if the very best government schools are *willing* to offer is only a *weak* approximation of the leadership style of St. Paul's or Groton. What fascinates me most is the cold-blooded quality of this shortfall because Groton's expectations cost almost nothing to meet on a different playing field—say a home school setting or even in John Gatto's classroom—while the therapeutic community of psychologized public schooling is extremely expensive to maintain. Virtually everyone could be educated the Groton way for less money than the average public school costs.

The Planetary Management Corporation

Who governs? And to what degree may rule be exercised arbitrarily? These are the political questions of forced schooling. In a free society tension must always exist between external governance and the other possibility seeking to replace it. This conflict extended indefinitely is our personal guarantee there will always be a way out of being suffocated by the will of another.

In a free society, the power situation must always be kept fluid, even though a high price in inefficiency, instability, and frustration is paid by the ruling group or coalition for that fluidity. As long as liberty is cherished beyond efficiency, the price will be willingly paid. *From the above it is only a short leap to deduce the political crime of mass forced schooling: it amputates the full argument and replaces it with engineered consensus.* Once such a peace-making apparatus is built, its interior drive to self-preservation and growth will organize its line and staff personnel around a single-minded logic of orthodoxy. But that orthodoxy will always be committed to the service of the economy, not to the interests of its nominal clientele.

As schooling encroaches further and further into family and personal life, monopolizing the development of mind and character, children must become human resources at the disposal of whatever form of governance is dominant at the moment. That, in turn, confers a huge advantage on the leadership of the moment, allowing it to successfully reproduce itself and foreclose the strength of its competitors. Schooling becomes an overwhelming subsidy for what is the ultimate form of corporate and status welfare, a destroyer of the free market.

Without opposition made possible by education (rather than schooling) of children, a Planetary Management Corporation is our certain destiny—and just as certain to be followed sometime after its birth by a dissolution into chaos, the fate of all empires. Our school tragedies are an early warning of something inherent in the laws of human thermodynamics. Chaos increases steadily in closed systems cut off from the outside, over-organization precipitates disorganization. Where the developing consciousness of children cries out for a jazz approach, what they get instead are scale exercises.

A FEW

MORE PAGES FROM THE

SCRAPBOOK IN MY HEART

CHAPTER EIGHTEEN

Breaking Out

Of The Trap

*We have a choice to make once and for all: between the empire
and the spiritual and physical salvation of our people. No road
for the people will ever be open unless the government completely
gives up control over us or any aspect of our lives. It has led the
country into an abyss and it does not know the way out.*
— Aleksandr Solzhenitsyn, *Pravda* (1986)

To hell with the cheese, let's get out of this trap!
— A mouse

Silicon Valley

To reform our treatment of the young, we must force the center of gravity of the school world to change. In this chapter I'll try to show you what I mean, but my method will be largely indirect, to fashion the beginnings of a solution from these materials will require your active engagement in an imaginative partnership with me, one that shall commence in Silicon Valley.

I went to Silicon Valley in the middle of 1999 to speak to some computer executives at Cypress Semiconductor on the general topic of school reform. The 50 or 60 who showed up to my talk directly from work were dressed so informally they might easily have been mistaken for pizza delivery men or taxicab drivers. The CEO of the corporation, its founder T.J. Rodgers, was similarly turned out. I didn't recognize him as the same famous man portrayed on a large photo mural mounted on the wall outside until he introduced me to the audience and the audience to me.

To let me know who my auditors were, Rodgers said that everyone there was a millionaire, none needed to work for him because all were self-sufficient and could find work all over the place simply by walking into a different company. They worked for Cypress because they wanted to, just as he did himself, and like him, they were usually hard at it from very early morning until long after five o'clock. Because they wanted to.

The thesis of my talk was that the history of forced schooling in America, as elsewhere, is the history of the requirements of business. School can't be satisfactorily explained by studying the careers of ideologues like Horace Mann or anyone else. The problem of American education from a personal or a family perspective isn't really a problem at all from the vantage point of big business, big finance, and big government. What's a problem to me is a solution for them. An insufficient incentive exists to change things much, otherwise things would change. I learned that from Adam Smith.

Think of it this way: in our present system, those abstract bignesses are saddled with the endless responsibility of finding a place for hundreds of millions of people, and the even more daunting challenge of creating demand for products and services which, historically viewed, few of us need or want. Because of this anomaly, a Procrustean discipline emerges in which the entire population must continually be cut or stretched to fit the momentary convenience of the economy. This is a free market only in fantasy; it seems free because ceaseless behind-the-scenes efforts maintain the illusion, but its reality is much different. Prodigies of psychological and political insight and wisdom gathered painfully over the centuries are refined into principles, taught in elite colleges, and consecrated in the service of this colossal *tour de force* of appearances.

Let me illustrate: people love to work, but they must be convinced that work is a kind of curse, that they must arrange the maximum of leisure and labor-saving devices in their lives upon which belief many corporations depend; people love to invent solutions, to be resourceful, to make do with what they have, but resourcefulness and frugality are criminal behaviors to a mass production economy, such examples threaten to infect others with the same fatal sedition; similarly, people love to attach themselves to favored possessions, even to grow old and die with them, but such indulgence is dangerous lunacy in a machine economy whose costly tools are continually renewed by enormous borrowings; people like to stay put but must be convinced they lead pinched and barren existences without travel; people love to walk but the built world is now laid out so they have to drive. Worst of all are those who yearn for productive, independent livelihoods like the Amish have, and nearly all Americans once had. If that vision spreads a consumer economy is sunk.

For all these and other reasons, the form of schooling we have is largely a kind of consumer and employee training. This isn't just incidentally true. Common sense should tell you it's necessarily so if the economy is to survive in any recognizable form.

Every principal institution in our culture is a partner with the particular form of corporatism which has come to dominate America since the end of WWII. Call it paternal corporatism, a wise elite can be trained to provide for the rest of us who will be kept as children. Unlike Plato's Guardians whom they otherwise resemble, this meritorious elite is not kept poor but is guaranteed prosperity and status in exchange for its oversight. An essential feature of this kind of central management is that the population remain mystified, specialized, and dependent.

The school institution is clearly a key partner in this arrangement: it suppresses the productive impulse in favor of consumption; redefines Work as a job someone will eventually give you if you behave habituates a large clientele to sloth, envy, and boredom; and accustoms individuals to think of themselves as members of a class with various distinguishing features. More than anything else, school is about class consciousness. In addition, it makes intellectual work and creative thinking appear like distasteful or difficult labor to most of us. None of this is done to oppress, but because the economy would dissolve into something else if those attitudes didn't become ingrained in childhood.

We have evolved a subtly architected, delicately balanced command economy and class-based society upon which huge efforts are lavished to make it appear like something else. The illusion has been wearing thin for years; that's a principal reason why so many people don't bother to vote. In such a bargain, the quality of schooling is distinctly secondary; other values are uppermost. A great many children see through the fraud in elementary school but lack the language and education to come to proper terms with their feelings. In this system, a fraction of the kids are slowly over time let in on a part of this managerial reality because they are eventually intended to be made into Guardians themselves, or Guardian's assistants.

School is a place where a comprehensive social vision is learned. Without a contrary vision to offer, the term "school reform" is only a misnomer describing trivial changes. Any large alteration of forced schooling which might jeopardize the continuity of workers and customers the corporate economy depends upon is unthinkable without some radical change in popular perception preceding it. Business/School partnerships and School-to-Work legislation aren't positive developments but the end of any pretense that ordinary children should be educated. That, in any case, was the burden of my talk at Cypress.

When I finished, Mr. Rodgers briefly took me to task for seeming to include the high tech group he led in the indictment. Later I learned that he had challenged Washington to stop government subsidies to the Valley on the grounds that such tampering destroyed the very principle that provided it with energy—open competition and risk-taking. Thinking about his criticism on the road home, I accepted the justice of his complaint against me and as penance, thought about the significance of what he had said.

A century ago mass production stifled the individualism which was the real American Dream. Big business, big government, and big labor couldn't deal with individuals but only with people in bulk. Now computers seem to be shifting the balance of power from collective entities like corporations back to people. The cult of individual effort is found all over Silicon Valley, standing in sharp contrast to leadership practices based on high SAT scores, elite college degrees, and sponsorship by prominent patrons.

The Valley judges people on their tangible contributions rather than on sex, seniority, old-school ties, club memberships, or family. About half the millionaires in my Cypress audience had been foreign-born, not rich at all just a few years earlier. Many new Internet firms are headed by people in their mid-twenties who never wear a suit except to costume parties. Six thousand high tech firms exist there in a nonstop entrepreneurial environment, the world's best example of Adam Smith's competitive capitalism. Companies are mostly small, personal, and fast on their feet. Traditional organization men are nowhere to be seen; they are a luxury none can afford and still remain competitive. Company mortality is high but so is the startup rate for new firms; when unsuccessful companies die their people and resources are recycled somewhere else.

Information technology creates an economy close to the model capitalism in Adam Smith's mind, a model which assumes the world to be composed not of childish and incompetent masses, but of individuals who can be trusted to pursue their own interests competently—if they are first given access to accurate information and then left relatively free of interference to make something of it. The Internet advances Smith's case dramatically. Computerization is pushing political debate in a libertarian direction, linking free markets to the necessary personal freedoms which markets need to work, threatening countries who fail to follow this course of streamlining government with disaster.

It can only be a matter of time before America rides on the back of the computer age into a new form of educational schooling once called for by Adam Smith, that and a general reincorporation of children back into the greater social body from which they were excised a century and more ago will cure the problem of modern schooling. We can't afford to waste the resources young lives represent much longer. Nobody's *that* rich. Nor is anybody smart enough to marshal those resources and use them most efficiently. Individuals have to do that for themselves.

On October 30, 1999, the *Economist* printed a warning that decision-making was being dispersed around global networks of individuals that fall beyond the control of national governments and nothing could be done about it. Innovation is now so fast and furious that "big organizations increasingly look like dinosaurs while wired individuals race past them." That critique encompasses the problem of modern schooling, which cannot educate for fear the social order will explode. Yet the Siliconizing of the industrial world is up-ending hierarchies based on a few knowing inside information and a mass knowing relatively less in descending layers, right on down to schoolchildren given propaganda and fairy tales in place of knowledge.

The full significance of what Adam Smith saw several centuries ago is hardly well understood today, even among those who claim to be his descendants. He saw that human potential, once educated, was far beyond the reach of any system of analysis to comprehend or predict, or of any system of regulation to enhance. Fixed orders of social hierarchy and economic destiny are barricades put up to stem the surprising human inventiveness which would surely turn the world inside out if unleashed; they secure privilege by holding individuals in place.

Smith saw that over time wealth would follow the release of constraints on human inventiveness and imagination. The larger the group invited to play the more spectacular the results. For all the ignorance and untrustworthiness in the world, he correctly perceived that the overwhelming majority of human beings could indeed be trusted to act in a way that over time is good for all. The only kind of education this system needs to be efficient is intellectual schooling for all, schooling to enlarge the imagination and strengthen the natural abilities to analyze, experiment, and communicate. Bringing the young up in somebody else's grand socialization scheme, or bringing them up to play a fixed role in the existing economy and society, and nothing more, is like setting fire to a fortune and burning it up because you don't understand money.

Smith would recognize our current public schools as the same kind of indoctrination project for the masses, albeit infinitely subtler, that the Hindus employed for centuries, a project whose attention is directed to the stability of the social order through constraint of opportunity. What a hideous waste! he might exclaim.

The great achievement of *Wealth of Nations* resides in its conviction and demonstration that people individually do best for everyone when they do best for themselves, when they aren't commanded too much or protected against the consequences of their own folly. As long as we have a free market and a free society, Smith trusts us to be able to manage any problems that appear. It's only when we vest authority and the problem-solving ability in a few that we become caught in a trap of our own making. The wild world of Silicon Valley and its outriggers is a hint of a dynamic America to come where responsibility, trust, and great expectations are once again given to the young as they were in Ben Franklin's day. That is how we will break out of the school trap. Ask yourself where and how these Silicon kids really learned what they know; the answer isn't found in memorizing a script.

Selling From Your Truck

In the northeast corner of an island a long way from here, a woman sells plates of cooked shrimp and rice from out of an old white truck. Her truck is worth $5,000 at most. She sells only that one thing plus hot dogs for the kids and canned soda. The license to do this costs $500 a year, or $43.25 a month, a little over a dollar a day. The shrimp lady is 59 years old. She has a high school diploma and a nice smile. Her truck parks on a gravel pull-off from the main highway in a nondescript location. No one else is around, not because the shrimp lady has a protected location but because no one else wants to be there. A hand-lettered sign advertises, "$9.95 Shrimp and Rice. Soda $1.00. Hot Dogs $1.25."

The day I stood in line for a shrimp plate, five customers were in front of me. They bought 14 plates among them and 14 sodas. I bought two and two when it came my turn, and by that time five new customers had arrived behind me. I was intrigued.

The next day Janet and I returned. We parked across the road where we could watch the truck but not make the shrimp lady nervous. In two hours, 41 plates and 41 sodas were handed out of the old truck, and maybe 10 hot dogs. A week later we came back and watched again as nearly the same thing happened. Janet, a graduate of the Culinary Institute of America, estimated that $7 of the $10.95 for shrimp and soda was profit, after all costs.

Later we chatted with the lady in a quiet moment. The truck sits there eight hours a day, seven days a week, 364 days a year (the island is warm year round). It averages 100 to 150 shrimp sales a day, but has sold as many as 300. When the owner-proprietress isn't there, one of her three daughters takes over. Each is only a high school graduate. For all I know, the only thing saleable any of them knows how to do is cook shrimp and rice, but they do that very well. The family earns in excess of a quarter million dollars a year selling shrimp plates out of an old truck. They have no interest in expanding or franchising the business. Another thing I noticed: all the customers seemed pleased; many were friendly and joked with the lady, myself included. She looked happy to be alive.

Mudsill Theory

A prophetic article entitled "The Working Classes," appeared in *The Boston Quarterly Review* in 1840 at the very moment Horace Mann's crowd was beating the drum loudest for compulsion schooling. Its author, Orestes Brownson, charged that Horace Mann was trying to establish a state church in America like the one England had and to impose a merchant/industrialist world-view as its gospel. "A system of education, [so constituted] may as well be a religion established by law," said Brownson. Mann's business backers were trying, he thought, to set up a new division of labor giving licensed professional specialists a monopoly to teach, weakening people's capacity to educate themselves, making them child-like.

Teaching in a democracy belongs to the whole community, not to any centralized monopoly,[1] said Brownson, and children were far better educated by "the general pursuits, habits, and moral tone of the community," than by a privileged class. The mission of this country, according to Brownson, was "to raise up the laboring classes, and make every man really free and independent." Whatever schooling should be admitted to society under the auspices of government should be dedicated to the principle of independent livelihoods and close self-reliant families. Brownson's *freedom* and *independence* are still the goals that represent a consensus of working class opinion in America, although they have receded out of reach for all but a small fraction, *like the shrimp lady*. How close was the nation in 1840 to realizing such a dream of equality before forced schooling converted our working classes into "human resources" or a "workforce" for the convenience of the industrial order? The answer is very close, as significant clues testify.

A century and a half after "The Working Classes" was published, Cornell labor scholar Chris Clarke investigated and corroborated the reality of Brownson's world. In his book, *Roots of Rural Capitalism*, Clarke found that the general labor market in the Connecticut Valley was highly undependable in the 1840s by employer standards because it was shaped by family concerns. Outside work could only be fitted into what available free time farming allowed (for farming took priority), and work was adapted to the homespun character of rural manufacture in a system we find alive even today among the Amish. Wage labor was not dependent on a boss's whim. It had a mind of its own and was always only a supplement to a broad strategy of household economy.

A successful tradition of self-reliance requires an optimistic theory of human nature to bolster it. Revolutionary America had a belief in common people never seen anywhere in the past. Before such an independent economy could be broken apart and scavenged for its labor units, people had to be brought to believe in a different, more pessimistic appraisal of human possibility. Abe Lincoln once called this contempt for ordinary people "mudsill theory," an attitude that the education of working men and women was useless and dangerous. It was the same argument, not incidentally, that the British state and church made and enforced for centuries, German principalities and *their* official church, too.

Lincoln said in a speech to the Wisconsin Agricultural Association in September 1859, that the goal of government planning should be independent livelihoods. He thought everyone capable of reaching that goal, as it is reached in Amish households today. Lincoln characterized mudsill theory as a distortion of human nature, cynical and self-serving in its central contention that:

> Nobody labors, unless someone else, owning capital, by the use of that capital,
> induces him to it. Having assumed this, they proceed to consider whether it is
> best that capital shall *hire* laborers, and thus induce them to work by their own

---

[1] By "community" Brownson meant a confederation of individual families who knew one another; he would have been outraged by a federation of welfare agencies masquerading as a human settlement, as described in Hillary Clinton's *It Takes A Village*, in which the village in question is suspiciously devoid of butcher, baker, and candlestick maker joining their voices in deciding child-care policies.

consent; or *buy* them, and drive them to it without their consent. Having proceeded so far, they naturally conclude that *all* laborers are necessarily either *hired* laborers, or *slaves*. They further assume that whoever is once a hired laborer is fatally fixed in the condition for life, and thence again that his condition is as bad as or worse than that of a slave. This is the mudsill theory.

This notion was contradicted, said Lincoln, by an inconvenient fact: a large majority in the free states were "neither hirers nor hired," and wage labor served only as a temporary condition leading to small proprietorship. This was Abraham Lincoln's perception of the matter. Even more important, it was his *affirmation*. He testified to the rightness of this policy as a national mission, and the evidence that he thought himself onto something important was that he repeated this mudsill analysis in his first State of the Union speech to Congress in December, 1861.

Here in the twenty-first century it hardly seems possible, this conceit of Lincoln's. Yet there is the baffling example of the Amish experiment, its families holding nearly universal proprietorship in farms or small enterprises, a fact which looms larger and larger in my own thinking about schools, school curricula, and the national mission of pedagogy as I grow old. That Amish prosperity wasn't handed to them but achieved in the face of daunting odds, against active enmity from the states of Pennsylvania, Wisconsin, Ohio, and elsewhere, and hordes of government agencies seeking to de-Amish them. That the Amish have survived and prevailed against high odds puts a base of realistic possibility under Lincoln and Brownson's small-market perspective as the proper goal for schooling. An anti-mudsill curriculum once again, one worthy of another civil war if need be.

It takes no great intellect to see that such a curriculum taught in today's economic environment would directly attack the dominant economy. Not intentionally, but lack of malice would be poor compensation for those whose businesses would inevitably wither and die as the idea spread. How many micro-breweries would it take to ruin Budweiser? How many solar cells and methane-gas home generators to bring Exxon to its knees? This is one reason, I think, that many alternative school ideas which work, and are cheap and easy to administer, fizzle rather than catching fire in the public imagination. The incentive to support projects wholeheartedly when they would incidentally eliminate your livelihood, or indeed eliminate the familiar society and relationships you hold dear, just isn't there. Nor is it easy to see how it could ever be.

Why would anyone who makes a living selling goods or services be enthusiastic about schools that teach "less is more"? Or teach that television, even PBS, alters the mind for the worse? When I see the dense concentration of big business names associated with school reform I get a little crazy, not because they are bad people—most are no worse than you are or I—but because humanity's best interests and corporate interests cannot really ever be a good fit except by accident.

The souls of free and independent men and women is mutilated by the *necessary* soullessness of corporate organization and decision-making. Think of cigarettes as a classic case in point. The truth is that even if all corporate production were pure and faultless, it is still an excess of *organization*—where the few make decisions for the many—that is choking us to death. Strength, joy, wisdom are only available to those who *produce* their own lives; never to those who merely *consume* the production of others. Nothing good can come from inviting global corporations to design our schools, any more than leaving a hungry dog to guard ham sandwiches is a good way to protect lunch.

All training except the most basic either secures or disestablishes things as they are. The familiar government school curriculum represents enshrined mudsill theory telling us people would do nothing if they weren't tricked, bribed, or intimidated, proving scientifically that labor is for the most part biologically incompetent, strung out along a bell curve. Mudsill theory has become institutionalized with buzzers, routines, standardized assessments, and terminal rankings interleaved with an interminable presentation of carrots and sticks, the positive and negative reinforcement schedules of behavioral psychology, screening children for a corporate order.

Mudsillism is deeply ingrained in the whole work/school/media constellation. Getting rid of it will be a devilish task with no painless transition formula. This is going to hurt when it happens. And it will happen. The current order is too far off the track of human nature, too dis-spirited, to survive. Any economy in which the most common tasks are the shuffling of paper, the punching of buttons, and the running of mouths isn't an order into which we should be pushing kids as if such jobs there were the avenue to a good life.

At the heart of any school reforms that aren't simply tuning the mudsill mechanism lie two beliefs: 1) That talent, intelligence, grace, and high accomplishment are within the reach of every kid, and 2) That we are better off working for ourselves than for a boss.[2] But how on earth can you believe these things in the face of a century of institution-shaping/economy-shaping/ monopoly schooling which claims something different? Or in the face of a constant stream of media menace that jobs are vanishing, that the workplace demands more regulation and discipline, that "foreign competition" will bury us if we don't comply with expert prescriptions in the years ahead? One powerful antidote to such propaganda comes from looking at evidence which contradicts official propaganda—like women who earn as much as doctors by selling shrimp from old white trucks parked beside the road, or 13-year-old boys who don't have time to waste in school because they expect to be independent businessmen before most kids are out of college. Meet Stanley:

I once had a 13-year-old Greek boy named Stanley who only came to school one day a month and got away with it because I was his home room teacher and doctored the records. I did it because Stanley explained to me where he spent the time instead. It seems Stanley had five aunts and uncles, all in business for themselves before they were 21. A florist, an unfinished furniture builder, a delicatessen owner, a small restaurateur, and a delivery service operator. Stanley was passed from store to store doing free labor in exchange for opportunity to learn the business. "This way I decide which business I like well enough to set up for myself," he told me. "You tell me what books to read and I'll read them, but I don't have time to waste in school unless I want to end up like the rest of these people, working for somebody else." After I heard that I couldn't in good conscience keep him locked up. Could you? If you say yes, tell me why.

---

[2] The *Boston Globe* for September 8, 1999 carried this dismal information: if all the households in the U.S. are divided into five equal fractions, and the household incomes in each fifth averaged together, the economic classes of the country look like this compared to one another: the bottom fifth earns $8,800 a year, the second fifth $20,000 a year, the third fifth $31,400 a year, and the fourth fifth $45,100 a year. The balance of the fruits of our managed society have been reserved for the upper 20 percent of its households, and even there the lion's share drops on the plate of a relatively small fraction of the fat cats. This is the structure our pyramidal, *centrally* controlled corporate economy has imposed after a century in close partnership with government and its schools.

Look at those 150,000 Old Order Amish in 22 states and several foreign countries: nearly crime-free, prosperous, employed almost totally at independent livelihoods; proprietors with only a five percent rate of failure compared to 85 percent for businesses in non-Amish hands. I hope that makes you think a little. Amish success isn't even *possible* according to mudsill theory. They couldn't have happened and yet they did. While they are still around they give the lie to everything you think you know about the inevitability of anything. Focus on the Amish the next time you hear some jerk say your children better shape up and toe the corporate line if they hope to be among the lucky survivors in the coming world economy. Why do they need to be hired hands at all, you should ask yourself. Indeed, why do you?

Autonomous Technology

The simple truth is there is no way to control this massive corporate/school thing from the human end. It has to be broken up. It has become a piece of autonomous technology. Its leadership is bankrupt in ideas. Merchants are merchants, not moral leaders or political ones. It surely is a sign of retrogression, not advance, that we have forgotten what the world's peoples knew forever. A merchant has the same right to offer his opinion as I do, but it makes little sense for people who buy and sell soap and cigarettes to tell you how to raise your kid or what to believe in. No more sense than it does for a *pedagogue* to do the same. How would a huckster who pushes toothpaste, a joker who vends cigarettes, or a video dream peddler know anything about leading nations or raising children correctly? Are these to be the Washingtons, Jacksons, and Lincolns of the twenty-first century?

The timeless core of Western tradition, which only the cowardly and corrupt would wish to surrender, shows that we can't grow into the truth of our own nature without local traditions and values at the center of things. We do not do well as human beings in those abstract associations for material advantage favored by merchants called networks, or in megalithic systems, whether governmental, institutional, or corporate. Joseph Campbell put his finger on the heart of the matter:

> [It is] an Oriental model. One of the typical things of the Orient is that any criticism disqualifies you for the guru's instruction. Well in heaven's name, is that appropriate for a Western mind? It's simply a transferring of your submission to a childhood father onto a father for your adulthood. Which means you're not growing up.... *The thing about the guru in the West is that he represents an alien principle*, namely, that you don't follow your own path, you follow a given path. And that's totally contrary to the Western spirit! Our spirituality is of the individual quest, individual realization—authenticity in your own life out of your own center.
>
> *— An Open Life*

Mario Savio, the 1960s campus radical, stood once on the steps of Sproul Hall, Berkeley, and screamed:

> There is a time when the operation of the machine becomes so odious, makes you so sick at heart that you can't take part; you can't even passively take part,

and you've got to put your bodies upon the gears and upon the wheels, upon
the levers, upon all the apparatus and you've got to make it stop. And you've
got to indicate to the people who own it that unless you are free the machine
will be prevented from working at all.

Limiting the power of government to liberate the individual was the great American
revolutionary insight. Too much cooperation, avoiding conflict from ordinary people, these things
aren't acceptable in America although they may suit China, Indonesia, Britain, or Germany just fine.
In America the absence of conflict is a sign of regression toward a global mean, hardly progress by
our lights if you've seen much of the governance of the rest of the world where common people are
crushed like annoying insects if they argue.

Carl Schurz, the German immigrant, said upon seeing America for the first time in 1848,
"Here you can see how slightly a people needs to be governed." What it will take to break
collectively out of this trap is a change in the nature of forced schooling, one which alters the balance
of power between societies and systems in favor of societies again. We need once more to debate
angrily the *purpose* of public education. The power of elites to set the agenda for public schooling
has to be challenged, an agenda which includes totalitarian labeling of the ordinary population,
unwarranted official prerogatives, and near total control of work. Until such a change happens, we
need to individually withhold excessive allegiance from any and all forms of abstract, remotely
displaced, political and economic leadership; we need to trust ourselves and our children to remake
the future locally, demand that intellectual and character development once again be the mission of
schools; we need to smash the government monopoly over the upbringing of our young by forcing
it to compete for funds whose commitments should rest largely on the judgment of parents and local
associations. Where argument, court action, foot-dragging, and polite subversion can't derail this
judgment then we must find the courage to be saboteurs, as the *maquis* did in occupied France during
WWII.

It isn't difficult, someone once said, to imagine young Bill Clinton sitting at the feet of his
favorite old professor, Dr. Carroll Quigley of Georgetown. As Quigley approached death, he came
back to Georgetown one last time in 1976 to deliver the Oscar Iden Lecture Series. The Quigley of
the Iden lectures said many things which anticipate the argument of my own book. His words often
turn to the modern predicament, the sense of impending doom many of us feel:

> The fundamental, all-pervasive cause of world instability is the destruction of
> communities by the commercialization of all human relationships and the resultant
> neuroses and psychoses. Another cause of instability is that the world is dominated
> by elements of sovereignty outside the structure of the state. Banks and corporations
> are free of political controls and social responsibility, and they have largely
> monopolized power in Western civilization and in American society. They are
> ruthlessly going forward to eliminate land, labor, entrepreneurial-managerial skills,
> and everything else economists once told us were the chief elements of production.
> The only element they are concerned with is the one they can control: capital.

Quigley alludes to a startling ultimate solution to our problems with school and with much else in
our now state-obsessed lives, a drawing of critical awareness:

Out of the Dark Age that followed the collapse of the Carolingian Empire came the most magnificent thing...*the recognition that people can have a society without having a state*. In other words, this experience wiped out the assumption that is found throughout Classical Antiquity, except among unorthodox and heretical thinkers, that the state and the society are identical, and therefore you can desire nothing more than to be a citizen. [Emphasis mine]

A society without a state. If the only value hard reading had was to be able to tune in on minds like Quigley's, minds free of fetters, sharp axes with which to strike off chains, that alone would be reason enough to put such reading at the heart of a new kind of schooling which might strongly resemble the education America offered 150 years ago—a movement to ennoble common people, freeing them from the clutches of masters, experts, and those terrifying true believers whose eyes gleam in the dark. Quigley thought such a transformation was inevitable:

Now I come to my last statement. I'm not personally pessimistic. The final result will be that the American people will ultimately opt out of the system. Today everything is a bureaucratic structure, and brainwashed people who are not personalities are trained to fit into this bureaucratic structure and say it is a great life—although I would assume that many on their death beds must feel otherwise.

The process of copping out will take a long time, but notice: we are already copping out of military service on a wholesale basis; we are already copping out of voting on a large scale basis.... People are also copping out by refusing to pay any attention to newspapers or to what's going on in the world, and by increasing emphasis on the growth of localism, what is happening in their own neighborhoods....When Rome fell, the Christian answer was, "Create our own communities."

We shall do that again. When we want better families, better neighbors, better friends, and better schools we shall turn our backs on national and global systems, on expert experts and specialist specialties and begin to make our own schools one by one, far from the reach of systems.

Did you know that Lear of LearJet fame was a dropout? Pierre Cardin, Liz Claiborne, the founder of McDonald's, the founder of Wendy's, Ben Franklin, one in every fifteen American millionaires?

The Bell Curve

We still have to face the propaganda barrier set up by statistical psychology—I mean the scam which demonstrates *mathematically* that most people don't have the stuff to do it. This is the rocket driving School at breakneck speed across the barren land it traverses as a mobile hospital for the detritus of evolution. Could it be that all the pedagogical scientists have gotten it wrong? Are ordinary people better than they think?

I found a telling clue in Charles Murray's bestseller, *The Bell Curve*, at the spot when Murray pauses to politely denounce black schoolteacher Marva Collins' fantastic claim that ghetto black children had real enthusiasm for difficult intellectual work. Oddly enough that was exactly my own experience as a white schoolteacher with black 13-year-olds from Harlem. I was curious why Dr. Murray or Dr. Herrnstein, or both became so exercised, since Marva Collins otherwise doesn't figure in the book. So certain were the authors, that Collins *couldn't* be telling the truth, that they dismissed her data *while admitting they hadn't examined* the situation firsthand. That is contempt of a very high order, however decorously phrased.

The anomaly struck me even as I lay in the idyllic setting of a beach on the northern coast of Oahu, watched over by sea turtles, where I had gone to do research for this book in America's most far-flung corporate colony, Hawaii. Bell curve theory has been around since Methuselah under different names, just as theories of multiple intelligence have, why get out of sorts because a woman of color argued from her practice a dissent? Finally the light went on: bell curve mudsill theory loses its credibility if Marva Collins is telling the truth. Trillions of dollars and the whole social order are at stake. Marva Collins has to be lying.

Is Marva telling the truth?

Thirty years of public school teaching whisper to me that she is.

George Meegan

George Meegan was 25 years old and an elementary school dropout, a British merchant seaman when he decided to take the longest walk in human history, without any special equipment, foundation bankroll or backing of any kind. Leaving his ship in South America he made his way to Tierra del Fuego alone and just began to walk. Seven years later after crossing the Andes, making his way through the trackless Darien Gap, and after taking a long detour on foot to see Washington, D.C., he arrived at the Arctic Ocean with a wife he met and married along the way, and their two children. In that instant, part of the high academic story of human migrations received its death blow from a dropout. His book was published in 1892.

Necking In The Guardhouse

About an hour out of Philadelphia there was once (and may still be) a large U.S. Air Force base from which officers being sent overseas to Germany, Crete, and elsewhere, were transshipped like California cabbages. During the early 1980s I drove a relative there, a freshly minted lieutenant, late on the night before she flew to Europe for her first assignment and the first real job of her life. She was young, tense, bursting with Air Force protocols. Who could blame her for taking the rulebook as the final authority?

By happenstance I took a civilian highway outside the eastern perimeter of the base when her billet was on the western side. Irritated, I checked a map and discovered to my disgust that the only public connection to the right road on the far side of the base (where the motel sat) was miles away. It was late, I was tired. To make matters worse, I knew this prim young lady would need to be sharp in the morning so guilt prodded me. There was just one way to avoid the long detour and that was to take the military road through the center of the base leading directly to where we wanted to be. Well then, we would take it! But the lieutenant was aghast. It was not possible. I wasn't authorized, had no tag, had no permit, had no rank. No! No! Not permitted! *Listen to me, Uncle Jack, the young woman demanded, security is maniacal on SAC bases; we will have to take the long way around.* What she said was perfectly reasonable, but quite wrong.

One of the genuine advantages of living as long as I have is that you eventually come to see the gaps between man-made systems and human reality. Even in a perfect system, functions must be assigned to *people*, and people find a way to sabotage their system functions even if they don't want to. Systems violate some profound inner equilibrium, call it the soul if you like. Systems are inhuman, people are not.

On the principle nothing ventured, nothing gained, I drove toward the guard post sitting astride the transverse road, all the while listening to my passenger, increasingly nervous, shrilly informing me there was "No way" I would be "allowed" to pass. "And don't play games," she further told me ominously, "MP's have instructions to shoot people acting suspiciously."

We pulled up to the guard booth. No one was in sight so I proceeded down the transverse like a justified sinner smiling, but the lieutenant beside me was so agitated, I stopped and I backed up quite a long way to the lighted hut again and blew the horn. This time a guard emerged, his tie askew, lipstick all over his face. Before he could fully collect himself I shouted out the window, "Okay if I drive through to the motel? The lieutenant here is leaving for Germany tomorrow. I'd like to get her to bed."

"Sure, go ahead," he waved and went back to whatever paramilitary pursuit he was engaged in, repopulating the world or whatever. The temptation to gloat over my officious kinswoman was strong but I fought it down in light of her tender age.

Just outside the far gate across the base was the ghastly two-story cinder-block motel, a type favored by military personnel in transit, where a reservation waited in the young woman's name. As we pulled into the front parking lot a terrible sight greeted my young relative, a sight that reminded me of nothing so much as Monongahela on a bad Saturday night around New Year's Eve. At least two dozen men, some half in uniform, some bare-chested and bloody, were fistfighting all over the first floor walkway and on the little balcony that paralleled the second floor. Dozens more watched, hooting and howling, beer cans in hand. Grunts and the sounds of fists smacking heads and bodies filled the air. They were all enlisted men, apparently indifferent to official disapproval, for all the world as if they had been Chechens or Hmong instead of obedient American soldiers.

At first I couldn't believe my eyes. The combat clearly had been raging for awhile, but no Air Force or local police had moved to stop it. Suddenly to my dismay, from the new officer's uniform beside me with a girl inside came something like these words: "*I'll stop this, let me out of the car. When they see an officer's uniform they'll take off running.*"

"Don't do it," I begged. "They *should* take off running but what if they don't? What if that pack of fighting drunks goes for *you* because they like to fight and thinks it's none of your business? Why don't we just find another place for you to sleep? You've got a plane to Germany in the morning. Let's keep our eye on the ball." Driving to another motel, I said cautiously, "You know, what they write in rule books and how things really work are never the same. We all learn that as we get older." She was too angry to hear, I think.

It's fairly clear to me by now that we engage in our endless foreign adventures, bombing tiny islands and vast deserts, and our reckless social experimentation, too, patenting human genes, forcing kids to be dumb, because our leadership classes are worn out from the long strain of organizing everything over the centuries. Our leadership has degenerated dramatically, just as British leadership did after Ladysmith, Kimberley, and Mafeking. Recently I read of an American newsman who walked unchallenged into a nuclear weapons storage facility near Moscow watched over by a single guard without a weapon. It tends to make me skeptical about any orderly scientific future. Is it possible that those who sit atop the social bell curve represent the *worst* of evolution's products, not its best? Have the fools among us who just don't get it risen up and taken command?

Think of the valent symbols of our time: Coca-Cola, the Marlboro Man, disposable diapers, disposable children, Dolly, the cloned sheep, Verdun, Auschwitz, Hiroshima, the national highway system, My Lai, fiat money, the space program, Chernobyl, Waco, the Highway of Death, welfare, Bhopal, hordes of homeless, psychopathic kids filling the corridors of the schools put out of sight and mind until their morale is deteriorated; think of Princess Di and the Ponzi scheme we call Social Security, the invasion of Grenada, the naval blockade of Haiti. The *naval blockade* of Haiti??! Is any of this real? Ordinary people who walk the dogs and kiss the grandchildren are all so tired of grandiose schemes and restless utopians I doubt if too many would really care if the planet exploded tomorrow.

Think of the never-ending stream of manufactured crises like the bombings of Panama or the cremation of Iraq, principal products of a spent leadership trying to buy itself time while the grail search for a destiny worth having goes on in laboratories and conference rooms instead of in homes and villages where it belongs. Did the people who arrange this sorry soap opera ever take note how green the world really is, how worthwhile the minds and hearts of average men and women, how particular the hue of each blade of grass? It's the terrible *idleness* of the social engineering classes that drives them mad, I think. They have nothing worthwhile to do. So they do us.

Tania Aebi

Tania Aebi was a 17-year-old New York City school dropout bicycle messenger in 1987 when she decided to become the first known woman to sail around the world alone. She had a 26-foot boat and no nautical tradition when she set out. She admits to cheating on her Coast Guard navigation exam. In a hurricane off Bermuda, generator gone, her life in peril, she taught herself navigation in a hurry by flashlight and made port. Two years later her record-making circuit of Planet Earth was complete.

A Fool's Bargain

A recent analysis of American diet by the Harvard school of public health disclosed the curious fact that the extremely poor eat healthier diets than upper-middle class Americans. If that doesn't break you up, consider the lesson of the 232-year-old aristocratic merchant bank of Barings, destroyed in the wink of an eye through the wild speculations of an executive who turned out to have been the son of a plasterer bereft of any college degree! The poor man's schemes were too impenetrable for company management to understand, but they needed his vitality badly so they were afraid to challenge his decisions.

"They never dared ask any basic questions," said the young felon who gambled away $1.3 billion on parlays so fanciful you might think only a rube would attempt them. "They were afraid of looking stupid about not understanding futures and options. They knew nothing at all." *Quis custodiet ipsos custodes?*

You can't help but smile at the justice of it. Having procured a Leviathan state finally, its architects and their children seem certain to be flattened by it, too, soon after the rest of us become linoleum. No walled or gated compound is safe from the whirring systems rationalizing everything, squeezing children of social engineers just as readily as yours and mine. "They knew nothing," said the criminal. Nothing. That's the feeling I frequently got while tracking the leaders of American schooling at every stage of the game while they mutilated their own lives as fantastically as they did the lives of others. All that sneaking, scheming, plotting, lying. It ruined the grand designers as it ruined their victims. The Big Schoolhouse testifies more to the folly of human arrogance, what the Greeks called *hubris*, than anything else.

So many of the builders of School were churchmen or the sons of churchmen. We need to grasp the irony that they ruined the churches as well, the official churches anyway. That probably explains the mighty religious hunger loose in the land as I write; having slipped the bonds of establishment churches as it became clear those vassal bodies were only sub-systems of something quite unholy, the drive to contemplate things beyond the reach of technology or accountants is far from extinct as the social engineers thought it was going to be. Such an important part of the mystery of coal-nation schooling is locked up in the assassination of religion and the attempted conversion of its principles of faith into serviceable secular wisdom and 12-step programs, that we will never understand our failure with schools if we become impatient when religion is discussed because School is the civil religion meant to replace Faith.

American Protestantism, once our national genius, left its pulpit behind, began to barter and trade in the marketplace, refashioning God and gospel to sustain a social service vision of life; in doing so it ruined itself while betraying us all, Protestants and non-Protestants alike. A legacy of this is the fiefdom of Hawaii, saddest American territory of all, an occupied nation we pretend is an American state, its land area and economy owned to an astonishing degree by the descendants of a few missionary families, managed by government agencies. The original population has been wiped away. Under the veneer of a vacation paradise, which wears thin almost at once, one finds the saddest congregations on earth, parishioners held prisoner by barren ministers without any rejuvenating sermons to preach. Hawaiian society is the Chautauqua forced schooling aims toward.

The privileges of leadership shouldn't rest on the shaky foundation of wealth, property and armed guards but on the allegiance, respect, and love of those led. Leadership involves providing some purpose for getting out of bed in the morning, some reason to lay about with the claymore or drop seeds in the dirt. Wealth is a fair trade to grant to leaders in exchange for a purpose but the leader's end of the bargain must be kept. In the United States the pledge has been broken, the break flaunted for an entire century through the mass schooling institution.

Here is the crux of the dilemma: *modern schooling has no lasting value to exchange for the spectacular chunk of living time it wastes or the possibilities it destroys*. The kids know it, their parents know it, you know it, I know it, and the folks who administer the medicine know it. School is a fool's bargain, we are fools for accepting its dry beans in exchange for our children.

Roland Legiardi-Laura

In 1966 I taught the novel Moby Dick, film theory, and versification to a 13-year-old kid named Roland Legiardi-Laura. Both his parents died shortly afterwards, leaving him orphaned and nearly penniless. Roland was memorable in many ways, but two I remember best were him reeking *of garlic at nine in the morning, every morning, and his determination never to work at a "job" but to be a poet. Twenty years later, while living on a shoestring, he organized a mobile band of poet-terrorists who raced around the state in a candy-striped truck, delivering poetry spontaneously in bars and on street corners; shortly afterwards, while living in a building without secure stairs or an intact roof, he flew to Nicaragua where poetry is the national sport and convinced the government to allow him to make a poetry documentary. When I advanced him $50 out of the 300 grand he would need I told him he was nuts. But somehow he raised the money, made the film, and won nine international film awards. Meanwhile he had learned to support himself doing carpentry and odd jobs, the oddest of which was to help to rehabilitate a shambles of a slum building near Hell's Angels headquarters in lower Manhattan and convert it into a poetry nightclub. Who would go to a poetry nightclub? It turns out a lot of people, and as the Nuyorican Poet's Cafe expanded to include Roland's unique creation, a live reading of original film scripts using top professional actors, I saw the unfolding of a life useful to thousands of fellow human beings, full of distinction, thoroughly "scholarly," which would simply not have been possible, or even foreseeable, to a government school-to-work project.*

The Squeeze

Of course when you cheat people good you start to worry about your victims getting even. David Gordon's 1996 book *Fat and Mean*: *The Corporate Squeeze of Working Americans and the Myth of Managerial Downsizing*, catches the spirit of the national guilty conscience this way:

> Can't trust your workers when left to their own devices? Peer over their shoulders. Watch behind their backs. Record their movements. Monitor them. Supervise them. Boss them. Above all else, don't leave them alone. As one recent study observed, "American companies tend, fundamentally, to mistrust workers, whether they are salaried employees or blue collar workers."

And American schools tend, fundamentally, to mistrust students. One way to deal with danger from the middle and bottom of the evolutionary order is to buy off the people's natural leaders, to deal Zapata in for his share. We've seen this principle as it downloaded into "gifted and talented" classrooms from the lofty abstractions of Pareto and Mosca, now it's time to regard those de-fanged "gifted" children grown up, waiting at the trough like the others. What do they in their turn have to teach anyone?

David Gordon says 13 percent of U.S. non-farm workers are managerial and administrative. That's one boss for every seven and a half workers! And the percentage of non-teaching school personnel is twice that. Compare those numbers to a manager/worker ratio of 4.2 percent in Japan, 3.9 percent in Germany, 2.6 percent in Sweden. Since 1947, when the employment-hierarchy egg laid during the American Civil War finally hatched after incubating for a century, the number of managers and supervisors in America has exploded 360 percent (if only *titled* ones are counted) and at least twice that if de facto administrators—like teachers without teaching programs—are added in. All this entails a massive income shift from men and women who produce things to managers and supervisors who do not.

What does this add up to in human terms? Well, for one thing, if our managerial burden was held to the Japanese ratio, somewhere in the neighborhood of 20 million production level jobs could be paid for. That would mean the end of unemployment. Totally. An economy arranged as ours is could not tolerate such a condition, I understand. Let me disabuse you next of any silly notion the pain of downsizing is being spread out by an even-handed political management, touching comfortable and hard-pressed alike. While it is true, as James Fallows says, that the media pay disproportionate attention to downsizing toward the top rungs of the occupational hierarchy, the sobering facts are these: from 1991 to 1996 the percentage of *managers* among non-farm employees *rose* about 12 percent. For each fat cat kicked off the gravy train, 1.12 new ones climbed aboard. All this is evidence not of generosity, I think, but of a growing fear of ordinary people.

Is this all just more of the same scare talk you've heard until you're sick of it? I don't know; what do you make of these figures? From 1790 until 1930 America incarcerated 50 people for every 100,000 in the population; for 140 years the ratio held steady. Then suddenly the figure doubled between 1930 and 1940. The Depression, you say? Maybe, but there had been depressions before, and anyway by 1960 it doubled again to 200 per 100,000. The shock of WWII could have caused that, but there had been wars before. Between 1960 and 1970 the figure jogged higher once again to 300 per 100,000. And 400 per 100,000 by 1980. And near 500 per 100,000 where it hovers at the new century's beginning.

Has this escalation anything to do in a family way with the odd remark attributed to Marine Major Craig Tucker of Ft. Leavenworth's Battle Command Training Program by a national magazine that "a time may come when the military may have to go domestic"? I guess that's what he was taught at Ft. Leavenworth.

Wendy Zeigler/Amy Halpern

How would pedagogical theory explain Wendy Zeigler, my prize student out of Roland's class at 13 but fairly anonymous (as most of us are) ever after, springing into action in her fifth decade, converting her flat in the funky Bernal Heights section of San Francisco to the day school code through her own labor, and suddenly opening a magnificently creative place for kids, 2½ to 6, called "Wendy Z's Room to Grow" which did land-office business from the first. How would it explain Amy Halpern devoting a substantial chunk of her life to fine-tuning a personal film, "Falling Lessons," which she knew in advance would never earn a penny and might not even be shown? What drives an artist like Amy to strive for an uncommercial masterpiece? We have no business imposing a simplistic template on the human spirit. That makes a mockery of Smith's brilliant free market.

A Magnificent Memory

When I get most gloomy about this I summon up a picture of a noble British general with powdered hair and pipe-clay leggings sitting astride a white stallion directing troop movements across the green river Monongahela, his brilliant columns all in red stretching far behind him. "The most magnificent sight I ever saw," said George Washington many years later when he remembered it. Who could blame all those ordinary men for betting their lives on an invincible military machine, all glittering and disciplined? All they had to do was to ride down naked American savages from the stone age; all they had to do was take their orders and obey them.

General Braddock and British tradition dictated common soldiers should be treated like dumb children, as a tough, unsentimental shepherd treats sheep. It isn't even very hard to imagine these lowly soldiers so well gotten up feeling proud to submerge their little destinies in the awesome collective will of the British empire.

But as things turned out, a day of reckoning was at hand for the empire. Exposed in full pretension, the collapse of the British expedition under Braddock sent a shock of wild surmise through the minds of other common men in the colonies and their leaders. If Braddock didn't know what *he* was doing, was it possible German King George back in London could be taken, too?

Prince Charles Visits Steel Valley High

An important counter-revolutionary event with a bearing on the changes going on in our schools happened quietly not so long ago just a stone's throw from where Braddock fell. Bill Serrin tells of it in his book *Homestead*. By 1988 the Monongahela valley had been stripped bare of its mines and mills by Pittsburgh financial interests and their hired experts who had no place in profit/loss equations for people and communities, whatever rhetoric said to the contrary.

As a consequence, Monongahela, Charleroi, Donora, Homestead, Monessen, all were dying, places that had "been on fire once, had possessed vibrancy and life." Now they were falling into the aimless emptiness of the unemployed after a century as the world's steelmakers. Not idle of their own choice, not even unproductive—the mills still made a profit—yet not a profit large enough to please important financial interests.

In the bleak winter of 1988 Charles of the blood royal came to visit Steel Valley High in Homestead nominally to talk about turning dead steel mills into *arboretums*. Why Charles? He was "the world's leading architecture buff," so why not? His Highness' fleet of two dozen Chinese red Jaguars crossed the Homestead High Bridge only minutes from the spot where Braddock died on the Monongahela. Perhaps the Prince had been informed of this, perhaps he was making a statement for history.

In a motorcade of scarlet he roared over the bridge. Residents who had gathered to wave at the prince and his entourage "saw only a whir of scarlet as he whizzed into Homestead." Charles was too preoccupied with his own agenda to wave back at the offspring of Europe's industrial proletariat, thrice removed. Victory as always comes to those who abide. We had only one Washington, only one Jackson, only one Lincoln to lead us against the Imperial Mind. After they were gone only the people remembered what America was about.

Serrin writes, "A handful of activist ministers gathered along Charles' way holding tomatoes, and police Chief Kelley assumed, not without reason, they were going to throw them at the prince. Or in Monongahela vernacular, 'tomato him.' " The motive for this bad hospitality was a growing anger at the text of the prince's speech to a group of architects assembled in Pittsburgh for a "Remaking Cities Conference." The conference had been co-sponsored by the Royal Institute of British Architects. Andrew Carnegie's dream of reuniting with the mother country was coming true in the very town Carnegie's name was most associated with. The British have a grand sense of history, they do.

The assembled architects had been studying the settlements of my valley and recommending replacement uses for its mills. They proposed conversion of empty steel plants into exhibition halls for flower shows. At the public hearing, valley residents shouted, "*We don't want flowers, we want jobs. We want the valley back. This was the steel center of the world.*" Prince Charles spoke to the crowd as one might speak to children, just as he might have spoken had Braddock *won* and the Revolution never taken place. The upshot was a grand coalition of elites formed to revitalize the valley. I see a parallel in the formation of the New American Schools Committee, whose 18 members counted 15 corporate CEOs including the R.J. Reynolds Tobacco Company's descendent form, RJR Nabisco, announcing revitalization of our schools.

The effort to save Homestead looked like this through the eyes of *New York Times* labor reporter Bill Serrin:

> In its tragedy Homestead became fashionable.... Homestead was the rage. There
> were study groups and committees, historical exhibits, film proposals, lectures,
> brown-bag lunches, dinners, economic analyses, historical surveys, oral histories,
> a case study of disinvestment and redevelopment plans in the Monongahela
> Valley done by the Harvard Business School, architects, city planners, historians,
> economists, anthropologists, sociologists, social workers, foundation experts—all
> these and others became involved.

An echo of the great transformational days when we got factory schooling, the same buzz and hubbub, fashionable people with their shirt sleeves metaphorically rolled up. Then suddenly the attention was over. All the paraphernalia of concern resulted in:

> Little effort on Homestead or the other steel towns. There never was a plan to
> redevelop Homestead. The goal had been to ensure there were no more protests
> like the ones earlier in the decade. If there was a master plan it was death and
> highways. Homestead would be gone. A highway through the valley would
> eliminate even the houses, perhaps obliterate Homestead and the other steel
> towns. One more thing...the training programs. They were bullshit.

So here we are. In order to clean the social canvas, a reduction in the maximum levels of maturity to be allowed grown men and women has been ordered from somewhere. We are to be made and kept as nervous, whining adolescents. This is a job best begun and ended while we are little children, hence the kind of schools we have—a governor put on our growth through which we are denied the understandings needed to escape childhood. Don't blame schools. Schools only follow orders. Schoolmen are as grateful as grenadiers to wear a pretty paycheck and be part of Braddock's invincible army. Theirs not to reason why...if they know what's good for them.

Empty Children

Not far to go now. Here is my recipe for empty children. If you want to cook whole children, as I suspect we all do, just contradict these stages in the formula:

1.   Remove children from the business of the world until time has passed for them to learn how to self-teach.

2.   Age-grade them so that past and future both are muted and become irrelevant.

3.   Take all religion out of their lives except the hidden civil religion of appetite, and positive/negative reinforcement schedules.

4.   Remove all significant functions from home and family life except its role as dormitory and casual companionship. Make parents unpaid agents of the state, recruit them into partnerships to monitor the conformity of children to an official agenda.

5.   Keep children under surveillance every minute from dawn to dusk. Give no private space or time. Fill time with collective activities. Record behavior quantitatively.

6.   Addict the young to machinery and electronic displays. Teach that these are desirable to recreation and learning both.

7.   Use designed games and commercial entertainments to teach preplanned habits, attitudes and language usages.

8.   Pair the selling of merchandise with attractive females in their prime childbearing years so that the valences of lovemaking and mothering can be transferred intact to the goods vended.

9.   Remove as much private ritual as possible from young lives, such as the rituals of food preparation and family dining.

10.   Keep both parents employed with the business of strangers. Discourage independent livelihoods with low start-up costs. Make labor for others and outside obligations first priority; self-development second.

11.   Grade, evaluate, and assess children constantly and publicly. Begin early. Make sure everyone knows his or her rank.

12.   Honor the highly graded. Keep grading and real world accomplishment as strictly separated as possible so that a false meritocracy, dependent on the support of authority to continue, is created. Push the most independent kids to the margin, do not tolerate real argument.

13.   Forbid the efficient transmission of useful knowledge, such as how to build a house, repair a car, make a dress.

14.   Reward dependency in many forms. Call it "teamwork."

15.   Establish visually degraded group environments called "schools" and arrange mass movements through these environments at regular intervals. Encourage a level of fluctuating noise (aperiodic negative reinforcement) so that concentration, habits of civil discourse, and intellectual investigation are gradually extinguished from the behavioral repertoire.

Schoolbooks

Until his death in an accident a few years ago, the president of Macmillan Publishing company, one of the largest school material suppliers in the world, was a third-grade dropout. He was also president of Berlitz Language Schools.

Almost The End

And so we arrive at the end of our journey together. You have seen the trap conceived, the trap built, the trap sprung, and its quarry turning in panic within until the bright light of living spirit goes dull behind its eyes and it grows indifferent to its banal fate in a comprehensively planned society and economy without any hope of escape. You have watched the trap grow like Arch Oboler's demonic chicken heart,[3] maintained by an army of behaviorally adjusted functionaries reproducing its own mechanistic encoding in the lives of schoolchildren. You have watched the listless creatures caught in the trap pressing a bar to get their food while they await instructions to their final meaningless destiny. How the trap was conceived hardly makes much difference at this point except to warn us we are not dealing with any ordinary mistake; this trap was intended to be as it is. It is a work of great human genius.

Mass schooling cannot be altered or reformed because any palliative from its killing religion will only be short-lived as long as the massification machinery it represents remains in place. That's why all the well-publicized "this-time-we-have-it-right" alternatives to factory schooling fizzle out a decade after launch. Most sooner.

Nothing in human history gives us any reason to be optimistic that powerful social machinery, *through its very existence*, doesn't lead to gross forms of oppression. If engines of mass control exist, the wrong hands will find the switches sooner or later. That's why standing armies like the enormous one we now maintain are an invitation to serfdom. They will always, sooner or later, go domestic. The more rationally engineered the machinery, the more certain its eventual corruption; that's a bitter pill rationalists still haven't learned to swallow.

We are, I think, at one of those great choice points in the human record where society gets to select from among widely divergent futures. It's customary to say there will be no turning back from our choice but that is wrong. It would be more accurate to say that we will not be able to turn

---

[3] My reference is to the greatest of the old "Lights Out" radio shows I heard long ago in Monongahela in which university scientists messing around with a chicken heart find a way to make it grow indefinitely, sort of like what schools are doing. It bursts from the laboratory and extends across the entire planet, suffocating every other living thing. The show is purportedly broadcast from an airplane flying over the global chicken heart until it runs out of fuel, crashes into the throbbing organ and is devoured with a giant sucking sound.

back from our next choice without a great and dreadful grief. It is best to heed the Amish counsel not to jump until you know where you're going to land.

Not jumping at this moment in time means rejecting further centralization of children in government schooling. It means rejecting every attempt to nationalize the religious enterprise of institutional schooling. If centralizers prevail, the connection between schooling and work will become total; if decentralizers prevail it will be diffuse, irregular, and for many kinds of work, utterly insignificant as it should be. Experts have consistently misdiagnosed and misdefined the problem of schooling. The problem is not that children don't learn to read, write, and do arithmetic well—the problem is that kids hardly learn at all the way schools insist on teaching. Schools desperately need a vision of their own purpose. It was never factually true that all young people learn to read or do arithmetic by being "taught" these things—though for many decades that has been the masquerade.

When children are stripped of a primary experience base as confinement schooling must do to justify its existence, the natural sequence of learning is destroyed, a sequence which puts experience first. Only much later, after a long bath in experience, does the thin gruel of abstraction *mean* very much. We haven't "forgotten" this, there is just no profit in remembering it for the businesses and people who make their bread and butter from monopoly schooling.

The relentless rationalization of the school world has left the modern student a prisoner of low-grade vocational activities. He lives in a disenchanted world without meaning. Our cultural dilemma here in the United States has little to do with children who don't read, it lies instead in finding a way to restore meaning and purpose to modern life. Any system of values that accepts the transformation of the world into machinery, and the construction of pens for the young called schools necessarily rejects this search for meaning.

Schools at present are the occupation of children; children have become employees, pensioners of the government at an early age. But government jobs are frequently not really jobs at all—that certainly is the case in the matter of being a schoolchild. There is nothing or very little to do in school, but one thing is demanded —that children must attend, condemned to hours of desperation, pretending to do a job that doesn't exist. At the end of the day, tired, fed up, full of aggression, their families feel the accumulated tedium of their pinched lives. Government jobs for children have broken the spirit of our people. They don't know their own history, nor would they care to.

In a short time such a system becomes addictive. Even when efforts are made to find real work for children to do, they often drift back to meaningless busywork. Anyone who has ever tried to lead students into generating lines of meaning in their own lives will have felt the resistance, the hostility even, with which broken children fight to be left alone. They prefer the illness they have become accustomed to. As the school day and year enlarges, students may be seen as people forbidden to leave their offices, as people hemmed in by an invisible fence, complaining but timid. Schools thus consume most of the people they incarcerate.

School curricula are like unwholesome economies. They don't deal in basic industries of mind, instead they try to be "popular," they deal in the light stuff in an effort to hold down rebellion. That's why we can't read Paine's *Common Sense* anymore, often can't read at all. Only one person in every sixteen, I'm told, reads more than one book a year after graduation from high school. Kids and teachers live day by day. That's all you *can* do when you have a runaway inflation of expectations fueled by false promissory notes on the future issued by teachers and television and other mythmakers in our culture. In the inflationary economy of mass schooling—with its "A's" and gold-stars and handshakes and trophies tied to nothing real—you cease to plan. You're just happy to make it to the weekend.

Once the inflation of dishonesty is perceived, the curriculum can only be imposed by intimidation, by a dizzapie of bells and horns, by confusion. With inflation of the school variety, a gun is held to your head by the state, demanding you acknowledge that school time is valuable, otherwise everyone would leave except the teachers who are being paid.

I Would Prefer Not To

What to do?

Take Melville's insight "I would prefer not to," from *Bartleby, the Scrivener* and make it your own watchword. Read Tolstoy's *Death of Ivan Ilych* for a shock of inspiration about what really matters. Breaking the hold of fear on your life is the necessary first step. If you can keep your kid out of any part of the school sequence at all, *keep him or her out of kindergarten*, then first, second, and maybe third grade. Home-school them at least that far through the zone where most of the damage is done. If you can manage that, they'll be OK.

Don't let a world of funny animals, dancing alphabet letters, pastel colors, and treacly music suffocate your little boy or girl's consciousness at exactly the moment when big questions about the world beckon. Funny animals were invented by North German social engineers; they knew something important about fantasy and social engineering that you should teach yourself.

Your four-year-old want to play? Let him help you cook dinner *for real*, fix the toilet, clean the house, build a wall, sing "Eine Feste Burg." Give her a map, a mirror, and a wristwatch, let her chart the world in which she really lives. You will be able to tell from the joy she displays that becoming strong and useful is the best play of all. Pure games are okay, too, but not day in, day out. Not a prison of games. There isn't a single *formula* for breaking out of the trap, only a general one you tailor to your own specifications.

No two escape routes are exactly alike, Stanley, my absentee pupil, found one. Two magnificent American teenagers, Tara Lipinski and Michelle Kwan, who enchanted the world with a display of physical artistry and mental discipline on ice skates in the Olympic games in Japan, found another. Neither went to school and both received wealth and prominence for their accomplishments. For me they show again what stories might be written out of ordinary lives if our time to learn wasn't so lavishly wasted. Are your children less than these?

At least nine major assumptions about the importance of government schooling need to be seen as false before you can get beyond the fog of ideology into the clear air of education. Here they are:

1) Universal government schooling is the essential force for social cohesion. There is no other way. A heavily bureaucratized public order is our defense against chaos and anarchy. Right, and if you don't wipe your bum properly the toilet monster will rise out of the bowl and get you.

2) The socialization of children in age-graded groups monitored by state agents is essential to learn to get along with others in a pluralistic society. The actual truth is that the rigid

compartmentalizations of schooling teach a crippling form of social relation: wait passively until you are told what to do, never judge your own work or confer with associates, have contempt for those younger than yourself and fear of those older. Behave according to the meaning assigned to your class label. These are the rules of a nuthouse. No wonder kids cry and become fretful after first grade.

3) Children from different backgrounds and from families with different beliefs must be mixed together. The unexamined inference here is that in this fashion they enlarge their understanding, but the actual management of classrooms everywhere makes only the most superficial obeisance to human difference—from the first a radical turn toward some unitarian golden mean is taken, along the way of which different backgrounds and different beliefs are subtly but steadily discredited.

4) The certified expertise of official schoolteachers is superior in its knowledge of children to the accomplishments of lay people, including parents. Protecting children from the uncertified is a compelling public concern. Actually, the enforced long-term segregation of children from the working world does them great damage, and the general body of men and women certified by the State as fit to teach is nearly the least fit occupational body in the entire economy if college performance is the standard.

5) Coercion in the name of education is a valid use of state power: compelling assemblies of children into specified groupings for prescribed intervals and sequences with appointed overseers does not interfere with academic learning. Were you born yesterday? Plato said, "Nothing of value to the individual happens by coercion."

6) Children will inevitably grow apart from their parents in belief, and this process must be encouraged by diluting parental influence and disabusing children of the idea their parents are sovereign in mind or morality. That prescription alone has been enough to cripple the American family. The effects of forced disloyalty on family are hideously destructive, removing the only certain support the growing spirit has to refer to. In place of family the school offers phantoms like "ambition," "advancement," and "fun," nightmare harbingers of the hollow life ahead.

7) An overriding concern of schooling is to protect children from bad parents. No wonder G. Stanley Hall, the father of school administration, invited Sigmund Freud to the United States in 1909—it was urgent business to establish a "scientific" basis upon which to justify the anti-family stance of State schooling, and the programmatic State in general.

8) It is not appropriate for any family to unduly concern itself with the education of its own children, although it is appropriate to sacrifice for the general education of everyone in the hands of state experts. This is the standard formula for all forms of socialism and the universal foundation of utopian promises.

9) The State is the proper parent and has predominant responsibility for training, morals, and beliefs. This is the *parens patriae* doctrine of Louis, King of France, a tale unsuited to a republic.

Nuts And Bolts

Let me end this book, my testament, with a warning: only the fresh air from millions upon millions of freely made choices will create the educational climate we need to realize a better destiny. No team of experts can possibly possess the wisdom to impose a successful solution to the problem inherent in a philosophy of centralized social management, solutions that endure are always local, always personal. Universal prescriptions are the problem of modern schooling.

If we closed all government schools, made free libraries universal, encouraged public discussion groups everywhere, sponsored apprenticeships for every young person who wanted one, let any person or group who asked to open a school do so—*without government oversight*—paid parents (if we have to pay anyone) to school their kids at home using the money we currently spend to confine them in school factories, and launched a national crash program in family revival and local economies, Amish and Mondragon style, the American school nightmare would recede.

That isn't going to happen, I know.

The next best thing, then, is to deconstruct forced schooling, minimizing its school aspect, indoctrination, and maximizing its potential to educate through access to tools, models, and mentors. To go down this path requires the courage to challenge deeply rooted assumptions. We need to kill the poison plant we created. School reform is not enough. The notion of schooling itself must be challenged. Do this as an individual if your group won't go along.

Here is a preliminary list of strategies to change the schools we have. I intend to develop the theme of change further in a future book, *How To Get An Education In Spite of School*, but I'm out of time and breath so the brief agenda which follows will have to suffice for the moment. As you read my ideas maintain a lively awareness of the implicit irony that to impose them as a counter system would require as dictatorial a central management as the current dismal reality. The trick then is not to impose them. My own belief based on long experience is that people given a degree of choice arrive without coercion at arrangements somewhat like these, and even improve upon them with ideas beyond my own imagination to conceive. Such is the genius of liberty:

Dismiss the army of reading and arithmetic specialists and the commercial empire they represent. Allow all contracts with colleges, publishers, consultants, and materials suppliers in these areas to lapse. Reading and arithmetic are easy things to learn, although nearly impossible to "teach." By the use of common sense, and proven methods that don't cost much, we can solve a problem which is artificially induced and wholly imaginary. Take the profit out of these things and the disease will cure itself.

Let no school exceed a few hundred in size. Even that's far too big. And make them local. End all unnecessary transportation of students at once; transportation is what the British used to do with hardened criminals. We don't need it, we need neighborhood schools. Time to shut the school factories, profitable to the building and maintenance industries and to bus companies, but disaster for children. Neighborhoods *need* their own children and vice versa; it's a reciprocating good, providing surprising service to both. The factory school doesn't work anywhere—not in Harlem and not in Hollywood Hills, either. Education is always individualized, and individualization requires absolute trust and split-second flexibility. This should save taxpayers a bundle, too.

Make everybody teach. Don't let anybody get paid for schooling kids without actually spending time with them. The industrial model, with pyramidal management and plenty of horizontal featherbedding niches, is based on ignorance of how things get done, or indifference to results. The administrative racket that gave New York City more administrators than all the nations of Europe combined in 1991 has got to die. It wastes billions, demoralizes teachers, parents, and students, and corrupts the common enterprise.

Measure performance with individualized instruments. Standardized tests, like schools themselves, have lost their moral legitimacy. They correlate with nothing of human value and their very existence perverts curriculum into a preparation for these extravagant rituals. Indeed, all paper and pencil tests are a waste of time, useless as predictors of anything important unless the competition is rigged. As a casual guide they are probably harmless, as a sorting tool they are corrupt and deceitful. A test of whether you can drive is driving. Performance testing is where genuine evaluation will always be found. There surely can't be a normal parent on Earth who doesn't judge his or her child's progress by performance.

Shut down district school boards. Families need control over the professionals in their lives. *Decentralize schooling down to the neighborhood school building level*, each school with its own citizen managing board. School corruption, like the national school milk price-rigging scandal of the 1990s, will cease when the temptations of bulk purchasing, job giveaways, and remote decision-making are ended.

Install permanent parent facilities in every school with appropriate equipment to allow parent partnerships with their own kids and others. Frequently take kids out of school to work with their own parents. School policies must deliberately aim to strengthen families.

Restore the primary experience base we stole from childhood by a slavish adherence to a utopian school diet of steady abstraction, or an equally slavish adherence to play as the exclusive obligation of children. Define primary experience as the essential core of early education, secondary data processing a supplement of substantial importance. But be sure the concepts of work, duty, obligation, loyalty, and service are strong components of the mix. Let them stand shoulder to shoulder with "fun." Let children engage in real tasks as Amish children do, not synthetic games and simulations that set them up for commercial variants of more-of-the-same for the rest of their lives.

Recognize that total schooling is psychologically and procedurally unsound. Wasteful and horrendously expensive. Give children some private time and space, some choice of subjects, methods, and associations, and freedom from constant surveillance. A strong element of volition, of choice, of anti-compulsion, is essential to education. That *doesn't* mean granting a license to do anything. Anyway, whatever is chosen as "curriculum," the vital assistance that old can grant young is to demand that personal second or third best will not do—the favor you can bestow on your children is to show by your own example that hard, painstaking work is the toll an independent spirit charges itself for self-respect. Our colleges work somewhat better than our other schools because they understand this better.

Admit there is no one right way to grow up successfully. One-system schooling has had a century and a half to prove itself. It is a ghastly failure. Children need the widest possible range of roads in order to find the right one to accommodate themselves. The premise upon which mass compulsion schooling is based is dead wrong. It tries to shoehorn every style, culture, and personality into one ugly boot that fits nobody. Tax credits, vouchers, and other more sophisticated means are necessary to encourage a diverse mix of different school logics of growing up. Only sharp competition can reform the present mess; this needs to be an overriding goal of public policy.

Neither national nor state government oversight is necessary to make a voucher/tax credit plan work: a modicum of local control, a disclosure law with teeth, and a policy of client satisfaction or else is all the citizen protection needed. It works for supermarkets and doctors. It will work for schools, too, without national testing.

Teach children to think dialectically so they can challenge the hidden assumptions of the world about them, including school assumptions, so they can eventually generate much of their own personal curriculum and oversight. But teach them, too, that dialectical thinking is unsuited to many important things like love and family. Dialectical analysis is radically inappropriate outside its purview.

Arrange much of schooling around complex themes instead of subjects. "Subjects" have a real value, too, but subject study as an exclusive diet was a Prussian secret weapon to produce social layerings. Substantial amounts of interdisciplinary work are needed as a corrective.

Force the school structure to provide flex-time, flex-space, flex-sequencing, and flex-content so that every study can be personalized to fit the whole range of individual styles and performance.

Break the teacher certification monopoly so anyone with something valuable to teach can teach it. Nothing is more important than this.

Our form of schooling has turned us into dependent, emotionally needy, excessively childish people who wait for a teacher to tell them what to do. Our national dilemma is that too many of us are now homeless and mindless in the deepest sense—at the mercy of strangers.

The beginning of answers will come only when people force government to return educational choice to everyone. But choice is meaningless without an absolute right to have progress monitored locally, too, not by an agency of the central government. Solzhenitsyn was right. The American founding documents didn't mention school because the authors foresaw the path school would inevitably set us upon, and rejected it.

The best way to start offering some choice *immediately* is to give each public school the independence that private schools have. De-systematize them, grant each private, parochial, and home school equal access to public funds through vouchers administered as a loan program, along with tax credits. In time the need for even this would diminish, but my warning stands—if these keys to choice are tied to intrusive government oversight, as some would argue they must be, they will only hasten the end of the American libertarian experiment. Vouchers are only a transition to what is really called for: an economy of independent livelihoods, a resurrection of principles over pragmatism, and restoration of the private obligation, self-imposed, to provide a living wage to all who work for you.

School can never deal with really important things. Only education can teach us that quests don't always work, that even worthy lives most often end in tragedy, that money can't prevent this; that failure is a regular part of the human condition; that you will never understand evil; that serious pursuits are almost always lonely; that you can't negotiate love; that money can't buy much that really matters; that happiness is free.

A 25-year-old school dropout walked the length of the planet without help, a 17-year-old school dropout worked a 26-foot sailboat all by herself around the girdle of the globe. What else does it take to realize the horrifying limitations we have inflicted on our children? School is a liar's world. Let us be done with it.

Epilogue

Only one nation refused to accept the psychology of submission. The Chechens never sought to please, to ingratiate themselves with the bosses; their attitude was always haughty and indeed openly hostile.... And here is the extraordinary thing—everyone was afraid of them. No one could stop them from living as they did. The regime which had ruled the land for thirty years could not force them to respect its laws.

> — Aleksandr Solzhenitsyn, *The Gulag Archipelago*

The history of the Hmong yields several lessons that anyone who deals with them might do well to remember. Among the most obvious are that the Hmong do not like to take orders; that they do not like to lose; that they would rather flee, fight, or die than surrender; that they are not intimidated by being outnumbered, that they are rarely persuaded that the customs of other cultures, even those more powerful than their own are superior; that they are capable of getting very angry....Those who have tried to defeat, deceive, govern, regulate, constrain, assimilate, or patronize the Hmong have, as a rule, disliked them intensely.

> — Anne Fadiman: *The Spirit Catches You and You Fall Down*

If they mean to have a war, let it begin here.

> — Captain John Parker, commanding the American militia against the British. Said at first light, Lexington, Massachusetts, April 19, 1775

I see two ghosts appear out of the mist on the morning river that runs into our green future, each wraith beckons me follow him down a different path. One I recognize by his arrogant bearing as the imperial spirit of Major General Edward Braddock calling all of us to follow him to the end of history just across the river.

Braddock is a bold man, proud, indifferent to fear. He has scorn for danger, because to him, all answers are already known; he demands to be our shepherd on this last regression to the royal destiny we escaped three lifetimes ago. If we go with him, the whole world will follow, the British Empire reconnected will be invincible. Come home, says Braddock, you are children who cannot care for yourselves properly. We shall give you a secure place in the bell curve pyramid of state. Together we shall witness the final evolution of the favored races, though many will be unable to participate in the triumph. Still, there will be for them the satisfaction of serving the fortunate who have inherited the Earth at the end of history.

The other ghost is a familiar one, too. A tall, muscular Virginian, just as compelling as Braddock but without his haughtiness, a man dressed in the browns and greens of nature, a brace of pistols at his waist, on a horse he calls Blueskin. He stands straight as an arrow. His powerful presence in combination with the delicate feet of a dancer mark him unmistakably as Major George Washington.

As a boy he learned the hard things: duty, piety, courage, self-reliance, to have a mind of his own, to refuse to accept the psychology of submission. His head was stocked with Cato, Fielding, Euclid, Newton, surveying, Caesar, Tacitus, the Testaments, horsemanship, dancing, how to tell a bawdy joke, how to comfort the weak, how to brace the strong, how to endure hardship, how to give men a reason to die, or one to live.

Once this same colonial frontiersman rode in a dream together with the English general, across an angry green river they rode into the deeps of the further forest. Braddock and his army died on the Monongahela that day but this American lived because he had learned to think for himself. The men who followed Washington lived, too, because the leader they chose was not a function of some greater abstraction. The loyalty they gave him was freely given, not imposed by intimidation or trickery.

Washington's greatest mistake in judgment, I think, was remembering Braddock's army as the most brilliant thing his eyes had ever seen, for surely that must have been his own reflection in the mirror. In that first moment after he refused to become King George I of America, brilliance never lived inside a more brilliant human vehicle. Behind the hero mask of Washington a real hero reposed. America is his legacy to us. Because of Washington we owe nothing to empires, not even to the one building in America today. We owe empires the same rude salute we gave them at Bunker Hill, Saratoga, and Yorktown.

Time to take our schools back. If they mean to have a war, let it begin now.

About The Books I Used

Four hundred odd books, articles, and monographs are cited in the text, usually by author and title. With the coming of Internet search engines, locating books by author and title is fairly easy to do. And these 400 citations are only the tip of an iceberg consisting of somewhat more than 2,500 similar documents I consulted to ground myself thoroughly in the minds, deeds, and biographies of those who gave us institutional schooling, as well as in the history of the ideas they represented. My reading odyssey expanded to include journals, meetings, conferences, interviews, extensive travel, letters, phone calls, faxes, and computer print-outs, too, though I drew the line at using or accepting e-mail, a personal prejudice, nothing more.

Should I now attempt to dazzle you with this grotesque assemblage arranged into a formal bibliography? I'll concede it would hardly have been possible to see School whole without reading my way there, nobody's personal experience is broad enough to allow otherwise, and yet my argument doesn't depend on this reference or that, it derives mostly from 30 years of classroom teaching, my own experience as a student, and a decade of non-stop reflection on these things informed by constant reading and discussion. All my critical conclusions will stand or fall on the discernment of the individual holding this book, and that is as it should be for an essay. *Underground History* is written for real people with real lives, people struggling to comprehend a menacing institution bent on processing their children, not for tenure committees or any aspect of the vast school establishment. So no formal bibliography.

The method I used was a simple one: I asked myself a question such as how to explain the ubiquitous presence of psychologists, social workers, lawyers, politicians, and government agents in every school in which I worked, and then set out to answer it. This accounts for the mosaic nature of the book you just read. It was my intention, eventually, to convert these bits into a unified narrative, but one day I realized that such a synthesis, however tempting it was to perform, would mislead the reader: School is like an enormous circus tent housing many different acts, a brilliant work of social engineering so sophisticated that none of its individual parts (or authors) really matters any more.

Once schooling was yoked to the new industrial economy of the early twentieth century, it advanced largely through the logic of rewards and punishments—those who helped to enlarge or maintain the system were paid off, those who opposed it were punished. Once the thing matured, its nominal leadership became irrelevant, expendable, interchangeable, human masks over a complex social mechanism, one out of control since the end of WWII. The programmed assumptions of this mechanism are that people cannot be trusted, that they are dangerous (and dangerously stupid) with few exceptions. School is a hospital where young people are prepared for lives of endless tutelage, "lifelong learning" in the current Newspeak.

I won't waste any more trees with a full Bibliography which would be useless to you, but I can easily put you on the road to further productive reading beyond my own book. Each of the following twelve recommendations is a work of genius. I've deliberately kept the list short to lure you into reading them all. Each, except Hoffer's, has an extensive Bibliography which mine, had I given it to you, would importantly have echoed; reading them all in the space of several months will certainly change the way you see things. Try it.

The List

Charles Glenn	The Myth of the Common School
Ray Callahan	Education and the Cult of Efficiency
Daniel Kevles	In the Name of Eugenics
David Rothman	The Discovery of the Asylum
John Harrison	Quest for a New Moral World
Christopher Lasch	The True and Only Heaven
John Higham	Strangers in the Land
David Hackett Fischer	Albion's Seed
James H. Billington	Fire in the Minds of Men
Eric Hoffer	The True Believer
Carroll Quigley	Tragedy and Hope
Langdon Winner	Autonomous Technology

Looking at my list, I'm tempted to double its size, then redouble it again. How can I leave off, E.G. West's books, and Joel Spring's, or any of a hundred other writers to whom I'm personally indebted? Only by a strict act of self-discipline I can tell you. But enough. Read these and you will be well on the way to the region I found myself in when I wrote this book. I wish you the same pleasure and profit I discovered there.

Index

Acknowledgments

This book was inspired by Janet, my wife, and also by the other women in my life: Frances Virginia, my beautiful mother; Lucrezia Calabro and Marian Moss Zimmer, my striking grandmothers; Joan, my fierce sister; Briseis, my brilliant daughter; Gudrun Moss, my Icelander granddaughter; Laura Ziriak, Virginia Gatto, Josephine Alexander, Helen VanArnam, my loving aunts; Susan, my resolute niece; Moss, Patty, Carol, Nancy, Delaney, Harper and Lauren, my patient and talented cousins; Doris, my indomitable mother-in-law; Mary MacAdam, my no-nonsense sister-in-law; and my friends Judith Kirsch Kovach, Virginia Hitchon, Barbara Loose, Marilyn Way, Sue Brown, Jane Howard, Ann Ritchey, Polly Smith, Holly Robinson, Mabel Anne Hutchinson, JoAnne Everly, Liz Cable, Breta Colanero, Wendy Zeigler, Janet Griffin, Chersteen Anderson and Amy Halpern, Hana Lamb, Lana Hamb, Diane Goldberg, Vanessa Killeen, Miyo Kono, Jennie Jerome, Luisa Fanto, and Claudia Patricia Vitallia Weiss. And including all those unknown Gattos, Calabros, D'Agostinos, Zimmers, Hoffmans, McManuses, Blairs, Browns, and MacAdams I hope to meet in the clouds one day. It is also for a few men: for my father, Angelo Mario Gatto who became Andrew Michael Gatto, for my mysterious son, Raven, named so that he could fly back home when he needed a sanctuary, for the intrepid Scot, Commander Thomas James McAdam, Janet's father, for the Harry Zimmers, Senior and Junior, without whom I never would have grown up, for uncle Frank and uncle Will who taught me many things, Colonel Ed O'Brien , and for an immortal friend, Ron Hitchon.

And this book is for Mary Leue, Pat Montgomery, Peg Luksik, Kathleen McCurdy, Mary Foley, Mary Pride, Becky Elder, Helen Hegener, Martha Mishoe, Susannah Scheffer, Day Farenga, Grace Llewellyn, Mimsy Sadowsky, Hanna Greenberg, Connie Frisbee Houde, Jackie Orsi, Betsy Mercogliano, Ellen Becker, Cathy Duffy, Debbie Caldwell, Linda Winklereid Dobson, Mary Leppert, Alethea Cheng, Carmen Wong, Lorraine Mollahan, Brenda Coman, Birgitta Erika Olsen, Cindy Wade, Roshanah Rothberg, Susan Rollins, Dulce Chicon, Luisa and Melly Fanto, Wilma Amaro, Mindy Bilgrey, Diane Flynn Keith, Terri Endsley, Laurie Lee, Devorah Weinman, Mary Pride, Alicia Katz, the Lappe ladies, Josette Piacetti, Norma Lynn, Nancy Stevenson, Dolores Burns, Elizabeth Cameron, Connie Brezina, and all the grand army of American women who went to the mat to wrestle children free from the state. You all were my inspiration. It's also for Debbie Meier who was the only official school person I ever knew worth listening to twice although there are many fundamentals on which we would disagree, for Julie Bennack who sweated through the preparation of the manuscript too many times to count, for Sylvia McNitt who finished it in grand style, and for all the gracious ladies my rotten memory has overlooked.

Thanks also to the Josephine Bay Paul and C. Michael Paul Foundation for resources to prepare a documentary film treatment based on this book. And thanks to the Separation Of School And State Alliance for its consistent support.

— John Taylor Gatto

ABOUT THE AUTHOR

John Taylor Gatto was born in Monongahela, Pennsylvania, a river town near Pittsburgh. He attended public schools in Swissvale, Monongahela, and Uniontown, and private boarding school in Latrobe, all towns in Pennsylvania. As a boy he held many jobs: sweeper in his grandfathers's printing office, snow shoveler, lawn mower, Kool-Aid salesman, and delivery boy for the Pittsburgh *Sun-Telegraph* and Uniontown *Morning Herald*, among others. He did undergraduate work at Cornell, University of Pittsburgh, and Columbia, and graduate work at Cornell, Yeshiva, Hunter College, and the University of California. After college, Mr. Gatto worked as a scriptwriter in the film business, was an advertising writer, a jewelry designer, an ASCAP songwriter, and a cab driver—before becoming a schoolteacher for 30 years, a career he climaxed as New York State Teacher of the Year. In 1992, he was named Secretary of Education in the Libertarian Party Shadow Cabinet, and in 1997, he was given the Alexis de Tocqueville Award for his contributions to the cause of Liberty. His other books are *Dumbing Us Down: The Hidden Curriculum of Compulsory Schooling* (1992), *The Exhausted School* (1993), and *A Different Kind of Teacher* (2000). Mr. Gatto lives in Oxford, New York, and is currently at work on a documentary film about the nature of modern schooling entitled, "The Fourth Purpose".

Phone orders: (212) 529-9397; Fax: (212) 529-3555
Mail: The Odysseus Group, 295 E. 8th Street,
Suite 3W, New York, New York 10009
$4 shipping/handling any number of items.

New York State residents add applicable tax.

En Ombra Radiant

The Odysseus Group, Inc.

We accept all major credit cards

THE ODYSSEUS GROUP SPONSORS JOHN TAYLOR GATTO'S LECTURES AND IS CURRENTLY ENGAGED IN TWO OTHER PROJECTS OF EDUCATIONAL REFORM FOR WHICH IT SEEKS ASSISTANCE (BOOK AND TAPE SALES ARE DEVOTED TO THESE ENDS):

Purchase our audio cassettes, videotapes and books:

I. AUDIO CASSETTES $8 EACH, cassettes contain approximately one hour of programming

1. <u>What Is An Education?</u> An examination of Three Ideas About the Business of Learning, Schooling and Education. Gatto reflects on his own curriculum and definition of an educated person.
2. <u>Bianica, You Animal, Shut up!</u> Gatto's Keynote address at the 20th Anniversary Conference of Growing Without Schooling. A discussion of humiliation. The dramatic environment of class-based schooling, and the common need to take action against the structure of forced schooling.
3. <u>On The Scientific Management of Children: A Short Angry History.</u> Tracks the rise of 4th Purpose in schooling which supplanted the traditional purposes to make good people, good citizens, and good lives.
4. <u>The Congregational Principle.</u> Locates the essential core of a free society in a fundamental principle brought to America by British Dissenters and Independents, and shows how this is subverted by schooling.
5. <u>A Schooling Is Not An Education.</u> An hour-long conversation between Barbara Dunlop of Pacifica Radio and John Taylor Gatto just after he left schoolteaching.
6. <u>The Logical Tragedy of Benson, Vermont.</u> The true tale of a tiny community driven to the verge of bankruptcy by the growth and articulation of systematic schooling. Why a school district with only 130 pupils "requires" a Superintendent, <u>and</u> an Assistant Superintendent, and all the rest.
7. <u>Mudsill Theory-Jaime Escalante and the Lancaster Amish.</u> An attempt to ground modern schooling in a negative theory of human nature, and in a British class-based social ideal, and to refute the theory with current examples.
8. <u>The Neglected Genius of American Spirituality.</u> Given at the Conference on Spirituality in Boulder, Colorado at which Dalai Lama delivered the Keynote. A profound analysis of pedagogy inherent to Western religion and the modern attempt to deliver its equivalent through forced schooling, an attempt which has failed.
9. <u>Beyond Money.</u> An analysis of how money devalues services which were once done charitably, how grades devalue independent learning, and why the things that matter will always be beyond money.
10. <u>Th Guerrilla Curriculum.</u> Recorded live in a Gatto workshop. Some of the things he did with kids that worked. (This selection is two 60-minute tapes ($16.00)).

II. VIDEOTAPES $29.95 EACH

1. <u>Classrooms Of The Heart.</u> Filmed by the Christian Science Monitor in John Gatto's last New York City classroom, and shown a number of times on the Discovery Channel.
2. <u>Absolute Absolution.</u> Filmed at the yearly meeting of the Utah Home Education Association. Covers some of the same ground contained in the cassette numbered #8 above, but delves much more deeply into the plan substituting science for religion in American Schools.

III. BOOKS

1. <u>Dumbing Us Down.</u> This book by John Taylor Gatto that started it all—has five key essays by Gatto including the famous: The Seven-Lesson Schoolteacher and The Psychopathic School. $9.95.
2. <u>The Exhausted School.</u> Complete text of the First National Grassroots Speakout On The Right To School Choice, held at Carnegie Hall. Includes essays by Gatto, Pat Farenga, Mary Leue, and Dave Lehman. $10.95.
3. <u>The Underground History Of American Education.</u> Gatto's opus. Buy a copy for a friend or your local library. $30.
4. <u>A Different Kind Of Teacher.</u> By John Taylor Gatto, due out October 2000. Contains never before published essays by Gatto on the art of teaching. $24.95.

THE ODYSSEUS GROUP LIBRARY AND RETREAT: The Odysseus Group, a 501 (c) (3) seeks tax-deductible contributions in order to build a library and retreat center for the use of private groups, which will include families and individuals, interested in the topic of school reform. We have acquired an option on 128 acres of wooded and open land in upstate New York, rich in wildlife with a structurally sound old barn, suitable for conversion into a place for reading and research. Together with necessary wells, septic tanks, and cabins, the Library and Retreat Center is estimated to require $250,000 to complete.

The Odysseus Group is producing a Documentary Film: THE FOURTH PURPOSE: The Deadly Paradox of **American Public Schooling,** projected as three to six 2-hour episodes to be aired on television and made available on home video. It is scheduled to begin shooting in late Fall, 2000.

If You would like to contribute to this project...

If You would like to invest in this project...

If You would like to offer your services to this project...Contact Us.

FAILED!

and a
school might have saved him!